SOCIOLOGICAL
METHODOLOGY
1992

SOCIOLOGICAL METHODOLOGY ❧ 1992 ❧

VOLUME 22

EDITOR Peter V. Marsden

ADVISORY EDITORS Gerhard Arminger

Aaron Cicourel

Glenn Firebaugh

Jan Hoem

Margaret M. Marini

Ronald Schoenberg

Michael E. Sobel

Christopher Winship

An official publication by Blackwell Publishers for

THE AMERICAN SOCIOLOGICAL ASSOCIATION

FELICE LEVINE, *Executive Officer*

Library of Congress Catalog Card Information
Sociological Methodology. 1969–85
 San Francisco, Jossey-Bass. 15 v. illus. 24 cm. annual. (Jossey-Bass behavioral science
 series)
  Editor: 1969, 1970: E. F. Borgatta; 1971, 1972, 1973–74: H. L. Costner;
  1975, 1976, 1977: D. R. Heise; 1978, 1979, 1980: K. F. Schuessler;
  1981, 1982, 1983–84: S. Leinhardt; 1985: N. B. Tuma

Sociological Methodology, 1986–88
 Washington, DC, American Sociological Association. 3 v. illus. 24 cm. annual.
  Editor: 1986: N. B. Tuma; 1987, 1988: C. C. Clogg

Sociological Methodology. 1989–1992
 Oxford, Basil Blackwell. 4 v. illus. 24 cm. annual.
  Editor: 1989, 1990: C. C. Clogg; 1991, 1992: P. V. Marsden
  "An official publication of the American Sociological Association."
  1. Sociology—Methodology—Year books. I. American Sociological
  Association. II. Borgatta, Edgar F., 1924– ed.

HM24.S55   301'.01'8   68-54940
                         rev.
Library of Congress   [r71h2]

British Cataloguing in Publication Data
Sociological Methodology. Vol. 22
  1. Sociology. Methodology
  301'.01'8

ISBN 1-557-86356-3
ISSN 0081-1750

Typeset by Huron Valley Graphics, Ann Arbor, MI
Printed by Edwards Brothers, Ann Arbor, MI

CONSULTANTS

Alan Agresti
Phipps Arabie
Gerhard Arminger
Mark Becker
Richard A. Berk
William T. Bielby
Kenneth Bollen
Phillip Bonacich
Richard T. Campbell
Glenn R. Carroll
Aaron Cicourel
Clifford C. Clogg
Charles Denk
Patrick Doreian
Malcolm Dow
Scott R. Eliason
Barbara Entwisle
Bonnie Erickson
Roberto Franzosi
Noah E. Friedkin
Mark Granovetter
Robert M. Hauser
David R. Heise
Ronald C. Kessler
Gary King

Tim Futing Liao
Allan L. McCutcheon
Margaret M. Marini
Stanley Presser
George Rabinowitz
Adrian Raftery
Mark Reiser
Ronald Schoenberg
Karl F. Schuessler
Joseph E. Schwartz
James Shockey
Michael E. Sobel
Aage B. Sørensen
Kenneth Spenner
Gillian Stevens
Tony Tam
Jay Teachman
Stanley Wasserman
Jeroen Weesie
Michael J. White
Christopher Winship
Lawrence Wu
Yu Xie
Kazuo Yamaguchi

CONTENTS

CONTRIBUTORS

Duane F. Alwin, Institute for Social Research and Department of Sociology, University of Michigan

David N. Barron, Department of Sociology, Cornell University

Stephen P. Borgatti, Department of Sociology, University of South Carolina

Larry S. Corder, Center for Demographic Studies, Duke University

Jan de Leeuw, Departments of Psychology and Statistics, University of California, Los Angeles

Glenn Deane, Department of Sociology, State University of New York, Albany

Martin G. Everett, School of Mathematics, Statistics and Computing, Thames Polytechnic, London

Donald P. Green, Department of Political Science, Yale University

Kenneth C. Land, Department of Sociology, Duke University

Kenneth G. Manton, Center for Demographic Studies, Duke University

Ab Mooijaart, Department of Psychometrics and Research Methods, University of Leiden

Bradley Palmquist, Department of Political Science, University of California, Berkeley

Albert Satorra, Department of Economics, Universitat Pompeu Fabra, Barcelona

Nora Cate Schaeffer, Department of Sociology, University of Wisconsin, Madison

Eric Stallard, Center for Demographic Studies, Duke University

Elizabeth Thomson, Department of Sociology, University of Wisconsin, Madison

Peter G. M. van der Heijden, Department of Empirical Theoretical Sociology, University of Utrecht

David L. Weakliem, Department of Sociology, Indiana University

Max A. Woodbury, Center for Demographic Studies, Duke University

INFORMATION FOR AUTHORS

Sociological Methodology is an annual volume on methods of research in the social sciences. Sponsored by the American Sociological Association, *Sociological Methodology*'s mission is to disseminate material that advances empirical research in sociology and related disciplines. Chapters present original methodological contributions, expository statements on and illustrations of recently developed techniques, and critical discussions of research practice. *Sociological Methodology* seeks contributions that address the full range of problems confronted by empirical work in the contemporary social sciences, including conceptualization and modeling, research design, data collection, measurement, and data analysis. Work on the methodological problems involved in any approach to empirical social science is appropriate for *Sociological Methodology*.

The content of each annual volume of *Sociological Methodology* is driven by submissions initiated by authors; the volumes do not have specific annual themes. Editorial decisions regarding manuscripts submitted are based heavily on the advice of expert referees; each article submitted for consideration is read by two or more editorial consultants. Criteria for evaluation include originality, breadth of interest and applicability, and expository clarity. Discussions of implications for research practice are vital, and authors are urged to include empirical illustrations of the methods they discuss.

Authors should submit four copies of manuscripts to the Editor (see below). Manuscripts should include an informative abstract of not more than one double-spaced page, and should not identify the author within the text. Submission of a manuscript for review by *Sociological Methodology* implies that it has not been previously published and that it is not under review elsewhere.

Inquiries concerning the appropriateness of material and other aspects of editorial policies and procedures are welcome; prospective authors should correspond with:

Peter V. Marsden, Editor
Sociological Methodology
Department of Sociology
Harvard University
616 William James Hall
33 Kirkland Street
Cambridge, MA 02138
Electronic mail address:
SOCMETH@HARVUNXT.BITNET

To Hubert M. Blalock, Jr. (1926–1991)

PROLOGUE

The topics covered in the chapters of the twenty-second volume of *Sociological Methodology* span virtually all phases of the research process. The volume begins with an essay on conceptual models. Three chapters on measurement follow; their subjects range from the design of research instruments to the assessment of the quality of available indicators. The final six chapters present statistical methods of data analysis that enable analysts to address such problems as comparing the goodness of fit of non-nested models, adjusting for spatial or temporal interdependence of observations, or estimating models that involve diverse types of latent variables. The authors give both abstract discussions and concrete empirical illustrations of the approaches they cover.

The introductory chapter, by Stephen Borgatti and Martin Everett, presents an expository discussion of models for "positions" in social networks. Structural models of this kind have been among the central concerns of social network analysts for the past 15 years or so. Borgatti and Everett focus on the contrast between models based on the concept of *structural equivalence* (which treats two nodes or actors as equivalent if and only if they are related to an identical set of nodes or actors) and models that draw on a more abstract concept of *isomorphic equivalence* (which regards actors as equivalent if and only if they are connected in the same way to identically situated nodes or actors). A related chapter, by Christopher Winship and Michael Mandel, appeared in *Sociological Methodology 1983–84*. Here, Borgatti and Everett observe that structurally equivalent nodes must be relatively closely connected to one another and that this form of equivalence thus embodies a certain amount of "cohesion" or direct interconnectedness. They contend that structural equivalence reflects the "surface" or "local" structure of a network, while isomorphic equivalence represents the "deep" or "global" structure.

After articulating the distinction between structural and isomorphic equivalence, Borgatti and Everett review the use of these concepts of position in three lines of substantive sociological research: representing distinctions between statuses and/or roles; explaining differences in power in experimental network studies; and specifying alternative mechanisms for social homogeneity in diffusion studies. They observe that some researchers theorize in terms of abstract or isomorphic equivalence, but then use operational procedures designed to measure structural equivalence. Borgatti and Everett also discuss theoretical mechanisms that are consistent with one or another of these positional concepts.

The first of the chapters on measurement, written by Nora Cate Schaeffer and Elizabeth Thomson, is about questionnaire development. The authors are especially concerned with the measurement of uncertain responses, distinguishing between "task" uncertainty due to the design of a research instrument and "state" uncertainty intrinsic to the construct under study. Schaeffer and Thomson seek questions that can capture distinct types of state uncertainty while minimizing task uncertainty. They point to the various forms that state uncertainty may take: These include neutrality, in which a respondent is genuinely indifferent between offered response categories; ambivalence, in which the respondent finds that his or her true state combines more than one response category, or recognizes that the true state varies from time to time; and lack of clarity, which could reflect insufficient knowledge about the feeling or subject under study.

Schaeffer and Thomson present a case study that reports on their efforts to develop a set of standardized questionnaire items about fertility motivation in a way that allows interviewers to record different types of state uncertainty. They begin with semi-structured interviews, which they subsequently content-analyze in an effort to abstract distinct expressions of uncertainty. The results of this inform the development of structured questions together with detailed inter-

viewer instructions that provide guidance about how to code different expressions of uncertainty. The end of the chapter presents evidence that the way in which respondents express uncertainty about
future fertility motivation varies with marital and parental status as
well as with the desire for (additional) children.

Schaeffer and Thomson's chapter can be read as an example
of how "qualitative" and "quantitative" research methods can be
combined, by allowing variations in respondent meaning to be discovered and incorporated into the design of structured questionnaire
items. Though the chapter is focused on expressions of uncertainty,
the approach they illustrate is certainly applicable to many other
concepts of interest to social scientists.

In Chapter 3, Duane Alwin examines how the reliability of
attitude items in surveys varies with the number of response categories offered to respondents. He draws on information theory and
recent work on the cognitive aspects of survey responses in formulat-
ing hypotheses about this. In general Alwin expects reliability to
increase with the number of categories provided; he argues, however, that the purpose of measurement must be considered in assessing reliability. For example, the direction of attitudes may be quite
reliably measured by dichotomous items, while ambiguities associated with middle-position responses for three-category items may
reduce their reliability for this purpose. Larger numbers of categories arguably provide better measures of attitude intensity, but very
large numbers of categories may pose respondent burdens that compromise both reliability and validity.

Alwin then presents results of his analyses of five three-wave
panel surveys containing a total of 99 attitude items, using a measurement model related to that discussed in the subsequent chapter by
Palmquist and Green. Alwin's findings are largely consistent with his
hypotheses: Reliability is generally higher when questions provide
many response categories, but is lower for three-category than for
two-category items. Thus, economical dichotomous-response items
can reliably assess the valence of attitudes, but finer distinctions are
useful for measuring intensity. Alwin introduces the caveat that differences in scale length and substantive content are confounded in
the data available to him; further, he is unable to assess the conjec-
ture that very large numbers of categories reduce the precision of
measurement, since none of the items measured in the studies he

analyzes has more than nine categories. Nonetheless, Alwin's results provide valuable guidance to researchers designing attitude surveys.

The reliability of measurements may be estimated when an analyst has multiple indicators of a concept—either multiple measurements obtained at a single point in time, which make it possible to assess internal consistency, or one or more measures repeated at several points in time, which allow the estimation of both the reliability and the stability of measures. The focus of Chapter 4 by Bradley Palmquist and Donald Green is on the latter type of reliability assessment. They study models for the analysis of single-indicator, multi-wave panel designs. They give special attention to one such model, the "correlated error" model, in which there is over-time stability not only in true scores on the concept to be measured but also in errors of measurement. Palmquist and Green point to important practical difficulties in the estimation of this model with three waves of data: In applications reported to date, parameter estimates have very large standard errors, while estimates of reliability and stability are correspondingly imprecise, and often implausible. They demonstrate that this occurs because the model is empirically underidentified. While it meets the formal criteria required for identification, its estimates vary substantially due to sampling fluctuations in the estimation of variances and covariances of observed variables. In fact, some parameters are identified only *because of* such fluctuations. Palmquist and Green's chapter demonstrates that this sampling variation can be much reduced if additional waves of data are available; these provide substantial enhancements in statistical power. Several examples illustrate the problems encountered with three waves of data, and the advantages of a fourth or fifth panel of measurements.

Chapters 5 through 7 cover problems of estimation and inference that arise with models or types of data that sociologists often encounter. David Weakliem, in Chapter 5, addresses the problem of comparing "non-nested" models for contingency tables. Two models are said to be nested when one is a special case of the other, that is, when it can be obtained by placing restrictions on the parameters of a second, more general, model. When models are nested, well-known likelihood-ratio tests can be used for comparing them. When they are not nested, however, analysts generally have been forced to resort to more informal comparisons.

The problem of comparing non-nested models arises frequently in the study of cross-classified data, for which so many different models have been proposed over the past two decades. These include hierarchical loglinear models, "topological" models that isolate association in levels or regions of a table, loglinear and log-multiplicative association models, and latent class models, among others. Analysts frequently find that two or more models resting on different substantive assumptions describe a table well, but are unable to judge between them since the models are not nested.

Weakliem's chapter begins by reviewing developments in the econometric literature that lead to tests for comparing non-nested pairs of linear regression models; many researchers will find this review informative in and of itself. The tests examine the assumptions built in to the specification of a model. The central intuition is that if a given model is consistent with the data, then its estimated residuals—which by assumption are random—should not be systematically related to the predicted values from alternative models. Weakliem relates these tests to Lagrange multiplier or score tests. Next, he develops versions of them suitable for cross-classified data. Use of these can lead to the conclusion that either, neither, or both of a given pair of models are consistent with the data; notably, the tests may signal that a model that fits poorly nonetheless explains features of the data that a better-fitting one misses. Weakliem illustrates the use of the tests by comparing four non-nested models for the well-known 8-by-8 Glass mobility table; though three of these models fit the data reasonably well by conventional criteria, Weakliem's results identify one of them as preferable to the others.

Chapter 6, by David Barron, is on models for the analysis of event-count data. Such data record the number of events experienced by some analytic unit (e.g. individual, organization) within an interval of time; examples are the number of times a corporation is cited for legal violations within a year, or the number of spells of unemployment experienced by an individual within a year. Event-count data differ from event-history data in that they do not record the specific times at which the events of interest take place.

Barron begins by discussing the most commonly used model for studying event-count data, the Poisson regression model. This assumes that the rate at which events occur is constant within time intervals, and that there is no over-time heterogeneity in the rate that is not captured by the differences between units that have been mea-

sured. Such assumptions may be violated in social science data for
many reasons; Barron highlights time dependence, social contagion
processes, omitted variables, and arbitrary time intervals. When these
assumptions are false, problems of overdispersion and autocorrelation can arise. These conditions make estimates from the Poisson
regression model problematic. Barron reviews different forms of the
negative binomial regression model and a quasi-likelihood (QL) approach that address the problem of overdispersion; he also covers
generalized quasi-likelihood (GQL) techniques that can take autocorrelation into account. Since the small-sample properties of the QL and
GQL techniques are not especially well-understood, Barron presents
the results of some Monte Carlo studies of their performance. He illustrates the use of all four estimators by analyzing data on the founding
of national labor unions in the U.S. (See related analyses presented in
Michael Hannan's chapter in *Sociological Methodology 1991*.)

    Kenneth C. Land and Glenn Deane reconsider the estimation
of the spatial- or network-effects model in Chapter 7. This model
posits that the value of an outcome variable for a focal unit of
analysis is affected not only by its own properties, but also by the
values of the outcome for spatially or socially proximate units. It is
used by geographers, sociologists, economists, and others who study
spatial data; it is also used in the study of diffusion or contagion
processes mediated by social networks. A maximum likelihood
(ML) estimator for this model was discussed in Patrick Doreian's
chapter in *Sociological Methodology 1981*. Land and Deane note
some limitations of this estimator, which has been the typical technique used in applications: It requires the development of special
software, and its computational demands for a large sample can
strain the limitations of even large computers. They present an
alternative two-stage least-squares (2SLS) estimator suitable for
large-sample work which makes much more modest computational
demands; moreover, it does not require some of the distributional
assumptions necessary for deriving the ML estimator. Land and
Deane illustrate the performance of their estimator with an analysis
of church adherence rates in U.S. counties; they also provide comparisons of the statistical and computational efficiency of their estimator, the ML estimator, and another 2SLS estimator developed for
the spatial-effects model by Luc Anselin.

    The final three chapters are on different latent variable models used in the analysis of continuous and discrete data. Many contributions to previous editions of *Sociological Methodology* have used covariance structure models that combine a measurement model for relationships of continuous latent variables to continuous observed ones with a structural equation model for relationships among the latent variables (see, among others, the chapter by Blair Wheaton and others in *Sociological Methodology 1977* and that by Michael Sobel and George Bohrnstedt in *Sociological Methodology 1985*). The best-known estimation methods for such models make the assumption that observed variables follow a multivariate normal distribution, which is unrealistic for many forms of data commonly studied by social scientists. In recent years much effort has gone into the development of "distribution-free" estimators that relax the normality assumption.

Albert Satorra contributes to the literature on distribution-free estimation in Chapter 8. He is concerned with models that place restrictions on the means, as well as on the covariances, of observed variables. Satorra notes that point estimates of parameters obtained under the normality assumption are robust to its violation, but that inferential statistics and interval estimates can be quite misleading when the assumption fails. His chapter discusses distribution-free approaches to estimating mean and covariance structure models, as well as techniques for obtaining inferential statistics that are robust to the violation of the normality assumption—both standard errors for individual parameters and goodness-of-fit statistics for assessing the correspondence between an estimated model and the observed means and covariances. Notably, Satorra shows how to obtain these statistics for the multistage sampling designs that social scientists often encounter. He presents a Monte Carlo simulation study to illustrate the advantages of the methods he proposes; one clearly risks drawing faulty inferences by using statistics that incorrectly assume normality. Use of the robust inferential statistics that Satorra proposes will yield much more reliable hypothesis tests and confidence intervals when the normality assumption is false.

In Chapter 9, Peter G.M. van der Heijden, Ab Mooijaart and Jan de Leeuw discuss their latent budget model for two-way cross-classifications. In this model, the conditional probability distribution (or "observed budget") in each row of a contingency table is modeled as a mixture of a number of latent conditional probability distri-

butions, or "latent budgets." These give one or more underlying
probability distributions across the column categories; the distribution in each row of the observed table is modeled by combining them
with parameters that reflect association between the observed row
variable and the discrete latent variable that differentiates the underlying distributions. Van der Heijden and colleagues begin by reviewing the general latent budget model and its relationship to latent class
analysis as presented, for example, by Clifford Clogg and Leo Goodman in *Sociological Methodology 1985*. Indeed, Chapter 9 demonstrates that unconstrained latent budget analysis is a reparameterization of the latent class model for a two-way table in which one
manifest (observed) variable is treated as an independent or explanatory variable while the other is regarded as a dependent or response
variable; in the usual parameterization of the latent class model all
manifest variables are treated as mutually dependent.

Chapter 9 goes on to discuss the imposition of various constraints on the parameters of the latent budget model. Some of these,
fixed-value and equality constraints, will be relatively familiar to
readers of *Sociological Methodology*. Van der Heijden and colleagues show, however, that multinomial logit constraints can be
imposed as well. These can make use of additional information that a
researcher may have about the row and column variables of the
observed cross-classification. A circumstance in which it is especially
useful to do this arises when the row or column variable is a joint
variable formed by cross-classifying two or more observed variables;
in this case multinomial logit constraints on the latent budget model
can reflect the factorial structure of the joint variable—that is, they
can separate associations that involve the joint variable into main
and interaction effects involving its components. This allows researchers to formulate more parsimonious latent budget models that
often have simpler interpretations than the unconstrained versions.
Van der Heijden, Mooijaart and de Leeuw illustrate the models they
propose with two examples, one on age and sex differences in methods of committing suicide, the other on age and ethnic differences in
crime patterns.

In the final chapter of *Sociological Methodology 1992*, Kenneth Manton, Max Woodbury, Eric Stallard and Larry Corder present their Grade-of-Membership (GOM) model for multivariate analysis, and compare it to other latent variable models including the

factor analytic model (for both continuous and discrete variables) and the latent class model. Three of the authors contributed to a related presentation on this model in the 1987 volume of *Sociological Methodology*. The GOM model abstracts a set of discrete latent "types" from a set of categorical indicator variables; for example, Manton and colleagues identify four latent health and functional types using a set of 56 indicators. These types, however, will rarely describe an individual observed case. Instead, each case is represented as a *mixture* of the basic types; the GOM model includes individual-specific "grade of membership" parameters that tell the degree to which a case's response profile is based on the pattern associated with one of the pure types.

There are many parallels between the GOM approach and latent class models for categorical data, and Manton and colleagues compare and contrast these methods at length, dealing with the models themselves as well as techniques for estimation. A contrast of interest is that the latent class approach assumes that each individual is of one of the pure types and estimates the a posteriori probability of each possibility, while the GOM approach models each individual as a unique mixture of types. Another difference is that GOM estimates its grade of membership parameters for individual cases simultaneously with other model parameters, instead of conditioning them on estimates of parameters that relate the latent types to observed variables.

After introducing the GOM model, Manton and colleagues show how it can be used to study successive sets of indicator variables, in a manner analogous to recursive structural equation models. They do this by examining the way in which latent types defined by a prior ("exogenous") set of variables are related to a new ("endogenous") set of variables, and abstracting new latent types from relationships among endogenous variables not accounted for by the exogenous types. Moreover, the authors examine relationships among the individual parameters indexing grades of membership, showing the exogenous types that tend to compose the endogenous types. They illustrate their approach with a three-stage analysis of health service utilization based on the National Long Term Care Surveys.

The *Sociological Methodology* editorial board has dedicated this volume to the memory of Hubert M. Blalock, Jr., who died on

February 8, 1991. Many contemporary sociologists—those engaged in
substantive studies as well as those who pursue methodological
research—were introduced to statistical methods by Blalock's *Social
Statistics*. His *Causal Inferences in Nonexperimental Research* called
attention to difficult methodological problems entailed in making
causal interpretations. Among these are considerations of research
design, model specification, measurement, omitted variables, and unmeasured or latent variables. Blalock continually reminded social researchers of these methodological challenges—which remain with
us—in books including *Conceptualization and Measurement in the
Social Sciences* and *Basic Dilemmas in the Social Sciences;* one of his
last statements about them appeared in *Sociological Methodology
1991*. Beyond his methodological work, Blalock was actively engaged
in substantive work, particularly the study of intergroup relations.
Fuller appreciations of his many contributions to sociology appear in
the April 1991 issue of *Footnotes,* the newsletter of the American
Sociological Association. By dedicating *Sociological Methodology
1992* to him, we recognize Blalock's central role in advancing both
methodology and theory construction in social research.

ACKNOWLEDGEMENTS

A large number of people have collaborated with me in developing this edition of *Sociological Methodology*. The 49 editorial consultants listed on page v have made especially important contributions by commenting on one or more manuscripts submitted for this
volume. They have given much wise and free advice; while maintaining high standards of scholarship, they have been generous and con-
structive in sharing both their technical expertise and their expository suggestions with authors and me. Their thoughtful reviews have
had major influences on the chapters that appear here. In addition I
am grateful to advisory editors who have given me guidance about
editorial matters that go beyond particular manuscripts, and to authors who have been tolerant of repeated requests for revision, some
of which have had rather short deadlines.

The copyediting and assembly of *Sociological Methodology
1992* has once again been managed with care and dedication by Ann
Kremers. Katsch Belash, Sandra Leonard, and Suzanne Washington
at Harvard have provided prompt and competent staff assistance to

editorial operations while this volume was prepared. Colleen Doyle
at Blackwell Publishers managed the production schedule and the
design of the cover.

   Sociological Methodology is an official publication of the
American Sociological Association, which provides essential financial support for it. In addition I am grateful to Harvard University for
providing office facilities, equipment, and other aid.

Peter V. Marsden
Harvard University
November 1991

1

NOTIONS OF POSITION IN SOCIAL NETWORK ANALYSIS

Stephen P. Borgatti*
Martin G. Everett†

The notion of position is fundamental in structural theory. However, at least two profoundly different conceptions of position exist. The two basic types of position have radically different characteristics, making them appropriate for different theoretical applications. We present examples in which scholars have operationalized one type of position but drawn conclusions as if the other type had been used. We compare the two notions of position in terms of their applicability in several research areas, including power in exchange networks, role theory, world-system theory, and social homogeneity.

One of the most central concepts in social network analysis and structural theory in general is the notion of position. Position is utilized as a dependent or independent variable in a variety of empirical and theoretical works. For example, position plays a critical role in the study of world systems (Snyder and Kick 1979; Breiger 1981; Nemeth and Smith 1985); adoption of innovation, diffusion, and other social homogeneity phenomena (Burt 1978, 1987; Rogers 1979; Friedkin 1984; Anderson and Jay 1985); and power in exchange networks (Cook et al. 1983; Markovsky, Willer, and Patton

We thank Katherine Faust, Linton Freeman, Noah Friedkin, Peter Marsden, and John Skvoretz for helpful comments on earlier drafts. We also thank the anonymous reviewers for many excellent suggestions.
*University of South Carolina
†Thames Polytechnic, London

1

1988). Position has also been related to similarity in attitudes (Erickson 1988); mental health (Kadushin 1982); economic success in interorganizational networks (Burt 1979); perception of leadership (Leavitt 1951); political solidarity (White, Boorman, and Breiger 1976); job changes (Krackhardt and Porter 1986); production of scientific knowledge (Brym 1988); growth of cities (Pitts 1978); organizational influence (Galaskiewicz and Krohn 1984); and many others.

However, the term *position* refers to more than one concept. A variety of different formal definitions exist, and an even greater variety of operational implementations of these definitions may be found in the form of relaxed definitions, algorithms, procedures, computer programs, and the like. These myriad variants can yield more than just different numerical results: Many must be interpreted quite differently and demand that different causal mechanisms be posited. Yet, as a rule, the substantive and theoretical literature that has utilized the notion of position has not done this. In fact, as we shall demonstrate, published works frequently define position one way and then proceed to draw conclusions as if a different definition had been used.

In this paper, we suggest that there are two fundamental types of positional notions that underlie the observed variety. To simplify the exposition, we select a single prototypical representative of each type to describe in detail. We then compare the applicability of each across several areas of research, including power in exchange networks, world-systems theory, roles and social structure, and social homogeneity. We conclude with a look at the deeper notions of structure that underlie the different approaches to the concept of position.

It should be emphasized that our discussion pertains to the idealized, mathematical formalizations of the positional notions, not to the actual algorithms and computer programs that implement them. This distinction is not problematic, however, since all valid algorithms and programs reach the same solutions when applied to perfect, error-free data; they differ only in the way they handle departures from mathematical ideals.

1. BASIC NOTIONS

The fundamental idea underlying the notion of position is that of structural correspondence or similarity. Actors who are connected in the same way to the rest of the network are said to be equivalent and to occupy the same position. In general, the objective of positional analyses is to partition actors into mutually exclusive classes of equivalent actors who have similar relational patterns. This positional approach to network analysis is intended to contrast with the relational or cohesive approach (Burt 1978; Friedkin 1984), which attempts to find subsets of actors who are strongly or closely related to each other. In the first case the underlying clustering principle is similarity; in the second, it is cohesion or proximity.

However, there are at least two fundamentally different ways of interpreting the phrase *connected in the same way to the rest of the network,* which depend on whether one wishes to take the phrase literally or metaphorically. The distinction is illustrated by the following problem, adapted from Hofstadter (1985). Consider the following two abstract structures:

$$A = \langle\, 1\ 2\ 3\ 4\ 5\ 5\ 4\ 3\ 2\ 1\, \rangle \quad \text{and} \quad B = \langle\, 0\ 1\ 2\ 3\ 4\ 4\ 3\ 2\ 1\ 0\, \rangle .$$

Hofstadter asks, "What is to B as 4 is to A? Or, to use the language of roles: What plays the role in B that 4 plays in A?" (p. 549). According to Hofstadter, an overly literal, concrete answer is 4, whereas a more natural, more analogical response is 3. More formally, the distinction is analogous to the distinction made in mathematics and logic between identity/equality and isomorphism/similarity. For example, in algebra, two binary relations are equal or identical if they contain the same ordered pairs, but they are isomorphic if there is a one-to-one correspondence between the pairs of each relation. Similarly, two semigroups are the same if they relate the same compound relations in the same ways, but they are isomorphic if there is a one-to-one correspondence between their multiplication tables. In geometry, two triangles are equal if corresponding sides are the same length, but they are similar if they are proportional to each other. In the case of networks, the distinction corresponds to Faust's (1988) distinction between *structural equivalence*[1] (Lorrain and White 1971; Burt 1976;

[1]It is unfortunate that Lorrain and White used the term *structural equivalence* to name their particular species of positional concept, because the term connotes a much broader notion of position than was actually defined. As will become apparent, their concept would have been more aptly named *structural equality* or *structural identity* or even *label equivalence*. It is important to keep in mind that despite appearances, *structural equivalence* refers to a specific definition of position, not to the general principle of structural similarity.

Breiger, Boorman, and Arabie 1975) and *general equivalences,* and to Pattison's (1988) distinction between structural equivalence and *abstract equivalences.* The general or abstract equivalences referred to include *automorphic equivalence* or *structural isomorphism* (Everett 1985; Winship 1988), *regular equivalence* (White and Reitz 1983; Borgatti and Everett 1989), and a variety of others (Winship and Mandel 1983; Breiger and Pattison 1986; Hummell and Sodeur 1987). The concepts of structural, automorphic, and regular equivalence are listed in order of increasing generalization: Any pair of nodes that is structurally equivalent is also necessarily automorphically and regularly equivalent, and any pair of automorphically equivalent nodes is also regularly equivalent.[2]

As Pattison (1988) noted, there are important differences among all the abstract equivalences, but the fundamental distinction is between structural equivalence and all the others. Of the others, the one most comparable to structural equivalence in definition and application is structural isomorphism (automorphic equivalence). For this reason, in the interests of clarity and simplicity, we focus our discussion only on the contrast between structural equivalence and automorphic equivalence.

2. TECHNICAL DEFINITIONS AND NOTATION

For convenience, all examples in this paper concern nonvalued networks defined by a single relation. The restriction is not necessary but significantly simplifies the exposition. Networks are represented as graphs denoted $G(V,E)$, where V refers to a set of vertices, nodes, points, or actors, and E refers to a set of edges, lines, links, ties, or relationships. When discussing the vertex sets of two graphs, G and H, we use $V(G)$ to refer to the vertex set of graph G and $V(H)$ to refer to the vertex set of graph H. Similarly, $E(G)$ refers to the edge set of graph G and $E(H)$ to the edge set of graph H.

The notation $P(a)$ is used to denote the position of node a in a network. The position of a node is a categorical attribute of that node, which can be thought of as its color (Everett and Borgatti

---

[2]It should also be noted that regular equivalence actually defines a lattice of distinct equivalences (Borgatti and Everett 1989), which includes structural and automorphic equivalence.

1990) or flavor. By a slight abuse of notation, we also let $P(\{a,b \ . \ .\})$ = $\{P(a) \cup P(b) \cup \ . \ . \ .\}$. In other words, if S is a set of nodes, $P(S)$ is the set of distinct positions occupied by the nodes in S.

In a directed graph, the notation $N^i(a)$ denotes the set of nodes that a receives ties from and is defined as $N^i(a) = \{ c: (c,a) \in E)$. The notation $N^o(a)$ denotes the set of nodes that a sends ties to and is defined as $N^o(a) = \{ c: (a,c) \in E)$. We refer to $N^i(a)$ and $N^o(a)$ as the *in-neighborhood* and *out-neighborhood* of a, respectively. The neighborhood of a point, $N(a)$, is defined as the ordered pair $N(a) = (N^i(a), N^o(a))$.

In an undirected graph, the neighborhood $N(a)$ is defined as the set of nodes directly connected to node a, so that $N(a) = \{ c:(a,c) \in E\} = \{ c: (c,a) \in E\}$.

A *structural* or *graph-theoretic attribute* is any attribute of a node or graph that makes no reference to the names or labels of the nodes in the graph. For example, in an undirected graph representing friendships among a set of people, the property of being no more than three links distant from any node is a structural attribute of a node, but the property of being no more than three links distant from Mary is not a structural attribute. The centrality of a point is a structural attribute, as is the property of belonging to seven cliques of size 4, but belonging to three cliques that include Bill as a member is not a structural attribute.

3. POSITION AS STRUCTURAL EQUIVALENCE

The term *structural equivalence* was coined by Lorrain and White (1971), who defined it this way:

> Objects a,b of a category C are *structurally equivalent* if, for any morphism M and any object x of C, aMx if and only if bMx, and xMa if and only if xMb. In other words, a is structurally equivalent to b if a relates to every object x of C in exactly the same ways as b does. From the point of view of the logic of the structure, then, a and b are absolutely equivalent, they are substitutable. (P. 81)

Today, however, the term is used to refer to a much simpler[3] concept. The modern usage is due to Burt (1976), who defined a set of structurally equivalent nodes as a set of nodes connected by the same relations to exactly the same people. Thus, an actor's position is defined by *who* he or she is connected to. It is literally and concretely the set of actors with whom he or she has direct contact. In the notation given in the previous section, $P(v) = N(v)$ for all $v \in V$. If we ask, What is Bill's position in the network?, we are asking nothing more than, Who is Bill directly connected to?

Applied to nonvalued graphs, Burt's definition can be elegantly stated as follows: If $G = \langle V,E \rangle$ is a graph and $a,b \in V$, then $P(a) = P(b)$ iff $N(a) = N(b)$. The definition says that two actors in a network occupy the same position if and only if they have perfectly overlapping neighborhoods. In other words, they have identical ego networks. By *identical* we mean not only that the ego networks contain the same individuals, but that, consequently, they also contain the same relationships among them. As shown in Figure 1, the only difference between the ego networks of structurally equivalent actors like Bill and Joe is the name or label of the two egos.

It should be noted that our rewritten definition reproduces a small but important shortcoming in Burt's definition, which also occurs in Lorrain and White's original. The problem is that for graphs without reflexive loops, none of these definitions allows nodes that are connected to each other to occupy the same position. Thus, in Figure 1a, Mary and Jane are not structurally equivalent by these definitions. A better definition is $P(a) = P(b)$ iff $N(a) - \{a,b\} = N(b) - \{a,b\}$. However, this version fails when a single directed arc links a and b. For example, in Figure 2, nodes a and b would be considered

---

[3]The difference between the formulations may not be apparent from the definitions. What Lorrain and White intended is something akin to the following simplified recipe. Start with a handful of observed relations. Call these generators. Using relational composition and some rules for determining when two relational products are the same, create a semigroup of relations. Determine which nodes have ties to the same actors on these new compound relations (not necessarily the generators). Call these structurally equivalent. It is important to realize that in Lorrain and White's formulation, structurally equivalent nodes need not have ties to the same alters on the *observed* relations, as Burt's definition requires, but they must always have ties to the same alters on certain derived relations.

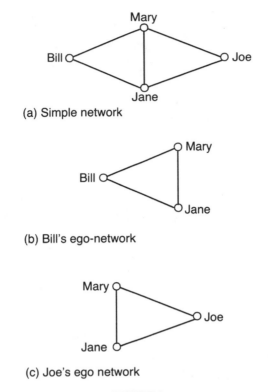

(a) Simple network

(b) Bill's ego-network

(c) Joe's ego network

FIGURE 1.

structurally equivalent by this definition. The definition also fails to distinguish nodes with reflexive loops from ones without.[4]

Since structurally equivalent actors are connected to exactly the same nodes, they are identical with respect to all structural variables. They have the same centrality, eccentricity (Harary 1969), degree, prestige, etc. In fact, any graph-theoretic statement that can be said about one actor can be said about the other. The converse, however, is not true. Actors who are indistinguishable on absolutely all graph-theoretic attributes are not necessarily structurally equivalent. For example, in Figure 3, nodes a and h are absolutely identical with respect to all possible graph-theoretic variables, but they are not structurally equivalent because they do not have the same neighborhoods.

[4]A definition that works in most cases was given by Burt (1987, p. 1330). A definition that works in all cases was given by Everett, Boyd, and Borgatti (1990). In their definition, $P(a) = P(b)$ iff $\exists\, \pi \in$ Aut (G) such that $\pi = (a\,b)$ and $\pi(a) = b$, where Aut (G) denotes the automorphism group of a graph G.

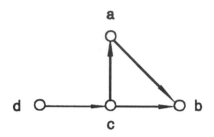

FIGURE 2. Graph containing no structurally equivalent nodes.

As Lorrain and White (1971, p. 82) pointed out, for a given set of relations, the notion of structural equivalence is a wholly *local* concept: To know whether two actors are equivalent, we only need to know who they are directly connected to. We do not require any knowledge of the rest of the network. Consequently, an actor's position is utterly unaffected by any changes in the network that occur more than one link away.[5] As a practical matter, this means that structural equivalence can be calculated on incomplete data sets, provided that no data that pertains to a given pair of individuals' ego networks is missing. In contrast, global variables, such as betweenness centrality (Freeman 1978) or abstract equivalences, are miscalculated if any ties, no matter how distal, are missing.

It also means that structural equivalence is not truly a relational concept in the sense of Wellman (1988) or a structural concept in the sense of Krippendorff (1971), because the entire network need

[5]Of course, if the researcher computes structural equivalence not on the raw data but on a derived dataset that encodes more than simple adjacency, then even remote changes in the original network could affect the measurement of the degree of structural equivalence of a given pair of actors. For example, Burt (1976) suggested computing structural equivalence on the geodesic distances among actors in a network. However, three points should be noted. First, this is not a theoretical issue: No changes in the network at more than two links away can ever affect the determination of whether a given pair of actors is equivalent or not equivalent in the ideal sense given by the definition of structural equivalence. It is only practical algorithms intended to detect structural equivalence in imperfect empirical data that are affected. Second, perfectly equivalent actors will not be affected by remote changes. The issue arises only when we compute a measure of the extent of structural equivalence *among actors who are not structurally equivalent*. Third, and most important, using derived datasets such as geodesic distance matrices can change results but not the essential nature of structural equivalence: It remains a local concept even if the data are somehow "global."

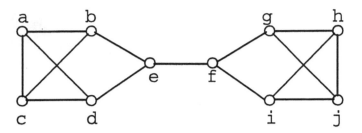

FIGURE 3. Graph in which all points have equal degree.

not be involved for one to evaluate the status of a given actor. Instead, one need collect only ego network data, which is not fundamentally different from collecting traditional "attribute" data (Wellman 1988) like marital status or number of children.

A consequence of the local nature of structural equivalence is that sets of structurally equivalent actors are always fully contained within components of a graph. That is, actors located in different components of a disconnected graph (or in different graphs) can never be structurally equivalent (except isolates). In fact, as a general rule, nodes cannot be structurally equivalent if they are more than two links apart. Exceptions occur only for isolates, which satisfy structural equivalence vacuously, and for directed graphs, in which case the rule refers to links without regard for direction (i.e., to semipaths). Hence, cohesion/proximity is part and parcel of the notion of structural equivalence. For undirected graphs, this means that sets of structurally equivalent actors form a cohesive subset, specifically a 2-clique (Luce 1950), which is a well-known formalization of the general notion of a cohesive subset.[6] Although the fact that structurally equivalent actors form cohesive subsets has often been noticed empirically (Friedkin 1984; Burt 1978, 1987), the literature has in general regarded sets of structurally equivalent actors as fundamentally different from cohesive subsets (e.g., DiMaggio 1986; Hartman and Johnson 1990), rather than as a special type of cohesive subset, which, mathematically, they are.

[6]Another method of detecting subgroups in graphs, which also succeeds in finding sets of structurally equivalent actors, is based on multidimensional scaling of the graph-theoretic distance matrix of a graph (Burt 1982, p. 71). Because structurally equivalent actors are the same distances from all other nodes, this method assigns the same map coordinates to all structurally equivalent nodes.

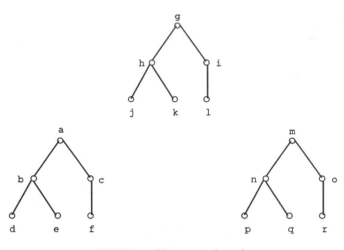

FIGURE 4. Disconnected graph.

Ultimately, the structural equivalence conception of position is about the *location* of an actor in a labeled graph. Structurally equivalent actors share the same location. From this perspective, it is not difficult to see why sets of structurally equivalent actors form cohesive subsets: Both concepts are based on detecting actors who occupy the same or nearly the same locations, neighborhoods, or regions of a network. It is also obvious that two nodes occupying the same location in a labeled graph share two fundamental and logically distinct properties: proximity and similarity. The difference is illustrated in Figure 4, in which a disconnected graph represents certain relations among coworkers in a formal organization. Each component is a different office or subsidiary. While points *a*, *g*, and *m* are similar in their patterns of connection, they are not at all proximate. Conversely, the points *a*, *b*, *c*, *d*, *e*, and *f* are relatively proximate, but they are not similar. However, points *d* and *e*, which are structurally equivalent, are both proximate and similar.

4. POSITION AS STRUCTURAL ISOMORPHISM

Since automorphic equivalence depends crucially on the notion of isomorphism, we use the terms *automorphic equivalence* and *structural isomorphism* interchangeably. The notion of isomorphism is fundamental in many branches of mathematics, including graph

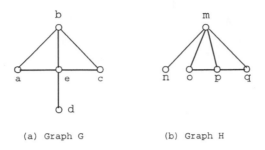

(a) Graph G   (b) Graph H

FIGURE 5. Graphs *G* and *H* are isomorphic.

theory. An isomorphism is a one-to-one mapping of one set of objects to another such that the relationships among the objects are also preserved. A graph isomorphism between two graphs *G* and *H* is a mapping $\pi:G{\rightarrow}H$ such that for all $a,b \in V(G)$, $(a,b) \in E(G) \leftrightarrow (\pi(a),\pi(b)) \in E(H)$. In other words, a graph isomorphism is a mapping of the nodes in one graph to corresponding nodes in another graph such that if two nodes are connected in one graph, then their correspondents in the second graph must also be connected. Two graphs are isomorphic if there exists an isomorphism that relates them. For example, the two graphs in Figure 5 are isomorphic because the mapping $\pi_1:G{\rightarrow}H$ (Table 1) is an isomorphism.

Isomorphic graphs are identical with respect to all graph-theoretic attributes. If a graph has twelve cliques of size 3 and ten cliques of size 4, then all graphs isomorphic to it also have twelve cliques of size 3 and ten cliques of size 4. The only possible differences between isomorphic graphs are the labels of the nodes and edges (if any).

TABLE 1
The Graph Isomorphism
$\pi_1:G{\rightarrow}H$, Relating the
Graphs in Figure 5

g	$\pi_1(g)$
a	*o*
b	*p*
c	*q*
d	*n*
e	*m*

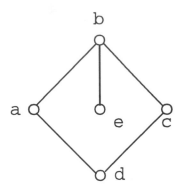

Graph K

FIGURE 6. Graph *K* is not isomorphic with any graph in Figure 5.

In fact, one way to think about isomorphic graphs is that without labels on the nodes or edges, they would be indistinguishable. If we removed the labels on the graphs in Figure 5, then picked the graphs up off the paper, shuffled them randomly, and then put them back on the paper, we would not be able to tell which graph was which. Nor, from a structural point of view, would it matter, since the graphs have the same structure.

On the other hand, graph *K* in Figure 6 is distinguishable from the graphs in Figure 5, even without the labels. Graphs *H* and *G* have a node with degree 4 while graph *K* does not. Note that it is not an issue of how the graphs are drawn (since the way a graph is drawn is arbitrary), but how they are structured, the pattern of their connections.

All graphs are isomorphic with themselves. That is, for all graphs, we can find a mapping $\pi:G \rightarrow G$ such that π is an isomorphism. An isomorphism of a structure with itself is known as an *automorphism*. Obviously, π can always be the identity mapping, where for all $v \in V$, $\pi(v) = v$. However, it is often the case that there exists an automorphism of *G* that is not the identity. For example, the graph in Figure 3 has three nontrivial automorphisms, which are visible as symmetries of the graph. One can see that if the labels were removed from the graph, a 180° rotation of the graph along the horizontal axis would be indistinguishable from the original. Similarly, a 180° rotation around the vertical axis would also leave the

TABLE 2

All Automorphisms of the Graph in Figure 3

v	$\pi1(v)$	$\pi2(v)$	$\pi3(v)$	$\pi4(v)$
a	h	c	j	a
b	g	d	i	b
c	j	a	h	c
d	i	b	g	d
e	f	e	f	e
f	e	f	e	f
g	b	i	d	g
h	a	j	c	h
i	d	g	b	i
j	c	h	a	j

graph unchanged. The third automorphism is a composition of the other two. Table 2 gives all automorphisms of the graph.

Two nodes a and b in a graph G are *structurally isomorphic* or *automorphically equivalent* if there exists an isomorphism $\pi:G{\to}G$ such that $\pi(a) = b$. Two actors occupy the same position if they are isomorphic. Sets of isomorphic actors are called *orbits*. In Figure 3, the orbits are $\{a,c,h,j\}$, $\{b,d,g,i\}$, and $\{e,f\}$. In contrast, the set of structurally equivalent points are $\{a,c\}$, $\{b,d\}$, $\{g,i\}$, and $\{h,j\}$.

Whereas the structural equivalence approach views two actors as occupying the same position only if they are connected to the same alters, the structural isomorphism approach (like regular equivalence) views actors as occupying the same position if they are connected to corresponding others. That is, if actors a and b are isomorphic, then for all $c \in V$, $(a,c) \in E$ implies there exists a node d isomorphic to c such that $(b,d) \in E$. Putting it another way, whereas the neighborhoods of structurally equivalent points contain the same actors, the neighborhoods of isomorphic actors contain the same positions. Technically, in the structural equivalence approach,

$$P(a) = P(b) \to N(a) = N(b),$$

whereas in the isomorphic and regular equivalence approaches,[7]

___

[7]It should be noted that this equation is true of structurally isomorphic nodes, but it is not a definition of automorphic equivalence. See Everett and Borgatti (1990) for details.

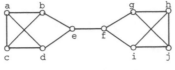

(a) Labels identify nodes

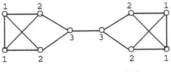

(b) Labels identify positions

FIGURE 7. Neighborhoods of isomorphic nodes contain the same positions, not the same nodes. $N(a) = \{b,c,d\}$, while $N(h) = \{g,i,j\}$, yet $P(N(a)) = P(N)(h)) = \{1,2\}$.

$$P(a) = P(b) \rightarrow P(N(a)) = P(N(b)).$$

Thus, in this approach, if actor a occupies the same position as actor b, then the set of positions that a's alters occupy is the same as the set of positions that b's alters occupy. An illustration is provided in Figure 7. Furthermore, the ego networks of isomorphic actors are also isomorphic. Not only is there a one-to-one correspondence between the nodes of each ego network, there is another one-to-one correspondence between the lines among them.

Like structurally equivalent nodes, isomorphic nodes are absolutely identical with respect to all structural variables. For example, in Figure 7a, nodes a, c, h, and j all have the same closeness centrality (Freeman 1978), graph-theoretic power index (Markovsky, Willer, and Patton 1988), prestige (Knoke and Burt 1983), and eccentricity (Harary 1969). They participate in exactly the same number of 2-clans, 3-cliques, and 4-clubs (Mokken 1979). They are connected to precisely the same number of nodes at distance 3. Unlike the case of structural equivalence, the converse is also true: All nodes that are identical with respect to all possible structural variables are necessarily isomorphic.

One way to think about isomorphic nodes is to remove the node labels from a graph, as in Figure 8a, to get an unlabeled graph, as in Figure 8b. Then imagine picking the unlabeled graph up off the

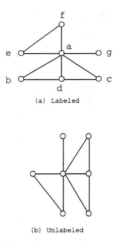

(a) Labeled

(b) Unlabeled

FIGURE 8. Labeled graph and underlying unlabeled graph.

paper, spinning it around a few times, and putting it down on a fresh piece of paper. Could we tell which node is which? Some nodes are obvious. Node *a*, for example, is easy to identify because it is the only node incident with six lines. Nodes *b* and *c*, in turn, are impossible to distinguish from each other but easy to distinguish from other nodes. A more interesting example is the graph in Figure 7a. In this graph, all nodes have equal degree. But no matter how the graph is drawn, certain structural differences among the nodes will be apparent. For example, whereas some nodes (*a*, *c*, *h*, and *j*) are five links distant from other nodes, two nodes (*e* and *f*) are no more than three links distant from any other nodes.

Unlike structural equivalence, structural isomorphism is independent of proximity. Isomorphic nodes may be adjacent, distant, or completely unreachable from each other. In a disconnected graph, nodes located in different components can be isomorphic, as shown in Figure 4. If the data in Figure 4 refer to relationships among coworkers in a formal organization, the components may refer to different offices or subsidiaries. Using structural isomorphism we can detect the similarity in position held by points *a* and *g*, or *b* and *h*.

In sum, structural equivalence and structural isomorphism are fundamentally different approaches to the notion of position. In the structural equivalence approach, position is seen quite literally as a location in a labeled graph. It is about identifying *who* an actor is directly connected to. In contrast, the structural isomorphism approach sees position as a location in an unlabeled graph. Since, by definition, nodes are not identifiable in an unlabeled graph except by the pattern of connections in which they are embedded, the location of a node in an unlabeled graph is the sum total of all structural characteristics that can be calculated for that node. It is, ultimately, the *way* in which the node is connected to others. If structurally equivalent actors occupy the same location, structurally isomorphic actors occupy analogous or isomorphic locations.

Abstracting a bit, we could say that in the structural equivalence approach, the network or labeled graph represents the underlying structure of a group; hence, an actor's location in that structure represents his or her position in the group. In contrast, in the structural isomorphism approach, the structure of interest is not the labeled graph itself, which is seen as the observed or "surface structure," but the structure of the surface structure, which is the unlabeled graph that underlies the labeled graph. It is the actor's location in this "deep structure," then, that represents his or her position in the group. Thus, structural equivalence is to labeled graphs what structural isomorphism is to unlabeled graphs. In the absence of a particular substantive application, we suggest that the choice between structural equivalence and structural isomorphism as measures of position rests entirely on which of the labeled or unlabeled representations best corresponds to one's intuitive concept of what *structure* means.

It is important to note that the difference between automorphic and structural equivalence is conceptual, theoretical, and fundamental: It is not that one is an approximation or computer-implementation of the other. We have found in informal discussions with colleagues that some believe that the purpose of algorithms like CONCOR (Breiger, Boorman, and Arabie 1975) and computer programs like STRUCTURE (Burt 1989) is to relax structural equivalence to get something akin to automorphic equivalence. This is not the case, as is easily verified by running a network such as Figure 3 through all these programs. Such programs do relax the definition of structural equivalence, but only to allow nodes that are not perfectly equivalent (i.e., that do not share absolutely every alter) to be considered equivalent; they will not find such points as *a* and *h* at all equivalent. Similarly, programs for computing regular equivalence, such as REGE (D. R. White 1984), and automorphic equivalence, such as MAXCORR (Borgatti 1987) or NSIM (Everett and Borgatti 1988), also relax their respective definitions, but the results will not resemble the output of CONCOR or STRUCTURE.

5. THE USE OF POSITION IN STRUCTURAL THEORY

In this section we consider ways in which the notion of position has been used in structural theory and discuss which type of position is best suited for each specific application. In the process, we give examples where the literature has confounded the two types of position, using structural equivalence for data analysis but interpreting results as if structural isomorphism had been used instead.

5.1. *Status/Role Systems*

Many authors (Lorrain and White 1971; Burt 1982; Sailer 1978; Winship and Mandel 1983; Faust 1988) have seen network equivalences as formalizations of the hallowed sociological concepts of status, position, role, and role-set.[8] Nadel (1957), Merton (1959), and Linton (1936) have all discussed social structure in terms of a "pattern or network (or 'system') of relationships obtaining between actors in their capacity of playing roles relative to one another" (Nadel 1957, p. 12). This relational approach to social structure, as distinguished from a normative approach, emphasizes that what defines a role, such as that of nurse, is precisely the characteristic set of relationships that actors who are nurses have with actors who are doctors, patients, suppliers, secretaries, other nurses, and so on, just as doctors are defined by their relationships with actors playing all the other roles. Society is a network of relationships among individuals, and social structure is an underlying network of relationships among roles or positions.

An illustration is given in Figure 9. Figure 9a records advice/order-giving relations among individuals in a doctor's office. Figure 9b collapses structurally similar actors (under both structural equivalence and isomorphism) into positions and records relations among the positions. Figure 9a describes the manifest society, while Figure 9b describes the underlying social structure.

---

[8]We use the terms *role, status,* and *role-set* synonymously, since their differences do not bear on the issues of this paper.

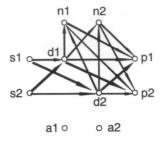

(a) The "gives information about medicine" relation

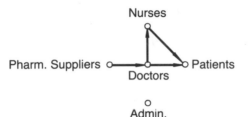

(b) Relations among positions

FIGURE 9. Relations in a doctor's office.

Note that in this example, both structural equivalence and isomorphism yield the same position, so they are equally applicable. In Figure 10, however, we have a slightly different doctor's office in which each doctor has his or her own nurse and patients. Now the doctors are no longer structurally equivalent, although they remain isomorphic. Figure 11a collapses structurally equivalent nodes into positions. Note that we no longer have a single position corresponding to the role of doctor, nor a single position corresponding to the role of secretary. In contrast, Figure 11b collapses structurally isomorphic nodes, yielding the same social structure as in Figure 9b.

As models of roles and social structure in general, structural equivalence and isomorphism are clearly different: According to structural equivalence, two actors must have the same relationships with the same *individuals* to be regarded as playing the same role, whereas according to structural isomorphism, they must have the same relationships with counterparts who are playing the same roles.

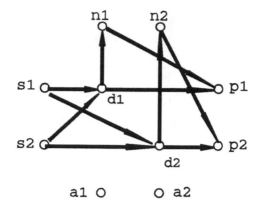

FIGURE 10. The "gives information about medicine" relation.

In other words, structural equivalence requires that two mothers have the *same* children to both be called mothers, and that two doctors have the same patients, nurses, and secretaries to both be doctors. Structural isomorphism, on the other hand, requires only that two mothers have the same relationships with their own children, and that two doctors have the same relationships with their own patients, nurses, and secretaries.

Hence, if we are interested in modeling social roles in the sense of Nadel and Merton, we must choose structural isomorphism over structural equivalence.[9] Even better, we should prefer a generalization of structural isomorphism, such as iterated automorphic equivalence (Everett et al. 1990) or regular equivalence. Substantively, the principal difference between structural isomorphism and regular equivalence is in the way in which quantities of ties are handled. For example, according to structural isomorphism, a mother with one child is different from a mother with 10 children, but according to regular equivalence, they are the same. Thus, regular equivalence can be used to get at more abstract aspects of roles. Which specific abstract equivalence is needed is not the issue here: The important point is that

---

[9]However, if one is interested in a more circumscribed notion of role, structural equivalence may be the most appropriate. For example, mothers and fathers of the same children jointly play the role of parent to those particular children, and they are structurally equivalent. Similarly, siblings are children of the same parent and are structurally equivalent.

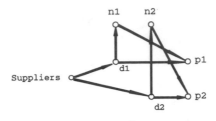

(a) Structurally equivalent positions

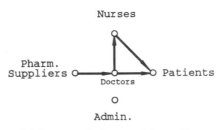

(b) Structurally isomorphic positions

FIGURE 11. Relations among positions in a doctor's office.

all are preferable to structural equivalence, which is not designed to model this sort of phenomenon.

Historically, however, researchers needing to operationalize concepts of social role, status, and role-set have employed structural equivalence. For example, in analyzing networks of supreme courts, Caldeira (1988, p. 46) claimed, "Even more important, if a researcher uses structural equivalence as a criterion, he can identify positions, or sets of individuals, that correspond to social roles in the network of communication." This misidentification of structural equivalence with social roles and positions is particularly unfortunate because role theory is often used as a template for building theory about a variety of social phenomena. Studies relying upon such concepts then mistakenly use structural equivalence to operationalize the key variable. For example, several authors (Evan 1966; Burt 1979; Galaskiewicz and Krohn 1984; DiMaggio 1986; H. C. White 1988) have seen economic systems and interorganizational networks as role systems. As Galaskiewicz and Krohn (1984) put it,

> A key concept in our study is the social role. . . .
> Two actors are in the same relative position in social
> space, i.e., have the same role, to the extent that
> they have similar relationships to others in the social
> arena or fields. . . . To phrase this in the context of
> resource dependency theory, two actors occupy the
> same structural position, i.e., role in the network, to
> the extent that they are dependent upon the same
> organizations for the procurement of needed input
> resources and the same actors are dependent upon
> them for their output resources. (Pp. 528–29)

Galaskiewicz and Krohn went on to use structural equivalence
to identify organizational roles (p. 532). Another example is provided by Burt (1979), who described economic sectors as sets of
structurally equivalent positions:

> An economy can be discussed as a network of eco-
> nomic transactions, relations, between corporate ac-
> tors; an interorganizational network of sales and pur-
> chases. The division of labor ensures a high level of
> redundancy in this network. Those actors engaged in
> the production of similar goods will have similar rela-
> tions from other actors (i.e., will require similar propor-
> tions of goods as inputs from suppliers) and will have
> similar relations to other actors (i.e., will offer similar
> types of goods as outputs to consumers). Viewing
> the economy as an interorganizational network, those
> firms producing similar types of goods are structurally
> equivalent and so jointly occupy a single "position" in
> the economy. The economic transactions between indi-
> vidual firms therefore can be aggregated into relations
> between groups of structurally equivalent firms so as to
> create a topological model of the economy. In the termi-
> nology of the Bureau of the Census, these structurally
> equivalent firms constitute "sectors" of the economy,
> or "industries" in the economy. (P. 417)

However, since firms in a given sector may purchase from
similar suppliers but not necessarily from the *same* suppliers, and

since they may sell to similar clients but not necessarily to the *same* clients, structurally equivalent firms cannot possibly constitute sectors, though structurally isomorphic (and particularly regularly equivalent) firms might. Empirical studies hoping to confirm hypotheses based on the kind of reasoning used by Burt will fail if they operationalize position as structural equivalence. It is important to note that there is nothing wrong with either the proposed image of an economy or the notion of structural equivalence in themselves: It is merely that the latter cannot be used as a model for the former.

Similarly, Snyder and Kick (1979) used role theory to justify their use of structural equivalence to define positions of nations in the world economy. Since world system/dependency theory uses concepts of position and role (Wallerstein 1974), and since structural equivalence has been claimed to find positions and roles, it is not surprising that someone would use structural equivalence to operationalize world system theory. The problem, of course, is that two nations that occupy the same position (say, "core") may have similar relations with other positions (say, "periphery"), but not necessarily the same nations. This point is also made by Smith and White (1986). For example, nation A might purchase certain agricultural products from Guatemala, electronic products from Japan, and engineering expertise from Germany. Nation B might purchase agricultural products from Honduras, electronic goods from Taiwan, and engineering from France. If it happens that Guatemala and Honduras occupy the same position in the world system, and Japan and Taiwan and, separately, Germany and France do as well, then from the point of view of a role system, A and B exhibit the same relational pattern and so play the same role. But from the point of view of structural equivalence, A and B are completely unalike.

It is not unusual in the literature for researchers to use structural equivalence programs to process their data but then to justify and explain the method as if structural isomorphism were used instead. For example, DiMaggio (1986) used structural equivalence to identify organizations with similar organizational fields:

> The alternative means of partitioning a population on the basis of observed relations among the population's members is to divide the population into structurally equivalent positions: Organizations in each

subset (or block) share similar relations with organizations in other blocks whether or not they are connected to one another. Imagine a population of organizations connected by flows of personnel and information. One subset of this population (A) recruits
personnel from and provides information to another
subset of the population (B). Organizations in Subset A never exchange information or personnel with
one another, nor do organizations in Subset B. Organizations in each subset exchange only with organizations in the other; but, within the subset with
which they exchange, their choices of partners are
random. (P. 344)

It is DiMaggio's final sentence that is of particular interest,
since it is certainly false if applied to structural equivalence but potentially true if applied to structural isomorphism. From the perspective
of philosophy of science, it is interesting to note that three types of
systems are implied by DiMaggio's discussion. First, there is the
"real" interorganizational network in which individual organizations
have links of various kinds with other individual organizations. Second, there is the simplified model of the researcher, in which underlying types of organizations (positions) are hypothesized such that all
organizations of one type have the same set of relations with organizations of other types, though not necessarily with the same individual organizations. Third, there is the operationalization of this model
via structural equivalence. In most scientific research, the deepest
problems probably occur in the generation of the second system,
which is essentially a theory or explanation of the observed relationships. However, in DiMaggio's case, the problem occurs with the
third system, in which the theory is incorrectly operationalized.

5.2. Power in Experimental Exchange Networks

There are two well-known streams of work in this area, represented by the work of Cook et al. (1983), on the one hand, and the
work of Markovsky et al. (1988), on the other. Since both use the
notion of position in the same way, for our purposes it suffices to
describe only the first approach.

The explicit objective of Cook et al. is to investigate structural power: The power that one individual has over another is a function of the extent to which each is dependent on the other for unnamed goods (Emerson 1962). Dependency is a function of demand (how much each individual needs the goods that others can provide) and supply (the number of individuals who can supply the goods). In the context of network analysis, demand may be viewed as an internal, individualistic, nonstructural attribute of actors. In contrast, supply may be viewed as an external function of the structural position of a node in the network. To investigate only the structural, supply-side of power, Cook et al. designed their experiments so that all actors had equal demand.

The appropriate notion of position in this context is structural isomorphism. If power, as expressed in these particular experimental designs, is a purely structural attribute, then sets of isomorphic actors must have equal power, since isomorphic actors are by definition identical with respect to all structural attributes. We can think of power in this context as the outcome of a purely structural process (exchange), which cannot contradict the classification of actors by automorphism classes. If it does, then the experimental design has not succeeded in filtering out all the nonstructural elements of the process, such as individual variations in competence, motivation, and resources, of which the latter two are components of the demand side of dependency. In this sense, the notion of structural isomorphism can be used to diagnose the presence of nonstructural elements in a process, in the "same" way that models based on the marginals of contingency tables can diagnose the presence of interactions among variables.

We can infer that both sets of researchers have recognized intuitively that structural isomorphism is the appropriate notion of position in this context because they invariably label positions in a way consistent with isomorphism and inconsistent with structural equivalence. However, this must remain an inference, since they do not address the issue directly. Markovsky et al. (1988) defined position (rather vaguely) as follows:

> Positions are network locations occupied by actors.
> A relation between two positions is an exchange opportunity for actors in those positions. In short,

actors occupy positions linked by relations. We will index both actors and position using uppercase letters and at times refer to them interchangeably. (P. 223)

Similarly, Cook and Emerson (1978) provided the following anti-definition:

People in structurally similar locations are said to occupy the same position. We will provide no explicit definition of position until the theory becomes more formal, at which point it will be given a graph-theoretic definition. (P. 725n)

A later paper (Cook et al. 1983) defined position as "a set of one or more points whose residual graphs are isomorphic." The reason for defining position in this way is left unstated, but as Everett et al. (1990) have shown, it can be regarded as an (inaccurate) approximation to structural isomorphism. Substituting structural isomorphism for their *ad hoc* definition would put that portion of their work on a more solid mathematical foundation.

Structural equivalence would not be an appropriate approach to this position in this case because there is nothing in the (present) theoretical formulation of power in exchange networks that demands that nodes of equal power be connected to precisely the same others. For example, in Figure 12, equal power is predicted by both major theories for all points labeled E, even though they are quite distant from each other. It is not that structural equivalence yields wrong predictions (it does not), but that it fails to make most of the predictions that can be made. In this example, all nodes F have equal power, but since some are more than one intermediary apart, they are not structurally equivalent, and structural equivalence cannot predict the observed power homogeneity of all Fs. Similarly, all E nodes have equal power, but again structural equivalence cannot predict this, this time because each is connected to nodes that the others are not connected to. In general, structural equivalence reacts to nonstructural elements and hence fails to predict homogeneity for the outcome of any truly structural process.

It is important to note that what makes structural isomor-

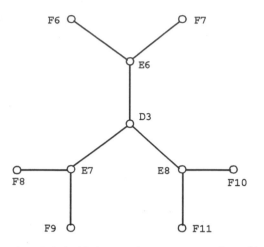

FIGURE 12. All nodes labeled with the same letter are expected to achieve similar levels of power. Adapted from Cook et al. (1983, p. 280).

phism the right concept here and structural equivalence the wrong concept is not the phenomenon of power: It may well be that equality of power in natural exchange networks is better predicted by structural equivalence than by structural isomorphism. That is, it may be that collections of actors who are both proximate and structurally similar are the most likely to achieve similar power levels for a host of substantive reasons, including the opportunity for alliance formation. But the way Cook et al. and Markovsky et al. have designed their experiments, the only components of power that are availabe to the subjects are the purely structural aspects. The aptness of this description is particularly evident in the work of Markovsky et al. They argued that power is a positive function of the number of odd-length, nonintersecting paths, and a negative function of the number of even-length, nonintersecting paths. These are entirely structural attributes. Consequently, in these experiments it does not matter *who* actors are connected to, but *how* they are connected.[10]

[10]A key implication of their results is that a node's power in an exchange network is a global, structural property that depends, recursively, on the power of the node's potential trading partners, which in turn depends on the power of their set of partners, and so on. If a node is connected only to powerful others, it cannot be powerful. This contrasts with Emerson's (1962) simple dependency theory, which implies that the more trading partners an actor has, the greater his or her power.

This is precisely the difference between structural equivalence and structural isomorphism.

More broadly, the important difference between structural isomorphism and structural equivalence is that each implies a different type of mechanism by which homogeneity across subsets of actors with respect to a key substantive outcome is achieved. Structural isomorphism is the right concept for modeling power in experimental exchange networks because the mechanism by which equality of power is achieved is entirely structural and unrelated to proximity. In contrast, structural isomorphism is the wrong concept for modeling the outcome of any kind of infectious process, such as homogeneity with respect to gossip heard or diseases suffered, because such processes are not entirely structural and depend crucially on proximity. Conversely, structural equivalence is wrong for modeling any homogeneity that is achieved by a noninfectious type of mechanism.

5.3. *Social Homogeneity*

In their classic study of innovation, Coleman, Katz, and Menzel (1957) used a network approach to explain adoption of a new drug among physicians. The idea was that while any given physician has a certain probability of adopting a new drug using information he or she may have gathered from manufacturers and published studies, the probability is increased if he or she knows another physician who has already adopted the drug. This relational or cohesive approach asserts that at least one causal mechanism underlying social homogeneity is a process of direct infection or transmission similar to the spread of gossip or disease. This assertion implies that groups of physicians who are closely connected are likely to be more homogeneous with respect to adoption of the new drug than are collections of physicians who are not closely connected. Consequently, we expect co-membership in cohesive subsets such as cliques to predict similar outcomes with respect to adoption.

There has been some interest in the literature (Burt 1978; Burt and Doreian 1982; Friedkin 1984; DiMaggio 1986; Burt 1987; Erickson 1988; Hartman and Johnson 1990) in evaluating whether the cohesive or the positional approach is the better predictor of certain forms of social homogeneity. At the substantive level, the question is which is the most effective mechanism of achieving homogeneity: person-to-person infection or some other mechanism such as imitation of one's peers. However, the debate is clouded by the use of structural equivalence as the definition of position. One problem with this choice is the assumption that structural equivalence is conceptually and empirically different from cohesion. It is not. As we have discussed earlier, sets of structurally equivalent actors form a kind of cohesive subset known as a 2-clique. Hence, if we take a structural equivalence approach to defining position, we cannot logically test whether position is a better predictor than cohesive subset membership. At best, we can choose between two kinds of cohesive subsets.[11]

Another problem concerns the linkage between the choice of network models (cohesion versus structural equivalence) and the choice of theoretical explanatory mechanisms (direct infection versus imitation or other mechanisms). At first glance it might appear that we could statistically partial out the cohesive component of structural equivalence. Friedkin (1984) attempted exactly this. Noting that direct connections among structurally equivalent actors confound the comparison with cohesive subsets, Friedkin partialed out these effects and found that structural equivalence loses a great deal of its predictive power. However, as Friedkin noted, removing the effects of direct connections is not nearly enough, since structurally equivalent actors will still share all of their contacts. If any or all of these contacts are infected, we would still expect structurally equivalent actors to be homogeneous. Consequently, both cohesive/relational and structural equivalence approaches are consistent with the mechanism of infection/transmission, and choosing one over the other does not necessitate a different explanatory mechanism.[12]

Friedkin also attempted to control for the number of shared contacts or two-step paths connecting equivalent actors. However, it is

[11]See Borgatti, Everett, and Shirey (1990) for a discussion of the different definitions of cohesive subsets.

[12]On the other hand, relational and structural equivalence approaches do not necessarily imply the same causal mechanisms. This point was made convincingly by Burt (1987, p. 1293n), who realized that "a vulgar understanding of structural equivalence views [diffusion] by structural equivalence to be no more than an indirect effect of cohesion." He dismissed this view on empirical grounds because, unlike Friedkin (1984), Burt found no evidence in the *Medical Innovation* data for diffusion via direct connections. He therefore concluded that the ability of structural equivalence to predict homogeneity could not be due to an infection-type mechanism.

impossible to control for all two-step paths because no actors (except isolates) can be structurally equivalent and yet share no contacts! Ultimately, the notion of structural equivalence without proximity is meaningless: It is an inseparable part of the concept.[13] Therefore, if we are truly interested in noncohesive (or, substantively, noninfectious) determinants of social homogeneity, we cannot use structural equivalence. Instead, we should use structural isomorphism, which measures structural similarity unconfounded by proximity.

Unlike structural equivalence, isomorphism entails a different theoretical explanation for diffusion than that posited by the relational or cohesion-based approach. In particular, the mechanism cannot depend upon interpersonal transmission of any kind, since isomorphic actors need not be connected even indirectly. An example is a centrality-based explanation, on the hunch that physicians who are peripheral to the medical community might be more likely to adopt than physicians who are more central. Adopting the latest medical advances might be a way for marginal physicians to gain prestige and attention and thereby move toward the center. Similarly, central physicians might be slow to adopt innovations that could make unwelcome changes to the status quo. Another mechanism might be the similar responses we expect from similarly constructed organisms to similar environments. For example, if certain respondents achieve similar scores in a psychometric test that measures, let's say, authoritarianism, it might be because they have the same combinations of relationships with their respective parents, bosses, and spouses, yielding similar experiences and opportunities and ultimately similar personality characteristics.

In reality, non-transmission-based mechanisms of the sort illustrated above might not exist, or if they do exist, their effects might be negligible compared with the powerful forces of person-to-person transmission. If so, cohesive subsets of actors will evince greater homogeneity than sets of isomorphic actors, and we shall be able to conclude that the relational approach predicts better than a posi-

[13]However, this is not to say that there aren't kinds of cohesive subgroups that are more cohesive than structural equivalence. Sets of structurally equivalent actors are 2-cliques, which were introduced by Luce (1950) with the express purpose of relaxing the extreme cohesiveness required by the clique concept (Luce and Perry 1949). Since that time, other cohesive subset definitions have appeared, which are intermediate in cohesiveness between true cliques and n-cliques (Alba 1973; Mokken 1979; Seidman and Foster 1978).

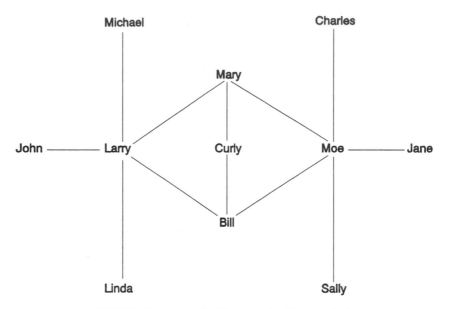

FIGURE 13. Mary and Bill are structurally equivalent.

tional approach. If both structural similarity and cohesion are important determinants of diffusion, then structural equivalence could well
emerge as the more powerful predictor.

From the point of view of building structural theory in general, however, we must be careful when using structural equivalence as an independent variable. Because it necessarily confounds
structural similarity with proximity, it is conceptually inelegant.
Moreover, it prevents evaluation of the relative contributions of
structural similarity and cohesion to predicting the outcome variable. A cleaner and more useful alternative is to use both cohesion
and structural isomorphism as theoretically orthogonal independent
variables, thereby separating the components of structural equivalence while not losing the benefits of either.

There is another advantage of structural isomorphism over
structural equivalence in building structural theory. Suppose we expect actors occupying the same position to have similar outcomes
with respect to a particular variable of interest. For example, we are
interested in testing the hypothesis that position in the social-support
network at a nursing home predicts the number of visits required by a

doctor. Suppose we operationalize position as structural equivalence, check the correspondence between position and outcome, and find that the hypothesis is supported. For example, suppose it turns out that Bill and Mary in Figure 13 both require a great deal of medical attention. The critical question from the point of view of structural theory is whether the similar result is due to some structural feature of their position (such as being the only bridges between two sets of actors) or to their being connected to the same three maddening individuals, named Moe, Curly, and Larry, and only these three. With structural equivalence, we cannot distinguish between these two possibilities because every member of a set of structurally equivalent actors is connected to the same unique combination of individuals. In this sense, structural equivalence is highly particularistic and individualistic and not, in this sense, structural. Isomorphism, in contrast, is purely structural. The effects of structural similarity are never confounded with the effects of specific individuals. For example, if in Figure 13 the isomorphic actors Michael, John, Linda, Charles, Jane, and Sally all have the same medical outcomes, then we can reasonably infer that it is due to some structural attribute of their common position, such as being peripheral.

6. SUMMARY

We have attempted to detail the differences between structural equivalence and more-abstract equivalences, focusing on the abstract equivalence most comparable to structural equivalence, which is structural isomorphism. Whereas structural equivalence defines position in terms of who an actor knows, structural isomorphism defines it in terms of the way an actor is connected. Whereas structurally equivalent actors are both proximate and similar, structurally isomorphic actors are only similar. Among methodologists, these distinctions have long been understood. However, the implications for building sociological theory have not previously been drawn out. For example, we have pointed out that while cohesive/relational and structural equivalence approaches to social homogeneity do not demand that different causal mechanisms be posited, cohesion and structural isomorphism almost always do. We have also pointed out, echoing Sailer (1978), that structural equivalence should not be used to model role systems, despite numerous studies that do just that.

REFERENCES

Alba, R. D. 1973. "A Graph-Theoretic Definition of a Sociometric Clique." *Journal of Mathematical Sociology* 3:133–26.

Anderson, J. G., and S. J. Jay. 1985. "The Diffusion of Medical Terminology: Social Network Analysis and Policy Research." *Sociological Quarterly* 26: 49–64.

Borgatti, S. P. 1987. *User's Manual for AL: Analytic Language.* Irvine: University of California, School of Social Sciences.

Borgatti, S. P., J. P. Boyd, and M. G. Everett. 1989. "Iterated Roles: Mathematics and Application." *Social Networks* 11:159–72.

Borgatti, S. P., and M. G. Everett. 1989. "The Class of All Regular Equivalences: Algebraic Structure and Computation." *Social Networks* 11:65–88.

Borgatti, S. P., M. G. Everett, and P. R. Shirey. 1990. "LS Sets, Lambda Sets and Other Cohesive Subsets." *Social Networks* 12:337–57.

Breiger, R. L. 1981. "Structures of Economic Interdependence Among Nations." Pp. 353–80 in *Continuities in Structural Inquiry,* edited by P. M. Blau and R. Merton. New York: Free Press.

Breiger, R. L., S. Boorman, and P. Arabie. 1975. "An Algorithm for Clustering Relational Data with Applications to Social Network Analysis." *Journal of Mathematical Psychology* 12:329–83.

Breiger, R. L., and P. E. Pattison. 1986. "Cumulated Social Roles: The Duality of Persons and their Algebras." *Social Networks* 8:215–56.

Brym, R. J. 1988. "Structural Location and Ideological Divergence: Jewish Marxist Intellectuals in Turn-of-the-Century Russia." Pp. 359–79 in *Social Structures,* edited by B. Wellman and S. D. Berkowitz. Cambridge: Cambridge University Press.

Burt, R. S. 1976. "Positions in Networks." *Social Forces* 55:93–122.

———. 1978. "Cohesion Versus Structural Equivalence as a Basis for Network Subgroups." *Sociological Methods and Research* 7:189–212.

———. 1979. "A Structural Theory of Interlocking Corporate Directorates." *Social Networks* 1:415–35.

———. 1982. *Toward a Structural Theory of Action.* New York: Academic Press.

———. 1987. "Social Contagion and Innovation: Cohesion Versus Structural Equivalence." *American Journal of Sociology* 92:1287–1335.

———. 1989. STRUCTURE Version 4.0. New York: Columbia University, Research Program in Structural Analysis.

Burt, R. S., and P. Doreian. 1982. "Testing a Structural Model of Perception: Conformity and Deviance with Respect to Journal Norms in Elite Sociological Methodology." *Quality and Quantity* 16:109–50.

Caldeira, G. A. 1988. "Legal Precedent: Structures of Communication Between State Supreme Courts." *Social Networks* 10:29–55.

Coleman, J., E. Katz, and H. Menzel. 1957. "The Diffusion of an Innovation Among Physicians." *Sociometry* 20:253–70.

Cook, K. S., and R. M. Emerson. 1978. "Power, Equity and Commitment in Exchange Networks." *American Sociological Review* 43:721–39.

Cook, K. S., R. M. Emerson, M. R. Gillmore, and T. Yamagishi. 1983. "The Distribution of Power in Exchange Networks: Theory and Experimental Results." *American Journal of Sociology* 89:275–305.

DiMaggio, P. 1986. "Structural Analysis of Organizational Fields: A Blockmodel Approach." *Research in Organizational Behavior* 8:335–70.

Emerson, R. M. 1962. "Power-Dependence Relations." *American Sociological Review* 27:31–40.

Erickson, B. H. 1988. "The Relational Basis of Attitudes." Pp. 99–122 in *Social Structures*, edited by B. Wellman and S. D. Berkowitz. Cambridge: Cambridge University Press.

Evan, W. M. 1966. "The Organization-Set: Toward a Theory of Interorganizational Relations." Pp. 173–91 in *Approaches to Organizational Design*, edited by J. D. Thompson. New York: McGraw Hill.

Everett, M. G. 1985. "Role Similarity and Complexity in Social Networks." *Social Networks* 7:353–59.

Everett, M. G., and S. P. Borgatti. 1988. "Calculating Role Similarities: An Algorithm that Helps Determine the Orbits of a Graph." *Social Networks* 10:77–92.

―――. 1990. "Any Colour You Like It." *Connections* 13:19–22.

Everett, M. G., J. P. Boyd, and S. P. Borgatti. 1990. "Ego-Centered and Local Roles: A Graph-Theoretic Approach." *Journal of Mathematical Sociology* 15:163–72.

Faust, K. 1988. "Comparison of Methods for Positional Analysis: Structural and General Equivalences." *Social Networks* 10:313–41.

Freeman, L. C. 1978. "Centrality in Social Networks: Conceptual Clarification." *Social Networks* 1:215–39.

Friedkin, N. E. 1984. "Structural Cohesion and Equivalence Explanations of Social Homogeneity." *Sociological Methods and Research* 12:235–61.

Galaskiewicz, J., and K. R. Krohn. 1984. "Positions, Roles, and Dependencies in a Community Integration System." *Sociological Quarterly* 25:527–50.

Harary, F. 1969. *Graph Theory.* Reading, MA: Addison-Wesley.

Hartman, R. L., and J. D. Johnson. 1990. "Social Contagion and Multiplexity: Communication Networks as Predictors of Commitment and Role Ambiguity," *Human Communication Research* 15:523–48.

Hofstadter, D. R. 1985. *Metamagical Themas: Questing for the Essence of Mind and Pattern.* New York: Basic Books.

Hummell, H., and W. Sodeur. 1987. "Strukturbeschreibung von Positionen in sozialen Beziehungsnetzen." Pp. 1–21 in *Methoden der Netzwerkanalayse,* edited by F. U. Pappi. Munich: Oldenbourg.

Kadushin, C. 1982. "Social Density and Mental Health." Pp. 147–58 in *Social Structure and Network Analysis,* edited by P. V. Marsden and N. Lin. Beverly Hills: Sage Publications.

Knoke, D., and R. S. Burt. 1983. "Prominence." Pp. 195–222 in *Applied Network Analysis,* edited by R. S. Burt and M. J. Minor. Newbury Park, CA: Sage Publications.

Krackhardt, D., and L. W. Porter. 1986. "The Snowball Effect: Turnover

Embedded in Communication Networks." *Journal of Applied Psychology* 71:50–55.

Krippendorff, K. 1971. "Communication and the Genesis of Structure." *General Systems* 16:171–85.

Leavitt, H. J. 1951. "Some Effects of Certain Communication Patterns on Group Performance." *Journal of Abnormal and Social Psychology* 46:38–50.

Linton, Ralph. 1936. *The Study of Man.* New York: Appleton-Century.

Lorrain, F. P., and H. C. White. 1971. "Structural Equivalence of Individuals in Networks." *Journal of Mathematical Sociology* 1:49–80.

Luce, R. D. 1950. "Connectivity and Generalized Cliques in Sociometric Group Structure." *Psychometrika* 15:169–90.

Luce, R. D., and A. D. Perry. 1949. "A Method of Matrix Analysis of Group Structure." *Psychometrika* 14:95–116.

Markovsky, B., D. Willer, and T. Patton. 1988. "Power Relations in Exchange Networks." *American Sociological Review* 53:220–36.

Merton, R. K. 1959. *Social Theory and Social Structure.* Glencoe, IL: Free Press.

Mokken, R. J. 1979. "Cliques, Clubs and Clans." *Quality and Quantity* 13:161–73.

Nadel, S. F. 1957. *The Theory of Social Structure.* London: Cohen and West.

Nemeth, R., and D. Smith. 1985. "International Trade and World-System Structure: A Multiple Network Analysis." *Review* 8:517–60.

Pattison, P. E. 1988. "Network Models: Some Comments on Papers in this Special Issue." *Social Networks* 10:383–411.

Pitts, F. R. 1978. "The Medieval River Trade Network of Russia Revisited." *Social Networks* 1:285–92.

Rogers, E. M. 1979. "Network Analysis of the Diffusion of Innovations." Pp. 137–64 in *Perspectives in Social Network Research,* edited by P. W. Holland and S.Leinhardt. New York: Academic Press.

Sailer, L. D. 1978. "Structural Equivalence: Meaning and Definition, Computation and Application." *Social Networks* 1:73–90.

Seidman, S. B., and B. L. Foster 1978. "A Graph-Theoretic Generalization of the Clique Concept." *Journal of Mathematical Sociology* 6:139–54.

Smith, D. A., and D. R. White. 1986. "Dynamic Analysis of International Trade and World-System Structure 1965–1980." Paper presented at the *Sunbelt International Network Conference,* San Diego.

Snyder, D., and E. L. Kick. 1979. "Structural Position in the World System and Economic Growth, 1955–1970: A Multiple-Network Analysis of Transnational Interactions." *American Journal of Sociology* 84:1096–1126.

Wallerstein, Immanuel. 1974. *The Modern World System.* New York: Academic Press.

Wellman, B. 1988. "Structural Analysis: From Method and Metaphor to Theory and Substance." Pp. 19–61 in *Social Structures,* edited by B. Wellman and S. D. Berkowitz. Cambridge: Cambridge University Press.

White, D. R. 1984. "REGGE: A Regular Graph Equivalence Algorithm for

Computing Role Distances Prior to Blockmodeling." Unpublished manuscript, University of California, Irvine.

White, D. R., and K. P. Reitz. 1983. "Graph and Semigroup Homomorphisms on Networks of Relations." *Social Networks* 5:193–235.

White, H. C. 1988. "Varieties of Markets." Pp. 226–60 in *Social Structures,* edited by B. Wellman and S. D. Berkowitz. Cambridge: Cambridge University Press.

White, H. C., S. A. Boorman, and R. L. Breiger. 1976. "Social Structure from Multiple Networks: I. Blockmodels of Roles and Positions." *American Journal of Sociology* 81: 730–80.

Winship, Christopher. 1988. "Thoughts about Roles and Relations: An Old Document Revisited." *Social Networks* 10:209–31.

Winship, Christopher, and M.J. Mandel. 1983. "Roles and Positions: A Critique and Extension of the Blockmodeling Approach." Pp. 314–44 in *Sociological Methodology 1983–84,* edited by S. Leinhardt. San Francisco: Jossey-Bass.

❦ 2 ❦

THE DISCOVERY OF GROUNDED UNCERTAINTY: DEVELOPING STANDARDIZED QUESTIONS ABOUT STRENGTH OF FERTILITY MOTIVATION

Nora Cate Schaeffer*
Elizabeth Thomson*

In survey interviews, expressions of uncertainty about subjective phenomena result from the interaction between the respondent's "true" answer and the structure of the survey task. The first kind of uncertainty, state uncertainty, is important in conceptualizing the theoretical construct under study. Task uncertainty raises operational issues, such as whether to use filter questions and which response alternatives to offer respondents. Analysis of a series of answers to open questions concerning feelings about having and not having children reveals that re-

This research was supported in part by National Institutes of Health grant HD-23898. Computing was provided by the University of Wisconsin Center for Demography and Ecology, which receives core support from the Center for Population Research of the National Institute for Child Health and Human Development (HD-5876). We thank Kristin Barker, James L. Baughman, Mary Lou Brady, Peter Marsden, Douglas Maynard, and the reviewers for their very helpful comments and suggestions; Kristin Barker, Chuck Benesh, Debbie Buettner, Pascale Carayon, Michael Carman, Wendy Manning, Raka Ray, and Emily Read for their help in conducting this research; and Corey Keyes for his assistance in the final stages. An earlier version of this paper was presented at the Annual Meetings of the American Association for Public Opinion Research, St. Petersburg, Florida, May 1989. Opinions expressed herein are solely those of the authors.

*University of Wisconsin, Madison

spondents' feelings may have low intensity or be unclear, and that respondents may be ambivalent or indecisive. Any of these states may lead respondents to express uncertainty. We propose standardized response categories to record spontaneous expressions of uncertainty as well as questions to measure these uncertainty dimensions directly. Data are provided by face-to-face semistructured interviews with a randomly selected sample of 18 and by CATI interviews with approximately 440. Both samples were Wisconsin adults aged 18-34.

1. INTRODUCTION

Standardized survey questions for measuring feelings or other subjective states frequently elicit respondent uncertainty. In interviews, respondents may express uncertainty by saying "I don't know" or by commenting "I don't really have any feelings about that," "that doesn't apply to me," "I'm not sure how to answer," or "it depends." Respondents may express uncertainty in a self-administered questionnaire by simply skipping the item. Such responses are usually lumped together in a "don't know" (DK), middle, or low-intensity category, depending on the type of question. In most cases, they are excluded from analysis, and only sometimes are their methodological or substantive implications examined.

Most respondents who express uncertainty are uncertain of their "true" state (state uncertainty) or are not sure how to communicate their true state using the standardized response categories (task uncertainty). State uncertainty is important for conceptualizing the construct under study. The theory of the construct should specify the role of uncertainty and distinguish among different states that may generate uncertainty, such as neutrality, lack of clarity, or ambivalence. Task uncertainty indicates problems with the survey instrument.

State and task uncertainty are not independent of each other. Expressions of uncertainty are produced by the interaction between the respondent's true state and the content and format of a question. Since most structured survey items and interviewer instructions discourage expressions of uncertainty, respondents whose true state is uncertain may experience even more task uncertainty than those whose known states cannot be easily expressed by using the structured items. Accurate measurement using standardized questions requires that researchers (a) identify types of state uncertainty that are relevant for a construct, (b) incorporate these states in the conceptualization of the construct, and (c) develop standardized questions that allow respondents to express relevant types of state uncertainty and that minimize task uncertainty.

We know something about state uncertainty (and resulting task uncertainty) from studies of DK and middle response categories of standardized questions. Several investigators found that these responses can have several meanings and have attempted to identify them (see Coombs and Coombs 1976; DuBois and Burns 1975; Duncan and Stenbeck 1988; Edwards 1946; Faulkenberry and Mason 1978; Goldberg 1981; Kaplan 1972; Klopfer and Madden 1980; Schuman and Presser 1981, pp. 143–45, 177–78). For example, Edwards (1946, p. 162) found that a statement rated neutral could be any of the following: ambiguous (statements with different interpretations), irrelevant (statements extraneous to the dimension being measured), indifferent (statements expressing lack of concern with the issue), and ambivalent (statements expressing indecision). Similarly, Klopfer and Madden (1980, p. 98) distinguished four different states that could be placed in the middle of the response continuum: ambivalence ("sometimes you feel one way and sometimes you feel another"), uncertainty ("you are just not able to identify your feelings"), neutrality ("you don't care one way or the other"), and nonspecific ("you just cannot decide").

Research with standardized surveys also illustrates several ways uncertainty may be integrated, either explicitly or implicitly, into the conceptualization and operationalization of a construct. If the construct is modeled as a set of classes, uncertainty classes may be added. For example, respondents may be offered the choices "yes," "no," and "uncertain." If the construct is thought of as a continuum, the continuum may be modeled as contingent on an uncertainty dimension. This is essentially what filter questions for opinion items do (e.g., Schuman and Presser 1981; Bishop, Oldendick, and Tuchfarber 1983). Filter questions imply that there is a separate opinion or knowledge dimension that conditions evaluations of an object, and they supply a substantive interpretation for the conditioning dimension. (Converse [1970, p. 180] made a similar proposal in a discussion of nonattitudes.) For example, the "no opinion" filter identifies a group distinct from those who say "not sure" to the subsequent opinion item (Duncan and Stenbeck 1988). A different strategy is to conceptualize uncertainty as a property distinct from—but parallel to—an individual's position on a subjective continuum. Then, describing an individual's true state requires simultaneously describing both that person's position on the continuum and the certainty with which that person knows or holds it (e.g., Schuman and Presser 1981).

Although these studies offer some insights, they begin with answers to standardized questions, thereby limiting respondents' expressions of state or task uncertainty. Talk that is less constrained may display varieties of uncertainty, and thus make it available for discovery and subsequently for incorporation into standardized questions. In other words, issues of ecological validity are potentially as central for uncertainty as for a substantive dimension being measured (Cicourel 1974, 1982; Briggs 1986; Mishler 1986; Suchman and Jordan 1990). Studies that begin with standardized questions also make it difficult to observe the impact of respondents' uncertainty, because these questions limit responses in ways that make expressions of uncertainty particularly difficult for interviewers to handle consistently. (For illustrative passing comments on interviewer variability in dealing with DKs, see Duncan and Stenbeck [1988, p. 515] and Schuman and Presser [1981, p. 146].)

In principle, an investigator refines the conceptualizations of the constructs, explores the implications of various operationalizations of the constructs, and resolves issues of ecological validity in the early stages of developing a standardized instrument. This work includes identifying important dimensions in the domain under study; locating the similarities and differences that define the dimensions; learning the vocabulary respondents use to discuss the domain; and making a preliminary assessment of whether the topic is accessible by self-reports. Unstructured interviews are frequently recommended for this phase of instrument development (e.g., Converse and Presser 1986; DeMaio 1983; McKennell 1974; Morton-Williams 1978). Such general recommendations provide investigators little guidance for this phase of research, but techniques include adapting ethnographic interviewing techniques (e.g., Spradley 1979; Werner and Schoepfle 1987; Brenner, Brown, and Canter 1985) and focus groups (Merton, Fiske, and Kendall 1990; Morgan 1988). Standardized questions, once developed, can be evaluated using focus groups (e.g., Joseph et al. 1984), intensive interviews (Belson 1986), or cognitive laboratory techniques, such as paraphrasing and "think-alouds" (e.g., Jabine et al. 1984). Completed instruments can be further polished during pretesting by coding the interviewer's and respondent's behaviors (Oksenberg, Cannell, and Kalton 1991; Morton-Williams and Sykes 1984).

Although techniques for evaluating and revising standardized questions have become better developed in recent years, less attention has been given to the earliest stage in developing new standardized questions (but see Morgan 1988). The traditional advice to use unstructured interviews in initial exploration of a domain is often ignored for lack of time and funds. Some guides to question development do not even mention such interviews as a possible step in the process (e.g., Sudman and Bradburn 1982, pp. 281–86). The standard sources on standardized questionnaire development (cited above) do not include detailed case studies, and few published descriptions of actual developmental procedures exist to guide the researcher (but see DeMaio 1983; Wilson 1985).

This paper presents a case study of the use of semistructured interviews in question development. The study allowed us to identify uncertainties and incorporate them into structured survey instruments. Although we did not rigorously follow the grounded theory method, we developed our distinctions among types of uncertainty by searching for the structure in our data, an approach that characterizes grounded theory (Glaser and Strauss 1967; Strauss 1987). Drawing on a content analysis of semistructured interviews, we suggest two methods for incorporating uncertainty in structured surveys: (a) expanding possible DK categories to reduce task uncertainty, and (b) directly measuring relevant types of state uncertainty. We also present illustrative analyses from a telephone survey in which these methods were applied.

2. UNCERTAINTY IN FERTILITY MOTIVATION: A CASE STUDY

Fertility motivation in previous fertility research has been conceptualized as demand for or subjective utility of children, that is, as a desire for children (e.g., Davidson and Jaccard 1975; McClelland

1983). But researchers do not always distinguish clearly among wanting, intending, or expecting to have a child.[1] Fertility research has paid more attention to the certainty of fertility intentions or decisions (Morgan 1981, 1982, 1985; Westoff and Ryder 1977; Silka and Kiesler 1977) than to the certainty of desires. However, intentions are not the same as motivations or desires; it is not surprising that respondents' intentions may be uncertain, because intentions must respond to circumstances and contingencies as well as desires.

Research on fertility motivation measures motivation either directly (e.g., by asking how many children one wants) or indirectly. In an indirect approach, a model-based measure is constructed using responses to questions about, for example, possible consequences of having children and their subjective probability (e.g., the subjective expected utility (SEU) model used by Beach et al. [1982]). In neither direct nor indirect approaches has the conceptualization of different kinds of uncertainty been comprehensive. Furthermore, this research has not explored the distinction between direct measurement of subjectively experienced uncertainty and an analyst's inference or assertion that some constructed score indicates "uncertainty."

Direct questions about fertility demand (how many children one wants) rarely tap uncertainty (but see Williams 1986). A partial exception, perhaps, is when there is a separate category for respondents who have no fertility preferences because the number of children they will have is "up to God." But a separate category is used only in societies where such responses are too common to ignore (Jensen 1985). An influential example of the indirect measurement of fertility motivation (or "expectation") is the SEU model. The model's operationalization includes explicit questions about the relative certainty of the benefits and costs of having children (e.g., respondents' reports of the subjective probability that a given positive or negative outcome will occur [see, for example, Beach et al. 1982, p. 96]). Uncertainty is also incorporated by interpreting an estimated SEU of 0.5 as ambivalence (e.g., Davidson and Beach 1981, p. 478).[2]

[1]Our interviews suggest that respondents recognize that these are different concepts, but exploring the distinction here would take us too far from our principal focus (see Schaeffer and Thomson 1989).

[2]See also their definition of "an empirically defined neutral" point in the components of the Fishbein model applied to fertility behavior (Davidson and Beach 1981, p. 484).

Even though the SEU handling of uncertainty does not elicit reports of the subjective *experience* of ambivalence, Beach and his colleagues (Beach et al. 1982; Davidson and Beach 1981) found that "ambivalent" SEU scores were distinctive: Respondents with such scores are unlikely to have children. The results of SEU research are particularly relevant here because they suggest that there are potential benefits (e.g., improvements in prediction) in expanding both conceptualizations and operationalizations of uncertainty. The research we report differs from previous research in its focus on the measurement of subjectively experienced desires and uncertainties. If fertility motivation is defined as a subjectively experienced desire for children, then it seems reasonable to explore the varieties of subjectively experienced uncertainties attached to those desires and the implications of those uncertainties for fertility behavior. If there are varieties of uncertainty, they may have different implications for fertility behavior.

We view motivation as a force toward a goal, stimulating goal-directed behaviors, and expressed as demand or subjective utility. Drawing on discussions of attitude intensity (Raden 1985), we identified potential dimensions of motivation, including (un)certainty as well as intensity and centrality. We further conceptualized motivation to achieve an outcome (having another child) as distinct from motivation to avoid the outcome (not having the child). These initial theoretical ideas are reflected in the structure and content of our semistructured interviews, but we did not anticipate the variety of expressions of uncertainty we report below. Furthermore, we based our strategy for incorporating uncertainty into our structured questions on materials provided by respondents.

2.1. *Developmental Interviews*

We conducted three types of interviews in the process of developing a structured survey instrument: (a) semistructured interviews, with standardized open questions and an agenda of topics to probe if respondents did not discuss the topics spontaneously; (b) feedback interviews, in which standardized closed questions were tried out and respondents were given an opportunity to comment on their meaning; and (c) pretest interviews using a complete instrument with standardized closed questions. In this paper, we present results from the semistructured interviews and from the end-product of the developmental process, the structured survey questions.

In designing the semistructured questionnaire, our goal was to create an instrument that was standardized enough to help a team of inexperienced interviewers cover essentially the same material, but unstructured enough that it did not impose our theoretical assumptions on respondents' answers. We deliberately gave respondents an opportunity to describe the relevance of our topic by beginning with questions about how often the respondent thought about or talked about having children, then exploring what the respondent thought or talked about, and with whom (see questions 4–8 in Appendix A). By this procedure, we also wished to give respondents for whom the topic was not relevant several opportunities to say so early in the interview; we expected that this would strengthen respondents against the "demand character" of later questions.[3] An agenda was provided for each question as the basis for neutral probes, because the respondent might initially cover some, all, or none of the topics (see, for example, the discussion in Brown and Sime [1981, p. 165]). The standardized open questions were deliberately long and somewhat repetitive in order to model lengthy responses and to give respondents time to collect their thoughts (Bradburn, Sudman, and Associates 1979; Mishler 1986; Spradley 1979).

The two investigators and eight students in a graduate survey research methods class conducted the interviews. Because the number of interviewers is large, which is probably relatively rare in such developmental work, the data cannot be overly influenced by the preconceptions or technique of any one interviewer; in other words, correlated "response deviations" from "true values" (insofar as these concepts can be applied to such interviews) should be small (e.g., O'Muircheartaigh 1977, p. 216). This is important, since less-structured interviews may be particularly susceptible to interviewer effects (Groves 1989). For both the semistructured and feedback interviews, each interviewer had to complete two practice interviews and two interviews with members of the sample drawn for the

---

[3]Only two respondents, one who was pregnant with her second child (respondent 18) and another who had a vasectomy (respondent 37) had no recent thoughts or conversations about having or not having children to report. Even the most determinedly neutral respondent reported having thought about having more children (respondent 40, question 4).

study (described below). Interviewers completed their first practice interview with another interviewer; thus, each interviewer was interviewed at least once. The second practice interview was usually completed with a graduate student not in the class. The instrument was discussed and revised after each round of interviewing.

2.2. Sample

Random-digit dialing was used to identify households with eligible respondents (aged 18–34) from telephone exchanges in the Madison, Wisconsin, metropolitan area. In later stages of sampling, exchanges near the university were omitted to increase the likelihood of finding married respondents. We attempted to select approximately equal numbers of all combinations of male and female, married and single, parent and nonparent respondents. To facilitate scheduling, those who refused to provide an address at the time of the initial screening were not pursued. Respondents were assigned to semistructured or structured feedback interviews, depending on when they entered the sample and when they could be interviewed.

Although the resulting sample is probably better described as haphazard than random, we avoided most of the selection biases that would have resulted had we relied on our own acquaintance networks or student populations. Of the 18 respondents to the semistructured interviews, 10 are women; 12 are married, 1 is divorced, and 5 have never been married; 3 have high school degrees, 2 are currently enrolled in college, and 13 have at least some college; 9 have no children; a few were foreign-born. (See Appendix B for a summary of respondents' characteristics.)

2.3. Analysis

This is a content analysis, the units of which are primarily meanings (e.g., Lofland and Lofland 1984, pp. 71–75; Mostyn 1985). Our analytic task involves pattern recognition. It is similar to developing codes for open questions or to a task sometimes presented to respondents: Sort a set of statements into categories using whatever principles you like and describe the dimensions you used (see e.g., Canter, Brown, and Groat 1985; Weller and Romney 1988). The two parts to this task are identifying a relevant dimension and determining similarities and differences along this dimension. The similarity-difference judgments sort statements into classes; if the classes can be ordered, a model of the dimension as a continuum may be reasonable.

Researchers sorting statements (or instructing computer programs to do so) are guided by the cognitive organization of their world, just as respondents are. In the case of the researcher, that organization incorporates theory and previous research. Both the perception of relevant dimensions and judgments of similarity and difference are potentially subject to reliability checks, but the meaning of reliability in identifying dimensions is less clear than for classes within a dimension. To some extent, the identification of dimensions is irreducible: They are validated by their performance in research and studies of construct validity. In research "as in life" (Schuman and Ludwig 1983), the dimensions one retains are those that successfully summarize past experience or guide later decisions.[4]

A primary problem in using open responses to create closed categories is what to infer from the absence or presence of a possible response. If person A raises issue X but person B does not, one cannot infer that X is not a concern for person B. B may have temporarily forgotten about X or may have decided not to mention it.[5] Similarly, issues that *are* raised may be partly a function of the interview method or interviewer behavior. In an effort to be helpful, for example, a respondent may dredge up many issues that are not personally important; or the inflection of an interviewer's probe may suggest that the respondent elaborate on one aspect of an answer rather than another.

Issues of comparability become more complex as interviews become less structured. The semistructured interview consisted of open standardized questions with neutral probes contingent on the

[4]We do not have verbatim transcripts of the interviews, so identification of dimensions and categories cannot depend on the *exact* choice of expression. Interviews recorded the respondents' exact words as much as possible, and the records of the interview suggest that most interviewers did this very well, but some abbreviations (such as omitting "I") necessarily occurred.

[5]Standardized questions increase the comparability of respondents' answers by asking all respondents to explicitly accept or reject the same set of choices. Thus, fully standardized questions provide stronger evidence than open questions of the absence of a category, and relying on typologies developed only from open answers (e.g., Lofland and Lofland 1984, pp. 96–97) is risky unless the presence or absence of each possible category in the typology is explicitly verified.

initial response. When interviewers encountered the relatively rare situations that were not handled easily by the interview schedule, they sometimes adapted questions.[6] Research indicates that the stimuli presented by interviewers in standardized interviews are somewhat variable (e.g., Fowler and Mangione 1985); but there is probably more variability in the present study, and we do not know its exact extent. The greater variability in interviewer behavior in less structured interviewing arises largely because the behavior of respondents is less constrained, and interviewers need to respond to the behavior of respondents. Like most samples of such interview material, our sample of responses has unknown properties and is produced by diverse processes, some of which are related to the constructs under consideration and some of which are not. For these reasons, our analysis provides not inferences, but hypotheses embodied in the categories we identify.

Having seen that expressions of uncertainty were very common in the interviews, we identified uncertainty dimensions and classes within the dimensions by (a) reviewing the content of responses for expressions of uncertainty about having or not having children and (b) searching for evidence of task uncertainty and for ways of expressing fertility desires that might lead to task uncertainty in a fully standardized interview. We tried out categories, reexamined the interviews, revised the classes we used, and examined the interviews again, repeating the process several times. The classification was reviewed by both investigators and an assistant (who was also one of the graduate student interviewers), and discrepancies were discussed and resolved.

The problems mentioned above are common to most unstructured or semistructured interviewing and to focus groups. None is particularly limiting for our purpose, which is to deepen our understanding of subjective expressions of uncertainty and to find ways of incorporating this understanding into standardized questions. After describing the results of our analysis of the semistructured interviews, we present preliminary data on the prevalence of uncertain answers to the standardized survey items we developed.

[6]For example, one respondent changed her mind about the number of children she wished to have in the course of the interview; since the interview was structured to ask differently worded questions of those who wanted and did not want more children, the interviewer had to adapt subsequent questions.

3. SPONTANEOUS EXPRESSIONS OF
STATE UNCERTAINTY

We first illustrate the salience and prevalence of uncertainty with one of the few fully structured items in our semistructured interviews. Approximately two-thirds of the way through the interview, we presented respondents with 22 pairs of words and asked them to choose *any* that reflected their feelings about having a (or another) child (Appendix A, q. 45). Five word pairs expressed uncertainty-certainty; *clear-unclear, stable-changing, certain-uncertain, unsure-definite, variable-constant.* Five respondents chose only words indicating certainty, five chose only words indicating uncertainty, seven chose both types of words. Only one chose no uncertainty-certainty words. The mean number of words from these pairs selected by those choosing such words was 3.5, and the most commonly chosen words were *unclear, changing, certain, definite,* and *variable.* Because all respondents had an opportunity to explicitly accept or reject these words, respondents' choices offer strong confirmation of the prevalence of an uncertainty-certainty dimension.

Other expressions of state uncertainty appeared throughout the interviews in responses to questions about feelings, goals, and conditions that might influence them.[7] Appendix C presents quotations from the semistructured interviews. Each quotation is followed by a respondent identification number and the number of the question or questions from which the quoted material was taken (e.g., [04-10] indicates the material is from respondent 4's answer to question 10). This notation allows the reader to determine the characteristics of the respondent making a particular statement by referring to Appendix B and to verify that the material contributing to our conclusions was drawn from all our respondents and from answers to a wide range of questions. Because some quotations are referred to several times in the text, tables display the quotations in order by respondent number so that the quotation being referred to can be easily located. Each of panels 1 through 4 in Appendix C illustrates a different

[7]Only one respondent (respondent 25, who was trying to conceive) made no statements suggesting uncertainty about the direction of fertility goals or their timing. We examined the answers in each category for patterns by sex, number of children, and number of children desired, but given the small number of cases, no patterns emerged.

variety of uncertainty. Panel 5 presents expressions that combine more than one kind of uncertainty; because the material in panel 5 illustrates several kinds of uncertainty, it is referred to throughout the discussion. The material from the interviews has been edited slightly for easier reading, and brackets indicate words added in editing. (Appendix A presents the exact wording of all questions cited in the text and tables.)

3.1. *Neutrality*

Neutral answers describe very low intensity feelings or feelings that cannot be perceived. The respondents know how they feel; they just do not experience a particular feeling, they are indifferent to fertility outcomes, they perceive having a preference as irrelevant, or their feelings are of very low intensity. As the data in Appendix C, panel 1, indicate, respondents expressed neutrality about the timing of the children [04-10], about the number of children desired [14-25], and about the relevance of fertility preferences [40-04, -18, -24, -40, -47, -55]. Respondent 40 even used the word *neutral*. His repeated statements indicate what a definite state neutrality can be. Panel 5 presents expressions of mixed feelings—including expressions of neutrality as a postulated state in the recent past [panel 5, 13-40] or expressions that combine neutrality with other forms of uncertainty, such as ambivalence [panel 5, 09-04].

3.2. *Lack of Clarity*

Feelings may be unclear for various reasons (see panel 2). For example, the respondent may not have thought much about an issue [panel 2: 08-40, 14-10, 18-17], he or she may be in the process of making or revising a decision [panel 5: 19-12], or his or her feelings may be contradictory and difficult to summarize [panel 5: 13-40, 26-21]. Two respondents said their feelings became unclear during the interview as they listened to their own answers [panel 2, 08-40; panel 5, 13-40]. How a respondent expresses unclear feelings depends partly on the question he or she is answering. For example, conflicting feelings may be expressed as a lack of clarity only if a person is asked to summarize them on a single positive-negative dimension.

3.3. *Ambivalence*

An ambivalent person has opposing or mixed feelings—moderate or strong—toward an object. These opposing feelings may appear as a combination of positive and negative feelings or as vacillation (panel 3). Because it is inherently a compound state, ambivalence presents unique problems. Although we did not begin by looking for expressions of ambivalence, we were attempting to compile lists of relevant positive and negative feelings. For this reason, the initial questions in the interview included probes for negative and positive feelings if both were not mentioned spontaneously. This use of probes provided either stronger evidence for the *absence* or ambivalence because respondents had to deny competing feelings or weaker evidence for the *presence* of ambivalence because respondents were encouraged to express competing feelings.[8] Statements of positive and negative feelings, however, also appeared in response to neutral probes following a single structured question or in response to different structured questions, sometimes at very different points in the interview.

Another problem in identifying ambivalence in these responses is that we could not evaluate the intensity or balance of competing feelings. The expression of some feelings in both directions does not necessarily mean a person feels ambivalent overall. For example, we cannot tell if a respondent's discussion of costs and benefits communicates conflicted feelings or simply a recognition of the complexities of trade-offs and choices. Similarly, any judgments we make about the intensity of competing positive and negative feelings would necessarily be tentative. For example, a woman who said she would feel both panicked and excited if she got pregnant communicated intense feelings, but the relative balance of positive and negative feelings is not clear [panel 3, 19-16]. Because of these

---

[8]The assumption that spontaneity indicates depth, intensity, relevance, or importance is common, but largely untested. Few studies have examined whether the importance of the content to the respondent—and the validity of the answer, in some sense—is greater if the answer is relatively unprompted. Arguments hinging on spontaneity suggest that questions without response categories provide more valid answers than questions with categories, that material provided before a probe is more valid than material provided after a probe, etc. (e.g., Kane and Schuman 1991).

complications, the category of ambivalent statements is less well-defined than the others.[9]

Almost all respondents expressed awareness of both positive and negative feelings about having children, either in response to one or to several questions. Only one respondent said he had "no negative thoughts" about having children [04-36, not in appendix]. The clearest expression of simple ambivalence came from a married man who was unsure whether he wanted a fifth child: "I wonder why I will have another child. It's hard to explain. Can't live with them, can't live without them" [panel 5, 39-33].

But ambivalence may be communicated in more complicated ways or involve answers to more than one question. Respondent 8's description of her feelings about having a child presented both positive and negative feelings in a single answer: She did not want to be pregnant or to have the sole responsibility for a child, but she thought that having children had rewards [panel 3, 08-11]. In contrast, respondent 26 said her feelings were mixed ("both good and bad" [panel 3, 26-19]), but describing her feelings more fully requires comparing answers to different questions [panel 3, 26-18; see also panel 5, 26-21]. These two respondents also illustrate how the contrast between someone's stated fertility goal and other statements may suggest ambivalence: Respondent 8 was definite about *not* wanting a child (at least until the interview). In contrast, respondent 26 repeatedly expressed negative feelings but also seemed to have definitely decided to have another child: "It is important. I am 27, and I want to have it before I am 30. I really do not want [my daughter] to be alone anymore" [26-22, not in appendix]. Some descriptions of positive and negative feelings are ambiguous: Is a person who recognizes that parental love is positive but that the stress of parenting is negative [panel 3, 07-27] or that the first two years of childrearing are disruptive [panel 3, 42-33] expressing ambivalence?

When respondents directly assert that feelings are variable, they are more clearly ambivalent (see panel 3). Variability in feelings may be seen as a possibility [14-21] or as the current state of things: "It really depends. Sometimes I really want to have a child, and

[9]These materials suggest some of the complex issues involved in conceptualizing ambivalence. The results from standardized questions, presented in Appendix D, confirm that recognition of positive and negative feelings associated with having children is widespread.

other times I don't" [09-34]. Variable feelings also appear with other expressions of uncertainty "When I'm around kids I enjoy it, but when I'm home in my peaceful surroundings, I'm glad I don't have them. . . . If I have a baby that's fine. If I don't, that's fine too" [panel 5: 09-04]. "If we have another, we'll have one more. Not sure if I want anymore. I don't know. I go back and forth. The kids are out of diapers. Do I want to get involved in having a newborn again?" [panel 5: 39-09]. But variable feelings do not necessarily indicate indecision; the balance may be tipped in one direction [panel 3, 01-19].

3.4. *Indecision*

When a person perceives that it is time to try to have a child, uncertainty about *desires* may be expressed as indecision (see panel 4). Some of the statements of variable feelings just reviewed implicitly express indecision. Circumstances may determine when the time of decision arrives, and indecision may be linked to the likelihood of these circumstances. For example, job and financial uncertainties may lead to indecision about fertility matters [panel 4, 03-51, 22-30; panel 5, 39-34]. A woman who expressed neutrality, ambivalence, and lack of clarity suggested the relationship between indecisiveness and other forms of uncertainty: "In spite of my uncertainties, it's important that they come at this point. Uncertainty comes before decision. I'll come to a point where I'm sure and all the plans come into place. . . . Somehow my husband and I will at some point have done enough talking to each other so that we'll both be sure and a baby will be conceived" [panel 4, 13-55]. Others also expressed indecision along with other forms of uncertainty [panel 5, 19-12, 26-21, 39-34]. The stress attached to uncertainty and indecision may be such that even an "unwanted" pregnancy can be a relief [panel 3, 19-16].

3.5. *Mixed Expressions*

The mixed expressions in panel 5 illustrate how our analytic distinctions appeared in respondents' talk and how respondents experienced the relationships among different kinds of uncertainty. The close relationship between neutrality and uncertainty is illustrated by respondent 9's statement, which suggests that she used neutrality to resolve her variable feelings about having a child [09-04]. The remaining examples illustrate various reasons feelings may be unclear. A simple statement that feelings are not clear—"I wonder if I do want a child" [13-40]—can summarize complex considerations. This respondent, who wanted a child, thought she was neutral about having a child, that "it would be OK either way, fine" [13-40]. But during the interview, she implicitly contrasted her positive *feelings* of wanting a child with her negative *actions:* "People who do want children have them, and I still don't have one" [13-40]. This contrast suggests ambivalence, apparently also to the respondent, who reconsidered her previous use of neutrality to balance positive and negative orientations to having children. Other respondents also summarized ambivalent or variable feelings by describing their feelings as unclear: "Not sure if I want any more. I don't know. I go back and forth" [39-09]. By saying that the desire for another child was "sometimes . . . not that strong" or that she felt "scared" when the decision got close [26-21], this respondent implied that stronger and more positive feelings were sometimes present, that her feelings were mixed. This woman's desire for another child coexisted with negative feelings, resulting in variable feelings and a lack of clarity: "I just do not know how I feel all the time" [26-21], which implies that sometimes she *does* know how she feels.[10]

4. REDUCING TASK UNCERTAINTY: RECORDING STATE UNCERTAINTY

All of these types of state uncertainty are potential sources of task uncertainty in a standardized interview. Our findings suggest that a simple DK category would not solve the problems respondents and interviewers would face with standardized questions about fertility motivation. Many of these respondents knew how they felt, but feelings depended on uncertain circumstances, varied over time, or

[10]These interview materials also indicate that respondents recognized that circumstances shaped their feelings and fertility goals and introduced uncertainty into their fertility plans. Furthermore, some respondents showed how fertility desires can be adapted to ultimate outcomes, how people come to want what they get. Because ultimate outcomes are uncertain, some uncertainty in desires may maintain adaptive flexibility. For a preliminary discussion of these aspects of uncertainty, see Schaeffer and Thomson (1989).

were not experienced at all.[11] To provide a more accurate description
of fertility motivation and to reduce the task uncertainty that could
result from not providing for expressions of uncertainty, we developed categories to record spontaneous expressions of uncertainty,
rules for training interviewers in recording these answers, and direct
questions about strength or uncertainty dimensions.[12]

4.1. *"Uncertainty" Categories*

Using the analysis presented above, we distinguish three
states that either constitute an uncertain condition or are likely to
generate task uncertainty: neutrality, ambivalence, and lack of clarity.[13] The training materials for interviewers define these categories
as follows:

Neutral. These respondents know how they feel about having
or not having a child, and their feelings are pretty much in the middle
or of very low intensity. Neutral or indifferent feelings are sometimes
difficult to express, so they may also cause the respondent to be
uncertain about how to answer the question, and therefore to say
"don't know." It is important to distinguish between being "in the

[11]This was confirmed in the subsequent feedback interviews, which are
not discussed in any detail here, but which informed the design of the standardized questions in Appendix D. For example, when we obtained feedback on
early versions of the questions about feelings, some respondents remarked that
whether or not they would feel content if they had a child depended on whether
they were "ready" for the event. These respondents "knew" how they would
feel, and how they would feel simply depended on circumstances they could not
guarantee. In the standardized interview, interviewers were explicitly trained to
expect such answers, and were provided a category in which to record them.
Respondents were told that such answers were adequate for the task.

[12]After developing these training materials, we found that Faulkenberry
and Mason (1978) had experimented with having interviewers distinguish between "no opinion" and "lack of knowledge." The attitude they studied is simpler than strength of fertility motivation and has a different structure, but their
basic approach has much in common with ours.

[13]We did not include a category for indecision because, as the material
presented earlier indicates, it is usually associated with one of the other categories, and we wanted to keep the number of uncertainty categories small. We
expected most expressions of indecision to be accompanied by descriptions of
variable feelings (see Edwards 1946, described above) or ambivalence. We did
ask whether the respondent had made a decision about having a child, but the
question did not focus on decisiveness: "Have you (and your wife/husband as a
couple) made a decision not to try to have (a/another) child (after this one)?"

middle" and being "on both sides" of the question. The first response is neutral; the second is ambivalent. There is one other type of response we classify as "neutral": The respondent says the question is irrelevant to her/his feelings, that it just does not describe the way she/he feels or thinks about the issue.

Ambivalent. The respondent expresses two or more conflicting feelings. For example, she/he feels both happy and unhappy at different times, about different aspects of having a child, or under different circumstances: If X happens I'll feel happy, if not I'll feel sad.[14]

Not sure of feelings (lack of clarity). The respondent doesn't really know how she/he feels; she/he cannot find or sort out her/his feelings, or has not tried to. This is *not* the same as a simple "not sure" response to a question, because that response could also indicate that the respondent knows her/his feelings but does not know which answer best expresses them.

For each question in the standardized interview, we determined whether any of the categories we offered respondents expressed neutrality, ambivalence, or lack of clarity (e.g., a question about strength of feelings might offer a "not at all" category, that is, a neutral category). We then added categories for recording *volunteered* expressions of the other types of neutrality or uncertainty. Appendix D provides examples of questions and the instructions used in training interviewers. In the first example in Appendix D, panel A, neutral and "not sure" categories were offered as part of the question, but a category for recording ambivalent answers was also available.

Our experience in feedback interviews (not reported in detail here) suggests that respondents who express uncertainty frequently cannot easily choose one of the offered categories even after probing. For this reason, interviewers were trained to code clear expressions of uncertainty without probing. Interviewers told respondents what they were doing, so that the respondents could clarify or change

[14]If the respondent predicted different feelings depending on the circumstances, we classified the reponse as "ambivalent." In pretesting the standardized questions, such answers were most common when we asked about feelings. For example, we asked how respondents would feel if they had a child, and the respondents replied that they would be excited if they were "ready," but not otherwise. We considered respondents who could only express feelings by referring to contingencies as exhibiting a "structural" or "circumstantial" ambivalence.

their answers if they wanted to, and so that the respondents knew that they could express uncertainty in the remainder of the interview. If the respondent expressed ambivalence, for example, the interviewer said "I can put down that you have mixed feelings" and entered the code for ambivalent. If the respondent gave a vague answer, such as "I don't know" or "I'm not sure," the interviewer used a single neutral probe (e.g., "How do you think you would feel?") and recorded the subsequent response. The mixed expressions reported earlier suggest that respondents' initial "don't know" may have really referred to more specific types of uncertainty that could only be elicited by giving respondents an opportunity to make their uncertainties clear to the interviewer. Answers that could not be classified after probing were recorded in a residual DK category.

These procedures provided interviewers with guidelines for responding to and recording answers that were unpredictable and that could be problematic for both respondents and interviewers, but that were conceptually distinct from each other. Task uncertainty should be reduced when the interviewer indicates that he or she will attempt to record the respondent's answer even when it does not fit the offered categories precisely. Although interviewers may vary in how well they execute these procedures, interviewer handling of respondents' expressions of uncertainty appear to be highly variable in any case, and explicit training should reduce interviewer variability in probing and recording uncertain answers.[15]

4.2. Direct Questions

Because of the potential importance of these dimensions for understanding fertility motivation, as Appendix D illustrates, we also included direct measures of neutrality (in the context of inten-

[15]An alternative strategy would be to use filter questions for uncertainty dimensions. We did not think this strategy was feasible, given the number of uncertainty dimensions we identified, our ignorance of the frequency with which they might occur for different items, and the large increase in the number of items that would be very tedious for respondents to answer. Similarly, it is impractical to offer a full menu of uncertainty categories for each item because the number of response categories respondents can process in a telephone interview is fairly limited (Sudman and Bradburn 1982). Offering all uncertainty categories for all questions would almost certainly have increased their use (e.g., Schuman and Presser 1981).

sity, panel B), clarity (sureness, panel C), and ambivalence (including simultaneous mixed and changeable feelings, panels D and E). Each of these questions also included categories for other types of uncertainty the respondent might volunteer.

5. EXPRESSIONS OF STATE UNCERTAINTY IN STANDARDIZED INTERVIEWS

Evaluating both the role of uncertain desires in predicting fertility behavior and the usefulness of distinguishing among varieties of uncertainty in these predictions are extensive projects in themselves. But the potential usefulness of the approach taken here—at least in distinguishing among kinds of uncertainty—can be illustrated with a brief descriptive analysis. The data are taken from structured interviews conducted with a sample of Wisconsin residents aged 18–34, identified through random-digit dialing. Oversamples were selected of single parents and married nonparents. Computer-assisted telephone interviews began in December 1989 and were completed in February 1990. The final response rate is estimated to be 62 percent.

The results show that respondents did express considerable uncertainty about fertility desires. The first panel of Table 1 summarizes answers to the four direct questions about fertility goals (in Appendix D, panels B through E). We show results separately for parents and nonparents who do and do not want (more) children because we expect three general factors to interact with goals in influencing uncertainty: pressures to achieve the parental role, previous experience with parenting, and the inertia of the status quo (continuing without another child). The results suggest that both parental status and fertility goals sometimes influence the type and strength of uncertainty expressed. Significance tests reported in the text for the effects of parental status and fertility goals are from logistic regressions in which the dependent variables are the dichotomies that are presented as proportions in Table 1.[16]

Partly because the most extreme responses to the questions about the strength and sureness of fertility desires are rare, there

[16]The models also included marital status, one of the sample stratification variables. The interaction between parental status and fertility goal was not significant (alpha = .05) in any of the models and was omitted from the model when the tests reported in the text were computed.

TABLE 1

Percentage of Respondents Indicating Uncertainty, by Parental Status
and Fertility Goals

	Nonparents		Parents	
	Want No Children	Want Child	Want No More Children	Want Child
Direct questions about goal				
Not at all strong	11.1	5.0	1.3	3.7
Not at all sure	11.1	6.4	0.0	7.4
Equally mixed	25.9	20.1	21.5	19.4
Changing	3.7	27.9	20.3	39.8
Feeling questions				
About having a child				
Any "not sure" (offered)	59.3	36.1	50.6	25.0
Any "ambivalent"	7.4	3.7	5.1	7.4
Any "don't know"	0.0	0.5	2.5	0.9
About not having child				
Any "not sure" (offered)	44.4	62.6	46.8	49.1
Any "ambivalent"	3.7	3.2	10.1	8.3
Any "don't know"	0.0	0.5	1.3	0.0
Number of respondents	27	219	79	108

Source: Wisconsin residents, 18–34 years old, telephone survey, December 1989–February 1990.

appear to be no significant (alpha = .05) differences between respondents by parental status or fertility goals in the probability that they will say that their fertility goals are "not at all strong" (which may make them less certain in response to other questions) or that they are "not at all sure" about their fertility goals. But the two different conceptualizations of ambivalence suggested by the developmental interviews are reported more frequently and give strikingly different results. It appears, as the analysis of the semistructured interviews found, that many respondents recognized equally mixed positive and negative feelings about their fertility goals regardless of parental status or fertility goals; that is, it was relatively easy for respondents to recognize that there are both costs and benefits to any fertility decision. But the frequency of reports of changing feelings varied substantially among these groups. Parents were significantly more likely than nonparents to say that their feelings changed ($b = .63, t =$

2.67). Those who wanted children were more likely to say that their feelings changed than those who did not want children ($b = 1.21, t = 3.88$). Parents' involvement with their children may act as an external stimulus that causes their feelings to vacillate, and those who are considering having a child may also be more likely to vacillate, because they experience the inertia of the status quo as they rehearse their fertility desires.

Other evidence that the varieties of uncertainty may differ from each other is provided by the uncertainty categories in a series of questions about feelings associated with fertility goals. The first question in the series is illustrated in Appendix D, panel A.[17] The second panel of Table 1 gives the percentage of respondents who chose the offered "not sure" response, who volunteered an "ambivalent" response, and who were coded (after probing) in a residual DK category for any of the six feelings presented. The proportion of respondents who chose the "ambivalent" category at least once is small but substantial, particularly given that these questions were "quasi-filtered" (Schuman and Presser 1981). The additional work required of respondents and interviewers to use the "ambivalent" category when "not sure" was offered suggests that the distinction between the kinds of uncertainty was salient. For questions both about having and about not having children, a similar pattern emerges: Parents were less likely than nonparents to say they were not sure (about having children, $b = -.47, t = -2.06$; about not having children, $b = -.38, t = -1.78$) and more likely than nonparents to say they were ambivalent (about having children, $b = .54, t = 1.15$; about not having children, $b = .97, t = 2.07$). If the distinction between being not sure and ambivalent is ignored and the two answers are treated similarly, parents appear less likely to express uncertainty, but the effect is not significant for either set of questions (about having children, $b = -.32, t = -1.45$; about not having children, $b = -.19, t = -.93$). Moreover, although the differ-

[17]The series of questions about feelings was asked twice, first about the respondent's fertility goal (e.g., having a child) and then about the opposite of the respondent's goal (e.g., not having a child). The feelings asked about were delighted, thrilled, content, sad, disappointed, and miserable. The questions were intended to determine the presence or absence of each of these feelings. Because the absence of a feeling could include both neutral feelings and the presence of opposite feelings, the "not feel (*feeling*)" category does not include *only* neutral responses.

ence is not always significant, the direction of the relationship observed for "not sure" and "ambivalent" answers to the feeling questions is the same as that observed for the direct questions about "sureness" and "changing feelings": Parents appear less likely to say they are not sure, but more likely to say they are ambivalent.

6. CONCLUSION

The case study presented here illustrates how responses to relatively unstructured interviews are used to conceptualize and operationalize constructs in standardized survey questions. The content analysis offers a fuller understanding of uncertainty and its potential role in the construct under study than could have been gained by beginning with standardized questions. The material we presented describes the idiom respondents use to express their uncertainties and the different ways uncertainty is experienced. It also suggests that the subjective experience of attitude strength is often expressed using the language of uncertainty rather than certainty. The domain we examined, expressions of uncertainty, and the wide range of expressions we found are potentially relevant not only to fertility motivation, but to a wide range of subjective phenomena.

The method of instrument development we describe is traditional and rudimentary in some ways, but it attempts to contribute to establishing public procedures for this phase of instrument design, as recent developments in pretesting have for that phase (see e.g., Oksenberg et al. 1991). How investigators make decisions in the early stages of instrument design, and the evidence that informs those decisions, is rarely well-documented, but these decisions may be crucial to the success of a research project. The style of developmental work reported here could clearly be improved by tape recording interviews at all stages of developmental work (e.g., unstructured, semistructured interviews, intensive interviews, cognitive interviews, etc.). Analysis of details of the interaction in the interviews could improve our understanding of the impact of the interviewer on the results of such interviews (see, e.g., Schaeffer 1991). In addition, experimentation with improved techniques of content analysis (e.g., Carley 1988) is needed, and these require tape recordings. Finally, we attempted to obtain a relatively heterogeneous sample for our semistructured interviews; we were thus not able to make group comparisons, because of the small number of cases in any group of interest. Most instrument development work is restricted to fairly small samples, but in some cases, sampling to increase the strength of comparisons on some variables for which a content analysis might give different results (e.g., race) may be desirable.

Comprehensive distinctions among different kinds of uncertainty and certainty and appropriate measurement approaches are only slowly cumulating (see e.g., Raden 1985; Schuman and Presser 1981). The frequency with which respondents in the semistructured interviews expressed various kinds of uncertainty suggested that to reduce task uncertainty, we needed to be able to record information about subjective states of uncertainty and explore the role of uncertainty systematically in the full survey. The results from the standardized interviews confirm that substantial minorities of respondents express some uncertainty, either in response to direct questions about uncertainty or by volunteering some variety of uncertainty when asked about their feelings. Whether direct or indirect methods of assessing subjectively perceived uncertainty will make a difference in the long-term goal of predicting and understanding fertility behavior is an empirical question for future analyses, but the SEU research described above gives good reason to believe that taking uncertainty into account could improve predictions of fertility behavior. In addition, the findings of psychologists and survey researchers reviewed earlier, and the importance of uncertainty in decision theory generally, suggest that conceptualizing and measuring uncertainty may be important to research in many substantive domains.

In general, the sensitivity of operationalized constructs and research results is limited by the sensitivity of data collection: We can only examine the categories we record. DK categories are often poorly defined, and the procedures used to record DK answers are difficult to reconstruct. DK responses are then often omitted from analysis, a practice that may affect our understanding of constructs and the results of analyses. The techniques we suggest for standardized data collection are experimental, but they provide a method for systematically recording potentially important distinctions and a public procedure for dealing with some problematic answers in survey interviews (see, e.g., Freedman et al. [1988] on the importance of standard solutions to problems in data collection).

As always, adequate conceptualizations and operationalizations of a concept (e.g., subjectively experienced uncertainty) are needed before its role in governing some outcome can be demonstrated, and these have been underdeveloped for uncertainty. Just as important, but easier to forget, good operationalizations are needed before the *absence* of an effect can be demonstrated, since poor measurement is often blamed when no effect is found. Careful development procedures can increase researchers' confidence in negative as well as positive findings, and the materials assembled during the early phases of instrument design may provide a resource to use in discovering the reasons for failure of a hypothesis. Advances in both data collection and analytic techniques are needed to integrate an understanding of uncertainty into our constructs and reduce task uncertainty.

REFERENCES

Beach, Lee Roy, Alexandra Hope, Brenda B. Townes, and Frederick L. Campbell. 1982. "The Expectation-Threshold Model of Reproductive Decision Making." *Population and Environment* 5:95–108.

Belson, William A. 1986. *Validity in Survey Research*. Aldershot, Hants, England: Gower.

Bishop, George F., Robert W. Oldendick, and Alfred J. Tuchfarber. 1983. "Effects of Filter Questions in Public Opinion Surveys." *Public Opinion Quarterly* 47:528–46.

Bradburn, Norman M., Seymour Sudman, and Associates. 1979. *Improving Interview Method and Questionnaire Design*. San Francisco: Jossey-Bass.

Brenner, Michael, Jennifer Brown, and David Canter, eds. 1985. *The Research Interview: Uses and Approaches*. London: Academic Press.

Briggs, Charles L. 1986. *Learning How to Ask*. Cambridge: Cambridge University Press.

Brown, Jennifer, and Jonathan Sime. 1981. "A Methodology for Accounts." Pp. 159–88 in *Social Method and Social Life,* edited by Michael Brenner. London: Academic Press.

Canter, David, Jennifer Brown, and Linda Groat. 1985. "A Multiple Sorting Procedure for Studying Conceptual Systems." Pp. 79–114 in *The Research Interview: Uses and Approaches,* edited by Michael Brenner, Jennifer Brown, and David Canter. London: Academic Press.

Carley, Kathleen. 1988. "Formalizing the Social Expert's Knowledge." *Sociological Methods and Research* 17:165–232.

Cicourel, Aaron V. 1974. *Theory and Method in a Study of Argentine Fertility*. New York: Wiley.

———. 1982. "Interviews, Surveys, and the Problem of Ecological Validity." *American Sociologist* 17:11–20.

Converse, Jean M., and Stanley Presser. 1986. *Survey Questions: Handcrafting the Standardized Questionnaire.* Sage University Paper Series on Quantitative Applications in the Social Sciences, No. 007-063. Beverly Hills: Sage.

Converse, Philip E. 1970. "Attitudes and Non-Attitudes: Continuation of a Dialogue." Pp. 168–89 in *The Quantitative Analysis of Social Problems,* edited by Edward R. Tufte. Reading, MA: Addison-Wesley.

Coombs, Clyde H., and Lolagene C. Coombs. 1976. " 'Don't Know': Item Ambiguity or Respondent Uncertainty?" *Public Opinion Quarterly* 40:497–514.

Davidson, Andrew R., and Lee Roy Beach. 1981. "Error Patterns in the Prediction of Fertility Behavior." *Journal of Applied Social Psychology* 11:475–88.

Davidson, Andrew R., and James J. Jaccard. 1975. "Population Psychology: A New Look at an Old Problem." *Journal of Personality and Social Psychology* 31:1073–82.

DeMaio, Theresa. 1983. "Approaches to Developing Questionnaires." Statistical Policy Working Paper No. 10. Prepared by Subcommittee on Questionnaire Design, Federal Committee on Statistical Methodology. Washington, DC: U.S. Government Printing Office.

DuBois, Bernard, and John A. Burns. 1975. "An Analysis of the Meaning of the Question Mark Response Category in Attitude Scales." *Educational and Psychological Measurement* 35:869–84.

Duncan, Otis Dudley, and Magnus Stenbeck. 1988. "No Opinion or Not Sure?" *Public Opinion Quarterly* 52:513–25.

Edwards, Allen L. 1946. "A Critique of 'Neutral' Items in Attitude Scales Constructed by the Method of Equal Appearing Intervals." *Psychological Review* 53:159–69.

Faulkenberry, G. David, and Robert Mason. 1978. "Characteristics of Non-Opinion and No Opinion Response Groups." *Public Opinion Quarterly* 42:533–43.

Fowler, Floyd J., and Thomas Mangione. 1985. *The Value of Interviewer Training and Supervision.* Final Report to the National Center for Health Services Research, Grant No. 3-R18-HS04189. Washington, DC: NCHSR.

Freedman, Deborah, Arland Thornton, Donald Camburn, Duane Alwin, and Linda Young-DeMarco. 1988. "The Life History Calendar: A Technique for Collecting Retrospective Data." Pp. 37–68 in *Sociological Methodology 1988,* edited by Clifford C. Clogg. Washington, DC: American Sociological Association.

Glaser, Barney G., and Anselm Strauss. 1967. *The Discovery of Grounded Theory.* Chicago: Aldine.

Goldberg, Lewis R. 1981. "Unconfounding Situational Attributions from Uncertain, Neutral, and Ambiguous Ones: A Psychometric Analysis of Descriptions of Oneself and Various Types of Others." *Journal of Personality and Social Psychology* 41:517–52.

Groves, Robert M. 1989. *Survey Errors and Survey Costs.* New York: Wiley.

Jabine, Thomas B., Miron L. Straf, Judith M. Tanur, and Roger Tourangeau, eds. 1984. *Cognitive Aspects of Survey Methodology: Building a Bridge Be-*

tween Disciplines. Report of the Advanced Research Seminar on Cognitive Aspects of Survey Methodology. Washington, DC: National Academy Press.

Jensen, Eric. 1985. "Desired Fertility, the 'Up to God' Response, and Sample Selection Bias." *Demography* 22:445–54.

Joseph, Jill G., Carol-Ann Emmons, Ronald C. Kessler, Camille B. Wortman, Kerth O'Brien, William T. Hocker, and Catherine Schaefer. 1984. "Coping with the Threat of AIDS: An Approach to Psychosocial Assessment." *American Psychologist* 39:1297–1302.

Kane, Emily, and Howard Schuman. 1991. "Open Survey Questions as Measures of Personal Concern with Issues: A Reanalysis of Stouffer's *Communism, Conformity, and Civil Liberties.*" Pp. 81–96 in *Sociological Methodology 1991,* edited by Peter Marsden. Oxford: Basil Blackwell.

Kaplan, Kalman J. 1972. "On the Ambivalence-Indifference Problem in Attitude Theory and Measurement: A Suggested Modification of the Semantic Differential Technique." *Psychological Bulletin* 77:361–72.

Klopfer, Frederick J., and Theodore M. Madden. 1980. "The Middlemost Choice on Attitude Items: Ambivalence, Neutrality, or Uncertainty." *Personality and Social Psychology Bulletin* 6:91–101.

Lofland, John, and Lyn H. Lofland. 1984. *Analyzing Social Settings.* Belmont, CA: Wadsworth.

McClelland, Gary H. 1983. "Family-Size Desires as Measures of Demand." Pp. 288–343 in *Determinants of Fertility in Developing Countries.* Vol. 1, *Supply and Demand for Children,* edited by Ronald D. Lee and Rodolfo A. Bulatao. New York: Academic Press.

McKennell, Aubrey C. 1974. "Surveying Attitude Structures: A Discussion of Principles and Procedures." *Quality and Quantity* 7:203–93.

Merton, Robert K., Marjorie Fiske, and Patricia L. Kendall. 1990. *The Focused Interview.* 2d ed. New York: Free Press.

Mishler, Elliot G. 1986. *Research Interviewing.* Cambridge, MA: Harvard University Press.

Morgan, David L. 1988. *Focus Groups as Qualitative Research.* Sage University Paper Series on Qualitative Research Methods, Vol. 16. Newbury Park, CA: Sage.

Morgan, S. Philip. 1981. "Intention and Uncertainty at Later Stages of Childbearing in the United States, 1965 and 1970." *Demography* 18:267–85.

———. 1982. "Family-Specific Fertility Intentions and Uncertainty: The United States, 1970–1976." *Demography* 19:315–34.

———. 1985. "Individual and Couple Intentions for More Children: A Research Note." *Demography* 22:125–32.

Morton-Williams, Jean. 1978. "Unstructured Design Work." Pp. 10–26 in *Survey Research Practice,* edited by Gerald Hoinville and Roger Jowell. London: Heinemann Educational Books.

Morton-Williams, Jean, and Wendy Sykes. 1984. "The Use of Interaction Coding and Follow-Up Interview to Investigate Comprehension of Survey Questions. *Journal of the Market Research Society* 26:109–27.

Mostyn, Barbara. 1985. "The Content Analysis of Qualitative Research Data: A Dynamic Approach." Pp. 115–45 in *The Research Interview: Uses and Approaches,* edited by Michael Brenner, Jennifer Brown, and David Canter. London: Academic Press.

Oksenberg, Lois, Charles Cannell, and Graham Kalton. 1991. "New Strategies of Pretesting Survey Questions." *Journal of Official Statistics* 7:349–69.

O'Muircheartaigh, C. A. 1977. "Response Errors." Pp. 193–239 in *Analysis of Survey Data.* Vol. 2, *Model Fitting,* edited by C. A. O'Muircheartaigh and C. Payne. London: Wiley.

Raden, David. 1985. "Strength-Related Attitude Dimensions." *Social Psychology Quarterly* 48:312–30.

Schaeffer, Nora Cate. 1991. "Conversation with a Purpose—Or Conversation? Interaction in the Standardized Interview." Forthcoming in *Measurement Errors in Surveys,* edited by Paul P. Biemer, Robert M. Groves, Lars E. Lyberg, Nancy A. Mathiowetz, and Seymour Sudman. New York: Wiley.

Schaeffer, Nora Cate, and Elizabeth Thomson. 1989. "The Discovery of Grounded Uncertainty: Developing Questions about Strength of Fertility Motivation." Working Paper No. 89-16. Madison: University of Wisconsin, Center for Demography and Ecology.

Schuman, Howard, and Jacob Ludwig. 1983. "The Norm of Even-Handedness in Surveys as in Life." *American Sociological Review* 48:112–20.

Schuman, Howard, and Stanley Presser. 1981. *Questions and Answers in Attitude Surveys: Experiments on Question Form, Wording, and Context.* Orlando: Academic Press.

Silka, Linda, and Sara Kiesler. 1977. "Couples Who Choose to Remain Childless." *Family Planning Perspectives* 9:16–25.

Spradley, James P. 1979. *The Ethnographic Interview.* New York: Holt, Rinehart, and Winston.

Strauss, Anselm. 1987. *Qualitative Analysis for Social Scientists.* Cambridge: Cambridge University Press.

Suchman, Lucy, and Brigitte Jordan. 1990. "Interactional Troubles in Face-to-Face Survey Interviews." *Journal of the American Statistical Association* 85:232–41.

Sudman, Seymour, and Norman M. Bradburn. 1982. *Asking Questions: A Practical Guide to Questionnaire Design.* San Francisco: Jossey-Bass.

Weller, Susan C., and A. Kimball Romney. 1988. *Systematic Data Collection.* Sage University Paper Series on Qualitative Research Methods, Vol. 10. Newbury Park, CA: Sage.

Werner, Oswald, and Mark Schoepfle. 1987. *Systematic Fieldwork.* Vol. 1, *Foundations of Ethnography and Interviewing.* Newbury Park, CA: Sage.

Westoff, Charles F., and Norman B. Ryder. 1977. "The Predictive Validity of Reproductive Intentions." *Demography* 14:431–53.

Williams, Richard A. 1986. "Indianapolis Revisited: A New Look at Social and Psychological Factors Affecting Fertility." Ph.D. diss., University of Wisconsin, Madison, Department of Sociology.

Wilson, T. D. 1985. "Questionnaire Design in the Context of Information Research." Pp. 79–144 in *The Research Interview: Uses and Approaches,* edited by Michael Brenner, Jennifer Brown, and David Canter. London: Academic Press.

APPENDIX A: INTERVIEW QUESTIONS

4. To begin with, I'd like to find out whether having a child or not having a child is something that's been on your mind recently, say in the last six months or so. In other words, in the last few months, how often have you thought about YOUR having or not having (a/ another) child, or is that something that you don't really think about? (AGENDA: what brings the subject up or triggers the thoughts; when does it come up: is it regular or irregular events or both; cover both having and not having; how often: occasional, periodic, frequent; how often: absolute frequency estimate)

5. IF R HAS BEGUN TO DESCRIBE TALK, GO TO Q. 6. Now I'd like to find out whether or not you TALK with others about these things, and the kinds of things you say. Have you ever talked with someone about YOUR having (a/another) child or about your NOT having (a/another) child?

6. IF R HAS DESCRIBED MOST RECENT CONVERSATION, CHECK AGENDA. GO TO Q. 7. When was the last time you talked to someone about this, and with whom did you talk? (AGENDA: probe for most recent or a recent conversation; what brought the subject up; what was said; was conversation long or short, detailed or not)

7. Who else have you talked with about these things, about having or not having (a/another) child? (AGENDA: what brings the subject up or triggers the talk; is it regular, or irregular events or both; how often: occasional, periodic, frequent; are conversations long or short, detailed or not)

8. ASK IF MOST RECENT CONVERSATION WAS 6 MONTHS AGO OR LESS (Q. 6). Overall, in the last six months, about how often have you talked with someone about having or about not having (a/another) child? (AGENDA: probe for best absolute frequency estimate from relative frequency)

9. Now I'd like you to think about having (a/another) child, not having a child right away, but just sometime. Thinking about your life the way it is and the way you think it will be in the future, how many (more) children do you want to have, or would you prefer not to have any (more) children?

10. ASK IF R (WANTS/MIGHT WANT) 1 OR MORE (ADDI-TIONAL) CHILDREN. If you were to have (a/another) child, would you like that to happen NOW, that is in the next year or so, or would you rather wait until later?

11. ASK IF R WANTS NO (MORE) CHILDREN. I'd like you to think about YOUR (not having/having no more) children and what that would be like. When you think about (not having/having no more) children, what things do you think about? (AGENDA: what consequences does R see; anyone else important; probe for negative/positive events; "anything else?")

12. ASK IF R HAS NOT DISCUSSED FEELINGS. I'd like you to focus on your FEELINGS about (not having/having no more) children. When you think about (not having/having no more) children, how does this make you feel? (AGENDA: focus on "feeling" words; focus on words that describe levels or intensity of feelings; probe for negative and positive feelings; "anything else?")

16. ASK IF R WANTS NO (MORE) CHILDREN. You've said that you prefer not to have (a/another) child, but now I'd like you to suppose that you DID have (a/another) child now, that is, in the next year or two. If that were to happen, how would you FEEL about it? (That is, what would be your FEELINGS about having (a/another) child now?) (AGENDA: focus on "feeling" words; focus on words that describe levels or intensity of feelings; probe for negative and positive feelings; "anything else?")

17. ASK IF R WANTS NO (MORE) CHILDREN. And what if it happened later on, that is, what if you had (a/another) child sometime in the future? Do you have any other feelings about having (a/another) child later on? (AGENDA: focus on similarities and differences by timing; probe for both positive and negative changes; probe for changes in intensity of feelings)

18. ASK IF R WANTS (A/ANOTHER) CHILD NOW. Now, I'd like you to think about YOUR having (a/another) child, and what it would be like. Not necessarily having a child now, but just sometime. When you think about having (a/another) child, what things do you think about? (AGENDA: thinking about ever vs. never; what consequences does R see; is anyone else important; probe for negative as well as positive aspects; "anything else?")

19 ASK IF R WANTS (A/ANOTHER) CHILD NOW. ASK IF R HAS NOT DISCUSSED FEELINGS IN Q. 18. Now I'd like you to focus on your FEELINGS about having (a/another) child. When you think about having (a/another) child, how does that make you feel? (AGENDA: focus on "feeling" words; focus on words that describe levels or intensity of feelings; probe for negative and positive feelings; "anything else?")

20. You've indicated you'd like to have (a/another) child in the next year or two. When you think about having (a/another) child during THIS TIME rather than later, are there any other feelings or thoughts that come up? (AGENDA: focus on similarities and differences by timing; probe for both positive and negative changes; probe for changes in intensity of feelings; "anything else?")

21. ASK IF R WANTS (A/ANOTHER) CHILD NOW. I would like to know how strong that feeling is for you, that is, how MUCH do you want to have (a/another) child in the next year or two? (AGENDA: ask R to expand, PROBE: Can you tell me more about that? focus on intensity words)

22. ASK IF R WANTS (A/ANOTHER) CHILD NOW. And how IMPORTANT is it to you to have (a/another) child in the next year or two? (AGENDA: Ask R to expand, PROBE: Can you tell me more about that? focus on intensity words)

24. ASK IF R WANTS (A/ANOTHER) CHILD NOW. You've said that you'd like to have (a/another) child within the next year or two. Now I'd like you to suppose that you DO NOT have (a/another) child within the next year or two. If that were to happen, how would you FEEL? (That is, how would you feel about NOT having (a/another) child within the next year or two?)

25. ASK IF R WANTS (A/ANOTHER) CHILD NOW. Now, I'd like you to suppose that you DO NOT have (a/another) child, even though you might like to. If that were to happen, how would you FEEL? (That is, how would you feel about NOT having (a/another) child?) (AGENDA: think about ever vs. never)

26. ASK IF R WANTS (A/ANOTHER) CHILD LATER, BUT NOT NOW. Now, I'd like you to think about YOUR having (a/another) child, and what that would be like. Not necessarily having a child now, but just sometime. When you think about having (a/another) child, what things do you think about? (AGENDA: thinking about ever vs. never; what consequences does R see; anyone else important; probe for negative as well as positive aspects; "anything else?")

27. Now I'd like you to focus on your FEELINGS about having (a/another) child. When you think about having (a/another) child, how does that make you feel? (AGENDA: focus on "feeling" words; focus on words that describe levels or intensity of feelings; probe for negative and positive feelings; "anything else?")

29. How IMPORTANT is it to you to have (a/another) child? (AGENDA: ask R to expand, PROBE: Can you tell me more about that? focus on intensity words)

30. ASK IF R WANTS (A/ANOTHER) CHILD LATER, BUT NOT NOW. Are there things that you have done, that you do now, or that you plan to do soon to help make sure that you have (a/another) child? (AGENDA: things R does to reach goal: past, now, future)

32. ASK IF R WANTS (A/ANOTHER) CHILD LATER, BUT NOT NOW. You've also said that you would (probably) rather not have (a/another) child in the next year or two. Now, I'd like you to suppose that you DO HAVE (a/another) child within the next year or two. If that were to happen, how would you FEEL? (That is, how would you feel about having (a/another) child within the next year or two?)

33. ASK IF R IS NOT SURE WHEN R WANTS (A/ANOTHER) CHILD. I'd like you to think about YOUR having (a/another) child

and what that would be like. Not necessarily having a child now, but just sometime. When you think about having (a/another) child, what things do you think about? (AGENDA: thinking about ever vs. never; what consequences does R see; is anyone else important; probe for negative as well as positive aspects; "anything else?")

34. ASK IF R IS NOT SURE WHEN R WANTS (A/ANOTHER) CHILD. ASK IF R HAS NOT DISCUSSED FEELINGS IN Q. 18. I'd like you to focus on your FEELINGS about having (a/another) child. When you think about having (a/another) child, how does that make you feel? (AGENDA: focus on "feeling" words; focus on words that describe levels or intensity of feelings; probe for negative and positive feelings; "anything else?")

35. ASK IF R IS NOT SURE WHEN R WANTS (A/ANOTHER) CHILD. Now, I'd like you to think about YOUR (not having/having no more) children and what that would be like. When you think about (not having/having no more) children, what things do you think about? (AGENDA: thinking about ever vs. never, whether or not R is sure about wanting; what consequences does R see; is anyone else important; probe for negative as well as positive aspects; "anything else?")

36. ASK IF R HAS NOT DISCUSSED FEELINGS. I'd like you to focus on your FEELINGS about (not having/having no more) children. When you think about (not having/having no more) children, how does that make you feel? (AGENDA: focus on "feeling" words; focus on words that describe levels or intensity of feelings; probe for negative and positive feelings; "anything else?")

40. Now, is there anything we've left out, or any other feelings or thoughts about having or not having (a/another) child that occurred to you as we talked? (AGENDA: "Can you describe them for me?" probe for feelings both about having and not having)

41. The next questions are somewhat different from those I've been asking. Now I need to know some specific words or phrases that you might use in describing your feelings about your having or not having children. I am going to read you some sentences, and I'd like you to fill in the blanks. If you can think of more than one word to fill in the blank, tell me all the words you think of. Some of the sentences

sound similar to each other, but they ARE different. Here is the first sentence. For me, having (a/another) child would be ____. REPEAT SENTENCE UNTIL R HAS NO MORE WORDS.

43. Here is the next sentence. For me, NOT having (a/another) child would be ____.

45. Next, I'd like you to look at this list of words that people might use to express their feelings about things. Would you please tell me which words describe your feelings about (having/not having) (a/another) child? Take your time to look over the list and pick out all the words YOU might use to describe your own feelings. CARD LISTS: not central-central; clear-unclear; not real-real; big-small; stable-changing; unimportant-important; mine-others; weak-strong; large-small; empty-full; new-long-standing; deep-shallow; certain-uncertain; dim-bright; intense-not intense; unsure-definite; genuine-not genuine; cold-hot; inside-outside; heavy-light; a little-much, a lot; variable-constant.

47. And here is the last sentence. NOT having (a/another) child would make me ____. REPEAT SENTENCE UNTIL R HAS NO MORE WORDS.

48. Now I'd like you to think about your life THE WAY IT IS NOW and the things in your life that would make it difficult or easy to have (a/another) child in the next year or two, if you WERE to have one. Let's start with the difficulties. What things in your life would make it difficult to have (a/another) child in the next year or two? (AGENDA: "anything else?")

50. Now think about the way you EXPECT YOUR LIFE TO BE in the future. Given the way you think your life will be, what things would make it difficult for you to have (a/another) child later on? (AGENDA: "anything else?")

51. And what things would make it easy for you to have (a/another) child at some later time?

52. You've said that you (would/would not/are not sure whether or not you would) like to have (a/another) child. Can you think of anything that might happen, some change in your life, that would

make you feel differently about wanting (a/another child/no more children)? (AGENDA: changes in ever vs. never; what might make R feel differently)

53. ASK IF R IS SURE R WANTS OR DOES NOT WANT (A/ ANOTHER) CHILD. Given that you want (a/another child/no more children), what might keep that from turning out the way you want? That is, is there anything that stands in the way or might make things turn out differently from the way you want?

55. Why do you think you'll end up having (that number of children/ no children)?

APPENDIX B: RESPONDENTS FOR SEMISTRUCTURED INTERVIEWS

Case Number	Sex	Age	Marital Status	Education	Occupation	Number of Children	Number of (Additional) Children Wanted
01	F	30	Married	B.A.	Housewife	1, pregnant	0-1 more
02	M	28	Never married	M.A.	Not available	0	2
03	M	33	Married	Doctoral student	Graduate teaching assistant	0	2-3
04	M	19	Never married	High school graduate	Loader at drugstore	0	2-3
07	M	22	Never married	College senior	Student	0	2-3
08	F	28	Never married	Some college	Student	0	0, 2[a]
09	F	32	Never married	14 years	Clerical worker	0	0, 2
13	F	34	Married	B.A.	Employment counselor	0	2
14	F	30	Married	M.A.	Housewife (speech pathologist)	2	1-2
18	F	35	Married	B.A.	Head nurse	1, pregnant	0
19	F	30	Married	M.A.	Marketing research	0	0
22	M	28	Married	3 years of college	Unemployed employment counselor	4	0, 1
25	F	28	Married	B.A.	Project coordinator	0	2
26	F	28	Married	B.A.	Housewife	1	1
37	M	34	Married	Not available	Construction worker	3	0
39	M	33	Married	B.A.	Landscape architect	2	0, 1
40	M	30	Married	High school graduate	Executive chef	1	1
42	F	32	Divorced	High school graduate	Accounting clerk	2	1, 2

[a]Respondent said she wanted no children at the beginning of the interview. She became unsure of what she wanted during the interview, and at the end of the interview she said that if she had any children, she would want two.

73

APPENDIX C: QUOTATIONS FROM THE INTERVIEWS

1. *Expressions of Neutrality: Low Intensity, Indifference, Irrelevance*

Either way [now or later]. If it was meant to be it will be. I'll take it if it comes. If it didn't, I'd wait. [04-10]

Satisfied with things as they are. Ultimately, if no more, OK. [14-25]

I've thought about it. My wife doesn't want a child, has a career going now. It really doesn't matter to me. If we had another child it would be great. If we didn't, it's fine. [40-04] Don't really think [about having a child] that much. It's destiny. If it happens it does. If it don't, it don't. [40-18] Not trying to have one or not have one. It's fate. [40-24] Don't really [have anything to add]. I'm very neutral. If we have a child, it's up to my wife. She's the one that has to be pregnant. [40-40] [Not having another child] wouldn't matter. I've read that only children are smarter and more adjusted, I think. Wouldn't make me unhappy or happy. I guess I'm neutral there. [40-47] [Will have] one probably. Why not. I guess I feel like I had to come up with a number. It would just as likely be zero. It's God's will. It's nature. We're not planning to have one or planning not to have one. If it happens it does; if it don't, it don't. I'd say one. I guess neither of us wants to have more than one. That's plenty. [40-55]

2. *Expressions of Confusion*

I hadn't really thought about this stuff until you asked me. Now I'm confused. How do I really feel? [08-40]

Not sure [how I'd feel about having a child] in the next year. Perhaps in next two years. Wouldn't wait five years. [14-10]

Don't know how we'd feel about starting this 7 or 8 years from now. There are advantages . . . to having them together. You have images of where you'll be at different ages. [18-17]

Not sure when or whether I will have a child. [42-10]

3. *Expressions of Ambivalence*

A. Ambivalence expressed as presence of positive and negative feelings

Positively, love shared between me and a child. Negatively, certain stressful times. [07-27]

I'd don't want to carry a child—the morning sickness, getting larger and larger, the physical things. . . . I wouldn't want to give a handicapped child up for adoption, but would really not be prepared to meet that demand in my life. On the other hand, I'm in education and children are an important part of my life. I enjoy kids and would like to see them and participate in their raising. I just don't want the primary and sole responsibility. Yet there are rewards—seeing it grow, giving it love and care. The baby's first step and the accomplishments and achievements throughout its life. That would be rewarding. [08-11] [If I had a child] I would be really scared. Confused. Probably also really excited. [08-16]

[If I had a child in the next two years] it probably would be the last child. Turning point—to be done. Sad. Enjoyed phase of life. But also a relief. [14-20]

[If I had a child in the next two years, I would be] panicked. Distressed. Relieved I wouldn't have to make a decision. Pretty upset. Get excited once I got used to the idea. Wonder if it would change my career or work. [19-16]

It is tradition for a woman to have children with her husband. I am, though, not happy about having to be pregnant and delivering and the first four months of the baby. I would like to just get one that is eight months old, but is my own child and not someone else's. Having a baby is painful and terrible. I do not like staying at home. I love clothes and I like dressing in fashion, but sometimes I think that a woman who is a mother is not supposed to look like young people. There is supposed to be some way that a woman is supposed to look when she is a mother. [26-18] [My feelings about having another child are] both good and bad. Sometimes when I was pregnant, my husband would do everything for me. I like to be taken care of that way. Everyone worries about you and likes to know that you are OK. My husband would call me three times a day when I was pregnant. I like being the focus. I like everyone being worried about me. There is more love between my husband and I. It is fun. [26-19]

[I think about] dirty diapers, toilet training, the joys of watching them grow. Those first two years seem to go on forever. Then comes the fun. It's fascinating to watch. [42-33] I've always had an easy labor. My kids were a delight to me. One of the biggest highs I've ever had. They felt so good. They were so beautiful. I breast fed both of them. They are a burden sometimes though. [42-34]

B. Ambivalence expressed as changing feelings

I feel really good about having another child. I enjoy having kids and love babies. At the end of the day when the place looks like a tornado hit it, I have my doubts, but I get over those pretty fast. [01-19]

I'm emotionally ready now [to have a child], but I'd like to stay home, and if I had to have a job, then I'd take in babysitting. [Thoughts about having children are] sometimes negative, especially when I see a little kid running around loose and their mom or dad, their parents, let them do it. That's when I'm glad that I don't have any. Or when I see an older child with a pacifier. [09-33] It really depends. Sometimes I really want to have another child, and other times I don't. [09-34] Like I said, sometimes I'm glad I don't have them. [09-35]

Probably trying soon means very much, almost, determination. I know I want to, but if I think too much, I may change. [14-21]

4. *Expressions of Indecision*

Yes, one thing [more]. If I don't find a job within the not too distant future, my wife and I will be doing a joint search in December. She might be throwing up while we're interviewing. [Having a child could complicate that second job search?] Yes. I'm not sure if it will change our decision. It will require much more thought. [03-20] That's interesting, as opposed to lack of financial security now. Would make it easier to postpone the decision. [03-51]

I'm presently unsure about my commitment to my marriage. We may be incompatible. We may figure out why we're fighting and decide not to be married. [13-53] I want them very much. If I have one child I'll have two. I want them to grow up healthy and happy. Better to grow up with another child. It isn't fair to the child. It's better for the parents to have two children. In spite of my uncertainties, it's important that they come in this point. Uncertainty comes before decision. I'll come to a point where I'm sure and all the plans come into place.

I'll survive with whatever money is available. It's relative. Families make it on less. Somehow my husband and I will at some point have done enough talking to each other so that we'll both be sure and a baby will be conceived. [13-55]

When I want to have one, it's a matter [I] control. If [I don't get a job], I may change my mind. If I find a job, the decision will come closer. [22-30]

Irregularly. I'm not obsessed. Haven't had the time to think or talk about it. In the next few months we'll have to decide. Wife is watching neighbor's 6-month-old baby. It's getting to that time. If we're going to accomplish our goal, got to do it now. Just got present children out of diapers and now have to get back into it. [39-04]

5. *Expressions Combining Different Types of Uncertainty*

Yes. When I'm around kids I enjoy it, but when I'm at home in my peaceful surroundings, I'm glad I don't have them. Only kids trigger [conversations about having children]. If I have a baby, that's fine. If I don't, that's fine, too. [09-04]

I've noticed more than I realized how much I've talked about not having children scares me. Not having a child is a big issue for me. I'm aware as we talk that it seems to make a big difference to me that I do it soon. I thought it would be OK either way, fine. I'm surprised how negative I sound to myself. I've been so careful in not having a child, I wonder if I do want a child. People who do want children have them, and I still don't have one. This is a sensitive area, but I feel like adding that my husband and I have had lots of sex issues. I wonder if that isn't related to our thoughts about having children. Since my marriage a year ago, we've had increased sexual problems, and I think it might be around having children. That's where the negativism and fear come from. It's really possible that it's not going to happen. [13-40]

[If I don't have children I'll feel] guilty. In a way, mad at myself because I can't make a decision, and I wish I would quit thinking about one or the other. Regretful. I don't know. Guilty came pretty quickly, didn't it? [19-12]

Sometimes it is not that strong. When I come close to having one, I get scared. It gets too close. After the first baby, it is a much more difficult decision about having another one. After we got married, just three months after, we wanted a baby and we were so happy about it. But now to have another one is a big decision, and many things count. Like I said, being able to leave the house to go shopping. If I had a baby, who would get [my daughter] to school? I would have to sit at home, and I do not like that at all. [My daughter] is just now the age where it is easy for me to take her along with me. Some people love children. I just do not know how I feel all the time. Two children for when we grow old and then we can have grandchildren over and it will be fun. Mostly, [my daughter] would not be alone anymore if we had a baby. [26-21]

If we have another, we'll have one more. Not sure if I want any more. I don't know. I go back and forth. The kids are out of diapers. Do I want to get involved in having a newborn again? You also think about the financial end. [39-09]

[I think about] changing diapers. How nice children are. I enjoy my children. I wonder why I will have another child. It's hard to explain. Can't live with them, can't live without them. I think about the responsibility. Is it worth it? [39-33] Overall, I'd like to. Anxious is the wrong word. The thought brings anxiety because I'm not sure. If I had my choice we would have had another child two years ago. Initially wanted three. I'm being wishy-washy. [Thought of having a child] makes me feel good. One way [about having a child] and then the other. I usually don't [feel anxious]. . . . I don't sit up at night thinking about it. It's not that intense. Just wondering. Once we have time to talk, make the decision, that's it. This may take a month. It's not a five-minute decision. [I think about] what it's going to do to my wife's career more than anything. Having another child is not going to affect me. The care of a new child is no big deal. I don't want the baby to affect my wife's job. If she has a baby, she'll have to stay home. Do we chance her being out of the job market for two or three years? [39-34]

APPENDIX D: SAMPLE QUESTIONS

A. Neutrality and lack of clarity as offered categories

Now I'm going to read a list of feelings that you might have, about having no (more) children (after this one). For each feeling, please tell me if it is a feeling you would have, you would NOT have, or if you are not sure. The first feeling is "content." If you have no more children (after this one), would you feel content, NOT feel content, or are you not sure?

1.   Content/probably content
2.   Not content/probably not content
3.   Not sure of feelings

4.   AMBIVALENT/DEPENDS/OPPOSING FEELINGS
7.   DON'T KNOW
9.   REFUSED

Interviewer instructions:

NEUTRAL: NOT CONTENT

"Content" just isn't a relevant word. It's not how I think about it.

AMBIVALENT: In some ways I'd be content, in other ways wouldn't.

NOT SURE OF
FEELINGS: NOT SURE

I'd have to say I'm unsure.

I just don't know how it would feel; it's too hard to imagine.

TO BE
PROBED: I might feel content.

B. Direct measure of intensity

Overall, are your feelings of NOT wanting to have (a/another) child very strong, moderately strong, a little strong, or not at all strong?

1.   Very strong
2.   Moderately strong
3.   A little strong
4.   Not at all strong

5. AMBIVALENT/DEPENDS/OPPOSING FEELINGS
6. NOT SURE OF FEELINGS
7. DON'T KNOW
9. REFUSED

Interviewer instructions:

NEUTRAL: NOT AT ALL STRONG

                  I just don't have any feelings one way or the
                  other.

AMBIVALENT: Sometimes my feelings are strong, other
                  times, they aren't.

                  They are strong in some ways, not in others.

                  Some of my feelings are strong, but others
                  aren't.

NOT SURE OF
FEELINGS: I just don't know how I feel.

TO BE
PROBED: I'm not sure.

                  That's hard to say.

C. Direct measure of lack of clarity

How sure are you that you do not want to have (a/another) child?
Are you very sure, moderately sure, slightly sure, or not at all sure?

1. Very sure
2. Moderately sure
3. Slightly sure
4. Not at all sure

5. AMBIVALENT /DEPENDS /OPPOSING FEELINGS
7. DON'T KNOW
9. REFUSED

Interviewer instructions:

NEUTRAL: (There is no 'neutral' point for this measure.)

AMBIVALENT: Sometimes I'm sure and sometimes I'm not.

NOT SURE OF
FEELINGS: NOT AT ALL SURE

I just haven't thought it through or made up my mind.

I don't know how sure I am because I just never thought about it before.

I don't know. I am just not that sure.

TO BE
PROBED: I don't know how sure I am.

I can't answer that question.

D. Direct measure of ambivalence—variable feelings

Would you say your feelings about having no (more) children have gone back and forth from day to day, week to week, month to month, or haven't they gone back and forth at all?

1. Day to day
2. Week to week
3. Month to month
4. Haven't gone back and forth at all

5. CONSTANTLY GOING BACK AND FORTH
6. NEUTRAL/NO FEELINGS
7. NOT SURE OF FEELINGS
8. DON'T KNOW
9. REFUSED

Interviewer instructions:

NEUTRAL: I just don't have any feelings about it.

I know I'm not going to have a child, so I don't have any feelings to change.

AMBIVALENT: DAY TO DAY, WEEK TO WEEK, etc.

CONSTANTLY (category available for separate coding)

NOT SURE OF
FEELINGS: I just don't know how I feel.

TO BE
PROBED: That's too hard to answer. I can't remember.

E. Direct measure of ambivalence—mixed feelings

Would you say your feelings about having no (more) children are only positive, mostly positive, or equally mixed with negative feelings?

1. Only positive
2. Mostly positive
3. Equally mixed with negative feelings

4. NEUTRAL/NO FEELINGS
5. NOT SURE OF FEELINGS
7. DON'T KNOW
9. REFUSED

Interviewer instructions:

NEUTRAL: I don't really feel either positive or negative about it.

I just don't think about it that way.

AMBIVALENT: MIXED FEELINGS

Sometimes my feelings are positive, sometimes they're negative.

My feelings depend on which day it is.

NOT SURE OF
FEELINGS: I just haven't thought about it, so I don't know.

DON'T KNOW: Maybe I would feel positive.

It's really hard to say.

3

INFORMATION TRANSMISSION IN THE SURVEY INTERVIEW: NUMBER OF RESPONSE CATEGORIES AND THE RELIABILITY OF ATTITUDE MEASUREMENT

Duane F. Alwin*

This paper examines the relation between the number of response categories used to measure attitudes in survey interviews and the reliability of such attitude measurements. I review and criticize the hypothesis that reliability increases with the "information carrying capacity" of a response scale. I also review the literature on the relationship between the number of scale points and measurement reliability. This leads to a set of predictions regarding the relationship between the number of scale points and reliability of measurement, which I then examine using results obtained from three-wave panel studies conducted by the General Social Survey and the National Election Study. Reliability estimates were obtained via several procedures (LISREL, EQS, and LISCOMP) employing a vari-

This research was supported in part by a grant from the National Institute on Aging (R01-AG04743-04). Earlier versions of this paper were presented at the International Conference on Social Science Methodology, Dubrovnik, June 1988, and at the Annual Meetings of the American Sociological Association, Cincinnati, August 1991. I gratefully acknowledge Lynn Dielman, Frank Mierzwa, Jessica Sansone, and Susan Sherry for research assistance, and Richard Campbell, Bengt Muthén, Willard Rodgers, Joseph Woelfel, and Yu Xie for useful advice while the paper was being written.
*University of Michigan

*ety of statistical-estimation approaches: maximum likelihood
(Jöreskog 1979), generalized least squares based on Browne's
(1984) asymptotically distribution-free (ADF) approach, and
estimation based on categorical variable methods (CVM) (Jöreskog 1990; Muthén 1984). With one important exception,
reliability is generally higher for attitudes measured using
more response categories. Reliability is relatively higher when
attitudes are assessed using two-category rather than three-
category response scales, but evidence consistently supports
the view that for four or more category scales, reliability increases with the number of response categories, but at a decreasing rate. I also examine the hypothesis that reliability can
be enhanced by combining three-category response forms with
other types of questions to measure the direction and intensity
of attitudes, i.e., via unfolding methods. Support for this hypothesis is lacking, but more research is necessary before firm
conclusions can be drawn.*

1. INTRODUCTION

There is a wide variety of views on the optimal number of
response categories to use in the measurement of attitudes in survey
research. Some have argued that the best approach is to construct
composite scales based on responses to dichotomous questions (e.g.
McKennell 1974). Such questions are easy for respondents, and the
use of such composite scales, as in the psychological testing tradition,
makes up for whatever lack of precision might result from such
coarse categorization at the level of the survey question. Other researchers have suggested that 3-category response scales may yield
the desired level of precision in social measurement (Benson 1971;
Jacoby and Matell 1971; Lehmann and Hulbert 1972). By contrast,
the well-known Likert-type scale uses a 4- or 5-category agree-
disagree format (see Likert 1932), containing information on both
direction and intensity, which may be important for attitude measurement. The use of 6- or 7-point bipolar rating scales, e.g. the semantic
differential, is also frequently advocated (e.g. Green and Rao 1970;
Heise 1969; Osgood, Suci, and Tannenbaum 1957; Peabody 1962).
Recently, a number of authors have suggested that 5- or 7-point
scales are more advantageous for obtaining responses to survey questions, since they allow for the discrimination of both direction and
intensity, and they permit a neutral or "middle" response (e.g. Alwin

and Krosnick 1991). Finally, several examples exist of rating scales with more than 7 response categories, including a variety of scales with 9, 10, 11, or more categories—for example, the well-known Michigan "feeling thermometers" (see Weisberg and Miller n.d.).

It is obvious from this brief review that there is an enormously wide range of opinions on this issue, each typically justified in terms of increasing the level of measurement precision. Interestingly, however, there is little attention to this topic in the survey methods research literature. Surprisingly, a recent two-volume set, *Surveying Subjective Phenomena* (Turner and Martin 1984), intended as a comprehensive review of important issues in the survey measurement of subjective phenomena, did not cover this subject.[1] Similarly, an early review of the literature on cognitive aspects of survey methods, written as a report to the National Research Council (Jabine et al. 1984), also gave very little attention to this issue.[2] And, recent efforts (e.g. Hippler, Schwarz, and Sudman 1987) to apply cognitive theories to survey measurement have shown a significant lack of concern with this issue. Yet this is one of the most basic and practical issues of measurement, raising a number of important questions regarding the quality of information transmission in survey interviews.

In an effort to remedy the lack of data on this topic, this paper investigates the relationship between the information transmitted by a set of response categories and the reliability of measurement. Specifically, I focus on the relationship between measurement reliability and the amount and nature of information transmitted by response scales differing in the number of categories. I limit the discussion to survey questions that deal with attitudes, but I assume that there may be some similarities to measures of other subjective phenomena, involving evaluations of satisfaction, preferences, judgments, and the like.

---

[1]Converse and Schuman (1984) in Turner and Martin (1984) deal with the issue of question form. They describe the main types of measures used in survey research, including open-ended questions, various types of closed questions, rating formats, and so forth. They do not address the question of the optimal number of response categories.

[2]In their contribution to the Jabine et al. (1984) report, Bradburn and Danis (1984, pp. 113–16) review open versus closed-form questions, the use of a "don't know" response category, and the use of middle alternatives (or odd numbers of response categories), but they do not address the question of the optimal number of response categories.

I begin by reviewing the accumulated research literature bearing on the relationship between reliability and the number of response categories. Then I present several hypotheses based on a theory of information transmission and examine these hypotheses using estimates of reliability for attitude measures from three-wave panel studies conducted by the General Social Survey and the National Election Study.

2. RESPONSE SCALES, INFORMATION THEORY, AND RELIABILITY OF MEASUREMENT

As noted, there is little consensus regarding the optimal number of response categories in rating tasks assessing subjective quantities. On the one hand, information theorists have argued that the more categories the better, since more categories can convey more bits of information. Cognitive theorists, on the other hand, suggest there is some practical upper limit to the number of categories, given the potential difficulties respondents may have in discriminating among a larger number of categories and in selecting the response category that reflects the latent attitude. Further, motivational theorists have argued that respondents may not be interested in making optimal distinctions in the rating of attitude objects or in making judgments or preferences. It has been suggested that many respondents may tend to "satisfice" rather than "optimize" (Alwin 1991; Krosnick and Alwin 1989; Tourangeau 1984).

The essential question from a measurement point of view, as Garner (1960) and others (see Cox 1980; Komorita and Graham 1965; Miller 1956) have noted, is whether, for any particular survey question or other type of rating task, there is an *optimal* number of response categories or scale points, or at least some point beyond which there are no further improvements in discrimination along an attitudinal continuum. On the one hand, too few categories may not permit the survey respondent to adequately express her/his attitude or rate her/his level of satisfaction, or make some other form of judgment. On the other hand, too many categories may go beyond the ability of the respondent to distinguish alternatives in terms of the categories used. In the latter case it may be that respondents will selectively employ just part of the response scale to make their judgments rather the full range intended by the investigator (Alwin and Krosnick 1985).

Before I review these hypotheses in greater detail, I point out that, although there has been some effort to address this question in the survey methods literature (see Andrews 1984; Andrews and Withey 1976; Alwin and Krosnick 1991), most of the existing research is in the fields of marketing and psychological testing. Much of that work was stimulated by *information theory* (see Shannon and Weaver 1949) and early research on the amount of information transmitted by judgment scales of differing lengths (Garner and Hake 1951; Bendig and Hughes 1953; Bendig 1954a, 1954b; Garner 1960; Coombs 1964). Although there seems to be little evidence supporting it, the literature is filled with the hypothesis that scales with more categories produce more reliable data. This is buttressed by several simulation studies suggesting that a large number of response options decrease the chances of categorization error (e.g. Bollen and Barb 1981; O'Brien 1979).

2.1. *Information Theory and Number of Scale Points*

Since the 1940s and 1950s it has been suggested that information theory may be profitably applied to the construction of rating scales. One argument is that the amount of information conveyed in a formal coding system is a positive monotonic function of the number of categories available for coding the information (Woelfel and Fink 1980). Assuming a rectilinear distribution of alternatives, the information carrying capacity of a set of categories is given by the function

$$H = \log_2 (x) = \ln (x) / \ln (2),$$

where H is the maximum number of bits of transmitted information, and x is the number of scale (or response) categories (see Woelfel and Fink 1980, pp. 20–21).

Despite the theoretical elegance of this formulation, little evidence exists that the information value of responses to survey questions would be enhanced by an increase in the number of response categories. Indeed, in one of the most famous citations on this issue, Miller (1956) argued the merits of the 7-category scale and the diminished utility of questions with more than 7 categories. He argued (p. 95) that the "span of absolute judgment and the span of immediate memory impose severe limitations" on the ability of humans to work with lengthy sets of response categories. Tasks that demand the processing of large amounts of information, the retention of critical pieces of that information, and the translation of complex linguistic information by humans often exceed their abilities. Miller's conclusions rest primarily on a series of experimental studies in which subjects were given a set of objective stimuli and a set of numeric response categories to identify stimuli. The purpose of the experiments was to identify the number of correct discriminations. Miller found an incredible degree of similarity in the average number of response categories that subjects could use effectively in making discriminations among stimuli.[3] The average across these several experiments was 2.6 bits of information, with a standard deviation of 0.6 bits. This translates roughly into an average of 6.5 response categories, with the range 4 to 10 containing plus or minus 1 standard deviation.

While such findings can potentially be applied to the question of the number of response categories to use in survey measurement of subjective phenomena, there are several problems in doing so. First, survey measurements of attitudes and other subjective responses are not comparable to objective stimulus-centered response scales. They essentially involve assessments of internal states rather than perceptions of external physical absolutes. Second, according to social judgment theory, variables like attitudes may not be best represented by single points on a latent continuum. They are best thought of in terms of "latitudes" or "regions" on a scale (e.g. Sherif, Sherif, and Nebergall 1965). Third, the response categories used as scale points in survey research are often given explicit verbal and numeric labels, and the meaning of categories so labeled may be enhanced from the perspective of the information conveyed (see Saris 1988). Still, most people are unable to make precise discriminations among attitudinal stimuli using large numbers of response categories, and

[3]These experiments synthesized by Miller (1956) rely exclusively on absolute, unidimensional, perceptual judgments, involving loudness; saltiness of a solution; position of a pointer on a linear interval; sizes of squares; intensity, duration, or position of vibrations on the skin; and the curvature, direction, and length of lines.

when confronted with too many categories, respondents may differ in the way they use the response categories provided, whether those categories are labeled or not (see Alwin 1992a).

2.2. Number of Scale Points and Reliability

One way to address the question of the optimal number of response categories is in terms of the *reliability* of measurement. The reliability of measurement is a *psychometric* concept defined as the proportion of the response variance due to true-score variance, where the response variable y (normally defined as continuous) is defined as the sum of two components: the true value (defined as the expectation of a hypothetical propensity distribution for a fixed person) and a random error score. The population model for the random variables y, τ, and ϵ is a follows:

$$y = \tau + \epsilon$$

where $E(\tau) = E(y)$, $E(\epsilon) = 0$ and $E(\tau\epsilon) = 0$. Derived from these assumptions, reliability is defined as $\rho_{y\tau}^2 = \sigma_\tau^2 \div \sigma_y^2$ (see Lord and Novick 1968).

It is often stated that the reliability of measurement increases with the number of response categories used (e.g. Jahoda, Deutsch, and Cook 1951). And although there is considerable opinion in favor of this principle (e.g. Symonds 1924; Champney and Marshall 1939; Ferguson 1941; Murphy and Likert 1938), the evidence to support it is virtually nonexistent. Bendig (1953) found that inter-rater reliabilities (computed by intraclass methods) were equal for rating scales with 3, 5, 7, or 9 categories but decreased for scales with 11 categories. Komorita (1963) analyzed internal consistency reliabilities for 14-item composite indexes that used 2-point versus 6-point scales and found no difference in the composite reliabilities. Matell and Jacoby (1971) found that reliability and criterion-validity are independent of the number of scale points used for Likert-type items. They argued that regardless of the number of response categories employed, "conversion to dichotomous or trichotomous measures does not result in any significant decrement in reliability or validity" (p. 672). Komorita and Graham (1965) found that for relatively homogeneous items, composite reliability does not increase with the number of scale points, but among sets of heterogeneous items, a gain in composite reliability can be obtained by using 6 scale points instead of 2. Using simulated data, Lissitz and Green (1975) reproduced the Komorita and Graham results, but suggested that 7 scale points may not be optimal. They found that after 5 scale points, the increase in reliability levels off. Similar results were obtained by Jenkins and Taber (1977). Birkett (1986) compared differences in reliability for scales employing 2, 6, and 14 response categories and found that reliability tended to be highest for those items with 6 response categories.

3. THE RESEARCH PROBLEM

All of the research reviewed above has focused on the effects of number of response categories on the reliability of linear composites or on inter-rater reliability in nonsurvey measurement settings. While this type of research is of interest (see Cox 1980), it is less pertinent to the question of the reliability of single survey items. Currently, there is considerably more interest in single survey questions under different conditions of measurement, and the study of items individually may be much more relevant to discussions of response errors in surveys (Alwin 1989; Bartholomew and Schuessler 1991). Of course, most of the above-cited research was published before the development of routine methods for estimating the reliability of single items, so there is little information on this question.

Some survey research evidence exists on this topic. Andrews and Withey (1976), for example, compared 7- and 3-category response options in the measurement of well-being, noting that "7-point scales provide more sensitive indications of respondent's feelings" than 3-point scales. They concluded that 3-category scales "capture only 80–90 percent of the total variation, whereas 7-category scales capture virtually 100 percent of it." Andrews (1984, p. 230) compared the estimated reliability, validity, and method variance of response scales with 2, 3, 4–5, 7, 9–19, and 20+ categories. He concluded that the number of response categories had larger effects on data quality than other aspects of question design. Specifically, he concluded that "as the number of answer categories goes up, data quality goes up, i.e., validity tends to increase and residual error tends to decrease." While he found that reliability generally increased with more response categories, he also found that 3-category scales were less reliable than scales with 2 or 4–5 categories. Also, he reported that there was no clear tendency for method variance to increase with the use of more response categories. Unfortunately, these results are less informative than desirable because Andrews analyzed a pool of survey questions measuring a wide range of content, including subjective variables as well as reports of factual information. Several of the questions he studied requested the frequency of certain behaviors (i.e., the number of days per month such behaviors occurred) and provided roughly 30 response alternatives. Thus, these results may not bear on the question of interest here.

Finally, in an experimental study carried out in the 1984 General Social Survey on the measurement of confidence in social institutions, Smith and Peterson (1985) reported that when compared with 3-category scales, 7-category scales do not produce higher inter-item correlations. In fact, they argued that 7-category scales produce greater amounts of respondent error than 3-category scales. Smith and Peterson did not, however, estimate the reliabilities of their two types of scales.

4. HYPOTHESES

As indicated above, there are several reasons why the amount of reliable information extracted from a set of response categories may not be a simple positive monotonic function of their number. Cox (1980, p. 409) noted that as the number of response categories increases beyond some hypothetical minimum, respondent burden also increases. The result of more response categories, he argued, is an increasing number of discrepancies between "the true scale value and the value reported by the respondent." Thus, although it may appear that the information carrying capacity of the scale is improved by increasing the number of scale points, "response error seems to increase concomitantly." If Cox is correct, scales with large numbers of categories will show less reliability than those with fewer. He is not specific about what is large or small, but we can reasonably infer that reliability of response may increase up to some point, say up to 7 response categories, and decrease thereafter (see Alwin and Krosnick 1991).

On the other hand, according to Cronbach (1946, 1950) more response categories may encourage response sets or rating-scale biases. Rating scales are known to be susceptible to problems of response style or response sets (e.g. Block 1965; Messick 1968). Rating scales have been shown to produce method variance (Alwin and Krosnick 1985). If more response categories exaggerate this tendency of rating scales, producing greater method variance, then more response categories will create higher levels of reliability. One can imagine the following possibility. If, as suggested earlier, respondents do not use all the response categories in making discriminations with respect to attitude objects but instead rely on a subportion of the response categories provided, then individual differences in the tendency to use one part of the scale versus another will produce "invalid" portions of reliable variance (see Alwin 1992a).

Of course, interpretations of the relationship between number of response categories and reliability of response must take into account the extent of verbal labeling. Saris (1988) found that unless the end points and midpoints of response scales are labeled, reliability of measurement is quite low for a range of scale types. Other evidence also suggests that verbal labeling of response categories enhances reliability. Bendig (1953), Madden and Bourdon (1964), Finn (1972), Peters and McCormick (1966), and Zaller (1988) all found that increasing the relative amount of verbal labeling increases estimated reliability. Surprisingly, Andrews (1984) found that partially labeled scales are more reliable than fully labeled scales.

4.1. Attitude Measurement

An *attitude* is a latent, unobserved tendency to behave positively or negatively (e.g., to approve or disapprove, approach or avoid, agree or disagree, favor or oppose, etc.) toward an attitude object.[4] Attitudes are often assumed to have both direction and intensity (also refered to as extremity of response or attitude strength). In the measurement of attitudes, researchers often attempt to obtain an attitude response on a continuum expressing both direction and intensity. Most approaches to measuring an attitude conceptualize the response scale as representing this underlying latent attitude continuum, and

[4]It is very important that *attitude* (a latent tendency to behave in a particular way) not be confused with a response on an attitude measure. Such a response is a behavior and should not be confused with the latent predisposition thought to underlie it (see Alwin 1973).

the response categories are intended to "map" this attitude contin-uum. In other words, the response scale is typically intended to be (at least) bi-dimensional, expressing both direction and intensity. Obvi-ously, 2- and 3-category scales cannot assess intensity, but they can as-sess direction, and in the case of the 3-category scale, a "neutral" point can be identified. In all other cases, both direction and intensity can be obtained from the typical approaches to attitude measurement.

It seems plausible that the *direction* of the attitude may be less difficult to measure reliably than the *intensity* of attitudes, especially when vague terms (or numbers) are used to express degrees of inten-sity. This suggests that questions with two categories of responses may be more reliable than questions with a greater number of catego-ries. Such a hypothesis obviously contradicts the predictions based on information theory, reinforcing the notion that there is no intrin-sic link between the number of bits of information transmitted and reliability of measurement. Indeed, measurement precision has as much to do with the fit between the purpose of measurement and the response scale as the number of categories used in the question.

The reliability of attitude measurement, thus, depends on how well the question and the response scale permit the transmission of information about the direction and intensity of the latent attitude. I hypothesize that to the extent that survey questions clearly communi-cate the attitude direction and intensity of response categories, mea-surement reliability will be improved. Thus, I expect that it is not just the amount of information conveyed that affects measurement reli-ability, but the quality of that information as well, evaluated in terms of the purpose of measurement.

I hypothesize that 2-category attitude scales have higher reliabilities than scales with greater numbers of categories. Moreover, 3-category scales may actually promote more unreliable measurement than 2-category scales, because the introduction of a middle alterna-tive or a neutral point between positive and negative options often causes ambiguity and confusion (Schuman and Presser 1981). Two types of ambiguity may exist. First, at the level of the latent attitude, the individual's region of neutrality may vary and in some cases may be quite wide. In other words, neutrality is not necessarily a discrete point on an attitude continuum. It may be a region between acceptabil-ity and unacceptability of the attitude object, and there may be consid-erable ambiguity about the difference between neutrality and weak

positive and negative attitudes. The respondent may resolve this ambiguity by chance; thus, 3-category scales may introduce more randomness in responses. Second, as others have observed, the response scale
itself may produce certain ambiguities. Even if the internal attitude
cues are clear, the respondent may find it difficult to translate the
attitude into the language of the response categories. Middle alternatives are more often chosen when they are explicitly offered than when
they are not (Schuman and Presser 1981), suggesting that the meaning
of the response categories may stimulate the response. In some cases
the respondent may choose a middle category because it requires less
effort and may provide an option in the face of uncertainty (Alwin
1991; Krosnick and Alwin 1989). Because of the strong potential for
these ambiguities, I hypothesize that 3-category scales are less reliable
than 2- and 4-category scales. On the other hand, 5-category scales do
not create the same problems because they provide weak positive and
weak negative categories, thereby giving the respondent a better opportunity to distinguish between neutrality and weak forms of positive
and negative attitudes. With the exception of 2-category scales, and in
keeping with the predictions of information theory, I hypothesize that
reliability increases as the number of response categories increases,
but at a decreasing rate.

5. METHODS

Using panel-based reliability estimates for a large number of
attitude measures from five 3-wave reinterview surveys, I examine
the relationship between the number of response categories and measurement reliability. In this section I (a) describe the samples, (b)
briefly describe the nature of attitude measures available in these
sources, and (c) describe how reliability is estimated. After presenting the results, I discuss several problems concerning the interpretation of these estimates of attitude measurement reliability.

5.1. The Samples

I draw upon five 3-wave panel surveys conducted in two sets of
studies. First, I use data from the 1973 and 1974 reinterview studies
conducted by the General Social Survey (see Smith and Stephenson
1979). Second, I use data from three 3-wave panel studies conducted

by the National Election Study: the 1956-58-60 NES panel (Campbell et al. 1971), the 1972-74-76 NES panel (see Converse and Markus 1979), and the 1980 NES panel (see Markus 1982). The numbers of cases and attrition rates across waves for these panels are given in Table 1.

The General Social Survey reinterview studies. The GSS is an annual cross-sectional survey of the noninstitutionalized residential population of the continental United States aged 18 and over (NORC 1990). It has been conducted nearly every year since 1972 on approximately 1,500 respondents per year. The purpose of the GSS has been to monitor social trends in attitudes and behavior. The GSS does not ordinarily include a panel component; however, in 1972, 1973, 1974, 1978, and 1987 such a design was included. In the 1973 and 1974 reinterview studies, three waves were included, making it possible to estimate the components of variance discussed above (see Smith and Stephenson 1979). In the 1973 study, the GSS attempted to reinterview a random subset of 315 respondents to the initial survey; 227 of these respondents completed a second interview, and 195 of those completed a third (see Table 1). In the 1974 study,

TABLE 1
Information on Panel Attrition for NES and GSS

Study	Sample Size				Retention Rates		
	Base N	t_1	t_2	t_3	t_1-t_2	t_2-t_3	t_1-t_3
NES 1956, 1958, 1960	2,475	1,752	1,356	1,132	77.0%	89.7%	69.1%
		(71.2%)					
NES 1972, 1974, 1976	—[a]	2,705	1,624	1,320	60.0%	81.3%	48.8%
		—					
NES 1980s	1,514	1,008	843	746	83.6%	88.5%	74.0%
		(74.6%)					
GSS 1973	—[b]	315	227	195	72.1%	85.9%	61.9%
		—					
GSS 1974	—[b]	291	210	195	72.2%	92.8%	67.0%
		—					

Note: Figures in parentheses are response rates.
[a]Base sample information was not available.
[b]Base sample is not applicable.

attempts were made to reinterview 291 of the original GSS respondents; 210 of these completed a second interview, and 195 of those completed a third. I analyze the data from the 195 cases surviving each of the 1973 and 1974 studies, 62 percent and 67 percent of the original target samples, respectively. The average interval between the first and second waves of the 1973 study was 46.9 days, the average interval between the first and third waves was 80.2 days. In the 1974 study, the average interval between the first and second waves was 46.4 days, and the average interval between the first and third waves was 78.9 days. The initial GSS interviews were conducted face-to-face; reinterviews were conducted by telephone (see Smith and Stephenson 1979). The 1973 reinterview study included 44 questions that were common across all three waves, 14 of which were attitude measures. In 1974, 19 questions were repeated in the second and third waves, 5 of which are attitude measures (see Alwin 1989).

The National Election Panel Studies. Every two years since 1952 (except 1954), the Survey Research Center of the University of Michigan's Institute for Social Research has interviewed a representative cross section of Americans to track national political participation. In presidential election years, a sample is interviewed before the election and immediately afterward. In nonpresidential election years, only postelection surveys are conducted. Data are obtained from face-to-face interviews with national full-probability samples of all citizens of voting age in the continental United States, exclusive of military reservations, using the Survey Research Center's multistage area sample (see Miller, Miller, and Schneider 1980).[5] The sample sizes typically range between 1,500 and 2,000.

Of the respondents interviewed in 1956, 1,132 were reinterviewed in 1958 and again in 1960 (see Campbell et al. 1971). The questionnaires used in the 1958 and 1960 panel studies were the same as those used in the 1958 and 1960 cross-sectional studies, respectively. With this design, only a small number of items could be replicated in all three studies. Of the respondents interviewed in 1972, 1,320 were successfully reinterviewed in 1974 and again in 1976. Again, the questionnaires used in these reinterview surveys were the same as those used for the cross-sectional samples interviewed at

[5]In 1978 the primary sampling units were changed from SMSAs and counties to fit congressional district lines, but this change should have no appreciable effect on the representativeness of the full sample.

those times. The data from the 1970s panel design, however, yielded many more replicate attitude questions. In the 1980 National Election Panel Study, 769 respondents were reinterviewed at roughly four-month intervals, beginning in January and ending in November (see Markus 1982).[6]

5.2. *The Measures*

The analysis is restricted to attitude measures, excluding measures of perceptions and beliefs, self-evaluations, and factual material (see Alwin 1989). For these purposes, 99 attitude measures are available from these studies. The types of questions used in these studies range from agree-disagree questions (which vary in number of response options, the extent of labeling, etc.) to questions with a variety of scale points. The longest scales are the "feeling thermometers," which have 9 scale points.[7] There is a fair number of 7-category scales and several scales with 2, 3, 4, or 5 categories. In all response scales, the extreme categories have verbal labels, but scales vary in the extent to which more than the extreme categories are labeled. The relationship between measurement reliability and the extent of category labeling is not studied here (but see Alwin and Krosnick 1991; Saris 1988).

Table 2 presents information on the substantive content assessed by these attitude measures. Content is classified according to a scheme developed to analyze life-span processes of stability and change in attitudes (see Alwin 1992c).[8] This scheme codes the mea-

[6]In all of the panel data analyzed here, respondents must have complete data at all three waves to be included in the analysis. In other words our analysis of covariance/correlation data for the measures described below is based on respondents with data present at all three waves for a particular variable.

[7]Feeling thermometers are sometimes thought of as having 101 scale points because the codes range from 0 to 100. In fact, in the NES, the respondents are shown a card that labels nine specific scores (0, 15, 30, 40, 50, 60, 70, 85, and 100), along with explicit verbal labels for each of these nine scale points (see Weisberg and Miller n.d.). Scores between these labeled scale-points, e.g. a score of 20 or 55, were recorded; however, our analysis indicates that rarely more than 3 percent to 5 percent of respondents gave responses other than the 9 labeled numeric options. Thus, for all intents and purposes, this is a 9-point scale. Our analysis of these data preserves the coding of finer gradations when they exist.

[8]A complete list of measures used in this analysis—including the questions, the response categories, and coding—is available from the author upon request.

TABLE 2
Mean Reliability Estimates by Attitude Content and Study

Content	NES 1950s	NES 1970s	NES 1980s	GSS 1973–1974
Political identification	.885 (1)	.699 (2)	.707 (1)	—
Ideology	—	.572 (3)	—	—
Parties	—	.496 (6)	.630 (3)	—
Racial categories	—	.549 (3)	—	—
Racial policies	.540 (2)	.569 (2)	—	—
Political institutions	—	.424 (6)	—	—
Role of government	.456 (6)	.463 (2)	.630 (7)	.789 (19)
Government officials	—	.475 (6)	—	—
Political processes	—	.432 (4)	—	—
Political candidates	—	.701 (5)	.747 (11)	—
Social groups	—	.492 (12)	—	—
Total	.477 (9)	.509 (51)	.691 (22)	.789 (19)

Note: Figures in parentheses are numbers of items in each category.

sures in terms of the domain of content reflected by the attitude object to which the attitude question was directed. Content domains are as follows: (a) political self-identification (party identification and rating as liberal or conservative),[9] (b) attitudes toward ideological categories (liberal and conservative), (c) attitude toward political parties (Democrats, Republicans, or parties in general), (d) attitude toward racial categories (black and white), (e) attitude toward racial policies (desegregation of schools, busing, civil rights), (f) attitude toward government as a political institution (most such measures evaluate the government as an attitude object), (g) attitude toward the role of government or social policies, (h) attitude toward government officials (members of Congress, people in government, or public officials), (i) attitude toward political processes (elections, voting, rights of the accused, demonstrations), (j) attitude toward political

[9]In fact the political self-identification measures are not attitudes in a strict sense. Personal identification with a political party or an ideological category does involve some attitudinal information, but as measures of identities they are conceptually distinct from measures of attitudes. Although presented here for comparative purposes, the party identification measures are not included in subsequent analyses of single-item measures because they involve two questions. These items—one from each of the NES studies—are treated subsequently in a discussion of the utility of "unfolding" questions.

candidates, and (k) attitude toward social groups (women, unions, big business, older people, etc.), which either are (or represent) political actors. Table 2 gives two pieces of information for each of these categories for each study: (1) the number of such items in each content category, and (2) the mean reliability of the items within a particular content category within a given study.[10]

These results suggest that a factor that may need to be taken into account when interpreting the results is the relationship between the number of response categories and the content of the attitude question. But attitude content and response scale length are almost hopelessly confounded. For example, in the NES data, measures of candidate ratings and political self-identifications are the most reliable, whereas measures of attitudes toward the government as a political institution and attitudes toward political procedures are less reliable. However, the items in the first set are measured with 7- and 9-point rating scales, whereas those in the second set are measured with 3-, 5-, and 7-point scales. Thus, it is difficult to conclude from these data whether higher reliabilities are due to the response scale or to the content being measured, or both. More research is clearly needed on this issue, but for present purposes I ignore this confounding (see Alwin and Krosnick 1991).

There is also a confounding of design and content in these results. The GSS measures attitudes primarily with 2-category response scales, whereas the NES routinely uses 3-, 5-, 7-, and 9-category scales (see Table 3 below). Unfortunately, there is only one 4-category scale in the GSS, so our main comparison there is of 2- and 3-category scales. However, because the GSS measures all fall within the same content category, namely policy attitudes, the nature of the attitude is controlled in this comparison. In the NES, by contrast, there are relatively few 2-category scales. In the panels from the 1950s and 1970s, there are sufficient numbers of 3-, 5-, 7-, and 9-category scales to allow some comparisons regarding our main hypotheses. In the 1980s panel there is only one 3-category scale, but there are several 4-, 7-, and 9-category scales. The 1980s panel, thus, provides an additional set of comparisons regarding reliability and number of scale points.

[10]In this table I present the GLS-ADF estimator of reliability from Bentler's (1989) EQS program (see below).

5.3. Statistical Design and Estimation

One approach to estimating reliability, possibly the preferred approach (see Alwin 1989), is to rely on reinterview measurement or panel designs. Such designs have several advantages but several problematic features, as well. In the test-retest approach using a single reinterview, we must assume that there is no change in the underlying trait being measured (Lord and Novick 1968; Siegel and Hodge 1968). This is problematic in many situations, because in a two-wave panel study, the assumption of perfect (correlational) stability may be unrealistic; but without this assumption, little purchase can be made on the question of reliability in such designs. Because of the problematic nature of this assumption, however, several efforts have been made to analyze panel surveys involving three waves, where reliability can be estimated under certain assumptions about the properties of the error distributions (Achen 1975; Erickson 1978; Heise 1969; Wiley and Wiley 1970; Werts, Jöreskog, and Linn 1971). This is the approach taken here.

Estimation of reliability from panel surveys makes sense only if there is enough time between measurements to make bias due to memory unlikely (Moser and Kalton 1972, p. 353). When the remeasurement interval is too close, the estimate of the amount of true stability in response will be biased. In such a case the measures appear to be more reliable than they are. This issue can be assessed by comparing reliability estimates from panel studies with varying remeasurement intervals.[11]

Given that these problems can be surmounted, there are several advantages of this approach. One advantage is that it lets us analyze reliability for single items, without having to restrict the examination of reliability to that of composite scores.[12] A second

[11]Unless one knows the sign of the covariance among the errors over occasions of measurement, it is not possible to predict the nature of the bias. Our experience, however, indicates that over shorter time intervals, reliability is estimated to be higher than over longer time intervals, suggesting that memory or consistency effects produce an upward bias in reliability (see Alwin 1989).

[12]Composite reliability is also of interest (see Cronbach 1951; Greene and Carmines 1979; Jöreskog 1971), but it does not provide clear-cut information on the link between reliability and the characteristics of survey questions. Composite-score reliability is a function of item-level reliabilities, so information pertaining to reliability of single items is relevant to issues of internal consistency of scores.

important advantage is that this approach does not require the *univocal* assumption of congeneric measurement, that is, the assumption that the true score of a given measure assesses just one latent variable (see Alwin 1989; Jöreskog 1971). And third, this approach does not relegate reliable and stable specific variance to the error term, thus producing bias in the estimation of reliability (see Alwin and Jackson [1979] for a discussion of this issue).

Reliability estimation. As indicated above, the approach I take here is *psychometric:* I assume that there are latent attitude variables that can be defined as more or less continuously distributed predispositions to respond to attitude stimuli.[13] This approach falls within the tradition of *classical true-score theory* (Lord and Novick 1968). However, in applying this approach to survey measurement, we may view the categoric nature of the measures as problematic, especially when the concern is differing numbers of categories. The definition of reliability typically assumes that the variables are continuous at both the observed and unobserved levels. Thus, to estimate reliability, as defined above, we must address the discrete nature of survey response categories.[14] This problem has two aspects. First, the use of simple product-moment correlations (and associated covariance structures) as input to reliability assessment (e.g., in LISREL maximum likelihood estimation) confounds the magnitude of correlation with the skewness of variables, especially when categoric variables are severely skewed and kurtotic (see Muthén and Kaplan 1985). Thus, simple Pearson product-moment correlations for 2- and 3-category scales may in some cases be attenuated by the marginal distributions. Second, statistical estimation approaches that assume continuously observed variables that are distributed as multivariate normal (e.g. maximum likelihood) are problematic to the extent that survey measures depart from this assumption. It is ordinarily assumed that this aspect of the problem is more serious for variables with fewer response cate-

[13]Defining attitudes as "latent" variables does not imply that they are not real or that their validity is questionable and indeterminable. This simple means that they are unobservable and therefore must exist as hypothetical quantities in our models.

[14]There are other approaches to the estimation of measurement error that fall outside the traditional psychometric approach. One is the latent class model; a second is the Rasch model (see Andrich 1985). Further work is necessary to bring these models to bear on the traditional psychometric issue of measurement reliability as conceptualized here.

gories.[15] In any case, the approach I take to statistical estimation (described below) attempts to deal with the problems stemming from the categoric nature of survey data.

Given data from the type of panel designs discussed above, reliability information can be obtained by estimating a simplex structure for a single variable measured at three time-points (Jöreskog 1970, 1974). Such models include a series of measures of the same variable separated in time and posit a Markovian (lag-1) process to account for change and stability in the underlying latent variable. This type of model has been useful in analyzing reliability of survey reinterview measures because it controls for true change in the underlying variable. This estimation strategy for three time-points is based on a class of just-identified *simplex* models that specify two structural equations for a set of three over-time measures of a given variable y_t (where the subscript t indexes the occasion of measurement):

$$y_t = \tau_t + \epsilon_t,$$

$$\tau_t = \beta_{t,t-1} \tau_{t-1} + v_t.$$

The first equation represents a set of measurement assumptions. The over-time measures are assumed to be *tau-equivalent* except for true attitude change and measurement error is assumed to be random (see Alwin 1988, 1989). The second equation specifies that the causal processes involved in attitude change over time follow a Markovian or lag-1 process. The assumptions for the underlying process of attitude change are not taken as problematic here, since I focus on the measurement model. However, I note that the model assumes a Markovian process in which the distribution of the true attitude at time t is dependent only on the distribution of the true attitude at time $t-1$ and a stochastic error term, v_t, and is not dependent on distributions of the true attitude at earlier times.

The above model is well known, and within this framework there are several defensible approaches to reliability estimation. Using this model and several estimation approaches, I obtained estimates of reliability, the proportion of response variance that can be attributed to "true" attitudes, i.e., $\sigma_\tau^2 / \sigma_y^2$. These reliability estimates

[15]Using Muthén and Hofacker's (1988) triplet-testing approach, I was unable to reject the normality assumptions for the NES dichotomous data used here.

were obtained using several different estimation approaches (described below). I then used these reliability estimates as input to a secondary analysis of the relationship of number of response categories to reporting reliability. Briefly, there are two ways to identify the model: One makes the assumption that error-variance components in the measures are constant over time (Wiley and Wiley 1970), and the other assumes constant reliabilities of measures over time (Heise 1969).[16] These approaches are discussed in sufficient detail in the statistical literature, so extensive discussion here would be redundant. Moreover, the various approaches to estimation are sufficiently similar to discourage any lengthy consideration of their differences. The key difference devolves to the nature of the covariance structure analyzed. It can be readily shown that when the Wiley and Wiley model is applied to correlational data, Heise's estimates are produced, whereas when covariance data are analyzed, the Wiley and Wiley estimates result. In general it may be advisable to implement the most general form of the model, which is essentially the approach described by Wiley and Wiley.[17]

Given the assumptions of these various approaches to identifying the simplex model, different amounts of reliability information are produced. Heise's approach produces one reliability estimate, since reliability is assumed to be constant over time. The Wiley and Wiley approach, on the other hand, produces a separate reliability estimate for each occasion of measurement. When developmental processes are the focus of study, there are some serious risks in using the Wiley and Wiley approach, since assumptions about equivalence of measurement-error variances without regard to heterogeneity in true-score variances over time can result in artificial changes in reliability with time (see Alwin 1988). By contrast, when the processes studied are in *dynamic equilibrium,* that is, when there is homogeneity in observed variances over time (see Lord 1963), the Heise and Wiley and Wiley approaches are identical.

Thus, except in the case noted, for all measures I estimated reliability both ways, that is, using Heise's (1969) constant reliability

---

[16]A third approach, which makes neither assumption but estimates only limited information, is also possible, but it is not pursued here because it gives the same information (Werts, Jöreskog, and Linn 1971).

[17]Further discussion of this issue is contained in Alwin (1989, pp. 297–305).

assumption and Wiley and Wiley's (1970) constant error-variance assumption. The processes of attitude change underlying the measures studied in this analysis all seem to be virtually in a state of *dynamic equilibrium,* and the Wiley and Wiley approach yields only trivial differences in reliability estimates across time. Moreover, the differences between the reliability estimates produced by these two approaches are trivial, since it can be shown (see Alwin 1989) that the reliability of the second time point estimated in the Wiley and Wiley approach equals the single reliability estimated in the Heise model. Thus, I report only this time 2 estimate here.[18] Of course, the "categoric" approach described in the next section, wherein tetrachoric and polychoric correlations are used as input in the estimation of this model, must rely on correlational data, and it is therefore not possible to obtain more than one reliability estimate; i.e., only the Heise approach can be implemented in that case.

Statistical estimation and categoric data. There are several ways to estimate the above model. One approach is to estimate the model parameters by maximum likelihood (Jöreskog and Sörbom 1989), assuming that variables are jointly normally distributed and thus ignoring the categoric nature of the data (e.g. see Alwin 1989; Alwin and Krosnick 1991). Such an approach may not always be justified for survey data, however, because of the nature of the distributional assumptions and the potential biases of the product-moment correlation as an estimator of the true underlying correlation. A second approach is to use an estimation strategy that is not based on such distributional assumptions, for example, a strategy that is based on arbitrary distribution theory (see Browne 1984; Bentler 1989, pp. 1–7). Both of these approaches, however, are geared to continuous observed variables and may not be viewed as appropriate estimation strategies, given the categoric nature of survey responses. Thus, a third option is to estimate the above model using correlations that attempt to deal with the categoric nature of the data, for example, using tetrachoric and polychoric correlations as input into conventional estimation routines (see Jöreskog 1990; Jöreskog and Sörbom 1988; Muthén 1988).

One could argue that the third approach represents an inadequate assessment of measurement reliability (see Alwin 1992*b*). Polychoric and tetrachoric correlations provide an estimate of the

---

[18]All of the reliability information is available from the author upon request.

relationships between continuous-level variables assumed to underlie categoric measures; therefore, model parameters express relationships among these hypothetical continuous-level variables and *not* the observed categoric variables. Reliability interpretations in this case should be applied to the hypothetical continuous-level variables (see Muthén 1988, pp. 4-3). However, so that issues of statistical estimation do not detract from the substantive methodological issues raised in this paper, I rely on all three methods of reliability estimation. These three methods of estimation produce very similar results regarding the hypothesis at issue.[19]

6. RESULTS

Table 3 presents mean reliability estimates by number of response categories for each of the three major design categories. Even though these average reliability estimates are often based on just a few items, it is advisable to present them separately rather than combine them across designs because the nature of the reinterview design influences the reliability (see Alwin 1989, pp. 318–20). This table presents the average reliability estimates from (a) LISREL maximum likelihood estimation (Jöreskog and Sörbom 1989),[20] (b) the EQS generalized least squares distribution-free approach based on arbitrary distribution theory (GLS-ADF estimates) (Bentler 1989),[21] and (c) the

[19]It is sometimes suggested that percent-agreement coefficients may inform questions of reliability (e.g. Krosnick and Berent 1990). In fact percent agreement is generally not related to reliability for some rather obvious reasons. In the case of *number of scale points* this measure is virtually worthless because there is a built-in tendency for such agreement coefficients to show greater agreement when there are fewer response categories. Indeed, percent agreement is a monotonically decreasing function of the number of response categories.

[20]For this model the LISREL program gives exactly the same figures for maximum likelihood estimation and any of the least squares approaches.

[21]Because this model is just-identified, in virtually all cases the results of the GLS-ADF approach were identical to those provided by LISREL maximum likelihood estimation. The only differences occurred when a negative variance was encountered in any of the disturbances of the model. This happened in 34 cases. In these cases EQS fixes the offending variance to zero on the assumption that variance cannot (by definition) be negative. LISREL and LISCOMP allow the model to be estimated with a negative variance. Such negative variances were not encountered in the measurement structure of the observed variables, but rather were due to negative disturbance variances in the underlying structural equation model. Experience indicates that misspecification at the level of the underlying structural equation model does not create severe distortion in estimates of measurement error variances.

TABLE 3
Reliability Information By Design of Study and Number of Response
Categories: GSS and NES Panel Data

Sample	Number of Categories	Number of Items	Mean Reliability		
			(1)[a]	(2)[b]	(3)[c]
GSS 1973–1974	2	15	.746	.807	.916
	3	3	.670	.685	.755
	4	1	(.663)	(.826)	(.754)
Total		19	.734	.786	.889
F ratio			0.77	3.20	7.33
p value			.40	.09	.01
NES 1950s and 1970s	2	6	.480	.480	.692
	3	22	.409	.430	.536
	4	1	(.435)	(.435)	(.579)
	5	8	.458	.477	.579
	7	6	.557	.599	.611
	9	15	.619	.630	.—[d]
Total		58	.494	.509	.577[e]
F ratio			12.73	13.15	3.79
p value			.00	.00	.02
NES 1980s	3	1	(.722)	(.752)	(.823)
	4	3	.559	.582	.697
	7	4	.635	.655	.690
	9	14	.722	.722	.—[d]
Total		22	.682	.689	.693[f]
F ratio			2.95	2.23	0.01
p value			.08	.14	.94

Note: Estimates in parentheses are based on one item and are not included in the ANOVA estimations.
[a]LISREL maximum likelihood estimates.
[b]EQS generalized least squares ADF estimates.
[c]LISCOMP/PRELIS-LISREL polychoric correlation-based estimates.
[d]PRELIS recommends LISREL analysis.
[e]Based on 42 items.
[f]Based on 7 items.

LISREL analysis of polychoric (or in the case of dichotomous variables, tetrachoric) correlations.[22]

In this table I also present the p values from one-way ANOVAs predicting reliability from the number of response categories. Of course, statistical tests on these category differences in reliability are not technically appropriate, since questions are neither randomly selected from some known universe of questions nor independent in a sampling sense. I present this information not as a basis for generalizing to some known universe of questions but as a potentially useful heuristic in evaluating the magnitude of the observed differences. I rely mainly on the observed differences themselves to draw conclusions regarding differences in reliability.

These results show that reliability is generally higher for measures involving more response categories, although there are some important exceptions. As hypothesized, the 2-category items represent the major exception to this trend. Indeed, in the GSS and in the NES of the 1950s and 1970s, the 2-category items have somewhat higher estimated reliabilities than the 3-category items, regardless of the method of estimation.[23] With this exception, there does seem to be a relationship between the number of scale categories and reliability. In general, beyond the dichotomous case, reliability increases monotonically with the number of response categories, thus supporting the general hypothesis given above from information theory. Figure 1 reinforces this conclusion. The GLS-ADF reliability estimates are plotted with the maximum bits of information by number

---

[22]The polychoric correlations produced by PRELIS and LISCOMP were the same in virtually every case, but in a few cases they were slightly different because of different bases for calculation. When they were different I used Muthén's (1988) correlations. These tend to be internally consistent and estimation does not encounter admissibility problems linked to inconsistent estimation of polychoric correlations. I present results obtained from the analysis of these polychoric correlations using weighted least squares (see Jöreskog 1990). I tried to reproduce these results using LISCOMP but was unable to do so. Using the same polychoric correlations, the LISCOMP program consistently produced incorrect estimates with uninterpretable standard errors and likelihood ratio statistics.

[23]As indicated above, percent agreement is likely to be naturally confounded with the number of response scale categories, since fewer categories increase the chances of agreement. The figures for percent agreement (not shown) indicate a very clear monotonic relationship with the number of scale categories, but in the direction opposite of the theoretical predictions.

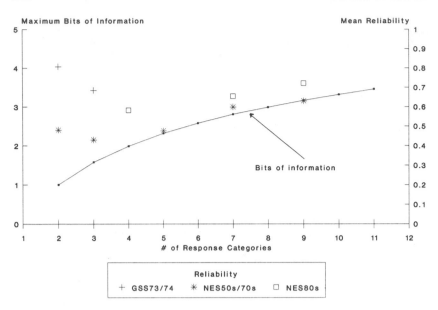

FIGURE 1. Relationship of number of response categories, information transmission, and reliability of rating scales.

of response categories. These results illustrate that the reliability estimates for 4- to 9-category measures follow the logarithmic functional form quite closely.

While the different estimation approaches provide different reliability estimates, the relationship between reliability and number of response categories is generally the same regardless of estimation strategy. The only exception to this is in the 1980s NES panel, where there are no significant differences between the polychoric-based reliability estimates for 4- and 7-category scales, whereas the maximum likelihood and GLS-ADF estimates produce a pattern of increasing reliability across 4-, 7-, and 9-category scales. To gauge the extent of similarity of reliability estimates across the three statistical estimation strategies, I calculated simple product-moment correlations among the three sets of estimates (see Table 4). I was looking not for absolute agreement between these estimates, but for general consistency across measures. As expected, the maximum likelihood and GLS-ADF estimates are quite similar, and both correlate highly (in the 0.8 to 0.9 range) with the PRELIS/LISCOMP polychoric/ tetrachoric-based estimates.

TABLE 4
Product-Moment Correlations Among Reliability Estimates

	1	2	3
1. LISREL maximum likelihood	1.00		
2. EQS GLS-ADF	.956	1.00	
	(99)		
3. LISCOMP/PRELIS-LISREL	.844	.839	1.00
	(70)	(70)	

Note. Pair-wise sample sizes are in parentheses.

6.1. *Unfolding Techniques*

The above analysis involved single questions wherein the response scales were read to the respondent. For questions with 4 or more response categories, an alternative is to combine questions in a manner that unfolds the response possibilities, first assessing the direction of the attitude, then assessing intensity. Here I briefly consider the possibility that unfolding techniques improve measurement reliability.

Although there are no unfolding questions available in these studies for comparison with the questions used above, I report results of reliability estimation for a set of such questions used in the NES panels to measure party loyalty. The two-part NES measure of party loyalty begins with the question, "Generally speaking, do you usually think of yourself as a Republican, a Democrat, an Independent, or what?" This is essentially a 3-category response scale. A second question is then asked of Republicans and Democrats: "Would you call yourself a strong (Republican/Democrat) or a not very strong (Republican/Democrat)?" If Independent, the respondent is asked, "Do you think of yourself as closer to the Republican or to the Democratic party?" These follow-up questions permit the assessment of *intensity* (or strength) of party loyalty.[24]

For present purposes I consider (a) the reliability of the 3-category party-loyalty question, (b) the reliability of a 4-category measure of *intensity* (in which 0 is assigned to Independents expressing no closeness to either major party, 1 is assigned to Independents

[24]These questions were not included in the analysis presented in Tables 3 and 4.

TABLE 5
Reliability Estimates for Unfolding Questions Measuring Direction and
Intensity of Party Identification: NES Panels

Year of Study	Direction	Intensity	Combined
1950s NES (1,045)	.869	.789	.889
1970s NES (1,237)	.780	.785	.837
1980s NES (754)	.846	.824	.848

Note: Sample sizes are in parentheses.

expressing some closeness to either party, 2 is assigned to "weak" Republicans and Democrats, and 3 is assigned to "strong" Republicans and Democrats), and (c) the reliability of the conventional 7-point party-loyalty scale (1 = strong Democrat, 2 = weak Democrat, 3 = Independent-leaning Democrat, 4 = Independent, 5 = Independent-leaning Republican, 6 = weak Republican, and 7 = strong Republican) (see Converse and Markus 1979). For this analysis "no preference," "uncertain," and "other" responses were considered missing data and were thus omitted from the analysis.

Table 5 presents the estimates of reliability obtained for these three measures of party loyalty for the NES 3-wave panels from the 1950s, 1970s, and 1980s.[25] These measures show relatively high reliabilities—all in the 0.8 range—well above those typically obtained for attitude measures. This indicates either that unfolding techniques can produce higher reliabilities, or that party loyalty is a trait that can be measured reliably, or both. The issue here, however, is whether the combined scale is more reliable than the component questions. Here the answer is clearly no, reliability does not seem to be enhanced through the use of the unfolding technique.

I argue that because they separate the issues of direction and intensity of attitudes, unfolding techniques may actually enhance the measurement reliability of attitudes. Such techniques capitalize on the relative ability of 2-category (and in some cases 3-category) response scales to reliably capture the direction of attitude and the proven effectiveness of longer response scales for measuring intensity. Such techniques are also relatively uncomplicated and do not place a great deal of cognitive burden on the respondent. This consideration may

[25]The estimates presented in Table 5 were obtained by using Bentler's (1989) GLS-ADF approach.

be important when visual aids cannot be used in the interviews—for example, in telephone surveys. Still, as indicated here, there is little basis for concluding that unfolding techniques enhance the reliability of measurement because adequate comparisons that control for the topic of measurement have not been carried out. Thus, more research is necessary for such a conclusion to be reached.

7. CONCLUSIONS

In this analysis I have presented data relevant to the hypothesis drawn from information theory, which suggests that the reliability of measuring subjective phenomena is in part a function of the number of response categories provided. This hypothesis is based on the idea that since more information can be transmitted via response scales of greater length, respondents can more reliably convey their subjective states using scales with more categories. I have examined this issue with respect to the transmission of attitudinal information in survey interviews. With one important exception, the analysis presented here provides support for this hypothesis. Generally those attitude measures with more response categories have systematically higher reliabilities. The major exception to this pattern is the 2-category response scale, which shows higher reliability than expected.

With the exception noted, one can conclude on the basis of these results that greater reliability in attitude measurement can be achieved by using questions with more response categories. The nonlinear nature of these results may account in part for results from previous studies that found no differences in reliability across questions differing in numbers of categories. While I believe these findings are robust, there are several important caveats. First, the 2-category response scale has shown itself to measure attitude direction as reliably as other response scales—in particular, 2-category response scales exceed 3-category scales in estimated reliability. Thus, if the purpose of measurement is to assess only the direction of attitudes, the 2-category scale seems to do as well or better than other forms. Longer response scales assess intensity as well as direction, which is in keeping with the assumptions of information theory, that longer response scales can transmit more information. And in keeping with the predictions of information theory, I report that longer response scales have higher estimated reliability. However, any conclusions regarding response-scale length (or number of categories) and reliability need to take the purpose of measurement into account. When measuring direction of attitude, 2-category scales are superior to 3-category scales, thus contradicting the predictions of information theory. On the other hand, when measuring intensity, reliability increases with the number of response categories.

Second, while these results may apply generally to attitude measurement, they may not generalize to other areas of subjective measurement. I have shown elsewhere (Alwin 1992*a*) that similar results obtain in the measurement of life satisfaction. But more research needs to be carried out in ways that will improve this knowledge base. A third, related issue was mentioned earlier, namely, that I have not attempted to control for substantive content in the measurement of differences in estimated reliability. Elsewhere (see Alwin and Krosnick 1991) I report an effort to estimate the relationship of response-scale length to reliability of measurement, while controlling statistically for the substantive content of the measures. Those results are consistent with the results presented here, thus reducing the potential threat to my conclusions.

Fourth, there are several reasons why the amount of reliable information extracted from response categories may be positively related to estimated reliability. One obvious possibility is that more response categories improve the quality of information transmission, but as I indicated earlier, more response categories may also encourage response sets or rating-scale biases (Cronbach 1946, 1950). Rating scales are known to produce method variance, and if more response categories exaggerate this tendency, then some of the improvement in reliability may represent the "reliable" assessment of response styles and not simply improved measures of the true latent attitude of interest. My decomposition of variance in life satisfaction measures, however, does not support this hypothesis (Alwin 1992*a*).

Finally, the above analysis has not taken into account other aspects of the survey questions. As my previous work indicates, there are theoretical reasons to expect that the amount of unreliability of measurement in attitudes is due to the ambiguity of response alternatives linked to differential labeling of response options, or differences in reponse due to the explicit offering of "don't know" options (see Alwin and Krosnick 1991). However, in the present analysis the questions employed use enough verbal labeling to make it doubtful that labeling produces much variation in reliability. Furthermore, very few of the NES and GSS questions actually provide "don't know" options, and it is doubtful that such differences could be confounded with response-scale length in this analysis. In this regard, a recent study by McClendon and Alwin (1990) found few differences in response variance that could be linked to the use of "don't know" filters.

REFERENCES

Achen, Christopher H. 1975. "Mass Political Attitudes and the Survey Response." *American Political Science Review* 69:1218–31.

Alwin, Duane F. 1973. "Making Inferences from Attitude-Behavior Correlations." *Sociometry* 36:253–78.

———. 1988. "Structural Equation Models in Research on Human Development and Aging." Pp. 71–170 in *Methodological Advances in Aging Research,* edited by K. Warner Schaie et al. New York: Springer-Verlag.

———. 1989. "Problems in the Estimation and Interpretation of the Reliability of Survey Data." *Quality and Quantity* 23:277–331.

———. 1991. "Research on Survey Quality." *Sociological Methods and Research* 20:3–29.

———. 1992a. "Are 'Feeling Thermometers' More Reliable Than 7-Point Scales?" Unpublished paper. Ann Arbor: University of Michigan, Institute for Social Research.

———. 1992b. "The Reliability of Attitudinal Survey Data." Unpublished paper. Ann Arbor: University of Michigan, Institute for Social Research.

———. 1992c. "The Life-Span Stability of Symbolic vs. Nonsymbolic Attitudes." Unpublished paper. Ann Arbor: University of Michigan, Institute for Social Research.

Alwin, Duane F., and David J. Jackson. 1979. "Measurement Models for Response Errors in Surveys: Issues and Applications." Pp. 68–119 in *Sociological Methodology 1980,* edited by Karl F. Schuessler. San Francisco: Jossey-Bass.

Alwin, Duane F., and Jon A. Krosnick. 1985. "The Measurement of Values in Surveys: A Comparison of Ratings and Rankings." *Public Opinion Quarterly* 48:409–42.

———. 1991. "The Reliability of Survey Attitude Measurement: The Influence of Question and Respondent Attributes." *Sociological Methods and Research* 20:139–81.

Andrews, Frank M. 1984. "Construct Validity and Error Components of Survey Measures: A Structural Modeling Approach." *Public Opinion Quarterly* 46:409–42.

Andrews, Frank M., and Stephen B. Withey. 1976. *Social Indicators of Well-Being: Americans' Perceptions of Life Quality.* New York: Plenum.

Andrich, David. 1985. "An Elaboration of Guttman Scaling with Rasch Models for Measurement." Pp. 33–88 in *Sociological Methodology 1985,* edited by Nancy Brandon Tuma. San Francisco: Jossey-Bass.

Bartholomew, David J., and Karl F. Schuessler. 1991. "Reliability of Attitude Scores Based on a Latent-Trait Model." Pp. 97–123 in *Sociological Methodology 1991,* edited by Peter V. Marsden. Oxford: Basil Blackwell.

Bendig, A. W. 1953. "The Reliability of Self-Ratings as a Function of the Amount of Verbal Anchoring and the Number of Categories on the Scale." *Journal of Applied Psychology* 37:38–41.

Bendig, A. W. 1954a. "Reliability and the Number of Rating Categories." *Journal of Applied Psychology* 38:38–40.

Bendig, A. W. 1954b. "Transmitted Information and the Length of Rating Scales." *Journal of Experimental Psychology* 47:303–308.

Bendig, A. W., and J. B. Hughes. 1953. "Effect of Amount of Verbal Anchoring and Number of Rating Scale Categories upon Transmitted Information." *Journal of Experimental Psychology* 46:87–90.

Benson, Purnell H. 1971. "How Many Scales and How Many Categories Shall We Use in Consumer Research?—A Comment." *Journal of Marketing* 35:59–61.

Bentler, Peter M. 1989. *EQS—Structural Equations Program Manual.* Los Angeles: BMDP Statistical Software Inc.

Birkett, Nicholas J. 1986. *Selecting the Number of Response Categories for a Likert-Type Scale.* Proceedings of the American Statistical Association. Section on Survey Research Methods. Washington, DC: American Statistical Association.

Block, Jack. 1965. *The Challenge of Response Sets.* New York: Appleton-Century-Crofts.

Bollen, Kenneth A., and Kenney H. Barb. 1981. "Pearson's *r* and Coarsely Categorized Measures." *American Sociological Review* 46:232–39.

Bradburn, Norman M., and Catalina Danis. 1984. "Potential Contributions of Cognitive Research to Questionnaire Design." Pp. 104–29 in *Cognitive Aspects of Survey Methodology: Building a Bridge Between Disciplines,* edited by T. B. Jabine et al. Washington, DC: National Academy Press.

Browne, M. W. 1984. "Asymptotically Distribution Free Methods for the Analysis of Covariance Structures." *British Journal of Mathematical and Statistical Psychology* 37:62–83.

Campbell, Angus, Philip Converse, Warren Miller, and Donald Stokes. 1971. *American Panel Study: 1956, 1958, 1960.* Ann Arbor: Inter-University Consortium for Political and Social Research.

Champney, Horace, and Helen Marshall. 1939. "Optimal Refinement of the Rating Scale." *Journal of Applied Psychology* 23:323–31.

Converse, Jean M., and Howard Schuman. 1984. "The Manner of Inquiry: An Analysis of Survey Question Form Across Organizations and Over Time." Pp. 283–316 in *Surveying Subjective Phenomena,* vol. 2, edited by Charles F. Turner and Elizabeth Martin. New York: Russell Sage Foundation.

Converse, Philip E., and Gregory B. Markus. 1979. "Plus ca Change . . .: The New CPS Election Panel Study." *American Political Science Review* 73:32–49.

Coombs, Clyde H. 1964. *A Theory of Data.* New York: Wiley.

Cox, Eli P. 1980. "The Optimal Number of Response Alternatives for a Scale: A Review." *Journal of Marketing Research* 17:407–22.

Cronbach, Lee J. 1946. "Response Sets and Test Validity." *Educational and Psychological Measurement* 6:475–94.

———. 1950. "Further Evidence on Response Sets and Test Design." *Educational and Psychological Measurement* 10:3–31.

———. 1951. "Coefficient Alpha and Internal Structure of Tests." *Psychometrika* 16:297–334.

Erikson, R. S. 1978. "Analyzing One-Variable, Three-Wave Panel Data: A Comparison of Two Models." *Political Methodology* 5:151–61.

Ferguson, Leonard W. 1941. "A Study of the Likert Technique of Attitude Scale Construction." *Journal of Social Psychology* 13:51–57.

Finn, R. H. 1972. "Effects of Some Variations in Rating Scale Characteristics on Means and Reliabilities of Ratings." *Educational and Psychological Measurement* 32:255–65.

Garner, W. R. 1960. "Rating Scales, Discriminability, and Information Transmission." *The Psychological Review* 67:343–52.

Garner, W. R., and H. W. Hake. 1951. "The Amount of Information in Absolute Judgments." *Psychological Review* 58:446–59.

Green, Paul E., and Vithala R. Rao. 1970. "Rating Scales and Information Recovery—How Many Scales and Response Categories to Use." *Journal of Marketing* 34:33–39.

Greene, Vernon L., and Edward G. Carmines. 1979. "Assessing the Reliability of Linear Composites." Pp. 160–75 in *Sociological Methodology 1980,* edited by Karl F. Schuessler. San Francisco: Jossey-Bass.

Heise, David R. 1969. "Some Methodological Issues in Semantic Differential Research." *Psychological Bulletin* 72:406–22.

Hippler, Hans-Jurgen, Norbert Schwarz, and Seymour Sudman, eds. 1987. *Social Information Processing and Survey Methodology.* New York: Springer.

Jabine, Thomas B., Miron L. Straf, Judith M. Tanur, and Roger Tourangeau. 1984. *Cognitive Aspects of Survey Methodology: Building a Bridge Between Disciplines.* Report of the Advanced Research Seminar on Cognitive Aspects of Survey Methodology. Washington, DC: National Academy Press.

Jacoby, Jacob, and Michael S. Matell. 1971. "Three-Point Scales Are Good Enough." *Journal of Marketing Research* 8:495–500.

Jahoda, Marie, Morton Deutsch, and Stuart W. ⌐ook. 1951. *Research Methods in Social Relations.* New York: Dryden Press.

Jenkins, G. Douglas Jr., and Thomas D. Taber. 1977. "A Monte Carlo Study of Factors Affecting Three Indices of Composite Scale Reliability." *Journal of Applied Psychology* 62:392–98.

Jöreskog, Karl G. 1970. "Estimation and Testing of Simplex Models." *British Journal of Mathematical and Statistical Psychology* 23:121–45.

———. 1971. "Statistical Analysis of Sets of Congeneric Tests." *Psychometrika* 36:109–33.

———. 1974. "Analyzing Psychological Data by Structural Analysis of Covariance Matrices." Pp. 1–56 in *Measurement, Psychophysics and Neural Information Processing,* edited by D. H. Kranz, R. C. Atkinson, R. D. Luce, and P. Suppes. San Francisco: Freeman.

―――. 1979. "Basic Ideas of Factor and Component Analysis." Chapter 1 in *Advances in Factor Analysis and Structural Equation Models,* edited by Karl G. Jöreskog and Dag Sörbom. Cambridge, MA: Abt Associates.

―――. 1990. "New Developments in LISREL—Analysis of Ordinal Variables Using Polychoric Correlations and Weighted Least-Squares." *Quality and Quantity* 24:387–404.

Jöreskog, Karl G., and Dag Sörbom. 1988. *PRELIS—A Program for Multivariate Data Screening and Data Summarization (A Preprocesser for LISREL).* 2d ed. Chicago: Scientific Software.

―――. 1989. *LISREL7—Analysis of Linear Structural Relationships By the Method of Maximum Likelihood.* User's Guide, Version 6. Chicago: Scientific Software.

Komorita, S. S. 1963. "Attitude Content, Intensity, and the Neutral Point on a Likert Scale." *Journal of Social Psychology* 61:327–34. t

Komorita, S. S., and William K. Graham. 1965. "Number of Scale Points and the Reliability of Scales." *Educational and Psychological Measurement* 25: 987–95.

Krosnick, Jon A., and Duane F. Alwin. 1989. "Response Strategies for Coping with the Cognitive Demands of Attitude Measures in Surveys." Unpublished paper. Ann Arbor: University of Michigan, Institute for Social Research.

Krosnick, Jon A., and Matthew K. Berent. 1990. "The Impact of Verbal Labeling of Response Alternatives and Branching on Attitude Measurement Reliability in Surveys." Paper presented at the Annual Meetings of the American Association for Public Opinion Research, Lancaster, PA.

Lehmann, Donald R., and James Hulbert. 1972. "Are Three-Point Scales Always Good Enough?" *Journal of Marketing Research* 9:444–46.

Likert, Rensis. 1932. "A Technique for the Measurement of Attitudes." *Archives of General Psychology* 140:5–55.

Lissitz, Robert W., and Samuel B. Green. 1975. "Effect of the Number of Scale Points on Reliability: A Monte Carlo Approach." *Journal of Applied Psychology* 60:10–13.

Lord, Frederick M. 1963. "Elementary Models for Measuring Change." Pp. 21–38 in *Problems in the Measurement of Change,* edited by Chester W. Harris. Madison: University of Wisconsin Press.

Lord, Frederick M., and Melvin R. Novick. 1968. *Statistical Theories of Mental Test Scores.* Reading, MA: Addison-Wesley.

Madden, Joseph M., and Roger D. Bourdon. 1964. "Effects of Variations in Scale Format on Judgment." *Journal of Applied Psychology* 48:147–51.

Markus, Gregory B. 1982. "Political Attitudes During an Election Year: A Report of the 1980 NES Panel Study." *American Political Science Review* 76:538–60.

Matell, Michael S., and Jacob Jacoby. 1971. "Is There an Optimal Number of

Alternatives for Likert Scale Items? Study I: Reliability and Validity." *Educational and Psychological Measurement* 31:657–74.

McClendon, McKee J., and Duane F. Alwin. 1990. "No Opinion Filters and Attitude Reliability." Paper presented at the Annual Meetings of the American Association for Public Opinion Research. Lancaster, PA.

McKennell, Aubrey. 1973. "Surveying Attitude Structures." *Quality and Quantity* 7:203–96.

Messick, Samuel. 1968. "Response Sets." Pp. 492–96 in *International Encyclopedia of the Social Sciences,* vol. 13, edited by David L. Sills. New York: Macmillan.

Miller, George A. 1956. "The Magical Number Seven, Plus or Minus Two: Some Limits on Our Capacity for Processing Information." *The Psychological Review* 63:81–97.

Miller, Warren E., Arthur H. Miller, and Edward J. Schneider. 1980. *American National Election Studies Data Sourcebook.* Cambridge, MA: Harvard University Press.

Moser, C. A., and G. J. Kalton. 1972. *Survey Methods in Social Investigation.* New York: Basic Books.

Murphy, Gardner, and Rensis Likert. 1938. *Public Opinion and the Individual: A Psychological Study of Student Attitudes on Public Questions, with a Retest Five Years Later.* New York: Russell and Russell.

Muthén, Bengt O. 1984. "A General Structural Equation Model with Dichotomous, Ordered Categorical and Continuous Latent Variable Indicators." *Psychometrika* 49:115–32.

———. 1988. *LISCOMP—Analysis of Linear Structural Equations with a Comprehensive Measurement Model: A Program for Advanced Research.* Fairplay, CO: Scientific Software.

Muthén, Bengt O., and Charles Hofacker. 1988. "Testing the Assumptions Underlying Tetrachoric Correlations." *Psychometrika* 53:563–78.

Muthén, Bengt, and David Kaplan. 1985. "A Comparison of Some Methodologies for the Factor Analysis of Non-Normal Likert Variables." *British Journal of Mathematical and Statistical Psychology* 38:171–89.

National Opinion Research Center. 1990. *General Social Surveys, 1972–88: Cumulative Codebook.* Chicago: NORC.

O'Brien, Robert. 1979. "The Use of Pearson's *r* With Ordinal Data." *American Sociological Review* 44:851–57.

Osgood, Charles E., George J. Suci, and Percy H. Tannenbaum. 1957. *The Measurement of Meaning.* Urbana: University of Illinois Press.

Peabody, Dean. 1962. "Two Components in Bi-Polar Scales: Direction and Extremeness." *Psychological Review* 69:65–73.

Peters, David L., and Ernest J. McCormick. 1966. "Comparative Reliability of Numerically Anchored Versus Job-Task Anchored Rating Scales." *Journal of Applied Psychology* 50:92–96.

Saris, Willem E. 1988. *Variation in Response Functions: A Source of Measurement Error in Attitude Research.* Amsterdam: Sociometric Research Foundation.

Schuman, Howard, and Stanley Presser. 1981. *Questions and Answers in Attitude Surveys.* New York: Academic Press.

Shannon, Claude, and Warren Weaver. 1949. *The Mathematical Theory of Communication.* Urbana: University of Illinois Press.

Sherif, Carolyn W., Muzafer Sherif, and Roger E. Nebergall. 1965. *Attitude and Attitude Change.* Philadelphia: W. B. Saunders.

Siegel, Paul M., and Robert W. Hodge. 1968. "A Causal Approach to the Study of Measurement Error." Pp. 28–59 in *Methodology in Social Research,* edited by Hubert M. Blalock, Jr., and Ann B. Blalock. New York: McGraw-Hill.

Smith, Tom W., and Bruce L. Peterson. 1985. "The Impact of Number of Response Categories on Inter-Item Associations: Experimental and Simulated Results." Paper presented at the Annual Meetings of the American Sociological Association, Washington, DC.

Smith, Tom W., and C. Bruce Stephenson. 1979. *An Analysis of Test/Retest Experiments on the 1972, 1973, 1974, and 1978 General Social Surveys.* GSS Technical Report No. 14. Chicago: NORC.

Symonds, Percival M. 1924. "On the Loss of Reliability in Ratings Due to Coarseness of the Scale." *Journal of Experimental Psychology* 7:456–61.

Tourangeau, Roger. 1984. "Cognitive Sciences and Survey Methods." Pp. 73–100 in *Cognitive Aspects of Survey Methodology: Building a Bridge Between Disciplines,* edited by T. B. Jabine et al. Washington, DC: National Academy Press.

Turner, Charles F., and Elizabeth Martin. 1984. *Surveying Subjective Phenomena.* New York: Russell Sage Foundation.

Weisberg, Herbert, and Arthur H. Miller. n.d. "Evaluation of the Feeling Thermometer: A Report to the National Election Study Board Based on Data from the 1979 Pilot Survey." Ann Arbor: University of Michigan, Institute for Social Research.

Werts, Charles E., Karl G. Jöreskog, and Robert L. Linn. 1971. "Comment on 'The Estimation of Measurement Error in Panel Data.' " *American Sociological Review* 36:110–13.

Wiley, David E., and James A. Wiley. 1970. "Estimating Measurement Error Using Multiple Indicators and Several Points in Time." *American Sociological Review* 35:112–17.

Woelfel, Joseph, and Edward Fink. 1980. *The Measurement of Communication Processes: Galileo Theory and Method.* New York: Academic Press.

Zaller, John. 1988. "Vague Minds vs. Vague Questions: An Experimental Attempt to Reduce Measurement Error." Paper presented at the Annual Meetings of the American Political Science Association, Washington, DC.

☙ 4 ☙

ESTIMATION OF MODELS WITH CORRELATED MEASUREMENT ERRORS FROM PANEL DATA

*Bradley Palmquist**
Donald P. Green†

Single-indicator multiwave models provide one way to estimate the error variance of survey items. Two influential papers in the early 1970s (Wiley and Wiley 1970; Wiley and Wiley 1974) presented variations of such models for three waves of data. The first assumes that the only measurement error present is random (RE model). The second allows for correlated errors (CE model). The RE model has frequently been applied with useful results. The CE model, on the contrary, has rarely been used and tends to produce anomalous results. CE estimates based on only three waves of data are shown to be generally so sensitive to sampling error that they are uninformative. The standard errors of the CE model improve substantially when panels of four or more waves are used. This improvement, however, is contingent on the appropriateness of extending the rigid assumptions underlying the three-wave CE model to longer panels.

An earlier version of this paper was presented at the Annual Meetings of the American Political Science Association, Atlanta, 1989. The presidential campaign data were originally collected by Thomas E. Patterson. These data, as well as the National Election Study data, were made available to us by the Inter-University Consortium for Political and Social Research, with the help of UC DATA at the University of California, Berkeley. We thank James Wiley and J. Merrill Shanks for helpful comments. The analysis and any remaining errors are the responsibility of the authors.

*University of California, Berkeley
†Yale University

One of the attractions of panel data is that they provide an opportunity to assess the stability of respondents' attitudes or behavior. These estimates of stability can be greatly affected by the presence of measurement error, however. Furthermore, since in such cases we are explicitly interested in the amount of change in the underlying attribute, some of the methods of classical test theory—namely, those that postulate identical true scores—are not feasible.

The key requirement for learning about measurement error is more than one measure of the attitude, trait, or behavior of interest. Thus, at a minimum, the analyst must have either multiple indicators at a given point in time (see, e.g., Sullivan and Feldman 1979) or multiple instances of a single item across time. In this paper we focus on single-indicator multiwave models.

Around 1970, a series of articles in the sociological measurement literature presented a way to estimate attitude stability measured with error by a single indicator at three points in time (Heise 1969; Wiley and Wiley 1970; Jöreskog 1970; Werts, Jöreskog, and Linn 1971; Wiley and Wiley 1974).[1] A detailed description of the model in two versions is given below, but the essential feature of both is the postulation of an autoregressive process linking the true scores. This, along with slightly varying assumptions regarding the connections among the several errors-in-variables and errors-in-equations terms, constrains the expected covariances and allows the estimation of stabilities and reliabilities through analysis of covariance structures.

The focus of this paper is on the particular variant proposed by Wiley and Wiley (1974), which considers the case of *correlated* measurement errors. We refer to this model as the correlated errors (CE) model to distinguish it from the 1970 random errors (RE) model.[2] The

---

[1]Structural equation models like this are not the only way to proceed. Perhaps the main alternative method is that of growth curves. See McArdle and Epstein (1987) and Rogosa, Brandt, and Zimowski (1982).

[2]Heise's (1969) paper on the subject of separating stability and reliability with single-indicator models appears to have inspired the Wiley and Wiley (1970) paper. We focus on the Wiley's formulation because their use of the covariance matrix rather than the correlation matrix provides more information and makes possible, in theory, the extension to correlated measurement errors proposed in Wiley and Wiley's (1974) CE model, the main concern of this discussion. The Heise model also differs in its identification restriction that reliabilities, rather than measurement-error variances, be equal.

CE model seems to give the researcher the option, even when limited to a single indicator at three waves in a panel study, of modeling either simple random error or systematic error with a component of over-time correlations. The analyst's conclusions, of course, depend on which model is deemed more appropriate. Since correlated errors have been shown to contaminate observers' ratings and grades (Werts, Jöreskog, and Linn 1976), responses to agree/disagree items (Couch and Keniston 1960), and self-placements along "thermometer" scales (Green 1988), the CE model might sometimes be preferable.

Wiley and Wiley (1974) compared the results one obtains from the RE model and the CE model. For the verbal-ability data they analyzed, the differences are not striking.[3] It is our belief that such comparability was merely fortuitous. In our own work, on both real data sets and simulated data, we have found that the CE model with three waves generally produces implausible results. As we report, our experience has apparently been shared by others. (To our knowledge, other than the analysis in the original paper there is not a single obviously successful application in the literature, even though the model's appeal is mentioned by several authors.) We find that with only three waves, the CE model is untenable because of the extreme sensitivity of the estimates to sampling error. We believe sampling variance accounts for the previously published anomalous results.

Although a useful warning, this negative conclusion is not fully satisfying, since the possibility of correlated measurement errors remains a potential threat to valid estimation. Our second goal is to demonstrate how additional waves of data provide more reliable estimates of the CE model parameters. With more than three waves of data, the standard errors decline to the point where the CE model can be utilized profitably. This finding may have implications for how time and expense are traded off in panel survey designs. We must add, however, that even with more than three waves of data, the CE model is not a general method. It rests heavily on the particular assumptions of how the correlated errors were generated.

---

[3]The data were first reported in Werts et al. (1971). Students were given the School and College Ability Test in grades 5, 7, 9, and 11. Thus we have longitudinal data of both verbal and quantitative scores. For the verbal data, the Wileys' estimated reliabilities of .914–.938 with the RE model and .795–.851 with the CE model. They estimated stabilities of .858–.922 with the RE model and .943–.940 with the CE model.

The paper is divided into five sections. In section 1, we describe the two measurement models (RE and CE) in detail and include a brief discussion of why an analyst might want to use a single-indicator model. In section 2, we describe some anomalous results that applications of the CE model have turned up. Here we also discuss the asymptotic standard errors for the model with three waves of data to show their variability. In the third section, we demonstrate how more waves of data can make the model useful. In the fourth section we present the results of an analysis of a five-wave panel study, which shows that we can determine the degree to which measurement errors are correlated. Finally, we conclude with a few comments about the utility of the CE model.

1. TWO MEASUREMENT-ERROR MODELS

Multiwave single-indicator models can be useful for various reasons. Practical considerations may preclude the use of multiple-indicator techniques to uncover the degree of measurement error. The physical side effects of certain medical tests, for example, may make it impossible or undesirable to obtain two or more independent readings during each observation period. Access to multiple indicators is especially problematic for secondary data analysis, since cost considerations (and a certain amount of indifference to methodological concerns) lead government data-gathering organizations to collect a single set of statistics on infant mortality, housing starts, and the like.

Preference for a single-indicator approach, however, is not always a matter of necessity. Even when more than one indicator of a latent construct is available, the researcher may be confident about the validity of only one of the measures. Since the use of invalid indicators in the assessment of reliability may produce seriously misleading results, the researcher may elect to discard the additional, suspect measures in favor of a single-indicator approach (Jagodzinski and Kühnel 1987).

The RE model proposed by Wiley and Wiley (1970) includes a specific model of trait stability and change along with a specific model of the impact of measurement errors. See Figure 1 for a path diagram of the RE model. The model can also be described by a set of recursive equations in which all variables have mean zero:

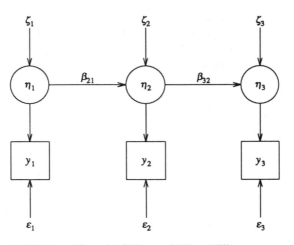

FIGURE 1. RE model (Wiley and Wiley 1970).

$$y_t = \eta_t + \epsilon_t, \qquad t = 1,2,3, \tag{1a}$$

$$\eta_1 = \zeta_1, \tag{1b}$$

$$\eta_t = \beta_{t,t-1}\eta_{t-1} + \zeta_t, \qquad t = 2,3. \tag{1c}$$

The y_t are the observed indicators of the latent η_t, the ζ_t are the disturbance or errors-in-equation terms, the ε_t are the measurement errors, and the β_{tu} are the effect coefficients linking the latent traits. We denote the covariance between any two measurement-error terms as θ_{tu} and the covariance between any two disturbances as ψ_{tu}. The restrictions on the error terms are

$$E(\zeta_t\zeta_u) = \psi_{tu} = 0, \qquad t, u = 1,2,3, t \neq u, \tag{2a}$$
$$E(\varepsilon_t\varepsilon_u) = \theta_{tu} = 0, \qquad t, u = 1,2,3, t \neq u, \tag{2b}$$
$$E(\varepsilon_t\zeta_u) = 0, \qquad t, u = 1,2,3, \tag{2c}$$
$$E(\zeta_t\eta_u) = 0, \qquad t > u, \tag{2d}$$
$$E(\varepsilon_t\eta_u) = 0, \qquad t, u = 1,2,3, \tag{2e}$$
$$\theta_{tt} = \theta_\varepsilon, \qquad t = 1,2,3. \tag{2f}$$

The last specification of homogeneous measurement-error variance is an identifying restriction. Werts et al. (1971) point out that the time-2 reliability can still be estimated even without this restriction. The six model parameters to be estimated given these restrictions are $\beta_{21}, \beta_{32}, \theta_\varepsilon, \psi_{11}, \psi_{22}$, and ψ_{33}.

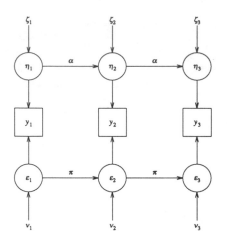

FIGURE 2. CE model (Wiley and Wiley 1974).

The setup is much the same for the CE model (see Figure 2). The key distinction is, of course, that in the CE model, the measurement errors are assumed to be systematic rather than purely random.

In both the RE and CE models, the "true," unobserved trait at time t (η_t) is specified to be a function only of the true trait at time $t - 1$ and a contemporaneous disturbance variable (ζ_t).[4] This lag-1 autoregressive process is Markovian in that only the just-previous time period has an effect.[5] Other models for describing trait change are imaginable (Anderson 1954). Indeed, in some cases these autoregressive models should not be applied. If it is thought that there are persistent "memory" effects in the process, such that the impact of previous positions is not wholly contained in the immediately preceding time period, then a Markov model is inappropriate. Also, if an attitude or behavior is thought to arise anew at each time period, a different model should be specified (see Hargens, Reskin, and Allison 1976). Nevertheless, there are situations in which a fair degree of trait stability is plausible and the effects of previous positions can reasonably be assumed to be summarized by the previous time period. Note that the model specifications do *not* "assume" or force the

[4]As may be apparent to the reader, we have labeled the variables according to the usual LISREL conventions.

[5]Jöreskog (1970) calls it a *quasi*-Markov simplex model because the latent variables follow a Markov process and the observed variables are error-laden.

finding of high stability. If the data are not consistent with such a hypothesis, the parameter estimates will show this.

Although a general formulation might allow for correlations among the disturbance terms, we join the original authors in specifying zero covariances among these errors-in-equation terms ($E(\zeta_t \zeta_u) = 0$, $t \neq u$).[6] All latent variables are considered to have mean zero, but no variances are prespecified. Rather, the model is implicitly normalized by setting each latent variable's scale equal to that of its indicator. The observed measurement variables (y_i) are considered in their mean deviate forms and hence $E(y_i) = 0$ also. For purposes of analysis, the observed variables are regarded as interval-level measures.[7]

With three waves, the RE model is just-identified (Wiley and Wiley 1970) and closed-form solutions are available for parameter estimates. With more than three waves, some maximum likelihood estimation technique is needed. We have used the programs LISREL 7 (Jöreskog and Sörbom 1989), GAUSS (1988), and LINCS (Schoenberg and Arminger 1989).

The CE model, a modification of the original RE multiwave single-indicator model, was proposed by Wiley and Wiley (1974). In this version allowance for correlated measurement errors is explicitly built into the assumed error structure. A second lag-1 autoregressive process connects the measurement errors, and thus another parameter, π, is estimated. As a result, for the CE model to be identified, another restriction must be made elsewhere in the model. The compensating restriction specifies that the β-effect coefficients between adjacent time periods are equal.[8] To indicate this change, the β_{tu} are relabeled α.

The definition of this model in terms of recursive equations follows, where only those equations that differ from the CE model are listed:

---

[6]In fact, of course, it is quite possible for this assumption to be violated. In situations we have analyzed, ignoring correlation among the disturbances when it exists causes one to underestimate the measurement-error variance and therefore underestimate the stability of the true score.

[7]Related latent Markov chain techniques are available for categorical data (Anderson 1954; Dobson and Meeter 1974; van de Pol and de Leeuw 1986).

[8]In many cases this is not an unreasonable assumption, but its plausibility should, of course, be assessed. It makes most sense if the time intervals are equal. In any case, unequal time intervals (or systematically varing effects) can be modeled by using powers of α.

$$\eta_t = \alpha\eta_{t-1} + \zeta_t, \qquad t = 2,3, \tag{1c'}$$

$$\varepsilon_1 = \nu_1, \tag{1d'}$$

$$\varepsilon_t = \pi\varepsilon_{t-1} + \nu_t, \qquad t = 2,3. \tag{1e'}$$

All the restrictions on the error terms in equations (2) still hold except for (2b), which becomes

$$\theta_{tu} = E(\varepsilon_t\varepsilon_u) = \pi^{|t-u|}\theta_\varepsilon, \qquad t, u = 1,2,3. \tag{2b'}$$

Allowing correlated measurement error means that θ_{tu} will not in general equal zero. With one indicator we cannot model completely arbitrary covariances among the measurement errors. The possible relationships are constrained by the stipulated autoregressive process. The six parameters to be estimated in the CE model are α, π, θ_ε, ψ_{11}, ψ_{22}, and ψ_{33}. Like the RE model, the CE model with three waves of data is just-identified and estimates can be calculated from closed-form expressions.

   With these two models to choose from, we seem to be able to estimate not only measurement-error variance but also the degree to which measurement errors are correlated across time periods—all with a single indicator. In practice, this is not so easy.

2. SENSITIVITY OF THE CE MODEL ESTIMATES

   A quick perusal of the *Social Sciences Citation Index* (Institute for Scientific Information 1975–1990) for all the years since publication of the CE model (Wiley and Wiley 1974) turns up only eight references to the paper. Yet as of 1990, there were more than 90 citations of the paper that introduced the RE model (Wiley and Wiley 1970). The RE model has been fruitfully applied by many researchers (see, e.g., Asher 1974; Erikson 1978; Markus 1979; Krosnick 1988; Green and Palmquist 1990), but as mentioned above, except for the example presented in Wiley and Wiley (1974), we can locate no successful implementation of the CE model. Although in many cases the RE model may be entirely appropriate, in others the question of correlation among the errors arises quite naturally. Why have there been so few applications of the CE model?

   One reason for the neglect of the CE model could be the general tendency of researchers to disregard the complications of correlated measurement errors, whether for substantively defensible reasons or not. Nevertheless, even if more researchers had attempted to use the CE model *with only three waves*, as originally presented in Wiley and Wiley (1974), we believe the results would almost always have been anomalous. Indeed, the few attempts we have found in the literature seem all to have ended in failure. Heyns (1978, p. 34) gave up trying to estimate error correlation even though she believes it is present in her data, because the Wiley models of measurement error produced unreasonable variances.[9] Jagodzinski and Kühnel (1987, p. 253*n*) report that the CE model *"always* led to anomalous results."

Achen (1983) explicitly compares the results of the RE and CE models. He is interested in the reliability and stability estimates that can be derived from the six primary parameters of the models.[10] Analyzing the stability of two attitudes toward government aid from the 1956–60 National Election Studies panel study, Achen finds reliabilities of .36 to .46, which result in disattenuated correlation coefficients of .96 to .99 under the assumptions of the RE model, indicating very high attitude stability. The CE model applied to the same data, however, gives estimates of .84 to .88 for the reliabilities and .03 to .27 for the stability coefficients. The implications of the two models differ drastically. Achen's conclusion is worth noting:

> Both models fit the data exactly, in the sense of reproducing the variance matrix with perfect accuracy. Yet their conclusions are astonishingly different. . . . With present knowledge, no grounds exist for choosing between these competing models. The rather dreary conclusion follows that even in the most heavily studied case, no confidence about the error variances is possible. (1983, p. 80)

Wiley and Wiley (1974) themselves report that in their attempt to reanalyze the data from Wiley and Wiley (1970), inadmissi-

[9]We found negative $\hat{\alpha}$ when we reanalyzed some of her data with the CE model.

[10]Reliability is true-score variance ($V(\eta_i)$) divided by observed-score variance (σ_i^2), where $V(\eta_i) = \sigma_i^2 - \theta_\varepsilon$. Under the RE model, correlation coefficients are disattenuated by dividing by the square roots of the two corresponding reliabilities. Under the CE model, direct calculation of stability coefficients is based on true-score covariances ($C(\eta_i \eta_j)$) and variances, where $C(\eta_i \eta_j) = \sigma_{ij} - \theta_{ij}$.

ble results were obtained. Why is it that the only successful application of the CE model is that published in the paper in which the method was originally presented? We are able to report that much of the puzzlement about the anomalous results of three-wave CE model analysis can be explained by examining the standard errors of the estimates. The standard errors of the measurement-error parameters are typically so large that it is not hard to see how implausible values could result simply from sampling error.

As far as we know, no one else has discussed standard errors for the parameter estimates of the CE model. It may seem odd that the sensitivity of these estimates has not been emphasized before. The reason may be that analysts have simply tended to use the closed-form equations as they were presented in the 1974 article, where standard errors were not discussed. Furthermore, although now there are packaged programs that can provide standard errors of the estimates, the reparameterization of the CE model is not straightforward.[11]

We limit the discussion in this section to the situation as originally presented, in which the analyst has three waves of data. In this case the model is just-identified, each of the six parameters of the model can be written as an explicit nonlinear function of the original variances and covariances, and thus closed-form expressions are available for computing the parameter estimates. These expressions are derived fairly simply by first representing the variances and covariances of y_i as functions of the six parameters. This is done by considering the six distinct $E(y_t y_u)$, then substituting and simplifying based on the definitions and restrictions of equations (1') and (2') (see Wiley and Wiley 1974, Table 1). Finally, the system of equations can be inverted to give the parameters in terms of the variances and covariances:

[11]Early on, analysis of covariance-structure methods were used to estimate RE models (Jöreskog 1970; Werts et al. 1971). The constraints for CE models, however, are more difficult to define. Wiley and Wiley (1974) expressed regret at not being able to use the then-current ACOVS program to calculate CE model estimates. Even now, to use the currently most popular program, LISREL 7, the analyst is forced to use somewhat convoluted specifications to program around design limitations (Green and Palmquist 1991). An example setup is given in Appendix A. Note that β_{47} in the LISREL output is an estimate of $\sqrt{\theta}$. The standard error of θ can be approximated by $2\beta_{47}\text{SE}(\beta_{47})$.

$$\alpha = \frac{\sigma_{23} - \sigma_{12}}{\sigma_{22} - \sigma_{11}}, \tag{3a}$$

$$\pi = \frac{\sigma_{13} - \alpha\sigma_{12}}{\sigma_{12} - \alpha\sigma_{11}}, \tag{3b}$$

$$\theta_\varepsilon = \frac{\sigma_{12} - \alpha\sigma_{11}}{\pi - \alpha}, \tag{3c}$$

$$\psi_1 = \sigma_{11} - \theta_\varepsilon, \tag{3d}$$

$$\psi_2 = \sigma_{22} - \alpha^2\psi_1 - \theta_\varepsilon, \tag{3e}$$

$$\psi_3 = \sigma_{33} - \alpha^2[\alpha^2\psi_1 + \psi_2] - \theta_\varepsilon. \tag{3f}$$

Except for a minor difference in equation (3b), this list corresponds exactly to Table 2 of Wiley and Wiley (1974).

Because we can avail ourselves of standard results concerning the asymptotic distribution of moments and their functions (Cramér 1946; Rao 1973; Serfling 1980), closed-form expressions can also be derived for estimates of the asymptotic standard errors by means of the so-called delta method.[12] Thus, the analysis can be executed without resource to reparameterized LISREL models. In practice this technique is useful for models in which convergence is difficult. It can also be helpful in trying to understand analytically the sources of the sampling fluctuations.

However the standard errors are calculated, they allow us to

---

[12]In this method, for parameters that are differentiable functions of other parameters, the asymptotic covariance matrix of the derived parameter estimates is in turn a function of the asymptotic covariance of the original parameter estimates. In this case the original parameters are the six unique elements of the population covariance matrix. Let G be the matrix of first derivatives of the derived parameters with respect to the original variances and covariances of the parent distribution, and let Ω be the covariance matrix of the estimates of these six central moments. The asymptotic covariance matrix of the *derived* parameter estimates can then be written as $1/N G\Omega G'$. For convenience we assume multivariate normality of the parent distribution, in both the delta method and the LISREL 7 analysis. The assumption of multivariate normality merely simplifies the calculations because we can ignore moments higher than the second, or more precisely, all higher moments can be expressed in terms of the first two. Neither method requires this assumption, because when the raw data are available, consistent estimates of fourth moments can be obtained and these can be used to calculate asymptotically distribution-free results. In any case, although the precise numeric estimates will differ, the general thrust of the results is not affected by this assumption.

TABLE 1
Replication of Wiley and Wiley's (1974) Analysis of
Verbal Ability Data, with Standard Errors

	CE Model	RE Model
α	1.069	1.010
	(.224)	(.018)
π	.333	
	(.731)	
θ	28.236	11.844
	(64.784)	(1.948)
ψ_{11}	109.780	125.887
	(63.908)	(7.510)
ψ_{22}	7.814	22.282
	(48.351)	(3.861)
ψ_{33}	8.960	23.628
	(49.342)	(3.946)
χ^2	0	.08
df	0	1
p		.71
N of cases	703	

Note: Asymptotic standard errors are in parentheses.

assess the specific estimates presented in Wiley and Wiley (1974). The values and their standard errors are found in Table 1. (Our notation departs slightly from the Wileys'.) Refer back to section 1 for the meaning of the parameter labels. The corresponding values for the RE model estimates are also included in Table 1. Note that β_{21} and β_{32} are constrained to be equal for comparison with the α of the CE model. Of course, there is no π parameter for the RE model.

The results are quite revealing. Looking at the CE model results, we find that not only is the π value of .333 not statistically significant, it is less than half its standard error of .731. Similarly, the error-variance estimate, θ_ε, of 28.2 is less than half its standard error of 64.8. Although the estimates have plausible values, we can have little confidence in them.

The story is much the same for other three-wave data we have analyzed. Often, clearly unacceptable parameter estimates are found (for example, the near-zero stabilities in the Achen analysis, a near-zero α coefficient in the Heyns (1978) model, and large negative π in applying the CE model to NES 1980 party identification). Even

TABLE 2
Replication of Achen's (1983) Analysis of Political Attitudes, with
Standard Errors

	Housing and Power		Government Jobs	
	CE Model	RE Model	CE Model	RE Model
α	.170	.997	.262	.948
	(1.265)	(.106)	(.575)	(.065)
π	1.608		1.515	
	(8.022)		(3.189)	
θ	.340	1.619	.407	1.354
	(3.838)	(.140)	(2.050)	(.111)
ψ_{11}	2.254	.957	2.127	1.216
	(3.893)	(.178)	(2.044)	(.149)
ψ_{22}	2.098	−.027	2.141	.191
	(2.819)	(.187)	(1.236)	(.154)
ψ_{33}	2.159	.020	1.947	.019
	(2.786)	(.225)	(1.268)	(.177)
χ^2	0	.13	0	.52
df	0	1	0	1
p		.72		.47
N of cases		596		868

Note: Asymptotic standard errors are in parentheses.

when estimates give plausible parameter values, the large standard errors suggest that the plausibility may be due to chance alone. We have replicated Achen's analysis and report in Table 2 the parameter estimates upon which his estimates of stability and reliability were based. This serves as another example of how large the CE model standard errors generally are.

On the other hand, the RE model results also listed in Tables 1 and 2 are characteristic of our experience with that model in a variety of circumstances. For the RE model, the standard errors are relatively small in comparison to the magnitude of the parameter estimates. The striking contrast in the size of the standard errors can be illustrated by noting that the standard error of the estimated error variance (θ_ε) is 20 to 30 times larger in the CE models than in the corresponding RE models (see Tables 1 and 2). To be sure, these estimates are meaningful only insofar as the model specifications are appropriate. But the main point is that given an equal number of cases, sampling error for the RE model estimates will not typically have the deleterious effects it has for the CE model.

How are we to explain this instability of the CE model estimates? The problem is not one of defective data. It is also not a question of an unstable estimation algorithm. The closed-form expressions can be evaluated with arbitrarily high precision and still the estimates are subject to high sampling variability. The difficulties are inherent in the structure of the model. With three waves of data, the problem itself is ill-conditioned in the sense that small perturbations in the "input" parameters result in large changes in the "output" parameters. In transforming the parameter space of the original variances and convariances to that made up of α, β, θ_ε, and the ψ's, stable estimates are unobtainable in most regions of the new parameter space with reasonable sample sizes. Although formally identified, estimates of the transformed parameters vary greatly as the result of small sampling fluctuations in the estimates of the original parameters (the variances and covariances of the parent distribution), even though the original parameters themselves are well identified and reliably estimated. This is an example of empirical underidentification. Formal identification conditions are met, but in practice the parameters cannot be estimated with precision (Rindskopf 1984).

Some instances of empirical underidentification in the CE model are easy to understand. The CE model accounts for the observed covariances among the three waves of data by the combination of a true-score process and an error process. (This contrasts with the RE model, in which the measurement errors are assumed to make no contribution to the covariances.) The assumption of constant error variance, θ_ε, makes the identification of the true-score regression parameter, α, easy. Regardless of the amount of measurement error and the degree to which it is correlated across waves, the effects can be cancelled out by taking the differences of variances and covariances from adjacent waves. Hence, α can be computed with relatively greater precision. What the formula for α (equation (3a)) requires is nonconstant observed variances to avoid a denominator of zero. Since the measurement-error variance is stipulated to be constant, the true-score variances must be the source of the increase or decrease. This seems natural, since without this requirement there is no distinction between the true-score regressive process and the measurement-error process. When σ_{11} and σ_{22} are exactly equal, the model is unidentified. When the two variances are nearly identical, the model is empirically underidentified. Although exactly equal variances constitute a measure-zero set of the parameter space, in practice near equality does occur and results in exceedingly large standard errors of some of the estimates. The model could be valid, but its estimation requires an increasingly large number of cases as σ_{11} and σ_{22} approach each other.

Another situation that is easy to understand analytically occurs when α and π just happen to be nearly equal. Exceedingly small perturbations in the sample estimate of the original covariance matrix produce wide swings in the estimates of π, θ_ε, ψ_1, and ψ_2. The formula for θ_ε (equation (3c)) clearly becomes unstable as the denominator approaches zero. Only α is unaffected by this fluctuation; all of the other parameter estimates are as unstable as θ_ε. In practice, of course, we will not necessarily know that the source of the problem is nearly equal true π and α parameters, because the estimate of π is likely to be quite different from its true value.

If empirical underidentification were caused only by nearly equal true-score variances or by nearly equal α and π, it would not be a serious limitation on the usefulness of three-wave CE models. We would simply have to be cautious with such data and use the size of the estimated standard errors as an indicator of when close is *too* close. However, even when the assumptions of the model are not violated, even when extreme empirical underidentification is not obvious from the original covariance matrix, the standard errors of the estimates other than α are often so large that they render the estimates too unreliable. Both our survey of empirical applications and our analysis of the estimation procedure indicate that most regions of the parameter space result in estimates of low precision for the parameters other than α. Since such apparent empirical underidentification is typical, except in particularly fortuitous circumstances, there is little chance of obtaining precise estimates of the parameters of the three-wave CE model.

If the parameters of the CE model were calculated as a linear transformation of the original covariance matrix, understanding why the estimates are typically so unstable would be easy. Standard results exist for characterizing sensitivity in terms of the condition number of a linear transformation matrix. The highly nonlinear nature of the transformations in the CE model, however, makes simple characterizations difficult. One way to see the vulnerability of the estimates to sampling fluctuations is to regard the estimation of the model as carried out in two steps, the first step being the estimate of α. To the extent that the observed off-diagonal elements deviate from a pattern producible by α and the true-score variances alone, the model attributes an additional effect to the product of π and θ_ε. The identifying assumption of constant θ makes possible a relatively reliable estimate of the true-score regression coefficient, α, but most of the uncertainty is then shifted to the measurement-error process.

We should note that under certain fortuitous empirical circumstances, π, the measurement-error correlation, may be estimated with reasonable precision. For example, if α and π are not too close, if σ_{11} and σ_{22} are not too close, and if the value of π comes close to being a particular function of α, ψ_1, and ψ_2, then a reasonably precise estimate of π can be expected.[13] But this situation is not general. The last condition is satisfied only by a fairly narrow range of π values even in favorable situations. For some combinations of parameters, this range may consist of inadmissible values. Furthermore, even in the range of smallest standard errors, the precision can still be quite low.

With these results in hand, we can now modify Achen's (1983) assessment of the RE and CE models of stability and measurement error. Achen asserts that "no grounds exist for choosing between these two competing models" (p. 80). Our revised view is that given the large standard errors for the CE model estimates (see Table 2), with only three waves of data, the results of this model have to be greatly discounted. Although both models do reproduce the observed *sample* covariance matrix "with perfect accuracy" (p. 80), minor departures in this matrix from the population covariances can cause much larger fluctuations in the CE parameter estimates than in the RE estimates. In the cases Achen discusses, as in most, the three-wave CE model is not able to provide clear evidence for or against the appropriateness of the RE model. Perhaps the clearest way to see this is to consider the power of a test that π is zero against alterna-

---

[13]The function that π must approach is $\alpha\psi_1/(\alpha^2\psi_1 + \psi_2)$. In such a situation the contributions of the true-score process and the error process line up so that π becomes simply the ratio of σ_{13}/σ_{23} or σ_{12}/σ_{22}. As an example, take the estimates in Table 1 as true parameter values. If $\pi = .88$, the standard error of its estimate is only .103.

tives. We do this in the next section, where we are also able to go beyond the cautionary warnings of this section to more-positive results with longer panels.

3. MAKING THE CE MODEL FEASIBLE BY USING LONGER PANELS

In the previous section, we saw that when the correlation among errors is assessed with three waves of panel data, the standard errors of the estimates are generally quite large. One way of handling this problem of sampling variability is to collect more data. However, it should be clear from the estimates presented in the preceding section that simply collecting more observations will not suffice. This is because with only three waves of data, minor deviations from the population covariance matrix lead to dramatic changes in the parameter estimates. Even samples containing thousands of observations will fail to provide reasonably precise estimates. In the case of the verbal-ability data the Wileys analyzed, for example, if the sample size were 10,000 instead of 703, the estimate of π would have a t statistic of just 1.72.

A more effective way to improve the precision of the estimates is to utilize additional waves of panel data. The fact that longer panels tend to produce parameter estimates with smaller sampling variability means that the test for positive π has much greater power. To illustrate this point, we consider a simulation based on the verbal-ability data.[14] Taking all but the value of π to be true as given, we varied π from 0 to 1.00, calculated the implied population covariance matrix, and computed the power of a level-.05 one-tailed test that π was zero against the alternative for three, four, and five waves of data.[15]

The results, presented in Figure 3, indicate the weakness of

[14]To set the values of the five parameters other than π to plausible values, we used estimates obtained from the CE model with four, rather than three, waves of data. Although Wiley and Wiley (1970) used only the first three waves, the covariances for the fourth wave can be obtained from Werts et al. (1971). Since the estimates are used for illustrative purposes as representative true parameter values, any choice is somewhat arbitrary.

[15]These are, of course, *simulated* waves, in which we have analyzed the population covariance matrices that would obtain if the true parameter values were as postulated.

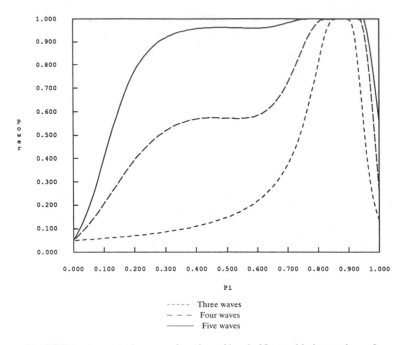

FIGURE 3. Asymptotic power function of level-.05 one-sided test of $\pi = 0$.

the three-wave model. Even when the error correlation is moderately high by social science standards (e.g., the Wileys' estimate, $\pi = .33$), the power of the test is a very low .15 or less. Only when π is in a narrow range around .89 does the power of the test increase noticeably. Still it remains disappointingly low, and as π approaches the value of α, the power actually declines again because of the increasing standard error.

Four waves of data yield a considerable increase in power. Against the alternative of $\pi = .33$, the power of the test in our four-wave simulation is .5. This level of power still leaves much to be desired. Hence, analysts using the four-wave model may wish to restrict their attention to relatively large data sets. Nevertheless, the confidence intervals provided by a four-wave analysis can shed light where the three-wave model cannot.

Only when at least five waves of data can be utilized does the single-indicator design allow a powerful test of the CE model against the RE alternative for a wide range of potential π values. Against an alternative of $\pi = .33$, the power of the test climbs above .9. It should be noted, however, that the improvement in power is purchased with some relatively strong structural constraints. Recall that the CE model assumes that α, π, and θ_ε remain constant over time. When the panel is extended, it may be more difficult to accept the continued validity of these restrictions.[16]

4. EMPIRICAL APPLICATION

Although the CE model requires the researcher to make a number of strong assumptions, it can be a valuable method for detecting correlated measurement error in panels with at least four waves of data. In this section we present an analysis, the results of which conform with what we expect from previous research on nonrandom measurement error. We consider two measures: one thought to be susceptible to nonrandom error and the other not. In the first case, π is indeed estimated to be large and statistically significant, and in the second case, the estimate of π is smaller and statistically insignificant.

4.1. Data

The data set comes from a study carried out during the 1976 presidential campaign by Patterson (1980). Residents of Los Angeles and Erie County, Pennsylvania, were interviewed in person every other month between February and October, resulting in a five-wave panel. For our purposes, the study has a couple of attractive features. Most crucial is that the study goes beyond the more common two or three waves. Furthermore, the study contains items of varying question formats, providing a chance to see if the CE model can distinguish between two items, one with nonrandom error and one without.

Previous research suggests that questions asked in an agree/ disagree format elicit responses that are contaminated by acquiescence bias, one source of nonrandom error (Couch and Keniston

---

[16]To some extent, these constraints may be loosened to allow for variation in π and θ_ε over time. For example, the following restrictions suffice: $\theta_1 = \theta_2$ and $\theta_3 = \theta_4 = \theta_5$ and $\pi_1 = \pi_2$ and $\pi_3 = \pi_4 = \pi_5$. Comparing the χ^2 of this less-restricted model with that obtained under the strict CE model is one way to test the plausibility of the CE constraints. It is important to note, however, that even under these relaxed restrictions, the CE model still imposes a rigid set of assumptions on the error process and the structural coefficients.

1960). Similarly, questions that ask respondents to describe their opinions by locating themselves on an unmarked continuum, such as a "feeling thermometer," cause nonrandom errors because respondents anchor themselves differently (Green 1988). It follows that survey questions that employ an agree/disagree format and that invite respondents to place themselves along a seven-point continuum that is labeled only at the endpoints are especially susceptible to nonrandom error. On the other hand, branched question formations, which present respondents with a series of labeled alternatives, might be thought more immune to nonrandom error because of the anchoring provided.

We have chosen two measures from the Patterson (1980) study that allow us to examine these suggested effects of question format. The first question, which is expected to contain nonrandom measurement error, assesses the respondent's overall approval of the incumbent president's performance in office. Respondents were asked to express their agreement with the statement "All in all, I feel that Gerald Ford has done a good job while in office" by choosing a point on a seven-point continuum, ranging from *agree* to *disagree*. By contrast, the standard Michigan party-identification measure (Campbell et al. 1960) is thought to be less susceptible to correlated measurement error.[17] That these two items entail such different effects is fortunate, because they are measures of substantively interesting variables in voting behavior.[18] The low level of nonresponse for these two questions also recommends them as good test cases.

4.2. Results

Both the Ford approval item and party-identification scale were analyzed using three-, four-, and five-wave CE models. The three-wave CE model, as usual, produces implausible and imprecise parameter estimates and does not allow us to evaluate the contrast between the two measures. In the party-identification analysis, $\pi =$

[17]Respondents were asked, "Generally speaking, do you usually think of yourself as a Republican, a Democrat, an independent, or what?" This first question was followed by, "Would you call yourself a strong Republican/ Democrat or a not very strong Republican/Democrat?" for the partisan respondents to the first question and by "Do you think of yourself as closer to the Republican party or to the Democratic party?" for the independents.

[18]In Green and Palmquist (1990), we studied party identification and incumbent performance, but we did not use the Patterson data.

.829. (Table 3), whereas in the Ford approval analysis, $\pi = .674$ (Table 4). The addition of a fourth wave, however, suggests that the two measures are subject to different kinds of measurement error. Now in the party-identification analysis, $\pi = -.003$, whereas in the Ford approval analysis, $\pi = .223$. There appears to be little error correlation in the party-identification analysis but some error correlation in the Ford approval analysis, even though the latter estimate of π falls below conventional levels of statistical significance.

With the inclusion of a fifth wave of data, the contrast between the two items becomes more conclusive. The estimate of π for party identification is implausibly negative $(-.106)$ and statistically insignificant according to the usual standards. Furthermore, if the π parameter is constrained to be zero, making the RE model a nested submodel, we can evaluate the χ^2 difference. For party identification this difference equals 2.72 $(df = 1)$, with a probability of approximately .1. That this difference is insignificant is just another way of showing that the data do not provide evidence for a nonzero value of π and hence do not support the supposition of correlated measurement error.

The picture that emerges for the presidential approval item is just the opposite. With five waves of data, $\pi = .238$, which is approximately 2.7 times its standard error of .088. If we again constrain π to be zero, we find a χ^2 difference of 6.88 $(df = 1)$, reflecting the nested model's significantly $(p < .01)$ decreased ability to fit the data.

The utility of the CE model in evaluating these two items with just three waves of data corresponds to what we have observed with other data sets. When the estimates are not implausible, the results are ambiguous because of large standard errors for one or more of the parameter estimates. In this case, however, because more than three waves of data are available, we have been able to extend the analysis so that the CE model can be fruitfully applied. The CE model is able to distinguish between two items—providing evidence for correlated measurement error in one and failing to do so for the other—in the manner predicted.

5. CONCLUSIONS

With three waves of data, the results of the CE model typically cannot be trusted. In such cases, if only a single indicator is available, the cautious approach is to use the RE model if the assumption of

TABLE 3

Correlated Errors Model of Party Identification, Three, Four, and Five Waves

	Three Waves	Four Waves	Five Waves
β	3.117	.995	.995
	(6.324)	(.012)	(.007)
π	.829	−.003	−.106
	(.120)	(.119)	(.063)
θ	4.276	.407	.364
	(.677)	(.086)	(.035)
ψ_{11}	.101	3.925	3.947
	(.539)	(.283)	(.269)
ψ_{22}	−.795	.304	.336
	(.524)	(.091)	(.064)
ψ_{33}	−1.432	.065	.120
	(.990)	(.089)	(.045)
ψ_{44}		.148	.142
		(.087)	(.045)
ψ_{55}			.110
			(.054)
χ^2	0	1.46	5.95
df	0	3	7
p		.692	.546
N of cases		494	

Source: Patterson 1980.

Note: Asymptotic standard errors are in parentheses.

uncorrelated errors is reasonable. Indeed, despite concern about nonrandom measurement error, as we have shown above, party identification provides just one example of a measure that does not obviously suffer from correlated measurement error. Like party identification, measures of such things as family income and verbal ability are also likely to be less problematic than observers' ratings (Werts et al. 1976); items that are based on thermometers, with responses anchored independently by each respondent (Green 1988); and agree/disagree questions or other formats that suffer from acquiescence bias (Couch and Keniston 1960).

If the RE model is applied when correlated errors are present, the stability estimate will be biased. Despite the perhaps natural intuition that neglecting correlation among the measurement errors implies an overestimate of the stability, this need not be so if the assumptions of the CE model are in fact valid.

TABLE 4

Correlated Errors Model of Ford Approval, Three, Four, and Five Waves

	Three Waves	Four Waves	Five Waves
β	36.731	.965	.977
	(919.879)	(.070)	(.030)
π	.674	.223	.238
	(.096)	(.179)	(.088)
θ	3.318	1.045	1.029
	(.219)	(.465)	(.207)
ψ_{11}	0	2.172	2.138
	(.021)	(.494)	(.270)
ψ_{22}	−.556	.498	.476
	(.242)	(.355)	(.167)
ψ_{33}	−12.087	−.057	−.030
	(286.006)	(.360)	(.148)
ψ_{44}		.180	.259
		(.338)	(.160)
ψ_{55}			.058
			(.154)
χ^2	0	3.54	8.53
df	0	3	7
p		.316	.288
N of cases		512	

Source: Patterson 1980.
Note: Asymptotic standard errors are in parentheses.

For panels of four or more waves, our conclusions regarding the CE model are more optimistic. If the assumption of stable parameters can be plausibly made, the CE model can be useful, as we have shown in analyzing the Patterson data. But under what conditions might the CE model produce misleading or unreliable results? There are at least two possibilities. First, and most critical, the particular error process specified by the model may simply be unrealistic. Recall that two assumptions are made simultaneously about the error variances. The variances are specified to follow a lag-1 autoregressive process while the amount, θ_i, is held constant across time periods. Second, four waves may not be enough to ascertain reliably whether the particular form of correlated errors is present. As we saw in the power discussion, five waves of data were required before the variability of the estimate of π was reduced to reasonable levels. Given the difficulty of obtaining panel studies of this length, this finding underscores the practical limitations of the CE model. Because of the cost, researchers will not typically design a multiwave study for the sole purpose of estimating measurement error, particularly when multiple indicators, test-restest methods, or validation procedures are feasible. Allison and Hauser (1991) suggested a trade-off. They showed how measurement models based on repeated measurements for only a small subsample can be efficiently combined with a structural model using the entire sample.

To go beyond this level of understanding of measurement error, we suggest two paths. First, if a second indicator of the latent trait is available at each wave, the simplex model may be expanded to include correlated errors between similar measures at different points in time (e.g., Werts et al. 1980). Because of the increase in degrees of freedom, this kind of model permits the researcher to make much more flexible assumptions about the covariances among the measurement errors. This approach is not without drawbacks, however. Correlated measurement errors between the two measures at each wave cannot be taken into account. In addition, if the second indicator is an invalid measure of the latent trait, even though combined with a presumably valid measure, the multiple-indicator model may perform badly.

Alternatively, social scientists might improve their understanding of measurement error in panel data by studying it more directly. Although relying upon analysis of covariance structures in studying the properties of measurement error has considerable merit, it generally requires fairly restrictive a priori assumptions about the relationships among the measurement errors and between the errors and the other latent variables. The principal way to evaluate the veracity of these assumptions is to examine the fit between theory and data. But this is of no help when, as is often the case, the comparison is between competing nonnested models that fit the data equally well. Although the related RE and CE models we discussed in section 4 were tested, other variants were not. A χ^2 difference test indicates that the CE model may outperform a constrained RE model—suggesting that the RE model incorrectly assumes merely random measurement error— while it compares badly to an RE model with relaxed assumptions regarding the constancy of β and θ. In these situations as well as others, it would be helpful if we could assess measurement errors more directly. In the social sciences, the problem of obtaining highly

precise measures of latent variables against which other measures can
be compared is difficult but not insurmountable.

APPENDIX A: LISREL CONTROL STATEMENTS FOR ESTIMATING THE THREE-WAVE CE MODEL

[insert data specifications here]
MO NY=3 NE=13 LY=FU,FI BE=FU,FI TE=ZE,FI PS=DI,FI
FR BE(2,1) BE(3,2)
EQ BE(2,1) BE(3,2)
FR BE(5,4) BE(6,5) BE(5,9) BE(6,11)
EQ BE(5,4) BE(6,5) BE(5,9) BE(6,11)
FR BE(4,7) BE(5,8) BE(6,10) BE(9,12) BE(11,13)
EQ BE(4,7) BE(5,8) BE(6,10) (BE(9,12) BE(11,13)
FR PS(1) − PS(3)
VA 1 PS(7) PS(8) PS(10)
VA −1 PS(12) PS(13)
VA 1 LY(1,1) LY(1,4) LY(2,2) LY(2,5) LY(3,3) LY(3,6)
[insert starting values and OUTPUT line which includes AD=OFF here]

APPENDIX B: SAMPLE COVARIANCE MATRICES

Housing and Power (NES 1956–1960)

	1956	1958	1960
1956	2.599997		
1958	0.941309	2.509737	
1960	0.960792	0.925137	2.567300

Source: Wiley and Wiley 1970.

Government Jobs (NES 1956–1960)

	1956	1958	1960
1956	2.534013		
1958	1.174197	2.694384	
1960	1.080445	1.216246	2.511179

Source: Wiley and Wiley 1970.

SCAT Verbal-Ability Test

	Grade 5	Grade 7	Grade 9	Grade 11
Grade 5	138.016			
Grade 7	126.710	161.392		
Grade 9	128.476	151.688	189.228	
Grade 11	131.592	153.078	170.106	206.756

Source: Wiley and Wiley 1974.

Party Identification—Erie and Los Angeles 1976

	February	April	June	August	October
February	4.3775119				
April	3.8617158	4.4642485			
June	3.9240706	4.1321086	4.6700487		
August	3.8663885	4.0697210	4.1940117	4.6893760	
October	3.8848248	4.1376847	4.3085053	4.3009994	4.8739355

Source: Patterson 1980.

Ford Approval—Erie and Los Angeles 1976

	February	April	June	August	October
February	3.3180039				
April	2.2518346	3.3265503			
June	2.0725294	2.5657565	3.3264280		
August	1.9473459	2.3186690	2.4232280	3.3361019	
October	2.0118028	2.2622080	2.2978764	2.6763278	3.5513966

Source: Patterson 1980.

REFERENCES

Achen, Christopher H. 1983. "Toward Theories of Data: The State of Political Methodology." Pp. 69–93 in *Political Science: The State of the Discipline,* edited by Ada W. Finifter. Washington, DC: American Political Science Association.

Allison, Paul D., and Robert M. Hauser. 1991. "Reducing Bias in Estimates of Linear Models by Remeasurement of a Random Sample." *Sociological Methods and Research* 19:466–92.

Anderson, T. W. 1954. "Probability Models for Analyzing Time Changes in Attitudes." Pp. 17–66 in *Mathematical Thinking in the Social Sciences,* edited by Paul F. Lazarsfeld. Glencoe, IL: Free Press.

Asher, Herbert B. 1974. "Some Consequences of Measurement Error in Survey Data." *American Journal of Political Science* 18:469–85.

Campbell, Agnus, Philip E. Converse, Warren E. Miller, and Donald E. Stokes. 1960. *The American Voter.* Chicago: University of Chicago Press.

Couch, Arthur, and Kenneth Keniston. 1960. "Yeasayers and Naysayers: Agreeing Response Set as a Personality Variable." *Journal of Abnormal and Social Psychology* 60:151–74.

Cramér, Harald. 1946. *Mathematical Methods of Statistics.* Princeton: Princeton University Press.

Dobson, Douglas, and Duane A. Meeter. 1974. "Alternative Markov Models for Describing Change in Party Identification." *American Journal of Political Science* 18:487–500.

Erikson, Robert S. 1978. "Analyzing One Variable—Three-Wave Panel Data: A Comparison of Two Models." *Political Methodology* 5:151–66.

GAUSS. 1988. Version 2.0. Kent, WA: Aptech Systems.

Green, Donald Philip. 1988. "On the Dimensionality of Public Sentiment Toward Partisan and Ideological Groups." *American Journal of Political Science* 32:758–77.

Green, Donald Philip, and Bradley Palmquist. 1990. "Of Artifacts and Partisan Stability." *American Journal of Political Science* 34:872–902.

———. 1991. "More Tricks of the Trade: Reparameterizing LISREL Models Using Negative Variances." *Psychometrika* 56:137–45.

Hargens, Lowell L., Barbara F. Reskin, and Paul D. Allison. 1976. "Problems in Estimating Measurement Error from Panel Data: An Example Involving the Measurement of Scientific Productivity." *Sociological Methods and Research* 4:439–58.

Heise, David R. 1969. "Separating Reliability and Stability in Test-Retest Correlation." *American Sociological Review* 34:93–101.

Heyns, Barbara. 1978. *Summer Learning and the Effects of Schooling.* New York: Academic Press.

Institute for Scientific Information 1975–1990. *Social Sciences Citation Index.* Philadelphia: Institute for Scientific Information Inc.

Jagodzinski, Wolfgang, and Steffen M. Kühnel. 1987. "Estimation of Reliability and Stability in Single-Indicator Multiple-Wave Models." *Sociological Methods and Research* 15:219–58.

Jöreskog, Karl G. 1970. "Estimation and Testing of Simplex Models." *British Journal of Mathematical and Statistical Psychology* 23:121–45.

Jöreskog, Karl G., and Dag Sörbom. 1989. *LISREL 7. A Guide to the Program and Applications.* Chicago: SPSS Inc.

Krosnick, Jon A. 1988. "Attitude Importance and Attitude Change." *Journal of Experimental Social Psychology* 24:240–55.

Markus, Gregory B. 1979. *Analyzing Panel Data.* Quantitative Applications in the Social Sciences Series, No. 18. Beverly Hills: Sage.

McArdle, J. J., and David Epstein. 1987. "Latent Growth Curves within Developmental Structural Equation Models." *Child Development* 58:110–33.

Patterson, Thomas E. 1980. *The Mass Media Election: How Americans Choose Their President.* New York: Praeger.

Rao, C. R. 1973. *Linear Statistical Inference and Its Applications.* 2d ed. New York: Wiley.

Rogosa, D., D. Brandt, and M. Zimowski. 1982. "A Growth Curve Approach to the Measurement of Change." *Psychological Bulletin* 90:726–48.

Rindskopf, David. 1984. "Structural Equation Models: Empirical Identification, Heywood Cases, and Related Problems." *Sociological Methods and Research* 13:109–19.

Schoenberg, Ronald, and Gerhard Arminger. 1989. *LINCS 2.0. User's Guide.* Kensington, MD: RJS Software.

Serfling, Robert J. 1980. *Approximation Theorems of Mathematical Statistics.* New York: Wiley.

Sullivan, John L., and Stanley Feldman. 1979. *Multiple Indicators: An Introduction.* Quantitative Applications in the Social Sciences Series, No. 15. Beverly Hills: Sage.

van de Pol, Frank, and Jan de Leeuw. 1986. "A Latent Markov Model to Correct for Measurement Error." *Sociological Methods and Research* 15:219–58.

Werts, Charles E., H. M. Breland, J. Grandy, and D. R. Rock 1980. "Using Longitudinal Data to Estimate Reliability in the Presence of Correlated Measurement Errors." *Educational and Psychological Measurement* 40:19–29.

Werts, Charles E., Karl G. Jöreskog, and Robert L. Linn. 1971. "Comment on 'The Estimation of Measurement Error in Panel Data.'" *American Sociological Review* 36:110–13.

———. 1976. "Analyzing Ratings with Correlated Intrajudge Measurement Errors." *Educational and Psychological Measurement* 36:319–28.

Wiley, David E., and James A. Wiley. 1970. "The Estimation of Measurement Error in Panel Data." *American Sociological Review* 35:112–17.

Wiley, James A., and Mary Glenn Wiley. 1974. "A Note on Correlated Errors in Repeated Measurements." *Sociological Methods and Research* 3:172–88.

5

COMPARING NON-NESTED MODELS FOR CONTINGENCY TABLES

David L. Weakliem*

Many different models of contingency tables have been developed in recent years. Standard nested hypothesis tests are based on combining the alternatives in a comprehensive model. This is often difficult to accomplish, in which case standard hypothesis tests are unusable. This paper discusses an alternative approach, non-nested hypothesis tests, and extends the tests that have been developed for normal regression models to models for count data. Four models of the Glass mobility table are compared, including both loglinear and latent class models. The non-nested tests yield definite conclusions that are not possible using conventional tests, suggesting that they are of practical value in the analysis of contingency tables and other count data.

1. INTRODUCTION

Sociological theory often suggests several distinct alternative explanations of a phenomenon. Conventional approaches to hypothesis testing, however, involve parameter restrictions within a general model. If models are separate, or non-nested, meaning that neither is a special case of the other, standard hypothesis tests cannot be used to compare them directly.

I thank Charles Halaby for introducing me to non-nested tests. I also thank Victor Nee, Michael Hannan, Ronald Breiger, Peter Marsden, and the reviewers for helpful comments.
*Indiana University

In the framework of nested hypothesis testing, separate models are handled by forming a comprehensive model that includes both competing models as special cases. In the case of two linear regression equations, for example, the comprehensive model simply includes all independent variables in both models as predictors. Each model is then a restricted version of the comprehensive model, and the restrictions can be tested by standard methods. Artificially nesting the alternatives within a comprehensive model is easy to understand and often easy to implement, but it has several limitations. On an intuitive level, it seems unnatural to construct a substantively meaningless comprehensive model rather than to compare the competing models directly. There are statistical problems as well: Most fundamentally, it may be impractical to construct a comprehensive model. Although it is always possible to artificially combine the alternatives into a general model, the resulting model is often very difficult to estimate. In the analysis of contingency tables, both latent class and loglinear models are widely used, but it is usually not feasible to estimate a comprehensive model including both as special cases. Even when estimation is possible, collinearity may reduce the power of the test; and in small samples, fitting the comprehensive model may exhaust the degrees of freedom.

In the analysis of contingency tables, it is common practice to form a hierarchy of nested models and select among them by using likelihood ratio tests (Bishop, Fienberg, and Holland 1975, pp. 320–24). Often the hierarchical procedure can lead to several different "final" models, none of which is nested in any other. Comparisons among these non-nested models are likely to be of particular substantive interest, because the models may represent fundamentally different theories about the process generating the data. Unfortunately, the conventional strategy is of no use in this case, so comparisons between separate models are made informally, if at all. Clogg (1981, p. 855), for example, in applying a latent class model to Glass's (1954) 8-by-8 British mobility rate, noted that "Duncan (1979) obtained a somewhat better fit . . . with his row-effects and his uniform-association model . . . but his model is developed from an entirely different point of view than the models considered here." Marsden (1985, p. 1019), in proposing a different latent class model, concluded that "a precise comparison . . . to Clogg's model is inappropriate, in that neither model is nested in the other." Duncan, Stenbeck, and Brody (1988, p. 1315), in a study of latent class and Rasch models for panel data, reported that "none of the Rasch models . . . may be compared with Brody's [latent class] BGW model."[1]

Although one might not want to choose a model solely on the basis of statistical performance, it is clearly desirable to test alternatives against each other. The tests of non-nested hypotheses discussed here make this possible. Following the theoretical work of Cox (1961, 1962), several tests have been proposed for linear and nonlinear regression models with normal errors (Pesaran 1974; Pesaran and Deaton 1978; Davidson and MacKinnon 1981). Although they are not difficult to implement, they have not seen much use in applied econometric work and are still virtually unknown among sociologists.

As it has become easier to fit complex models to data, distinct models have proliferated in areas such as the analysis of contingency tables, making the need for non-nested tests more apparent. This paper extends the tests to count data. The basis for this work is the recognition that existing non-nested tests are part of the general class of Lagrange multiplier or score tests. I illustrate the use of the tests by comparing four models of the 8-by-8 British mobility table: the loglinear crossings model (Goodman 1984), the logbilinear association model (Goodman 1979), and the latent class models of Clogg (1981) and Marsden (1985). Non-nested tests make it possible to accept one of the models and reject all others. This definite conclusion cannot be obtained by standard tests, illustrating the value of the present approach.

2. NON-NESTED HYPOTHESIS TESTS IN REGRESSION MODELS

It is useful to consider non-nested tests for regression models before turning to models for count data. Suppose that two models, H_0 and H_1, have been proposed for the dependent variable Y. The models are assumed to be non-nested, meaning that neither can be expressed as a special case of the other. Cox (1961) proposed an

---

[1]Lindsay, Clogg, and Grego (1991) showed that Rasch models can be represented as latent class models. Nevertheless, the general point that the alternatives are not easily combined into a comprehensive model remains true.

intuitively appealing way of testing the alternatives. First, take H_0 as the maintained model and calculate how well H_1 *ought* to fit if H_0 is in fact true. If the alternative actually performs significantly better than expected under the maintained hypothesis, then H_0 is rejected. Then reverse the role of the two hypotheses, and compare the actual performance of H_0 with its expected performance if H_1 is true. There are four possible outcomes: only H_1 is rejected, only H_0 is rejected, neither is rejected, or both are rejected. In the first two cases, one model is clearly to be preferred over the other. In the third, both are consistent with the data. In the fourth case, neither can be taken as true, and a new model must be developed.

More precisely, define

$$T_0 = (L_0 - L_1) - E_0(L_0 - L_1),$$

where L_0 and L_1 are maximized loglikelihoods of the two models, and E_0 is the expectation conditional on the truth of H_0. The observed difference in loglikelihoods is compared with the expected difference under the null hypothesis. A negative value indicates that H_1 performs better than is expected on the assumption that H_0 is true. Therefore, a sufficiently large negative value counts as evidence against H_0. Cox (1961, pp. 112–13) provided the basis for a test by showing that under the null hypothesis, the statistic T_0 is asymptotically normally distributed with mean zero. The two problematic steps in constructing a test statistic are finding the expectation of $(L_0 - L_1)$ and the variance of T_0. Cox did not give special consideration to regression models, but his results apply very generally.

Pesaran (1974), however, found an expression for Cox's statistic in the case of linear regression models with normal errors.[2] Suppose that the two alternatives are classical regression models:

$$H_0: Y = W\beta_0 + \varepsilon_0, \qquad \varepsilon_0 \sim N(0,\sigma_0^2),$$

$$H_1: Y = Z\beta_1 + \varepsilon_1, \qquad \varepsilon_1 \sim N(0,\sigma_1^2).$$

[2]Several notational conventions are followed throughout this paper. When used without a subscript, σ^2 refers to variances generally, so that statements that include σ^2 apply to all models. X refers to covariates in general, W and Z to the covariates in the maintained and alternative models. Hence, any statements about X apply to both W and Z. The estimates of β and ϵ are designated b and e, respectively. The predicted values Wb_0 and Zb_1 are referred to as f and g.

Define an auxiliary regression of the systematic part of H_0 on the predictors in H_1:

$$Wb_0 = Zb_{10} + \varepsilon_a, \qquad \varepsilon_a \sim N(0, \sigma_a^2).$$

The natural estimator of $E_0(L_0)$ is the observed loglikelihood L_0, so T_0 reduces to $E(L_1) - L_1$, i.e., to the difference between the expected and observed values of L_1. The loglikelihood of a regression with normally distributed errors is asymptotically equal to $K - (N/2) \log(\sigma^2)$, where N is the number of cases and K is a constant depending on sample size. Hence, T_0 is

$$T_0 = (N/2)\log(\sigma_1^2/\sigma_{10}^2), \tag{1}$$

where σ_{10}^2 is the expected value of σ_1^2 under the assumption that H_0 is true. Pesaran (1974, pp. 156–57) showed that $\sigma_{10}^2 = \sigma_0^2 + \sigma_a^2$: that is, the variance from H_0 plus the variance from the regression of the predicted values from H_0 on Z.

Intuitively, the idea of the statistic is that if H_0 is true, only the variance in Y explained by W is systematic. Because the variance due to ε_0 is random by assumption, the alternative model should not be able to explain any of it. The expected residual variance from H_1 will therefore equal the true error variance due to ε_0 plus whatever part of the systematic variance in Y that H_1 cannot explain. In other words, H_1 should account for the variance in Y only to the extent that it accounts for the variance in Wb_0. An estimate of T_0 is obtained by substituting consistent estimates of σ_0, σ_1, and σ_a in (1). That is, one obtains ordinary least squares estimates for H_0 and H_1 and uses the predicted values from H_0 as the dependent variable in the auxiliary regression.

The variance of T_0 is estimated by

$$V(T_0) = (\hat{\sigma}_0^2/\hat{\sigma}_{10}^4)b_0'W'M_zM_wM_zWb_0,$$

where M_x is the idempotent matrix $(I - X(X'X)^{-1}X')$, sometimes known as the hat matrix. The predicted values from the regression of Y on X are equal to $Y - M_xY$, while the regression residuals are equal to M_xY and to $M_x\varepsilon$, where the ε are the true disturbances. Consequently, M_zWb_0 is the vector of residuals from the regression of Wb_0 on Z, and $b_0'W'M_zM_wM_zWb_0$ is the estimated residual variance, σ_{100}^2, from the regression of those residuals on W. The variance of T_0 can therefore be expressed more simply as

$$V(T_0) = \hat{\sigma}_0^2 \hat{\sigma}_{100}^2 / \hat{\sigma}_{10}^4. \tag{2}$$

Thus, a regression of Wb_0 on Z is needed to calculate T_0, and a second regression of e_a on W is needed to calculate its variance. The test statistic for maintained hypothesis H_1 is computed in a parallel fashion. Pesaran called $T_0/(V(T_0))^{1/2}$ the N statistic because of its standard normal distribution under the null hypothesis. For nonlinear regressions, the only change is that the matrix M is defined as $(I - F(F'F)^{-1}F')$, where F is a matrix of derivatives of the loglikelihood of the individual observations with respect to the parameters. The expression for M in linear regressions is a special case of this general form.

Davidson and MacKinnon (1981) proposed a test that, although superficially quite different, is asymptotically equivalent to the N test. Like the standard F test, it is based on the idea of artificially combining the two alternatives into a single model. A simple way of testing H_0 would be to estimate the regression

$$y = (1 - a)f + ag + e$$

and test for the significance of a. This equation could be more conveniently rewritten as

$$y - f = a(g - f) + e. \tag{3}$$

In other words, the residuals from H_0 are regressed on the difference in the predicted values from H_0 and H_1, and the t statistic for a is taken as the test of the null hypothesis. If H_0 is true, its residuals should be entirely random and it should be impossible to explain their values by using the predictions of an alternative model. Davidson and MacKinnon (1981, p. 787) showed, however, that the variance of the t statistic for a is *not* asymptotically equal to one under the null hypothesis.

The strategy of artificial nesting may be used to obtain a consistent estimate of the standard error of a by estimating the regression

$$y - f = a(g - f) + W\delta + e. \tag{4}$$

The t statistic for a has an asymptotic standard normal distribution under the null hypothesis. The test requires only a regression of the residuals from H_0 on the original covariates and a new variable defined as the difference in the predicted values. The parameters δ are of no interest in themselves, but the original covariates must be included to obtain an accurate estimate of the standard error of a. For a nonlinear regression, the only difference is that the partial derivatives F are used in place of the covariates: That is, $y - f$ is regressed on F and $g - f$. Davidson and MacKinnon called (4) the P test and the simpler version (3) the C test. They pointed out (1981, p. 787) that the C test "will be valid in the sense that the true (asymptotic) probability of Type I error will be no greater than the size of the test." That is, the C test will be overly conservative in rejecting the null hypothesis.

The asymptotic equivalence of the P and N tests can be seen by writing the residuals from H_1 as $(y - f) + (f - g)$. Then,

$$\hat{\sigma}_1^2 = (1/N)[(y - f)'(y - f) + (f - g)'(f - g) + 2(y - f)'(f - g)]$$
$$= \hat{\sigma}_0^2 + \hat{\sigma}_a^2 + 2\hat{\sigma}_{y -f,f-g}.$$

The first term is the variance from H_0, and under the maintained hypothesis, the second is asymptotically equal to the variance from the regression of f on Z. Thus, the sum of the first two terms converges to the expected value of σ_1^2 under the null hypothesis, and whether the actual value differs from its expectation depends only on the last term. As MacKinnon (1983, p. 93) pointed out, "What the Cox test [i.e., the N test] is really testing . . . is whether $(y-f)$ is asymptotically uncorrelated with $(f - g)$," which the P test does directly.

The P and N tests are asymptotically equivalent but generally differ in finite samples. Neither seems unambiguously superior in small-sample performance, so the consensus is that both are worth using in practice (McAleer 1987, pp. 179–83).[3] The simplicity of the C test makes it appealing despite its incorrect size, and it has occasionally been used in empirical work (Quandt and Rosen 1988, p. 89).

[3] If the alternative is nested in the maintained model, both tests become unusable. In the P test, the predicted values of the restricted model will be an exact linear function of the independent variables in the unrestricted model, so no parameter estimate will be obtained. In the N test, the estimate of σ_{100}^2 will equal zero. Both tests could be used if the maintained model is nested in the alternative, although theoretical discussions generally exclude this case by definition (e.g. Pesaran 1974, p. 156). The tests also break down if the covariates unique to each model are orthogonal to each other and to the variables the models have in common. In this case, $\hat{\sigma}_{100}^2$ in (2) will equal zero and the N statistic will be undefined.

3. NON-NESTED TESTS AS SCORE TESTS

The P test is a member of the general class of Lagrange multiplier or score tests, which are asymptotically equivalent to likelihood ratio tests (Rao 1973; Breusch and Pagan 1980). This point will be important in developing the tests for contingency tables, so it is worth taking some time to review the general principles of these tests.[4] Likelihood ratio tests for nested models are constructed by comparing the likelihoods of the restricted and unrestricted models. Score tests are based on fitting only the restricted model. Suppose that the parameter estimates from the unrestricted model are called $\hat{\theta}$, the estimates from the restricted model are $\bar{\theta}$, and the vector of partial derivatives of the loglikelihood with respect to θ (often called the efficient score) is designated $d(\theta)$. At the maximum likelihood estimates of the unrestricted model, $d(\hat{\theta})$ will equal zero. Consequently, when $d(\bar{\theta})$ is close to zero, the restricted model will be close to the unrestricted model, and the hypothesis should be accepted.

More precisely, consider the likelihood ratio test: LR $=$ $2\{L(\hat{\theta}) - L(\bar{\theta})\}$. If we approximate $L(\bar{\theta})$ by taking a Taylor series expansion of the likelihood around the unrestricted parameter values $\hat{\theta}$,

$$L(\bar{\theta}) \approx L(\hat{\theta}) + (\bar{\theta} - \hat{\theta})d(\hat{\theta}) - \frac{1}{2}(\bar{\theta} - \hat{\theta})'\frac{\partial^2 L(\hat{\theta})}{\partial\hat{\theta}\,\partial\hat{\theta}'}(\bar{\theta} - \hat{\theta}).$$

The efficient score $d(\hat{\theta})$ is zero at the maximum likelihood estimates of the unrestricted model. The expectation of the matrix of second derivatives of the loglikelihood with respect to the parameter estimates, usually known as the information matrix, can be estimated by $F'F$ (Silvey 1975, pp. 37–40; Cox and Hinkley 1974, pp. 108–10). If the estimated information matrix is designated $i(\theta)$, it follows that

$$\text{LR} \stackrel{a}{=} (\bar{\theta} - \hat{\theta})'i(\hat{\theta})(\bar{\theta} - \hat{\theta}). \tag{5}$$

[4]More detailed discussion of the general principles of likelihood ratio and score tests can be found in many sources, including Rao (1973), Cox and Hinkley (1974), and Silvey (1975). Godfrey (1988) discussed applications of the Lagrange multiplier principle in model-specification tests.

The expression on the right-hand side is generally known as the Wald statistic, or W (Silvey 1975, pp. 113–14).[5] This statistic provides a large sample alternative to the likelihood ratio test; the most familiar form of the Wald test is the t test for a single parameter. A statistic based on the efficient score of the restricted model alone can be shown to be asymptotically equal to W and therefore to LR as well. A Taylor series expansion of the score $d(\bar{\theta})$ about the unrestricted estimates $d(\hat{\theta})$ gives

$$d(\bar{\theta}) \approx d(\hat{\theta}) + \frac{\partial^2 L(\hat{\theta})}{\partial \hat{\theta} \partial \hat{\theta}'} (\bar{\theta} - \hat{\theta}).$$

Again substituting the information matrix for the matrix of second derivatives and recalling that the efficient score equals zero at the maximum likelihood estimates of the unrestricted model,

$$d(\bar{\theta}) = i(\hat{\theta})(\bar{\theta} - \hat{\theta}). \tag{6}$$

The Lagrange multiplier or score test statistic is based on the efficient score at the restricted estimates:

$$\text{LM} = d(\bar{\theta})' i(\bar{\theta})^{-1} d(\bar{\theta}). \tag{7}$$

Substituting the expression for $d(\bar{\theta})$ in (6) into (7), we obtain

$$\text{LM} \stackrel{a}{=} (\bar{\theta} - \hat{\theta})' i(\hat{\theta}) i(\bar{\theta})^{-1} i(\hat{\theta})(\bar{\theta} - \hat{\theta}).$$

Under the null hypothesis, $i(\hat{\theta})$ and $i(\bar{\theta})$ are asymptotically equal. Hence, LM is asymptotically equal to W (Cox and Hinkley 1974, pp. 313–15).

The score test is closely related to the Newton-Raphson method of maximum likelihood estimation, which updates the parameter vector by taking a Taylor series expansion of the score around a set of trial parameter values. If an estimate of the information matrix is substituted for the matrix of second derivatives that appears in the expansion, we have the method of "scoring" (Rao 1973, pp. 366–74) in which parameter estimates are updated by

$$\bar{\theta}_{t+1} = \bar{\theta}_t + i(\bar{\theta}_t)^{-1} d(\bar{\theta}_t),$$

[5]The Wald statistic is sometimes expressed in terms of the estimated covariance matrix of the parameters. Because the covariance matrix is estimated as the inverse of the information matrix, the expressions are equivalent.

where $\bar{\theta}$ is an estimate of θ, and the subscripts refer to the iteration number. A computationally convenient form of the score test is obtained by using the method of scoring with the restricted parameter estimates $\bar{\theta}$ as starting values. If (7) is combined with (6) and substituted into the definition of LM, we obtain

$$\begin{aligned} \text{LM} &= (\bar{\theta}_1 - \bar{\theta})i(\bar{\theta}_1)i(\bar{\theta})^{-1}i(\bar{\theta}_1)(\bar{\theta}_1 - \bar{\theta}) \\ &\stackrel{a}{=} (\bar{\theta}_1 - \bar{\theta})i(\bar{\theta}_1)(\bar{\theta}_1 - \bar{\theta}).^6 \end{aligned} \tag{8}$$

This expression has the same form as the W statistic (5). Unlike the Wald test, however, it is not based on the unrestricted maximum likelihood estimates but on a single iteration of the scoring algorithm starting at the restricted parameter estimates. The P test (4) involves only one degree of freedom, so it is simply the t test for the hypothesis that $a = 0$ after one iteration starting from the parameter estimates of H_0.

Although the N test statistic takes the form of a likelihood ratio, it can also be derived as a score test. The two hypotheses H_0 and H_1 imply distinct conditional probability density functions (pdf) for the random variable y, which I call $f_0(y;w)$ and $f_1(y;z)$. If we consider the family of distributions with pdf proportional to

$$\{f_0(y;w)\}^a\{f_1(y;z)\}^{1-a}, \tag{9}$$

H_0 implies $a = 1$ and H_1 implies $a = 0$. Cox and Hinkley (1974, p. 327) showed that the score statistic (7) for testing the hypothesis $a = 1$ is identical to the square of the N statistic (see also Breusch and Pagan 1980; pp. 248–49). As with the P test, the two separate models are combined in a comprehensive model. In principle, we could find the maximum likelihood estimate of a in (9) and carry out a likelihood ratio test against H_0 and H_1, but the score test is computationally much simpler.

4. NON-NESTED TESTS FOR COUNT DATA

One preliminary point in applying non-nested tests to count data concerns the asymptotic normality of the N and P statistics. This quality does not depend on an assumption of normally distributed

---

[6]$\bar{\theta}_1$ is the vector of updated parameter estimates after one iteration of the scoring algorithm.

errors but on the central limit theorem (White 1982, p. 312). Because the statistic T_0 is the sum of the contributions of independent observations, it will approach normality as the number of observations increases. This is essentially the same argument used to prove the asymptotic normality of the maximum likelihood estimates, which provides the basis for all large-sample tests (Cramer 1946, p. 503). Hence, there is no obstacle to applying non-nested tests to data with non-normal error distributions, such as count data. In general, the tests do not require any special assumptions beyond those normally made in maximum likelihood estimation (see White 1982 for a detailed discussion).

Count data are usually assumed to have a Poisson distribution with an unobserved mean parameter, here designated μ. Both latent class and loglinear models share this assumpton about the relation between the mean and the observed count. The difference between latent class and loglinear models is in their specification of the model for the mean, making it fairly simple to apply non-nested tests. Development of non-nested tests for models with different error structures is possible in principle but much more difficult in practice and will not be considered here.

For the distributions from the exponential family, including the Poisson distribution, the method of scoring is equivalent to an iteratively reweighted least squares procedure in which $y - \hat{\mu}$ is regressed on $\partial\hat{\mu}/\partial b$ (Nelder and Wedderburn 1972; Jorgensen 1984). In the case of the Poisson distribution, the weights are $1/\hat{\mu}$. The parameter estimates from the previous iteration are updated by

$$b_{t+1} = b_t + \delta_t,$$

where δ is the vector of parameter estimates from the regression of $y - \hat{\mu}$ on $\partial\hat{\mu}/\partial b$. The updated parameter estimates are then used to compute a new estimate of $\hat{\mu}$, and the regression is repeated using the new estimates of $y - \hat{\mu}$ and $\partial\hat{\mu}/\partial b$. At convergence, the weighted sum of squares will be the sum of the squared Pearson residuals.

To implement the procedure, we must calculate the partial derivatives of $\hat{\mu}$ with respect to the parameter estimates b. For loglinear models, $\hat{\mu} = \exp(\Sigma bx)$. To find the partial derivative with respect to a parameter, say b_1, rewrite $\hat{\mu}$ as $\exp(b_1 x_1)\Sigma_{i \neq 1} b_i x_i)$. The second part of the expression does not contain b_1 and is therefore a constant with respect to that parameter. The derivative of $\exp(b_1 x_1)$

with respect to b_1 is $x_1 \exp(b_1 x_1)$, so $\partial \hat{\mu} / \partial b_1 = x_1 \exp(b_1 x_1) \exp(\Sigma_{i \neq 1} b_i x_i)$ $= x_1 \hat{\mu}$. In other words, in loglinear models the partial derivatives $\partial \hat{\mu} / \partial b$ are the original covariates multiplied by the current estimated value of μ. The estimation procedure can be simplified by recalling that weighted least squares regression is equivalent to ordinary least squares regression of transformed variables. If both sides of the regression are divided (elementwise) by $\hat{\mu}$, the result is a regression of a modified dependent variable $(y - \hat{\mu}) / \hat{\mu}$ on the original covariates X with weight $\hat{\mu}$.

The logbilinear association model is closely related to standard loglinear models, since the only nonlinearity is the multiplicative combination of row and column scores. The model may be written $\hat{\mu}_{ij} = \exp(r_i + c_j + u_i v_j)$, where $\hat{\mu}_{ij}$ is the estimated count, r and c are row and column parameters, u_i is an estimated row score, and v_j is an estimated column score. To find the partial derivative of $\hat{\mu}$ with respect to the row score, we must treat v as a constant. That is, v plays the role of x in the discussion of loglinear models in the last paragraph. Hence, the partial derivative with respect to a particular row score, say u_k, will be $v_j \hat{\mu}$ in that row (i.e., for $j = k$) and zero otherwise. Similarly, the partial derivative with respect to a particular column score will be $u_i \hat{\mu}$ in that column and zero otherwise.

The latent class model makes the predicted values an additive function of several loglinear models of independence. Suppose we have a two-class model $\mu = p_1 \exp(bx) + p_2 \exp(cx)$, where x is a set of dummy variables for the rows and columns, p_1 and p_2 are the proportions in each latent class, and b and c are the logs of the conditional row and column proportions in the latent classes. Notice that the parameter estimates b do not appear in the second part of the expression, so $\partial \hat{\mu} / \partial b$ is the partial derivative of $p_1 \exp(bx)$ with respect to b. By the reasoning above, $\partial \hat{\mu} / \partial b = p_1 x \exp(bx)$. To obtain the partial derivatives for a latent class model, we must calculate the predicted values in the subtables corresponding to each latent class. This information is not usually provided by latent class programs, but it is easy to reconstruct from the parameter estimates.[7]

[7]The most popular program for latent class analysis, MLLSA (Eliason 1989), uses an estimation method that does not involve calculation of the partial derivatives. Recent versions, however, do give the partial derivatives as optional output. Latent class models can also be estimated by scoring or closely related methods (Haberman 1988).

Since the maximum likelihood method of scoring is equivalent to a series of weighted least squares regressions, the P test is easily applied to count data. It is performed by starting from the maximum likelihood estimates of the parameters in the maintained model and performing the linear regression in (4) with weights $1/f$. Except for its use of iterative weights, the P test is identical to nonlinear regressions with normal errors:

1. Fit H_0 and H_1 and call the predicted counts f and g respectively.
2. Calculate the partial derivatives of f with respect to the parameters of H_0.
3. Define a variable $h = g - f$. Regress $(y-f)$ on h and $\partial\hat{\mu}/\partial b_0$, using $1/f$ as the weight.[8]
4. Divide the parameter estimate for h by its standard error to get the P-test statistic.

The P-test statistic has (asymptotically) a standard normal distribution. A significant value implies rejection of the null hypothesis. Although a significant negative value is possible in principle, significant values are usually positive.

The C test is identical except that the partial derivatives are omitted in step 3. That is, the residuals $y - f$ are regressed on the difference between the predictions of the maintained and alternative models, with $1/f$ as the weight.

The N test can also be extended to models for count data, although not quite as straightforwardly. As pointed out above, the P and N tests are score tests and consequently should be based on the score statistic (7). To obtain this, consider a single observation with parameter μ. The loglikelihood for a single observation from the Poisson distribution is $n \log(n/\hat{\mu}) - n + \hat{\mu}$ (Nelder and Wedderburn 1972, p. 375). The efficient score $d(\theta)$ is thus

$$\partial L/\partial\hat{\mu} = -n/\hat{\mu} + 1 = (\hat{\mu} - n)/\hat{\mu}.$$

The information or expected value of the second derivative is equal to the expected value of the square of $\partial L/\partial\hat{\mu}$ (Silvey 1975, p. 37). The

[8]It may be more convenient, particularly when H_0 is a loglinear model, to perform the weighted least squares analysis after dividing through by f and using f as the weight. For loglinear models, this will result in a regression of $(y - f)/f$ on h/f and the original covariates (see the appendix for an example).

square of $(\hat{\mu} - n)/\hat{\mu}$ is the Pearson X^2 statistic divided by $\sqrt{\hat{\mu}}$, so its expected value is $1/\mu$. Substituting these quantities into the formula for the score test statistic (7) produces the Pearson X^2 (Cox and Hinkley 1974, pp. 315–16). Although the non-nested tests could be carried out with likelihood ratio chi squares, the Pearson X^2 is the natural test statistic to use.[9] The assumption that H_0 is true nevertheless suggests a modification in the calculation of the Pearson X^2 for the alternative model. The usual denominator in the statistic is the estimated count under that model. Assuming that H_0 is true, however, its estimates should be used to calculate the fit of H_1. That is, the fit of H_1 is evaluated as if the estimates from the maintained model were the true expectations of the counts. Rather than using the Pearson X^2, we must calculate $\Sigma(y - g)^2/f$.

We must make one important modification before we can apply the N statistic to models for count data. As discussed above, the numerator of the statistic is the difference between the observed and expected loglikelihoods of the alternative model. For Poisson regressions, the loglikelihood is asymptotically equal to the sum of squares of the Pearson residuals. To preserve continuity with the previous discussion, I use the symbol σ^2 to denote the sum of squares of Pearson residuals divided by N. A version of T_0 applicable to data from a Poisson distribution, which I designated as T_0^*, is then

$$T_0^* = (N/2)\, (\hat{\sigma}_1^2 - \hat{\sigma}_{10}^2).$$

We can find the variance of T_0^* by noting that the estimator of T_0 in regressions with normal errors (1) may be linearized to obtain an asymptotically equivalent form:

$$TL_0 \approx (N/2)(\hat{\sigma}_1^2 - \hat{\sigma}_{10}^2)/\hat{\sigma}_{10}^2.$$

Since TL_0 is asymptotically equivalent to T_0, it has the same asymptotic variance, given in (2). Note that $T_0^* = TL_0\hat{\sigma}_{10}^2$. Because f is a consistent estimator under the null hypothesis, $\hat{\sigma}_{10}^2$ is a consistent estimator of σ_{10}^2. Cramer (1946, pp. 254–55) showed that if x and y are random variables and y converges in probability to a constant c, then the distribution of xy tends to the distribution of xc. The asymptotic variance of xy is thus $c^2\mathrm{Var}(x)$. Taking σ_{10}^2 to be c and TL_0 to be x, we obtain

[9]This is implicitly true for the P test as well, because the estimated standard errors are based on the Pearson X^2 statistic.

$$\text{Var}(T_0^*) = \sigma_0^2 \sigma_{100}^2.$$

The expected value of σ_0 for a correctly specified model is known to be one, so the variance simplifies further, and the N statistic is

$$N_0 = (N/2) \, (\hat{\sigma}_1^2 - \hat{\sigma}_{10}^2)/\hat{\sigma}_{100}. \tag{10}$$

The N test for H_0 is therefore carried out as follows:

1. Fit H_0 and H_1 to the data. Obtain the Pearson X^2 from H_0 and calculate $\hat{\sigma}_1^2 = (1/N)\Sigma[(y - g)^2/f]$ for H_1.
2. Fit H_1 to f and call the predicted values $\hat{\sigma}_{10}$. Calculate $\hat{\sigma}_a^2 = (1/N)\Sigma[(f - \mu_{10})^2/f]$.
3. Regress $(f - \hat{\sigma}_{10})$ on $\partial\mu/\partial b_0$ using $1/f$ as weights and take the weighted mean square error as the estimate of σ_{100}^2.
4. Calculate the N statistic according to (10) and compare it with a standard normal distribution.

A significant negative value for the N statistic indicates a substantially better fit for H_1 than expected and therefore rejection of H_0. As with the P test, the fit of the alternative can be significantly worse than expected, but this rarely occurs in practice.

The P test is computationally simpler than the N test, because after H_0 and H_1 have been estimated, it requires only a single linear regression of the residuals from H_0 on $\partial\hat{\mu}/\partial b_0$ and $(f - g)$. The N test requires one linear regression and one re-estimation of the alternative model. Although calculation of the derivatives is straightforward, the C test is even simpler and may be useful in some situations. Since nothing is known about the actual performance of any of the tests for contingency tables, all three are used in the example below.

One potentially important issue is the use of the tests when some of the estimates are on the borders of the parameter space and constrained to equal zero. This is fairly common in latent class models, and it occurs with one parameter in Clogg's model, estimated below. Strictly speaking, the estimates for such models are not maximum likelihood estimates. In this case, the standard likelihood ratio test is not valid because it does not have an asymptotic chi-square distribution, but score tests are not affected (Godfrey 1988, p. 95). In fact, score tests are asymptotically optimal when we start from any consistent estimator of the restricted model (Breusch and Pagan

1980, pp. 249–50).[10] Under the hypothesis that the model is true, the true parameter values cannot be less than zero, so the constrained solution is consistent and there are no problems in using the tests.

A related but more general issue is the performance of the tests when latent class or mixture models are involved. Standard asymptotic theory is not generally valid for hypotheses that restrict parameters to values on the border of the parameter space, such as the hypothesis that a latent class probability equals zero (Titterington, Smith, and Makov 1985, pp. 152–59). The asymptotic behavior of the non-nested tests for comparison involving latent class models requires further investigation. For the purposes of this paper, however, I assume that these comparisons present no special problems.

5. AN EXAMPLE

I use these tests on the well-known 8-by-8 British mobility table (Glass 1954). I compare four models: the loglinear crossings model, the logbilinear association model, the latent class model proposed by Clogg (1981), and the restricted latent class model proposed by Marsden (1985).

The crossings and association models represent scales of social distance. The crossings model is based on a prior ordering of categories, and it includes a set of dummy variables that represent the movement between adjacent classes. If i is the index for rows and j is the index for columns, then the model can be written

$$\log(\mu_{ij}) = r_i + c_j + \Sigma_k \tau_k d_k,$$

where r_i and c_j are parameters for the row and column marginals and $d_k = 1$ if $\min(i,j) < k$ and $\max(i,j) \geq k$ and zero otherwise. Consequently, d_k is defined from $k = 2$ to $k = 8$ in an 8-by-8 table.[11] A person who moved from class 1 to class 3, for example, would be coded 1 on d_2 and d_3. The parameters τ_k represent the strength of the barrier between adjacent classes. Consequently, the log odds of a

[10] Tests in which consistent estimators are used are usually known as $C(a)$ tests. Score tests, in which maximum likelihood estimates are used, are a special case. See Moran (1970) for a general discussion and a proof of the asymptotic optimality of these tests.

[11] When dummy variables are used for the diagonal cells, as in these models, d_8 becomes redundant.

movement across several boundaries is equal to the sum of the log odds of movement across each individual boundary (Goodman 1984, pp. 368–70). The logbilinear association model does not require a prior ordering but estimates scores for each origin and destination category (Goodman 1979, pp. 73–74). A restricted version of the association model makes the origin and destination scores equal. This model can be written

$$\log(\mu_{ij}) = r_i + c_j + v_i v_j,$$

where v is the vector of estimated scores.[12] The restriction can be accepted using standard tests for nested models (Goodman 1979, p. 81), so the homogeneous association model will be used for the non-nested comparison.

The Clogg and Marsden models both posit the existence of latent classes within which individuals have identical mobility chances. Clogg (1981, p. 855) supposes that there are two classes: an upper class and a lower class. Marsden (1985, p. 1015) allows for three underlying classes but restricts them so that most observed categories are entirely within a single latent class. The model permits mobility between latent classes of origin and destination, so it includes nine latent classes, one for each combination of origin and destination. Marsden's model can be thought of as a measurement model relating observed groups to classes defined by mobility chances.

All of the models use dummy variables or latent classes of "stayers" to fit the diagonal cells exactly. Because they are fitted exactly, the diagonal cells have no bearing on the tests, which can be performed either by including the dummies as parameters or by excluding diagonal cells.

Table 1 shows the G^2 and X^2 fit statistics for each model and the p value of G^2.[13] Raftery's (1986) BIC statistic, which has become a popular criterion for model selection in contingency tables,

---

[12]The partial derivatives with respect to, say, v_1, are $\delta_{1.} v \hat{\mu} + \delta_{.1} v \hat{\mu}$, where $\delta_{1.}$ is a dummy variable equal to one for row 1 and zero otherwise, and $\delta_{.1}$ is equal to one for column 1 and zero otherwise.

[13]The latent class models were estimated in Clogg's MLLSA program as implemented in the CDAS package (Eliason 1989). The crossings and association models were estimated with GLIM. The fits of the Clogg and Marsden models reported here are slightly different from the fits reported in the original sources, apparently because of differences in convergence criteria.

TABLE 1
Fit Statistics for Models of the Glass Mobility Table

Model	G^2	X^2	df	BIC	p
Clogg	60.56	61.26	28	−167.9	.0003
Crossings	45.63	43.02	36	−248.1	.130
Marsden	38.01	36.45	33	−231.3	.251
Association	29.15	27.97	28	−199.3	.404
Homogeneous association	32.56	31.21	34	−244.9	.538
Clogg + Marsden	7.45	7.41	3	−17.0	.059
Crossings + Homogeneous association	27.42	24.75	29	−209.2	.549

is also displayed. The difference between the Bayesian approach to model selection represented by Raftery's statistic and the classical hypothesis-testing approach represented by the non-nested tests is discussed in a later section.

   None of the four models is nested in any of the others. The crossings and association models can be artificially nested to allow a conventional likelihood ratio test, although no one has done this.[14] The two latent class models can also be combined into a general model. Results for these two general models are displayed in the last two lines of the table. Using the standard nested tests, we reject the crossings model against the comprehensive loglinear model, but we do not reject the homogeneous association model. We reject the Clogg model against the comprehensive latent class model, but we do not reject the Marsden model. By testing nested models, we are left with two final alternatives, the Marsden and association models, which cannot be compared.

   In addition to nested hypothesis tests, several other ways of comparing models are sometimes used. These approaches involve some trade-off of parsimony against fit. The choice among models naturally depends on the particular standard used for the trade-off. In this case, the two criteria considered lead to different conclusions: The BIC statistic favors the crossings model, and the p value favors the homogeneous association model.

[14]Although specifying the comprehensive model is simple in principle, making the estimates converge was difficult. In this case, like many others, the conventional test was too inconvenient to be of much practical use.

A difference between all selection criteria and classical testing procedures is that selection criteria are designed to pick one best model, while in both nested and non-nested tests, it's possible that no model is acceptable. For example, the association model appears to fit better than the Clogg model by most standards. Nevertheless, it is possible that the Clogg model explains some features of the data that are not fully explained by the association model. If this is the case, the association model cannot be accepted, despite its apparently good fit. If, however, the Clogg model adds nothing, the association model should be accepted. When the purpose of an investigation is to find a true model, it is desirable to be able to make this distinction.

The results of tests of the Clogg model are shown in Table 2. The C and P test statistics have a standard normal distribution under the hypothesis that the Clogg model is true; a positive value indicates rejection in the direction of the alternative. The N test also has a standard normal distribution, but with the opposite sign. Regardless of which test is used, the Clogg model is rejected against all of the alternatives. This is not surprising, since it fits less well than any of the other models. In general, non-nested tests cannot accept a maintained model that fits substantially less well than an alternative. Table 2 is of interest mainly because it establishes that all of the non-nested tests arrive at the same conclusion in this case.

Results of tests of the crossings model are shown in Table 3. Once again, all tests agree that this model should be rejected against all of the others. The fact that it is rejected against the Clogg model is worth noting. The Clogg model, despite its worse fit, appears to

TABLE 2
Tests of Clogg Model Against Non-Nested Alternatives

	Test		
Alternative Model	C	P	N
Crossings	4.64*	5.65*	−9.22*
Marsden	4.80*	5.54*	−12.82*
Homogeneous association	4.91*	6.19*	−43.13*

Note: Statistics have asymptotic standard normal distribution under the hypothesis that the Clogg model is true.
*Maintained hypothesis rejected at 1 percent level.

TABLE 3
Tests of Crossings Model Against Non-Nested Alternatives

Alternative Model	Test		
	C	P	N
Clogg	3.18*	4.16*	−4.39*
Marsden	2.88*	3.28*	−12.09*
Homogeneous association	3.88*	3.91*	−7.66*

Note: Statistics have asymptotic standard normal distribution under the hypothesis that the crossings model is true.
*Maintained hypothesis rejected at 1 percent level.

explain some aspects of the table that the crossings model cannot explain. Using the non-nested tests, an investigator considering only the Clogg and crossings models would conclude that it was necessary to search further for a satisfactory model. An investigator relying on the p value, however, could conclude that the crossings model was satisfactory.

The corresponding results for the Marsden model are shown in Table 4. Here, there is disagreement among the tests. According to the C test, the Marsden model can be accepted against both the Clogg and crossings models. The P test, however, rejects it against the Clogg model, and the N test rejects it against both the Clogg and crossings models. Although the C and P tests produce identical conclusions for all other comparisons, the difference in this case is large enough to cast doubt on the acceptability of the C test as an approximation of the P test.

Because the P and N tests disagree in the comparison of the Marsden model against the crossings model, they must be taken as ambiguous. Davidson and MacKinnon (1982, p. 561), in a simulation study of regressions with normal errors, found that both the P and N tests reject a true null too often in small samples but that this tendency is stronger for the N test.[15] There is no particular reason to

[15]In these tests, the N statistics are usually larger in absolute value than the P statistics, particularly in testing the Clogg and Marsden models against the association model. Davidson and MacKinnon (1981, p. 792) noted the same tendency in comparing linear regression models. Their simulation results, however, showed no consistent differences in power after they adjusted for the greater tendency of the N statistic to over-reject a true null in small samples (Davidson and MacKinnon 1982, p. 563). That is, the N statistic does not appear

TABLE 4
Tests of Marsden Model Against Non-Nested Alternatives

Alternative Model	Test		
	C	P	N
Clogg	1.63	3.99*	−5.29*
Crossings	0.70	1.36	−2.62*
Homogeneous association	2.53*	3.15*	−63.54*

Note: Statistics have asymptotic standard normal distribution under the hypothesis that the Marsden model is true.
*Maintained hypothesis rejected at 1 percent level.

expect the tests to behave differently for Poisson regressions. If Davidson and MacKinnon's findings hold generally, the P test is probably reliable in cases of disagreement in small samples. It is not clear, however, what should be regarded as a small sample in count data. This issue is discussed further in the conclusion.

The most interesting finding is that according to both the P and N test, the Marsden model should be strongly rejected against the Clogg model. This was not the result of the nested test of Table 1. That test, however, had limited power because it required a large number of parameters to be filled. The results of the non-nested tests suggest that the Marsden and Clogg models explain different aspects of the observed contingency table. This is an unexpected finding, since on the surface the Marsden and Clogg models seem to have more in common than the Marsden and crossings models. The result suggests that a more elaborate latent class model combining features of both models might fit substantially better.

Finally, tests of the homogeneous association model are displayed in Table 5. According to the C and P tests, the association model cannot be rejected against any of the others. The results for the N test are more puzzling: They indicate that all other models fit significantly *worse* than expected under the hypothesis that the association model is true. Significant positive values have not been reported in other applications of non-nested tests, so it is difficult to interpret these results. They could indicate that the association

to be systematically larger than the P statistic in the range of reasonable critical values. Rather, the N statistic tends to be larger than the P statistic when both agree in strongly rejecting the maintained model.

TABLE 5

Tests of Homogeneous Association Model Against Non-Nested Alternatives

Alternative Model	Test		
	C	P	N
Clogg	0.25	0.35	14.45*
Crossings	1.39	1.53	46.04*
Marsden	1.00	1.18	14.47*

Note: Statistics have asymptotic standard normal distribution under the hypothesis that the homogeneous association model is true.

*Maintained hypothesis rejected at 1 percent level (two-sided test only).

model should be rejected in the direction away from the alternatives, meaning roughly that the model should be revised to make it less like the alternatives. On the other hand, the N test could be treated as a one-sided hypothesis test, in which case the association model could be accepted. The large positive test statistics seem to be related to the breakdown of the N test in the case of orthogonal regressors: the regression of $f - \hat{\mu}_{10}$ on $\partial\hat{\mu}/\partial b_0$ gives a nearly perfect fit, resulting in a very small estimate of σ_{100}^2 and a correspondingly large N statistic. The models are not exactly orthogonal, of course, but the unique parts of the association and other models may be close to orthogonal with these data. Although the N test should still be valid in principle, this could cause it to be unstable in practice. The extremely large statistics for the tests of the Clogg and Marsden models against homogeneous association in Tables 2 and 4 probably have a similar explanation. Consequently, the results of the N test should be regarded with some caution. It is impossible to know whether the present case is typical, but if it is, the N test is likely to be less useful than the P test.[16]

　　If we rely on the P test, we can reach an unambiguous conclusion: Of these models, the homogeneous association model provides

[16]White (1982, p. 316) and MacKinnon (1983, p. 92) point out that an N test using b_1 in place of b_{10} (and therefore eliminating the auxiliary regression of Wb_0 on Z) is asymptotically equivalent to the standard test. When this alternative version of the N test is applied to the homogeneous association model, the test statistics are nearly identical (except for sign) to those obtained in the P test. The alternative version of the N test has not previously been implemented, but this example suggests that it might prove more useful than the standard version in practice.

the best fit to the Glass mobility table. The N test yields the same conclusion if it is treated as a one-sided test. If the association model is omitted, the results of the P and N tests indicate that none of the models should be accepted, since each is rejected against at least one of the alternatives. This illustrates the value of the tests, because by conventional standards both the Marsden and the crossings models have acceptable fits. The p value tests a model against a saturated model, which understandably is less powerful than testing it against a meaningful alternative. The non-nested tests can be useful even if neither the maintained nor the alternative model is true: A false alternative can sometimes lead to rejection of a false maintained model. This is not always the case; it depends on how closely the predictions of each false model are associated with the predictions of the true model. Nevertheless, it is an important aid in the search for a satisfactory model.

6. DISCUSSION

The preceding section has illustrated the use and interpretation of non-nested hypothesis tests for contingency tables. This section compares non-nested tests to other methods of model selection and considers some unresolved issues and possible objections.

In many tests, such as the comparison of two loglinear models, it is possible to form a comprehensive model and carry out standard likelihood ratio tests. The degrees of freedom for the standard tests are then equal to the number of parameters in the competing models. The non-nested tests, in contrast, use only one degree of freedom regardless of the number of parameters in each model. In effect, the non-nested test takes each model as a single unit, rather than as a collection of parameters. This approach seems intuitively sensible if the models are taken as having distinct theoretical interpretations. It is also plausible to think that because they use only one degree of freedom, the non-nested tests have greater power. This is not invariably the case, but it has been proved for some special situations, and simulations suggest that it is often true (McAleer 1987, pp. 159–61). In the analysis of contingency tables, there are usually relatively few degrees of freedom to start with, so non-nested tests may be preferable even where nesting is possible. In the present case, the nested test of the Marsden and Clogg models did not reject the Marsden model, and in fact could not have rejected it even if the comprehensive model had fit perfectly, but the P and N tests rejected it decisively.

This characteristic of the non-nested tests, however, might be regarded as a defect rather than a virtue. Because there is no penalty for using degrees of freedom, one could make any model unbeatable by adding enough parameters. One response to this problem would be to modify the tests to include some penalty for degrees of freedom. It would be easy to adjust the denominator of the N test. The P test could also be modified, although in a less straightforward manner. Many of the possible adjustments, however, have no clear theoretical basis, and others make the test much more difficult to implement.[17] An alternative response is to see non-nested tests as a complement to, not a substitute for, standard hierarchical tests. If one takes each model as a representative of a distinct theoretical outlook, then it is necessary to choose models that are theoretically acceptable. This means, among other things, that superfluous parameters should be eliminated. The preliminary selection can be accomplished by using standard nested hypothesis tests, and non-nested tests can be performed on the resulting models. In the present case, for example, the homogeneous association model was used in the comparisons because it could be accepted against the unrestricted association model.

Assuming that neither model contains any superfluous parameters, it is less apparent that there should be an adjustment for degrees of freedom. The textbook answer is that we should prefer simplicity in a model, on the grounds that a simpler theory is inherently more plausible than a complex one. It is not clear, however, that theoretical simplicity corresponds to the number of parameters estimated.[18] For example, is Marsden's model simpler than Clogg's? It fits fewer parameters, but it involves three latent classes rather than two, and it implies a more complex structure of relations between them. Clogg

[17]See Godfrey and Pesaran (1983) for a discussion of adjustments to the N test in normal regression models. Some of the adjustments do seem to produce considerable improvement in small-sample performance, so their application to count data merits further investigation.

[18]Good (1975, p. 47) proposes an alternative definition of complexity based on the "linguistic expression that defines the theory." Although there are some difficulties with the specific measure he uses, Good's general approach corresponds more closely to the notion of theoretical complexity than does a definition in terms of the number of parameters.

presented his model as a straightforward representation of the "traditional sociological concepts of class" (1981, pp. 866–67), while Marsden (1985, pp. 1002–3) motivated his by the more recent and less familiar idea "of internal homogeneity" (Breiger 1981). One could plausibly argue that the idea represented by Clogg's model is simpler than the one represented by Marsden's when they are considered as theories of social mobility. The point is not that Clogg's model is objectively simpler, but that judgements on this point depend on the investigator's theoretical beliefs, so that there is no uncontroversial measure of simplicity. If the goal is to make a choice among competing theories, theoretical simplicity is desirable, but it is not equivalent to the number of parameters.[19]

As mentioned above, the non-nested tests are classical hypothesis tests. The Bayesian model-selection criterion known as the BIC (Raftery 1986) has become popular in recent years. Since it can be applied to both nested and non-nested models, the non-nested tests may seem unnecessary because a simpler alternative is already at hand. This is true if one accepts the theoretical rationale for the BIC. The popularity of the BIC in the analysis of contingency tables, however, seems to follow from the practical problems encountered in the analysis of large samples rather than from a general acceptance of the theory behind it. As the sample size increases, the power of classical tests increases, so a misspecified model tends to be rejected with certainty. In large samples, it is often impossible to find any reasonably simple model that can be accepted with classical tests.[20] Like standard tests, non-nested tests gain power as sample size increases, so the same issue arises. In effect, the tests become too powerful, and investigators prefer to use a weaker criterion. Investigators working with small or medium-size samples, however, usually encounter the opposite problem and try to use the most powerful test possible. Using the BIC in small and medium-size samples generally forces investigators to accept models that they might find too sim-

---

[19] These remarks are intended to apply to non-nested models. In nested models, we can say that imposing a restriction simplifies the model.

[20] This is also true for the BIC. The chi-square statistic for a misspecified model increases with N, while the penalty for degrees of freedom in the BIC increases with $\log(N)$. As the sample size increases, small discrepancies in fit therefore require the adoption of a more complicated model. Hence, one cannot argue for the BIC against the classical approach on these grounds, although the BIC does generally favor simpler models.

ple.[21] Hence, while there are arguments for the consistent use of the
BIC, most sociologists have employed it for model simplification in
large samples and still use classical tests in smaller samples. This is
not unreasonable: Small effects are sometimes discarded as substantively unimportant, especially in very large samples; but sometimes
small effects are of theoretical interest. It seems appropriate to use
different strategies in each case. Thus, the situations in which the
BIC should be used are different from those in which non-nested
hypothesis tests should be used, so the two are complements rather
than rivals.

There are, however, important theoretical differences in the
arguments underlying non-nested tests and the BIC. This is not the
place for a general discussion of classical and Bayesian approaches to
hypothesis testing, but a few theoretical issues deserve comment.
First, investigators usually carry out a large number of tests when
comparing models, so the probability of falsely rejecting at least one
hypothesis is greater than the nominal significance level. This suggests
the need to adjust probability values when considering a large number
of models, although there are few systematic rules for doing so. Non-
nested tests are not immune to this problem, but one appealing feature of the P test is that it is easily extended to the simultaneous testing
of multiple hypotheses (MacKinnon 1983, pp. 96–97).[22] The N test
can also be extended to multiple hypotheses, although not as easily
(Sawyer 1984). Constructing the comprehensive model necessary for
nested hypothesis tests is even more difficult when more than two
models are involved, so non-nested tests are likely to be especially
useful in this case. Second, it has often been pointed out that even a
model that seems to fit well may be seriously defective, and a variety
of specification tests have been developed to aid in the evaluation of

---

[21]In a sample of 1,000, for example, a restriction involving four degrees
of freedom would be acceptable by the BIC criterion if it increased the L^2 by any
amount less than 27.6. The 5 percent critical value for the chi-square test is 9.49.

[22]We simply calculate the difference between each of the alternatives and
the maintained model and include them all simultaneously in the regression. For
example, if the predictions from the alternative models are designated g_1, g_2, and
g_3, we regress $y - f$ on $g_1 - f$, $g_2 - f$, $g_3 - f$, and $\partial \hat{\mu}/\partial b_0$ and test the hypothesis
that the parameters of all three of the differences in predictions are zero. In the
models considered here, the joint test fails to reject the homogeneous association model at the 5 percent level, although the statistic is close to the critical
value.

regression models (Godfrey 1988). Non-nested tests can be regarded as a kind of specification test, and as such they can reveal problems that might go unnoticed if we rely entirely on model-selection criteria such as the BIC.

7. CONCLUSION

In this paper I have discussed non-nested hypothesis tests for models of count data. They are not difficult to apply, and P tests can even be calculated from published data using any regression program. Because there are many theoretically interesting non-nested models for cross-classified data, these tests are widely applicable. Even when artificial nesting and use of standard tests is possible, the non-nested tests may have an advantage in both power and ease of use, as in the models considered here.

Because the non-nested tests are asymptotic rather than exact, it would be useful to know more about their performance in small samples. Simulations for regressions with normal errors have found that the P and N tests reject the null too often in very small samples but are quite accurate in samples of more than about 50 cases (Pesaran 1974, pp. 161–63; Davidson and MacKinnon 1982, pp. 559–63). For count data, however, a significantly larger sample is likely to be necessary. Since the tests are based on Pearson's X^2 statistic, they require a sample size at least as large as that necessary for chi-square tests of nested models. It is not clear whether non-nested tests require a substantially larger sample size than nested chi-square tests, and investigation of their small-sample performance is in order.

The results reported here appear to favor the P test over the N test. The P test is simpler to compute and is more stable, especially when the association model is included. More experience is needed before we can reach definite conclusions on this point, however. The substantial divergence between the results of the C and P tests for one pair of models casts doubt on the value of the C test. Because it is not especially difficult to calculate partial derivatives for either loglinear or latent class models, it seems better to use the P test.

In recent years, researchers have devoted considerable attention to specification analysis in regression models (see the survey in Godfrey 1988). Few of these techniques, however, have been extended to other models, and analyses of contingency tables often do not go beyond reporting basic indices of fit. The techniques reported here make it possible to test competing models. No technique can or should make model selection an automatic process, but the tests discussed here promise to be useful tools in analyses of contingency tables and other count data.

APPENDIX

This appendix describes how to perform the non-nested hypothesis tests. The examples were computed in GLIM, but they could have been carried out in any weighted least squares program. Commands are preceded by a dollar-sign ($). Other lines represent program output.

Performing the P Test

This example gives the test of the maintained homogeneous association model against the alternative Marsden model. A macro fitting the homogeneous association model has been invoked, and the covariates and fit statistics are shown below. The iterative weight, WT, is equal to the current predicted values. The predicted values from other models are read from another data file. In the notation used in the paper, $RESI = (y - f)/f$ and $AMARS = h/f$. A weighted least squares regression of RESI on AMARS and the original terms in the model is then performed. The standard error shown in the output must be divided by the square root of the scale parameter before the P statistic can be calculated because GLIM normalizes standard errors by the sum of the weights. Thus the P statistic is $.3828/(.30762/\sqrt{.9033}) = 1.18$. Note that the test statistic is also equal to the square root of the difference in the weighted sum of squares (Pearson's X^2) between the association model and the model including AMARS.

Results at iteration 9.00000
Pearson chisquare is 31.2072
ML chisquare is 32.5624
$disp m
Current model:

number of units is 64
y-variate WV
weight WT
offset *

probability distribution is NORMAL
link function is IDENTITY
scale parameter is to be estimated by the mean deviance

terms = 1 + ROW + COL + P1 + P2 + P3 + P4 + P5 + P6 +
  P7 + P8 + DIAG

```
$calc resi=(n − wt)/wt
$data pclogg pcross pmars prc prch
$dinput 20
$calc amars = (pmars − wt)/wt
$fit + amars $
```
deviance = 29.80836 (change = −1.39897)
d.f. = 33 (change = −1)

```
$disp e
```
estimate s.e. parameter
[OMITTED TO SAVE SPACE]
32 0.382825 0.307616 AMAR
scale parameter taken as 0.903284

GLIM Macro for the N Test

```
$macro coxx
$c Macro HO contains linearized equation for maintained hypothe-
$c sis. You need to input predicted values from HO (xb), H1 (zg),
$c and H1 fit to xb (zge). Note: 'actual' fit of zg is computed with
$c xb as denominator in the Pearson statistic.
$c Note: For loglinear models, partial derivatives assumed to be
$c x*xb Can use with original x's by setting scalar %l=1 before
$cuse
$calc %r = −1*%cu(((n − xb)**2/xb)/2)
$calc %q = −1*%cu(((n − zg)**2/xb)/2) : %s = −1*%cu(((xb −
  zge)**2/xb)/2)
```

```
$calc %t = (%s + %r − %q) : wt = %if(%eq(%l,1),xb,1/xb)
$calc u = xb − zge : u = %if(%eq(%l,1),u/xb,u)
$yvar u
$error n
$weight wt
$fit #h0
$calc %v = %cu((u − %fv)*(u − %fv)*wt) : %z = %t/%sqrt(%v)
  : %p = %le(%z,−1.96) + 1
$print 'N test statistic is ' %z
$print 'Maintained hypothesis ' h0
$switch %p accept reject
$endmac
$macro reject
$print 'is rejected' ::
$endm
$macro accept
$print 'is not rejected' ::
$endm
$return
```

Invocation and Output of the N Test Macro

This example tests the maintained crossings model against the alternative Clogg model. The necessary data have been previously read in and assigned the names used in the macro. For convenience, the scalar %l can be set to perform the test using either weights *f* or 1/*f*. The former is usually more convenient when the maintained hypothesis is a loglinear model, the latter when it is a latent class model.

```
$calc %l = 1
$macro h0 row + col,cr2,cr3,cr4,cr5,cr6,cr7,diag $endm
$use coxx $
—model changed
deviance = 29.463
d.f. = 36
```

N test statistic is -4.387
Maintained hypothesis row + col,cr2,cr3,cr4,cr5,cr6,cr7,diag
is rejected

REFERENCES

Bishop, Yvonne M. M., Stephen E. Fienberg, and Paul W. Holland. 1975. *Discrete Multivariate Analysis.* Cambridge, MA: MIT Press.

Breiger, Ronald L. 1981. "The Social Class Structure of Occupational Mobility." *American Journal of Sociology* 87: 578–611.

Breusch, T. S., and A. R. Pagan. 1980. "The Lagrange Multiplier Test and its Applications to Model Specification in Econometrics." *Review of Economic Studies* 47: 239–53.

Clogg, Clifford C. 1981. "Latent Structure Models of Mobility." *American Journal of Sociology* 86: 836–68.

Cox, D. R. 1961. "Tests of Separate Families of Hypotheses." Pp. 105–23 in *Proceedings of the Fourth Berkeley Symposium on Mathematical Statistics and Probability,* vol. 1, edited by J. Neyman. Berkeley: University of California Press.

———. "Further Results on Tests of Separate Families of Hypotheses." *Journal of the Royal Statistical Society,* ser. B, 24: 406–24.

Cox, D. R., and D. V. Hinkley. 1974. *Theoretical Statistics.* London: Chapman and Hall.

Cramer, Harald. 1946. *Mathematical Methods of Statistics.* Princeton: Princeton University Press.

Davidson, Russell, and James G. MacKinnon. 1981. "Several Tests for Model Specification in the Presence of Alternative Hypotheses." *Econometrica* 49: 781–93.

———. 1982. "Some Non-Nested Hypothesis Tests and the Relations Among Them." *Review of Economic Studies* 49: 551–65.

Duncan, Otis Dudley. 1979. "How Destination Depends on Origin in the Occupational Mobility Table." *American Journal of Sociology* 84: 793–803.

Duncan, Otis Dudley, Magnus Stenbeck, and Charles J. Brody. 1988. "Discovering Heterogeneity: Continuous versus Discrete Latent Variables." *American Journal of Sociology* 93: 1305–21.

Eliason, Scott R. 1989. *The Categorical Data Analysis System: Version 3.00A User's Manual.* Iowa City: University of Iowa, Department of Sociology.

Glass, D. V., ed. 1954. *Social Mobility in Britain.* London: Routledge and Kegan Paul.

Godfrey, L. G. 1988. *Misspecification Tests in Econometrics.* Cambridge: Cambridge University Press.

Godfrey, L. G., and M. H. Pesaran. 1983. "Tests of Non-Nested Regression Models: Small Sample Adjustment and Monte Carlo Evidence." *Journal of Econometrics* 21: 133–54.

Good, I. J. 1975. "Explicativity, Corroboration, and the Relative Odds of Hypotheses." *Synthese* 30: 39–73.

Goodman, Leo. 1979. "Simple Models for the Analysis of Association in Cross-Classifications Having Ordered Categories. *Journal of the American Statistical Association* 74: 537–52. Reprinted in Goodman 1984.

Goodman, Leo. 1984. *The Analysis of Cross-Classified Data Having Ordered Categories.* Cambridge, MA: Harvard University Press.

Haberman, Shelby. 1988. "A Stabilized Newton-Raphson Algorithm for Log-Linear Models for Frequency Tables Derived by Indirect Observation." Pp. 193–211 in *Sociological Methodology 1988,* edited by C. C. Clogg. Washington, DC: American Sociological Association.

Jorgensen, Bent. 1984. "The Delta Algorithm and GLIM." *International Statistical Review* 52: 283–300.

Lindsay, Bruce, Clifford C. Clogg, and John Grego. 1991. "Semiparametric Estimation in the Rasch Model and Related Exponential Response Models." *Journal of the American Statistical Association* 86: 96–107.

McAleer, Michael. 1987. "Specification Tests for Separate Models: A Survey." Pp. 146–95 in *Specification Analysis in the Linear Model,* edited by M. L. King and D. E. A. Giles. London: Routledge and Kegan Paul.

MacKinnon, James G. 1983. "Model Specification Tests Against Non-nested Alternatives." *Econometric Reviews* 2: 85–110.

Marsden, Peter V. 1985. "Latent Structure Models for Relationally Defined Social Classes." *American Journal of Sociology* 90: 1002–21.

Moran, P. A. P. 1970. "On Asymptotically Optimal Tests of Composite Hypotheses." *Biometrika* 57: 47–55.

Nelder, J. A., and R. W. M. Wedderburn. 1972. "Generalized Linear Models." *Journal of the Royal Statistical Society,* ser. A, 135: 370–84.

Pesaran, M. H. 1974. "On the General Problem of Model Selection." *Review of Economic Studies* 41: 153–71.

Pesaran, M. H., and A. S. Deaton. 1978. "Testing Non-nested Nonlinear Regression Models." *Econometrica* 46: 677–94.

Quandt, Richard E., and Harvey S. Rosen. 1988. *The Conflict Between Equilibrium and Disequilibrium Theories.* Kalamazoo, MI: Upjohn Institute for Employment Research.

Raftery, Adrian E. 1986. "Choosing Models for Cross-Classifications." *American Sociological Review* 51: 145–46.

Rao, C. R. 1973. *Linear Statistical Inference and its Applications.* 2d ed. New York: Wiley.

Sawyer, K. R. 1984. "Multiple Hypothesis Testing." *Journal of the Royal Statistical Society,* ser. B, 46: 419–24.

Silvey, S. D. 1975. *Statistical Inference.* London: Chapman and Hall.

Titterington, D. M., A. F. M. Smith, and U. E. Makov. 1985. *Statistical Analysis of Finite Mixture Distributions.* Chichester, England: Wiley.

White, Halbert. 1982. "Regularity Conditions for Cox's Test of Non-nested Hypotheses." *Journal of Econometrics* 19: 301–18.

℀6℀

THE ANALYSIS OF COUNT DATA: OVERDISPERSION AND AUTOCORRELATION

*David N. Barron**

I begin this paper by describing several methods that can be used to analyze count data. Starting with relatively familiar maximum likelihood methods—Poisson and negative binomial regression—I then introduce the less well known (and less well understood) quasi-likelihood approach. This method (like negative binomial regression) allows one to model overdispersion, but it can also be generalized to deal with autocorrelation. I then investigate the small-sample properties of these estimators in the presence of overdispersion and autocorrelation by means of Monte Carlo simulations. Finally, I apply these methods to the analysis of data on the foundings of labor unions in the U.S. Quasi-likelihood methods are found to have some advantages over Poisson and negative binomial regression, especially in the presence of autocorrelation.

1. INTRODUCTION

The study of dynamic social processes often involves some form of event analysis. There are many instances in sociological research. For example, studies of collective action (Olzak 1989),

This research was supported by National Science Foundation grant SES-9008493. Michael Hannan, Miller McPherson, Elizabeth West, Peter Marsden, and the anonymous reviewers made helpful comments on earlier versions of the paper. I am particularly grateful to Michael Hannan for being so generous with his time and advice.

*Cornell University

179

organizational ecology (Hannan and Freeman 1989), and life course dynamics (Elder 1985) all rely on the analysis of events. An important feature of these three examples is their temporal focus. Indeed, event analysis is frequently associated with the study of processes or states that change over time. A wide variety of methods are appropriate for analyzing data of this kind (Tuma and Hannan 1984). The methods that go under the general heading of event history analysis are becoming increasingly common in sociological research, and they are perhaps the most powerful. However, event history analysis has the disadvantage of requiring very detailed data; usually a unique time of occurrence must be identified for each individual event.[1] Even when event history data can be collected in principle, the costs involved may be prohibitive. Often such detail is simply not available at any cost. However, in many situations it may well be feasible to obtain counts of the total number of events occurring in some time interval.

Sociologists have long been interested in methods for the analysis of event counts (Coleman 1964; Spilerman 1971). The most common is probably Poisson regression. In this paper I discuss the problems caused by violations of the assumptions that underlie this technique and some methods that circumvent these problems. I emphasize methods that are scarcely more complicated or costly to implement than Poisson regression but that provide a significantly more robust basis for statistical inference. Because so much event analysis is associated with the study of dynamic processes, I focus in particular on the use of time-series data. However, many of the methods described can in principle be applied in other contexts.[2]

Problems with the use of Poisson regression are associated particularly with two of the key assumptions that underlie the Poisson process: (a) the rate at which events occur is constant throughout a period of observation, and (b) there is no unobserved heterogeneity. Violation of either assumption can lead to biased esti-

---

[1]This information is required for at least the majority of events. There are some techniques that can cope with a limited number of ties. Alternatively, if we know the order in which events occurred, but not the exact time, we can use Cox's (1975) proportional hazards model.

[2]For example, analysis of count data from cross-sectional or panel research designs can also violate the Poisson assumptions. For discussions of count data methods in some of these contexts see Hausman, Hall, and Griliches (1984), Liang and Zeger (1986), and King (1989b).

mates of standard errors in Poisson regression. Such violations are likely to be common in sociological research. For example, contagion causes the rate of events to increase within periods of observation. Evidence of contagion has been found in studies of such dissimilar events as collective violence (Olzak 1989), aircraft high-jacking (Holden 1987), and the founding of organizations (Hannan and Freeman 1989). There are undoubtedly many other situations in which a previous event increases the chance of further incidents. Similarly, there can be no doubt that many sociological models omit some causal variables that vary over time. These complications can be dealt with by using a generalization of the Poisson model known as negative binomial regression. A major advantage of this approach is that it can cope with the presence of either, or both, time dependence in the rate or unobserved heterogeneity. Furthermore, estimates can be obtained relatively easily by the method of maximum likelihood (ML).

However, ML estimation of both Poisson and negative binomial regressions typically requires *independent* observations. This assumption will often not be true in time-series data, and Poisson and negative binomial regression are then problematic. We discuss a method of analyzing event count data by means of quasi-likelihood (QL) estimation and an extension of this method, which I call generalized quasi-likelihood (GQL) estimation (Wedderburn 1974; McCullagh 1983; Zeger 1988; McCullagh and Nelder 1989). The latter technique allows one to model autocorrelation in the rate caused by the operation of an unobserved disturbance term, in addition to the effects of variation in causal variables and unobserved heterogeneity, and it is as straightforward and cheap to implement as the more familiar methods based on ML. Of course, analyzing autocorrelation in this way is only one possible approach to dynamic model building. Alternatives, such as using the lagged count as an explanatory variable, may be appropriate in some circumstances. However, in this paper I concentrate on models that involve autocorrelated disturbances.

The GQL method has only recently been introduced. Although some asymptotic properties have been derived, its behavior in small samples has not yet been studied. To clarify the properties of this estimator, I present results of several Monte Carlo simulations. These simulations also allow comparisons of the GQL estimator with the more well known Poisson and negative binomial ML estimators.

I illustrate the advantages of the GQL estimator by analyzing data on the foundings of national labor unions in the U.S., using Poisson regression, three different negative binomial regressions, QL estimation assuming independence, and finally the GQL estimator.

2. THE POISSON PROCESS

Although this paper is about the analysis of event *counts,* bear in mind that the properties of a series of such counts depend on the nature of the process governing the occurrence of the individual (unobserved) events. The simplest such process, in which events occur "at random," is known as the Poisson process (Coleman 1964; Cox and Lewis 1978). Let $Y_{t,t+\delta}$ be a random variable defined as the number of events occurring in the interval of time $(t,t + \delta]$, where $\delta > 0$. If λ is the rate of occurrence of events in a time period that is longer than $(t,t + \delta]$, then the events are generated by a Poisson process if, as $\delta \to 0$,

$$\Pr(Y_{t,t+\delta} = 0) = 1 - \lambda\delta + o(\delta), \tag{1}$$

$$\Pr(Y_{t,t+\delta} = 1) = \lambda\delta + o(\delta), \tag{2}$$

and if $Y_{t,t+\delta}$ is independent of the history of the process in the period $(0,t]$, where $o(\delta)$ represents a quantity that tends to zero more rapidly than δ as $\delta \to 0$ (Cox and Lewis 1978). Equations (1) and (2) imply the following:

1. The probability of more than one event occurring in a short period of time is negligible.
2. The rate, λ, is constant.
3. The probability of an event in $(t,t + \delta]$ is not affected by the previous history of the series and, in particular, does not depend on the length of time since the previous event.

If events occur according to a Poisson process, then the distributions of times between events and of the number of events in a given time period have particular properties. If X_i is a random variable denoting the length of time between event $i - 1$ and event i, then X_i is exponentially distributed, and the mean length of time between events is $1/\lambda$. That is, X has a distribution $F(x)$ and density function $f(x)$ given by

$$\Pr(X_i \le x) = F(x) = 1 - \exp(-\lambda x), \qquad x \ge 0, \qquad (3)$$

$$f(x) = \frac{dF(x)}{dx} = \lambda \exp(-\lambda x), \qquad x \ge 0. \qquad (4)$$

If Y_t is the number of events occurring in an interval of length t, then Y_t is distributed as

$$\Pr(Y_t = y) = f(y) = \frac{\exp(-\lambda t)(\lambda t)^y}{y!}, \qquad y = 0,1,2,\ldots \qquad (5)$$

The first two moments of this distribution are

$$E(Y_t) = \lambda t \quad \text{and} \quad \text{Var}(Y_t) = \lambda t. \qquad (6)$$

Many event-generating processes—often known as point processes (Cox and Isham 1980)—are generalizations of the Poisson process. We are particularly interested in those that can lead to overdispersion (that is, those in which the variance of Y_t is greater than its mean) and autocorrelation in series of event counts. However, before discussing these processes, we need to understand how series of counts generated by Poisson processes can be analyzed by means of Poisson regression.

3. POISSON REGRESSION

The rationale for using Poisson regression is based in the first instance on the assumption that events are generated by a Poisson process. We observe a subject (say a country or a city) at the end of a given period of time (an hour, a day, a year, etc.) and record the total number of times a particular event (say the founding of a labor union, or a riot) occurred during this period, but not the times of the individual events. Alternatively, we observe the number of events in a single period of time for a number of different subjects; for example, the number of riots in a given year in various countries. In this paper I focus on the time-series observation plan, but similar methods may be used in the cross-sectional case. The Poisson conditions imply that events occur at a constant rate within a unit of observation, though of course the rate can vary across units.

Given that the Poisson assumption holds, it follows that the observed events in each time period ($t = 1,2, \ldots ,T$) are conditionally independent random variables, Y_t, with a probability distribution given by equation (5) and a parameter λ_t.[3] It is therefore easy to see that the joint distribution of all the random variables, Y_t, is given by

$$L = \prod_{t=1}^{T} \frac{\exp(-\lambda_t)\lambda_t^{y_t}}{y_t!}. \tag{7}$$

This is the likelihood function for independently Poisson-distributed random variables.[4] The loglikelihood function is, therefore,

$$l = \sum_{t=1}^{T} y_t \log(\lambda_t) - \lambda_t - \log(y_t!). \tag{8}$$

Since the factorial term is constant with respect to the parameters to be estimated, it is usually omitted in parameter estimation. In substantive applications, we naturally have to consider how to introduce covariates. A linear specification, $E(Y_t) = \lambda_t = x_t'\beta$, can certainly be used for Poisson regression (Cameron and Trivedi 1986), but it can be problematic because the expected number of events can be negative for some values of the covariates. A more commonly used formulation is a loglinear relationship between the expected number of events and the covariates:

$$E(Y_t) = \lambda_t = \exp(x_t'\beta), \tag{9}$$

which ensures that λ_t is positive. It also implies that the effect on λ_t of a change in a covariate x_{it} is given by

$$\frac{\partial \lambda_t}{\partial x_{it}} = \beta_i \lambda_t. \tag{10}$$

This means that the effect of a given change in x_{it} rises as λ_t gets larger. This will often be desirable. However, it should be borne in mind that this loglinear relationship is only one of many that are feasible: It is quite possible to estimate models using other relationships between covariates and λ_t.[5]

---

[3]To simplify notation, I make the additional assumption that all periods of observation are of unit length.
    [4]A useful introduction to likelihood theory, including discussions of Poisson and negative binomial regression, is provided by King (1989b).
    [5]For example, Hannan (1991) described models with a variety of different relationships between λ_t and covariates.

Given the simple form of the likelihood function in equation (7) and the fact that first and second derivatives of this function can easily be calculated, ML estimation of Poisson regression models is straightforward. A number of widely available computer packages, such as GLIM (Numerical Algorithms Group 1986), LIMDEP (Green 1990), and COUNT (King 1990), include routines for performing Poisson regression.[6] It is also easy to write programs in a matrix language such as GAUSS (Aptech Systems 1991), APL (STSC 1989) or SAS's Interactive Matrix Language (SAS Institute 1985), particularly given that ML estimates can be obtained by means of iterative weighted least squares for likelihood functions that, like equation (7), are members of the linear exponential family (Nelder and Wedderburn 1972; McCullagh 1983).

Poisson regression offers substantial advantages over least squares methods. If the data are Poisson distributed, then Poisson regression is more efficient. Even if the data are not so distributed, the ML estimator is fairly robust provided that the rate is correctly specified (Gourieroux, Monfort, and Trognon 1984).[7] Finally, estimated standard errors will be unbiased as long as the Poisson assumptions listed above are valid and λ_t is modeled correctly.

There are, however, a number of potential problems associated with Poisson regression. In many cases it is not realistic to assume that the rate at which events occur during a period of observation is constant. Violation of this assumption implies that the data cannot be Poisson distributed, that Poisson regression will therefore not be fully efficient, and that estimated standard errors will be biased and inconsistent.

The second problem associated with Poisson regression is the implicit assumption that there is no unobserved heterogeneity in the data. Notice that in equation (9) there is no error term in the relationship between the covariates and λ_t. This implies that the rate is completely determined only by observed covariates: There is no allowance for random error or unobserved variables.

If either time variation in the rate or heterogeneity are pres-

---

[6]All the functions that are available in COUNT can also be found in the Event Count and Duration Regression application module in GAUSS (Aptech Systems 1991).

[7]Specifically, ML estimates will be consistent if the true distribution is a member of the linear exponential family.

ent, then overdispersion can occur. That is, the variance of Y_t can be greater than its expected value. These two problems have led to the derivation of an alternative model: the negative binomial model. I consider this alternative below. First I discuss in more detail the sort of event-generating processes that can lead to overdispersion in series of counts.

4. SOURCES OF OVERDISPERSION IN COUNT DATA

Overdispersion in event count data is present when $\text{Var}(Y_t) > \text{E}(Y_t)$, in contrast to the equality of the first two moments of a Poisson-distributed random variable (equation (6)). Various deviations from the basic Poisson process can result in overdispersion. A detailed discussion of these can be found in Cox and Isham (1980). I will review some of the most important results here.

4.1. *Time Dependence in the Rate*

In the basic Poisson process, the rate λ is considered to be constant over a period of observation, t, though it can vary across periods. In the regression context, variation across periods is modeled by considering the rate to be a function of time-varying covariates, as discussed above in the context of Poisson regression. However, it is possible that λ is not constant during a period of observation. When λ is a function of time, we have what Cox and Isham (1980, p. 48) called a nonstationary Poisson process. We can consider this form of time dependence to be caused by one or more independent variables changing during a period of observation. Interestingly, in this situation the numbers of events in a set of periods are still independent Poisson variables, but the expected count is now given by

$$\text{E}(Y_t) = \int_{t-1}^{t} \lambda(s)ds. \tag{11}$$

The problem, of course, is that we typically do not have the information necessary to model such a process. That is, we do not know the time of occurrence of events within a period of observation unless we have event history data.

Consider the simplest possible case. Suppose that λ depends only on a single independent variable, X, and that this variable changes in value at the mid-point of a period of observation (say a year). Clearly, the number of events in each six-month period will be Poisson distributed with a constant rate. Furthermore, the number of events over the whole year is also Poisson distributed with an expected count $E(Y_t) = 1/2\{\exp(\beta x_1) + \exp(\beta x_2)\}$, where the x_i represent the values of X in the first and second halves of the year, respectively, and the rate and covariates have the usual loglinear relationship. However, we typically observe the value of independent variables only at the start of a year. If we assume that $X = x_1$ for the whole year, it is no longer necessarily the case that $\widehat{Var(Y_t)} = \widehat{E(Y_t)}$: There may be over-dispersion or underdispersion, depending on the relationship between the values of X in the two halves of the year.

4.2. Contagion

One particular cause of variation in the rate within a period of observation is contagion, which means that the rate of occurrence of events depends on the number of previous events. Positive contagion, which is more common, indicates that previous events increase the rate of occurrence. Negative contagion indicates that previous events reduce the rate. At this stage I am referring to the effect of prior events within a given period of observation. We will continue to assume that λ_t is independent of the number of events in previous periods.

Positive contagion leads to overdispersion (King 1989a,b). To see why, suppose that all observed causal variables have the same values for two periods. Imagine that an event occurs early in one period but later in the second period. This difference need not reflect any variation in the underlying rate of occurrence at the point when no events have occurred. It is a property of a Poisson process that an event is equally likely at any point in a period of observation. However, in a contagious process, as soon as the first event occurs, there is an increase in the probability of further events in the same period. But since this increased probability exists in more of the first time period, there is a greater chance of a second event occurring in the first period than in the second period. Of course, a second event increases the probability of more events, and so on. Thus, contagion

can be seen aś a special cause of variation in the rate within a period
of observation.[8]

4.3. Heterogeneity

Time dependence and contagion are forms of heterogeneity
within periods of observation. There can also be heterogeneity
across observations. There has been some discussion in the social
science literature on the relationship between unobserved heterogeneity of this type and overdispersion (Hausman et al. 1984; Cameron
and Trivedi 1986). Consider the relationship between the observed
covariates and the expected number of events in equation (9). Since
there is no error term in this relationship, the expected number of
events is the same for all periods for which the observed covariates
have the same values. Now suppose that an unobserved causal variable, z_t, affects the expected count and that the omitted variable has
different values at $t = 1$ and $t = 2$. The true expected numbers of
events are then $\lambda_1 = \exp(x'\beta + \pi z_1)$ and $\lambda_2 = \exp(x'\beta + \pi z_2)$, but the
estimates are $\hat{\lambda}_1 = \hat{\lambda}_2 = \exp(x'\hat{\beta})$. This level of unobserved heterogeneity means that on average, the observed counts are likely to differ
from the expected count more than they would if the model were
correctly specified. In other words, the variance of the observed
counts will be greater than the variance estimated by Poisson regression. Provided that z_2 is independent of z_1, the counts will still be
independent.

In this section I have reviewed some deviations from the
Poisson assumptions that lead to overdispersion. In event count data
it is often not possible to distinguish the cause of overdispersion.
Indeed, this is often problematic even in event history data (Coleman 1964; Heckman and Borjas 1980). If Poisson regression is used
in the presence of overdispersion, estimated standard errors are
likely to be too low (Cameron and Trivedi 1986). We can adjust these
estimates by using White's (1978) heteroskedastic consistent estimator, but as we'll see below, this tends to result in standard errors that

[8]There is an extensive literature on the explicit modeling of contagion.
Coleman's (1964) model is well known; Holden (1987) recently proposed a
generalization of this model. Coleman and Holden described sophisticated ways
of parameterizing contagion in the context of ML estimation. But they could
also be used with other estimators, such as the QL approach described below.

are too high. However, there is another solution to overdispersion that deals with the problem very well: the negative binomial model.

5. OVERDISPERSION AND THE NEGATIVE BINOMIAL MODEL

Although we cannot distinguish the source of overdispersion in event count data, we can adjust for its presence by introducing a stochastic component into the relationship between λ_t and the covariates in equation (9):

$$\lambda_t = \exp(x_t'\beta)\epsilon_t, \tag{12}$$

which makes λ_t into a random variable. If the probability density function of ϵ_t, or equivalently of λ_t, is denoted by $g(\epsilon_t)$, then the marginal distribution of Y_t given λ_t is defined as

$$\Pr(Y_t = y_t \mid \lambda_t) = \int \frac{\exp(-\lambda_t)\lambda_t^{y_t}}{y_t!} g(\epsilon_t)d\epsilon_t. \tag{13}$$

The solution to this integral equation depends on the form of the function $g(\epsilon_t)$. Ideally, the choice of this function reflects some knowledge or theory about the process that generates the overdispersion. However, such information is rarely, if ever, available. Furthermore, few functions will produce compound Poisson distributions that are computationally tractable. In practice, the gamma distribution is usually chosen. There are two main advantages to this choice. First, the solution to equation (13) that follows from this choice can easily be used to obtain parameter estimates. Second, the gamma distribution is quite flexible. It can vary from highly skewed to symmetric shapes, depending on the values of the two parameters that characterize it. However, this choice does represent an implicit assumption, albeit not a particularly restrictive one, about the nature of the underlying process.[9] Assuming then that $g(\epsilon_t)$ has a gamma distribution with parameters ϕ_t and v_t, the solution to the integral in equation (13) is

$$\Pr(Y_t = y_t \mid \phi_t, v_t) = \frac{\Gamma(y_t + v_t)}{\Gamma(y_t + 1)\Gamma(v_t)} \left(\frac{v_t}{v_t + \phi_t}\right)^{v_t} \left(\frac{\phi_t}{v_t + \phi_t}\right)^{y_t}, \tag{14}$$

[9]Other choices of the form of $g(\epsilon_t)$ are possible. Many of them are discussed in Johnson and Kotz (1969).

where $\Gamma(z) = \int_0^\infty t^{z-1}e^{-t}dt$ for $z > 0$. Then

$$E(Y_t) = \phi_t, \tag{15}$$

and

$$\text{Var}(Y_t) = \phi_t + \frac{1}{v_t}\phi_t^2. \tag{16}$$

This is the negative binomial bistribution, originally derived in this manner by Greenwood and Yule (1920).

Once again, we can specify a wide range of functions linking the paramenters ϕ_t and v_t with exogenous variables. As with Poisson regression, it is common to specify

$$E(Y_t) = \phi_t = \exp(x_t'\beta), \tag{17}$$

since this again ensures that the estimated expected value of Y_t will be non-negative and that the effect on ϕ_t of a change in an independent variable will be as given in equation (10).

We also have to specify a relationship between the second parameter, v_t, and covariates. This is a potentially important issue, since the parameterization we choose for v_t determines the form of heteroskedasticity we assume is present. Three forms of heteroskedasticity are most commonly specified. We have already seen the simplest case, where the mean and variance are equal, in the discussion of Poisson regression. The next most simple form specifies that the variance is a linear function of the mean. We can obtain the relationship

$$\text{Var}(Y_t) = (1 + \gamma)E(Y_t), \tag{18}$$

where γ is a constant, by setting $v_t = (1/\gamma)\exp(x_t'\beta)$ and substituting for v_t in equation (16). McCullagh and Nelder (1989) called this the *linear* negative binomial specification. Notice that the ratio of the variance to the mean is a constant.

The third specification that is commonly used is the logical next step from the linear specification, in which the variance is given by

$$\text{Var}(Y_t) = E(Y_t) + \gamma E^2(Y_t). \tag{19}$$

We can obtain this specification in practice by setting v_t equal to a constant: $v_t = 1/\gamma$. This form of the negative binomial model is called the *quadratic* specification (McCullagh and Nelder 1989). In this case the variance-to-mean ratio increases linearly as the rate increases.

Other parameterizations are possible. A more general case can be represented by

$$v_t = \frac{1}{\gamma}[\exp(x_t'\beta)]^k, \tag{20}$$

where k is an arbitrary constant. Clearly, we can obtain the linear specification by setting $k = 1$ and the quadratic specification by setting $k = 0$. These are the most commonly encountered versions of negative binomial regression found in standard statistical packages. For example, COUNT (King 1990) uses the linear specification, while LIMDEP (Greene 1990) follows the quadratic parameterization in equation (19). It is also easy to obtain estimates of either specification, and others as well, by using a general ML estimation package, such as that available in GAUSS (Aptech Systems 1991). And we can model the variance function by using a set of covariates different from those used to model the rate.[10]

As Cameron and Trivedi (1986) pointed out, the choice of functional form of heteroskedasticity is a choice between *different models*. Typically, however, we do not have a substantive reason for preferring one specification over another. One way to deal with the arbitrariness this implies is to treat k in equation (20) as a parameter to be estimated from the data. I call this parameterization the *unconstrained* negative binomial specification. A more common approach is to decide on the appropriate variance function after studying plots of generalized residuals. Below I report Monte Carlo simulations that allow comparisons of Poisson and negative binomial regression with QL methods. I also report analyses of data on labor union foundings based on Poisson regression and the three types of negative binomial regression discussed above. In the appendix I present a test for the presence of overdispersion that requires only the results of Poisson regression.

6. SOURCES OF AUTOCORRELATION IN COUNT DATA

In section 4 I discussed sources of overdispersion in count data. In this section I examine potential causes of autocorrelation. Cox and Isham (1980) also examined this issue in detail. Many of the

[10]This can be done easily in COUNT (King 1990).

sources of autocorrelation are related to sources of overdispersion. Remember that in the discussion of overdispersion, contagion and heterogeneity were restricted to a period of observation. However, these periods are usually entirely arbitrary. There is normally no reason to suppose that the process that generates events really changes only on, say, the first day of each year or at the start of each period. The periodization is normally imposed by the structure of the available data. Hence, in general the effects of contagion or heterogeneity are not likely to be restricted to a period of observation, particularly in time-series data.

6.1. *Time Dependence in the Rate*

We have already seen that time dependence in the rate, λ, can cause overdispersion. Certain types of time dependence can also cause autocorrelation. In particular, if the interval between two events depends on the length of the previous interval—that is, if there is duration dependence (Heckman and Borjas 1980)—then there will be autocorrelation in the counts if the rate in one period is affected by that part of the interval that falls in the previous period. Exact second-order properties are difficult to determine in most cases. However, unless the rate is very low, duration dependence will normally result in a negligible amount of autocorrelation, since most intervals will fall within periods of observation.[11]

6.2. *Contagion*

In section 4 I discussed contagion within periods of observation. Generally, it is unrealistic to assume that the rate within a period is affected by previous events within that period and not by events at earlier times, unless the contagious effect is short-lived relative to the length of units of observation. When contagion does occur across periods, autocorrelation will be present in the event counts.

Once again, the exact properties of a contagious process are difficult to work out even in the simplest of cases (Cox and Isham

[11]Overdispersion or underdispersion will result, of course, depending on whether there is positive or negative duration dependence.

1980). However, Oakes (1975) used numeric methods to show that successive *intervals* between events have relatively small serial correlations. Serial correlations between counts can be expected to have similar properties.[12]

6.3. *Heterogeneity*

I have already noted that unobserved heterogeneity across observations can cause overdispersion. If the cause of the heterogeneity is itself uncorrelated over time, then the event counts will be independent, although overdispersed. However, omitted variables are often correlated over time, causing autocorrelation in the rate. The form of this autocorrelation depends on the nature of the heterogeneity. Below I generate simulated data with this form of autocorrelation to investigate the properties of different types of estimator.

6.4. *Autoregressive and Moving-Average Point Processes*

Cox and Isham (1980) introduced a class of point processes in which sequences of *intervals* are autocorrelated. They showed how to derive second-order properties of counts for simple cases. However, the calculations become impractical when the autocorrelation is modeled by anything more complex than a first-order exponential moving-average process.

Some or all of these complications are likely to be present in much time-series data. Autocorrelation is the norm, not the exception. In the next section I present an estimator that can deal with this problem and that is as simple and cheap to implement as the ML estimators already discussed.

7. QUASI-LIKELIHOOD ESTIMATION

The models discussed in earlier sections can help solve the problem of overdispersion. If autocorrelation is present, however, use of the ML estimators is problematic, since the event counts are not independent and likelihood functions do not equal the product of the individual probability functions. These problems are particularly

[12]In any event, if contagion is of substantive interest it is better to model it explicitly. See footnote 8.

common in time-series data. However, the same issues can arise when spatial or network autocorrelation is found in cross-sectional data. Although ML methods for the analysis of count data in the presence of autocorrelation have been developed (Harvey and Fernandes 1989), they are computationally burdensome and consequently time consuming and costly. An alternative to ML estimation that is well suited to such situations is quasi-likelihood estimation.[13] This estimator is no more complicated than those already discussed, and it provides significant advantages.

There are important differences between ML and QL estimation. In ML estimation a probability law that is assumed to govern the observed data is specified. From this law we can derive expressions for the mean and variance. For example, we have seen that specifying that events occur according to a Poisson process implies that the mean and variance of each event count is equal to λ_t. The QL approach, on the other hand, starts from the premise that the first two moments are by far the most important properties of a probability distribution, at least as far as parameter estimation is concerned. Indeed, these moments are usually the only properties of a distribution to be explicitly modeled even in the ML framework. QL estimators are therefore derived by specifying only the first two moments, leaving the underlying probability distribution of the observed data undefined. Clearly, there are disadvantages to this approach in some circumstances. We cannot recover predicted probabilities, for example, and goodness-of-fit tests can sometimes be problematic. However, the QL approach allows considerable flexibility and greatly facilitates treatment of the autocorrelation issue, which is the focus of this paper.

Given first and second moments, the log quasi-likelihood function is

$$\frac{d\mathbf{Q}(\boldsymbol{\lambda})}{d\boldsymbol{\lambda}} = \mathbf{V}^{-1}(\mathbf{y} - \boldsymbol{\lambda}), \tag{21}$$

where $\mathbf{Q}(\boldsymbol{\lambda})$ is the log quasi-likelihood function, $\boldsymbol{\lambda}$ is a $(T \times 1)$ vector of predicted rates, $\mathbf{V}$ is a $(T \times T)$ diagonal variance matrix with

---

[13]This use of the term *quasi-likelihood* appears to have been introduced by Wedderburn (1974). The name is appropriate, since the quasi-likelihood function is closely related to the more familiar likelihood function employed in ML estimation.

elements that are functions of λ and (possibly) nuisance parameters, and y is a $(T \times 1)$ vector of observed counts. This seems reasonable because the right side of equation (21) is a vector of generalized residuals. Furthermore, the derivative of a standard loglikelihood with respect to λ has the same form as equation (21) when the likelihood is a member of the linear exponential family of distributions. Hence, this definition of the log quasi-likelihood function is intuitively appealing.

From equation (21) we can see that $d\mathbf{Q}(\lambda)/d\boldsymbol{\beta}$ is equal to

$$\mathbf{U}(\boldsymbol{\beta}) = \frac{d\lambda'}{d\boldsymbol{\beta}} \mathbf{V}^{-1}(\mathbf{y} - \lambda). \tag{22}$$

The function $\mathbf{U}(\boldsymbol{\beta})$ is sometimes called the quasi-score function because it is analogous to the score function that can be used to obtain ML estimates (McCullagh and Nelder 1989). It turns out that the properties of QL and ML estimators are very similar. McCullagh (1983) has demonstrated that the QL estimator is consistent, asymptotically Gaussian, and robust in the sense that consistent estimates of $\boldsymbol{\beta}$ can be obtained given only that $E(\mathbf{Y}) = \lambda$. Note that the condition that $\mathbf{V}$ is a diagonal matrix implies that there is no serial correlation.

As stated above, an important feature of QL estimation is that it requires no assumptions about the random process generating the observed data (McCullagh and Nelder 1989). To implement this estimator we only have to specify the relationship between the expected value of Y_t and causal variables and the relationship between the mean and variance of the dependent variable.[14]

The underlying rationale of the QL estimator is clearer when we recognize that the function $\mathbf{U}(\boldsymbol{\beta})$ has properties very similar to those of a derivative of a standard loglikelihood function. In particular, McCullagh (1983, p. 62) showed that

$$E[\mathbf{U}(\boldsymbol{\beta})] = \mathbf{0};$$

$$\mathrm{Cov}[\mathbf{U}(\boldsymbol{\beta})] = \frac{d\lambda'}{d\boldsymbol{\beta}} \mathbf{V}^{-1} \frac{d\lambda}{d\boldsymbol{\beta}}.$$

[14]Of course, when autocorrelation is present, we also have to specify the form this takes. The framework described below is extremely flexible in this respect.

Quasi-likelihood estimation is also related to the generalized linear model. Recall that in linear models, we want to find solutions to systems of equations of the form

$$Y = X\beta + \epsilon. \tag{23}$$

This is achieved by rearranging the equation so that ϵ is expressed as the difference between Y and $X\beta$, squaring both sides, and finding the partial derivatives of $\epsilon'\epsilon$ with respect to β. Setting this equal to zero to find the minimum gives

$$X'(Y - X\beta) = 0. \tag{24}$$

The QL equation (22) reduces to the OLS estimator in equation (24) in the linear case, since $\lambda = X\beta$. However, in general there is no closed-form solution to equation (22), and iterative methods have to be employed.

It is also interesting to note that the QL equation (22) gives the same estimates as ML estimation of Poisson models if $E(Y_t) = \lambda_t$, $\lambda_t = \exp(x_t'\beta)$, and $\text{Var}(Y_t) = \lambda_t$. To see this, notice that the partial derivative of λ_t with respect to β_i in this case is $x_{it} \exp(x_t'\beta)$ and that V^{-1} is a diagonal matrix with nonzero elements equal to $1/\lambda_t$. Substituting these terms into equation (22) and canceling yields

$$X'(Y - \lambda) = 0. \tag{25}$$

Exactly the same equation is obtained by differentiating the loglikelihood function of the Poisson regression model given in equation (8) with respect to β and setting this to zero. Therefore, the QL function and ordinary likelihood function are equivalent in this case. In fact, it can be shown that they are equivalent for all members of the linear exponential family (McCullagh and Nelder 1989). However, not all QL functions are equivalent to ordinary likelihoods. In some senses the QL approach is more flexible, since any relationship between the variance and the mean can be specified.

Suppose that the variance, V, involves an overdispersion parameter, γ, as well as λ. There are some important differences between ML estimation of negative binomial models of overdispersion and QL estimation of models of overdispersion. First, the estimates of γ obtained by quasi-likelihood methods are not in general the same as the estimates obtained by ML estimation of negative binomial regression models. Typically in QL estimation we obtain an estimate of γ by the method of moments. Second, the QL estimates of β are not *in general* the same as ML estimates, since in the QL approach no assumptions are made about the distribution of Y_t.

7.1. Quasi-Likelihood and Autocorrelation

The standard QL estimator does not deal with the problem of autocorrelation. That is, it specifies a diagonal variance matrix, $\mathbf{V}$, in equation (22). A generalization of the QL estimator (Zeger 1988) addresses this problem. I call this the generalized quasi-likelihood (GQL) estimator. To simplify notation, equation (22) can be written

$$\mathbf{D'V}^{-1}(\mathbf{y} - \boldsymbol{\lambda}) = \mathbf{0}, \tag{26}$$

where $\mathbf{D} = d\boldsymbol{\lambda}/d\boldsymbol{\beta}$. Zeger (1988) considered the case in which autocorrelation operates through a latent process ϵ_t (similar to the error term introduced in equation (12) in obtaining the negative binomial distribution). Assume that Y_t is a sequence of event counts that are independent of each other conditional on this latent process, and that their mean and variance are equal to

$$l_t = \exp(\mathbf{x}_t'\boldsymbol{\beta})\epsilon_t = \mathrm{E}(Y_t \mid \epsilon_t) = \mathrm{Var}(Y_t \mid \epsilon_t). \tag{27}$$

Further, assume that ϵ_t has an expected value of 1 and that its variance-covariance function can be written

$$\mathrm{Cov}(\epsilon_t, \epsilon_{t+\tau}) = \gamma_\epsilon(\tau), \tag{28}$$

where $0 \le \tau \le (T - 1)$, γ is an overdispersion parameter analogous to γ in equations (18) and (19), and the $\rho_\epsilon(\tau)$ are autocorrelation parameters.[15] Then, the unconditional expectation of Y_t is given by[16]

$$\begin{aligned}
\mathrm{E}(Y_t) &= \mathrm{E}[\mathrm{E}(Y_t \mid \epsilon_t)] \\
&= \mathrm{E}[\exp(\mathbf{x}_t'\boldsymbol{\beta})\epsilon_t] \\
&= \exp(\mathbf{x}_t'\boldsymbol{\beta})\mathrm{E}(\epsilon_t) \\
&= \exp(\mathbf{x}_t'\boldsymbol{\beta}) \\
&= \lambda_t.
\end{aligned} \tag{29}$$

[15] The assumption that $\mathrm{E}(\epsilon_t) = 1$ ensures that the unconditional expectation of Y_t depends only on λ_t. If this assumption is violated, only the constant is affected.

[16] This derivation uses the general result that $\mathrm{E}[\mathrm{E}(A \mid B)] = \mathrm{E}(A)$. See, for example, Ross (1985).

Similarly, the unconditional variance, $\text{Var}(Y_t)$, is derived thus:[17]

$$
\begin{aligned}
\text{Var}(Y_t) &= E[\text{Var}(Y_t|\epsilon_t)] + \text{Var}[E(Y_t|\epsilon_t)] \\
&= E[E(Y_t|\epsilon_t)] + \text{Var}[\exp(x_t'\beta)\varepsilon_t] \\
&= \exp(x_t'\beta) + \exp(x_t'\beta)^2\text{Var}(\epsilon_t) \\
&= \lambda_t + \gamma\lambda_t^2.
\end{aligned}
\tag{30}
$$

Notice that the relationship between the mean and variance in this model is the same as in the quadratic specification of the negative binomial model. However, even when $\rho_\epsilon(\tau) = 0$ (that is, when observations are uncorrelated), in general, estimates of β and γ obtained by ML negative binomial regression and QL methods differ, for the reasons discussed above.

Given this specification, how can we obtain estimates of β, γ, and ρ? Zeger (1988) suggested an approach to estimating β that is similar to QL for the case in which the off-diagonal elements of V are nonzero. In matrix form we can write $\text{Var}(Y) = V = \Lambda + \gamma\Lambda R_\epsilon\Lambda$, where

$$
\Lambda = \begin{pmatrix}
\lambda_1 & 0 & \dots & 0 \\
0 & \lambda_2 & \dots & 0 \\
\vdots & \vdots & \ddots & \vdots \\
0 & 0 & \dots & \lambda_T
\end{pmatrix},
\tag{31}
$$

and

$$
R_\epsilon = \begin{pmatrix}
1 & \rho_\epsilon(1) & \rho_\epsilon(2) & \dots & \rho_\epsilon(T-1) \\
\rho_\epsilon(1) & 1 & \rho_\epsilon(1) & \dots & \rho_\epsilon(T-2) \\
\vdots & \vdots & \vdots & \ddots & \vdots \\
\rho_\epsilon(T-1) & \rho_\epsilon(T-2) & \rho_\epsilon(T-3) & \dots & 1
\end{pmatrix}.
\tag{32}
$$

Notice that V depends on R_ϵ as well as on β and γ and that, therefore, the off-diagonal elements of V are nonzero. Zeger showed that the estimator of β obtained by using this specification of V in equation (22) is asymptotically normally distributed with zero mean and variance-covariance matrix given by

$$
V_{\hat{\beta}} = \lim_{T\to\infty} \left(\frac{D'V^{-1}D}{T}\right)^{-1}.
\tag{33}
$$

[17]This derivation uses another standard result that can also be found in Ross (1985): $\text{Var}(A) = E[\text{Var}(A \mid B)] + \text{Var}[E(A \mid B)]$.

7.2. *A Simplified Estimation Procedure*

Although estimates of $\hat{\beta}$ can in principle be obtained using iterative weighted least squares, calculation of $V_{\hat{\beta}}$ is difficult because it requires the inversion of a $T \times T$ matrix. Zeger (1988) therefore proposed a modification to the above method, in which the general autocorrelation scheme described above is simplified to a finite autoregressive process of a given order. To simplify the explanation I describe the specification of a first-order autoregressive (AR[1]) process. Generalization of the estimator to higher-order processes is straightforward. The AR(1) process is represented by a band-diagonal matrix, R_ω.[18] If $S = \text{diag}(\lambda_t + \gamma\lambda_t^2)$, then V is approximated by $V_R = S^{1/2}R_\omega S^{1/2}$. The inverse of V_R is much easier to calculate than the inverse of V, since it is given by

$$V_R^{-1} \approx S^{-1/2}L'LS^{-1/2}, \tag{34}$$

where L is a matrix that applies a linear filter to the data. For example, in the case of the first-order autoregressive scheme used here,

$$L_t y_t = y_t - \rho y_{t-1}.$$

Thus, L is a $(T - 1) \times T$ matrix of the form

$$L = \begin{pmatrix} -\rho & 1 & 0 & \dots & 0 \\ 0 & -\rho & 1 & \dots & 0 \\ \vdots & \vdots & \vdots & \ddots & \vdots \\ 0 & 0 & \dots & -\rho & 1 \end{pmatrix}. \tag{35}$$

Given this simplification, estimates of β at the $(p + 1)$th iteration of the process can be found by using the following equation:

$$\hat{\beta}_{p+1} = \left\{\left(LS^{-1/2}D\right)'\left(LS^{-1/2}D\right)\right\}^{-1}\left(LS^{-1/2}D\right)' \\ \left\{LS^{-1/2}\left(D'\hat{\beta}_p + (Y - \Lambda)\right)\right\}. \tag{36}$$

Moment estimates of γ and ρ can be obtained by using the following (Zeger 1988):

---

[18]A band-diagonal matrix has nonzero elements on the diagonal and in "bands" on both sides of the diagonal. The number of nonzero bands depends on the order of the autoregressive process being modeled. In the first-order scheme used here, there is one non-negative band on each side of the diagonal, each element of which is equal to ρ.

$$\hat{\gamma} = \frac{\sum_{t=1}^{T}\left\{\left(y_t - \hat{\lambda}_t\right)^2 - \hat{\lambda}_t\right\}}{\sum_{t=1}^{T}\hat{\lambda}_t^2} \tag{37}$$

and

$$\hat{\rho} = \frac{\hat{\gamma}^{-1}\sum_{t=2}^{T}\left\{\left(y_t - \hat{\lambda}_t\right)\left(y_{t-1} - \hat{\lambda}_{t-1}\right)\right\}}{\sum_{t=2}^{T}\hat{\lambda}_t\hat{\lambda}_{t-1}}. \tag{38}$$

To begin we must first select suitable starting values of $\hat{\boldsymbol{\beta}}$. A good procedure is to constrain $\hat{\rho}$ to be zero and obtain QL estimates of this model using OLS estimates as the starting values. These QL estimates can then be used as starting values with $\hat{\rho}$ unconstrained. Given an estimate of $\boldsymbol{\beta}$, we can obtain estimates of γ and ρ by using the moment estimators shown in (37) and (38), and we can calculate $\hat{\mathbf{D}}$, $\hat{\mathbf{S}}$, and $\hat{\mathbf{L}}$. These values are used in equation (36) to get new estimates of $\hat{\boldsymbol{\beta}}$. This procedure is then repeated until the process converges.[19] In practice, convergence is usually rapid. Indeed, results are often obtained more quickly in this procedure than in standard negative binomial regression packages.

The variance-covariance matrix of this estimator is given by (Zeger 1988):

$$\text{Var}(\hat{\boldsymbol{\beta}}) = \mathbf{I}_0^{-1}\mathbf{I}_1\mathbf{I}_0^{-1}, \tag{39}$$

where

$$\mathbf{I}_0 = \lim_{T\to\infty}\frac{(\mathbf{D}'\mathbf{V}_R^{-1}\mathbf{D})}{T}; \qquad \mathbf{I}_1 = \lim_{T\to\infty}\frac{(\mathbf{D}'\mathbf{V}_R^{-1}\mathbf{V}\mathbf{V}_R^{-1}\mathbf{D})}{T}. \tag{40}$$

The estimates obtained with this procedure have three strong advantages. First, they are fully compatible with the properties of count data (unlike least squares methods). Second, they can cope with autocorrelation as well as overdispersion. Third, they are obtained at low computational cost. The main drawback of the QL and GQL estimators is that they are likely to be less efficient than their ML counterparts *if* we can correctly specify the likelihood function. It remains to be seen whether the loss of efficiency in the QL estimators outweighs the inconsistency introduced in ML estimates of stan-

[19]A GAUSS program to implement this estimator is available from the author.

dard errors by failing to control for autocorrelation. Below I address this issue by means of Monte Carlo simulations.

8. MONTE CARLO SIMULATIONS

In this section I present the results of several sets of Monte Carlo simulations designed to clarify the properties of the estimators discussed above when they are used with different types of data. Data for the first three sets of simulations were generated according to the following equation:

$$\lambda_t = \exp(\beta_0 + \beta_1 X_{1t} + \beta_2 X_{2t}),$$

where X_1 is a normally distributed random variable with a mean of 4 and standard deviation of 1; X_2 is also normally distributed, but with a mean and standard deviation of 2; $\beta_0 = 0.25$, $\beta_1 = 0.3$, and $\beta_2 = -0.5$, which gives a mean rate of 1.57. Estimates were obtained from 100 samples with 150 observations in each. For the first set of simulations the counts were drawn from a negative binomial distribution with parameters λ_t and $\gamma = 0.75$ (see equation (18)).

There are two reasons for carrying out this set of simulations. First, we want to compare the performance of Poisson regression and negative binomial regression in the presence of overdispersion. Also of interest is the performance of estimated standard errors calculated from the inverse Hessian matrix and using White's (1978) heteroskedastic consistent estimator.[20] Second, we are interested to see how much efficiency is lost by using QL and GQL estimators. The results of the first set of simulations are shown in Table 1. The means and standard deviations of the parameter estimates are presented for each set of results. ML results also show the square root of the estimated variances obtained from the inverse Hessian and heteroskedastic consistent estimators, respectively. For the QL estimates, square roots of estimated variances obtained by applying equation (39) are shown.

Notice first that all four estimators provide good estimates of the parameters, the one exception being the estimate of β_0 obtained by Poisson regression. This is not surprising, since the relationship between the rate and covariates is correctly specified in all cases. Of

[20]An anonymous reviewer suggested that the strategy of using Poisson regression in conjunction with White's method of estimating standard errors is useful. These simulations can be used to compare such a strategy with negative binomial regression and QL methods.

TABLE 1

Monte Carlo Simulations of a Dependent Variable with a Negative Binomial
Distribution: ML, QL, and GQL Estimates

	Maximum Likelihood		Quasi-Likelihood	
Parameter	Poisson	Negative Binomial	QL	GQL
$\beta_0 = .25$				
Mean $\hat{\beta}_0$	.195	.229	.231	.242
Standard deviation	(.486)[a]	(.416)[a]	(.415)[a]	(.459)[a]
Square root mean variance	(.227)[b]	(.419)[b]	(.408)[d]	(.408)[d]
Square root mean HCV	(.450)[c]	(.407)[c]		
$\beta_1 = .3$				
Mean $\hat{\beta}_1$	.307	.301	.300	.298
Standard deviation	(.112)	(.097)	(.096)	(.104)
Square root mean variance	(.052)	(.099)	(.096)	(.096)
Square root mean HCV	(.106)	(.095)		
$\beta_2 = -.5$				
Mean $\hat{\beta}_2$	−.492	−.493	−.491	−.491
Standard deviation	(.077)	(.056)	(.054)	(.055)
Square root mean variance	(.028)	(.054)	(.052)	(.052)
Square root mean HCV	(.061)	(.053)		
$\gamma = .75$				
Mean $\hat{\gamma}$		.720	.696	.706
Standard deviation		(.157)	(.440)	(.450)
Square root mean variance		(.163)		
Square root mean HCV		(.162)		
$\rho = 0$				
Mean $\hat{\rho}$				−.012
Standard deviation				(.256)

[a]Standard deviation of the parameter estimates.

[b]Square root of the mean variance calculated by the inverse Hessian.

[c]Square root of the mean variance calculated by the heteroskedastic-consistent estimator.

[d]Square root of the mean variance calculated by equation (39).

more interest is the performance of the different standard error estimators. Notice that the heteroskedastic-consistent standard errors obtained by Poisson regression are twice as large as those obtained by the inverse Hessian—the more common way of obtaining standard errors in ML estimation. Furthermore, the heteroskedastic-consistent standard errors are somewhat smaller than the standard deviations of the parameter estimates over the 100 runs of the simulation.

The results for the standard errors of the negative binomial regressions are very different. Here there is very little difference between the standard deviations and both sets of estimated standard errors. This is as we expect, since this is the correctly specified model. However, it is interesting to note that the heteroskedastic-consistent standard errors obtained by negative binomial regression are *smaller* than those obtained by Poisson regression. This suggests that the strategy of obtaining parameter estimates by Poisson regression and then using the heteroskedastic-consistent standard errors is not optimal. This will be borne out by later results.

Finally, compare the results of the negative binomial regression with those of QL and GQL estimation. We can see that the standard errors of the structural parameter estimates are barely, if at all, different. This is somewhat surprising; we may have expected the QL methods to be much less efficient than ML estimation in this instance. These results suggest that we lose little efficiency by choosing QL over ML estimation even when the ML model is correctly specified. However, there are exceptions in the estimates of the overdispersion parameter, γ. The standard deviations of the moment estimates of γ obtained in the course of QL estimation are much higher than those of the ML estimates.

The second set of simulations tests the performance of each estimator in a particular kind of misspecification. For these simulations the rate was specified as before, but the counts were drawn from a Poisson distribution (that is, $\gamma = 0$). This time, however, the value of X_{2t} depended on its value in the previous period. The correlation between consecutive observations was 0.3. However, X_2 was omitted from the estimations. On the basis of the discussion in section 4, we should expect this to produce overdispersion and autocorrelation in the event counts. The results of this set of simulations are shown in Table 2.

The pattern of these results is similar to those found in the previous simulations, although estimates of the constant, β_0, are always much too high. All three estimates of γ indicate the presence of considerable overdispersion, while the GQL estimate of ρ shows evidence of autocorrelation of the expected magnitude. Perhaps the most interesting result from these simulations is that the GQL estimator appears to be *more efficient* than ML estimators in the presence of autocorrelation. These sets of simulations, then, suggest that al-

TABLE 2

Monte Carlo Simulations of a Dependent Variable with a Poisson Distribution, One Correlated Independent Variable Omitted: ML, QL, and GQL Estimates

	Maximum Likelihood		Quasi-Likelihood	
Parameter	Poisson	Negative Binomial	QL	GQL
$\beta_0 = .25$				
Mean $\hat{\beta}_0$	.977	.954	.954	.897
Standard deviation	(.530)[a]	(.527)[a]	(.528)[a]	(.493)[a]
Square root mean variance	(.126)[b]	(.405)[b]	(.507)[d]	(.474)[d]
Square root mean HCV	(.513)[c]	(.483)[c]		
$\beta_1 = .3$				
Mean $\hat{\beta}_1$	.279	.284	.284	.298
Standard deviation	(.123)	(.122)	(.122)	(.113)
Square root mean variance	(.029)	(.098)	(.122)	(.110)
Square root mean HCV	(.121)	(.115)		
$\gamma = 0$				
Mean $\hat{\gamma}$		1.232	2.051	2.040
Standard deviation		(.212)	(.887)	(.922)
Square root mean variance		(.154)		
Square root mean HCV		(.183)		
$\rho = .3$				
Mean $\hat{\rho}$				.344
Standard deviation				(.140)

[a]Standard deviation of the parameter estimates.

[b]Square root of the mean variance calculated by the inverse Hessian.

[c]Square root of the mean variance calculated by the heteroskedastic-consistent estimator.

[d]Square root of the mean variance calculated by equation (39).

though we lose nothing by using the GQL estimator where there is no autocorrelation, we gain efficiency by using it when there is autocorrelation.

To investigate the properties of these estimators in the presence of autocorrelation, I performed four more sets of simulations. There are several reasons why these are important. First, although Zeger (1988) showed that the GQL estimator is asymptotically normal and consistent, it has not yet been shown that the estimator has good small-sample properties. Second, the fact that the overdispersion and autocorrelation parameters are estimated by the method of moments is a potential source of difficulty. Notice in particular that estimates of ρ are not confined to the interval $[-1,1]$. Furthermore, Tuma and Hannan (1984) showed that moment estimators of autocorrelation parameters in other contexts are biased. Third, there is no guarantee that the GQL estimator will out-perform Poisson and negative binomial regression estimators in the presence of autocorrelation when the relationship between the rate and exogenous variables is correctly specified.

The values of λ_t were generated using the same approach as that used above, with the exception that β_0 was set equal to 1.0. The stationary process, ϵ_t, was generated by

$$\epsilon_t = \rho\epsilon_{t-1} + u_t, \tag{41}$$

where u_t is an independent random number picked from a gamma distribution. The parameters of the gamma distribution were selected so that for each value of ρ, $E(\epsilon_t) = 1$ and $Var(u_t) = 1$.

According to equation (27), $E(Y_t \mid \epsilon_t) = Var(Y_t \mid \epsilon_t) = \exp(x_t'\beta)\epsilon_t = \lambda_t\epsilon_t = l_t$. Each observation, y_t, was generated from a Poisson distribution with parameter l_t. Thus, each y_t is effectively drawn from a negative binomial distribution. Simulations were performed with values of ρ ranging from -0.75 to $+0.75$. As before, in each case 100 random samples of 150 observations were generated. Estimates were obtained using Poisson, quadratic negative binomial, QL, and GQL regression.

The results of these four sets of simulations are shown in Tables 3 and 4. To conserve space, complete results are shown in Table 3 for only one of the sets of simulations (with $\rho = -0.75$). Table 4 reports results of negative binomial and GQL regression for the other three sets of simulations.[21] These tables clearly show that the GQL estimator produces excellent estimates of the structural parameters. Kolmogorov-Smirnov (K-S) tests of the normality of these estimates have p values greater than 0.99 in eleven out of twelve cases.[22] Moment estimates of the overdispersion and autocorrelation parameters are also reasonable, although their standard de-

---

[21]Complete results from all simulations are available from the author.
[22]The remaining value is 0.19. The K-S statistic tests the hypothesis that a set of numbers are drawn from a particular distribution—in this case, the normal distribution. Thus, a high p value indicates a high probability that the observed set of estimates come from a normal distribution.

TABLE 3

Monte Carlo Simulations of an Autoregressive Process with $\rho = 0.75$:
ML, QL, and GQL Estimates

Parameter	Maximum Likelihood		Quasi-Likelihood	
	Poisson	Negative Binomial	QL	GQL
$\beta_0 = 1$				
Mean $\hat{\beta}_0$	.938	.872	.877	1.088
Standard deviation	(.834)[a]	(.647)[a]	(.640)[a]	(.565)[a]
Square root mean variance	(.641)[b]	(.509)[b]	(.506)[c]	(.985)[c]
$\beta_1 = .3$				
Mean $\hat{\beta}_1$	.296	.317	.315	.297
Standard deviation	(.176)	(.123)	(.122)	(.087)
Square root mean variance	(.150)	(.120)	(.119)	(.093)
$\beta_2 = -.5$				
Mean $\hat{\beta}_2$	−.499	−.502	−.499	−.492
Standard deviation	(.113)	(.075)	(.075)	(.055)
Square root mean variance	(.082)	(.064)	(.063)	(.055)
γ				
Mean $\hat{\gamma}$		1.502	1.591	1.672
Standard deviation		(.421)	(1.180)	(1.510)
Square root mean variance		(.250)		
$\rho = .75$				
Mean $\hat{\rho}$				.740
Standard deviation				(.219)

[a]Standard deviation of the parameter estimates.
[b]Square root of the mean variance calculated by the heteroskedastic-constant estimator.
[c]Square root of the mean variance calculated by equation (39).

viations are quite high. In particular, there is greater variation in the moment estimates of γ than in the ML estimates. The K-S test p values for the overdispersion parameter estimates are less than 0.05 in all cases. However, tests of the normality of the estimator of ρ had values greater than 0.99 in two out of four cases, the remaining scores being 0.34 and 0.09, respectively.

Perhaps most striking is that the estimated standard errors from GQL estimation are almost always smaller than those obtained by negative binomial regression. In many cases the difference is quite dramatic: Negative binomial standard errors are up to 25 percent

TABLE 4

Monte Carlo Simulations of Autoregressive Processes with $\rho = 0.25$ to -0.75: Negative Binomial and GQL Estimates

| Parameter | $\rho = 0.25$ | | $\rho = -{}^{m}s \times \pm$ | | $\rho = -0.75$ | |
	Negative Binomial	GQL	Negative Binomial	GQL	Negative Binomial	GQL
$\beta_0 = 1$						
Mean $\hat{\beta}_0$	.997	1.011	1.019	1.017	1.154	1.115
Standard deviation	(.390)[a]	(.373)[a]	(.353)[a]	(.394)[a]	(.409)[a]	(.336)[a]
Square root mean variance	(.403)[b]	(.395)[c]	(.390)[b]	(.368)[c]	(.398)[b]	(.317)[c]
$\beta_1 = .3$						
Mean $\hat{\beta}_1$	.293	.291	.297	.298	.306	.313
Standard deviation	(.087)	(.084)	(.083)	(.094)	(.094)	(.080)
Square root mean variance	(.095)	(.090)	(.092)	(.087)	(.093)	(.075)
$\beta_2 = -0.5$						
Mean $\hat{\beta}_1$	−.502	−.497	−.495	−.494	−.505	−.495
Standard deviation	(.057)	(.054)	(.050)	(.049)	(.045)	(.045)
Square root mean variance	(.050)	(.049)	(.049)	(.046)	(.050)	(.040)
γ						
Mean $\hat{\gamma}$	.895	.941	1.128	.828	1.576	.843
Standard deviation	(.182)	(.729)	(.189)	(.399)	(.219)	(.302)
Square root mean variance	(.153)		(.198)		(.283)	
ρ						
Mean $\hat{\rho}$		.281		−.262		−.655
Standard deviation		(.222)		(.244)		(.218)

[a]Standard deviation of the parameter estimates.

[b]Square root of the mean variance calculated by the heteroskedastic-consistent estimator.

[c]Square root of the mean variance calculated by equation (39).

higher.[23] Overall, these simulation results suggest that we lose nothing in accuracy or efficiency by using GQL estimation rather than Poisson or negative binomial regression, and we can gain considerable efficiency in the presence of autocorrelation. Additionally, of

[23]The difference between GQL and Poisson regression standard errors is even more dramatic. As we noticed in the first group of simulations, heteroskedastic-consistent standard errors from Poisson regression tend to be higher than those obtained by negative binomial regression.

course, we gain information about any autocorrelation that is present. As a final means of comparing the performance of these four estimators, we now turn to an empirical application: analysis of data on the founding rate of national labor unions.

9. AN EMPIRICAL APPLICATION: THE FOUNDING RATE OF NATIONAL LABOR UNIONS

We have discussed several different estimation strategies that could be used to analyze count data. To recapitulate:

1. ML estimation assuming no overdispersion (Poisson regression), assuming two different functional forms of overdispersion (the linear and quadratic negative binomial regression specifications), and allowing the functional form of the overdispersion to vary (unconstrained negative binomial regression)
2. QL regression allowing for overdispersion only, and a generalization of this method that allows for autocorrelation as well

In this section I discuss the results of using these methods in an analysis of real data. The data comprise information about every national labor union that existed in the U.S. between 1836 (the year of the first national unions) and 1985. A total of 621 unions are included in the dataset. The maximum number of unions in existence in any year was 211, in 1954. Since that time, the number of unions has been falling. These data are fully documented in Hannan (1988) and Hannan and Freeman (1989).

The dependent variable in the analyses reported here is the number of unions founded in each year. Eight independent variables are used. The first two are the natural logarithm of the total number of unions in existence at the start of the year (that is, the log of union density, denoted in the tables as $\log(N_t)$)[24] and the square of density $(N_t^2/1,000)$.[25] The third variable is the number of foundings in the

---

[24]In years with a density of zero, the log of 0.01 is used. Hannan (1991) showed that this adjustment does not affect the results of estimations in these data.

[25]This variable is divided by 1,000 to ensure that it, and the partial derivative of the various loglikelihood functions used with respect to this variable, are similar in order of magnitude to the other variables.

previous year (Fnd$_{t-1}$).[26] Next, four dummy variables are used to differentiate historical periods during which the labor unions' environment changed in important ways. The first period begins with the creation of the American Federation of Labor; the second starts with the New Deal; the Taft-Hartley variable represents the period following the passage of this important piece of labor legislation; and the fourth-period variable shows the effect of the formation of the AFL-CIO. Finally, another dummy variable (depression year) codes years of economic depression.

The interested reader should refer to Hannan and Freeman (1987, 1989) for a discussion of the theoretical significance of the models. It is sufficient to state that the important hypotheses to be tested are that the effect of the log of density (which I call α) is positive, that this parameter is less than one, that the effect of the square of density (which I call β) is negative, and that this parameter is of smaller magnitude than the effect of the log of density. The model is therefore

$$\lambda_t = N_t^{\alpha}\exp(\beta N_t^2)\exp(x_t'\pi),$$

where λ_t is the founding rate in year t, N_t is the number of unions in existence in year t (that is, the density), and x_t is a vector of the other covariates described above, as well as a constant term. The hypotheses are $0 < \alpha < 1$, $\beta < 0$, and $|\beta| < \alpha$.

The analyses reported here exclude the first year in which there were foundings. As Hannan (1991) pointed out, by definition the number of foundings must be positive. Since no other years are constrained in this way, it cannot be assumed that the process generating these events is the same as that operating in subsequent years. This is a special case of a general problem with the first observed event in a series (Cox and Lewis 1978). In general, we cannot assume that the distribution of the waiting time from an arbitrary time origin to the first event (known as the forward-recurrence time) is the same as the distribution of the intervals between subsequent events.

---

[26]As one reviewer pointed out, the use of the lagged number of foundings as an explanatory variable is potentially confusing. It is included here, following Delacroix and Carroll (1983), Hannan and Freeman (1989), and other similar research, for *substantive* reasons.

TABLE 5
Maximum Likelihood Estimates of the Founding Rate of National Labor
Unions (Heteroskedastic-Consistent Standard Errors in Parentheses)

Variable	Poisson	Negative Binomial		
		Linear	Quadratic	Unconstrained
Constant	−.798	−.446	−.534	−.564
	(.571)	(.436)	(.431)	(.481)
$\log(N_t)$	.548*	.448*	.431*	.430*
	(.183)	(.141)	(.143)	(.148)
$N_t^2/1,000$	−.040*	−.031*	−.036*	−.038*
	(.019)	(.019)	(.019)	(.022)
Fnd_{t-1}	.061*	.064*	.077*	.081*
	(.016)	(.016)	(.018)	(.026)
AFL	.245	.109	.353	.419
	(.479)	(.483)	(.473)	(.579)
New Deal	.320	.261	.215	.201
	(.283)	(.282)	(.290)	(.300)
Taft-Hartley	.018	.002	.151	.200
	(.304)	(.276)	(.325)	(.405)
AFL-CIO	−1.146*	−1.086*	−1.092*	−1.097*
	(.381)	(.367)	(.367)	(.369)
Depression year	.211	.175	.268*	.286*
	(.145)	(.142)	(.153)	(.164)
γ		.846*	.224*	.141
		(.263)	(.064)	(.314)
k				−.280
				(1.297)
Number of observations	149	149	149	149
Loglikelihood	−304.85	−290.03	−288.32	−288.28

*$p < .05$

9.1. Maximum Likelihood Methods

Table 5 contains ML estimates of Poisson and negative binomial regressions. The linear negative binomial specification has
$\text{Var}(Y_t) = (1+\gamma)\text{E}(Y_t)$, while the quadratic parameterization has
$\text{Var}(Y_t) = \text{E}(Y_t)[1+\gamma\text{E}(Y_t)]$ (as previously discussed). Poisson regression can be thought of as constraining γ to be zero, since this implies
that $\text{Var}(Y_t) = \text{E}(Y_t)$. Therefore, a t test of the hypothesis that γ is

significantly different from zero is a test of the hypothesis that overdispersion is present in the data. A likelihood ratio test can also be performed, since the Poisson and negative binomial models are nested.

It is clear from the results in Table 5 that there is indeed significant overdispersion in these data. Both the quadratic and linear specifications of the negative binomial model fit the data significantly better than the Poisson model. Although the two specifications of negative binomial regression are not nested, which means we cannot choose between them on the basis of a simple test, comparison of the two loglikelihoods suggests that the quadratic specification has the better fit. Inspection of some form of generalized residuals (McCullagh and Nelder 1989) often suggests an appropriate form for the variance function. Estimation of the parameter k in equation (20) confirms that the quadratic specification is appropriate in this case.[27]

9.2. Quasi-Likelihood Estimation

Estimates of the QL and GQL models are shown in Table 6. The first column contains estimates of a model in which overdispersion has the form $\text{Var}(Y_t) = \text{E}(Y_t)[1 + \gamma\text{E}(Y_t)]$; the second column assumes that a first-order autoregressive process is operating. Estimates of γ and ρ are obtained by the method of moments.[28] The estimates in the first column are similar to those obtained by ML estimation of the quadratic negative binomial regression model. This is not surprising, since they both assume the same variance-mean relationship. However, the QL estimates do not involve assumptions about distributional forms.

Although the two models are therefore not nested, a comparison of Pearson's X^2 statistic may give some indication of relative goodness of fit.[29] We must be cautious about such a comparison, since the properties of Pearson's X^2 statistic are not defined for comparisons of non-nested models or for the case in which the

[27]The value of $\hat{k}$ is not significantly different from zero. When $k = 0$ we have the quadratic specification.

[28] As previously shown, QL estimates when γ is assumed to be zero are identical to ML estimates of Poisson regression models; therefore, these results are not shown.

[29] Pearson's X^2 statistic is given by $\Sigma(y_t - \widehat{y_t})^2/\widehat{\text{Var}(y_t)}$. In other words, it is the sum of squared Pearson residuals.

TABLE 6
Quasi-Likelihood Estimates of the Founding Rate of
National Labor Unions (Standard Errors in Parentheses)

Variable	QL	GQL
Constant	−.510*	−.518*
	(.282)	(.248)
$\log(N_t)$	.419*	.326*
	(.087)	(.076)
$N_t^2/1000$	−.035*	−.028*
	(.016)	(.015)
Fnd_{t-1}	.079*	.156*
	(.019)	(.018)
AFL	.355	.290
	(.421)	(.375)
New Deal	.201	.069
	(.279)	(.251)
Taft-Hartley	.162	.372
	(.352)	(.319)
AFL-CIO	−1.083*	−.909*
	(.375)	(.337)
Depression year	.274*	.280*
	(.162)	(.155)
$\hat{\gamma}$	.270	.484
$\hat{\rho}$		−.572
Number of observations	149	149
Pearson's X^2	171.87	127.17

Note: Standard errors are not reported for $\hat{\gamma}$ or $\hat{\rho}$, because
these estimates are obtained by the method of moments.
*$p < .05$

distribution of the original data is unknown. However, in the absence
of any alternative method, this statistic can at least suggest relative
goodness of fit, especially when the differences in the value of the
statistic are large, as they are here. In fact, in ML estimation of a
quadratic negative binomial specification, $X^2 = 186.43$; in QL estimation, $X^2 = 171.87$. A difference of this magnitude suggests that the
QL estimates fit the data considerably better than the ML negative
binomial estimates, and it calls into question the distributional assumptions of the latter.

Examination of the GQL estimates assuming an AR(1) process brings to light an even more serious problem, however. The

estimates of the AR(1) specification in column 2 of Table 6 clearly fit the data a great deal better than the model with no autocorrelation.[30] This implies that the assumption of independence between observations required by the ML estimation methods we used is false.

Notice that there is evidence of *negative* autocorrelation. When this autocorrelation is taken into account, the effect of lagged foundings (that is, rate dependence) increases. On the other hand, the absolute values of $\hat{\alpha}$ and $\hat{\beta}$ *decrease*. In addition, the magnitude of the estimated overdispersion parameter, $\hat{\gamma}$, also increases substantially, from 0.27 (a figure that is comparable to the value of $\hat{\gamma}$ from the quadratic negative binomial specification) to 0.48. To see why this occurs, remember that negative autocorrelation implies that a year with a large number of foundings tends to be followed by a year with few foundings, other factors controlled.

Therefore, there is a tendency for the overdispersion to be "averaged out" when this factor is not taken into account. This also helps to explain why there is such a large improvement in the overall fit of the autocorrelation model. In most cases, the values of the independent variables do not vary much between successive years (with the exception of the lagged number of foundings). Therefore, those specifications that do not allow for autocorrelation predict similar numbers of foundings from one year to the next. Figure 1 shows a plot of the differences between the numbers of foundings in consecutive years. There is a clear pattern of high numbers of foundings followed by few foundings, and years when foundings were scarce preceding years when they were relatively abundant. Therefore, failing to control for autocorrelation results in substantially inferior fit.[31]

Figure 2 plots the Pearson residuals of the GQL estimator and ML estimates of quadratic negative binomial models with no autocorrelation. Notice that at high values of the dependent variable, the GQL model predicts much better than the negative binomial model. Interestingly, the GQL model also results in smaller residuals at low levels of founding. In particular, the two large outliers that occur in years with one and two foundings, respectively, are much smaller in

---

[30]The difference between the respective Pearson X^2 statistics is 44.7.

[31]I also estimated models with higher-order autoregressive processes, but their fit was not significantly better.

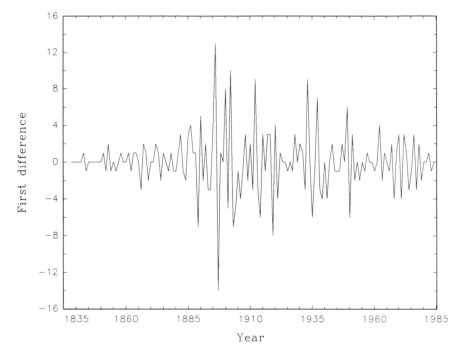

FIGURE 1. First difference in the number of labor union foundings in each year.

the autocorrelation model than in the quadratic negative binomial specification.[32]

We also see in Table 6 that the estimates of α and β (that is, the estimated effects of density on the founding rate) support the theoretical predictions of organizational ecologists even when we control for autocorrelation. Both estimates also remain significant at the 5 percent level. However, there is a substantial change—around 25 percent—in the magnitudes of these estimated effects, compared with ML negative binomial regression estimates and QL estimates that do not control autocorrelation.

Although the estimates of the sizes and statistical significance of the key parameters across all the ML and QL methods are quite stable in this case, the autocorrelation specification has uncovered

[32]Both of these outliers occur when the density is zero, a state that causes problems for the form of relationship between density and founding used here (Hannan 1991).

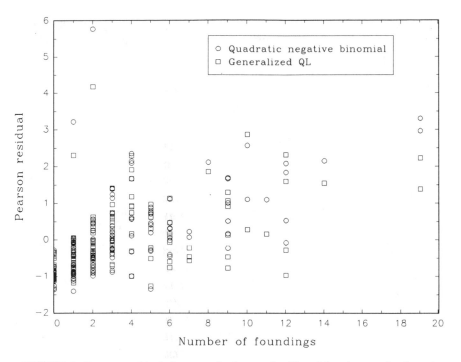

FIGURE 2. Pearson residuals from quadratic negative binomial and generalized quasi-likelihood regressions.

some interesting results. In particular, the estimate of the effect of rate dependence obtained in the autocorrelation specification is twice as large as that obtained in other methods. That this occurs despite the cyclical nature of the founding rate is powerful evidence of the importance of rate dependence independent of density dependence.

10. CONCLUSIONS

In this paper I have examined a range of methods that can be used to analyze count data. Many of the methods have something to recommend them. ML methods are widely available and are well understood. Since there is a simple test for the presence of overdispersion, there is no reason why Poisson regression should be applied inappropriately. Negative binomial estimation programs are becoming more widely available, and we need to be cautious about the use of heteroskedastic-consistent standard errors with Poisson regression in the presence of overdispersion. Unfortunately, the negative binomial regression packages that are currently available are restricted to either the linear or quadratic models. As we have seen, the most appropriate choice of form for the negative binomial is usually not obvious. Although the quadratic negative binomial model provided the best fit for the labor union data used here, analyses of data on the founding rates of other organizational forms not reported here have found that the constant model is as likely to be the better of the two common specifications. Perhaps the best strategy is to estimate the parameter k by ML methods and to carefully examine the residuals from this estimation.

We have seen that the GQL estimator provides accurate parameter estimates in small samples. Results from Monte Carlo simulations show that QL and GQL estimators are almost indistinguishable from ML methods in most respects when there is no autocorrelation. In particular, they are not noticeably less efficient, except in the estimation of the overdispersion parameter. Although this is often considered to be a nuisance parameter, there are occasions when the variance function is of substantive importance. In such circumstances use of QL methods may be problematic. The main advantage of the QL approach, however, is the ease with which it can be adapted to deal with autocorrelation. In such circumstances GQL estimates are considerably more efficient than those obtained by standard ML methods. This gain in efficiency is obtained at very little or no computational cost. Since autocorrelation is typically present in time-series data, this is a major advantage.

Some may question the need for the GQL estimator, arguing that one can deal with autocorrelation adequately by including lags of the count as explanatory variables. Such a strategy is not always appropriate, however. The GQL estimator can be used in situations where inclusion of the lagged count as an explanatory variable is technically problematic: for example, when observed counts are small (Harvey and Fernandes 1989). Perhaps more importantly, inclusion of the lagged count is not always justified on theoretical grounds. The GQL model implies autocorrelation in the *rate* due to an unobserved process. The lagged count model holds that it is the *actual number* of events that occurred in previous periods that affects the rate in the current period. Thus, there is an important *substantive* difference between the lagged count model and the GQL model.

And as we saw in the example on labor union foundings, the GQL model can encompass the lagged count model. In light of this, and given that the GQL estimator is no more complex or expensive to implement than well-known ML methods, QL methods deserve to become more widely known.

APPENDIX

It is sometimes useful to determine whether overdispersion is present without having to carry out negative binomial regressions. A useful test for overdispersion was proposed by Lee (1986).[33] This test is based on the relationship between the conditional expectation, $E(Y_t \mid \lambda_t)$, and the conditional variance, $Var(Y_t \mid \lambda_t)$, where $\lambda_t = \exp(x_t'\beta)$, as usual. Under the null hypothesis that Y_t has a Poisson distribution with parameter λ_t, the mean and variance are equal. This hypothesis can be tested against the alternative

$$H_A : E(y_t|\lambda_t) = \lambda_t;$$
$$Var(Y_t|\lambda_t) = \lambda_t + \gamma\lambda_t^\theta, \qquad \text{for given } \theta.$$

(42)

The test statistic is given by

$$\hat{T}_l = \frac{\sum_{t=1}^{T} \hat{\lambda}_t^{\theta-2}\left((y_t - \hat{\lambda}_t)^2 - y_t\right)}{\sqrt{2\sum_{t=1}^{T}(\hat{\lambda}_t^{\theta-1})^2}},$$

(43)

where $\hat{\lambda}_t = \exp(x_t'\hat{\beta})$ is evaluated using the estimates of β obtained under the null hypothesis (that is, assuming that the variables, Y_t, have Poisson distributions). The statistic $\hat{T}_l$ is distributed as $\mathcal{N}(0,1)$ under the null hypothesis. To test this hypothesis against the alternative that the data correspond to a particular parameterization of the negative binomial model, we have to select an appropriate value of θ. It is clear from equation (42) that setting $\theta = 1$ enables us to test the alternative that data fits the linear negative binomial specification, while setting $\theta = 2$ allows us to test the quadratic negative binomial model. A one-tailed test is appropriate, since overdispersion implies that $\hat{T}_l$ is positive.

The statistic $\hat{T}_l$ has the advantage of requiring only estimates

[33]This test is also discussed in Cameron and Trivedi (1986).

from Poisson regression. However, if obtaining ML estimates of negative binomial regression models is not a problem, we can use the estimated standard errors derived from the inverse Hessian matrix to test whether the overdispersion parameter is significantly different from zero. Similarly, since a Poisson model is nested within a negative binomial model (with the restriction that $\gamma = 0$), then under the null hypothesis, twice the loglikelihood ratio has an asymptotic χ^2 distribution with one degree of freedom.

REFERENCES

Aptech Systems. 1991. *GAUSS 2.1 System and Applications Manuals*. Kent, WA: Aptech Systems Inc.

Cameron, Colin A., and Pravin K. Trivedi. 1986. "Econometric Models Based on Count Data: Comparisons and Applications of Some Estimators and Tests." *Journal of Applied Econometrics* 1: 29–53.

Coleman, James S. 1964. *Introduction to Mathematical Sociology*. New York: Free Press.

Cox, David R. 1975. "Partial Likelihood." *Biometrika* 62: 269–76.

Cox, David R., and Valeris Isham. 1980. *Point Processes*. London: Chapman and Hall.

Cox, David R., and P. A. W. Lewis. 1978. *The Statistical Analysis of Series of Events*. London: Chapman and Hall.

Delacroix, Jacques, and Glenn R. Carroll. 1983. "Organizational Foundings: An Ecological Study of the Newspaper Industries of Argentina and Ireland." *Administrative Science Quarterly* 28: 274–91.

Elder, G. H., Jr., ed. 1985. *Life Course Dynamics: Trajectories and Transitions, 1968–1980*. Ithaca, NY: Cornell University Press.

Gourieroux, C., A. Monfort, and A. Trognon. 1984. "Pseudo Maximum Likelihood Methods: Theory." *Econometrica* 52: 681–700.

Greene, William H. 1990. *LIMDEP Version 5.1 Manual*. New York: Econometric Software Inc.

Greenwood, Maurice, and G. Udny Yule. 1920. "An Enquiry into the Nature of Frequency Distributions of Multiple Happenings, With Particular References to the Occurrence of Multiple Attacks of Disease or Repeated Accidents." *Journal of the Royal Statistical Society*, ser. A, 83: 255–79.

Hannan, Michael T. 1988. "Documentation of Public Use Data Set: Ecology of Labor Unions Project." Technical Report 88-2. Ithaca, NY: Cornell University, Department of Sociology.

———. 1991. "Theoretical and Methodological Issues in the Analysis of Density-Dependent Legitimation in Organizational Evolution." Pp. 1–42 in *Sociological Methodology 1991*, edited by Peter V. Marsden. Oxford: Basil Blackwell.

Hannan, Michael T., and John Freeman. 1987. "The Ecology of Organizational

Founding: American Labor Unions, 1836–1985." *American Journal of Sociology* 92: 910–43.

———. 1989. *Organizational Ecology*. Cambridge, MA: Harvard University Press.

Harvey, A. C., and C. Fernandes. 1989. "Time Series Models for Count or Qualitative Observations." *Journal of Business and Economic Statistics* 7: 407–17.

Hausman, J., B. H. Hall, and Z. Griliches. 1984. "Econometric Models for Count Data with an Application to the Patents-R. & D. Relationship." *Econometrica* 52: 909–38.

Heckman, J., and G. Borjas. 1980. "Does Unemployment Cause Future Unemployment? Definitions, Questions and Answers from a Continuous Time Model for Heterogeneity and State Dependence." *Econometrica* 47: 247–83.

Holden, Robert T. 1987. "Time Series Analysis of a Contagious Process." *Journal of the American Statistical Association* 82: 1019–26.

Johnson, N. L., and S. Kotz. 1969. *Discrete Distributions*. New York: Wiley.

King, Gary. 1989a. "Variance Specification in Event Count Models: From Restrictive Assumptions to a Generalized Estimator." *American Journal of Political Science* 33: 762–84.

———. 1989b. *Unifying Political Methodology: The Likelihood Theory of Statistical Inference*. Cambridge: Cambridge University Press.

———. 1990. "COUNT: A Program for Estimating Event Count and Duration Regressions." Unpublished mimeo. Cambridge, MA: Harvard University, John F. Kennedy School of Government.

Lee, Lung-Fei. 1986. "Specification Tests for Poisson Regression Models." *International Economic Review* 27: 689–706.

Liang, K.-Y., and S. L. Zeger. 1986. "Longitudinal Data Analysis Using Generalized Linear Models." *Biometrika* 73: 13–22.

McCullagh, Peter. 1983. "Quasi-Likelihood Functions." *The Annals of Statistics* 11: 59–67.

McCullagh, Peter, and J. A. Nelder. 1989. *Generalized Linear Models*. London: Chapman and Hall.

Nelder, J. A., and R. W. M. Wedderburn. 1972. "Generalized Linear Models." *Journal of the Royal Statistical Society*, ser. A, 135: 370–84.

Numerical Algorithms Group. 1986. *The GLIM System Release 3.77 Manual*. Downers Grove, IL: Numerical Algorithms Group.

Oakes, D. 1975. "The Markovian Self-Exciting Process." *Journal of Applied Probability* 12: 69–77.

Olzak, Susan. 1989. "Analysis of Events in Studies of Collective Action." *Annual Review of Sociology* 15: 119–41.

Ross, Seldon M. 1985. *Introduction to Probability Models*. San Diego: Academic Press.

SAS Institute. 1985. *SAS/IML User's Guide. Version 5 Edition*. Cary, NC: SAS Institute Inc.

Spilerman, Seymour. 1971. "The Causes of Racial Disturbances: Tests of an Explanation." *American Sociological Review* 36: 427–42.

STSC. 1989. *APL*PLUS System for the PC User's Manual.* Rockville, MD: STSC Inc.

Tuma, Nancy Brandon, and Michael T. Hannan. 1984. *Social Dynamics: Models and Methods.* New York: Academic Press.

Wedderburn, R. W. M. 1974. "Quasi-Likelihood Functions, Generalized Linear Models and the Gauss-Newton Method." *Biometrika* 61: 439–47.

White, H. 1978. "A Heteroskedasticity Consistent Covariance Matrix and a Direct Test for Heteroskedasticity." *Econometrica* 46: 817–38.

Zeger, Scott L. 1988. "A Regression Model for Time Series of Counts." *Biometrika* 75: 621–29.

ON THE LARGE-SAMPLE ESTIMATION OF REGRESSION MODELS WITH SPATIAL- OR NETWORK-EFFECTS TERMS: A TWO-STAGE LEAST SQUARES APPROACH

Kenneth C. Land*
Glenn Deane†

In this paper we apply the two-stage least squares (2SLS) estimation technique to produce regression estimators for linear models that incorporate spatial- or network-effects terms. Such models are often necessary to adequately represent social processes in data that have been aggregated for politically or administratively defined areas such as census tracts, cities, counties, or states. They are also necessary to represent data from individuals or organizations connected in explicit social networks. We review maximum likelihood (ML) estimators of the spatial-

This research was supported in part by National Science Foundation grant SES-8907665 and by the Yale University Program on Non-Profit Organizations. The paper was presented at the Annual Meetings of the American Sociological Association, Cincinnati, 1991. We thank Yu Xie, Noah E. Friedkin, Peter Marsden, and three anonymous reviewers for helpful comments on an earlier version. Members of the Applied Statistics Seminar organized by Kenneth A. Bollen at the Institute for Research in the Social Sciences of the University of North Carolina, Chapel Hill, also provided an insightful discussion of several issues in a presentation based on this paper.
*Duke University
†State University of New York, Albany

effects model (Ord 1975; Doreian 1981) and sample-size limitations thereto. We discuss Roncek and Montgomery's (1984) suggested use of generalized population potentials to measure spatial effects, and we demonstrate the inconsistency of ordinary least squares (OLS) estimators of spatial-effects models with potential variables. We use the 2SLS technique to derive consistent estimators in spatial-effects models with generalized potential variables. We derive the asymptotic (large-sample) variance of the 2SLS estimator and compare it with the ML estimator. We also compare the 2SLS estimator and its properties with similar estimators for spatial econometric models developed independently by Anselin (1988). We apply the 2SLS estimators to a large sample of county-level data on church adherence rates and find that our 2SLS estimator is much more computationally efficient than the ML estimator and yields numerical estimates of comparable statistical efficiency.

Sociologists and other social scientists study a diverse array of social, political, demographic, and economic phenomena that take place in geographical space. When the social processes that generate these phenomena are analyzed with data that have been aggregated for politically or administratively defined areas such as census tracts, cities, counties, or states, the geographical constraints and impacts of these arbitrary units on the social processes are implicitly retained. Yet standard applications of linear statistical models rarely take geographical dependency into account.[1] This point has been made most forcefully in the sociological methodology literature by Doreian (1980, 1981), who applied modifications of Ord's (1975) maximum likelihood (ML) estimation procedures for spatial-interaction models.

A shortcoming of Ord's estimators is that they become unwieldy or impossible to apply in larger samples, a point made by Roncek and Montgomery (1984). This—and the absence of computer software specifically written for Ord's procedures—may account for the few empirical applications in the sociological literature.

[1]Similar problems arise in the linear model analysis of data on individuals or organizations connected in explicit social networks when the network interdependencies are ignored. Because the empirical applications that motivated this paper involve spatially distributed rather than network data, however, the present discourse is limited to the spatial context. We briefly discuss applications of the methods developed herein to the related network-effects model in the "Conclusion."

To circumvent the sample-size limitations of ML estimators, Roncek and Montgomery (1984) introduced the generalized population-potential variable and recommended using this variable as a regressor in the conventional linear model. As we show below, a problem with this procedure is that the resulting regressor is correlated with the error term of the linear model, which means that the usual least squares regression estimator of its effect parameter is statistically inconsistent (i.e., biased in large samples).

In this paper we apply the two-stage least squares (2SLS) technique to produce a regression estimator for Ord's spatial-effects model that is statistically consistent and can accommodate large samples. In the following sections, we review the specification of the spatial-effects model, its ML estimators, and its sample-size limitations. We then discuss Roncek and Montgomery's (1984) suggested use of generalized population potentials in spatial-effects models and the inconsistency of ordinary least squares (OLS) estimation of linear models with potential variables. We use the 2SLS estimation technique to produce consistent estimators in spatial-effects models with potential variables. We derive the asymptotic (large-sample) variance of the 2SLS estimator and compare it with the ML estimator. We also compare similar 2SLS estimators developed by Anselin (1988) for spatial econometric models. Finally, we apply the 2SLS estimators to a large sample of county-level data on church adherence rates.

1. THE SPATIAL-EFFECTS MODEL: SPECIFICATION AND MAXIMUM LIKELIHOOD ESTIMATION

Ord (1975) developed two types of regression models for spatial interaction to accommodate situations in which spatially aggregated social data violate the standard linear model's assumption of random errors that are independently distributed among the sampled units. These violations are due either to errors that are correlated across some systematic ordering of the spatial units because of the influence of unmeasured variables or to spatial processes for the dependent variable that are not fully captured by the regressors included in the model. In the latter case, the values of the dependent variable in one spatial unit are systematically related to values of this variable in adjacent units. Doreian (1980, 1981) called a regression model of the former situation the *spatial-disturbances model* and a regression model of the latter the *spatial-effects model.*

The spatial-effects model is the focus of this paper. It is specified by

$$y = \rho Wy + X\beta + \epsilon, \tag{1}$$

with

$$E[\epsilon] = 0 \quad \text{and} \quad E[\epsilon\epsilon'] = \sigma_\epsilon^2 I,$$

where y is a column vector of n sample observations on a dependent or response variable, X is an n-by-k matrix of observations on k fixed exogenous or explanatory variables (including a unit vector), β is a k-row column vector of regression (intercept and slope) parameters, ϵ is an n-row column vector of unobserved random errors or disturbances with expected values of zero and variance σ_ϵ^2, W is an n-by-n matrix of weights with elements w_{ij} describing the "nearness" of sample units i and j and a zero principal diagonal (indicating that the distance of unit i to itself is zero), and I is an identity matrix of order n.

In the specification of the spatial-effects model, the random errors must be normally distributed with mean and variance as given above (Ord 1975; Doreian 1981). This assumption (or some suitable alternative parametric assumption) is necessary for the derivation of ML estimators. But only the weaker error specifications stated above are necessary for the 2SLS estimation techniques applied here. This adds substantial flexibility to the error processes permitted by model (1). All that is required is that the errors have zero expectation, have constant variance, and be independent (random). Even the latter two assumptions can be relaxed under suitable generalizations of 2SLS techniques (which are not pursued in this paper).

The parameter ρ is a *spatial-effects coefficient* that measures the relation of the value of y in any given geographical unit of analysis to the values of y in other areas. If ρ is significantly different from zero, a spatial-interaction or diffusion process is operating. Doreian (1981) described several empirical applications in which the estimation of regression models that do not contain the spatial-effects term results in coefficient estimates for the exogenous variables in the X matrix of model (1) that are inflated (biased upward) relative to their values when the spatial effects are taken into account. Thus, the accuracy of inferences may depend upon the incorporation of the spatial-effects term.

The statistical inference problem for the spatial-effects model is to develop statistically efficient estimators of ρ, $\boldsymbol{\beta}$, and σ^2, and the standard errors of these parameters. Ord (1975) developed ML estimators for this purpose, which Doreian (1981) exposited for sociologists, modified, and applied empirically. The ML estimators can be written as follows:

$$\hat{\boldsymbol{\beta}} = (\mathbf{X'X})^{-1}\mathbf{X'} \, (\mathbf{I} - \hat{\rho}\mathbf{W})\mathbf{y}$$
$$= (\mathbf{X'X})^{-1}\mathbf{X'z}, \tag{2}$$

where $\mathbf{z} = \mathbf{Ay} = (\mathbf{I} - \rho\mathbf{W})\mathbf{y}$,

$$\hat{\sigma}^2 = (1/n)\mathbf{z'Mz}, \tag{3}$$

where $\mathbf{M} = \mathbf{I} - \mathbf{X}(\mathbf{X'X})^{-1}\mathbf{X'}$, and $\hat{\rho}$ is the value of ρ that minimizes the quantity

$$-(2/n) \sum_{i=1}^{n} \ln(1 - \rho\lambda_i) + \ln [\mathbf{y'My} - 2\rho\mathbf{y'MWy} + \rho^2(\mathbf{Wy})'\mathbf{MWy}], \tag{4}$$

where the $(1 - \rho\lambda_i)$ are the eigenvalues of the matrix $\mathbf{A} = \mathbf{I} - \rho\mathbf{W}$.

When they are written in terms of the transformed dependent variable z, we can see that the ML estimators $\hat{\boldsymbol{\beta}}$ and $\hat{\sigma}^2$ in equations (2) and (3) look similar to the ML expressions for these parameters in the standard linear model. However, a numerical value of $\hat{\rho}$ is required to compute each of these estimators, and $\hat{\rho}$, in turn, must generally be computed by a direct-search numerical-minimization procedure applied to equation (4). For datasets of almost any realistic complexity, this requires a computer. In small to medium-size samples (up to 200, say), while computationally demanding, this should be feasible and relatively quick with current statistical packages (SAS, SPSS^x) and mainframe computers.

Roncek and Montgomery (1984) noted, however, that the ML estimators of the spatial-effects regression model can be increasingly difficult to compute in larger samples. The difficulties relate partly to the storage and processing capacity of computers and to the limitations of statistical software. The source of these difficulties is the spatial weight matrix $\mathbf{W}$ of model (1), which is an n-by-n matrix. This matrix is used in matrix addition and multiplication operations in the

ML estimators (2), (3), and (4) above. To obtain the variance-covariance matrix of these estimators (see Doreian 1981, pp. 383–84), which is necessary for hypothesis testing and the construction of confidence intervals, we must compute the inverse of the n-by-n matrix $\mathbf{A} = \mathbf{I} - \rho\mathbf{W}$.

Roncek and Montgomery (1984) observed that specifying a $\mathbf{W}$ matrix (and hence the corresponding $\mathbf{A}$ matrix) to analyze census-tract data from the city of Chicago would require approximately a 900-by-900 matrix, and that analyzing Chicago city blocks would require a 15,000-by-15,000 matrix. Using the double-precision arithmetic necessary for multiplying and inverting matrices would require 128 megabytes of main memory just to store the latter matrix. Large mainframe computers typically have about 100 megabytes of main memory. Thus, the addition, multiplication, and inversion of matrices of these sizes would require the use of supercomputers.[2]

2. GENERALIZED POPULATION POTENTIALS

To circumvent the sample-size limitations of ML procedures for the spatial-effects model, Roncek and Montgomery (1984) proposed an adaptation of the population-potential variable developed in population studies of migration and related spatial phenomena by Duncan, Cuzzort, and Duncan (1963). The population-potential variable measures the cumulative proximity of the populations of all the areas surrounding a particular place. The population potential for location i, PP_i, is defined by

$$PP_i = \sum_{j \neq i}^{n} (P_j/D_{ij}), \qquad i = 1, \ldots, n, \qquad (5)$$

[2]Standard computer software packages that perform regression analyses also limit the sizes of matrices on which matrix operations can be performed. For instance, generally available versions of SAS, one of the most powerful statistical packages used by social scientists, limit the number of elements that can be simultaneously processed in the main memory to 32,000, which equates to a maximum square matrix of 178 rows and columns. However, the recently released version 6 of SAS allows matrices with any number of rows and columns, provided there is enough main computer memory to store them. For an example of the space-conservation strategies necessary to apply the ML estimator—on a mainframe computer with eight megabytes of main memory—to social network data on a sample of approximately 1,000 high school students, see Duke (1991, App. A).

where P_j is the population of the jth location or place in the environment of location i, D_{ij} is the distance of location j from location i, and the summation is taken over all locations j other than i. To operationalize the denominator, Duncan et al. (1963) use the Euclidean or straight-line distance between geographical locations. Other measures such as travel distance are more difficult to measure. Compared with transformed distance measures such as the logarithm of Euclidean distance or the squared distance (as in gravity models), the simple Euclidean distance measure works well in practice (Roncek and Montgomery 1984).

In brief, to calculate the population potential for a set of n locations, each place is treated successively as the point of reference, and the sum of quotients of the population of every other place divided by its distance from the reference point is computed. In classical population models of migration among a set of locations (Duncan et al. 1963), it is sufficient to use the size of populations in other locations in the numerator, as in equation (5). When the substantive phenomenon being investigated is something other than the migratory exchange of individuals among the locations, variants of the potential concept, which we call *generalized population potentials,* can be defined by replacing the population sizes in the numerator of (5) with the values of the dependent variable being studied (Roncek and Montgomery 1984). For instance, Roncek and Robinson (1984) analyzed the effects of crime in the surroundings of census tracts in Cleveland by using a generalized population-potential variable they called the crime potential.

In the spatial-effects regression model (1), the generalized population-potential variable can be obtained by multiplying the weight matrix $\mathbf{W}$ (with elements suitably defined as inverses of Euclidean distances between the geographical units in an analysis) by the dependent variable (column vector) $\mathbf{y}$:

$$\mathbf{y}^* = \mathbf{W}\mathbf{y}. \tag{6}$$

For example, in the aforementioned census-tract crime study of Roncek and Robinson (1984), the dependent column vector $\mathbf{y}$ consists of the numbers of crimes reported to the police in the various census tracts, and the column vector $\mathbf{y}^*$ contains measures of the crime potential of each census tract relative to the numbers of crimes in the other census tracts of the city, each weighted by its distance from the focal tract.

Algebraically, Roncek and Montgomery's (1984) proposal to use generalized population potentials is the same as treating the product of the weight matrix $\mathbf{W}$ and the dependent variable vector $\mathbf{y}$ on the right side of model (1) as a new variable, $\mathbf{y}^*$, so that model (1) can be rewritten

$$\mathbf{y} = \rho\mathbf{y}^* + \mathbf{X}\boldsymbol{\beta} + \boldsymbol{\epsilon}. \tag{7}$$

This new variable can be entered as just another regressor variable in an OLS estimation of model (7), without creating problems in the estimates of the spatial-effects parameter ρ (Roncek and Montgomery 1984). In general adjacency weight matrices, $\mathbf{W}$ (i.e., in matrices with elements not necessarily restricted to inverses of physical distances), Doreian and Hummon (1976) similarly suggested that $\mathbf{y}^* = \mathbf{W}\mathbf{y}$ can simply be included as another exogenous variable in an OLS estimation of model (7).[3]

3. THE INCONSISTENCY OF ORDINARY LEAST SQUARES ESTIMATION

We agree with Roncek and Montgomery (1984) that the treatment of $\mathbf{y}^*$ as an ordinary regressor in the estimation of model (7) has the computational benefit in large samples of replacing the large n-by-n matrix $\mathbf{W}$ with an n-element column vector, but consistent estimates of ρ are not as easy to obtain as OLS estimates. As Ord (1975) pointed out, this requires that inferences be restricted to so-called conditional inferences in which the spatial effects are presumed to be determined prior to the dependent variable. But in spatial-effects models, the spatial diffusion or interaction processes are determined simultaneously with the dependent variable. This produces a nonzero correlation between the potential variable $\mathbf{y}^*$ and the error term $\boldsymbol{\epsilon}$, which violates the assumptions under which OLS produces unbiased (and therefore consistent) estimates of the regression coefficients.

This can be demonstrated as follows. Taking expectations of model (1), we see that for the ith case

[3]Doreian (1981, p. 373) recognized that the suggested OLS procedure of Doreian and Hummon (1976) was incorrect and compared numerical estimates of OLS with ML estimates.

$$E(y_i) = \rho\Sigma_j w_{ij}E(y_j) + \mathbf{X}_i\boldsymbol{\beta}, \tag{8}$$

where $\mathbf{X}_i$ denotes the row vector of observations on the k explanatory variables corresponding to the unit i. The appearance of the expected-value operator on both sides of this equation emphasizes the joint nature of the $\mathbf{y}$ and $\mathbf{y}^*$ variables. By contrast, as Ord (1975) noted, in a conditional spatial-effects specification,

$$E\{y_i \mid y_j, j \in J(i)\} = \rho\Sigma_j w_{ij}y_j + \mathbf{X}_i\boldsymbol{\beta}, \tag{9}$$

where $J(i)$ denotes the set of locations whose values on the dependent variable interact with the value of location i. The expectation on the left side of equation (9) is a conditional expectation, where the conditioning is on the observed values of the dependent variable y_j that fall within the set $J(i)$. Furthermore, the two equations are equivalent only if

$$E\{\epsilon_i \mid y_j, j \in J(i)\} = E\{\epsilon_i y_j^*\} = 0, \tag{10}$$

that is, only if ϵ_i and $y_i^* = \Sigma_k w_{jk}y_k$ are uncorrelated.

In some time-series models, the time-dependent, one-sided nature of the relationship may make equation (10) a natural restriction. But in spatial-effects models in which the dependent variable in a given location may be influenced by the dependent variable in all of the locations in a given set, equation (10) will generally not be satisfied (Ord 1975). The consequence, of course, is a violation of the assumption in the general linear regression model that the error term ϵ is distributed independently of the regressors. In turn, this implies that the OLS estimators will be biased in samples of any size and therefore asymptotically biased or inconsistent (Johnston 1984).

The foregoing can be intuitively expressed as follows. For any given location i in a set under consideration, assume that all $w_{ij} \geq 0$, although some of these coefficients may be quite small. Assume also that $\rho > 0$, so that spatial effects are operative among the locations. Then the value of the dependent variable for location i, y_i, will be influenced (i.e., will be a function of) the values of the dependent variable at all other locations through the generalized potential variable for location i, $y_i^* = \Sigma_j w_{ij}y_j$. But in turn, y_i and therefore its random component ϵ_i will enter into the determination of the values of y_j for each other location j through the contributions of y_i to the generalized potentials, y_j^*. This implies that the value of the generalized potential for location i, y_i^*, will be partly affected by its own random error, ϵ_i, and therefore that the two are correlated. Again, this violates the conditions necessary for unbiased and consistent OLS regression estimators.[4]

4. A TWO-STAGE LEAST SQUARES ESTIMATOR

In brief, direct OLS estimation of the spatial-effects model (7) will result in biased and inconsistent parameter estimates because of an unknown level of correlation of the generalized potential variable and the error term of the model. Theil (1953a, 1953b, 1961) and Basmann (1957) developed 2SLS estimation to produce consistent estimators in a similar context: simultaneous equation econometric models in which some regressors affecting the dependent or endogenous variable in a given equation (namely, those corresponding to other endogenous variables in the model) are correlated with the error term. In 2SLS estimation, the regressors in question are replaced by other regressors, which are purged of the stochastic elements that correlate with the error term of the equation, and then an OLS regression of the dependent variable of the equation on the purged and exogenous variables of the equation is performed.

The problem in this paper is to construct a variable, say $\hat{y}^*$, to replace the generalized potential variable y^* in model (7). This is similar to the problem for which the 2SLS technique was developed. It will be useful (for reasons explained below) to redefine and partition the matrix X of all fully exogenous variables as $[X_1\ X_2]$, where X_1 consists of a set of exogenous variables that enter into (7), and X_2 consists of those that do not enter.

In the 2SLS procedure (Johnston 1984, pp. 472–73), the column vector $\hat{y}^*$ is computed in the *first-stage:* The generalized

---

[4]Doreian, Teuter, and Wang (1984) provided a Monte Carlo simulation study of the consequences of direct application of OLS—which they called the QAD (quick and dirty) method—to model (7). In general, they found that as the size of the ρ parameter increases from .1 to .9, the bias of the OLS estimates of the ρ and β parameters increases, although not dramatically in all cases. More important for statistical inferences, as the size of ρ increases, the actual standard deviations of the OLS coefficient estimates (estimated by a simulation approximation to their true variation) are often much larger than those of the ML estimates.

population-potential column vector y^* is regressed on the complete set of fully exogenous variables (i.e., on the variables in the full matrix X), and the actual observations on the y^* variable are replaced by the corresponding regression (predicted) values:

$$\hat{y}^* = Xd = X[(X'X)^{-1}X'y^*] = X[(X'X)^{-1}X'Wy]. \qquad (11)$$

In the *second stage*, y is regressed on $\hat{y}^*$ and the submatrix X_1, yielding the following solution to the normal equations:

$$\begin{bmatrix} r \\ b \end{bmatrix} = \begin{bmatrix} \hat{y}^{*'}\hat{y}^* & \hat{y}^{*'}X_1 \\ X_1'\hat{y}^* & X_1'X_1 \end{bmatrix}\begin{bmatrix} \hat{y}^{*'}y \\ X_1'y \end{bmatrix}, \qquad (12)$$

where $[r\ b]'$ now denotes the 2SLS estimator of $[\rho\ \beta]'$.

Several comments will help to clarify this application of the 2SLS method to model (7). First, to estimate $[r\ b]'$, there is no need to compute the expected regression values in $\hat{y}^*$ and enter them explicitly in the matrix equation (12). An alternative form of the estimator (12), which involves only the matrices of actual observations, is available (Johnston 1984, p. 473). It is the latter form that is utilized in the 2SLS programs available in many computer packages. While not reproduced here, this form may be obtained by substituting equation (11) into equation (12).

Second, we indicated above that y^* should be regressed on all fully exogenous variables (contained in the matrix X) in the first stage. This produces a set of predicted values, the $\hat{y}^*$ of equation (11), for $y^* = Wy$ in the spatial-effects model (7). The logic here is to treat y^* the same way that endogenous variables are treated in simultaneous equation systems and compute predicted values of y^* via equation (11). Because the resulting $\hat{y}^*$ of equation (11) is a linear combination of all of the exogenous variables contained in the X matrix, the matrix to be inverted in equation (12) will be singular and not invertible unless equation (11) contains some exogenous variables that do not enter into the second-stage regression of equation (12).[5] Hence, we get the partition of the matrix X introduced above. Note that this partition requires that the analyst be able to sort exogenous variables into those (in X_1) that have direct effects on the

[5]We are grateful to an anonymous referee for pointing out this identifiability constraint and to Peter V. Marsden for providing a numerical demonstration of the requirement.

dependent variable $\mathbf{y}$ in model (7) and those (in $\mathbf{X}_2$, which often are called *instrumental variables* or *instruments*) suitable for the identification and estimation of the predicted variable $\hat{\mathbf{y}}^*$. (Additional suggestions for choosing instrumental variables are given in later sections of the paper.)

Third, as in a simultaneous equation system, the 2SLS estimator (12) is consistent. That is, this estimator $[r \; \mathbf{b}]'$ converges in probability (or has probability limit equal) to the population-parameter vector $[\rho \; \boldsymbol{\beta}]'$.

Consistency of the 2SLS estimator (12) requires that both the predicted variable $\hat{\mathbf{y}}^*$ and the exogenous variables $\mathbf{X}$ are uncorrelated with the error term $\boldsymbol{\epsilon}$ of model (7) in the probability limit. By their very definition as exogenous variables, the X variables are uncorrelated in the limit with the model's error term. For the predicted variable $\hat{\mathbf{y}}^*$, we have

$$
\begin{aligned}
\text{plim}[(l/n)\hat{\mathbf{y}}^{*\prime}\boldsymbol{\epsilon}] &= \text{plim}[(1/n)\mathbf{y}^{*\prime}\mathbf{X}(\mathbf{X}'\mathbf{X})^{-1}\mathbf{X}'\boldsymbol{\epsilon}] \\
&= [\text{plim}(1/n)\mathbf{y}^{*\prime}\mathbf{X}][\text{plim}(1/n)(\mathbf{X}'\mathbf{X})^{-1}][\text{plim}(1/n)\mathbf{X}'\boldsymbol{\epsilon}] \\
&= \mathbf{0}, \quad\quad\quad\quad\quad\quad\quad\quad\quad\quad\quad\quad\quad\quad\quad\quad (13)
\end{aligned}
$$

where $\mathbf{0}$ denotes a column vector of dimension n, and we have utilized standard properties of the probability limit operation (see, e.g., Johnston 1984, pp. 269–74). To see that this expression indeed equals a zero vector, first note that the last term in the second line pertains to the probability limit of the covariance of the exogenous variables and the error term of model (7), which we have just noted must be zero, otherwise the X variables would not be classified as exogenous. Second, note that for the equality to hold, the other two probability limits in (13) must converge to finite matrices and the middle term must be nonsingular.

These are fairly weak conditions on the cross-product matrices of these components that must be satisfied for any meaningful regression analysis. Essentially, they require that the cross products standardized for sample size (or, equivalently, the second moments) of the X variables with themselves and with the generalized population-potential variable $\mathbf{y}^*$ stabilize at finite levels as the sample size increases without bound. Under these conditions, and assuming that the exogenous variables are truly exogenous, the 2SLS estimator (12) is consistent.

5. THE ASYMPTOTIC VARIANCE OF THE TWO-STAGE LEAST SQUARES ESTIMATOR

Under similar conditions, it has been established that 2SLS estimators are generally asymptotically normally distributed with mean vector equal to the parameter vector and a specific form for the asymptotic variance-covariance matrix (see, e.g., Theil 1971, pp. 497–99). In the present case, the estimator of this matrix has the following form:

$$\text{asy var} \begin{bmatrix} r \\ b \end{bmatrix} = s_\epsilon^2 \begin{bmatrix} \hat{y}^{*\prime}\hat{y}^* & \hat{y}^{*\prime}X_1 \\ X_1'\hat{y}^* & X_1'X_1 \end{bmatrix}^{-1}, \tag{14}$$

where

$$s_\epsilon^2 = \frac{(y - \hat{y}^*r - X_1b)'(y - \hat{y}^*r - X_1b)}{n}$$

is a consistent estimator of σ_ϵ^2, the error variance of model (7).[6] Like the 2SLS estimator (12), the variance-matrix estimator (14) has a more computationally convenient expression that involves only the matrices of actual observations (see, e.g., Johnston 1984, p. 479), which can be obtained by substituting the expression for $\hat{y}^*$ from equation (11) into equation (14). We will compare the asymptotic variance matrix (14) of the 2SLS estimator (12) with that of Ord's (1975) ML estimator.

For this purpose, it is useful to transform expression (14) into another form. Note first that the observed population-potential vector y^* can be written as the sum of its predicted value from the first-stage regression, $\hat{y}^*$, and the OLS error vector, v:

$$y^* = \hat{y}^* + v. \tag{15}$$

Furthermore, premultiplying each side of this expression by its own transpose yields

$$\begin{aligned} y^{*\prime}y^* &= (\hat{y}^* + v)'(\hat{y}^* + v) \\ &= \hat{y}^{*\prime}\hat{y}^* + \hat{y}^{*\prime}v + v\hat{y}^{*\prime} + v'v \\ &= \hat{y}^{*\prime}\hat{y}^* + v'v, \end{aligned} \tag{16}$$

[6]No correction for loss of degrees of freedom is applied to the 2SLS estimator of the error variance because its known properties refer to large samples for which such corrections have no appreciable effect.

by the usual properties of OLS residuals.

Equation (16) can be substituted for the upper-left-hand submatrix in the 2SLS variance matrix (14). Then the expectation operator can be applied to asymptotic distributions of the random components, the generalized population-potential vectors, $\mathbf{y}^*$, and their predicted values, $\hat{\mathbf{y}}^*$, and functions thereof. This yields, for instance, $E(\mathbf{X}_1'\hat{\mathbf{y}}^*) = E(\mathbf{X}_1'\mathbf{y}^*) = X_1'E(\mathbf{y}^*)$, where the first equality follows from properties of OLS residuals and the second from factoring the fixed exogenous variables (constants) out of the expectation. This results in the following equivalences for the asymptotic variance matrix:

$$
\text{asy var} \begin{bmatrix} r \\ \mathbf{b} \end{bmatrix} = \sigma_\epsilon^2 \begin{bmatrix} \hat{\mathbf{y}}^{*\prime}\hat{\mathbf{y}}^* & \mathbf{X}_1'E(\hat{\mathbf{y}}^*) \\ \mathbf{X}_1'E(\hat{\mathbf{y}}^*) & \mathbf{X}_1'\mathbf{X}_1 \end{bmatrix}^{-1}
$$

$$
= \sigma_\epsilon^2 \begin{bmatrix} E(\mathbf{y}^{*\prime}\mathbf{y}^* - \mathbf{v}'\mathbf{v}) & \mathbf{X}_1'E(\mathbf{y}^*) \\ \mathbf{X}_1'E(\mathbf{y}^*) & \mathbf{X}_1'\mathbf{X}_1 \end{bmatrix}^{-1} \quad (17)
$$

$$
= \sigma_\epsilon^2 \begin{bmatrix} E(\mathbf{y}^{*\prime}\mathbf{y}^*) - E(\mathbf{v}'\mathbf{v}) & \mathbf{X}_1'E(\mathbf{y}^*) \\ \mathbf{X}_1'E(\mathbf{y}^*) & \mathbf{X}_1'\mathbf{X}_1 \end{bmatrix}^{-1}
$$

$$
= \sigma_\epsilon^2 \begin{bmatrix} E(\mathbf{y}^{*\prime}\mathbf{y}^*) - \sigma_v^2 & \mathbf{X}_1'E(\mathbf{y}^*) \\ \mathbf{X}_1'E(\mathbf{y}^*) & \mathbf{X}_1'\mathbf{X}_1 \end{bmatrix}^{-1}
$$

where σ_v^2 denotes the asymptotic variance of the error term of the first-stage regression of $\mathbf{y}^*$ on $\mathbf{X}$.

To compare expression (17) with the asymptotic variance matrix of the ML estimators (2) and (4) for model (1), we cannot use the final expression derived by Doreian (1981, p. 384), because it is written in terms of the parameters of model (1) rather than model (7). Stepping back in his derivations a few paces and using Ord's (1975) asymptotic expectation notation, however, we get the following equivalent expression:

$$
\text{asy var} \begin{bmatrix} \hat{\rho} \\ \hat{\boldsymbol{\beta}} \end{bmatrix} = \sigma_\epsilon^2 \begin{bmatrix} E(\mathbf{y}^{*\prime}\mathbf{y}^*) - \alpha\sigma_\epsilon^2 & \mathbf{X}_1'E(\mathbf{y}^*) \\ \mathbf{X}_1'E(\mathbf{y}^*) & \mathbf{X}_1'\mathbf{X}_1 \end{bmatrix}^{-1}, \quad (18)
$$

where $\alpha = \partial^2 \ln|\mathbf{A}|/\partial\rho^2 = \Sigma_{i=1}^n (\lambda_i^2)/(1 - \hat{\rho}\lambda_i)^2$, $|\mathbf{A}| = |\mathbf{I} - \rho\mathbf{W}|$, $\lambda_1, \ldots, \lambda_n$ are the eigenvalues of the weight matrix W, and

$$
\hat{\sigma}_\epsilon^2 = \frac{(\mathbf{y} - \hat{\rho}\mathbf{W}\mathbf{y} - \mathbf{X}\hat{\boldsymbol{\beta}})'(\mathbf{y} - \hat{\rho}\mathbf{W}\mathbf{y} - \mathbf{X}\hat{\boldsymbol{\beta}})}{n}
$$

is an alternative expression of the ML estimator (3) of the error variance of model (1).

Comparing the submatrix components of the asymptotic variance-covariance matrices (17) and (18), we see that three of them—namely, those in the lower-diagonal and off-diagonal positions—are identical. The first of these three, the $X_1'X_1$ component, is the usual matrix of cross products of the fixed exogenous variables, which enters into the calculation of the variances and covariances of the estimators of the regression coefficient vector, β, as in the conventional linear model. The off-diagonal elements in (17) and (18), $X_1'E(y^*)$, similarly enter into the calculation of the covariances of the estimators of the regression and spatial-effects coefficients (i.e., the elements of β and ρ). These submatrices have computational expressions that differ, because the parameterizations of model (1) and model (7) differ. When they are written in terms of the respective asymptotic expected values of the two models, as in expressions (17) and (18), however, we can see that they are indeed identical.

It is more difficult to compare the last component submatrices of the two asymptotic variance matrices (the upper-diagonal term), which represent the asymptotic variances of the respective estimators of the spatial-effects coefficient ρ. Again, because of the different parametric representations of models (1) and (7), these elements differ, even when they are written in terms of expected values of asymptotic distributions, as in (17) and (18). Nonetheless, they do have a common component—namely, the asymptotic expected value $E(y^{*'}y^*)$. But the 2SLS expression (17) subtracts from this the asymptotic variance of the error term of the first-stage regression of the 2SLS estimator, whereas the ML expression (18) subtracts a function of the asymptotic variance of the error term of the original model (1). The former is the error variance from the first-stage regression of the weighted $y^* = Wy$ on the full set of exogenous variables in X, while the latter error variance is scaled by the second partial derivative with respect to the spatial-effects parameter ρ of the log of the determinant of the matrix $A = I - \rho W$, which is one component of the loglikelihood function of the ML estimator of model (1). Informally, the scaling of the ML error variance by this second partial derivative is necessary to transform it to the scale of the error variance of the first-stage regression of the weighted $y^* = Wy$ on X in the 2SLS estimator.

Investigations comparing 2SLS and ML estimators of the parameters of single equations in classical simultaneous equation models have shown the equivalence of the variances of their asymptotic distributions (see, e.g., Theil 1971, pp. 500–507). The conditions necessary for the proof of this equivalence pertain to model accuracy (no misspecification) and stability of distributions of relevant variables. Because the spatial-effects model analyzed here is a special case of the classical model, asymptotic equivalence of the upper-diagonal components of expressions (17) and (18) follows under similar conditions.

6. COMPARISON WITH ANSELIN'S TWO-STAGE LEAST SQUARES ESTIMATORS

Anselin (1988) developed two 2SLS estimators in spatial econometrics models, one of which is identical to that developed herein.[7] Therefore, we call the estimator developed above and by Anselin the *Land-Deane/Anselin 2SLS estimator*. Anselin also described an alternative 2SLS estimator that is not identical to the estimator developed here. We call this *Anselin's alternative 2SLS estimator*. In this section we describe conceptual differences between the two estimators. In the next section, we investigate some numerical differences in a particular empirical application and discuss the relative computational efficiencies of the two estimators.

Anselin (1988, pp. 82–87) described a general instrumental variables (IV) approach to estimation that permits the specification of instruments for all variables in the regression model (7), i.e., for both the $\mathbf{X}$ and $\mathbf{y}^*$ variables. In practice, of course, the focus is on the $\mathbf{y}^*$ variable, which Anselin called a spatially lagged dependent variable. Anselin (1988, p. 84) showed that his general IV estimator can subsume an alternative 2SLS estimator in which $\mathbf{y}^*$ in the second-stage OLS regression is replaced by a transformation of the predicted values of the dependent variable $\mathbf{y}$ from a first-stage regression on a

---

[7]Anselin (1988), however, did not motivate the derivation of the 2SLS method in terms of the population-potential notions of spatial sociology, he did not give a detailed comparison of the variance-covariance matrix of the 2SLS estimator with that of the ML estimator, and he did not present numerical and computational efficiency comparisons of 2SLS and ML.

fixed set of exogenous variables, where the weight matrix $\mathbf{W}$ is used to perform the transformation.

Formally, Anselin's alternative 2SLS estimator proceeds by OLS estimation of the reduced form of model (7), in which the effects of the $\mathbf{y}^*$ variable are factored out and the dependent variable $\mathbf{y}$ is taken as dependent only on the fully exogenous variables $\mathbf{X}$. The predicted values of $\mathbf{y}$ from this first-stage regression are given by $\hat{\mathbf{y}} = \mathbf{X}(\mathbf{X}'\mathbf{X})^{-1}\mathbf{X}'\mathbf{y}$. Anselin's alternative estimator then transforms these predicted values by the weight matrix $\mathbf{W}$ to yield the following:

$$\bar{\mathbf{y}}^* = \mathbf{W}\hat{\mathbf{y}} = \mathbf{W}[\mathbf{X}(\mathbf{X}'\mathbf{X})^{-1}\mathbf{X}'\mathbf{y}], \tag{19}$$

where we use the notation $\bar{\mathbf{y}}^*$ to distinguish these predicted values for $\mathbf{y}^*$ from those introduced in equation (11). Anselin's alternative 2SLS estimator then is completed by inserting these predicted values into a second-stage OLS regression, as in equation (12).

Comparing the right sides of equations (11) and (19), we can see, first, that the predicted variables of the two 2SLS procedures differ in the way in which the weight matrix $\mathbf{W}$ enters. In equation (11), we enter $\mathbf{W}$ into the first-stage regression by scaling the dependent variable (regressand) of the regression. In equation (19), we enter $\mathbf{W}$ after the first-stage regression by scaling the predicted values computed after the regression of $\mathbf{y}$ on $\mathbf{X}$. In this alternative procedure, the predicted value of $\mathbf{y}^*$ is not a linear combination of $\mathbf{X}$, because it is premultiplied by $\mathbf{W}$, which varies across observations, so there is no perfect collinearity between $\mathbf{X}$ and the instrument.

Accordingly, if we use this alternative 2SLS estimator, we can avoid the exclusion restrictions (which can be hard to justify) required by the estimator of equation (11). On the other hand, equation (19) requires that we premultiply the predicted values of y by $\mathbf{W}$, which can yield a very large matrix in large samples. Indeed, standard computer packages (e.g., SAS) typically require that one save the predicted values of y from the first stage, premultiply these by $\mathbf{W}$ in an auxiliary routine (e.g., in SAS/IML), and then move back into a regression program. Alternatively, one can trick SAS into performing matrix multiplication.[8] This, of course, means that the 2SLS

---

[8]The numerical application of Anselin's method described in the next section was programmed in both ways. The code used to perform the analyses in SAS without resort to an auxiliary routine is available from the authors on request.

estimator of equation (19) in the spatial-effects model, like the ML estimator, is not easily applicable in large samples, which is a primary motivation for the 2SLS estimator developed herein.

7. EMPIRICAL APPLICATION AND COMPARISON OF ESTIMATORS

The 2SLS estimator of equations (11), (12), and (14) was developed by Land, Deane, and Blau (1991) in a study of the effects of religious pluralism and social conditions on church membership in the U.S. in the early decades of this century. The debate on the effect of religious pluralism has recently been enlivened by Finke and Stark (1988, 1989) and Breault (1989a,b). Their findings, however, are contradictory: Finke and Stark reported that religious pluralism has a positive effect on the rate of church membership (church adherence), but Breault found a negative effect.

Land et al. (1991) recently entered this debate with an analysis of church adherence rates in U.S. counties or county groups for three decennial census periods in the early twentieth century: 1910, 1920, and 1930. County-level analyses, especially those that use data from the period before World War II, are plagued by problems of boundary comparability, because counties may split, merge, or emerge in places where there had been no internal political boundaries. To overcome this difficulty, Land et al. grouped counties involved in any kind of boundary shift with other counties implicated in the boundary change by using a county longitudinal template compiled by Horan and Hargis (1989). Consequently, the unit of analysis is a county or county group, depending on whether or not boundaries changed.

The Horan and Hargis (1989) template includes approximately 1,600 counties and county groups, from which Land et al. (1991) drew a 50 percent random sample stratified by percentage urban in 1910: 0 percent, 1 percent to 22 percent, 23 percent to 40 percent, and over 40 percent. Initial statistical analyses and models were estimated on this 50 percent sample. To assess whether inferences from these analyses were unduly influenced by statistical overfitting on this initial sample, Land et al. used the remaining 50 percent sample of county groups for replication analyses.

Explanatory variables in the Land et al. (1991) study were

aggregated to county groups from the Inter-University Consortium for Political and Social Research (ICPSR, no date) collection of demographic, economic, and social data based on county-level counts from the U.S. decennial censuses of 1910, 1920, and 1930. Church membership data were obtained from ICPSR files reporting the 1906, 1916, and 1926 censuses of religious bodies. Although the religious censuses were carried out four years before each of the population censuses, this is not considered problematic because of the high stability of church membership counts for geographical units over time (Bainbridge and Hatch 1982, p. 244; Christiano 1987, p. 40). For convenience, we describe the analyses in terms of the census dates.

Variables in the Land et al. (1991) study were defined as follows. The dependent or endogenous variable to be explained is the percentage of the county group's population that are church members, as recorded in the religious censuses. The explanatory or exogenous variables include the county group's religious diversity, the percentage of the county group's population that is Catholic, ethnic diversity, population change (computed as the percentage change in total population size from the previous decade), the percentage of the population that is living in an urban area, the percentage of the adult population that is illiterate, and the average county crop value in 1910, which was used as an indicator of economic well-being. The religious and ethnic diversity variables were measured by applying the Gibbs-Martin index (Christiano 1987; Lieberson 1969; Gibbs and Martin 1962) to sets of religious denominations and ethnic groups, respectively.

In addition, Land et al. (1991) included a variable for *church-adherence potential*, which is like the generalized population-potential variables described above: It is a product of a geographical distance weight matrix **W** and a vector of county adherence rates. This generalized potential variable was introduced to capture the impact on the rate of church adherence in a given county of higher or lower rates of adherence in neighboring and more-distant counties. Land et al.'s (1991) collective influence/social diffusion interpretation of the church-adherence potential is based on the models of Granovetter (1978) and Granovetter and Soong (1983). The presence of the potential variable combined with relatively large samples (on the order of 700, depending on the decade and the number of counties with missing data) and the inability of the mainframe computer available for regression analyses to handle weight matrices larger than 300 rows by 300 columns limited the applicability of the ML estimators described above. Accordingly, Land et al. (1991) applied the 2SLS estimators (11), (12), and (14) of model (7).

To illustrate the numerical application of the 2SLS estimators derived above and compare them with Anselin's alternative 2SLS estimators (based on equation (19) in the first stage) and with the ML estimators, we draw upon the Land et al. (1991) analysis for a random subsample of 300 county groups for 1910. (Corresponding calculations for 1920 and 1930 are available from the authors on request.) The number of cases in this subsample is limited only by the aforementioned limits of the mainframe computer.

Table 1 reports the first-stage regression (based on equation (11)) of the church-adherence potential/spatial-effects variable on a set of fully exogenous variables. In addition to the explanatory variables listed above, this set of exogenous variables includes (as instrumental variables) eight regional dummy variables (the Northeast region is the baseline region against which the effects of the other regions are estimated) and the county group's total population size (logged). The coefficient of determination, 0.68, shows that the first stage is quite successful in determining the values of the potential variable for county groups. In particular, several of the regional control variables are significantly related to the dependent variable, although the total population variable does not reach statistical significance. Our experience with applications of the 2SLS method to

TABLE 1

First-Stage Least Squares Estimates for Model of Church Adherence Rates; Random Sample of County Groups, 1910 (Metric Coefficients, Standardized Coefficients in Brackets, t Ratios in Parentheses

Intercept	13.92
	(3.22)**
Religious diversity	2.50
	[.07]
	(1.37)
Percentage Catholic	−.03
	[−.05]
	(−1.03)

Log total population	.29
	[.05]
	(1.08)
Ethnic diversity	−4.16
	[−.08]
	(−2.17)*
Percentage urban	−.02
	[−.07]
	(−1.39)
Log percentage illiterate	.03
	[.01]
	(.08)
Log economic conditions[a]	.95
	[.09]
	(1.95)
Middle Atlantic[b]	1.00
	[.04]
	(.82)
South Atlantic[b]	1.78
	[.10]
	(1.39)
East South-Central[b]	1.98
	[.08]
	(1.39)
West South-Central[b]	−5.32
	[−.23]
	(−4.01)**
East North-Central[b]	6.02
	[.37]
	(5.55)**
West North-Central[b]	.56
	[.04]
	(.49)
West Mountain[b]	−10.81
	[−.40]
	(−7.55)**
Pacific[b]	−14.16
	[−.41]
	(−9.21)**
N	287
R^2	.68

[a]Average crop value
[b]The reference category for regional dummy variables is Northeast.
*$p < .05$
**$p < .01$

these data, however, and the fact that potential variables will often capture regional or population size effects on generalized potential variables suggest that these are useful instrumental variables for entry in the first-stage regressions.

Table 2 reports the second-stage regressions of the county-group church-adherence rates on the predicted values of the church-adherence potential/spatial-effects variable and the set of explanatory regressors identified above. For Land-Deane/Anselin's and Anselin's alternative 2SLS estimators (recall that the former are based on equation (11) in the first-stage regressions and that the latter use equation (19) in the first stage), the estimated 2SLS metric regression coefficients, standardized coefficients, and t ratios are given in the second and third columns of the table, respectively. Sample sizes after loss of cases due to incomplete data and measures of fit are given at the bottom of the table.[9] For comparison, the corresponding ML estimates are reported in the fourth column. To assess the extent to which the spatial-effects corrections of each of these reduces bias in the estimated coefficients and increases explanatory power, we also display the OLS estimates of a nonspatial model (i.e., a regression model that ignores the spatial-effects term) in the first column of the table.

Several comments concerning these results are in order. First, the OLS estimates for the nonspatial model are clearly inferior to the 2SLS and ML estimates. In particular, the magnitude of the coefficient of religious diversity and its t ratio (the key variable in the debate on the effects of religious diversity described above) are greatly underestimated by the nonspatial OLS estimators. Coefficients and t ratios of several of the other variables also are substantially affected by omission of the spatial term. Specifically, the coefficients tend to be inflated in the nonspatial OLS model, while the t ratios tend to be deflated (see Doreian 1981).

Second, the magnitudes of the metric regression coefficient estimates from both 2SLS methods are generally quite close to those of the ML estimates. The only exception is the spatial-effects coeffi-

---

[9]The measures of fit reported in Table 2 are the squares of the correlation between **y** and the fitted values **ŷ** in each model. While this appears similar to the standard coefficient of determination of regression models, it cannot strictly be interpreted as the proportion of variance explained due to the interdependence of the observations (Doreian 1981, p. 368).

TABLE 2
Alternative Estimates for Model of Church Adherence Rates; Random Sample
of County Groups, 1910. Metric coefficients, standardized coefficients [in
brackets], and *t*-ratios (in parentheses).

| | OLS | 2SLS | | ML |
		Land-Deane Anselin	Anselin Alternative	
Intercept	60.75	41.82	41.16	42.13
	(6.09)**	(4.92)**	(4.74)**	(5.04)**
Spatial effects	—	.94	1.03	.92
	—	[.49]	[.47]	[.48]
	—	(11.10)**	(10.43)**	(11.08)**
Religious diversity	−9.31	−22.17	−22.52	−21.96
	[−.14]	[−.32]	[−.33]	[−.32]
	(−2.31)*	(−6.23)**	(−6.16)**	(−6.27)**
Percentage Catholic	.36	.38	.36	.38
	[.33]	[.34]	[.33]	[.34]
	(5.59)**	(7.09)**	(6.60)**	(7.17)**
Population change	−2.10	−1.39	−1.47	−1.40
	[−.20]	[−.13]	[−.14]	[−.13]
	(−4.20)**	(−3.30)*	(−3.42)**	(−3.37)*
Ethnic diversity	−25.24	−14.85	−15.72	−15.02
	[−.27]	[−.16]	[−.17]	[−.16]
	(−4.74)**	(−3.66)**	(−3.81)**	(−3.76)**
Percentage urban	.08	.07	.08	.07
	[.15]	[.15]	[.16]	[.14]
	(2.86)*	(3.28)*	(3.54)**	(3.18)*
Log percentage illiterate	2.14	1.66	1.79	1.67
	[.19]	[.15]	[.16]	[.15]
	(3.11)*	(2.88)*	(3.06)*	(2.94)*
Log economic conditions[a]	−1.23	−1.18	−1.16	−1.18
	[−.06]	[−.05]	[−.05]	[−.05]
	(−1.02)	(−1.17)	(−1.14)	(−1.19)
N	287	287	287	287
R^2	.39	.58	.56	.58

[a]Average crop value
*$p < .01$
**$p < .001$

cient, for which Anselin's alternative 2SLS point estimate is considerably larger than the ML and Land-Deane/Anselin 2SLS estimates. Both the Land-Deane/Anselin 2SLS and the ML estimators suggest strong spatial-diffusion effects, with highly statistically significant metric regression coefficients of 0.94 and 0.92, respectively. By comparison, Anselin's alternative 2SLS estimate of this coefficient is greater than one, a value that certainly indicates strong spatial effects but that also differs substantially from the ML estimate.

Third, the Land-Deane/Anselin 2SLS metric regression coefficient estimates for the other regressor variables are uniformly closer to the ML estimates than the Anselin alternative 2SLS estimates. The former often agree with the ML estimate to two or three digits.

Fourth, the Land-Deane/Anselin 2SLS method yields t ratios that are closer to those of the ML estimates than are the Anselin alternative estimates for seven of the eight regressors. The measure of fit (see footnote 9) of the Land-Deane/Anselin estimates is also identical to that of the ML estimates, while that of the Anselin alternative estimates differs slightly.

In addition to the greater accuracy and statistical efficiency of the 2SLS and ML estimators compared with nonspatial OLS, the Land-Deane/Anselin 2SLS estimator is much more computationally efficient than both the Anselin alternative 2SLS estimator and the ML estimator. Specifically, as noted above, the Land-Deane/Anselin 2SLS estimator can handle a wider range of sample sizes in standard computer packages than the other two estimators. This, of course, affects the amount of computer processing time required to compute the estimates. In particular, for calculations executed in SAS batch mode on an IBM 3090 mainframe computer with a vector processor, the ML estimates in Table 2 required 43.08 seconds of CPU time, about 55 times more than the Land-Deane/Anselin 2SLS estimates, which required 0.78 second. The Anselin alternative 2SLS estimates required 16.36 seconds, about 21 times more than the Land-Deane/Anselin estimates.

8. CONCLUSION

Sociologists and other social scientists will undoubtedly continue to analyze data that are aggregated into arbitrary spatial configurations. In such analyses, incorporating spatial-effects terms into regression models is always an issue. The empirical results reported here and in Doreian (1981) indicate that when spatial effects are substantial and statistically significant, inferences can be greatly affected by the exclusion of spatial regression terms. Accordingly, analysts are well advised to take spatial-effects terms explicitly into account, especially when they can be substantively interpreted in terms of collective influences, social diffusion, or other processes.

Similar recommendations apply to analyses of data collected from individuals or organizations connected in well-defined (social, exchange, authority, communication, transportation, etc.) networks—when data on the network interrelationships (specified in the **W** matrix) are available. In such cases, the spatial-effects term of the spatial regression model is a network-effects term, and failure to estimate such effects in a regression model can have similarly deleterious effects on coefficient estimates and inferences (see, e.g., Duke's [1991] study of network effects in a high school student body).

Major limiting factors are the relatively computationally burdensome extant ML procedures and their sample-size limitations. In this paper, we have derived a corresponding 2SLS estimator for the spatial-effects regression model that is applicable to large samples. We have demonstrated that this estimator, which is equivalent to a 2SLS estimator previously derived in spatial econometrics by Anselin (1988), has desireable statistical and computational properties. Unlike the ML estimator, the 2SLS estimator does not require the assumption of normal random errors and yet is consistent and computationally efficient.

We also compared this 2SLS estimator with Anselin's alternative 2SLS estimator for the spatial regression model. In an empirical application to a moderately large sample, we found that Anselin's alternative 2SLS estimator is somewhat less computationally efficient. The Land-Dean/Anselin estimator also produced coefficient estimates closer to the ML estimates than Anselin's alternative 2SLS estimator, but evidence from other empirical applications is necessary before any generalizations can be stated. Based on the empirical analyses we have done and an empirical application[10] to data on electoral support for the Democratic presidential candidate in the 64

---

[10]This application was graciously provided by Peter V. Marsden.

Louisiana parishes analyzed in Doreian's (1981) article, we believe that the Land-Deane/Anselin method will perform relatively well in large samples when good exogenous identifying variables are available as predictors for the first-stage regressions.[11]

As noted earlier, the Land-Deane/Anselin 2SLS method requires such identifying variables, but Anselin's does not. Thus, we believe that when such identifying variables are available and sample sizes are large (say, 200 or more cases), the method has much to recommend it. When sample sizes are large but exogenous identifiers are unavailable, the analyst must cope with the computational complications of ML or Anselin's alternative 2SLS. In the case of small samples with or without identifying exogenous variables, ML may be the preferred method, provided that the errors are reasonably well approximated by the normal distribution assumption.

Given that appropriate estimators are now available for these various contingencies, future regression analyses of spatially distributed or network-related social data may be more likely to estimate the effects of spatial- or network-effects terms. All existing methods have been developed for the estimation of a single linear (in parameters) equation. Extensions to more-complicated error processes, nonlinear equations, and systems of simultaneous linear or nonlinear equations have yet to be fully explored.

REFERENCES

Anselin, Luc. 1988. *Spatial Econometrics: Methods and Models*. Dordrecht, The Netherlands: Kluwer Academic Publishers.
Bainbridge, William Sims, and Laurie Russell Hatch. 1982. *The Churches and the American Experience*. Grand Rapids, MI: Baker Book House.

[11]The proper choice of instruments with which to construct predicted values in the first stage is always problematic in two-stage and instrumental variables estimators. Although these estimators are consistent, their efficiency is effectively only asymptotic (i.e., applicable to large samples) and depends on the exogenous variables used as regressors in the first stage. The general textbook advice is that these variables should be highly correlated with the endogenous variable for which predicted values are sought and uncorrelated with the error term of the model. In practice, we believe that the former criterion means that the coefficient of determination obtained in the first-stage regression should be reasonably large in comparison to the amount of association in the variables being analyzed. For instance, if the variables being analyzed yield a measure of fit in the second-stage regression of approximately 0.5, then the first-stage regression should produce a coefficient of determination of greater magnitude.

Basmann, R. L. 1957. "A Generalized Classical Method of Linear Estimation of Coefficients in a Structural Equation." *Econometrica* 25:77–83.

Breault, Kevin D. 1989*a*. "New Evidence on Religious Pluralism, Urbanism, and Religious Participation." *American Sociological Review* 54:1048–53.

———. 1989*b*. "Reply to Finke and Stark." *American Sociological Review* 54:1056–59.

Christiano, Kevin J. 1987. *Religious Diversity and Social Change*. Cambridge: Cambridge University Press.

Doreian, Patrick. 1980. "Linear Models with Spatially Distributed Data: Spatial Disturbances or Spatial Effects?" *Sociological Methods and Research* 9:29–60.

———. 1981. "Estimating Linear Models with Spatially Distributed Data." Pp. 359–88 in *Sociological Methodology 1981*, edited by Samuel Leinhardt. San Francisco: Jossey-Bass.

Doreian, Patrick, and Norman P. Hummon. 1976. *Modeling Social Processes*. New York: Elsevier.

Doreian, Patrick, Klaus Teuter, and Chi-Hsein Wang. 1984. "Network Autocorrelation Models: Some Monte Carlo Results." *Sociological Methods and Research* 13:155–200.

Duke, James Brian. 1991. "The Peer Context and the Adolescent Society: Making Sense of the Context Effects Paradox." Ph.D. diss., Harvard University, Department of Sociology.

Duncan, Otis Dudley, Ray P. Cuzzort, and Beverly A. Duncan. 1963. *Statistical Geography*. New York: Free Press.

Finke, Roger, and Rodney Stark. 1988. "Religious Economies and Sacred Canopies." *American Sociological Review* 53:41–49.

———. 1989. "Comment on Breault." *American Sociological Review* 54:1054–55.

Gibbs, Jack P., and Walter T. Martin. 1962. "Urbanization, Technology, and the Division of Labor." *American Sociological Review* 27:667–77.

Granovetter, Mark. 1978. "Threshold Models of Collective Behavior." *American Journal of Sociology* 83:1420–43.

Granovetter, Mark, and Roland Soong. 1983. "Threshold Models of Diffusion and Collective Behavior." *The Journal of Mathematical Sociology* 9: 165–80.

Horan, Patrick M., and Peggy G. Hargis. 1989. "The County Longitudinal Template." Paper presented at the Annual Meetings of the Social Science History Association, Chicago.

Inter-university Consortium for Political and Social Research. n.d. Historical, Demographic, Economic, and Social Data: The United States, 1790–1970. Ann Arbor: ICPSR [producer and distributor].

Johnston, J. 1984. *Econometric Methods*. 3d ed. New York: McGraw-Hill.

Land, Kenneth C., Glenn Deane, and Judith R. Blau. 1991. "Religious Pluralism and Church Membership: A Spatial Diffusion Model." *American Sociological Review* 56:237–49.

Lieberson, Stanley. 1969. "Measuring Population Diversity." *American Sociological Review* 34:850–62.

Ord, Keith. 1975. "Estimation Methods for Models of Spatial Interaction." *Journal of the American Statistical Association* 70:120–26.

Roncek, Dennis W., and Andrew Montgomery. 1984. "Spatial Autocorrelation: Diagnoses and Remedies for Large Samples." Paper presented at the Annual Meetings of the Midwest Sociological Society, Des Moines.

Roncek, Dennis W., and James Robinson. 1984. "The Effects of Crime in the Surroundings of Residential Areas." Paper presented at the Annual Meetings of the American Society of Criminology, Cincinnati.

Theil, H. 1953a. *Repeated Least-Squares Applied to Complete Equation Systems*. The Hague: Central Planning Bureau.

———. 1953b. *Estimation and Simultaneous Correlation in Complete Equation Systems*. The Hague: Central Planning Bureau.

———. 1961. *Economic Forecasts and Policy*. 2d ed. Amsterdam: North-Holland.

———. 1971. *Principles of Econometrics*. New York: Wiley.

𝕏 8 𝕏

ASYMPTOTIC ROBUST INFERENCES IN THE ANALYSIS OF MEAN AND COVARIANCE STRUCTURES

*Albert Satorra**

Structural equation models are widely used in economic, social, and behavioral studies to analyze linear interrelationships among variables, some of which may be unobservable or subject to measurement error. Alternative estimation methods that exploit different distributional assumptions are now available. This paper deals with issues of asymptotic statistical inferences, such as the evaluation of standard errors of estimates and chi-square goodness-of-fit statistics, in the general context of mean and covariance structures. The emphasis is on drawing correct statistical inferences regardless of the distribution of the data and the method of estimation employed. A simple expression for a consistent estimate (given any distribution of the data) of Γ, the matrix of asymptotic variances of the vector of sample second-order moments, is used to compute asymptotic robust standard errors and an asymptotic robust chi-square goodness-of-fit statistic. Simple modifications of the usual estimate of Γ

This research was supported by grant PS89-0040 from the Dirección General de la Investigación Científica y Técnica, Spanish Ministry of Education. A preliminary version of the paper was presented at the International Conference on Measurement Errors in Surveys, Tucson, 1990, and at the International Workshop: Statistical Modelling and Latent Variables, Trento, 1991. I thank two anonymous reviewers for their comments and suggestions, which greatly improved the paper, Peter Marsden for very valuable editorial comments and assistance, and Bengt Muthén for comments on an earlier draft. I also acknowledge the precious assistance of Maria Ollé in manuscript production.
*Universitat Pompeu Fabra, Barcelona

249

*also permit correct asymptotic inferences in multistage complex
samples. We also discuss the conditions under which, regardless of the distribution of the data, one can rely on the usual
(nonrobust) normal-theory inferential statistics. Finally, we use
a multivariate regression model with errors-in-variables to illustrate, by means of simulated data, various theoretical aspects of
the paper.*

1. INTRODUCTION

Structural equation models are widely used in economic, social, and behavioral studies to analyze the interrelationships among
variables, some of which may be unobservable (latent) or subject to
measurement error (see, e.g., Jöreskog 1981; Jöreskog and Sörbom
1989; Bentler 1983a, 1989; Muthén 1987; Bollen 1989, and references contained therein). Computer programs that use various estimation methods for a general class of structural equation models are
now available: LISREL (Jöreskog and Sörbom 1989), EQS (Bentler
1989), LISCOMP (Muthén 1987), LINCS (Schoenberg 1989), and
PROC CALIS (SAS 1990).

A general approach to inference in structural equation models
consists of fitting structured population moments to sample moments, usually variances and covariances, using minimum distance
(MD) methods (e.g., Malinvaud 1970, chapter 9; Chamberlain 1982;
Hansen 1982; Browne 1974, 1984; Bentler and Dijkstra 1985; Shapiro 1986; Fuller 1987, section 4.2). In the MD framework the estimator is obtained as the parameter value that minimizes a quadratic
form in the difference of population and sample moments. The
pseudo maximum likelihood (PML) approach, with normality as a
working assumption (which is a closest-moment estimation, in the
sense of Manski [1983]), is also asymptotically equivalent to MD
estimation with, say, a normal-theory (NT) weight matrix $\mathbf{W}_{NT}$ (cf.
Browne 1974; Newey 1988). For the precise definition of MD, PML,
and NT-MD analyses, see sections 3 and 5 below.

Traditional structural equation modeling has focused on models in which means are unrestricted, and hence only covariance structures needed to be considered. A notable exception to this, however,
is Bentler (1983b) and the recent work of Arminger and Schoenberg
(1989) and Arminger and Sobel (1990). In view of the growing num-

ber of applications involving models that restrict means as well as covariances, it seems natural to develop the theory of structural equation models in the general setting of mean and covariance structures.

Two distinct approaches can be distinguished to deal with mean and covariance structures. One approach (e.g., as in the recent versions of LISREL, EQS, and LISCOMP) considers a moment structure for a vector of means and covariances. In this approach, the usual fitting function for covariance structure analysis is modified, since a second term corresponding to the fit of the mean structure needs to be added to the usual term that fits the covariances. An alternative approach is to analyze the (uncentered) second-order moment structure of a vector of observable variables augmented with a constant equal to one. The latter approach is easy to put into practice, since it can be implemented without modifying the conventional software for covariance structures: One needs only to replace the covariance matrix to be analyzed with the corresponding augmented moment matrix. In fact, augmented moment structures have been analyzed in the context of normality and maximum likelihood estimation (see, e.g., Jöreskog and Sörbom 1984; Meredith and Tisak 1990). In this paper we develop the theory for the analysis of augmented moment structures for arbitrary distributions of the data, not only under normality.

It is widely known that parameter estimates are consistent whether or not the normality assumption holds (i.e., consistency is a robust quality of PML and MD estimation). This property of robustness, however, does not carry over to inferential statistics obtained under the normality assumption. For example, the usual standard errors of estimates and probability values of test statistics associated with PML and NT-MD estimation may be incorrect with non-normal data. Since in practice the distribution of the observable variables is often skewed with non-normal kurtosis, the lack of robustness of the normal-theory inferential statistics is of practical concern. See Satorra (1990) for a review of robustness issues in the analysis of covariance structures.

To remedy the problems associated with violation of distributional assumptions, the so-called asymptotic distribution-free (ADF) methods have been proposed for covariance structure analysis (Browne 1984) and, more recently, for the analysis of mean and covariance structures (Muthén 1989). The ADF approach is in fact an MD method in which the weight matrix is equal to the inverse of a matrix of sample fourth-order moments of the data. For moderate-size models, however, fourth-order sample moments are large in number and highly unstable in small samples. In fact, even though ADF methods are asymptotically optimal, the empirical evidence reported so far does not recommend their routine use, since they may lead to excessive computational burden and lack of robustness in small samples. See Muthén and Kaplan (1985, 1990) for Monte Carlo evidence on the small-sample performance of ADF methods.

An alternative to using an estimation method that requires inversion of a matrix of sample fourth-order moments is to equip usual estimation methods (e.g., the PML approach) with asymptotic standard errors of parameter estimates and asymptotic chi-square goodness-of-fit statistics, which are valid for any distribution of the data. These are called robust (asymptotic) inferential statistics. In fact, robust (asymptotic) standard errors of estimates in MD estimation have been available for many years (Ferguson 1958; Chiang 1956). Robust (asymptotic) standard errors for mean and covariance structures have also been deduced in PML estimation (White 1982; Arminger and Sobel 1990; Arminger and Schoenberg 1989). Recently, the EQS computer program (Bentler 1989) has made robust asymptotic standard errors for NT-MD available in practice, though they are confined to covariance structures with unrestricted means. LISREL 7 (Jöreskog and Sörbom 1989) also provides such standard errors but with an additional assumption of independence between sample means and sample variances and covariances. In fact, for PML estimation, robust asymptotic standard errors for mean and covariance structures are available in the program LINCS (Schoenberg 1989; see also Arminger and Schoenberg 1989). The work reported so far, however, lacks a robust asymptotic chi-square goodness-of-fit statistic for mean and covariance structures under general estimation methods. It also lacks a general approach within which the mentioned alternative proposals for robust standard errors can be related. Furthermore, to our knowledge, inferential statistics that are valid in the practically interesting case of data from multistage complex samples have not yet been developed.

Here we develop the asymptotic theory for the analysis of augmented moment structures for arbitrary distributions of the data. By analyzing mean and covariance structures under an augmented moment structure, we keep the theory as simple as the one for covariance structure analysis, and more important, most of the computations are readily available through standard software for covariance structure analysis. The so far incomplete theory for the analysis of augmented moment structures is now given full development, not only under normal-theory methods (section 5 below) but also under arbitrary distributions of the data. Robust asymptotic standard errors and a robust asymptotic chi-square statistic arise naturally, also in the case of data from multistage complex samples. In section 5 we relate the PML approach of Arminger and Schoenberg (1989) to corresponding MD methods. Further, Satorra and Bentler's (1990) results on asymptotic robustness of methods based on a normality assumption, which so far have been confined to models with unrestricted means, are extended to models that restrict means as well as covariances. The paper is self-contained, and the more involved analytics are confined to the appendices. Appendix A develops technical results needed for the normal-theory approach to the analysis of augmented moment matrices. A technical result derived in a research note of Satorra (1990), our lemma 2, is exploited in Appendix B.[1]

The rest of the paper is structured as follows. Section 2 presents the family of models to be dealt with. Section 3 develops asymptotic theory for augmented moment structures, summarizing the basic theory for MD estimation and developing a general type of chi-square goodness-of-fit statistic. Section 4 deals with the estimation of the asymptotic variance matrix of sample moments and the asymptotically optimal MD analysis. Section 5 presents robust standard errors and a robust chi-square goodness-of-fit statistic associated with PML and NT-MD. Section 6 deals with asymptotic robustness of normal-theory inferential statistics. Section 7 illustrates theoretical issues of the paper using a specific model context and simulated data, and section 8 is the conclusion.

2. LINEAR RELATION MODELS

We will deal with the following general latent variable model:

$$\begin{cases} z = \Lambda\eta + \epsilon, \\ \eta = B\eta + \xi, \end{cases} \tag{1}$$

---

[1]Here, however, we go beyond the mentioned technical note by developing a theory for the analysis of structural equation models. We also go beyond Satorra (1990) by including structural equation models that allow restrictions on the means.

where z is a $p \times 1$ vector of observable variables, η is an $m \times 1$ vector of (possibly) latent variables, ϵ is a $p \times 1$ vector of measurement errors having mean zero, and ξ is a random vector composed of disturbance terms of simultaneous equations and (possibly) unobservable exogenous variables. The vector ξ is assumed to have mean zero except for its last component, which is a constant equal to one, say, $c1$. The matrices Λ $(p \times m)$, $\mathbf{B}$ $(m \times m)$, $\boldsymbol{\Psi} \equiv \mathrm{E}\epsilon\epsilon'$, and $\boldsymbol{\Phi} \equiv \mathrm{E}\xi\xi'$, where E denotes mathematical expectation, are structured as continuously differentiable functions of, say, a q-dimensional parameter vector $\boldsymbol{\theta}$. Without loss of generality, the matrix $(\mathbf{I} - \mathbf{B})$ is assumed to be invertible, and the last component of ξ, η, and z is assumed to be $c1$. This model encompasses factor analysis, multivariate regression with (or without) measurement error, and structural equation models with measurement error (i.e., the family of so-called LISREL models). The gradient vector and Hessian matrix associated with model (1), for different fitting functions, are given in Neudecker and Satorra (1991).

The presence of the (pseudo) variable $c1$ allows us to impose structure on the means as well as on the covariances of z. For such an approach to encompassing mean and covariance structures see, for example, Jöreskog and Sörbom (1984) and Bentler (1989). In the computer program EQS (Bentler 1989), $c1$ is called the independent variable $V999$.

For the developments of this paper it is important to note that (1) can be rewritten as

$$z = \Lambda(\mathbf{I} - \mathbf{B})^{-1}\xi + \epsilon = [\Lambda(\mathbf{I} - \mathbf{B})^{-1},\mathbf{I}][\xi',\epsilon']' = \mathbf{A}\boldsymbol{\delta}, \qquad (2)$$

where $\mathbf{A} \equiv [\Lambda(\mathbf{I} - \mathbf{B})^{-1},\mathbf{I}]$, $\mathbf{I}$ is an identity matrix of appropriate dimensions, and $\boldsymbol{\delta}' \equiv [\xi',\epsilon']$. Therefore, model (1) is a specific case of a linear structure

$$z = \sum_{i=1}^{L} \mathbf{A}_i\boldsymbol{\delta}_i, \qquad (3)$$

where the $\boldsymbol{\delta}_i$'s are uncorrelated random vectors and the matrices $\mathbf{A}_i$ and $\boldsymbol{\Phi}_{ii} \equiv \mathrm{E}\boldsymbol{\delta}_i\boldsymbol{\delta}_i'$, $i = 1, \ldots, L$, are restricted to being functions of $\boldsymbol{\theta}$. Here the $\boldsymbol{\delta}_i$'s are assumed to be of zero mean except for $\boldsymbol{\delta}_L$, which is taken to be $c1$; hence, (3) can be written as

$$z = \sum_{i=1}^{L-1} \mathbf{A}_i\boldsymbol{\delta}_i + \mu c1, \qquad (4)$$

where $\mu \equiv Ez$, the mean of z, is also allowed to be a function of θ. The (pseudo) variance of the (pseudo) variable $c1$ is denoted as ϕ_c.

The linear structure (3), without the possibility of constraining the mean of z, has been considered recently by different authors (e.g., Anderson 1989; Browne and Shapiro 1988; and Satorra and Bentler 1990; see also Bentler 1983a).

As an illustration of the above model, consider the following multivariate regression model with measurement error

$$\begin{cases} Y_1 = \alpha + \beta x + \zeta_1, \\ Y_2 = \alpha + \beta x + \zeta_2, \\ X = x + u, \end{cases} \tag{5}$$

where α and β are parameters, and the ζ_i's, the Y_i's, X, x, and u are scalar random variables. The variables ζ_1, ζ_2, x, and u are assumed to be mutually uncorrelated. Since in model (5) the intercepts (and the slopes) of first and second equations are restricted to being equal, the model imposes restrictions on the means of the observable variables; hence, it implies a mean and covariance structure.

In fact (5) is a special case of (1), where $z \equiv (Y_1, Y_2, X, c1)'$, $\eta \equiv (Y_1, Y_2, x, c1)'$, $\epsilon \equiv (0, 0, u, 0)'$, and $\xi \equiv (\zeta_1, \zeta_2, x - \mu_x, c1)'$, $\Lambda \equiv I$,

$$B \equiv \begin{pmatrix} 0 & 0 & \beta & \alpha \\ 0 & 0 & \beta & \alpha \\ 0 & 0 & 0 & \mu_x \\ 0 & 0 & 0 & 0 \end{pmatrix}, \tag{6}$$

$\Phi \equiv \text{diag}(\phi_{11}, \phi_{22}, \phi_{33}, \phi_c)$, and $\Psi \equiv \text{diag}(0, 0, \psi, 0)$. In this example the variables ζ_1, ζ_2, x, and u take the role of the δ_i's of (4).

Note that in this example, $c1$ plays a crucial role, since its inclusion enables us to structure the intercepts. In the econometric literature, the model (5) is known as a seemingly unrelated regression (SUR) model with errors-in-variables.

3. MOMENT STRUCTURE ANALYSIS: ASYMPTOTIC INFERENCES

The structural equation model (1) implies a moment structure $\Sigma = \Sigma(\theta)$ for the matrix $\Sigma \equiv Ezz'$ of (population) second-order moments of z. Here $\Sigma(.)$ is a (continuously differentiable) symmetric matrix-valued function of $\boldsymbol{\theta}$, a (q-dimensional) vector of parameters. Since the last component of $\mathbf{z}$ is $c1$, $\boldsymbol{\Sigma}$ contains means and uncentered second-order moments; in fact, writing $\mathbf{z}' = (\mathbf{y}', c1)$,

$$\boldsymbol{\Sigma} = \begin{pmatrix} \text{Eyy}' & \text{Ey} \\ \text{Ey}' & 1 \end{pmatrix} \tag{7}$$

is the so-called (population) augmented moment matrix of $\mathbf{y}$.

Given a sample $\mathbf{z}_1, \mathbf{z}_2, \ldots, \mathbf{z}_n$ of n independent observations of $\mathbf{z}$, consider the following matrix of sample (uncentered) second-order moments of $\mathbf{z}$ (i.e., the [sample] augmented moment matrix of $\mathbf{y}$):

$$\mathbf{S} = \sum_{i=1}^{n} (\mathbf{z}_i \mathbf{z}_i')/n. \tag{8}$$

The MD estimator $\hat{\boldsymbol{\theta}}$ of $\boldsymbol{\theta}$ is defined as the minimizer of[2]

$$F = (\mathbf{s} - \boldsymbol{\sigma}(\boldsymbol{\theta}))'\hat{\mathbf{W}}(\mathbf{s} - \boldsymbol{\sigma}(\boldsymbol{\theta})), \tag{9}$$

where $\mathbf{s} = \text{vech } \mathbf{S}$ and $\boldsymbol{\sigma} = \text{vech } \boldsymbol{\Sigma}$ are the (reduced) vectors of sample and population moments, respectively, and $\hat{\mathbf{W}}$ is a matrix converging in probability to $\mathbf{W}$, a non-negative definite matrix. Here vech $(\mathbf{S})$ is the column vector formed by stacking the $p^* \equiv p(p + 1)/2$ different elements of $\mathbf{S}$. It holds that $\text{vec}(\mathbf{S}) = \mathbf{D}$ vech $(\mathbf{S})$, where vec(.) denotes the usual column vectorization of a matrix and $\mathbf{D}$ is the 0-1 duplication matrix; we can also write vech $(\mathbf{S}) = \mathbf{D}^+ \text{vec}(\mathbf{S})$, where $\mathbf{D}^+ \equiv (\mathbf{D}'\mathbf{D})^{-1}\mathbf{D}$ is the Moore-Penrose inverse of $\mathbf{D}$ (for further properties of $\mathbf{D}$ and $\mathbf{D}^+$ see Magnus and Neudecker [1988]). More generally, the estimator can be defined as the minimizer of $F = F(\mathbf{S},\boldsymbol{\Sigma}(\boldsymbol{\theta}))$, where $F = F(.,.)$ is a non-negative real-valued function that is continuous in both arguments and zero when $\mathbf{S} = \boldsymbol{\Sigma}$ (e.g., Browne 1984); such an estimator, however, is asymptotically equivalent to an MD estimator with a weight matrix $\mathbf{W}$ that is equal to the Hessian matrix $\partial^2 F/\partial\boldsymbol{\sigma}\partial\boldsymbol{\sigma}'$ evaluated at $(\boldsymbol{\Sigma},\boldsymbol{\Sigma})$ (cf. Shapiro 1985; see also Satorra 1989; and Newey 1988).

To include restrictions of the means, some computer programs (e.g., LISREL, EQS, and LISCOMP) recently incorporated a fitting

---

[2]Typical regularity assumptions, as, for example, $\boldsymbol{\theta}$ identifiable, are assumed to ensure that $\hat{\boldsymbol{\theta}}$ is well defined, consistent, and asymptotically normal. For a set of general regularity conditions see Satorra (1989).

function that is the sum of two parts: one corresponding to the fit of means and the other to the fit of variances and covariances. This approach requires basic modifications to conventional software for covariance structure analysis. In contrast, we adopt the simpler framework of fitting the matrix of sample moments S defined in (8) above to the corresponding matrix Σ of population moments given in (7), which is structured as a function of θ through the model (1). The structure on the means is imposed through $c1$. By adopting this approach we can use conventional software (without modification) to analyze mean and variance structures, where the role of the covariance matrix to be analyzed is assigned to the augmented moment matrix S.

The asymptotic variance matrix of estimates and test statistics can now be obtained. Under fairly general conditions, it holds that

$$\sqrt{n}(s - \sigma) \to_L N(0,\Gamma), \tag{10}$$

where $\to_L$ denotes convergence in distribution, and $N(0,\Gamma)$ denotes a normal distribution of zero mean and variance matrix Γ, a finite $p^* \times p^*$ matrix (remember that $p^* \equiv p(p + 1)/2$). From (10), and typical regularity conditions, it follows that the expression for the matrix of asymptotic variances of $\hat{\theta}$ is (e.g., Satorra 1989):

$$\operatorname{avar}(\hat{\theta}) = n^{-1}(\Delta'W\Delta)^{-1}\Delta'W\Gamma W\Delta(\Delta'W\Delta)^{-1}, \tag{11}$$

where $\Delta \equiv (\partial/\partial\theta')\sigma(\theta)$, a $p^* \times q$ matrix.

When W and Γ are such that $\Delta'W\Gamma W\Delta = \Delta'W\Delta$ then, obviously, (11) reduces to

$$\operatorname{avar}(\hat{\theta}) = n^{-1}(\Delta'W\Delta)^{-1}, \tag{12}$$

and in that case, the corresponding fitting function is said to be asymptotically optimal (AO) for the given model and distribution of the data (Satorra 1989).

A chi-square goodness-of-fit statistic based on the residuals of the fit of S to $\Sigma = \Sigma(\theta)$ can also be developed. Let $\hat{\sigma} = \operatorname{vech} \Sigma(\hat{\theta})$ and $\Delta_\perp$ be an orthogonal complement of Δ (i.e., $\Delta_\perp$ is a $p^* \times (p^* - q)$ matrix of full column rank such that $\Delta_\perp'\Delta = 0$).[3] In these conditions, it

---

[3]To compute such an orthogonal matrix, consider the $p^* \times p^*$ matrix $P \equiv I - \Delta(\Delta'\Delta)^{-1}\Delta'$, which is idempotent of rank $p^* - q$. Consider the singular value decomposition $P = HVH'$, where H is a $p^* \times (p^* - q)$ matrix of full column rank, and V is a $(p^* - q) \times (p^* - q)$ diagonal matrix. It is obvious that $H'\Delta = 0$; hence, H is the desired orthogonal complement. This method of constructing an orthogonal complement was proposed by Heinz Neudecker (1990, pers. comm.).

follows easily that the "residual" vector $\sqrt{n}(s - \hat{\sigma})$ is asymptotically normal with asymptotic variance matrix

$$
\begin{aligned}
\operatorname{avar}(\sqrt{n}(s - \hat{\sigma})) = {}& (\mathbf{I} - \boldsymbol{\Delta}(\boldsymbol{\Delta}'\mathbf{W}\boldsymbol{\Delta})^{-1}\boldsymbol{\Delta}'\mathbf{W}) \\
& \times \boldsymbol{\Gamma}(\mathbf{I} - \boldsymbol{\Delta}(\boldsymbol{\Delta}'\mathbf{W}\boldsymbol{\Delta})^{-1}\boldsymbol{\Delta}'\mathbf{W})';
\end{aligned} \tag{13}
$$

hence, $\sqrt{n}\boldsymbol{\Delta}'_{\perp}(s - \hat{\sigma})$ is asymptotically normal with asymptotic covariance matrix $\boldsymbol{\Delta}'_{\perp}\boldsymbol{\Gamma}\boldsymbol{\Delta}_{\perp}$. This implies that the generalized Wald statistic (Moore 1977),

$$
T = n(s - \hat{\sigma})'\hat{\mathbf{A}}(s - \hat{\sigma}), \tag{14}
$$

where $\hat{\mathbf{A}}$ is a consistent estimate of

$$
\boldsymbol{\Delta}_{\perp}(\boldsymbol{\Delta}'_{\perp}\boldsymbol{\Gamma}\boldsymbol{\Delta}_{\perp})^{-}\boldsymbol{\Delta}'_{\perp}, \tag{15}
$$

and the superscript $^{-}$ denotes g-inverse, is asymptotically chi-square distributed with degrees of freedom equal to $r \equiv \operatorname{rank}(\boldsymbol{\Delta}'_{\perp}\boldsymbol{\Gamma}\boldsymbol{\Delta}_{\perp})$. The goodness-of-fit statistic T is the generalization to moment structure analysis, with $\boldsymbol{\Gamma}$ possibly nonsingular, of a goodness-of-fit statistic developed by Browne (1984, p. 68) in the context of covariance structure analysis.

A more typical version of the goodness-of-fit statistic is n times the fitting function at its minimum, that is, $nF(\hat{\boldsymbol{\theta}})$. It can be shown (Satorra 1989) that when the fitting function is asymptotically optimal, that is, when $\mathbf{W}\boldsymbol{\Gamma}\mathbf{W} = \mathbf{W}$, then $nF(\hat{\boldsymbol{\theta}})$ is asymptotically equal to the test statistic T of (14); however, when asymptotic optimality does not hold, then $nF(\hat{\boldsymbol{\theta}})$ is in general not asymptotically chi square. Likelihood ratio, score, and Wald-type test statistics for testing a specific set of restrictions can also be developed in line with the arguments of Satorra (1989).

A scaled (adjusted-for-mean) goodness-of-fit statistic

$$
ST = nF(\hat{\boldsymbol{\theta}})/\kappa, \tag{16}
$$

where

$$
\begin{aligned}
\kappa \equiv {}& \operatorname{tr}[(\mathbf{W} - \mathbf{W}\boldsymbol{\Delta}(\boldsymbol{\Delta}'\mathbf{W}\boldsymbol{\Delta})^{-1}\boldsymbol{\Delta}'\mathbf{W})\boldsymbol{\Gamma}]/r \tag{17} \\
= {}& (\operatorname{tr}[(\boldsymbol{\Delta}'_{\perp}\mathbf{W}^{-1}\boldsymbol{\Delta}_{\perp})^{-1}(\boldsymbol{\Delta}'_{\perp}\boldsymbol{\Gamma}\boldsymbol{\Delta}_{\perp})])/r,
\end{aligned}
$$

has also been proposed in covariance structure analysis (cf. Satorra and Bentler 1988) on the grounds that it would improve the chi-square approximation under a general type of distribution of z. This is the so-called Satorra-Bentler chi-square statistic implemented in EQS (Bentler 1989).

An adjusted (for mean and variance) Satterthwaite-type of chi-square goodness-of-fit statistic could also be considered (Satterthwaite 1941). The adjusted test statistic, AT, is obtained by computing the integer, say d, nearest to $d^* = (\mathrm{tr}\mathbf{U}\boldsymbol{\Gamma})^2/\mathrm{tr}((\mathbf{U}\boldsymbol{\Gamma})^2)$, where $\mathbf{U} = (\mathbf{W} - \mathbf{W}\boldsymbol{\Delta}(\boldsymbol{\Delta}'\mathbf{W}\boldsymbol{\Delta})^{-1}\boldsymbol{\Delta}'\mathbf{W})$, and by setting $AT \equiv [d/\mathrm{tr}(\mathbf{U}\boldsymbol{\Gamma})]nF(\hat{\boldsymbol{\theta}})$. This statistic is referred to as a chi-square distribution with d degrees of freedom (cf. Satorra and Bentler 1988, p. 311).

4. CONSISTENT ESTIMATION OF $\boldsymbol{\Gamma}$ AND AO-MD ANALYSIS

The asymptotic variance matrix $\boldsymbol{\Gamma}$ of the vector of sample moments plays a fundamental role in assessing the sampling variability of statistics of interest (i.e., in drawing correct statistical inferences) and in defining the optimal MD analysis. For general types of distribution, $\boldsymbol{\Gamma}$ involves the third- and fourth-order moments of the observable variables. When the vector of observable variables is normally distributed, then, of course, $\boldsymbol{\Gamma}$ is expressed as a function of only first- and second-order moments (see (25) below).

To estimate the asymptotic variance matrix of estimates as well as to compute the goodness-of-fit statistic, we require an estimate of the matrix $\boldsymbol{\Gamma}$. As shown below, for general distributions of the observable variables, and also for complex samples, such a consistent estimator of $\boldsymbol{\Gamma}$ is readily available from standard theory.

Define $\mathbf{d}_i \equiv \mathrm{vech}(\mathbf{z}_i\mathbf{z}_i')$, $i = 1, 2, \ldots, n$; hence, $\mathbf{s} = \Sigma_{i=1}^n\mathbf{d}_i/n$. Since the $\mathbf{d}_i$'s are independent, an unbiased and consistent estimate of the variance matrix of $\sqrt{n}\mathbf{s} = \Sigma_{i=1}^n\mathbf{d}_i/\sqrt{n}$ is the following ($p^* \times p^*$) matrix of fourth-order sample moments:

$$\hat{\boldsymbol{\Gamma}} = \sum_{i=1}^n (\mathbf{d}_i - \mathbf{s})(\mathbf{d}_i - \mathbf{s})'/(n - 1). \tag{18}$$

In complex samples, a similar type of estimate of $\boldsymbol{\Gamma}$ can also be developed. Consider a population divided into H strata ($h = 1, 2, \ldots, H$) within each of which I_h primary sample units (PSUs) are randomly chosen (with replacement). Within each PSU further stages of sampling may be undertaken (consider, e.g., two further levels of sampling, with indexes c and t). Define

$$\mathbf{d}_{hi} \equiv \sum_{tc} vech(\mathbf{z}_{hict}\mathbf{z}'_{hict}), \tag{19}$$

where $\mathbf{z}_{hict}$ is the vector value associated with the tth third-stage unit of the cth second-stage unit of the ith PSU of stratum h, with the summation going over all the units within the ith PSU (of course, further levels of sampling could be considered by adding more sub-scripts, besides t and c).

Since within stratum h the $\mathbf{d}_{hi}$'s ($i = 1, \ldots, I_h$) are independent, by standard results (see, e.g., Wolter 1985, chapter 2) an unbiased and consistent estimate of matrix $\boldsymbol{\Gamma}$ is (cf. Skinner, Holt, and Smith 1989, p. 48)

$$\hat{\boldsymbol{\Gamma}} = \sum_{h=1}^{H} \left[\sum_{i=1}^{I_h}(I_h/(I_h - 1))(\mathbf{d}_{hi} - \mathbf{s}_h)(\mathbf{d}_{hi} - \mathbf{s}_h)' \right] /n, \tag{20}$$

where $\mathbf{s}_h \equiv \sum_{i=1}^{I_h}\mathbf{d}_{hi}/I_h$, and n is the total sample size (total number of last-stage sample units over all strata). Note that when $H = 1$ and $I_h = n$ (i.e., when there is only one stratum and each PSU is a final sample unit), then (20) reduces to (18). It should be noted that we require consistency of the above estimate of $\boldsymbol{\Gamma}$. Since consistency holds as the number of PSUs goes to infinity, we may require the number of PSUs to be large if we want the asymptotic approximation to be accurate in applications with large models. In fact, for a small number of PSUs, issues like the comparative quality of the alternative goodness-of-fit statistics T, ST, and AT defined in section 3 above can arise. Other estimates of $\boldsymbol{\Gamma}$, using, for example, Half-Samples or Jackknife methods, can be developed easily at this stage of the analysis (Wolter 1985; Skinner et al. 1989, section 2.13).

Note that since the last column of $\mathbf{z}$ is the constant $c\mathbf{1}$, $\hat{\boldsymbol{\Gamma}}$ is a singular matrix and partitions as

$$\begin{pmatrix} \hat{\boldsymbol{\Gamma}}^* & \mathbf{0} \\ \mathbf{0} & \mathbf{0} \end{pmatrix},$$

where $\hat{\boldsymbol{\Gamma}}^*$ is a matrix of dimensions $(p^* - 1) \times (p^* - 1)$ and $\mathbf{0}$ denotes a zero matrix of appropriate dimensions.

An asymptotically optimal MD analysis (AO-MD) is attained by using the weight matrix

$$\hat{\mathbf{W}}_{AO} = \begin{pmatrix} \hat{\boldsymbol{\Gamma}}^{*-1} & \mathbf{0} \\ \mathbf{0} & \mathbf{0} \end{pmatrix}, \tag{21}$$

since the probability limit of $\hat{\mathbf{W}}_{AO}$, say $\mathbf{W}_{AO}$, satisfies the asymptotic optimality condition of $\mathbf{W}_{AO} \boldsymbol{\Gamma} \mathbf{W}_{AO} = \mathbf{W}_{AO}$. Furthermore, (21) yields a goodness-of-fit statistic T of (14), which is asymptotically equal to $nF(\hat{\boldsymbol{\theta}})$; under the null hypothesis that the model holds, T (or $nF(\hat{\boldsymbol{\theta}})$) is asymptotically chi square with degrees of freedom given by[4] (Satorra 1989, theorem 4.2)

$$\text{rank } (\mathbf{W}) - q = p(p + 1)/2 - q - 1. \tag{22}$$

In the context of covariance structure analysis and independent observations, the AO-MD analysis just described is equivalent to the ADF approach of Browne (1984); for mean and covariance structures it should also be equivalent to the approach of Muthén (1989). Note that the above analysis is asymptotically efficient within the class of MD fitting functions (9); it involves, however, the inversion of a matrix of third- and fourth-order sample moments. This matrix inversion may turn out to be computationally expensive, or inaccurate, or it may not even exist because of small sample size (or a small number of PSUs per stratum). Specifically, $\hat{\boldsymbol{\Gamma}}^*$ is not invertible when n, or the number of PSUs, is lower than $(p^* - 1)p^*/2$.

In fact, as has been noted by a reviewer, there are two reasons to avoid the use of AO-MD analysis in practice. First, the amount of computation implied by AO-MD may be formidable and much more than the PML or NT-MD analyses discussed in the next section. For example, with 10 variables, $\boldsymbol{\Gamma}$ has $(55 \times 56)/2 = 1{,}540$ elements. The computation of this matrix from the sample usually takes much longer than the computation of the matrices involved in the PML analysis of Arminger and Schoenberg (1989). Second, since the matrix $\boldsymbol{\Gamma}$ contains so many elements, its estimate from small data sets is extremely unstable, and AO-MD may thus suffer from lack of robustness against small sample sizes (see Muthén and Kaplan 1985, 1990).

One analysis that may not be asymptotically efficient, but that is conputationally much more feasible than the AO-MD method described above, and that may also be more robust against small samples, consists of using PML or NT-MD together with robust standard errors and a robust goodness-of-fit test statistic. This more convenient approach is described in the next section.

[4]In this AO-MD analysis, to ensure a unique minimizer of (9), the "pseudo" variance ϕ_c should be "fixed" at 1; that is, ϕ_c should not be a free parameter of the model.

5. PML AND NT-MD ANALYSIS

Let $z' = (y', c1)$. Then, under the assumption that y is normally distributed, it can be shown that the loglikelihood function is an affine transformation of (see, e.g., Meredith and Tisak 1990, p. 109–10)

$$F_{ML} = \ln |\Sigma| + \text{tr}S\Sigma^{-1} - \ln |S| - p, \qquad (23)$$

such that the minimization of $F_{ML} = F(S, \Sigma(\theta))$ gives maximum likelihood estimation. The use of F_{ML} when the normality assumption does not necessarily hold is called pseudo maximum likelihood (PML) analysis.

It can be seen that the Hessian matrix $\partial^2 F_{ML}/\partial\sigma\partial\sigma'$ evaluated at (Σ, Σ) is equal to (see, e.g., Neudecker and Satorra 1991)

$$W_{NT} \equiv 2^{-1} D'(\Sigma^{-1} \otimes \Sigma^{-1})D. \qquad (24)$$

Since the asymptotic properties of statistics of interest are characterized by this Hessian matrix (Shapiro 1985; Satorra 1989; Newey 1988), PML is asymptotically equivalent to MD analysis with weight matrix W_{NT}, as given by (24). By NT-MD analysis we mean the use of an MD fitting function (9) with the asymptotic limit of $\hat{W}$ equal to W_{NT} of (24). Obviously, a specific choice for $\hat{W}$ is the matrix of (24) with S substituting for Σ. In the case of covariance structure analysis, this equivalence between PML and NT-MD was first proven by Browne (1974). In fact, the PML estimator can be obtained from a reweighted NT-MD analysis by substituting $\Sigma(\bar{\theta})$ for Σ in (24), where $\bar{\theta}$ is updated iteratively (Browne 1974; Lee and Jennrich 1979; Fuller 1987, section 4.2.2).

It should be noted that the PML and NT-MD analyses defined above are available in conventional software for covariance structure analysis. For example, in the program LISREL (Jöreskog and Sörbom 1989), the minimization of F_{ML} of (23) is invoked when ML is the estimation method, S is the covariance matrix to be analyzed, and model (1) is used.

The asymptotic efficiency of maximum likelihood analysis (e.g., Cox and Hinkley 1974) and the fact that PML is maximum likelihood when y is normally distributed guarantees the asymptotic optimality of PML in case of normality. The above-mentioned equivalence between PML and NT-MD implies that the asymptotic efficiency property of PML also extends to the NT-MD analysis. In fact, when $\mathbf{y}$ is normally distributed, this asymptotic optimality of NT-MD also follows directly from lemma 1 in Appendix A.

When $\mathbf{y}$ is normally distributed, it follows from lemma 2 in Appendix B that the asymptotic variance matrix of $\mathbf{s}$ is given by

$$\boldsymbol{\Gamma} = \boldsymbol{\Gamma}_{NT} \equiv \boldsymbol{\Omega} - 2\mathbf{D}^+(\boldsymbol{\mu}\boldsymbol{\mu}' \otimes \boldsymbol{\mu}\boldsymbol{\mu}')\mathbf{D}^{+'}, \tag{25}$$

where

$$\boldsymbol{\Omega} \equiv 2\mathbf{D}^+(\boldsymbol{\Sigma} \otimes \boldsymbol{\Sigma})\mathbf{D}^{+'} \quad (= \mathbf{W}_{NT}^{-1}). \tag{26}$$

Obviously a consistent estimate of $\boldsymbol{\Omega}$ is obtained by substituting $\mathbf{S}$ for $\boldsymbol{\Sigma}$ in (26). In this case, since it holds that (see lemma 1 in Appendix A)

$$\boldsymbol{\Delta}'\mathbf{W}_{NT}\boldsymbol{\Gamma}_{NT}\mathbf{W}_{NT}\boldsymbol{\Delta} = \boldsymbol{\Delta}'\mathbf{W}_{NT}\boldsymbol{\Delta}, \tag{27}$$

the general expression (11) of $\operatorname{avar}(\hat{\boldsymbol{\theta}})$ simplifies to (12). Further, when $\mathbf{y}$ is normally distributed and $\boldsymbol{\Delta}$ belongs to the space generated by $\boldsymbol{\Gamma}_{NT}$ (which is obviously the case when ϕ_c is set as a fixed parameter of the model), then it can easily be seen that

$$\operatorname{avar} \sqrt{n}(\mathbf{s} - \hat{\boldsymbol{\sigma}}) = (\boldsymbol{\Gamma}_{NT} - \boldsymbol{\Delta}(\boldsymbol{\Delta}'\mathbf{W}_{NT}\boldsymbol{\Delta})^{-1}\boldsymbol{\Delta}'). \tag{28}$$

Hence, the chi-square goodness-of-fit statistic of (14) can be written as (this follows from (A1) and (A3) of lemma 1 in Appendix A):

$$T = n(\mathbf{s} - \hat{\boldsymbol{\sigma}})'[\mathbf{W}_{NT} - \mathbf{W}_{NT}\boldsymbol{\Delta}(\boldsymbol{\Delta}'\mathbf{W}_{NT}\boldsymbol{\Delta})^{-1}\boldsymbol{\Delta}'\mathbf{W}_{NT}](\mathbf{s} - \hat{\boldsymbol{\sigma}}) \tag{29}$$

$$= n(\mathbf{s} - \hat{\boldsymbol{\sigma}})'\boldsymbol{\Delta}_\perp(\boldsymbol{\Delta}'_\perp\boldsymbol{\Omega}\boldsymbol{\Delta}_\perp)^{-1}\boldsymbol{\Delta}'_\perp(\mathbf{s} - \hat{\boldsymbol{\sigma}}),$$

where, in a specific analysis, obvious consistent estimates would replace population values. From the last expression of the equality above, it can be seen that T is asymptotically equivalent to $nF(\hat{\boldsymbol{\theta}})$ (e.g., Satorra 1989). Consequently, $nF(\hat{\boldsymbol{\theta}})$ is also asymptotically chi square when the model holds. That is, the conventional standard errors and goodness-of-fit statistics obtained by a computer program for the analysis of covariance structures when $\mathbf{S}$ is analyzed as the covariance matrix are correct when $\mathbf{y}$ is normally distributed.

For general distributions of $\mathbf{s}$ (i.e., when $\mathbf{y}$ is not normally distributed), it follows from the general theory of sections 3 and 4 that asymptotic robust (i.e., correct for any distribution of $\mathbf{y}$) standard errors and an asymptotic robust chi-square statistic are obtained by substituting $\hat{\Gamma}$ of (18) or (20) for Γ in (11) and (15). This approach produces what we call (asymptotic) robust standard errors of estimates and the robust chi-square goodness-of-fit statistic, respectively.

With regard to computational aspects of these robust standard errors and the robust chi-square goodness-of-fit statistic, substituting $\hat{\Gamma}$ of (18) for Γ in (11), the following variance matrix of estimates is obtained:

$$\widehat{\text{avar}}(\hat{\boldsymbol{\theta}}) = n^{-1}(\boldsymbol{\Delta}'\hat{\mathbf{W}}\boldsymbol{\Delta})^{-1}[\sum_{i=1}^{n} \boldsymbol{\ell}_i\boldsymbol{\ell}_i'/(n - 1)](\boldsymbol{\Delta}'\hat{\mathbf{W}}\boldsymbol{\Delta})^{-1}, \quad (30)$$

where

$$\boldsymbol{\ell}_i \equiv \boldsymbol{\Delta}'\hat{\mathbf{W}}(\mathbf{d}_i - \mathbf{s}), \quad (31)$$

$\mathbf{d}_i \equiv \text{vech}(\mathbf{z}_i\mathbf{z}_i')$, $i = 1, 2, \ldots, n$, and the derivative matrix $\boldsymbol{\Delta}$ is evaluated at $\hat{\boldsymbol{\theta}}$. Note that this step of computing standard errors requires a second pass through the data in order to compute the q-dimensional vectors $\boldsymbol{\ell}_i$. When $\mathbf{W} = \mathbf{W}_{NT}$, then the jth element ℓ_i, $j = 1, 2, \ldots, q$, can be expressed as

$$[\ell_i]_j = [\boldsymbol{\Delta}'\hat{\mathbf{W}}_{NT}(\mathbf{d}_i - \mathbf{s})]_j = 2^{-1}\text{tr}(\hat{\boldsymbol{\Sigma}}^{-1}(\mathbf{z}_i\mathbf{z}_i' - \mathbf{S})\hat{\boldsymbol{\Sigma}}^{-1}(\partial\boldsymbol{\Sigma}(\hat{\boldsymbol{\theta}})/\partial\theta_j)). \quad (32)$$

In fact, the consistent asymptotic variance matrix estimate given by the expression (32) above parallels Arminger and Schoenberg's (1989) computation of robust standard errors: "The asymptotic co-variance matrix can be estimated consistently without computing the empirical fourth-order moment matrix of the data" (p. 410; see also formula (24), p. 414). Arminger and Schoenberg's method of com-puting the variance of the estimates may be computationally faster than using expression (11) of section 3 with consistent estimates replacing population matrices (with $\hat{\Gamma}$ of (18) replacing Γ).

Further, another way to compute the test statistic T of (14) is as follows. Let $\hat{\boldsymbol{\Delta}}_\perp'$ denote the orthogonal complement of $\boldsymbol{\Delta}$ evaluated at $\hat{\boldsymbol{\theta}}$. Then in (14) one could use

$$\hat{\mathbf{A}} = \hat{\boldsymbol{\Delta}}_\perp\left[\sum_{i=1}^{n} \mathbf{b}_i\mathbf{b}_i'/(n - 1)\right]^{-}\hat{\boldsymbol{\Delta}}_\perp', \quad (33)$$

where $\mathbf{b}_i \equiv \hat{\boldsymbol{\Delta}}_\perp'(\mathbf{d}_i - \mathbf{s})$, $i = 1, 2, \ldots, n$. Note that the $\mathbf{b}_i$ are also of reduced dimension $((p^* - q)$-dimensional$)$, hence only the inversion of a matrix of dimension $(p^* - q) \times (p^* - q)$ is required to compute the chi-square goodness-of-fit statistic T. Finally, a consistent estimate of the scaling correction κ of (17) can easily be seen to be

$$\hat{\kappa} = [\sum_{i=1}^{n} \mathbf{b}_i'(\hat{\mathbf{\Delta}}_\perp'\hat{\mathbf{W}}^{-1}\hat{\mathbf{\Delta}}_\perp)^{-1}\mathbf{b}_i]/nr$$

$$= \text{tr}[(\hat{\mathbf{\Delta}}_\perp'\hat{\mathbf{W}}^{-1}\hat{\mathbf{\Delta}}_\perp)^{-1}(\sum_{i=1}^{n} \mathbf{b}_i\mathbf{b}_i'/n)]/r, \qquad (34)$$

and this computation requires only an inversion of a matrix of dimension $(p^* - q) \times (p^* - q)$.

In fact, the value $\mathbf{b}_i' (\hat{\mathbf{\Delta}}_\perp'\hat{\mathbf{W}}^{-1}\hat{\mathbf{\Delta}}_\perp)^{-1}\mathbf{b}_i$ can be interpreted as the "influence" of observation i on the departure of $nF(\hat{\boldsymbol{\theta}})$ from a chi-square distribution (the influence being nil when such a value equals r). Obviously, the same type of computational considerations apply in complex samples, where the estimate (20) for $\boldsymbol{\Gamma}$ is used instead of (18).

Note that the above computational considerations, and the fact that for NT-MD analysis the quadratic function (9) can be written as (Browne 1974) $F = 2^{-1}\text{tr}\{[(\mathbf{S} - \mathbf{\Sigma}(\boldsymbol{\theta}))\mathbf{\Sigma}^{-1}]^2\}$, where $\mathbf{\Sigma}$ is substituted by a consistent estimate, enable us to perform NT-MD analysis without explicitly computing the usually large $p^* \times p^*$ matrix $\boldsymbol{\Gamma}$.

The next section shows situations in which inferences based on the assumption that $\mathbf{y}$ is normally distributed can be trusted even when $\mathbf{y}$ is non-normally distributed.

6. ASYMPTOTIC ROBUSTNESS OF INFERENCES BASED ON SECOND-ORDER MOMENTS

Let the linear relation (4) be such that

$$\mathbf{z} = \sum_{i=1}^{L-1} \mathbf{A}_i(\tau)\boldsymbol{\delta}_i + \boldsymbol{\mu}(\tau)c\mathbf{1}, \qquad (35)$$

where $\mathbf{A}_i(\tau)$, $i = 1, 2, \ldots, L - 1$, and $\boldsymbol{\mu}(\tau)$ are (continuously differentiable) functions of τ, a t-dimensional subvector of the parameter vector $\boldsymbol{\theta}$. Let the moment matrices of non-normally distributed $\boldsymbol{\delta}_i$'s be unconstrained; that is, let

$$\boldsymbol{\theta} = [\tau', \omega']', \qquad (36)$$

where ω is the vector formed by stacking the second-order moments vech $\boldsymbol{\Phi}_{ii}$'s of non-normally distributed δ_i's. The moment matrices $\boldsymbol{\Phi}_{ii}$'s of normally distributed δ_i's are considered to be (continuously differentiable) symmetric matrix-valued functions of τ; that is, they may be constrained. Let the estimator $\hat{\boldsymbol{\theta}}$ be partitioned as $\hat{\boldsymbol{\theta}} = [\hat{\tau}', \hat{\omega}']'$, according to (36). The results of this section are summarized by the following theorem.

Theorem 1. Assume that the random variables δ_i in (35) above are mutually independent (not only uncorrelated). Then for PML and MD analyses (given any choice of weight matrix $\mathbf{W}$), it is verified that
(a) The goodness-of-fit statistic T of (14) and (15) with $\boldsymbol{\Omega}$ substituting for $\boldsymbol{\Gamma}$ is asymptotically chi square when the model holds;
(b) The $t \times t$ leading principal submatrix of avar($\hat{\boldsymbol{\theta}}$) of (11) with $\boldsymbol{\Omega}$ substituting for $\boldsymbol{\Gamma}$ gives the correct asymptotic variance matrix of the estimator $\hat{\tau}$ of τ.

Proof. See Appendix B.

In section 5 it was shown that when $\mathbf{z} = (\mathbf{y}', c1)'$ and $\mathbf{y}$ is normally distributed, using $\mathbf{S}$ as the covariance matrix in conventional software for covariance structure analysis produces correct asymptotic inferences. The theorem above shows that correct asymptotic inferences are also produced when $\mathbf{y}$ is non-normally distributed, provided that the conditions of the theorem hold and, in the case of standard errors, that attention is restricted to the estimate of the subvector of parameters τ. The theorem also shows the validity of the usual NT chi-square goodness-of-fit test statistic, $nF_{\mathrm{NT}}(\hat{\boldsymbol{\theta}})$, when the normality assumption is violated. (Remember that $nF_{\mathrm{NT}}(\hat{\boldsymbol{\theta}})$ is asymptotically equivalent to T of (29); hence, both have the same asymptotic robustness properties.)

A fundamental assumption turns out to be the independence, and not only zero correlation, between the basic random constituents of the model, the δ_i's. Restricted to covariance structure analysis and PML (or NT-MD) estimation, results similar to (a) and (b) were derived by Anderson (1987, 1989), Anderson and Amemiya (1988), Amemiya and Anderson (1990), Browne and Shapiro (1988), and Mooijaart and Bentler (1991). For the general type of discrepancy functions (such as PML and MD with any choice of W), but also confined to the context of covariance structure analysis, (a) and (b) were derived by Satorra and Bentler (1990).

More recently, Browne (1990) has considered asymptotic robustness in the context of mean and covariance structures, for PML and NT-MD estimation. For PML and NT-MD estimation, result (a) is in agreement with the corresponding results of Browne (1990). Result (b) of the theorem, however, is different from Browne's corresponding result, since we are concerned only with correctness of the standard errors of estimates of τ, and not with the asymptotic efficiency of the whole estimate of θ. Our result is more general in that we do not need to impose conditions on the third-order moment of the δ_i's (namely, zero third-order moments) to attain asymptotic robustness when means are restricted. In both (a) and (b) we deal with more general types of estimators than those considered by Browne.

Note that the theorem above applies to MD analysis with any choice of weight matrix $\mathbf{W}$. For example, $\mathbf{W}$ could in fact be the identity matrix, as in unweighted least squares (ULS) analysis. In this case of ULS, the theorem above says that the variance matrix of the estimate of τ, as well as the chi-square goodness-of-fit statistic, obtained under a normal-theory assumption (i.e., by using an estimate of Ω instead of the consistent estimate of Γ) is valid for general types of distribution of y when the conditions of the theorem hold.[5] In fact the current version of LISREL provides such normal-theory standard errors for ULS estimates, which are correct even for nonnormal data when the conditions of the theorem hold.

In the next section we provide a concrete illustration of theoretical aspects of the paper by considering different types of data in the context of the SUR model presented in section 2.

7. ILLUSTRATION

Consider the SUR model specified in (5) with the parameter values shown in the first column of Table 1. Remember that model (5) assumes that the variables ζ_1, ζ_2, x, and u are uncorrelated, and since intercepts are restricted to being equal, it implies restrictions on the means of the observable variables. Hence, this model restricts means and covariances of observable variables.

[5]Note that for the conditions of the theorem to hold, the pseudo parameter ϕ_c should be a free parameter of the model. See Appendix B.

Three cases are considered. The data in case 1 are non-normal but independence between ζ_1, ζ_2, x, and u (these are the δ_i's of theorem 1) cannot be assumed. (In fact, ζ_1, ζ_2, and u were heteroskedastic with variance changing with x.) In this case the AO methods of section 4 are required for an efficient statistical inference. In the generally nonoptimal PML or NT-MD analysis, robust standard errors and a robust goodness-of-fit statistic are required for correct asymptotic inferences.

In case 2, variables ζ_1, ζ_2, x, and u were chosen to be mutually independent centered chi-square distributions with one degree of freedom (rescaled to have variance equal to one). Here the data are non-normal, but the conditions for asymptotic robustness, like the independence between ζ_1, ζ_2, x, and u, hold. Consequently, usual PML (or NT-MD) analysis gives a correct chi-square goodness-of-fit statistic and correct standard errors for some of the parameters of interest.

The data in case 3 were clustered in 20 groups of size 25 with high intraclass correlation (0.8); that is, the observations are not independent.

The Monte Carlo study consisted of 1,000 simulations of a sample of size $n = 500$ from model (5), with (population) values of the parameters as shown in the first column of each table (same values in all tables) and three different distributions (cases 1–3). NT-MD analysis was performed with S substituting for Σ in (24). The robust standard errors and the robust chi-square statistic were computed as explained above in section 3. Summary statistics of the Monte Carlo results are presented in the corresponding tables. In each table, columns (1) and (2) provide information about the consistency of estimates, and columns (3), (4), and (5) provide information about the consistency of the NT and robust estimates of standard errors.

Table 1 summarizes the Monte Carlo results for case 1. The results clearly show that with this type of data, robust standard errors and a robust chi-square goodness-of-fit statistic are required for NT-MD analysis. In this table, the scaled goodness-of-fit statistic ST performs better than T.

Table 2 shows the results for case 2. In this case the basic random constituents of the model are independent, so theorem 1 above guarantees that the usual normal-theory chi-square test statis-

TABLE 1

Monte Carlo Results (1,000 Replications) for NT-MD Parameter Estimates and Different Types of Standard Errors and Test Statistics. Case 1: Non-Normal Data Produced by Heteroskedasticity on ζ_i's and ε ($n = 500$).

	True Values	Monte Carlo Mean of Parameter Estimates	Monte Carlo Standard Deviation of Parameter Estimates	Monte Carlo Mean of NT Standard Errors	Monte Carlo Mean of Robust Standard Errors
ϕ_{11}	1.00	0.97	0.70	0.22*	0.67
ϕ_{22}	1.00	0.97	0.67	0.22*	0.67
ϕ_{33}	8.00	7.84	0.71	0.54*	0.70
ψ	0.80	0.77	0.21	0.05*	0.18
β	4.00	4.00	0.12	0.06*	0.12
α	8.00	7.99	0.20	0.17*	0.20
μ	1.00	0.99	0.14	0.13*	0.13

Chi-Square Statistics

	Mean	Variance	Reject. Freq. 10%/5%/1%
Expected (χ^2, $df = 2$)	2.00	4.00	100/50/10
$nF(\hat{\theta})$	5.93*	41.73*	422*/340*/209*
T	1.96	3.18	83/32/6
ST	1.97	4.21	103/64/9
(κ)	(3.06)		

*Not necessarily robust

tic can be trusted and that the usual standard errors of estimates of β, α, and μ are asymptotically correct. However, the usual normal-theory standard errors of estimates of the ϕ's and ψ are not necessarily correct.

In case 3 the observations are not independent. In this case, the specific estimate (20) of Γ that takes into account the clustered structure of the observations was used. Note that here the number of groups is small; hence, the AO analysis of section 4 would have to face a singular matrix $\hat{\Gamma}^*$. The results of the simulation are described in Table 3. Clearly, robust standard errors as well as the robust chi-square statistics are required in this case. Note that in this table, the

TABLE 2
Monte Carlo Results (1,000 Replications) for NT-MD Parameter Estimates
and Different Types of Standard Errors and Test Statistics.
Case 2: Non-Normal Data Produced by Independent Chi-Square
Distributions of 1 df (n = 500)

	True Values	Monte Carlo Mean of Parameter Estimates	Monte Carlo Standard Deviation of Parameter Estimates	Monte Carlo Mean of NT Standard Errors	Monte Carlo Mean of Robust Standard Errors
ϕ_{11}	1.00	0.99	0.27	0.23*	0.27
ϕ_{22}	1.00	1.00	0.27	0.23*	0.27
ϕ_{33}	8.00	8.01	1.35	0.56*	1.29
ψ	0.80	0.80	0.13	0.05*	0.13
β	4.00	4.00	0.06	0.06	0.06
α	8.00	8.00	0.17	0.17	0.17
μ	1.00	1.00	0.14	0.13	0.13

Chi-Square Statistics

	Mean	Variance	Reject. Freq. 10%/5%/1%
Expected (χ^2, df = 2)	2.00	4.00	100/50/10
$nF(\hat{\theta})$	1.92	3.35	95/42/5
T	1.95	3.36	93/43/5
ST	1.95	3.42	94/45/7
(κ)	(1.00)		

*Not necessarily robust

scaled chi-square statistic ST shows slightly better performance than
the robust statistic T.

8. CONCLUSIONS

We have discussed general approaches to inference for structural equation models that impose restrictions on the means and
covariances of the vector z of observable variables. The emphasis has
been on drawing correct statistical inferences regardless of the distribution of z and the estimation method used. Asymptotic robust stan-

TABLE 3

Monte Carlo Results (1,000 Replications) for NT-MD Parameter Estimates and Different Types of Standard Errors and Test Statistics. Case 3: Non-Independent Observations ($n = 500$)

	True Values	Monte Carlo Mean of Parameter Estimates	Monte Carlo Standard Deviation of Parameter Estimates	Monte Carlo Mean of NT Standard Errors	Monte Carlo Mean of Robust Standard Errors
ϕ_{11}	1.00	0.88	0.42	0.23*	0.41
ϕ_{22}	1.00	0.88	0.42	0.23*	0.42
ϕ_{33}	8.00	7.14	1.90	0.51*	1.71
ψ	0.80	0.80	0.05	0.05*	0.05
β	4.00	4.02	0.08	0.06*	0.07
α	8.00	7.99	0.24	0.19*	0.24
μ	1.00	1.01	0.60	0.13*	0.57

Chi-Square Statistics

	Mean	Variance	Reject. Freq. 10%/5%/1%
Expected (χ^2, $df = 2$)	2.00	4.00	100/50/10
$nF(\hat{\theta})$	29.97*	668.83*	873*/848*/774*
T	2.27	5.54	137/73/17
ST	1.95	3.66	92/45/8
(κ)	(16.49)		

Note: The observations are clustered in 20 groups of size 25 with an intraclass correlation of 0.8.

*Not necessarily robust

dard errors and an (asymptotic) robust chi-square goodness-of-fit statistic have been derived for PML and MD analyses, encompassing the case of multistage complex samples.

Recent results on asymptotic robustness of normal-theory methods (Satorra and Bentler 1990) have been extended to a more general model in which restrictions on means are also allowed. In this more general context, the correct expression for Γ is replaced by a matrix Ω that is a function of second-order moments and does not equal Γ even under normality. When the usual assumption of uncorrelation among random constituents of the model is replaced by the stronger assumption of independence (and no restrictions are imposed on the variances and covariances of non-normally distributed constituents of the model), the robust inferential statistics are not required.

In practice, when the conditions for asymptotic robustness of theorem 1 hold, then in large samples the deviation between the usual (nonrobust) and robust standard errors, and between the robust and nonrobust chi-square goodness-of-fit statistics, indicate that the assumption of independence does not hold and that the robust inferential statistics should be trusted. Such a discrepancy between robust and nonrobust inferential statistics is to be expected, for example, when the variance of the error terms varies across cases (i.e., under heteroskedasticity), a situation in which robust inferential statistics are certainly required.

As argued at the end of section 4, AO-MD methods create excessive computational burden and suffer from lack of robustness against small samples. In fact, regardless of the distribution of the data, our general recommendation is to use PML or NT-MD analyses together with robust inferential statistics. As discussed in section 5, these methods imply a minimal increase in computational burden and require minimal modifications to the software currently in use.

APPENDIX A: RESULTS OF PML AND NT-MD ANALYSES

Lemma 1. Let $\mathbf{W}_{NT}$ and $\boldsymbol{\Gamma}_{NT}$ be the matrices defined in (24) and (25), respectively. It holds that

$$\boldsymbol{\Gamma}_{NT}\mathbf{W}_{Nt}\boldsymbol{\Gamma}_{NT} = \boldsymbol{\Gamma}_{NT}. \tag{A1}$$

If $\boldsymbol{\Delta}$ is in the column space of $\boldsymbol{\Gamma}_{NT}$, then

$$\boldsymbol{\Delta}'\mathbf{W}_{NT}\boldsymbol{\Gamma}_{NT}\mathbf{W}_{NT}\boldsymbol{\Delta} = \boldsymbol{\Delta}'\mathbf{W}_{NT}\boldsymbol{\Delta} \tag{A2}$$

and

$$(\boldsymbol{\Gamma}_{NT} - \boldsymbol{\Delta}(\boldsymbol{\Delta}'\mathbf{W}_{NT}\boldsymbol{\Delta})^{-1}\boldsymbol{\Delta}')\mathbf{Q}(\boldsymbol{\Gamma}_{NT} - \boldsymbol{\Delta}(\boldsymbol{\Delta}'\mathbf{W}_{NT}\boldsymbol{\Delta})^{-1}\boldsymbol{\Delta}')$$
$$= (\boldsymbol{\Gamma}_{NT} - \boldsymbol{\Delta}(\boldsymbol{\Delta}'\mathbf{W}_{NT}\boldsymbol{\Delta})^{-1}\boldsymbol{\Delta}'), \tag{A3}$$

where $\mathbf{Q} \equiv (\mathbf{W}_{NT} - \mathbf{W}_{NT}\boldsymbol{\Delta}(\boldsymbol{\Delta}'\mathbf{W}_{NT}\boldsymbol{\Delta})^{-1}\boldsymbol{\Delta}'\mathbf{W}_{NT})$.

If Δ and $(s - \sigma(\theta))$ are in the column space of Γ_{NT}, then the MD estimator associated with $W = W_{NT}$ is the same as that associated with $W = \Gamma_{NT}^-$ (for any choice of g-inverse).

Proof. Since it is verified that $\mu'\Sigma^{-1}\mu = 1$,

$$[2D^+(\mu\mu' \otimes mm')D^{+'}][(1/2)D'(\Sigma^{-1} \otimes \Sigma^{-1})D][2D^+(\mu\mu' \otimes \mu\mu')D^{+'}]$$

$$= 2D^+(\mu\mu' \otimes \mu\mu')D^{+'}.$$

Consequently,

$$\Gamma_{NT}W_{NT}\Gamma_{NT} = (W_{NT}^{-1} - Y)W_{NT}(W_{NT}^{-1} - Y)$$
$$= W_{NT}^{-1} - 2Y + YW_{NT}Y = (W_{NT}^{-1} - Y) = \Gamma_{NT},$$

where $Y \equiv 2D^+(\mu\mu' \otimes \mu\mu')D^{+'}$, which proves (A1) of the lemma.

Results (A2) and (A3) follow trivially from (A1) and the stated condition that Δ should be in the column space of Γ_{NT}.

Note that the MD estimator $\hat{\theta}$ is the root of the matrix equation $\Delta'W(s - \sigma(\theta)) = 0$. By hypothesis, there is a matrix R and a vector R^* such that $\Delta = \Gamma_{NT}R$ and $(s - \sigma(\theta)) = \Gamma_{NT}R^*$. Therefore,

$$\Delta'W(s - \sigma(\theta)) = R'\Gamma_{NT}W\Gamma_{NT}R^* = R'\Gamma_{NT}R^*.$$

Hence the root of $\Delta'W_{NT}(s - \sigma(\theta)) = 0$ does not depend on the choice of g-inverse. From (A1) note that a choice of g-inverse is in fact W_{NT}.

Note that the equality (A2) of lemma 1 is the condition 6* of Satorra (1989 p. 137), which guarantees the correctness of the simpler expression (12) for the variance matrix of estimates (see also Shapiro 1987). Note that in the models defined in section 2, the condition of Δ to be in the column space of Γ_{NT} is trivially verified when the pseudo variance ϕ_c is a fixed parameter.

APPENDIX B: PROOF OF THEOREM 1

Consider first the simple case in which each moment matrix $\Phi_{ii} \equiv E\delta_i\delta_i'$, $i = 1, 2, \ldots, L$, is a (symmetric) free matrix, thus the parameter vector θ partitions as

$$\theta = [\tau',(\text{vech } \Phi_{11})', \ldots,(\text{vech } \Phi_{ii})', \ldots,(\text{vech } \Phi_{LL})']',$$

as in (36). Since (3) implies

$$\boldsymbol{\sigma} \equiv \mathrm{E} \, \mathrm{vech} \, (\mathbf{z}\mathbf{z}') = \sum_{i=1}^{L} \mathbf{D}^+ (\mathbf{A}_i \otimes \mathbf{A}_i) \, \mathbf{D}\mathrm{vech} \, \boldsymbol{\Phi}_{ii},$$

the derivative matrix $\boldsymbol{\Delta} \equiv (\partial/\partial\boldsymbol{\theta}')\boldsymbol{\sigma}(\boldsymbol{\theta})$ partitions as

$$\boldsymbol{\Delta} = [\boldsymbol{\Delta}_1, \mathbf{D}^+ (\mathbf{A}_1 \otimes \mathbf{A}_1)\mathbf{D}, \ldots, \mathbf{D}^+ (\mathbf{A}_i \otimes \mathbf{A}_i)\mathbf{D}, \ldots, \mathbf{D}^+ (\mathbf{A}_L \otimes \mathbf{A}_L)\mathbf{D}]$$
$$= [\boldsymbol{\Delta}_1, \boldsymbol{\Delta}_2], \qquad\qquad (\mathrm{B1})$$

say, where $\boldsymbol{\Delta}_1 \equiv (\partial/\partial\boldsymbol{\tau}')\boldsymbol{\sigma}(\boldsymbol{\theta})$ is a $p^* \times t$ matrix.

The following results will be needed.

Lemma 2. (cf. Satorra 1991) Let $\mathbf{z} = \Sigma_{i=1}^{L} \mathbf{A}_i \boldsymbol{\delta}_i$, as in (3), where the $\boldsymbol{\delta}_i$'s are mutually independent and of zero mean, with the exception of $\boldsymbol{\delta}_L$, a scalar-variate constant equal to 1. Then

$$\boldsymbol{\Gamma} = \boldsymbol{\Omega} + \sum_{i=1}^{L-1} \{2\mathbf{D}^+ (\mathbf{A}_i \otimes \mathbf{A}_L)[\mathrm{E} \, \boldsymbol{\delta}_i(\mathrm{vech} \, \boldsymbol{\delta}_i\boldsymbol{\delta}_i')'] \, \mathbf{D}'(\mathbf{A}_i \otimes \mathbf{A}_i)'\mathbf{D}^{+\prime}$$
$$+ 2\mathbf{D}^+ (\mathbf{A}_i \otimes \mathbf{A}_i)\mathbf{D} \, [\mathrm{E}(\mathrm{vech} \, \boldsymbol{\delta}_i\boldsymbol{\delta}_i')\boldsymbol{\delta}_i'] \, (\mathbf{A}_i \otimes \mathbf{A}_L)'\mathbf{D}^{+\prime} \qquad (\mathrm{B2})$$
$$+ \mathbf{D}^+ (\mathbf{A}_i \otimes \mathbf{A}_i)\mathbf{D}[\mathrm{var}(\mathrm{vech}\boldsymbol{\delta}_i\boldsymbol{\delta}_i') - 2 \, \mathbf{D}^+\mathrm{E}(\boldsymbol{\delta}_i\boldsymbol{\delta}_i')\otimes$$
$$\mathrm{E}(\boldsymbol{\delta}_i\boldsymbol{\delta}_i')\mathbf{D}^{+\prime}] \, \mathbf{D}'(\mathbf{A}_i \otimes \mathbf{A}_i)'\mathbf{D}^{+\prime}\}$$
$$- 2\mathbf{D}^+ (\boldsymbol{\mu} \otimes \boldsymbol{\mu})(\boldsymbol{\mu} \otimes \boldsymbol{\mu})'\mathbf{D}^{+\prime},$$

where

$$\boldsymbol{\Omega} = 2\mathbf{D}^+ (\boldsymbol{\Sigma} \otimes \boldsymbol{\Sigma})\mathbf{D}^{+\prime}$$

and

$$\boldsymbol{\mu} = \mathrm{E}\mathbf{z} = \mathbf{A}_L.$$

Note. We could, of course, write $\mathbf{D}^+ (\boldsymbol{\mu} \otimes \boldsymbol{\mu})(\boldsymbol{\mu} \otimes \boldsymbol{\mu})'\mathbf{D}^{+\prime} = \mathbf{D}^+ (\boldsymbol{\mu}\boldsymbol{\mu}' \otimes \boldsymbol{\mu}\boldsymbol{\mu}')\mathbf{D}^{+\prime}$.

Proof. See Satorra (1991).

Since $\boldsymbol{\Delta}_\perp'\boldsymbol{\Delta} = 0$,

$$\boldsymbol{\Delta}_\perp'\mathbf{D}^+ (\mathbf{A}_i \otimes \mathbf{A}_i) \, \mathbf{D} = 0, \qquad\qquad (\mathrm{B3})$$

for $i = 1, 2, \ldots, L$. Consequently, given the form of $\boldsymbol{\Gamma}$ in (B2), it is verified that

$$\boldsymbol{\Delta}_\perp(\boldsymbol{\Delta}_\perp'\boldsymbol{\Gamma}\boldsymbol{\Delta}_\perp)^-\boldsymbol{\Delta}_\perp' = \boldsymbol{\Delta}_\perp(\boldsymbol{\Delta}_\perp'\boldsymbol{\Omega}\boldsymbol{\Delta}_\perp)^-\boldsymbol{\Delta}_\perp'. \qquad\qquad (\mathrm{B4})$$

Hence, result (a) of the theorem is proved. When the parameter ϕ_c is a fixed parameter, then $\Delta_\perp(\Delta_\perp'\Gamma_{NT}\Delta_\perp)^-\Delta_\perp' = \Delta_\perp(\Delta_\perp'\Omega\Delta_\perp)^-\Delta_\perp'$.

Clearly, when

$$\Gamma \equiv (\Omega + \Delta_2 C \Delta_2' + \Delta_2 B + B'\Delta_2'), \tag{B5}$$

which is the form of Γ given by (B2), for any matrix W it holds that the matrix

$$[(\Delta'W\Delta)^{-1}\Delta'W\Gamma W\Delta(\Delta'W\Delta)^{-1}]_{t \times t}, \tag{B6}$$

where t is the dimension of the subvector τ of θ, is free of the matrices B and C. Consequently, setting B and C equal to zero, it holds that

$$[(\Delta'W\Delta)^{-1}\Delta'W\Gamma W\Delta(\Delta'W\Delta)^{-1}]_{t \times t}$$
$$= [(\Delta'W\Delta)^{-1}\Delta'W\Omega W\Delta(\Delta'W\Delta)^{-1}]_{t \times t}, \tag{B7}$$

which, from the expression of the asymptotic variance matrix of estimates of (11), proves part (b) of the theorem.

It should be noted that the form (B5) of Γ corresponds to the case where the pseudo parameter ϕ_c is a free parameter of the model. When ϕ_c is a parameter fixed at 1, then (B5) changes to

$$\Gamma \equiv (\Gamma_{NT} + \Delta_2 C \Delta_2' + \Delta_2 B + B'\Delta_2'), \tag{B8}$$

in which case we get

$$[(\Delta'W\Delta)^{-1}\Delta'W\Gamma W\Delta(\Delta'W\Delta)^{-1}]_{t \times t}$$
$$= [(\Delta'W\Delta)^{-1}\Delta'W\Gamma_{NT}W\Delta(\Delta'W\Delta)^{-1}]_{t \times t}. \tag{B9}$$

Consequently, when ϕ_c is a fixed parameter, the correctness of the NT standard errors of estimates of τ, that is, those provided by the matrix

$$[(\Delta'W\Delta)^{-1}\Delta'W\Omega W\Delta(\Delta'W\Delta)^{-1}]_{t \times t},$$

is not guaranteed for arbitrary W. It is guaranteed when $W = W_{NT}$, since in that case it is verified that $\Delta'W\Gamma_{NT}W\Delta = \Delta'W\Omega W\Delta$. For arbitrary weight matrix W, the validity of the NT standard errors requires ϕ_c to be a free parameter of the model, which is of course estimated at the value 1. For example, in ULS analysis, where W is the identity matrix, the usual NT estimates of standard errors of $\hat{\tau}$ are correct when the analysis is performed specifying ϕ_c to be free (this prompts a note in section 6). It should be noted that setting ϕ_c as a free or fixed parameter has implications only for the computation of standard errors of estimates (parameter estimates and the chi-square goodness-of-fit statistic are the same).

Now suppose that the matrices $\boldsymbol{\Phi}_{ii}$ ($i \neq L$) corresponding to normally distributed $\boldsymbol{\delta}_i$'s are also restricted to being functions of $\boldsymbol{\tau}$. Note that if $\boldsymbol{\delta}_i$ is normally distributed, then $[\mathrm{E}\ \boldsymbol{\delta}_i(\mathrm{vech}\ \boldsymbol{\delta}_i\boldsymbol{\delta}_i')']$ and $[\mathrm{var}(\mathrm{vech}\ \boldsymbol{\delta}_i\boldsymbol{\delta}_i') - 2\mathbf{D}^+\mathrm{E}(\boldsymbol{\delta}_i\boldsymbol{\delta}_i') \otimes \mathrm{E}(\boldsymbol{\delta}_i\boldsymbol{\delta}_i')\mathbf{D}^{+'}]$ are zero matrices. Hence, there will be a correspondence between the elements of the partition (B1) of $\boldsymbol{\Delta}$ that drop out from $\boldsymbol{\Delta}_2$ (because some $\boldsymbol{\Phi}_{ii}$ are functions of $\boldsymbol{\tau}$) and the terms of (B2) that vanish (because some $\boldsymbol{\delta}_i$ are normally distributed). Consequently, the same results (a) and (b) of the theorem apply when the covariance matrices of normally distributed $\boldsymbol{\delta}_i$'s are restricted to being functions of $\boldsymbol{\tau}$.

REFERENCES

Amemiya, Y., and T. W. Anderson. 1990. "Asymptotic Chi-Square Tests for a Large Class of Factor Analysis Models." *The Annals of Statistics* 3: 1453–63.

Anderson, T. W. 1987. "Multivariate Linear Relations." Pp. 9–36 in *Proceedings of the Second International Conference in Statistics,* edited by T. Pukkila and S. Puntanen. Tampere, Finland: University of Tampere.

———. 1989. "Linear Latent Variable Models and Covariance Structures." *Journal of Econometrics* 41: 91–119.

Anderson, T. W., and Y. Amemiya. 1988. "The Asymptotic Normal Distribution of Estimators in Factor Analysis under General Conditions." *The Annals of Statistics* 16:759–71.

Arminger, G., and R. J. Schoenberg. 1989. "Pseudo-Maximum Likelihood Estimation and a Test for Misspecification in Mean and Covariance Structure Models." *Psychometrika* 54: 409–25.

Arminger, G., and M. E. Sobel. 1990. "Pseudo-Maximum Likelihood Estimation of Mean and Covariance Structures with Missing Data." *Journal of the American Statistical Association* 85: 195–203.

Bentler, P. M. 1983a. "Some Contributions to Efficient Statistics for Structural Models: Specification and Estimation of Moment Structures." *Psychometrika* 48: 493–517.

———. 1983b. "Simultaneous Equation Systems as Moment Structure Models." *Journal of Econometrics* 22: 13–42.

———. 1989. *EQS Structural Equations Program Manual.* Los Angeles: BMDP Statistical Software Inc.

Bentler, P. M., and T. Dijkstra. 1985. "Efficient Estimation via Linearization in Structural Models." Pp. 9–42 in *Multivariate Analysis VI,* edited by P. R. Krishnaiah. Amsterdam: North-Holland.

Bollen, K. A., 1989. *Structural Equations with Latent Variables.* New York: Wiley.

Browne, M. W. 1974. "Generalized Least Squares Estimators in the Analysis of Covariance Structures." *South African Statistical Journal* 8: 1–24.

―――. 1984. "Asymptotically Distribution-Free Methods for the Analysis of Covariance Structures." *British Journal of Mathematical and Statistical Psychology* 37: 62–83.

―――. 1990. "Asymptotic Robustness of Normal Theory Methods for the Analysis of Latent Curves." Pp. 211–225 in *Statistical Analysis of Measurement Errors and Applications,* edited by P. J. Brown and W. A. Fuller. Providence, RI: American Mathematical Society.

Browne, M. W., and A. Shapiro. 1988. "Robustness of Normal Theory Methods in the Analysis of Linear Latent Variable Models." *British Journal of Mathematical and Statistical Psychology* 41: 193–208.

Chamberlain, G. 1982. "Multivariate Regression Models for Panel Data." *Journal of Econometrics* 18: 5–46.

Chiang, C. L. 1956. "On Regular Best Asymptotically Normal Estimates." *Annals of Mathematical Statistics* 27: 336–351.

Cox, D., and D. V. Hinkley. 1974. *Theoretical Statistics*. London: Chapman and Hall.

Ferguson, T. 1958. "A Method of Generating Best Asymptotically Normal Estimates with Application to the Estimation of Bacterial Densities." *Annals of Mathematical Statistics* 29: 1046–62.

Fuller, W. A. 1987. *Measurement Error Models*. New York: Wiley.

Hansen, L. P. 1982. "Large Sample Properties of Generalized Method of Moments Estimators." *Econometrica* 50: 1029–54.

Jöreskog, K. 1981. "Analysis of Covariance Structures" *Scandinavian Journal of Statistics* 8: 65–92.

Jöreskog, K., and D. Sörbom. 1984. *LISREL IV: A Guide to the Program and Applications*. Chicago: International Testing Services.

―――. 1989. *LISREL 7: A Guide to the Program and Applications*. 2d ed. Chicago: SPSS Inc.

Lee, S. Y., and R. I. Jennrich. 1979. "A Study of Algorithms for Covariance Structure Analysis with Specific Comparisons using Factor Analysis." *Psychometrika* 44: 99–113.

Magnus J., and H. Neudecker. 1988. *Matrix Differential Calculus*. New York: Wiley.

Malinvaud, E. 1970. *Statistical Methods of Econometrics*. Amsterdam: North Holland.

Manski, C. 1983. "Closest Empirical Distribution Estimation." *Econometrica* 51:305–19.

Meredith, W., and J. Tisak. 1990. "Latent Curve Analysis." *Psychometrika* 53: 107–22.

Mooijaart, A., and P. M. Bentler. 1991. "Robustness of Normal Theory Statistics in Structural Equation Models." *Statistica Neerlandica* 45: 159–71.

Moore, D. S. 1977. "Generalized Inverses, Wald's Method, and the Construction of Chi-Squared Tests of Fit." *Journal of the American Statistical Association* 72: 131–37.

Muthén, B. 1987. *LISCOMP: Analysis of Linear Structural Equations with a Comprehensive Measurement Model. User's Guide*. Mooresville, IN: Scientific Software.

———. 1989. "Multiple Group Structural Modeling with Non-Normal Continuous Variables." *British Journal of Mathematical and Statistical Psychology* 42: 55–62.

Muthén, B., and D. Kaplan. 1985. "A Comparison of Some Methodologies for the Analysis of Non-Normal Likert Variables." *British Journal of Mathematical and Statistical Psychology* 38: 171–89.

———. 1990. "A Comparison of Some Methodologies for the Factor Analysis of Non-Normal Likert Variables: A Note on the Size of the Model." *British Journal of Mathematical and Statistical Psychology* (in press).

Neudecker, H., and A. Satorra. 1991. "Linear Structural Relations: Gradient and Hessian of the Fitting Function." *Statistics and Probability Letters* 11: 57–61.

Newey, W. K. 1988. "Asymptotic Equivalence of Closest Moments and GMM Estimators." *Econometric Theory* 4: 336–40.

SAS 1990. *Technical Report P-200. SAS/STAT Software: CALIS and LOGISTIC Procedures*. Cary, NC.: SAS Institute.

Satorra, A. 1989. "Alternative Test Criteria in Covariance Structure Analysis: A Unified Approach." *Psychometrika* 54: 131–51.

———. 1990. "Robustness Issues in Structural Equation Modeling: A Review of Recent Developments." *Quality and Quantity* 24: 367–86.

———. 1991. "On the Asymptotic Variance Matrix of Sample Second-Order Moments in Multivariate Linear Relations." Economics Working Paper No. 8. Barcelona: Universitat Pompeu Fabra.

Satorra, A., and P. M. Bentler. 1988. "Scaling Corrections for Chi-Square Statistics in Covariance Structure Analysis." Pp. 308–313 in *Proceedings of the Business and Economics Statistics Section*. Alexandria, VA: American Statistical Association.

———. 1990. "Model Conditions for Asymptotic Robustness in the Analysis of Linear Relations." *Computational Statistics and Data Analysis* 10: 235–49.

Satterthwaite, F. E. 1941. "Synthesis of Variance." *Psychometrika* 6: 309–16.

Schoenberg, R. J. 1989. *LINCS: Linear Covariance Structure Analysis. User's Guide*. Kent, WA: RJS Software.

Shapiro, A. 1985. "Asymptotic Equivalence of Minimum Discrepancy Function Estimators to G.L.S. Estimators." *South African Statistical Journal* 19: 73–81.

———. 1986. "Asymptotic Theory of Overparameterized Models." *Journal of the American Statistical Association* 81: 142–49.

———. 1987. "Robustness Properties of the MDF Analysis of Moment Structures." *South African Statistical Journal* 21: 39–62.

Skinner, C.J., D. Holt, and T. M. F. Smith. 1989. *Analysis of Complex Surveys*. New York: Wiley.

Wolter K. M. 1985. *Introduction to Variance Estimation*. New York: Springer Verlag.

White, H. 1982. "Maximum Likelihood Estimation of Misspecified Models." *Econometrica* 50: 1–25.

9

CONSTRAINED LATENT BUDGET ANALYSIS

Peter G. M. van der Heijden*
Ab Mooijaart†
Jan de Leeuw‡

A budget is defined as a row of a two-way table consisting of conditional probabilities adding up to one. The latent budget model approximates the observed budgets of a table by a lower number of underlying, or latent, budgets. The model was originally proposed by Clogg (1981) in the context of square social mobility tables. In this paper we discuss the model in the context of two-way contingency tables. We extend the latent budget model by imposing constraints upon the parameters. Special attention is given to imposing multinomial logit constraints on the latent budget parameters. We show what these constraints imply for the interpretation of the latent budget model as a loglinear model for the latent probabilities. We discuss two examples.

1. INTRODUCTION

In a two-way contingency table, the row and the column variables regularly play different roles: One can be considered an ex-

We gratefully acknowledge the comments of Peter Marsden and the reviewers on an earlier version of the paper. We also thank Ad Kerkhof, who helped us interpret the suicide example, and Murray Pearson, who corrected the English.

*University of Utrecht, The Netherlands
†University of Leiden, The Netherlands
‡University of California, Los Angeles

279

planatory variable and the other a response variable. In such a situation we are interested in the dependence of the response variable on the explanatory variable. One way to study this asymmetric relation between the two variables is by comparing the proportions conditional on each level of the explanatory variable.

In this paper we examine a model for the conditional probabilities, namely, the latent budget model (see van der Heijden, Mooijaart, and de Leeuw 1989; de Leeuw, van der Heijden, and Verboon 1990). A vector with conditional proportions that add up to one is called an *observed* budget; for each row there is an observed budget that specifies the observed proportions of the response variable for that row. The latent budget model approximates the observed budgets by a mixture of one or more unknown or *latent* budgets. There are two types of parameters in the latent budgets: (a) conditional probabilities that add up to one (probabilities which have to be estimated) and (b) mixing parameters that define how the latent budgets are mixed to approximate as closely as possible the observed budgets.

In the context of square social mobility tables, Clogg (1981) presented the latent budget model as a reparameterization of latent class analysis. Unaware of this earlier work de Leeuw and van der Heijden (1988) independently found the latent budget decomposition for the analysis of so-called time-budget data. Time-budget data are a specific type of constant row-sum data (also called compositional data) in which the matrix to be analyzed comprises (groups of) individuals in the rows, activities in the columns, and proportions of time spent by individuals on the activities in the cells. In the same context of time-budget analysis, de Leeuw et al. (1990) discussed the identifiability of the model in more detail and demonstrated the relation of latent budget analysis to logcontrast principal component analysis (Aitchison 1986), which is another method for the analysis of compositional data.

Preliminary results of latent budget analysis in the general context of contingency tables can be found in van der Heijden et al. (1989). De Leeuw and van der Heijden (1991) discussed the relationship between latent budget analysis, (simultaneous) latent class analysis, and (a maximum likelihood version of) correspondence analysis (Goodman 1985, 1986; Gilula and Haberman 1986, 1988). Van der Heijden (1991) discussed the relationship between versions of the latent budget model, the RC(M)-association model, and correspondence analysis, which deal with structural zero cells in two-way tables.

Van der Heijden et al. (1989) also showed how latent budget analysis can be used to analyze higher-way contingency tables. To analyze higher-way tables, one must subdivide the variables into two subgroups: explanatory variables and response variables. The variables in each subgroup are treated as a joint variable.

In this paper we extend the latent budget model by imposing constraints upon the parameters of the model. We consider fixed-value constraints, equality constraints, and linear-logistic constraints. Constraining parameters in models is important for several reasons. First, imposing further constraints (i.e., if they are legitimate) often simplifies the model because it reduces the number of parameters to be interpreted. Second, substantive research questions can sometimes be formulated as constraints on the latent budget model. Testing the admissibility of these constraints provides answers to the research questions. Third, constraining parameters reduces the standard errors of the unconstrained parameter estimates.

In section 2 we define the latent budget model and discuss its relevant properties. In section 3 we discuss the three types of constraints. Then we discuss the identifiability of the model when constraints are used and the degrees of freedom. In the examples, we give special attention to the analysis of higher-way tables, where by imposing constraints, we can use the factorial structure of joint variables.

2. UNCONSTRAINED LATENT BUDGET MODEL

2.1. *Introduction*

To present the latent budget model formally, we introduce some notation. Let observed proportions be denoted as p_{ij}, where i ($i = 1, \ldots, I$) indexes the levels of the explanatory (row) variable A, and j ($j = 1, \ldots, J$) indexes the levels of the response (column) variable B. If we sum over an index, we will replace the index by a plus sign: $p_{i+} = \Sigma_j p_{ij}$. The proportions p_{ij} are derived from frequencies n_{ij} as $p_{ij} = n_{ij}/N$, where $N = n_{++}$.

The conditional proportions we are interested in are p_{ij}/p_{i+}. The independence model is often used as a baseline in the study of the dependence of B on A. Independence implies for the theoretical

probabilities π_{ij} that $\pi_{ij}/\pi_{i+} = \pi_{+j}$, which shows that under independence, the conditional probability for column j is π_{+j} irrespective of
the level of the explanatory variable. Thus, the *dependence* of the
response variable on the explanatory variable can be studied by comparing values p_{ij}/p_{i+} for different i. The logit model can be used to
study the dependence of the response variable B on the explanatory
variable A if the response variable is dichotomous. The multinomial
logit model can be used if the response variable is polytomous (see,
for example, Bock 1975; Haberman 1979; Agresti 1990). The independence model is a special case of such models. The independence
model is also a special case of the latent budget model.

In an observed budget, with the conditional proportions ($p_{i1}/
p_{i+}, \ldots, p_{ij}/p_{i+}, \ldots, p_{iJ}/p_{i+}$), row budget i is the conditional distri-
bution of the column categories for row i. The latent budget model
describes the *theoretical* budgets with elements π_{ij}/π_{i+} as a mixture of
T *latent* budgets, indexed by t ($t = 1, \ldots, T$). Let the latent budget t
have parameters $\pi_{jt}^{\overline{B}X}$, where the bar over B shows that these latent
budget parameters are conditional probabilities interpreted as fol-
lows: The parameter $\pi_{jt}^{\overline{B}X}$ specifies the probability of level j for response variable B given latent budget t. Let the mixture be defined
by mixture parameters $\pi_{it}^{A\overline{X}}$, where the bar over variable X indicates
that the mixture parameters are conditional probabilities interpreted
as follows: The parameter $\pi_{it}^{A\overline{X}}$ specifies the probability that an observation falls into latent budget t given level i for the explanatory
variable A. The model is defined thus:

$$\frac{\pi_{ij}}{\pi_{i+}} = \sum_{t=1}^{T} \pi_{it}^{A\overline{X}} \pi_{jt}^{\overline{B}X}, \tag{1}$$

with constraints

$$\sum_{t=1}^{T} \pi_{it}^{A\overline{X}} = 1 \quad \text{for } i = 1, \ldots, I, \pi_{it}^{A\overline{X}} \geq 0,$$

$$\tag{2}$$

$$\sum_{j=1}^{J} \pi_{jt}^{\overline{B}X} = 1 \quad \text{for } t = 1, \ldots, T, \pi_{jt}^{\overline{B}X} \geq 0.$$

If the number of latent budgets T is 1, then (1) is equivalent to the
independence model: In this case, $\pi_{it}^{A\overline{X}} = 1$ for all i and $\pi_{jt}^{\overline{B}X} = \pi_{+j}$. If T

= min (I,J), then the model is equivalent to a saturated model: In this case it does not impose constraints.

On the assumption that the observations are distributed multi-nomially for each level of the explanatory variable A, maximum likelihood estimates can be derived (see below). The model can be tested against the unconstrained alternative using the Pearson chi-square test and the likelihood ratio chi-square test. If the model is true, then the test statistic follows asymptotically a chi-squared distri-bution with $(I - T)(J - T)$ degrees of freedom. The conditional test of the model with $T = n$ latent budgets, given that the model with $T = n + m$ latent budgets is true $(n,m \geq 1, n + m < \min(I,J))$, does *not* follow asymptotically a chi-squared distribution because we are work-ing in the domain of mixture models. (See Aitkin, Anderson, and Hinde [1981] and Everitt [1988] for discussions of this problem in latent class analysis.)

2.2. Example

To motivate the model, we analyze German suicide data. Van der Heijden and de Leeuw (1985) used correspondence analysis to analyze these data. The row variable is a cross-classification of two explanatory variables—namely, age group and sex—and the column variable, or response variable, is cause of death. The data are given in Table 1. They were collected by the German Office for Statistics in Western Germany for the years 1974 to 1977, and are provided by Heuer (1979, Table 1). The latent budget model aims to find the latent budgets of cause-of-death categories that have generated the 2 × 17 = 34 observed budgets of cause-of-death categories. The latent budgets can be interpreted as typical cause-of-death distributions.

For the model with one latent budget, $G^2 = 10,332.9$ ($df = 264$). For two latent budgets, $G^2 = 4,595.4$, $df = 224$; for three, $G^2 = 1,085.9$, $df = 186$; and for four, $G^2 = 465.7$, $df = 150$. We use the test statistics only as descriptive measures for three reasons. First, the sample size is large ($n = 53,210$). Second, we are analyzing popula-tion data, so we don't have to make inferences from the sample to the population. Third, the observations are most likely not com-pletely independent, since it is known that suicides generate new suicides with similar characteristics (here, suicides of the same age and sex and the same cause of death). We use the model with one

TABLE 1
Suicide Behavior: Age by Sex by Cause of Death

Age	Cause of Death[a]									Total
	1	2	3	4	5	6	7	8	9	
Males										
10–15	4	0	0	247	1	17	1	6	9	285
15–20	348	7	67	578	22	179	11	74	175	1,461
20–25	808	32	229	699	44	316	35	109	289	2,561
25–30	789	26	243	648	52	268	38	109	226	2,399
30–35	916	17	257	825	74	291	52	123	281	2,836
35–40	1,118	27	313	1,278	87	293	49	134	268	3,567
40–45	926	13	250	1,273	89	299	53	78	198	3,179
45–50	855	9	203	1,381	71	347	68	103	190	3,227
50–55	684	14	136	1,282	87	229	62	63	146	2,703
55–60	502	6	77	972	49	151	46	66	77	1,946
60–65	516	5	74	1,249	83	162	52	92	122	2,355
65–70	513	8	31	1,360	75	164	56	115	95	2,417
70–75	425	5	21	1,268	90	121	44	119	82	2,175
75–80	266	4	9	866	63	78	30	79	34	1,429
80–85	159	2	2	479	39	18	18	46	19	782
85–90	70	1	0	259	16	10	9	18	10	393
90+	18	0	1	76	4	2	4	6	2	113
Females										
10–15	28	0	3	20	0	1	0	10	6	68
15–20	353	2	11	81	6	15	2	43	47	560
20–25	540	4	20	111	24	9	9	78	67	862
25–30	454	6	27	125	33	26	7	86	75	839
30–35	530	2	29	178	42	14	20	92	78	985
35–40	688	5	44	272	64	24	14	98	110	1,319
40–45	566	4	24	343	76	18	22	103	86	1,242
45–50	716	6	24	447	94	13	21	95	88	1,504
50–55	942	7	26	691	184	21	37	129	131	2,168
55–60	723	3	14	527	163	14	30	92	92	1,658
60–65	820	8	8	702	245	11	35	140	114	2,083
65–70	740	8	4	785	271	4	38	156	90	2,096
70–75	624	6	4	610	244	1	27	129	46	1,691
75–80	495	8	1	420	161	2	29	129	35	1,279
80–85	292	3	2	223	78	0	10	84	23	715
85–90	113	4	0	83	14	0	6	34	2	256
90+	24	1	0	19	4	0	2	7	0	57
Total	17,565	253	2,154	20,377	2,649	3,118	937	2,845	3,313	53,211

[a]Cause-of-death categories: 1 = ingestion of solid or liquid matter; 2 = gas poisoning at home; 3 = poisoning by other gas; 4 = hanging, strangling, suffocation; 5 = drowning; 6 = guns or explosives; 7 = knives, etc.; 8 = jumping; 9 = other methods.

latent budget as the baseline model, which assumes that age-sex combinations are independent of the cause of death. Models with more than one latent budget describe the dependence of the response variable on the explanatory variables. The model with two latent budgets fits .555 of this dependence ([10,332.9 − 4,595.4] ÷ 10,332.9), the model with three latent budgets fits .895, and the model with four latent budgets fits .955 of this dependence. We focus on the solution with three latent budgets, keeping in mind that this solution shows only the main aspects of dependence. Including a fourth latent budget leads to a further gain of only 6 percent. The parameter estimates are given in Tables 2a and 2b.

We first study the latent budgets that have generated the expected budgets. The latent budget parameters $\hat{\pi}_{jt}^{\overline{B}X}$ can be interpreted cursorily by comparing them with their corresponding marginal probabilities $\hat{\pi}_{+j}$. If $\hat{\pi}_{jt}^{\overline{B}X} > \hat{\pi}_{+j}$, then latent budget t is characterized by category j (among others) in the sense that, given t, a much higher probability of j is observed than if we had no information about t. This shows that the first latent budget is characterized by relatively high conditional probabilities of suicide by ingestion of solid or liquid matter, including medicine ($\hat{\pi}_{jt}^{\overline{B}X} = .530$ versus $\hat{\pi}_{+j} = .330$), by gas poisoning (gas home, .011 versus .005; gas other, .135 versus .040), by guns and explosives (.104 versus .059), and by other methods (.141 versus .062). This latent budget is used relatively more often by younger adults: For example, for males aged 15–20, $\hat{\pi}_{it}^{A\overline{X}} = .519$; for males aged 20–25, $\hat{\pi}_{it}^{A\overline{X}} = .666$; for females aged 15–20, $\hat{\pi}_{it}^{A\overline{X}} = .458$, and so on).

The second latent budget, used mainly by females (see estimates $\hat{\pi}_{it}^{A\overline{X}}$ in second column for females), gives estimates relatively higher than marginal probabilities for drowning (.099 versus .050), ingestion of solid or liquid matter (.437 versus .330), and jumping (.084 versus .053), methods that are relatively less violent. The third latent budget is used mainly by males and gives relatively higher estimates for hanging (.840 versus .383), guns and explosives (.090 versus .059), knives (.029 versus .018), and so on.

To understand how the expected budgets are constructed from the latent budgets, we have to consider the row parameters. A cursory overview of all the row parameter estimates $\hat{\pi}_{it}^{A\overline{X}}$ can be obtained by comparing them with the parameter estimates $\hat{\pi}_{t}^{X}$: .296, .396, and .308. These are the probabilities of each of the latent

TABLE 2a
Latent Budget Analysis Parameter Estimates for Data in Table 1
(Row Parameters $\hat{\pi}_{it}^{A\overline{X}}$)

Age	Males			Females		
	$t = 1$	$t = 2$	$t = 3$	$t = 1$	$t = 2$	$t = 3$
10–15	.026	.000	.974	.278	.642	.081
15–20	.519	.000	.481	.458	.542	.000
20–25	.666	.000	.334	.408	.592	.000
25–30	.671	.000	.329	.428	.572	.000
30–35	.626	.031	.343	.300	.700	.000
35–40	.543	.060	.396	.303	.697	.000
40–45	.491	.054	.455	.154	.834	.012
45–50	.460	.033	.507	.109	.882	.009
50–55	.354	.128	.518	.080	.878	.042
55–60	.290	.187	.522	.056	.909	.036
60–65	.228	.229	.544	.016	.937	.047
65–70	.126	.318	.556	.000	.931	.069
70–75	.074	.374	.552	.000	.967	.033
75–80	.037	.391	.573	.000	.978	.022
80–85	.006	.482	.511	.000	1.000	.000
85–90	.000	.414	.586	.000	1.000	.000
90+	.029	.346	.625	.000	.999	.001
$\hat{\pi}_t^X$	.296	.396	.308			

budgets when there is no information about the level of the row variable. The parameter estimates $\hat{\pi}_t^X$ are the weighted averages of the row parameters $\hat{\pi}_{it}^{A\overline{X}}$. Comparison of $\hat{\pi}_{it}^{A\overline{X}}$ and $\hat{\pi}_t^X$ shows that the first latent budget is used predominantly by males aged 15 to 55 and by females aged 15 to 40. It is hardly used by young boys (aged 10–15) by males older than 70, or by women older than 40. The second latent budget is used mainly by males aged 80 to 90 and by females of all ages, but it is hardly used by males under 40. The third latent budget is predominantly used by males of all ages and is hardly used by females. Roughly speaking, then, the first latent budget is used mainly by younger adults, the second is used mainly by females and older males, and the third is used almost exclusively by males.

It is difficult to say whether the three latent budgets that we found can be considered generic types of suicide. Heudin (1982,

TABLE 2b
Latent Budget Analysis Parameter Estimates for Data in Table 1
(Column Parameters $\hat{\pi}_{jt}^{\bar{B}X}$)

Cause of Death[a]	$\hat{\pi}_{+j}$	$t = 1$	$t = 2$	$t = 3$
1	.330	.530	.437	.000
2	.005	.011	.004	.000
3	.040	.135	.002	.000
4	.383	.000	.315	.840
5	.050	.021	.099	.015
6	.059	.104	.000	.090
7	.018	.007	.017	.029
8	.053	.052	.084	.016
9	.062	.141	.044	.010
Total	1.000	1.000	1.000	1.000

[a]See note to Table 1.

Chapter 7) points out that there are many possible explanations for the suicide method chosen. For example, it is argued that women care what they will look like after their death. This could explain their preference for the methods overrepresented in the second budget, which do not lead to mutilation of the body. In the third budget we find overrepresentation of methods that do mutilate the body. Another theory emphasizes the importance of opportunity. Some of the methods overrepresented in the first budget are methods for which one must have opportunity; i.e., one needs medicine, a car, or a gun (which is not easy to obtain in Germany). Younger people may have more opportunity to use these methods. Psychoanalytic theories suggest that suicides represent sexual wish fulfillments: To poison oneself is to become pregnant; to drown is to bear a child; to throw oneself from a height is to be delivered of a child. Poisoning, drowning, and jumping are three methods that are overrepresented in the second latent budget. There are also individual factors involved: Psychoanalysts suggest that suicide is a message to relatives. All the above explanations are highly speculative, although evidence of regional differences in methods used supports the opportunity theory. For example, people in the United States are more likely to commit suicide by using guns than people in countries where guns are not easily obtained. More information is needed to understand the relation of age and sex to the method chosen.

2.3. Comparison with Latent Class Analysis

Clogg (1981) presented latent budget analysis as a reparameterization of latent class analysis, and as a result many properties of
latent class analysis also hold for latent budget analysis. Let π_t^X be the
probability of falling into latent class t; let $\pi_{it}^{\overline{A}X}$ be the conditional
probability of falling into level i of variable A given latent class t; and
let $\pi_{jt}^{\overline{B}X}$ be the conditional probability of falling into level j of variable
B given latent class t. Then the latent class model for two-way contin-
gency tables is defined as a model for the latent probabilities π_{ijt} of
falling into level i of variable A, level j of variable B, and level t of
the latent variable X:

$$\pi_{ijt} = \pi_t^X \pi_{it}^{\overline{A}X} \pi_{jt}^{\overline{B}X}. \tag{3a}$$

And the latent probabilities are related to the probabilities using
only the manifest variables A and B by

$$\pi_{ij} = \sum_{t=1}^{T} \pi_{ijt}. \tag{3b}$$

Latent budget analysis and latent class analysis have in common the
parameters $\pi_{jt}^{\overline{B}X}$. The latent budget analysis parameters $\pi_{it}^{A\overline{X}}$ are derived
from the latent class analysis parameters π_t^X and $\pi_{it}^{\overline{A}X}$ by using Bayes's
rule:

$$\pi_{it}^{A\overline{X}} = \frac{\pi_t^X \pi_{it}^{\overline{A}X}}{\sum_{t=1}^{T} \pi_t^X \pi_{it}^{\overline{A}X}}. \tag{4}$$

Latent budget analysis and latent class analysis are also readily
compared in terms of the latent probabilities π_{ijt}. For both models
the column parameters are related to the latent probabilities π_{ijt} as
$\pi_{jt}^{\overline{B}X} = \pi_{+jt}/\pi_{++t}$. For latent class analysis the row parameters are
related to the latent probabilities π_{ijt} as $\pi_{it}^{\overline{A}X} = \pi_{i+t}/\pi_{++t}$, whereas for
latent budget analysis the row parameters are related to the latent
probabilities π_{ijt} as $\pi_{it}^{A\overline{X}} = \pi_{i+t}/\pi_{i++}$. In terms of the latent probabilities, the observed variables A and B are conditionally independent
given the latent variable X for both models. From (3a) it follows
that latent class analysis can be defined as

$$\pi_{ijt} = \pi_{++t}\left(\frac{\pi_{i+t}}{\pi_{++t}}\right)\left(\frac{\pi_{+jt}}{\pi_{++t}}\right) = \frac{\pi_{i+t}\pi_{+jt}}{\pi_{++t}}. \tag{5}$$

Latent budget analysis implies that

$$\frac{\pi_{ijt}}{\pi_{i++}} = \left(\frac{\pi_{i+t}}{\pi_{i++}}\right)\left(\frac{\pi_{+jt}}{\pi_{++t}}\right) = \left(\frac{1}{\pi_{i++}}\right)\left(\frac{\pi_{i+t}\pi_{+jt}}{\pi_{++t}}\right).$$

Both the latent class model and the latent budget model can therefore be understood as a loglinear model with latent variables (see, e.g., Haberman 1979; Hagenaars 1986, 1988, 1990). This relation with loglinear analysis will be taken up later in the paper.

Latent class analysis is most often used to analyze contingency tables with more than two variables, where it aims to identify a latent variable that can explain the relations between the observed variables (see, e.g., Goodman 1974). Relatively little attention has been given to latent class analyses of two-way contingency tables, except in the theoretical contributions of Good (1969), Gilula (1979, 1983, 1984), Clogg (1981), Goodman (1987), and de Leeuw and van der Heijden (1991), and in the social mobility research of Marsden (1985), Grover (1987), Grover and Srinivasan (1987), and Luijkx (1987). As far as we know, the reparameterization (1) appears only in Clogg (1981) and in the references given in the introduction.

A choice between the latent class model and the latent budget model will depend on the research question at hand. If the question is about dependence, that is, how response variables depend on explanatory variables, then the latent budget model is more appropriate (see also section 2.4). If the question is about relations between variables, then latent class analysis is preferable. In this sense the distinction between latent class analysis and latent budget analysis is similar to the distinction between loglinear analysis and (multinomial) logit analysis. It will become apparent in section 3.2 that the distinction between explanatory variables and response variables suggests specific types of models for latent budget analysis that have not been considered thus far in the context of latent class analysis.

2.4. Graphical Representations of the Model

Figures 1 and 2 illustrate the usefulness of latent budget analysis with representations inspired by those used in covariance struc-

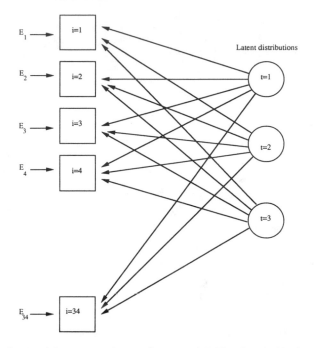

FIGURE 1. Latent budget model represented as a mixture model. The observed budgets are derived from three latent budgets plus error (E). Lines in the figure symbolize the mixing parameters

ture analysis. We have chosen two such representations, one emphasizing the interpretation as a mixture model, and one emphasizing the interpretation as a MIMIC model. In both, squares indicate observed entities, and circles latent entities.

In Figure 1, the latent budget model for Table 1 is represented as a mixture model. The observed contingency table is conceived as a matrix of I observed distributions (budgets), one for each row. These I observed distributions are generated by T latent distributions. The observed distributions have elements p_{ij}/p_{i+}, and the latent distributions have elements $\hat{\pi}_{jt}^{\overline{B}X}$. The 34 observed age-sex distributions of suicide types are represented by squares, and the latent distributions are represented by circles. The direction of the arrows in Figure 1 suggests that the mixtures of three latent distributions generate the observed distributions. The error E_i associated with each observed distribution represents the difference between the observed distribu-

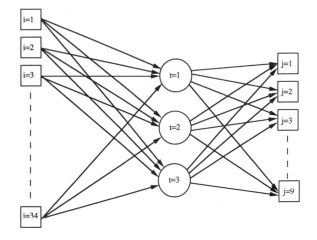

FIGURE 2. MIMIC model representation of the latent budget model.

tion elements p_{ij}/p_{i+} and the estimates of expected distribution elements $\hat{\pi}_{ij}/\hat{\pi}_{i+}$. Next to the arrows we could plot the parameter estimates $\hat{\pi}_{it}^{A\overline{X}}$, since they show how the mixture of the three latent budgets generates the estimates of the expected distributions. In the example in section 2.2, the latent distributions can be understood as typical distributions of cause-of-death categories, and our analysis has demonstrated that the observed distributions of the 34 age groups are relatively well approximated by three such typical distributions.

In Figure 2, the latent budget model is represented as a MIMIC model. In this case, the squares and circles do not denote distributions but categories of variables. This interpretation is due to Clogg (1981), who used it to represent a social mobility example. Here, it demonstrates that given a specific age-sex combination i ($i = 1, \ldots, 34$), there are probabilities associated with each of the three latent states t ($t = 1, 2, 3$); in each latent state there are nine probabilities ($j = 1, \ldots, 9$) corresponding to the nine cause-of-death categories. Now the estimates for the row parameters $\hat{\pi}_{it}^{A\overline{X}}$ as well as the estimates for the column parameters $\hat{\pi}_{jt}^{\overline{B}X}$ can be specified next to the arrows. The parameter estimates $\hat{\pi}_{it}^{A\overline{X}}$ can be placed beside the arrows from the age-sex group categories to the latent states. Beginning from a specific age-sex group, these estimates add up to one, showing that the probabilities associated with the latent states add up to one. The parameter estimates $\hat{\pi}_{jt}^{\overline{BX}}$ can be placed beside the arrows from the latent states to the cause-of-death categories. Starting from a given latent state, these estimates also add up to one, showing that the probability of falling in one of the cause-of-death categories is one. In the latent budget model in Figure 2, the squares and circles represent categories. In the usual covariance structure model, they represent *variables*. It is sometimes difficult to interpret the latent states. In the suicide example a latent state might stand for the experiences and influences that people have undergone, which might differ by age-sex group.

A latent class model would be similar to the model in Figure 2, except that the arrows would go from the latent classes to the row categories, and not from the row categories to the latent classes, as in the latent budget model. Latent budget analysis is the equivalent of latent class analysis, but the former is used to study asymmetric relations between variables and the latter is used to study symmetric relations. In this sense, the equivalence between latent class and latent budget analysis is similar to the equivalence between loglinear analysis and the (multinomial) logit model, the former intended in the first place for the study of symmetric relations between variables, the second for the study of asymmetric relations between variables.

2.5. *Identification*

For two observed variables, neither the unconstrained latent budget model nor the latent class model is identified, although the identification problem is rather well understood. For a detailed discussion of this identification problem in latent class analysis we refer to Goodman (1987); for latent budget analysis the problem is discussed in detail in de Leeuw et al. (1990). The latent budget analysis parameter estimates can be varied within a specific range without changing the estimates of expected frequencies for the model, suggesting enormous freedom for the parameter estimates. However, this freedom is smaller than it seems. The reason is that all parameter estimates covary, which means that interpretation remains rather stable over different choices of identifying restrictions for the model.

The identification problem is most easily explained by formalizing the latent budget model in matrix terms. Let $\mathbf{D}_r$ be a diagonal $I \times I$ matrix with marginal probabilities π_{i+} as elements; and let $\mathbf{\Pi}$ be the $I \times J$ matrix with probabilities π_{ij}. Collect the parameters $\pi_{it}^{A\overline{X}}$ in a $I \times T$ matrix **A**, and collect the parameters $\pi_{jt}^{\overline{B}X}$ in a $J \times T$ matrix **B**. Let **S** be a $T \times T$ square matrix with the property that $\mathbf{S1} = \mathbf{1}$, where **1** is a unit column vector of length T. Let $\mathbf{A^*} = \mathbf{AS}$ and $\mathbf{B^*} = \mathbf{B(S^{-1})'}$ be matrices with alternative parameters. Then the identification problem can be written as

$$\mathbf{D_r^{-1}}\boldsymbol{\Pi} = \mathbf{AB'} = \mathbf{(AS)(S^{-1}B')} = \mathbf{A^*B^{*'}}. \tag{6}$$

Since $\mathbf{S1} = \mathbf{1}$, the elements of $\mathbf{A^*}$ add up to 1 for each row and the elements of $\mathbf{B^*}$ add up to 1 for each column. **S** has to be chosen in such a way that all elements of $\mathbf{A^*}$ and $\mathbf{B^*}$ are non-negative, since these elements are probabilities.

The identification problem is very similar to the rotation problem in factor analysis, except that the abundance of solutions known for factor analysis is not yet available for latent budget analysis. De Leeuw et al. (1990) discuss some choices of **S** and suggest a way to obtain them. One possibility is to choose a matrix **S** that results in as many zeros in $\mathbf{A^*}$ or $\mathbf{B^*}$ as possible. This number of zeros is maximally $T(T - 1)$, the number of free elements of **S**. If we choose as many zeros in $\mathbf{A^*}$ as possible, interpretation is simplified, because if a parameter estimate $\hat{\pi}_{it}^{A\overline{X}}$ equals zero, then the estimates of the theoretical budget for row i are derived from less than T latent budgets. Of course, such a restriction would have to be sociologically justified. Many other details on the identification problem of the latent budget model can be found in de Leeuw et al. (1990).[1]

In the analysis of the suicide data the identification problem is negligible: Many row and column parameters are estimated at zero; therefore, no admissible matrix **S** will have a noticeable effect upon the parameter estimates (see de Leeuw et al. 1990).

The problem of identification is related to the derivation of the number of degrees of freedom:

df = No. of nonredundant cells − No. of independent parameters.

[1]This approach to identification emphasizes a choice of **S**, because by fitting the model with the EM algorithm, unidentified estimates **A** and **B** are obtained and are then transformed to some simple structure. It is also possible to start the other way around, i.e., to fix some parameters in **A** and **B**, try to prove that **S** can only be the identity matrix, and if this is the case, estimate the free parameters. The procedure advocated here has the advantage that the unidentified estimates suggest which elements of **A** and **B** can be fixed to zero without decreasing the fit of the model.

Given that the row totals n_{i+} are fixed, the number of nonredundant cells is $I(J - 1)$. In the unconstrained case with T latent budgets, the number of row parameters is $I(T - 1)$, and the number of column parameters is $(J - 1)T$. However, because these parameters are not independent, since $\mathbf{AB'} = \mathbf{ASS^{-1}B'}$, we must subtract the total number of free elements of $\mathbf{S}$ from the estimated parameters. This number is $T(T - 1)$. Hence, in the unconstrained case we get

$$df = I(J - 1) - [I(T - 1) + (J - 1)T - T(T - 1)] = (I - T)(J - T).$$

2.6. Maximum Likelihood Estimation

Here we discuss the estimation of the model. Readers who are not interested in this subject can skip this section without loss of continuity.

We estimate the model with the EM algorithm (Dempster, Laird, and Rubin 1977), which is also the algorithm most often employed for the estimation of latent class models (see Goodman [1974] for a description of the algorithm). Alternative algorithms used for the estimation of latent class models are provided by Haberman (1979, 1988) and by Formann (1978).

The EM algorithm is used to estimate missing values. In this paper the observations on the latent variable X are missing, and only the marginal frequencies n_{ij} of the three-way matrix with elements n_{ijt} are observed. For the unobserved three-way matrix with probabilities π_{ijt}, the latent budget model (1) is defined in terms of π_{ijt}/π_{i++} by $\pi_{ijt}/\pi_{i++} = \pi_{it}^{A\overline{X}}\pi_{jt}^{\overline{B}X}$. The loglikelihood for the unobserved matrix is

$$L = \sum_{i=1}^{I} \sum_{j=1}^{J} \sum_{t=1}^{T} n_{ijt} \ln \frac{\pi_{ijt}}{\pi_{i++}}. \tag{7}$$

The unobserved n_{ijt} and the parameter estimates for $\pi_{it}^{A\overline{X}}$ and $\pi_{jt}^{\overline{B}X}$ are unknown.

The EM algorithm consists of two steps: the expectation step (E-step) and the maximization step (M-step). In the E-step the expectation of the loglikelihood for the unobserved data n_{ijk} is found, conditional on the observed frequencies n_{ij} and the current parameter estimates. The expectations of the sufficient statistics of the complete data matrix therefore have to be expressed in terms of the model parameters, so we need an expression for n_{ijt}. For this step the current best estimates of $\pi_{it}^{A\overline{X}}$ and $\pi_{jt}^{B\overline{X}}$ are taken. Thus, updated estimates of the unobserved frequencies $\underline{n}_{ijt}$ are given by

$$\underline{n}_{ijt} = n_{ij}\frac{\pi_{ijt}}{\pi_{ij+}} = n_{ij}\frac{\pi_{ijt}/\pi_{i++}}{\pi_{ij}/\pi_{i+}} = n_{ij}\left(\frac{\pi_{it}^{A\overline{X}}\pi_{jt}^{B\overline{X}}}{\sum\limits_{t=1}^{T}\pi_{it}^{A\overline{X}}\pi_{jt}^{B\overline{X}}}\right). \qquad (8)$$

In the M-step the loglikelihood for the unobserved data is maximized as a function of the model parameters. Let γ_i and δ_t be Lagrange multipliers needed for the constraints (2). Then the following function is to be maximized over $\pi_{it}^{A\overline{X}}$ and $\pi_{jt}^{B\overline{X}}$:

$$f(\pi_{it}^{A\overline{X}},\pi_{jt}^{B\overline{X}},\gamma_i,\delta_t) = \sum_{i=1}^{I}\sum_{j=1}^{J}\sum_{t=1}^{T}\underline{n}_{ijkt}\ln(\pi_{it}^{A\overline{X}}\pi_{jt}^{B\overline{X}})$$

$$\qquad (9)$$

$$-\sum_{i=1}^{I}\gamma_i\left((\sum_{t=1}^{T}\pi_{it}^{A\overline{X}})-1\right)-\sum_{t=1}^{T}\delta_t\left((\sum_{j=1}^{J}\pi_{jt}^{B\overline{X}})-1\right).$$

To find the updated estimates $\underline{\pi}_{it}^{A\overline{X}}$ and $\underline{\pi}_{jt}^{B\overline{X}}$ that maximize $f(\pi_{it}^{A\overline{X}},\pi_{jt}^{B\overline{X}},\gamma_i,\delta_t)$, we can rewrite (9) as both (10a) and (10b) and maximize these over $\pi_{it}^{A\overline{X}}$ and $\pi_{jt}^{B\overline{X}}$ separately:

$$f(\pi_{it}^{A\overline{X}},\gamma_i) = \sum_{i=1}^{I}\sum_{t=1}^{T}\underline{n}_{i+t}\ln\pi_{it}^{A\overline{X}} - \sum_{i=1}^{I}\gamma_i\left((\sum_{t=1}^{T}\pi_{it}^{A\overline{X}})-1\right) + \text{constant}, \quad (10a)$$

$$f(\pi_{jt}^{B\overline{X}},\delta_t) = \sum_{j=1}^{J}\sum_{t=1}^{T}\underline{n}_{+jt}\ln\pi_{jt}^{B\overline{X}} - \sum_{t=1}^{T}\delta_t\left((\sum_{j=1}^{J}\pi_{jt}^{B\overline{X}})-1\right) + \text{constant}. \quad (10b)$$

This gives as updated estimates $\underline{\pi}_{it}^{A\overline{X}} = \underline{n}_{i+t}/\underline{n}_{i++}$ and $\underline{\pi}_{jt}^{B\overline{X}} = \underline{n}_{+jt}/\underline{n}_{++t}$. These updated estimates are used in (8) as current best estimates in the next E-step of the algorithm.

Initial parameter estimates should be consistent with the constraints (2). If initial estimates equal to zero are chosen, their values will not change throughout the algorithm. De Leeuw et al. (1990) prove that in this application of the EM algorithm, the likelihood increases in each step. Therefore, the algorithm converges. To investigate whether it converges to a global maximum, one should try different sets of initial estimates.

3. CONSTRAINING THE PARAMETERS

In this section we will describe and illustrate three types of constraints on parameters: fixed-value constraints, equality constraints, and multinomial logit constraints. Since latent budget analysis is closely related to latent class analysis, the procedure for constraining the parameters in latent budget analysis is similar to the procedure in latent class analysis. Fixed-value constraints and equality constraints are well known in that context, so they receive less attention in this paper. Langeheine (1989) gives an insightful overview of constraints in latent class analysis and relates the types of constraints to the different ways latent class analysis is presented— for example, as a product of conditional probabilities, as in (3a) and (3b) (Goodman 1974), and as a loglinear model with a latent variable (Haberman 1979). We use both representations in our discussion of constraints in latent budget analysis.

3.1. *Fixed-Value and Equality Constraints*

Theory. A fixed-value constraint on a parameter fixes this parameter to a prespecified value, for example, $\pi_{it}^{A\overline{X}} = c$, or $\pi_{jt}^{\overline{B}X} = c'$, where $0 \leq c, c' \leq 1$. It is important here to distinguish between identifying constraints and constraints that affect the fit of the model. In section 2.5, we chose a matrix $\mathbf{S}$ to resolve the identification problem. This choice of a specific $\mathbf{S}$ implies a choice of a specific solution, for example, a solution with as many parameters $\pi_{it}^{A\overline{X}}$ as possible fixed to zero, or as many parameters $\pi_{jt}^{\overline{B}X}$ as possible fixed to zero (see de Leeuw et al. 1990). Such fixed parameters are called identifying constraints. To impose these constraints, we first identify the model by choosing a matrix $\mathbf{S}$, thus implicitly constraining some of the parameters to certain values. We can then constrain one or more further parameters. The model with both the identifying constraints and the extra constraints can be estimated by considering both types of constrained parameters as fixed parameters.

Fixed-value constraints are useful for testing whether parameter estimates differ significantly from values that are of theoretical interest. In many circumstances such values will be zero or one. For the suicide data discussed in section 2, additional constraints could be imposed upon the parameters $\pi_{jt}^{\overline{B}X}$ for budget $t = 3$, for example, by constraining all probabilities to zero except those for hanging, stabbing, and shooting deaths. Thus, the third budget would be a budget consisting only of more-violent causes of death. Subsequently, the row parameters $\pi_{it}^{A\overline{X}}$ for women in the third latent budget could be constrained to zero, so that only males were in the third latent budget. Such fixed-value constraints would simplify the interpretation considerably.

An interesting example of a fixed-value constraint is $\pi_{j1}^{\overline{B}X}$ $= \ldots = \pi_{jt}^{\overline{B}X} = \ldots = \pi_{jT}^{\overline{B}X} = p_{+j}$; that is, element j of each latent budget is equal to the sample proportion that falls into category j. Thus, for all i and some category j, $\pi_{ij}/\pi_{i+} = \pi_{+j}$. This allows us to determine whether the differences between the budgets π_{ij}/π_{i+} are due to differences in column categories other than column category j. This hypothesis can be tested against the unconstrained model with T latent classes; since T parameters are constrained, the test statistic is asymptotically chi-square distributed with T degrees of freedom. If such a hypothesis cannot be rejected, the interpretation is simplified considerably: It is no longer necessary to characterize the groups (rows) in terms of differences in their use of column j. Equality constraints specify that certain row-parameter estimates $\pi_{it}^{A\overline{X}}$ or certain column-parameter estimates $\pi_{jt}^{\overline{B}X}$ are unknown but equal to one another. Such equality constraints can be used to test whether two parameter estimates really are different. If this is the case, the interpretation is again simplified considerably. As with fixed-value constraints, the model should first be identified by some choice of **S**. Then certain parameter estimates can be constrained to be equal.

An interesting test for equality constraints amounts to a test for the collapsibility of rows. If $\pi_{it}^{A\overline{X}} = \pi_{i't}^{A\overline{X}}$ for all t, then rows i and i' are related to the latent budgets in the same way. This implies for the theoretical budget elements in rows i and i' that $\pi_{ij}/\pi_{i+} = \pi_{i'j}/\pi_{i'+}$. The equality of theoretical row budgets was used earlier by Goodman (1981), Gilula (1986), and Gilula and Krieger (1989) as a criterion for the collapsibility of rows. In a similar way we can also interpret the test that $\pi_{it}^{A\overline{X}} = \pi_{i't}^{A\overline{X}}$ for all t as a test for collapsibility of rows i and i'. Gilula (1986) and Gilula and Krieger (1989) applied similar tests for equality of the parameters of two or more rows (or two or more columns) in a maximum likelihood version of correspondence analysis. The similarity between the work of Gilula and the procedure described here follows immediately in all cases in which correspondence analysis and latent budget analysis are equivalent (see de Leeuw and van der Heijden 1991). In cases in which correspondence analysis and latent budget analysis are not equivalent, the tests can give different results.

Derivation of the number of degrees of freedom for the unconstrained case was discussed above in section 2.5. In the unconstrained case we usually choose an **S** that gives us as many zero parameters in **A** or **B** as possible, thus simplifying the interpretation. This can also be done by constraining these estimates to zero. Each additional fixed-value constraint leads to a higher number of degrees of freedom. Similar remarks apply to equality constraints. First, we constrain $T(T - 1)$ parameters so that the model is identified. Then, after imposing equality constraints, we can easily derive the number of degrees of freedom.

We will not discuss examples of fixed-value or equality constraints. Some applications are suggested above, and examples can be found in the latent class analysis literature (see, e.g., McCutcheon 1987).

Estimation.[2] For the constraints discussed above, the loglikelihood can always be split into two parts, as in (10a) and (10b), which can be maximized separately to update parameter estimates.

We first introduce some notation. We denote parameters constrained to fixed values by adding a bar over the parameter symbol, that is, $\bar{\pi}_{it}^{A\overline{X}}$ and $\bar{\pi}_{jt}^{B\overline{X}}$. In the presence of fixed-value constraints, we denote free parameters by adding a tilde over the parameter symbol, that is, parameters to be estimated are $\tilde{\pi}_{it}^{A\overline{X}}$ and $\tilde{\pi}_{jt}^{B\overline{X}}$. From the parameters $\tilde{\pi}_{it}^{A\overline{X}}$, $\tilde{\pi}_{jt}^{B\overline{X}}$, $\bar{\pi}_{it}^{A\overline{X}}$, and $\bar{\pi}_{jt}^{B\overline{X}}$ we derive the elements $\pi_{it}^{A\overline{X}}$ and $\pi_{jt}^{B\overline{X}}$ of matrices **A** and **B**. For this purpose the current estimates of the parameters $\tilde{\pi}_{it}^{A\overline{X}}$ and $\tilde{\pi}_{jt}^{B\overline{X}}$ are sometimes rescaled so that estimates for the parameters $\pi_{it}^{A\overline{X}}$ and $\pi_{jt}^{B\overline{X}}$ follow constraints (2).

Fixed-value constraints for specific row and column parameters can be easily imposed. This is shown for fixed row parameters only. (The results for the column parameters can be derived in a similar way.) Let the parameter for row i in budget m be fixed to some constant c; that is, $\bar{\pi}_{im}^{A\overline{X}} = c, 0 \le c \le 1$. Since the elements $\pi_{it}^{A\overline{X}}$ of matrix **A** are constrained by (2), we have

$$\pi_{it}^{A\overline{X}} = (1 - \sum_m \bar{\pi}_{im}^{A\overline{X}})\tilde{\pi}_{it}^{A\overline{X}}, \quad \text{with} \sum_j \tilde{\pi}_{it}^{A\overline{X}} = 1, \tag{11}$$

[2]This section can be skipped without loss of continuity.

where $\Sigma_m \bar{\pi}_{im}^{A\overline{X}}$ implies that the sum is taken over the fixed parameters for row i, and $\Sigma_t \tilde{\pi}_{it}^{A\overline{X}}$ implies that the sum is taken over the free parameters for row i. To estimate the elements $\pi_{it}^{A\overline{X}}$ of matrix $\mathbf{A}$, we maximize the loglikelihood in the M-step over the parameters $\tilde{\pi}_{it}^{A\overline{X}}$:

$$f(\tilde{\pi}_{it}^{A\overline{X}}, \gamma_i) = \sum_{\substack{\text{index pairs } (i,t) \\ \text{corresponding with} \\ \text{free parameters}}} \left[n_{i+t} \ln \left(\left(1 - \sum_m \bar{\pi}_{im}^{A\overline{X}} \right) \tilde{\pi}_{it}^{A\overline{X}} \right) \right]$$

(12)

$$- \sum_{i=1}^{I} \gamma_i \left(\left(\sum_j \tilde{\pi}_{it}^{A\overline{X}} \right) - 1 \right) + \text{constant}.$$

Maximizing (12) over $\tilde{\pi}_{it}^{A\overline{X}}$, we find the estimate $\tilde{\pi}_{it}^{A\overline{X}} = n_{i+t}/n_{i++}$, where in obtaining n_{i++} and n_{i+t}, we use only those frequencies with index pairs (i,t) of free parameters. Having $\tilde{\pi}_{it}^{A\overline{X}}$ we can now find new estimates $\pi_{it}^{A\overline{X}}$ using (11).

We next consider both equality constraints and fixed-value constraints. A bar over the parameter symbol indicates that the parameter is again fixed to some specific value. A tilde indicates that the parameter is either completely free or constrained to be equal to other unknown parameters. These two types of parameter constitute the matrices $\mathbf{A}$ with elements $\pi_{it}^{A\overline{X}}$ and $\mathbf{B}$ with elements $\pi_{jt}^{B\overline{X}}$. We consider only equality constraints between row parameters and equality constraints between column parameters. We do not consider equality constraints between row and column parameters. Thus, the estimation problem in the M-step can be simplified because we can rewrite the loglikelihood, separating the parameters for $\mathbf{A}$ from the parameters for $\mathbf{B}$ and maximizing these parameters separately (compare (9), (10a), and (10b)).

We first consider constraints on row parameters $\pi_{it}^{A\overline{X}}$. Equation (12) represents the loglikelihood function to be maximized over the free parameters $\tilde{\pi}_{it}^{A\overline{X}}$, where there are only fixed-value constraints and no equality constraints. The updated estimates $\tilde{\pi}_{it}^{A\overline{X}}$ can be transformed into their corresponding $\pi_{it}^{A\overline{X}}$ via (11). Now let some parameters $\pi_{it}^{A\overline{X}}$ be restricted to be equal to one another. We introduce some extra notation. Let A_{it} be the set of pairs $\{(i,t)\}$ for which equality constraints are imposed; we denote this set by the first combination (i,t) encountered (the index i running faster than the index t). That is, if $\pi_{12}^{A\overline{X}} = \pi_{21}^{A\overline{X}}$, then the set $\{(1,2),(2,1)\}$ is A_{12}, and A_{21} is not defined.

If no equality constraint is imposed for some $\pi_{it}^{A\overline{X}}$, then A_{it} has as its only element (i,t). Let W be the set of existing index pairs (i,t) of the sets A_{it}. Let the number of parameters in each A_{it} be equal to c_{it}, and let $f_{it} = \Sigma_{\text{index pairs in } A_{it}} n_{i+t}$. Instead of (12) we find that

$$f(\tilde{\pi}_{it}^{A\overline{X}},\gamma_i) = \sum_{\substack{\text{index pairs } (i,t) \\ \text{in } W}} \left[f_{it} \ln \left((1 - \sum_m \tilde{\pi}_{im}^{A\overline{X}}) \tilde{\pi}_{it}^{A\overline{X}} \right) \right]$$

$$\tag{13}$$

$$- \sum_{i=1}^{I} \gamma_i \left((\sum_t c_{it} \tilde{\pi}_{it}^{A\overline{X}}) - 1 \right) + \text{constant.}$$

Now we maximize (13) over $\tilde{\pi}_{it}^{A\overline{X}}$ and use the updated estimate $\tilde{\pi}_{it}^{A\overline{X}}$ in (11) to find the updated parameter estimates $\pi_{it}^{A\overline{X}}$. For example, if the equality constraint is $\pi_{11}^{A\overline{X}} = \pi_{12}^{A\overline{X}}$, then the updated estimate found for $\pi_{11}^{A\overline{X}}$ is $\pi_{11}^{A\overline{X}} = (n_{1+1} + n_{2+1})/(n_{1++} + n_{2++})$, and the other parameters in rows 1 and 2 may be derived from n_{i+t}/n_{i++}, then adjusted in a way similar to (11) so that (2) holds. In most cases the maximization of (13) over $\tilde{\pi}_{it}^{A\overline{X}}$ gives direct solutions. There are cases, however, in which no direct solutions exist. In such a case, a Newton-Raphson or similar procedure should be applied in each M-step of the EM algorithm. This can make the algorithm very time-consuming. For a discussion of the existence of direct solutions in latent class analysis, see Mooijaart and van der Heijden (in press). Since latent class analysis and latent budget analysis are equivalent, their results can readily be applied to the latent budget model.

3.2. Multinomial Logit Constraints

If there is additional information about the rows and columns of the two-way table, it is possible to constrain the corresponding row and column parameters as a function of this additional information. One sort of additional information specifies that the row variable or the column variable is a joint variable. The suicide data analyzed in section 2 have a joint row variable, based on the separate variables age and sex. In section 3.5 we show how this type of additional information about the rows can be used in the model. Another sort of information that we can use is any available quantitative information relevant to the row or column categories. For example, consider a matrix of industry groups by years, in which the number of firms in each industry founded in each year are in the cells. The observed budgets give the proportions of types of firms founded in each year, and the latent budgets give typical distributions of new firms by industry. If the row categories of a matrix are specific years, then these years themselves could be used as additional information in the model. It is also possible to use other variables that describe the economic situation in these years to model the differences between the observed budgets.

The parameters $\pi_{it}^{A\overline{X}}$ and $\pi_{jt}^{\overline{B}X}$ are conditional probabilities; therefore, we use the multinomial logit model, which has been devised specifically for this situation. We use the version of the multinomial logit model discussed extensively by Bock (1975) to constrain both the row and column parameters.

The multinomial logit model has been used to constrain parameters in other contexts. Formann (1982, 1985, 1989) constrains latent class analysis in a manner very similar to our own but concentrates on latent class analysis of dichotomous variables (see also Langeheine 1989). Shigemasu and Sugiyama (1989) use this parameterization for latent class analysis of choice behavior. Takane (1987) uses the multinomial logit model to restrict the conditional probabilities in ideal point discriminant analysis.

Multinomial logit constraints on row parameters. Let the additional information for the rows i of the two-way contingency table be collected in an $I \times M$ matrix $\mathbf{V}$, where the columns are indexed by m ($m = 1, \ldots, M$). We can use this information by defining the following model for the (conditional) row parameters $\pi_{it}^{A\overline{X}}$.

$$\pi_{it}^{A\overline{X}} = \frac{\exp\left(\sum_{m=1}^{M} v_{im}\gamma_{mt}\right)}{\sum_{t=1}^{T}\exp\left(\sum_{m=1}^{M} v_{im}\gamma_{mt}\right)}. \tag{14}$$

Here, γ_{mt} is the (m,t)th element of the $M \times T$ parameter matrix $\boldsymbol{\Gamma}$. Model (14) can be identified by constraining $\gamma_{m1} = 0$, for all m.

Model (14) allows a large range of constraints to be defined by the matrix $\mathbf{V}$. We get more insight into this class of constraints by relating unconstrained latent budget analysis to loglinear analysis with latent variables. Let π_{ijt} be the latent probabilities. Then equation (5) shows that variables A and B are conditionally independent given the level of the latent variable X. Thus, using notation similar to that employed by Haberman (1979, Chapter 10), we get

$$\log \pi_{ijt} = \lambda + \lambda_i^A + \lambda_j^B + \lambda_t^X + \lambda_{it}^{AX} + \lambda_{jt}^{BX}. \tag{15}$$

From (14), the conditional probabilities $\pi_{i+t}/\pi_{i++} = \pi_{it}^{A\overline{X}}$ are further constrained. Thus, although the variables A and B remain conditionally independent given the level of the latent variable X, the interaction between A and X, λ_{it}^{AX}, is further constrained.

An important special case of (14) is when the row variable is itself a cross-classification of two or more variables, and the matrix **V** is a design matrix describing the factorial structure of the rows. In this case, we can define a multinomial logit model for the row parameters $\pi_{it}^{A\overline{X}}$ that is equivalent to a hierarchical loglinear model for unconditional marginal probabilities π_{i+t}. The hierarchical loglinear model to which it is equivalent has the same sets of parameters, which describe the relations between the explanatory and the response variables, as the multinomial logit model and additional sets of parameters that describe the relations between the explanatory variables (see Bock 1975; Haberman 1979). This is well known in the case of two latent budgets ($T = 2$), since then the multinomial logit model simplifies to the ordinary logit model (see, for example, Fienberg 1980, Chapter 6). In fact, if the loglinear parameter estimates are identified in the same way that the multinomial logit parameter estimates were identified above (i.e., by setting the first parameter of each set equal to zero), then estimates for the multinomial logit parameters are equal to estimates for the corresponding loglinear parameters.

The equivalence of the multinomial response model and the hierarchical loglinear model gives us further insight into the constrained latent budget model. Goodman (1971) showed that if the marginal probabilities π_{i+t} follow a restrictive hierarchical loglinear model including parameters for t (which correspond to a column of 1's in **V**), and if for the latent probabilities π_{ijt} the variables A and B are independent given the level of variable X, then the probabilities π_{ijt} still follow a hierarchical loglinear model. It follows from collapsibility properties in loglinear models that have conditional independence properties (see Whittaker 1990). Thus, constraining the latent budget model does not affect the relationship between latent budget analysis and loglinear analysis: The constrained latent budget model can still be considered a hierarchical loglinear model for the latent probabilities.

Consider an example. Let the rows of a two-way contingency

table be stratified by two variables, A and C, with categories of A indexed by i and categories of C indexed by k ($k = 1, \ldots, K$). The latent budget model can be written as

$$\frac{\pi_{ikj}}{\pi_{ik+}} = \sum_{t=1}^{T} \pi_{ikt}^{AC\overline{X}} \pi_{jt}^{\overline{B}X}. \tag{16}$$

Consider the case in which the matrix $\mathbf{V}$ in (14) does not constrain the row parameters; that is, it specifies a saturated multinomial logit model. Then the latent loglinear model is (compare (15))

$$\log \pi_{ikjt} = \lambda + \left(\lambda_i^A + \lambda_k^C + \lambda_{ik}^{AC}\right) + \lambda_j^B + \lambda_t^X$$
$$+ \left(\lambda_{it}^{AX} + \lambda_{kt}^{CX} + \lambda_{ikt}^{ACX}\right) + \lambda_{jt}^{BX}. \tag{17}$$

We can constrain $\pi_{ikt}^{AC\overline{X}}$ by omitting the columns of the matrix $\mathbf{V}$ corresponding to the two-factor interactions λ_{it}^{AX} and λ_{kt}^{CX} or the three-factor interaction λ_{ikt}^{ACX}. For example, we could constrain λ_{ikt}^{ACX} to equal zero for all i, k, and t by deleting the columns of $\mathbf{V}$ that describe the interaction between i and k: If a model with this constraint fits adequately, we can conclude that the row budgets cross-classified by variables A and C can be adequately approximated in terms of the latent budgets $\pi_{jt}^{\overline{B}X}$ by an effect of A and an effect of C, although in terms of the latent loglinear model, there is no interaction between these variables in their relation to the latent budgets. Thus, the latent budget model can still be understood as a loglinear model for the latent probabilities.

Although the multinomial logit parameters γ_{mt} (or the corresponding λ parameters) are the fundamental parameters of the model defined for the conditional probabilities $\pi_{it}^{A\overline{X}}$, these fundamental parameters are difficult to interpret. Usually we do not study the γ_{mt} parameters. Often we do not even calculate them. Instead, we study the conditional probabilities $\pi_{it}^{A\overline{X}}$ that they yield. A drawback of interpreting the conditional probabilities instead of the fundamental parameters is that the constraints imposed by the set of fundamental parameters are not always clearly revealed by the conditional probabilities $\pi_{it}^{A\overline{X}}$ used in latent budget analysis. The properties that hold for $\log \pi_{ijt}$ are affected by the way in which the conditional probabilities $\pi_{it}^{A\overline{X}}$ are defined in (14). However, in situations like model (17) with constraint $\lambda_{ikt}^{ACX} = 0$, it is possible to study marginal probability estimates $\hat{\pi}_{it}^{A\overline{X}} \equiv \hat{\pi}_{i++t}/\hat{\pi}_{i+++}$ and $\hat{\pi}_{kt}^{C\overline{X}} \equiv \hat{\pi}_{+k+t}/\hat{\pi}_{+k++}$ instead of estimates $\hat{\pi}_{ikt}^{AC\overline{X}} = \hat{\pi}_{ik+t}/\hat{\pi}_{ik++}$ because the margins $\hat{\pi}_{i++t}$ and $\hat{\pi}_{+k+t}$ are two of the margins that generated the hierarchical loglinear model for the latent probabilities π_{ikjt}. Interpreting parameter estimates $\hat{\pi}_{it}^{A\overline{X}}$ and $\hat{\pi}_{kt}^{C\overline{X}}$ instead of $\hat{\pi}_{ikt}^{AC\overline{X}}$ can simplify the interpretation considerably.

To illustrate the usefulness of multinomial logit constraints for the row parameters, we will discuss two examples below.

Multinomial logit constraints on column parameters. Using the multinomial logit model, we can define constraints on the column parameters (see Bock 1975). We assume that the information on the column categories of the two-way contingency table is collected in the matrix $\mathbf{W}$, which has J rows and H columns and is indexed by h ($h = 1, \ldots, H$). Let $\mathbf{\Psi}$ be an $H \times T$ matrix with parameters ψ_{ht}. Now we can constrain the $\pi_{jt}^{\overline{B}X}$ parameters by the multinomial logit model

$$\pi_{jt}^{\overline{B}X} = \frac{\exp\left(\sum_{h=1}^{H} w_{jh}\psi_{ht}\right)}{\sum_{n=1}^{J} \exp\left(\sum_{h=1}^{H} w_{nh}\psi_{ht}\right)}. \tag{18}$$

The matrix $\mathbf{W}$ defines a model that is fitted to each latent budget t separately.

If $\mathbf{W}$ is chosen in an appropriate way, then the multinomial logit model for $\pi_{jt}^{\overline{B}X}$ is equivalent to a hierarchical loglinear model for the marginal probabilities π_{+jt}. Goodman (1971) showed that if π_{+jt} follows a hierarchical loglinear model and variables A and B are independent given X, the latent probabilities π_{ijt} also follow a hierarchical loglinear model. The situation is therefore similar to that for multinomial logit constraints on the rows.

When the column categories are classified by more than one variable, we can use the matrix $\mathbf{W}$ to describe the factorial structure of the columns. In this situation, an important special case is a constrained version of the simultaneous latent class model. Let there be two variables for the column categories, B indexed by j and D indexed by m. Then the latent budget model is

$$\frac{\pi_{ijm}}{\pi_{i++}} = \sum_{t=1}^{T} \pi_{it}^{A\overline{X}} \pi_{jmt}^{\overline{BDX}}, \tag{19}$$

and the loglinear model for the latent probabilities π_{ijmt} is

$$\begin{aligned}
\log\pi_{ijmt} = &\lambda + \lambda_i^A + \left(\lambda_j^B + \lambda_m^D + \lambda_{jm}^{BD}\right) \\
&+ \lambda_t^X + \lambda_{it}^{AX} + \left(\lambda_{jt}^{BX} + \lambda_{mt}^{DX} + \lambda_{jmt}^{BDX}\right).
\end{aligned} \tag{20}$$

Let **W** constrain the variables B and D to be independent at each level of X. This is achieved when **W** consists of columns contrasting the categories of variable B and the categories of variable D but there are no contrasts linking them. Then in the loglinear model for the marginal probabilities π_{+jmt}, B and D are conditionally independent given X (see Bock 1975). This yields model (20) with additional constraints $\lambda_{jm}^{BD} = \lambda_{jmt}^{BDX} = 0$. Model (19) can then be rewritten as

$$\frac{\pi_{ijm}}{\pi_{i++}} = \sum_{t=1}^{T} \pi_{it}^{A\overline{X}} \pi_{jt}^{\overline{B}X} \pi_{mt}^{\overline{D}X} . \tag{21}$$

Thus we have obtained a constrained form of simultaneous latent class analysis. In this constrained version of the simultaneous latent class model, variables B and D are conditionally independent given X, and the relationship between variables B and D is identical for every level of the group variable A. This identity makes (21) a *constrained* version of the simultaneous latent class model (cf. Clogg and Goodman 1984). The levels of the group variable A may be related in different ways to the latent budgets, however.

To illustrate the usefulness of multinomial constraints for the column parameters, we analyze the suicide data that was discussed in section 2.

Degrees of freedom and identification. By imposing multinomial logit constraints on row and column parameters, we sometimes identify the model. If the model is identified by imposing constraints as in (14) and (18), then the matrix **S** in $\mathbf{AB'} = \mathbf{ASS^{-1}B'}$ can only be the identity matrix (cf. Mooijaart 1982), and we should not subtract $T(T - 1)$ from the number of estimated parameters. This occurs in many constrained models.

If there is uncertainty about the number of degrees of freedom, this number can be derived by standard methods, for example, by determining the rank of the matrix of partial derivatives of the probabilities with respect to the parameters (cf. Goodman 1974).

Maximum likelihood estimation. When there are multinomial logit models for both the row and column parameters, then a loglikelihood function that is similar to (9) can be defined, and as in (10a) and (10b), it can be split into two parts, one part for the row parameters and one part for the column parameters. These parts can be maximized separately. They are

$$f(\gamma_{tm}) = \sum_{i=1}^{I} \sum_{T=1}^{T} \underline{n}_{i+} t \ln \left(\frac{\exp \left(\sum_{m=1}^{M} v_{im}\gamma_{tm} \right)}{\sum_{n=1}^{T} \exp \left(\sum_{m=1}^{M} v_{im}\gamma_{nm} \right)} \right) + \text{constant} \quad (22a)$$

and

$$f(\psi_{th}) = \sum_{j=1}^{J} \sum_{t=1}^{T} \underline{n}_{+j} t \ln \left(\frac{\exp \left(\sum_{h=1}^{H} w_{jh}\psi_{th} \right)}{\sum_{n=1}^{J} \exp \left(\sum_{h=1}^{H} w_{nh}\psi_{th} \right)} \right) + \text{constant}, \quad (22b)$$

where (22a) is to be maximized over γ_{tm} and (22b) is to be maximized over ψ_{th}.

For the row parameters $\pi_{it}^{A\overline{X}}$, this amounts to fitting the multinomial logit model to the updated estimate of the margins of the latent frequencies $\underline{n}_{i+}t$, using these as if they were ordinary observed frequencies. For the column parameters $\pi_{jt}^{B\overline{X}}$, this amounts to fitting the multinomial logit model to the updated estimate of the margins of the latent frequencies $\underline{n}_{+jk}$, using these as if they were ordinary observed frequencies.

Bock (1975) shows how to find the estimates for the general multinomial logit model using the Newton-Raphson algorithm. He also explains how to fit the multinomial logit model in case of structural zeros, which can be used in our context whenever there are additional fixed-value constraints for some of the $\pi_{it}^{A\overline{X}}$.

We deal now with an important special case in which the multinomial logit model is equivalent to a hierarchical loglinear model. This might occur for the rows when the matrix $\mathbf{V}$ describes the factorial structure of the rows of the contingency table, and it might occur for the columns when the matrix $\mathbf{W}$ describes the factorial structure of the columns of the contingency table. In such cases, the multinomial logit model can be fitted using iterative proportional fitting (see Bishop, Fienberg, and Holland 1975; Fienberg 1980, Chapters 3 and 4). Iterative proportional fitting is computationally more efficient than the Newton-Raphson procedure either when the number of parameters to be estimated becomes large or when direct estimates for the expected frequencies exist.

When iterative proportional fitting is used to fit a multinomial logit model for the row parameters $\pi_{it}^{A\overline{X}}$, for example, then this procedure yields constrained estimates $\hat{\pi}_{it}^{A\overline{X}}$ but no estimates for the multinomial logit parameters γ_{mt} (compare (14)). However, the constrained estimates $\hat{\pi}_{it}^{A\overline{X}}$ can be used to obtain the multinomial logit parameters in the following way. Let the estimates of conditional probabilities $\hat{\pi}_{it}^{A\overline{X}}$ follow some multinomial logit model. In this case the unconditional estimates $p_{i+}\hat{\pi}_{it}^{A\overline{X}}$ follow a corresponding loglinear model. If the loglinear parameters are identified in the same way as the multinomial logit parameters, that is, by constraining the first of a set of parameters to be zero, then the estimates for the multinomial logit parameters γ_{mt} are identical to the corresponding estimates for the loglinear λ parameters. Thus, the estimates for the loglinear λ parameters can be derived easily from $\log p_{i+}\hat{\pi}_{it}^{A X}$, since $\log p_{1+}\hat{\pi}_{11}^{A X}$ $= \hat{\lambda}$, $\log p_{1+}\hat{\pi}_{12}^{A\overline{X}} = \hat{\lambda} + \hat{\lambda}_{2}^{X} = \log p_{1+}\hat{\pi}_{11}^{A\overline{X}} + \hat{\lambda}_{2}^{X}$, and so on.

Examples. For the suicide data analyzed in section 2, we chose the unconstrained model with $T = 3$. The fit of this model was $G^{2} = 1,085.9$, $df = 186$, although the fit measures were used as descriptive measures only.

Let the row variable age be A, indexed by i, and let the row variable sex be C, indexed by k. Then the unconstrained latent budget model is (16) or, as the equivalent loglinear model for the latent probabilities π_{ikjt}, (17). As discussed above, we will use the factorial structure of the rows to constrain the row parameters $\pi_{ikt}^{AC\overline{X}}$. The matrix **V** used to constrain these parameters has as its first column a unit vector, as its second column a dummy vector for sex, and then 16 dummy vectors for age. The unconstrained model would have 16 extra dummy vectors for the interaction between sex and age. We will investigate here whether this interaction is important by omitting these sixteen columns. In terms of the loglinear model for the latent probabilities π_{ikjt}, this corresponds to constraining the parameters $\lambda_{ikt}^{AC X}$ to be zero.

This constraint can be motivated as follows. In the unconstrained model the expected budgets of the age-sex groups are related to three latent budgets. There can be a sex effect, an age effect, and an age-sex interaction effect. If the interaction effect can be omitted, then the interpretation simplifies considerably: Only the age effect and the sex effect need to be interpreted. An individual's suicide behavior is then determined by that person's sex and age, but not by the specific age-sex combination.

The number of degrees of freedom for this constrained model is derived as follows. There are 34×8 independent cells, $18 \times (3 - 1)$ parameters γ_{mt} for the rows, and $T(J - 1) = 3 \times 8$ parameters for the columns; and the model is identified by constraining the row parameters $\hat{\pi}_{ikt}^{AC\overline{X}}$ by the matrix **V** described above. This gives $272 - (36 + 24) = 212df$.

The constrained model has a fit of $G^2 = 1,136.6$, $df = 212$, and the difference between it and the unconstrained three-budget model is relatively slight, given the large sample size ($G^2 = 1,136.6 - 1,085.9 = 50.6$, $df = 212 - 186 = 26$). The parameter estimates in Table 3[3] are similar to the parameter estimates in Table 2, especially the column parameters. To simplify the interpretation of the row parameters $\hat{\pi}_{ikt}^{AC\overline{X}}$, we also give average age-effect parameter estimates $\hat{\pi}_{it}^{A\overline{X}}$ and average sex-effect parameter estimates $\hat{\pi}_{kt}^{C\overline{X}}$. (For a derivation of these parameter estimates, see the section "Multinomial logit constraints on row parameters," above.)

The average sex-effect parameter estimates show that the expected budgets for males consist far more than average (i.e., much more than the probabilities given by the average) of latent budgets 1 and 3, whereas the expected budgets for females consist far more than average of latent budget 2. The average age-effect parameter estimates show that the first age group has an extremely high tendency to use the third latent budget, the younger age groups tend to use the first latent budget, and the older groups are most likely to use the second latent budget.

This application shows how the factorial structure of the row categories may be used to constrain the row parameters. We conclude that by constraining the row parameters with a multinomial logit model, the interpretation has been simplified considerably. Although this type of application is possible, by using the methodology of loglinear modeling with latent variables, it has not received attention thus far in the literature.

Crime among four ethnic groups. The Netherlands Ministry of Justice investigated the differences in involvement in crime among youth from four ethnic groups: Moroccans, Turks, Surinamese, and Dutch. To control for the generally lower socioeconomic status of the first three ethnic groups, the Dutch sample consisted of youngsters who lived on the same streets as the youngsters from the other ethnic groups. For more details, see Junger (1990). Among other things, three crime measures were gathered from the police registration:

---

[3]We do not give the multinomial logit parameters γ_{mt}, because these parameters are much harder to interpret than the conditional probabilities that they yield (see (14)).

TABLE 3
Parameter Estimates for Constrained Model

Age	Males $\hat{\pi}_{ikt}^{AC\overline{X}}$			Females $\hat{\pi}_{ikt}^{AC\overline{X}}$			Average Age Effect $\hat{\pi}_{it}^{A\overline{X}}$		
	$t=1$	$t=2$	$t=3$	$t=1$	$t=2$	$t=3$	$t=1$	$t=2$	$t=3$
10–15	.023	.002	.975	.268	.732	.000	.070	.143	.787
15–20	.498	.015	.486	.522	.478	.000	.505	.144	.352
20–25	.642	.022	.336	.497	.503	.000	.606	.143	.251
25–30	.648	.023	.329	.483	.517	.000	.605	.151	.244
30–35	.614	.038	.347	.352	.648	.000	.547	.195	.258
35–40	.552	.036	.412	.339	.661	.000	.494	.205	.301
40–45	.473	.071	.456	.183	.817	.000	.391	.281	.328
45–50	.420	.081	.499	.149	.851	.000	.334	.326	.340
50–55	.354	.121	.525	.090	.910	.000	.237	.472	.291
55–60	.304	.165	.532	.059	.941	.000	.191	.522	.287
60–65	.217	.247	.536	.029	.971	.000	.129	.587	.285
65–70	.104	.359	.537	.010	.990	.000	.060	.652	.288
70–75	.054	.417	.530	.004	.996	.000	.032	.670	.298
75–80	.017	.434	.549	.001	.999	.000	.009	.701	.289
80–85	.000	.518	.482	.000	1.000	.000	.000	.748	.252
85–90	.000	.442	.558	.000	1.000	.000	.000	.662	.338
90+	.005	.395	.600	.000	1.000	.000	.003	.598	.399

Cause of Death[a]	Column Parameters $\hat{\pi}_{jt}^{B\overline{X}}$					Average Sex Effect $\hat{\pi}_{kt}^{C\overline{X}}$		
	$\hat{\pi}_{+j}$	$t=1$	$t=2$	$t=3$		$t=1$	$t=2$	$t=3$
1	.330	.543	.416	.000	Males	.383	.151	.466
2	.005	.011	.003	.000	Females	.143	.857	.000
3	.040	.130	.001	.006				
4	.383	.000	.340	.823	Average	.296	.408	.296
5	.050	.021	.098	.012				
6	.059	.094	.001	.103				
7	.018	.006	.018	.029				
8	.053	.054	.082	.014				
9	.062	.141	.041	.013				
Total	1.000	1.000	1.000	1.000				

[a]See note to Table 1.

TABLE 4
Crime Among Four Ethnic Groups, by Age

Ethnicity	Age	Crime Pattern BDE[a]								Total
		000	100	010	110	001	101	001	111	
Moroccans	12–13	65	13	1	1	0	1	0	1	82
	14–15	43	12	0	4	2	2	0	2	65
	16–17	26	18	1	2	0	3	0	1	51
Turks	12–13	52	4	0	0	1	0	0	0	57
	14–15	73	16	1	2	3	0	0	0	95
	16–17	32	13	1	3	0	1	0	1	51
Surinamese	12–13	71	9	1	0	2	2	0	0	85
	14–15	54	10	0	1	0	1	1	1	68
	16–17	36	12	1	1	0	2	0	1	53
Dutch	12–13	78	5	0	0	2	3	0	0	88
	14–15	70	5	1	1	0	1	0	1	79
	16–17	26	3	1	1	3	1	0	2	37
Total		626	120	8	16	13	17	1	10	811

Note: Type of crime: B = property crime, D = aggression against persons, E = vandalism.

[a] 0 = not registered, 1 = registered.

property crime, aggression against persons, and vandalism. The age of the youngsters was coded into three categories: 12–13, 14–15, and 16–17. This led to the data in Table 4. The relevant questions are (1) Are there one or more underlying crime measures? (2) Are these underlying crime measures the same for each of the ethnic groups? (3) If so, how is group membership (i.e., ethnic-group and age-group membership) related to these underlying crime measures?

Since the table is sparse, the power of tests will be relatively low. Therefore, we will not use the test results as evidence for acceptance of models, but rather as evidence for not rejecting them.

The first two questions can be answered readily by a constrained form of simultaneous latent class analysis similar to (21). For the explanatory variables, let age be denoted by A, indexed by i, and ethnic group by C, indexed by k. For the response variables, let the three crime measures be denoted by B, D, and E, indexed by j, m, and n, respectively. Then the latent budget model is

$$\frac{\pi_{ikjmn}}{\pi_{ik+++}} = \sum_{t=1}^{T} \pi_{ikt}^{AC\overline{X}} \pi_{jmnt}^{\overline{BDEX}} , \tag{23}$$

with the parameters $\pi_{jmnt}^{\overline{BDEX}}$ constrained by a multinomial logit model (18) with fixed scores w_{jmnh} and parameters ψ_{ht}. The fixed scores w_{jmnh} can be collected in an 8×3 matrix $\mathbf{W}$, where 8 is the number of response combinations defined by j, m, and n, and 3 is the number of variables. The first column contrasts the two categories of variable B, the second column contrasts the two categories of variable D, and the third column contrasts the two categories of variable E. Thus, the three variables B, D, and E are unrelated in $\mathbf{W}$, and the variables B, D, and E are independent at each level of the latent variable X. Therefore, $\pi_{jmnt}^{\overline{BDEX}}$ can be rewritten as $\pi_{jmnt}^{\overline{BDEX}} = \pi_{jt}^{\overline{BX}} \pi_{mt}^{\overline{DX}} \pi_{nt}^{\overline{EX}}$ (compare (19) with (21)). The parameters ψ_{ht} are collected in a $3 \times T$ matrix, where T is the number of latent budgets. There are thus $3 \times T$ parameters to be estimated.

Model (23) with the above constraints corresponds to the following loglinear model for the latent probabilities π_{ikjmn}:

$$\pi_{ikjnmt} = \lambda + (\lambda_i^A + \lambda_k^C + \lambda_{ik}^{AC}) + (\lambda_j^B + \lambda_m^D + \lambda_n^E) + \lambda_t^X$$
$$+ (\lambda_{it}^{AX} + \lambda_{kt}^{CX} + \lambda_{ikt}^{ACX}) + (\lambda_{jt}^{BX} + \lambda_{mt}^{DX} + \lambda_{nt}^{EX}). \tag{24}$$

Therefore, because of the multinomial logit model for the parameters $\pi_{jmnt}^{\overline{BDEX}}$, there are no direct relations between the response variables B, D, and E.

Model (23) with two latent budgets, or classes, and constraint $\pi_{jmnt}^{\overline{BDEX}} = \pi_{jt}^{\overline{BX}} \pi_{mt}^{\overline{DX}} \pi_{nt}^{\overline{EX}}$ has an adequate fit: $G^2 = 65.93$, df is 66 (see Table 5). Since the Pearson chi-square statistic is better approximated by the chi-square distribution in case of small frequencies, we also give it here: $X = 72.14$. The parameters $\hat{\pi}_{ikt}^{A C\overline{X}}$, $\hat{\pi}_{jt}^{\overline{BX}}$, $\hat{\pi}_{mt}^{\overline{DX}}$, and $\hat{\pi}_{nt}^{\overline{EX}}$ are given in the first columns (model 1) of Table 6. In the first latent

TABLE 5
Fit of Models for Table 4

	G^2	X^2	df
Model 1, No constraints	65.93	72.15	66
Model 2, $\lambda_{ikt}^{ACX} = 0$	70.30	80.74	72
Model 3, $\lambda_{ikt}^{ACX} = 0$, $\lambda_{kt}^{CX} = 0$	104.87	131.38	74
Model 4, $\lambda_{ikt}^{ACX} = 0$, $\lambda_{it}^{AX} = 0$	86.70	85.60	75
Model 5, $\lambda_{ikt}^{ACX} = 0$, λ_{it}^{AX} is linear in age	70.31	80.81	73

Note: Models are defined in terms of constraints that they impose upon the conditional row probabilities $\pi_{ikt}^{AC\overline{X}}$.

TABLE 6a
Latent Budget Estimates for Table 4
(Parameter Estimates $\hat{\pi}_{ikt}^{AC\overline{X}}$)

Ethnicity	Age	Model 1		Model 2		Model 5	
		$t = 1$	$t = 2$	$t = 1$	$t = 2$	$t = 1$	$t = 2$
Moroccans	12–13	.851	.149	.853	.147	.855	.145
	14–15	.693	.307	.703	.297	.701	.299
	16–17	.510	.490	.482	.519	.483	.517
Turks	12–13	1.000	.000	.935	.065	.935	.065
	14–15	.858	.142	.852	.148	.852	.148
	16–17	.649	.351	.694	.306	.696	.304
Surinamese	12–13	.921	.079	.930	.070	.931	.069
	14–15	.836	.164	.844	.156	.843	.157
	16–17	.714	.286	.680	.320	.682	.318
Dutch	12–13	.944	.056	.959	.041	.960	.040
	14–15	.929	.071	.906	.094	.905	.095
	16–17	.779	.222	.790	.210	.792	.208

budget, children have estimated probabilities of .063, .006, and .017 of being arrested for crimes B, D, and E, whereas in the second latent budget, children have estimated probabilities of .859, .219, and .213 of being arrested for those crimes. The first budget is thus a budget for children who have a very low probability of being arrested, whereas these probabilities are high for B and moderate for D and E in the second budget. The parameters $\pi_{ikt}^{AC\overline{X}}$ show the estimated probabilities of each of the latent budgets for each of the age-ethnicity groups. It shows that for each ethnic group, the probability of the (more criminal) second budget increases as they get older, that Moroccans have the highest probability of the second budget in each age group, and that the Turks show a rapid increase in the probability of the second budget as they get older. The Dutch have relatively low probabilities of the criminal budget, especially as they get older. This analysis appears to answer the first two questions: (1) The data provide no evidence against the existence of only two latent types of criminality, and (2) all ethnic groups have these in common. The model with two latent budgets gives an adequate fit.

The third question is also partly answered by the above analysis. However, we may wonder whether there is in fact any evidence of an ethnic-group effect, of an age-group effect, and of an interac-

TABLE 6b
Latent Budget Estimates for Table 4
(Parameter Estimates $\hat{\pi}_{jt}^{BX}$, $\hat{\pi}_{mt}^{DX}$, $\hat{\pi}_{nt}^{EX}$)

Type of Crime[a]	Registration	Model 1		Model 2		Model 5	
		$t = 1$	$t = 2$	$t = 1$	$t = 2$	$t = 1$	$t = 2$
B	0	.937	.141	.942	.135	.941	.135
	1	.063	.859	.058	.865	.059	.865
D	0	.994	.781	.993	.787	.993	.786
	1	.006	.219	.007	.213	.007	.214
E	0	.983	.787	.983	.794	.983	.794
	1	.017	.213	.017	.206	.017	.206

[a]See note to Table 4.

tion between age and ethnic group. This can be tested by constraining the parameters π_{ikt}^{ACX} by using multinomial logit models. In terms of the latent loglinear model, we can constrain the parameters λ_{it}^{AX}, λ_{kt}^{CX}, and λ_{ikt}^{ACX} to be zero. Goodness-of-fit statistics for the models that we will discuss are given in Table 5.

Constraining the parameters λ_{ikt}^{ACX} to be zero implies that there are age-group and ethnic-group effects on the amount of criminality, but also that the age-group effect is the same for each ethnic group and that the ethnic-group effect is the same for each age group. This is Model 2 in Table 5. For this model the fit decreases to $G^2 = 70.30$, $df = 72$, $X^2 = 80.74$), which is still adequate. The difference between the fit of Model 2 and the fit of unconstrained Model 1 (see Table 5) is also not significant: $G^2 = 4.37$, $df = 6$. Therefore, there is insufficient evidence of any interaction between age and ethnic group in their relation to crime. The parameter estimates for Model 2 are given in the middle columns of Table 6. They differ only slightly from those for the unconstrained solution. A plot of the parameters $\hat{\pi}_{ik2}^{ACX}$, showing the probabilities for both the constrained and the unconstrained models of the criminal latent budget, is given in Figure 3. The lines connecting the different age points for the four ethnic groups are slightly more regular than those in the constrained solution.

A more restrictive model constrains both λ_{it}^{AX} and λ_{ikt}^{ACX} to be zero. This model (Model 3 in Table 5) assumes no direct relationship between age and crime, but only a direct relationship between ethnic group and crime (specified by the parameters λ_{kt}^{CX}). The fit of this

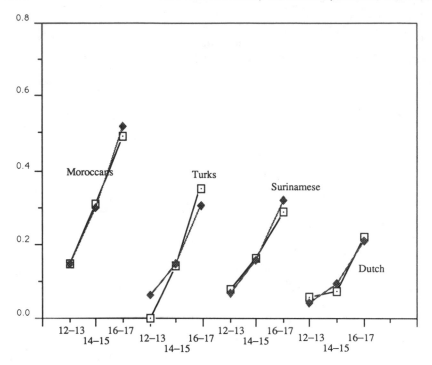

FIGURE 3. Plot of estimated row probabilities of the second (more criminal) latent budget. Open squares: unconstrained (Model 1, Table 4); solid squares: constrained (Model 2, Table 4).

model is poor: $G^2 = 104.87$, $df = 74$, $X^2 = 131.38$). Another model
(Model 4) constrains both λ_{kt}^{CX} and λ_{ikt}^{ACX} to be zero. No ethnic-group
effect is assumed, only an age-group effect. This model fits quite
well, but we reject this hypothesis because the difference between it
and Model 2 is significant: $G^2 = 86.70 - 70.30 = 16.40$, $df = 75 - 72$
$= 3$.

We therefore end up with Model 2. Model 2 can be constrained further by making use of the fact that the age categories are
ordered. We can model this by replacing the two columns for age in
the design matrix (one column for ages 12–13, and one for ages 14–
15) with one column with values −1, 0, and 1 for ages 12–13, 14–15,
and 16–17. Then, the age-group effect is assumed to be linear with
age (Model 5). The difference between Models 2 and 5 is extremely
small: $G^2 = 70.81$, $df = 73$, $X^2 = 80.81$.

The models used in this analysis are very similar to simultaneous latent class models. The example shows how multinomial logit constraints on the column parameters can be used to model conditional independence of three manifest variables given a latent variable. Assuming a latent variable that accounts for the association between manifest variables is standard in latent class analysis, but using the multinomial logit model for this purpose is new. The analysis shows that there is no evidence for more than two latent types of crime (the interpretation of the latent variable) and that all age-ethnic-group combinations have these two latent types of crime in common. Using the multinomial logit model to constrain the row parameters is also new. This turns out to be fruitful when there is additional information for the row variable. Here we can conclude that there is evidence of an age-group effect and of an ethnic-group effect, but not of age-ethnic-group interaction effects in the use of the criminal budgets. Furthermore, the age-group effect turns out to be linear in age.

4. CONCLUSION

Latent budget analysis is closely related to latent class analysis. In latent budget analysis the observed variables are considered to be either explanatory or response variables. In this sense latent budget analysis is different from latent class analysis, because in most applications of latent class analysis, all observed variables play the same role. However, the unconstrained models are equivalent, as shown in section 2. Latent class analysis of a two-way table is most often used when a latent variable should explain the association between the two manifest variables. Latent budget analysis can be used when the observed budgets are considered to be generated by a number of unknown latent budgets (see the mixture model in Figure 1) or when the latent variable is thought to intervene between two manifest variables (see the MIMIC model in Figure 2).

We have discussed constraints on the parameters of the latent budget model. The most interesting constraints discussed in the paper are the multinomial logit constraints. Our presentation emphasizes conditional independence of the rows and columns of a two-way table given a latent variable, and multinomial logit constraints imposed on the relations between the row variable and the latent variable and between the column variable and the latent variable. We showed that, just as for the unconstrained model, the constrained latent budget model can be understood as a loglinear model for the unobserved contingency table.

This conclusion suggests that constrained latent budget analysis is very similar to the loglinear model approach of latent class analysis as presented by, for example, Haberman (1979) and Hagenaars (1988, 1990). Indeed, although our models are different from the latent class models of Haberman and Hagenaars, our models can be fit using their methodology. However, the use of an explanatory variable for the rows and a response variable for the columns gives a specific interpretation to the parameters that is different from the interpretation in latent class analysis. In addition, the use of joint variables, and the exclusion of certain interaction effects, leads to interpretations that are different, and often more parsimonious, than those in latent class analysis. For example, Hagenaars (1988, 1990) discusses local dependence models as models with direct effects between manifest response variables and allows for these direct effects to account for correlated response error. In this paper direct effects between explanatory variables are included in the latent budget model because a multinomial distribution is assumed for each of the joint levels of the joint row variable. Both approaches can lead to the same loglinear model with latent variables, but with a different interpretation. The models given here allow us to answer questions previously unanswered by latent class models.

APPENDIX: SOFTWARE

The analysis in this paper has been performed with prototypes of programs written in APL. These prototypes can be obtained from the first author free of charge. However, it is also possible to use existing software.

Unconstrained latent budget analysis can be performed with existing programs for latent class analysis, such as MLLSA (Clogg 1977) or LCAG (Hagenaars and Luijkx 1990) or NEWTON, a program that replaces the earlier program LAT (see Haberman 1988). MLLSA and LCAG use the EM algorithm, while NEWTON uses a combination of the Newton-Raphson algorithm and the EM algorithm. After convergence of these programs, the row-parameter estimates of the latent budget model have to be derived using equation

(3). It is also possible to use the relation of latent budget analysis to simultaneous latent class analysis (see van der Heijden et al. 1989) or to mixed Markov latent class models (see van de Pol and Langeheine 1990). In programs that use the EM algorithm, simultaneous latent class models are fitted by using latent class models with so-called quasi-latent variables (see, for example, Hagenaars 1988, 1990). Then the row-parameter estimates are found directly. The program PAN-MARK (van de Pol, Langeheine, and de Jong 1989), used for mixed Markov latent class analysis, can be used if the latent budget model is considered as a mixed Markov latent class model for one variable with only one time point (see van de Pol and Langeheine 1990).

The above programs all allow for fixed-value and equality constraints in the latent budget model. Multinomial logit constraints can be fitted in NEWTON and LCAG by considering the latent budget model with multinomial logit constraints as a loglinear model with a latent variable. In NEWTON, design matrices are used to define the loglinear model for the unobserved matrix. Thus, all possible multinomial logit constraints can be fitted in NEWTON. In LCAG quasi-latent variables are used, and the program fits standard hierarchical loglinear models to the matrix with latent class probabilities (see Hagenaars 1988, 1990). Thus, all multinomial logit constraints that constrain loglinear interaction parameters to be zero can be fitted.

REFERENCES

Agresti, A. 1990. *Categorical Data Analysis.* New York: Wiley.

Aitchison, J. 1986. *The Statistical Analysis of Compositional Data.* London: Chapman and Hall.

Aitkin, M., D. Anderson, and J. Hinde. 1981. "Statistical Modeling of Data on Teaching Styles." *Journal of the Royal Statistical Society,* ser A., 144:419–61.

Bishop, Y. M. M., S. E. Fienberg, and P. W. Holland. 1975. *Discrete Multivariate Analysis.* Cambridge, MA: MIT Press.

Bock, R. D. 1975. *Multivariate Statistical Methods in Behavioral Research.* New York: McGraw-Hill.

Clogg, C. C. 1977. "Unrestricted and Restricted Maximum Likelihood Latent Structure Analysis: A Manual for Users." Working Paper No. 1977–9. State College, PA: Pennsylvania State University, Population Issues Research Office.

———. 1981. "Latent Structure Models of Mobility." *American Journal of Sociology* 86:836–68.

Clogg, C. C., and L. A. Goodman. 1984. "Latent Structure Analysis of a Set of Multidimensional Contingency Tables." *Journal of the American Statistical Association* 79:762–71.

de Leeuw, J., and P. G. M. van der Heijden. 1988. "The Analysis of Time Budgets with a Latent Time-Budget Model." Pp. 159–66 in *Data Analysis and Informatics 5,* edited by E. Diday et al. Amsterdam: North Holland.

———. 1991. "Reduced Rank Models for Contingency Tables." *Biometrika* 78:229–32.

de Leeuw, J., P. G. M. van der Heijden, and P. Verboon. 1990. "A Latent Time-Budget Model." *Statistica Neerlandica* 44:1–22.

Dempster, A. P., N. M. Laird, and D. B. Rubin. 1977. "Maximum Likelihood from Incomplete Data via the EM Algorithm." *Journal of the Royal Statistical Society,* ser. B, 39:1–38.

Everitt, B. S. 1988. "A Monte Carlo Investigation of the Likelihood Ratio Test for Number of Classes in Latent Class Analysis." *Multivariate Behavioral Research* 23:531–38.

Fienberg, S. E. 1980. *The Analysis of Cross-Classified Categorical Data.* 2d ed. Cambridge, MA: MIT Press.

Formann, A. K. 1978. "A Note on Parameter Estimation for Lazarsfeld's Latent Class Analysis." *Psychometrika* 43:123–26.

———. 1982. "Linear Logistic Latent Class Analysis." *Biometrical Journal* 24:171–90.

———. 1985. "Constrained Latent Class Models: Theory and Applications." *British Journal of Mathematical and Statistical Psychology* 38:87–111.

———. 1989. "Constrained Latent Class Models: Some Further Applications." *British Journal of Mathematical and Statistical Psychology* 42:37–54.

Gilula, Z. 1979. "Singular Value Decomposition of Probability Matrices: Probabilistic Aspects of Latent Dichotomous Variables." *Biometrics* 66:339–44.

———. 1983. "Latent Conditional Independence in Two-Way Contingency Tables: A Diagnostic Approach." *British Journal of Mathematical and Statistical Psychology* 36:114–22.

———. 1984. "On Some Similarities Between Canonical Correlation Models and Latent Class Models for Two-Way Contingency Tables." *Biometrika* 71:523–29.

———. 1986. "Grouping and Association in Contingency Tables: An Exploratory Canonical Correlation Approach." *Journal of the American Statistical Association* 81:773–79.

Gilula, Z., and S. J. Haberman. 1986. "Canonical Analysis of Contingency Tables by Maximum Likelihood." *Journal of the American Statistical Association* 81:780–88.

———. 1988. "The Analysis of Multivariate Contingency Tables by Restricted Canonical and Restricted Association Models." *Journal of the American Statistical Association* 83:760–71.

Gilula, Z., and A. M. Krieger. 1989. "Collapsed Two-Way Contingency Tables and the Chi-Square Reduction Principle." *Journal of the Royal Statistical Society,* ser. B, 51:425–33.

Good, I. J. 1969. "Some Applications of the Singular Decomposition of a Matrix." *Technometrics* 11:823–31.

Goodman, L. A. 1971. "Partitioning of Chi-Square, Analysis of Marginal Contingency Tables, and Estimation of Expected Frequencies in Multidimensional Contingency Tables." *Journal of the American Statistical Association* 66:339–44.

———. 1974. "Exploratory Latent Structure Analysis Using Both Identifiable and Unidentifiable Models." *Biometrika* 61:215–31.

———. 1981. "Criteria for Determining Whether Certain Categories in a Cross-Classification Table Should be Combined, with Special Reference to Occupational Categories in Occupational Mobility Tables." *American Journal of Sociology* 87:612–50.

———. 1985. "The Analysis of Cross-Classified Data Having Ordered and/or Unordered Categories: Association Models, Correlation Models, and Asymmetry Models for Contingency Tables With or Without Missing Entries." *Annals of Statistics* 13:10–69.

———. 1986. "Some Useful Extensions to the Usual Correspondence Analysis Approach and the Usual Loglinear Approach in the Analysis of Contingency Tables" (with comments). *International Statistical Review* 54:243–309.

———. 1987. "New Methods for Analyzing the Intrinsic Character of Qualitative Variables Using Cross-Classified Data." *American Journal of Sociology* 93:529–83.

Grover, R. 1987. "Estimation and Use of Standard Errors of Latent Class Model Parameters." *Journal of Marketing Research* 24:298–304.

Grover, R., and V. Srinivasan. 1987. "A Simultaneous Approach to Market Segmentation and to Market Structuring." *Journal of Marketing Research* 24:139–53.

Haberman, S. J. 1979. *Analysis of Qualitative Data*. 2 vols. New York: Academic Press.

———. 1988. "A Stabilized Newton-Raphson Algorithm for Log-Linear Models for Frequency Tables Derived by Indirect Observation." Pp. 193–212 in *Sociological Methodology 1988*, edited by C. C. Clogg. Washington, DC: American Sociological Association.

Hagenaars, J. A. 1986. "Symmetry, Quasi-Symmetry, and Marginal Homogeneity on the Latent Level." *Social Science Research* 15:241–55.

———. 1988. "Latent Structure Models with Direct Effects Between Indicators. Local Dependence Models." *Sociological Methods and Research* 16:379–405.

———. 1990. *Categorical Longitudinal Data. Log-Linear, Panel, Trend, and Cohort Analysis*. London: Sage.

Hagenaars, J. A., and R. Luijkx. 1990. "LCAG. A Program for Latent Class Models and Other Loglinear Models with Latent Variables With and Without Missing Data." Working Paper No. 17. Tilburg: Tilburg University, Department of Sociology.

Heudin, H. 1982. *Suicide in America*. New York: Norton.

Heuer, J. 1979. *Selbstmord bei Kinder und Jugendlichen* (Suicide of children and youth). Stuttgard, Germany: Ernst Klett Verlag.

Junger, M. 1990. *Delinquency and Ethnicity.* Deventer, The Netherlands: Kluwer.

Langeheine, R. 1989. "New Developments in Latent Class Theory." Pp. 77–108 in *Latent Trait and Latent Class Models,* edited by R. Langeheine and J. Rost. New York: Plenum.

Luijkx, R. 1987. "Loglinear Modeling with Latent Variables: The Case of Mobility Tables." In *Sociometrics Research,* vol. 2, edited by W. Saris and I. Gallhofer. London: MacMillan.

Marsden, P. V. 1985. "Latent Structure Models for Relationally Defined Social Classes." *American Journal of Sociology* 90:1002–21.

McCutcheon, A. L. 1987. *Latent Class Analysis.* No. 64 in *Quantitative Applications in the Social Sciences.* London: Sage.

Mooijaart, A. 1982. "Latent Structure Analysis for Categorical Variables." In *Systems Under Indirect Observation,* edited by K. G. Jöreskog and H. Wold. Amsterdam: North Holland.

Mooijaart, A., and P. G. M. van der Heijden. 1992. "The EM Algorithm for Latent Class Analysis with Constraints." *Psychometrika* (in press).

Shigemasu, K., and Sugiyama, N. 1989. "Latent Class Analysis of Choice Behavior." Paper presented at the Annual Meetings of the Psychometric Society, University of California at Los Angeles.

Takane, Y. 1987. "Analysis of Contingency Tables by Ideal Point Discriminant Analysis." *Psychometrika* 52:493–513.

van de Pol, F., and R. Langeheine. 1990. "Mixed Markov Latent Class Models: From Description Towards Explanation." Pp. 213–47 in *Sociological Methodology 1990,* edited by C. C. Clogg. Oxford: Basil Blackwell.

van de Pol, F., R. Langeheine, and W. de Jong. 1989. *PANMARK User Manual.* Voorburg: Netherlands Central Bureau of Statistics.

van der Heijden, P. G. M. 1991. "Three Approaches to Study the Departure from Quasi-Independence." *Statistics Applicata* (in press).

van der Heijden, P. G. M., and J. de Leeuw. 1985. "Correspondence Analysis Used Complementary to Loglinear Analysis." *Psychometrika* 50:429–47.

van der Heijden, P. G. M., A. Mooijaart, and J. de Leeuw. 1989. "Latent Budget Analysis. In *Statistical Modelling. Proceedings, Trento, 1989,* edited by A. Decarli et al. Berlin: Springer Verlag.

Whittaker, J. 1990. *Graphical Models in Applied Multivariate Statistics.* New York: Wiley.

✖ 10 ✖

THE USE OF GRADE-OF-MEMBERSHIP TECHNIQUES TO ESTIMATE REGRESSION RELATIONSHIPS

*Kenneth G. Manton**
*Max A. Woodbury**
*Eric Stallard**
*Larry S. Corder**

In this paper we describe the use of grade-of-membership (GOM) models to estimate multivariate regression relationships between multiple sets of discrete variables. A GOM model is a semiparametric latent structure model that represents state variables as a continuous mixture of fuzzy classes. The use of fuzzy classes allows representation of individual heterogeneity. We present conditions for identifiability and consistency of GOM estimators, and we present the generalization to conditionally dependent sets of variables, each represented by their own set of latent fuzzy classes. We discuss similarities and differences between GOM models and other latent structure models such as LISREL (and recent variants in which the observed variables may be discretely distributed). Finally we present an example from the 1982 and 1984 National Long Term Care Surveys, which found that health-service utilization is determined by medical conditions and functional status and that resources, attitudes, and behaviors act as mediating variables.

This research was supported by National Institute on Aging grants 1RO1AG07469, 5R37AG07198, and 5R01AG01159 and by HCFA grant 18-C-98641.

*Duke University

321

1. INTRODUCTION

Multivariate procedures to determine the structural relations of jointly normal latent state variables are well developed (e.g., Jöreskog and Sörbom 1979, 1988). Procedures are also available to identify latent normally distributed state variables, under certain conditions, from discrete variables (e.g., Muthén 1989; Jöreskog and Sörbom 1986). The *statistical* properties of these models are robust (e.g., even if latent variables are not normally distributed) if certain conditions hold (e.g., if data are described by the sample covariance matrix and if errors are independent) (Anderson and Amemiya 1988). We present a procedure based on "fuzzy set" principles (Zadeh 1965, 1968) to estimate structural relations from multivariate discrete response data in which *no* parametric assumptions are made about the distribution of the latent state variables. We compare this procedure, the grade of membership (GOM) model (e.g., Woodbury, Clive, and Garson 1978; Woodbury and Clive 1974; Clive, Woodbury, and Siegler 1983), to maximum likelihood (ML) factor analysis, ML factor analysis in which observed variables are discretely distributed, and the latent class model in which latent variables may be discretely distributed. Each model's parametric structure and statistical assumptions used in estimation are discussed.

In addition we illustrate the use of GOM techniques in structural equation modeling. Structural equations have been defined by their ability to explain either the structure of the covariance matrix (e.g., Bollen 1989, p. 1) or the structure of general simultaneous equation systems (Malinvaud 1970). The structural form of a simultaneous equation system represents the interdependency of endogenous variables conditioned on exogenous variables. This definition is not restricted to quadratic forms (i.e., covariance matrices) and is useful in dealing with general distributions (e.g., Johnston 1984). In both cases the structure of the equation system is defined by constraints on the parameter space designed to represent hypotheses about the causal relation of variables. We illustrate the use of GOM techniques in simultaneous equation systems in a model of health-service utilization and expenditures, based on data from the 1982 and 1984 National Long Term Care Surveys (U.S. Department of Health and Human Services 1988).

2. PRELIMINARIES: THE PARAMETRIC STRUCTURE OF THE GOM MODEL AND COMPARISONS WITH OTHER MULTIVARIATE MODELS

In this section we present the parametric structure of the GOM model, introduce the concept of set membership in a fuzzy partition, and extend this concept to joint membership functions to form a basis for representing joint dependency between sets of latent variables defined in the GOM model. We compare GOM techniques to other procedures in two stages. First, we describe the mathematical parameterization of ML factor analysis, discrete response factor analysis, and the latent class model. This allows comparison with the parametric structure of the GOM model and helps clarify what that model does and does not do. Second, in section 3, we compare each model's likelihood function, which relates data, through the probability structure assumed to generate the data, to model parameters. The likelihood function, and its statistical properties, is important in understanding the behavior of each model because it is the mechanism that separates total variation into components associated with model parameters and components due to stochastic error.

2.1. *The Parametric Structure of the GOM Model*

In the GOM model (e.g., Woodbury and Clive 1974) parameters are *simultaneously* optimized in case and variable spaces (Dempster 1969). This differs from most implementations of factor analysis, in which scores for individuals are calculated conditionally upon structural parameter estimates using Bayes' theorem. One set of GOM parameters describes how variables are associated with the latent fuzzy classes identified by the model. A second set describes how the individual's observed characteristics relate to each fuzzy class. Because individual state parameters are explicitly estimated, GOM is a classification methodology (e.g., Woodbury and Manton 1982; Davidson et al. 1989). The GOM model can also be used to estimate structural equations in which the fuzzy classes define a natural metric describing the structure (i.e., the moments of the joint distribution function) of the dependency of the distributions of theoretically distinct sets of discrete variables (Manton, Woodbury, and Stallard 1991).

More formally, assume that data $\{x_{ij}\}$ on I individuals are defined by one of L_j responses to each of J categorical variables. Associated with each response are binary variables, y_{ijl} ($i = 1, \ldots, I; j = 1, \ldots, J; l = 1, \ldots, L_j$), where $y_{ijl} = 1$ if $x_{ij} = l$, and $y_{ijl} = 0$ otherwise. $\{y_{ijl}\}$ refers to the *set* of responses indexed by i, j, and l. Lowercase y_{ijl} refers to either a random variable or its realization (i.e., the value observed), depending upon context. Continuous variables must be recoded into categories. The boundaries of the categories are selected to represent the most informative parts of the continuous distribution (e.g., where the curvature is greatest). Analyses of the approximation of continuous variables by categories indicate that the information in most continuous distributions can usually be captured by small numbers of categories, e.g., 12 to 15 (Scott 1985; Terrell and Scott 1985). Furthermore, in survey instruments, many "continuous" variables are coded as a small number of levels or as ranges (e.g., income in the NLTCS). Even if continuous responses are solicited, there is often a respondent preference for reporting round numbers, which restricts the information recorded. Thus, discrete coding of continuous variables may not lose significant information, may better reflect the information present, and because the information used in estimation is restricted to what can be reliably reported, may be more robust. The costs are (a) greater effort in recoding and (b) heavier computational burden. The computational burden is greater when continuous variables are coded into discrete categories than when they are used under parametric assumptions because more information from the continuous distribution is retained. For example, if a model describes the first two moments of the data (i.e., the covariance matrix), information on higher-order moments of the individual responses is ignored. In the GOM model, all moments and cross moments up to the Jth degree (J is the number of variables) may be retained.

After recoding $\{x_{ij}\}$ into $\{y_{ijl}\}$, the GOM model describes y_{ijl} by two types of parameters. First are the probabilities, λ_{kjl}, that a person exactly of the kth class ($k = 1, \ldots, K$) has the lth response to the jth variable. These are *continuously* mixed by a second coefficient, g_{ik}, to best reproduce the probability that $y_{ijl} = 1$. The g_{ik} terms are estimated with constraints that $0 \leq g_{ik} \leq 1$ and $\Sigma_k g_{ik} = 1$; i.e., the g_{ik} values are scores that generate probabilities of observed characteristics as convex combinations of the K sets of λ_{kjl} profiles. The model is written

$$\pi_{ijl} = \Pr(y_{ijl} = 1) = \sum_k g_{ik} \lambda_{kjl} \tag{1}$$

or

$$y_{ijl} = \left(\sum_k g_{ik} \lambda_{kjl}\right) + e_{ijl}, \tag{2}$$

where the e_{ijl} are errors in prediction.

The λ_{kjl} parameters define the position of the K vertices of a K-1–dimensional simplex in the J-dimensional measurement space. The g_{ik} are scores continuously distributed within the simplex. This distribution is not a priori constrained to a specific parametric form. The g_{ik} represent the degree to which a person's observed characteristics are represented by one (or more) of the K sets of response profiles, i.e., the vectors of λ_{kjl}. The g_{ik} are not probabilities but weights that combine the extreme points (vertices) defined by the λ_{kjl} in a convex set.

Formally, the g_{ik} are values of the membership function for case i in class C_k, where the family of classes $C = \{C_k\}$ forms a fuzzy partition of the sample S of all cases. In ordinary set theory, a partition of a set S is a disjoint family of nonempty subsets $D = \{D_k\}$ whose union is S. Set membership is defined by the indicator function $I_{D_k}(i)$, which is 1 if $i \in D_k$ and 0 if $i \notin D_k$. Joint membership is defined using $I_{D_k \cap D_l}(i) = I_{D_k}(i) \times I_{D_l}(i) = \min[I_{D_k}(i), I_{D_l}(i)]$, which is zero when $D_k \cap D_l = \varnothing$, the null set. Fuzzy set theory extends the range of the indicator function from the *set* $\{0, 1\}$ to the *interval* $[0, 1]$. Thus, the GOM model assumes that $I_{C_k}(i) = g_{ik}$, subject to the constraints that $0 \le g_{ik} \le 1$ and $\Sigma_k g_{ik} = 1$. To form a fuzzy partition C, the GOM model also assumes that $C_k \cap C_l = \varnothing$, for $k \ne l$, in which case $I_{C_k \cap C_l}(i) = 0$. Thus, the joint membership in two distinct sets is zero if the sets are classes of a fuzzy partition. The treatment of joint membership for the general case is given below.

The *vector* of the g_{ik} for the ith individual, denoted $\mathbf{g}_i$, is assumed to be a *state* vector. Loosely speaking, this means that $\mathbf{g}_i$ contains information on all dimensions of the individual that are relevant to the process under study. This is equivalent to the so-called local independence assumption. In particular, the vector $\mathbf{x}_i$ of observed variables contains elements that are independently distributed conditional on $\mathbf{g}_i$. This focuses attention on processes describing changes in $\mathbf{g}_i$ over time, or more generally over any set of variables that induces change in $\mathbf{g}_i$.

State variable changes. To describe changes in $\mathbf{g}_i$ over time, recall that probabilities of discrete state changes are described by the Chapman-Kolmogorov equations (Lipster and Shiryayev 1977), which represent changes in $\mathbf{g}_i$ under the restriction that $\mathbf{g}_i$ is a vertex of the K-1–dimensional simplex. To remove this restriction and allow $\mathbf{g}_i$ to be any point in the interior of the simplex (i.e., a fuzzy state vector), we need to modify the Chapman-Kolmogorov matrix $\mathbf{P} = \{p_{kl}\}$ of conditional probabilities that a person at vertex k "jumps" to vertex l over a fixed time interval. Denote this modified transition matrix as $\mathbf{T} = \{t_{kl}\}$. If $\mathbf{g}_i^{(1)}$ and $\mathbf{g}_i^{(2)}$ are the state (column) vectors for person i at times 1 and 2, the estimate of $\mathbf{g}_i^{(2)}$, denoted $\hat{\mathbf{g}}_i^{(2)}$, is

$$\hat{\mathbf{g}}_i^{(2)'} = \mathbf{g}_i^{(1)'}\, \mathbf{T}, \tag{3}$$

where superscript prime denotes transposition. Hence, we obtain

$$\mathbf{g}_i^{(2)} = \hat{\mathbf{g}}_i^{(2)} + \mathbf{e}_i^{(2)}, \tag{4}$$

where $\mathbf{e}_i^{(2)}$ is error and $\hat{\mathbf{g}}_i^{(2)}$ is a fuzzy state vector.

$\mathbf{T}$ describes the movement of cases within the fuzzy set simplex or state space. The coefficients of $\mathbf{T}$ are transition intensities of $g_{il}^{(2)}$ with respect to $g_{ik}^{(1)}$; i.e., they represent the tendency to move to a new position in the simplex given a prior position in the simplex. $\mathbf{T}$ is *not* a conditional probability matrix, since the g_{ik} are in the closed interval $[0, 1]$ rather than in a two-element set $\{0, 1\}$. One might estimate $\mathbf{T}$ in (3) by minimizing the sums of squares of the $e_{il}^{(2)}$, i.e., by treating (4) as an ordinary least squares regression equation. This does *not* guarantee that constraints on $\hat{g}_{il}$ (i.e., that $0 \le \hat{g}_{il} \le 1$ and $\Sigma_{l=1}^{K^{(2)}}\hat{g}_{il} = 1$) are fulfilled. To define the transition matrix for fuzzy states, with $g_{ik}^{(1)} \in [0, 1]$ and $g_{il}^{(2)} \in [0, 1]$, let t_{kl} be

$$t_{kl} = \mathrm{E}(g_{ikl}^{(1,2)})/\mathrm{E}(g_{ik}^{(1)}), \tag{5}$$

where $g_{ikl}^{(1,2)}$ is the joint membership function (defined below) for case i in states k and l at times 1 and 2, respectively, and $\mathrm{E}(\cdot)$ denotes mathematical expectation. t_{kl} satisfies conditions for the special case when fuzzy states collapse to discrete states, viz.,

$$t_{kl} = \Pr[(g_{ik}^{(1)} = 1) \cap (g_{il}^{(2)} = 1)]/\Pr(g_{ik}^{(1)} = 1) \tag{6a}$$

$$= \mathrm{E}\!\left(g_{ik}^{(1)} \times g_{il}^{(2)}\right)\!/\mathrm{E}\!\left(g_{ik}^{(1)}\right) \tag{6b}$$

$$= \mathrm{E}\!\left(g_{ikl}^{(1,2)}\right)\!/\mathrm{E}\!\left(g_{ik}^{(1)}\right), \tag{6c}$$

where $g_{ik}^{(1)} \in \{0, 1\}$, $g_{il}^{(2)} \in \{0, 1\}$, and the division by $E(g_{ik}^{(1)})$ ensures that t_{kl} reflects changes in state for persons initially in state k.

There are two methods to define $g_{ikl}^{(1,2)}$ and satisfy (3), i.e., to yield $\hat{g}_{il}^{(2)}$ such that $0 \le \hat{g}_{il}^{(2)} \le 1$ and $\Sigma_{l=1}^{K^{(2)}} \hat{g}_{il} = 1$. The first,

$$g_{ikl}^{(1,2)} = g_{ik}^{(1)} g_{il}^{(2)}, \tag{7}$$

reflects joint membership as the *product* of individual memberships. This satisfies (6b) for discrete states. However, in (7) even if $\mathbf{g}_i^{(1)}$ and $\mathbf{g}_i^{(2)}$ are identical, so that the same fuzzy partition C obtains at times 1 and 2, the product does not produce an identity matrix for $\mathbf{T}$. In addition, the entropy (defined below) of the matrix $\{g_{ikl}^{(1,2)}\}$ is a maximum (i.e., least informative) for (7).

An alternative defines $g_{ikl}^{(1,2)}$ as the minimum of each pair, $g_{ik}^{(1)}$ and $g_{il}^{(2)}$ (see Kaufmann and Gupta 1985, p. 14). This satisfies (6b) for discrete states. To ensure that the marginals of the joint membership table reproduce the $g_{ik}^{(1)}$ and $g_{il}^{(2)}$, i.e., that

$$\sum_l g_{ikl}^{(1,2)} = g_{ik}^{(1)} \quad \text{and} \quad \sum_k g_{ikl}^{(1,2)} = g_{il}^{(2)}, \tag{8}$$

we use an algorithm to generate a minimum entropy (i.e., maximum information) solution under marginal constraints. The minimum entropy $g_{ikl}^{(1,2)}$ estimates satisfy (8). Also, if $\mathbf{g}_i^{(1)}$ and $\mathbf{g}_i^{(2)}$ are identical, so that the same fuzzy partition C obtains at times 1 and 2, the resulting $g_{ikl}^{(1,2)}$ satisfies $g_{ikl}^{(1,2)} = g_{ik}^{(1)}$ for $k = l$ and $g_{ikl}^{(1,2)} = 0$ for $k \ne l$ so that $\{g_{ikl}^{(1,2)}\}$ yields an identity matrix for $\mathbf{T}$.

Properties of minimum entropy estimators. The entropy of the matrix $\{\Sigma_i \ g_{ikl}^{(1,2)}\}$, used to obtain the numerator of (5), is $H = \Sigma_i \ H_i$, where $0 \le H_i = -\Sigma_k \Sigma_l g_{ikl}^{(1,2)} \ln g_{ikl}^{(1,2)}$. For (7), individual entropies are sums of marginal entropies, i.e., $H_i = H_i^{(1)} + H_i^{(2)}$, where $H_i^{(1)} = -\Sigma_k g_{ik}^{(1)} \ln g_{ik}^{(1)}$ and $H_i^{(2)} = -\Sigma_l g_{il}^{(2)} \ln g_{il}^{(2)}$. Hence, if $\mathbf{g}_i^{(1)} = \mathbf{g}_i^{(2)}$, the entropy for (7) is *twice* that for the minimum entropy function. In the latter case, minimum entropy values are $g_{ikl}^{(1,2)} = g_{ik}^{(1)} = g_{ik}^{(2)}$.

Determining $\{g_{ikl}^{(1,2)}\}$ so that H_i is a minimum has the problem that $-g \times \ln(g)$ is concave downward (with a maximum of $e^{-1} = .368$ at $g = .368$), so that entropy may be reduced by changing *both* large and small values of g; i.e., H_i can have multiple local minima. The algorithm used to determine the minimum entropy for H_i produces the solution by selecting changes in a series of steps. At each step s, we determine $g_{ikl}^{(1,2)}(s)$, for the index pair (k, l), that yields the maximum reduction in entropy. Initially, when $s = 0$, $\{g_{ikl}^{(1,2)}(0)\}$ is set to zero, $\mathbf{g}_i^{(1)}(0) = \mathbf{g}_i^{(1)}$ and $\mathbf{g}_i^{(2)}(0) = \mathbf{g}_i^{(2)}$. The following are components of entropy: $H_i^{(0)}(s) = -\Sigma_k\Sigma_l\, g_{ikl}^{(1,2)}(s) \ln [g_{ikl}^{(1,2)}(s)]$, $H_i^{(1)}(s) = -\Sigma_k\, g_{ik}^{(1)}(s)$ $\ln [g_{ik}^{(1)}(s)]$, and $H_i^{(2)}(s) = -\Sigma_l g_{ik}^{(2)} \ln [g_{il}^{(2)}(s)]$. At step s, the entropy is computed using $H_i(s) = H_i^{(0)}(s) + H_i^{(1)}(s) + H_i^{(2)}(s)$. It follows that the initial entropy $H_i(0)$ is the maximum entropy obtained from (7). Thus, at each step, we maximize the reduction in entropy, measured by the difference $D_i(s) = H_i(s-1)-H_i(s)$, by choosing the index pair $(k,\ l)$ such that $D_i(s) = \underset{k,l}{\max} [D_{ikl}(s)]$, where $D_{ikl}(s)$ is the reduction associated with $g_{ikl}^{(1,2)}(s)$. This uses an "exchange" rule that shifts membership values from the marginals into the interior of the joint membership matrix. The rule has three parts:

1. $g_{ikl}^{(1,2)}(s) = \min (g_{ik}^{(1)}(s-1),\, g_{il}^{(2)}(s-1))$
2. $g_{ik}^{(1)}(s) = g_{ik}^{(1)}(s-1) - g_{ikl}^{(1,2)}(s)$
3. $g_{il}^{(2)}(s) = g_{il}^{(2)}(s-1) - g_{ikl}^{(1,2)}(s)$

Thus, at least one of $g_{ik}^{(1)}(s)$ and $g_{il}^{(2)}(s)$ must be zero, and either row k or column l is precluded from further exchanges. If $g_{ik}^{(1)}(s-1) \geq g_{il}^{(2)}(s-1)$, then $D_{ikl}(s) = -g_{ik}^{(1)}(s-1)\ln[g_{ik}^{(1)}(s-1)] + g_{ik}^{(1)}(s)\ln[g_{ik}^{(1)}(s)]$. Alternatively, if $g_{ik}^{(1)}(s-1) < g_{il}^{(2)}(s-1)$, then $D_{ikl}(s) = -g_{il}^{(2)}(s-1)\ln[g_{il}^{(2)}(s-1)] + g_{il}^{(2)}(s)$ $\ln [g_{il}^{(2)}(s)]$. Because of the concavity of $-g \times \ln(g)$, any exchange that sets $g_{ikl}^{(1,2)} < g_{ikl}^{(1,2)}(s)$ will have larger entropy. Thus, $D_i(s)$ is the maximum *one*-step reduction in entropy.

     The algorithm can be generalized so that the index pair $(k,\ l)$ selected at each step achieves the maximum *two*-step or *three*-step reduction in entropy. Frequently the index pair $(k,\ l)$ satisfies one or both of $g_{ik}^{(1)}(s) = \underset{m}{\max} [g_{im}^{(1)}(s)]$ and $g_{il}^{(2)}(s) = \underset{m}{\max} [g_{im}^{(2)}(s)]$. This reduces computational effort. The selection continues to a maximum of $2K-1$ nonzero joint $g_{ikl}^{(1,2)}$ terms, with the rest of the elements fixed at zero. Since the original marginals of the matrix are fixed, and modification of the matrix must change at least one zero to a nonzero, a change *increases* H_i. Because each step of the algorithm achieves the maximum possible reduction in entropy H_i at each step (or for a set of two or three steps), the solution will likely be the minimum, or very close to it. A fully simultaneous solution is not computationally practical because the number of exchanges increases as $(K!)^2$.

     In structural equations, dependencies between GOM classes are represented in the off diagonals of the joint membership matrix, where structure is imposed by constraining specific diagonals to zero.

If the entropy of the joint membership matrix is truly minimized, our structural coefficients are unique and have statistical properties related to maximum likelihood estimates (MLEs) (Kullback and Leibler 1951). In particular, since the structural coefficients obtained under the minimum entropy algorithm are functions of the g_{ik}, they are MLEs if the g_{ik} are MLEs, which they are. More generally, the ML algorithm used to obtain g_{ik} allows identification of all moments of g_{ik} up to the Jth degree, which involves both linear and nonlinear moments. A restricted form involves only linear moments of the fuzzy classes, i.e., the bivariate, trivariate, etc., joint moments of the g_{ik}. Though all of this information is resident in the MLEs of the g_{ik}, it is complex. Thus, below we restricted our examination of the transition matrix to only bivariate moments (or joint memberships) so that we could compare them with the coefficients estimated in other structural equation models.

2.2. Maximum Likelihood Factor Analysis

The factor analytic model (for J continuous variables, x_{ij}) is written

$$\hat{x}_{ij} = u_j + \sum_k \lambda_{jk} f_{ik} + e_{ij}. \tag{9}$$

In (9), x_i represents a vector of J observations on individual i; u is the constant vector, which may, or may not, be modeled; $\Lambda = \{\lambda_{jk}\}$ represents a $J \times K$ matrix of regression coefficients; f_i represents a vector of K factor scores; and e_i represents error.

Commonly, x_i is a vector of jointly normal continuous variables (Lawley and Maxwell 1971), so all significant information on the joint distribution function is contained in the first- and second-order moments. Higher-order moments are assumed to be non-informative, i.e., zero or functions of the first two moments. Because the f_i are unobserved, (9) cannot be directly estimated. Ignoring means, (9) produces (suppressing subscripts)

$$E(x\,x') = \Lambda\,E(f\,f')\,\Lambda' + E(e\,e'), \tag{10}$$

where $E\,(x\,x')$ contains the second-order central moments of x_i, Λ is the factor-loadings matrix as in (9), $E(f\,f')$ is a moments matrix of factor scores (i.e., the values for individuals on the latent state variable), and $E(\mathbf{e}\,\mathbf{e}')$ is the second-order moments matrix for residuals. Equation (10) is estimable, though we can estimate only as many parameters as there are unique moments in $E(\mathbf{x}\,\mathbf{x}')$; i.e., for J variables this is $(J^2 + J)/2$.

With appropriate scaling, (10) may be written as

$$\boldsymbol{\Sigma} = \boldsymbol{\Lambda}\,\boldsymbol{\phi}\,\boldsymbol{\Lambda}' + \boldsymbol{\Psi}, \tag{11}$$

where $\boldsymbol{\Sigma} = E(\mathbf{x}\,\mathbf{x}')$, $\boldsymbol{\phi} = E(\mathbf{f}\,\mathbf{f}')$, and $\boldsymbol{\Psi} = E(\mathbf{e}\,\mathbf{e}')$. If factors are assumed orthogonal (uncorrelated), then $\boldsymbol{\phi} = \mathbf{I}$ and the number of parameters is reduced. Scaling depends on the diagonal elements of $\boldsymbol{\Psi}$. If scaled to be equal and of unit length, the distribution is multivariate spherical and ML estimation can be used.

In (9) the factor scores, f_{ik}, are analogous to the g_{ik} parameters: Both represent latent states of individuals, and both are continuous. However, while the f_{ik} are generally assumed to be multivariate normally distributed, the g_{ik} are not restricted to a specific distribution. Furthermore, while the f_{ik} vary from plus to minus infinity, the vector of g_{ik} is constructed to fall in the K-1 dimensional simplex; i.e., the f_{ik} are unbounded, and the g_{ik} are bounded. Finally, the λ_{jk} represent the change in x_{ij} per unit change in f_{ik}. The scale of $\boldsymbol{\Lambda}$ depends upon constraints on $\boldsymbol{\Psi}$. In the GOM model the scale of the λ_{kjl} is fixed by the constraints of the observed discrete event space. A major difference is that factor analysis requires evaluation of the quadratic form (i.e., equation (10), restricted to second-order moments), with the f_{ik} *conditionally* estimated using a regression procedure (Saris, de Pijper, and Mulder 1978). The GOM model provides direct estimates of the g_{ik}.

2.3. Discrete Response Factor Analysis
(Normally Distributed Latent Variables)

Muthén (1978, 1987, 1989), Christoffersson (1975), Muthén and Christoffersson (1981), and Jöreskog and Sörbom (1986) proposed to estimate parameters of a factor model for discretely distributed data with normally distributed states (e.g., Muthén, 1989), e.g.,

$$\mathbf{x}_i^* = \boldsymbol{\Lambda}\,\mathbf{f}_i + \mathbf{e}_i. \tag{12}$$

If x_{ij}^* is continuous, then f_{ik} should be similarly scaled. For discrete variables, x_{ij}, there is a mathematical inconsistency. To resolve this,

x_{ij}^* can be viewed as a latent variable representing a "tendency" to express a specific response x_{ij}, which, for a dichotomous variable, is

$$x_{ij} = \begin{cases} 0, & x_{ij}^* \le \tau \\ 1, & x_{ij}^* > \tau \end{cases}. \tag{13}$$

Thus, persons at different distances from the threshold, τ, have the same observed discrete response, x_{ij}. This implies a nonlinear relation between x_{ij} and x_{ij}^*; i.e., the distribution of x_{ij}^* is normal with means linear in f_{ik}, but the relation between x_{ij} and f_{ik} is nonlinear, i.e.,

$$\Pr(x_{ij} = 0 \mid f_{ik}) = \Pr(x_{ij}^* \le \tau) = F(\tau - \sum_k \lambda_{jk} f_{ik}), \tag{14}$$

where F can be, e.g., the standard normal.

Discrete variable factor analysis allows non-normality only in observed variables. The latent state variables must still be normally distributed. Thus, the differences between the f_{ik} and the g_{ik} are essentially the same as for standard factor analysis. The x_{ij}^* are continuous normally distributed state variables, so the f_{ik} range from plus to minus infinity and are estimated from tetrachoric correlations. The g_{ik} are bounded, generally distributed, and estimated directly. The f_{ik} above are nonlinearly related to the data.

2.4. Discrete Response Factor Analysis (Non-Normal Latent Variables)

To deal with non-normal latent factors, Muthén (1989) proposed relating second-order factors to first-order factors by a linear regression. If there is a large number of binary items, their sum may be used as a "proxy" for second-order factors. If second-order factor scores are non-normally distributed, then because of the linear regression, the first-order factors are non-normally distributed. The first-order factors written as a function of the sum of binary items, say s_i, are

$$x_{ij}^* = \pi_j \times s_i + \delta_{ij}, \tag{15}$$

where $\boldsymbol{\Pi} = \{\pi_j\}$ is the vector of regression coefficients, $s_i = \Sigma_{j=1}^J x_{ij}$ (assuming that the x_{ij} are dichotomous), and δ_{ij} is a normally distributed residual. Connecting the "observed" second-order factors and the first-order latent factors is a probit function (Muthén 1989),

$$\mathbf{V(x^*)} = \boldsymbol{\Pi} \, V(s) \, \boldsymbol{\Pi}' + \boldsymbol{\Omega}, \qquad\qquad (16)$$

where $\boldsymbol{\Omega}$ is the covariance matrix of the residuals (δ), $V(s)$ is the variance of the summary score, and diagonal elements of $\boldsymbol{\Omega}$ are standardized to unity. Inserting $\boldsymbol{\Omega}$ and sample estimates of $V(s)$ gives the estimated covariance matrix of the first-order factors $\mathbf{V(x^*)}$. This produces estimates of "non-normal" tetrachoric correlations of the $\mathbf{x^*}$. Factor scores are calculated conditionally from model parameters by Bayes' theorem using a multivariate normal as the prior distribution.

When summary scores of binary items are used in a second-order factor analysis, first-order factors are made non-normal by making them functions of a non-normal second-order factor proxy. If the summary score, s, is used to represent the items, however, information is lost if there are meaningful covariances among the summands. Also, if items used to construct s are not substantively homogeneous (e.g., medical diagnosis and functional disability), then the scaling of s is unclear.

2.5. The Latent Class Model

The latent class model assumes that discrete data may be explained by a weighted combination of latent tables corresponding to K values of a latent discrete variable (e.g., Lazarsfeld and Henry 1968). Thus, in contrast to factor analysis, the latent *state* variables ($k_i = 1, \ldots, K; i = 1, \ldots, I$) may be discrete. In the latent profile model, continuous data are used to estimate latent discrete states.

Both the latent class and the latent profile models differ from the GOM model when the latent state variables, g_{ik}, vary *continuously* within the bounded space. In the latent class model, the latent variables, k_i, take only one nonzero value in the range $k = 1, \ldots, K$. This corresponds to a restricted, nonfuzzy form of the GOM model in which $g_{ik} = 1$ for $k = k_i$ and $g_{ik} = 0$ for $k \neq k_i$. The difference is that the g_{ik} are estimated in the GOM model so that these restrictions can be tested. If k_i is not estimated in the latent class model, the restriction cannot be tested.

The distribution of responses in the latent class model are a finite mixture of K discrete distributions, each satisfying local independence. To compare models, common notation is needed. Let $P_{ab\cdots e}^{AB\cdots E}$

be the joint probability that variables A, B, . . . , E have outcomes a, b, . . . , e; i.e.,

$$P^{AB\cdots E}_{ab\cdots e} = \Pr(A = a \cap B = b \cap \ldots \cap E = e). \tag{17}$$

Let P^K_k be the probability that a latent variable K has outcome k; i.e.,

$$P^K_k = \Pr(K = k). \tag{18}$$

Let $P^{\overline{A}K}_{ak}$ be the conditional probability of outcome a on variable A, given that $K = k$; i.e.,

$$P^{\overline{A}K}_{ak} = \Pr(A = a \mid K = k). \tag{19}$$

With these definitions, the latent class model can be expressed as

$$P^{AB\cdots E}_{ab\cdots e} = \sum_k P^{\overline{A}K}_{ak} P^{\overline{B}K}_{bk} \cdots P^{\overline{E}K}_{ek} P^K_k, \tag{20}$$

where each factor on the right is a parameter to be estimated.

The notation in (20) is standard for the latent class model, but it differs from GOM notation. For example, the GOM notation in (18) would be $P_k = \Pr(k_i = k)$ rather than $P^K_k = \Pr(K = k)$, because K is the number of classes rather than the name of the latent variable. We obtain consistent notation by using the posterior probability from (20):

$$p_{ik} = \Pr(k_i = k \mid A_i = a_i, B_i = b_i, \ldots, E_i = e_i) \tag{21a}$$

$$= P^K_{k_i} P^{\overline{A}K}_{a_ik_i} P^{\overline{B}K}_{b_ik_i} \cdots P^{\overline{E}K}_{e_ik_i} / P^{AB\cdots E}_{a_ib_i\cdots e_i}, \tag{21b}$$

where A_i, B_i, . . . , E_i are the data for individual i. Similarly, the analogue to the GOM probability λ_{kjl} obtains from (19), using

$$\lambda_{kjl} \equiv P^{\overline{A}K}_{ak} \mid {}^{A=j}_{a=l}, \tag{22a}$$

$$= \Pr(x_{ij} = l \mid k_i = k). \tag{22b}$$

The GOM model's prediction of $\pi_{ijl} = \Pr(y_{ijl} = 1)$ is obtained using (1); the latent class model's prediction is

$$\pi_{ijl} = \Pr(y_{ijl} = 1) = \sum_k p_{ik} \lambda_{kjl}, \tag{23}$$

where p_{ik} and λ_{kjl} derive from (21) and (22). Comparison of (1) and (23) shows that the differences involve use of $\mathbf{p}_i = (p_{i1}, \ldots, p_{ik})'$ in place of $\mathbf{g}_i$. Similarities involve use of λ_{kjl} to represent the conditional probability of response l to variable j. Thus, the λ_{kjl} are latent probabilities in both models.

TABLE 1
Comparisons of Latent Class and GOM Models

1. Computation of Individual Level Marginal Probabilities (%s)

	Class 1	Class 2	$\Pr(y_{ijl} = 1; \text{LC})$	$\Pr(y_{ijl} = 1; \text{GOM})$
Variable 1				
Yes	90.0	20.0	62.0	62.0
No	10.0	80.0	38.0	38.0
Variable 2				
Yes	70.0	40.0	58.0	58.0
No	30.0	60.0	42.0	42.0
p_{ik}	60.0	40.0		
g_{ik}	60.0	40.0		

2. Computation of Class-Specific Joint Probabilities (%s)

	Variable 2		Variable 2	
	Yes	No	Yes	No
	Class 1		Class 2	
Variable 1				
Yes	63.0	27.0	8.0	12.0
No	7.0	3.0	32.0	48.0

3. Computation of Joint Probabilities (%s), General Case

	Variable 2		Variable 2	
	Yes	No	Yes	No
	LC		GOM	
Variable 1				
Yes	41.0	21.0	36.0	26.0
No	17.0	21.0	22.0	16.0

We can distinguish the models based on the role of $\mathbf{p}_i$ as a posterior probability vector and $\mathbf{g}_i$ as a membership vector defined on a fuzzy partition. The mathematical properties of the g_{ik} and the p_{ik} are illustrated in Table 1. The comparison demonstrates that the g_{ik} *are* state variables and that the p_{ik} are *not*.

The top panel illustrates the computation of π_{ijl} for two variables with two latent classes. The numbers, expressed as percentages, are the probabilities of each response ("yes" and "no") for each class (λ_{kjl}) and for person i under the latent class and GOM models (π_{ijl}) using the latent class model's posterior probabilities $\mathbf{p}_i = (.6, .4)$ and the GOM model's scores $\mathbf{g}_i = (.6, .4)$. The GOM model's prediction of π_{ijl} is obtained by using (1). The latent class model's prediction is obtained by using (23). Since $\mathbf{p}_i = \mathbf{g}_i$, the π_{ijl} in the last two columns are identical. Thus, the latent class and GOM models yield identical predictions of the *marginal* probabilities for individuals with $\mathbf{p}_i = \mathbf{g}_i$.

The second panel illustrates the computation of class-specific *joint* probabilities of response for the latent class and GOM models. Both models assume local independence for latent discrete or fuzzy classes. Thus, the joint probabilities for classes 1 and 2 are obtained by multiplying the corresponding marginal probabilities. Let $\lambda_{kj_1l_1j_2l_2}$ denote the joint probability of response $(j_1\, l_1)$ and $(j_2\, l_2)$. Then,

$$\lambda_{kj_1l_1j_2l_2} = \Pr(y_{ij_1l_1} = 1 \mid \text{class}_i = k) \times \Pr(y_{ij_2l_2} = 1 \mid \text{class}_i = k) \quad (24a)$$

$$= \lambda_{kj_1l_1} \lambda_{kj_2l_2}, \quad (24b)$$

where $\text{class}_i = k$ implies $p_{ik} = 1$ or $g_{ik} = 1$, depending on the model.

The third panel illustrates the computation of joint probabilities of response for the general case. The models have different joint probabilities for individuals whose $\text{class}_i \neq k$, for $k = 1, \ldots, K$. Let

$$\pi_{ij_1l_1j_2l_2} = \Pr[(y_{ij_1l_1} = 1) \cap (y_{ij_2l_2} = 1)]. \quad (25)$$

For the latent class model,

$$\pi_{ij_1l_1j_2l_2} = \sum_k p_{ik} \lambda_{kj_1l_1j_2l_2}, \quad (26)$$

which is a weighted average of the joint probabilities for classes 1 and 2. For the GOM model,

$$\pi_{ij_1l_1j_2l_2} = \pi_{ij_1l_1} \pi_{ij_2l_2}, \quad (27)$$

which is a product of corresponding marginal probabilities. Comparison of the estimates in panel 3 shows that the models yield different estimates of the joint probabilities, even though $\mathbf{p}_i = \mathbf{g}_i$ and the marginal probabilities are identical.

The latent class model assumes that (26) is an appropriate generalization of (23), since the latent class model represents the population as a weighted average of latent "tables." The GOM model assumes that (27) is an appropriate generalization of (24). Since the GOM model identifies individual state vectors $(\mathbf{g}_i)$, the assumption of local independence is satisfied.

Local, or conditional, independence is a central assumption of both the GOM model *and* factor analysis. In factor analysis the residual covariances of the observed variables, conditional on the vector of factor scores $\mathbf{f}_i$, are zero (see (42)). Under normality, this means that the observed variables are independent, conditional on $\mathbf{f}_i$. In the GOM model observed variables are independent (i.e., cross moments are zero), conditional on $\mathbf{g}_i$, so that $\mathbf{g}_i$ is an analogue of $\mathbf{f}_i$. Both $\mathbf{f}_i$ and $\mathbf{g}_i$ are state vectors for their respective models.

The latent class model's posterior probability vector $\mathbf{p}_i$ is *not* a state vector; i.e., the observed variables are not independent (in general) conditional on $\mathbf{p}_i$. In Table 1 (panel 3) the joint distribution for the latent class model is different than for the independence (GOM) model. Thus, $\mathbf{p}_i$ is not analogous to $\mathbf{f}_i$ or $\mathbf{g}_i$, and the latent class model is *not* analogous to factor analysis.

It may be argued that focusing on $\mathbf{p}_i$ as a state vector for the latent class model is incorrect because the latent variable in the model is inherently categorical; i.e., one and *only* one of the K latent tables (say, k_i) characterizes individual i. In this case, local independence holds, conditional on k_i, so that k_i *is* analogous to $\mathbf{f}_i$. However, whereas factor analysis provides conditional estimates of $\mathbf{f}_i$, and the GOM model estimates $\mathbf{g}_i$ directly, the latent class model does *not* "typically" provide estimates of k_i; i.e., the k_i are assumed to be missing data (but see Madansky 1959; Everitt 1984).

In practice (from the usual implementation of the latest class model), k_i can be heuristically "assigned" by choosing the largest p_{ik}:

$$k_i = k \mid p_{ik} = \max(p_{i1}, \ldots, p_{ik}). \tag{28}$$

This *ad hoc* procedure assigns a state variable k_i for each individual i. The problem is that the π_{ijl} may be changed. In the example with $\text{class}_i = 1$, there is change in both the predicted marginal and the joint probabilities. Thus, if the latent class model is used for individual prognostication, the use of k_i in place of $\mathbf{p}_i$ may lead to different decisions. Furthermore, since the latent class model does not usually use k_i in its fitting algorithm, there is no way to test whether (28) fits the data. Interestingly, since setting $k_i = k$ in the latent class model corresponds to setting $g_{ik} = 1$ in the GOM model, such a test can be conducted using the GOM algorithm with additional constraints on the g_{ik}.

The need for a *post hoc* assignment rule like (28) for the latent class model illustrates the difference between a random state variable and a fuzzy state variable. In the latent class model, $p_{ik} = \Pr(k_i = k)$ so that selection of state k will be correct $p_{ik} \times 100\%$ of the time.

In the GOM model, g_{ik} is the value for individual i on the membership function for class k. As information is increased on individuals by adding variables (i.e., by increasing J), their g_{ik} are more precisely estimated. For example, if the "true" g_{ik} values for i are 0.6 and 0.4 for two dimensions, then as J is increased, the g_{ik} will approach 0.6 and 0.4 more closely (and the other $g_{ik} \rightarrow 0.0$). In general, as information increases, the estimated $\hat{g}_{ik}$ will approach the vector of the true scores for each individual.

As information is added to the latent class model, the posterior probability of classification, p_{ik}, approaches 1.0 for the single discrete class (or "state") k_i to which the person is assumed to belong. This implies g_{ik} scores whose true values can only be 0 or 1, since the person is resident in one homogenous class (see, e.g., Everitt 1984, p. 79). When the expectation maximization (EM) algorithm is applied to the latent class model, the k_i are not estimated (Everitt 1984). Instead, they are assumed to be missing data and assignment is made in probability terms (Woodbury, Manton, and Tolley 1990). The posterior probability of classification in class k can be viewed either as $p_{ik} = \Pr(k_i = k)$ or as $p_{ik} = \Pr(g_{ik} = 1.0)$. In the latent class model, the posterior probabilities are calculated conditionally upon the data and parameters estimated using Bayes' theorem. In the GOM model, the g_{ik} are parameters estimated simultaneously with the λ_{kjl}.

3. ESTIMATION

3.1. *The GOM Model*

To estimate parameters for the GOM model, we assume that observations for individuals are independent. The multinomial likelihood is

$$L = \prod_i \Pr(\mathbf{X}_i = \mathbf{x}_i \mid \mathbf{g}_i) \tag{29a}$$

$$= \prod_i \prod_j \prod_l [\Pr(Y_{ijl} = 1 \mid \mathbf{g}_i)]^{y_{ijl}} \tag{29b}$$

$$= \prod_i \prod_j \prod_l \left(\sum_k g_{ik} \lambda_{kjl} \right)^{y_{ijl}}, \tag{29c}$$

with (1) inserted for the probabilities (Woodbury and Clive 1974; Woodbury et al. 1978).

To optimize (29c) we use a Newton-Raphson algorithm with Kuhn-Tucker constraints (Kuhn and Tucker 1951). For a problem with fixed J, consistency can be demonstrated for the identifiable moments, the μ_k, of the g_{ik} distribution and for the λ_{kjl}. The g_{ik} in this case are an algorithmic device for determining the μ_k. Maximizing (29c) with respect to the g_{ik} for independent observations best approximates the distribution with the desired set of moments while maintaining the required constraints on the g_{ik}. Since the distribution of the g_{ik} is optimized, the moments of the distribution of the g_{ik} estimates are optimized, and the estimated g_{ik} provide MLEs of the moments and of the λ_{kjl}. The properties of the likelihood function help to ensure identifiability of parameters by selecting the broadest definition of the simplex defined by the λ_{kjl} consistent with the contribution of the g_{ik} to the likelihood.

The large number of g_{ik} means that the computational effort is significant and that the algorithm should be optimized to the machine employed. Shah (1990) programmed the procedure in a user-supplied SAS subroutine, which he modified for a SPARC workstation. Marini and Singer (1988) developed computer programs for a VAX minicomputer, and NIH has contracted to develop a version for their IBM mainframe. All of these procedures are based on methods developed by Woodbury and Clive (1974) and Woodbury et al. (1978).

The algorithm is a modification of Orchard and Woodbury's (1972) missing information principle (MIP). The score functions have π_{ijl} terms involving both the g_{ik} and the λ_{kjl}. The algorithm begins by using trial values for the g_{ik} to generate conditional expectations of the λ_{kjl}. After modifying those values to fit the data, it takes updated values of the λ_{kjl} to generate new expected values of the g_{ik}. This is performed iteratively until a solution is achieved to a required precision. Expressions for the score functions are presented in Woodbury and Clive (1974) and in Woodbury et al. (1978). Care must be taken in "stopping" calculations. Because of the large number of terms, a satisfactory solution may require changes in the g_{ik} and the λ_{kjl} to be "near" zero.

Identifiability. To evaluate the properties of the GOM model, we must describe the characteristics of the parameter space and show that the mapping of the moments of the observation space to that parameter space are unique (i.e., identifiable). The model is defined by a $K-1$–dimensional simplex with parameter space $\Omega \times \Gamma$ where Ω is the space of possible values of the λ_{kjl} and Γ is the space of possible distributions of the g_{ik}. Properties of $\Omega \times \Gamma$ are described in Tolley and Manton (1991).

Briefly, Γ is a metric space containing all $K-1$–dimensional distributions G, without singular subcomponents, of $\boldsymbol{\xi}_i = (\xi_{i1}, \ldots, \xi_{iK})$, where ξ_{ik} is a random variable, with realization g_{ik}, subject to constraints on the g_{ik}. The marginal distribution of y_{ijl} given the parameters $\boldsymbol{\gamma}$ (i.e., $h(\mathbf{y} \mid \boldsymbol{\gamma})$, where $\boldsymbol{\gamma} = (\boldsymbol{\lambda}, G)$) is *identifiable* if the following is true: When a measure of the distance (δ_R) between two sets of parameter estimates, $\boldsymbol{\gamma}_1$ and $\boldsymbol{\gamma}_2$, is nonzero (i.e., $\delta_R(\boldsymbol{\gamma}_1, \boldsymbol{\gamma}_2) \neq 0$), the distribution functions for each set of parameter estimates are *not* equal (i.e., $h(\mathbf{y} \mid \boldsymbol{\gamma}_1) \neq h(\mathbf{y} \mid \boldsymbol{\gamma}_2)$) for *at least* one value of $\mathbf{y}$. The distance, δ_R, between two sets of parameter estimates is a function of the differences of both the λ_{kjl} and the *moments* of the g_{ik}:

$$\delta_R(\boldsymbol{\gamma}_1, \boldsymbol{\gamma}_2) = \sum_k \sum_j \sum_l |\lambda_{kjl}^{(1)} - \lambda_{kjl}^{(2)}| + d_R(G_1, G_2), \tag{30}$$

where

$$d_R(G_1, G_2) = \sum |\mu_{a_1, \ldots, a_K}^{(1)} - \mu_{a_1, \ldots, a_K}^{(2)}|. \tag{31}$$

The sum in (31) is taken over all K-order combinations of nonnegative integers $(a_1, \ldots, a_K)$ $[(a_1 + \ldots + a_K = r \leq R \leq J)]$, where the μ are the raw moments of the $\boldsymbol{\xi}$, and r is their *degree*. Constraints on λ_{kjl} and ξ_{ik} determine that $\delta_R(\cdot, \cdot)$ is a bounded distance function satisfying Kiefer and Wolfowitz (1956, p. 890).

If the distance function $d_R(G_1, G_2) = 0$, then $G_1 = G_2$ up to moments of degree R or less. This defines a family of distributions $\Gamma_R = \{G_m: d_R(G_0, G_m) = 0\}$. No restrictions are placed on moments of degree greater than R. For technical reasons, Tolley and Manton (1991, 1990) restrict G to distributions with at most a countable number of jumps. This includes all continuous distributions of $\boldsymbol{\xi}$ and distributions with probability mass at the boundaries (i.e., 0 or 1) of the simplex. It is a minor limitation.

Let $\overline{\Gamma}$ be the completion of Γ under the pseudometric $d_R(\cdot, \cdot)$. Then $\overline{\Gamma}$ contains the limits of all Cauchy sequences measured using $d_R(\cdot, \cdot)$. Furthermore, $\Omega \times \overline{\Gamma}$ is a complete pseudometric space.

The limits to identifiability of $\boldsymbol{\gamma}$ are determined by counting the unique moments defined for J multinomial variables. This is equivalent to counting the unique parameters in the covariance matrix used in factor analysis to estimate factor loadings, correlations, and residuals. To determine the limits for the GOM model, we express $h(\mathbf{y}_i \mid \boldsymbol{\gamma})$ as a function of the parameters:

$$h(\mathbf{y}_i \mid \boldsymbol{\gamma}) = \int \cdots \int \prod_{j=1}^{J} \prod_{l=1}^{L_j} \left(\sum_{k=1}^{K} \lambda_{kjl} \xi_{ik} \right)^{y_{ijl}} dG_i(\xi_{i1}, \ldots, \xi_{iK}).$$

(32)

Because the y_{ijl} are discrete, (32) can be written

$$h(\mathbf{y}_i \mid \boldsymbol{\gamma}) = \sum_{k_1=1}^{K} \sum_{k_2=1}^{K} \sum_{k_J=1}^{K} \left(\prod_{j=1}^{J} \prod_{l=1}^{L_j} \lambda_{k_j jl}^{y_{ijl}} \right)$$

(33)

$$\times \left(\int \cdots \int \prod_{j=1}^{J} \prod_{l=1}^{L_j} \xi_{ik_j}^{y_{ijl}} dG_i(\xi_{i1}, \ldots, \xi_{iK}) \right),$$

where the distribution function G_i is identical over i. For any i and j, y_{ijl} has only one value equal to 1 (i.e., the distribution of the jth variable is multinomial). Therefore, (33) involves all raw moments up to degree J and simplifies to

$$h(\mathbf{y}_i \mid \boldsymbol{\gamma}) = \sum_{k_1=1}^{K} \sum_{k_2=1}^{K} \cdots \sum_{k_J=1}^{K} a(k_1, \ldots, k_J) \times b(k_1, \ldots, k_J),$$

(34)

where $a(k_1, \ldots, k_J)$ is a function of the λ_{kjl} and $b(k_1, \ldots, k_J)$ is a function of the moments of $(\xi_1, \ldots, \xi_K)$ up to degree J. Identifiability requires that $R \leq J$.

Thus, $\boldsymbol{\gamma}$ is uniquely estimated for distributions of responses where all *moments* of the g_{ik} to the Jth degree are identifiable. Identifiability is limited to this set of distributions because, though the g_{ik} can vary continuously (i.e., adopt any point within the simplex boundaries), the space is assumed complete (i.e., the realized g_{ik} are located at specific points). If J is increased, the resolution of the state space (i.e., the g_{ik} distribution) is improved and more features (and higher-order moments) can be determined.

Equation (34) defines the number of nonlinear equations available in the likelihood function to estimate parameters. The maximum number of equations, and hence parameters, is $\Pi_{j=1}^{J} L_j - 1$ (Tolley and Manton 1991). For a solution of order K, the number of λ_{kjl} parameters is $K \Sigma_{j=1}^{J} (L_j - 1)$; the number of moments for g_{ik} distributions of degree J or less is $\{(J + K-1)!/J!(K-1)!\} - 1$. The necessary condition for identifiability is

$$\prod_{j=1}^{J} L_j > K \sum_{j=1}^{J} (L_j - 1) + \frac{(J+K-1)!}{J!(K-1)!} - 1. \tag{35}$$

This compares the number of equations formed by varying the values of y_i in $h(y_i \mid \gamma)$ with the number of λ parameters and moments of ξ estimated for K classes. It is analogous to the necessary conditions for identifiability in confirmatory factor analysis (e.g., Bollen 1989) and in the latent class model (e.g., Everitt 1984).

Consistency. With (35), consistency of the MLEs of the λ_{kjl} and the moments of the g_{ik} (e.g., Tolley and Manton 1991) can be shown for the equivalence class of distributions (Γ_R) with equal moments up to degree J. Identifiability demonstrates that the relation of data to parameters is unique. It can be shown that information increases as both the number of cases and the number of variables increase. Given the Kiefer and Wolfowitz (1956) conditions, we can use the identifiability condition to demonstrate that if $\hat{\gamma}_I$ is *not* a consistent estimator of γ_0, then a sequence of MLEs can be obtained such that

$$\frac{\sup_{\gamma \in A(\rho)} \prod_{i=1}^{I} h(y_i \mid \gamma)}{\prod_{i=1}^{I} h(y_i \mid \gamma_0)} \geq \frac{\prod_{i=1}^{I} h(y_i \mid \hat{\gamma}_I)}{\prod_{i=1}^{I} h(y_i \mid \gamma_0)} \geq 1 \tag{36}$$

for infinitely many I, where $A(\rho)$ is exterior to a sphere of radius ρ centered at γ_0; i.e., $d_R(\gamma_0, \gamma) > \rho$. This event has probability zero. Hence, the λ_{kjl} and the ξ_{ik} moments of degree J or less are consistently estimated (see Tolley and Manton 1991 for proof).

The consistency theorem shows that information increases as a function of both I and J. As J increases, the number of moments of ξ_{ik} increases as $(J+K-1)!/J!(K-1)!$. The size of the family of distributions Γ_R *decreases* as J increases; i.e., the distribution of ξ_{ik}, G_0, is more precisely determined as J increases. Similarly, the number of parameters that may be estimated in factor analysis increases as a function of J, which determines the number of covariances.

The moments of G_0 are not directly estimated from (29c). Instead, the g_{ik} are estimated, along with the λ_{kjl}. Consistency under the proof above applies to the λ_{kjl} but not to the individual g_{ik}. The moments of G_0 are estimated as the empirical moments of the g_{ik}. The consistency results in (36) apply to these moments. The consistency of the moments of G_0 up to degree J, where J can range from 10 to 50 or more ($J=33$ in our first example in Table 3), implies that estimators of

$$\bar{\pi}_{jl}^{(S_0)} = \sum_{i \in S_0} \pi_{ijl} / \sum_{i \in S_0} 1 \tag{37a}$$

$$= \sum_k \bar{g}_k^{(S_0)} \lambda_{kjl}, \tag{37b}$$

where S_0 is any fixed subset of the population, are consistent. The term $\bar{g}_k^{(S_0)}$ is the mean of the g_{ik} for the specified subset. Thus, the GOM model can be consistently applied to predictions for groups of individuals with selected common characteristics or for problems in which J is large.

The advantage of having larger numbers of variables is threefold. First, as J increases (assuming that each new variable $J+1$ is not perfectly correlated with the first J measures), the number of estimable moments of G_0 increases. This applies to moment estimates for population subsets. As J increases, the number of potential subsets increases, as well as the ability to more precisely specify subsets of interest. Second, as J increases, the estimates of g_{ik} (for fixed K) exhibit greater stability. In addition to providing consistency of the individual g_{ik} (Woodbury 1963), increased stability (i.e., as J increases, the g_{ik} "averaged" over the J data elements become more stable and their variance declines) implies that the g_{ik} are closer on average to ξ_{ik}, which also improves efficiency (which is enhanced by the boundary constraints). Third, as J increases, the number of classes in the sample, K, is better determined.

Forming test statistics. Because the λ_{kjl} estimates (and implied moments of G_0) are consistent, the test statistic for judging whether the $(K+1)$th class extracts more information than expected by chance has the α critical region of the χ^2 approximation to the ratio of likelihoods from models with K and $K+1$ dimensions when no boundary constraints are imposed on γ. Since boundary constraints *are* imposed, the proof that the critical region for the test of χ^2 is more complicated. The proof involves examination of the distribution of (a) parameters introduced in the $K+1$–order model (set S_1), (b) parameters on the boundary in the K-order model (set S_2), and (c) nonzero parameters in the K-order model (set S_3). The null hypothesis is that the Kth-order model fits; i.e., parameters in S_1 are not significantly different than zero. The alternative is that S_1 is not zero. Evaluation of hypotheses about S_1 is conditioned upon S_2 and S_3, which are *not* nuisance parameters in the sense of case 8 in Self and Liang (1987), since boundary constraints are enforced. While parameters in S_2 and S_3 are of substantive interest, their values are not relevant for tests of S_1.

The distribution of the three sets is discussed in Tolley and Manton (1990). Briefly, if $Q(y)$ is derived from the likelihood ratio as

$$Q(\mathbf{y}) = -2(l_{NI}(\mathbf{y}, \boldsymbol{\gamma}_I) - l_{NII}(\mathbf{y}, \boldsymbol{\gamma}_{II})), \tag{38}$$

where l_{NI} and l_{NII} are loglikelihood values under two models, the test is

$$\phi(\mathbf{y}) = \begin{cases} 1 \text{ if } Q(\mathbf{y}) > \chi^2_{d,\,1-\alpha} & \text{(rejects model I)}, \\ 0 \text{ otherwise} & \text{(fails to reject model I)}, \end{cases} \tag{39}$$

where d is the degrees of freedom (df) and α is the size of the test.

The test $\phi(\mathbf{y})$ has size α, asymptotically, when model I is true, because (Tolley and Manton 1990)

$$\mathrm{E}(\phi(\mathbf{y})) = \Pr(\phi(\mathbf{y}) = 1) = \sum_R \Pr(Q(\mathbf{y}) \in CR_\alpha(R) \mid R) r_R = \alpha, \tag{40}$$

where R partitions parameters according to location on the boundary or interior, $CR_\alpha(R)$ is the critical region for a given α conditional on R, and r_R is the probability of R when model I holds. Thus, $\mathrm{E}(\phi(\mathbf{y})) = \alpha$, as required.

The df for the test are determined by the number of parameters estimated. The number of moments that can be determined is limited by the number of g_{ik} estimated at any step. Thus, the number of g_{ik} and λ_{kjl} define the df for the test. This is conservative because we penalize a df for each parameter on the boundary, since at any iteration, a parameter can move off the boundary. Their boundedness, however, means that they contribute less to χ^2 than would be expected for an unrestricted df. Counting them as a full df penalizes the test in a conservative way (i.e., "charges" too much information).

To go beyond "counting of parameters" to determine df, we must represent the dependency of parameters. This is done in time-series analyses where "equivalent" df are used (Blackman and Tukey 1958) and in models with sequential parameter fitting, for example, Mallows C_p criterion or Akiake's information criterion (AIC).

3.2. Factor Analysis

In factor analysis, local independence is implemented by relating the sample covariance (i.e., the second-order moments) matrix, S, of the data to a set of K latent dimensions by

$$S = \Lambda \, \phi \, \Lambda' + \Psi, \qquad (41)$$

where Λ is a matrix relating each of J observed variables to K latent factors, ϕ is the covariance matrix of the K factors, and Ψ is a diagonal error matrix. Though (41) may be estimated by least squares from data with any distribution, it is limited mathematically to describing only second-order moments: It reduces the residual covariance matrix to diagonal form; i.e.,

$$S - [\Lambda \, \phi \, \Lambda'] = \Psi, \qquad (42)$$

where the test of the $(K+1)$th factor is a test that off-diagonal elements of Ψ are zero.

Least squares estimation of (41) is difficult to implement when parameters are constrained. An alternative is ML factor analysis (Jöreskog 1969; Lawley and Maxwell 1971), based on the sample covariance matrix, S, the population covariance matrix, Σ, and its estimator, $\Sigma(\theta)$,

$$\Sigma(\theta) = \Lambda \, \phi \, \Lambda' + \Psi. \qquad (43)$$

Defining Λ, ϕ, and Ψ as in (41), the likelihood is

$$\ln L = -\frac{n}{2} \left[\ln | \Lambda \, \phi \, \Lambda' + \Psi | + \text{tr} \{ \Lambda \, \phi \, \Lambda' + \Psi^{-1} S \} \right] \quad (44a)$$

$$= -\frac{n}{2} \left[\ln | \Sigma(\theta) | + \text{tr}(\Sigma^{-1}(\theta) \, S) \right]. \qquad (44b)$$

Anderson and Amemiya (1988) showed that this estimator has robust properties. Specifically, the asymptotic standard errors of the factor loadings are valid even if factor scores and errors are non-normally distributed if disturbance terms are independent and the data are described by the sample covariance matrix. The result holds for structural equation models such as those estimated in LISREL.

The necessary condition for identifiability is

$$(J^2 + J)/2 > t, \qquad (45)$$

where t is the number of free parameters on the right of (43). For $J=30$, 465 parameters may be estimated. This constraint holds for models estimated in both LISREL and LISCOMP.

3.3. Discrete Factor Analysis (Full Information)

Estimation of (44) assumes that the observed variables have a multivariate normal distribution or, more precisely, that sample covariances are sufficient statistics for the distribution. For multiple discrete variables this may not hold. An alternate procedure assumes that the discrete density function, p, of the *observed* variables derives from a multivariate normal density of K continuous latent variables, each corresponding to an observed variable. The relation of discrete variables $\mathbf{x}$ to the K-dimensional normally distributed factor scores $\mathbf{y}$ is

$$p(\mathbf{x}) = \int_{a_1}^{b_1} \int_{a_2}^{b_2} \cdots \int_{a_K}^{b_K} f(\mathbf{y}) \, d\mathbf{y}, \tag{46}$$

where $f(\mathbf{y})$ is the K-dimensional multivariate normal density with covariance matrix Σ, and the limits of integration are response thresholds, h_j, defined as follows: If $x_j = 1$, then $a_j = h_j$ and $b_j = \infty$; if $x_j = 0$, then $a_j = -\infty$ and $b_j = h_j$. This generates a likelihood function with parameters $\mathbf{h}$ (thresholds), Λ (factor loadings), and ϕ (factor correlations):

$$L(\mathbf{h}, \Lambda, \phi) = \prod_{i=1}^{I} p(\mathbf{x}_i) \tag{47a}$$

$$= \prod_{i=1}^{I} \left[\int_{a_1}^{b_1} \int_{a_2}^{b_2} \cdots \int_{a_K}^{b_K} f(\mathbf{y}) \, d\mathbf{y} \right]. \tag{47b}$$

Evaluation of the K-dimensional multiple integral in (47b) is computationally burdensome. A limited information procedure is often used.

3.4. Discrete Factor Analysis (Limited Information)

Christofferson (1975) suggests use of the marginal frequency, M, for each item j,

$$M_j = \Pr(x_j = 1) = \int_{h_j}^{\infty} \frac{1}{\sqrt{2\pi\sigma_j^2}} \exp\left(-\frac{y^2}{2\,\sigma_j^2}\right) dy \tag{48}$$

and the joint occurrence of item pairs

$$M_{jl} = \Pr(x_j = 1, x_l = 1) = \int_{h_j}^{\infty} \int_{h_l}^{\infty} \frac{1}{2\pi |\Sigma_{jl}|^{1/2}} \exp\left(-\frac{1}{2} y' \Sigma_{jl}^{-1} y\right) dy. \quad (49)$$

This model is based on the multivariate normal distribution and extracts information only from the marginal distribution and second-order (two-way) interactions of the discrete responses. It is equivalent to applying ML analysis to tetrachoric or polychoric correlations. If the distribution deviates from the normal, then the model will not behave properly; e.g., the tetrachoric correlation matrix may not be positive definite.

3.5. The Latent Class Model

An alternate approach without the normality assumption is the latent class model. Let $N_{ab\cdots e}^{AB\cdots E}$ be the number of cases in cell $(a, b, \ldots, e)$ defined by variables $A, B, \ldots, E$. Let $P_{ab\cdots e}^{AB\cdots E}$ be the probability in (20). Then the likelihood is

$$L = \prod_{(a,b,\ldots,\, e)} [P_{ab\cdots e}^{AB\cdots E}]^{N_{ab\cdots e}^{AB\ldots E}}. \quad (50)$$

The necessary condition for identifiability is (Everitt 1984)

$$\prod_{j=1}^{J} L_j > K \sum_{j=1}^{J} (L_j - 1) + K - 1. \quad (51)$$

The likelihood ratio test statistic is

$$G^2 = 2 \sum_{(a,b,\ldots,\, e)} N_{ab\cdots e}^{AB\cdots E} \ln\left(\frac{N_{ab\cdots e}^{AB\cdots E}}{I \times P_{ab\cdots e}^{AB\cdots E}}\right), \quad (52)$$

where I is the sample size, and G^2 is asymptotically χ^2 distributed with df equal to the difference between the two sides of (51).

Since maximization of L is equivalent to minimization of G^2, the latter statistic is used for model evaluation. This is problematic when J is large, because even with large samples, there are many empty and nearly empty cells. Since G^2 requires, say, an expected cell size ≥ 5 for stability, the problem may have to be segmented (e.g., Eaton et al. 1989).

This is *not* inherent to (50). It arises because the likelihood ratio statistic G^2 compares the hypothesized and "saturated" models, i.e., models that have as many parameters as df. This is $\Pi_{j=1}^{J} L_j - 1$, so that if $J=10$, there are 1,023 parameters for 10 binary variables, but 1,048,575 for 10 variables with 4 categories. If $J=20$, there are 1,048,575 parameters if all variables are binary. The number of cells (and parameters in the saturated model) rapidly exceeds sample size as J increases, so that comparisons with the saturated model become vacuous.

As an alternative, (50) can be written (Everitt 1984)

$$L = \prod_i P_{a_i b_i \cdots e_i}^{AB \cdots E} \tag{53a}$$

$$= \prod_i \sum_k P_k \prod_j \prod_l \lambda_{kjl}^{y_{ijl}}, \tag{53b}$$

which differs from (29c) by interchange of summation and multiplication. Equation (53b) can be solved by the EM algorithm. In this algorithm trial values are inserted for the P_k and the λ_{kjl}. The p_{ik} (posterior probabilities) are estimated in the E (expectation step) conditional on the λ_{kjl}, giving rise to revised P_k. After the P_k are estimated, new λ_{kjl} are calculated in an M (maximization) step. Steps are repeated until convergence. The EM algorithm does not have the limitations of computations based on the G^2 statistic.

Let L_K and L_{K+1} be likelihood statistics associated with the latent class model with K and $K+1$ classes. The test statistic for judging if the $(K+1)$th class extracts more information than expected by chance is

$$G^2 = -2(\ln L_K - \ln L_{K+1}), \tag{54}$$

which is χ^2 distributed with $df = 1 + \Sigma_j (L_j - 1)$.

An alternative, conditional approach to (53b) for the latent class model (the CLC model in Woodbury et al. 1990) is based on the observation that setting $k_i = k$ in the latent class model corresponds to setting $g_{ik} = 1$ in the GOM model. Hence, conditional MLEs for the CLC model can be obtained from the likelihood (29c), subject to the constraint that $g_{ik} = 1$ for precisely one k and $g_{il} = 0$ for $l \neq k$. The CLC model is nested within the GOM model, so that the GOM properties of identifiability and consistency apply. The estimation strategy allows the CLC model to be used with larger numbers of variables than the latent class model. The additional variables help stabilize estimates of the restricted g_{ik}.

Comparison of identifiability conditions for the GOM model and the latent class model. In Table 2 the limits on the left of (35) and

TABLE 2
The Number of Parameters Required for Identifiability of GOM and Latent Class Models with K Classes

J	2	3	4	5	6	10	20	30
				All Binary Variables				
$\prod_{j=1}^{J} L_j$	4	8	16	32	64	1,024	1,048,576	1,073,741,824
K					Latent Class Model			
2	5*	7	9	11	13	21	41	61
3	—	11*	14	17	20	32	62	92
4	—	—	19*	23	27	43	83	123
5	—	—	—	29	34	54	104	154
6	—	—	—	35*	41	65	125	185
7	—	—	—	—	48	76	146	216
8	—	—	—	—	55	87	167	247
9	—	—	—	—	62	98	188	278
10	—	—	—	—	69*	109	209	309
					GOM Model			
2	6*	9*	12	15	18	30	60	90
3	—	—	26*	35*	45	95	290	585
4	—	—	—	—	107*	325	1,850	5,575
5	—	—	—	—	—	1,050*	10,725	46,525
6	—	—	—	—	—	—	53,249	324,811
7	—	—	—	—	—	—	230,369	1,948,001
8	—	—	—	—	—	—	888,189	10,295,711
9	—	—	—	—	—	—	3,108,284*	48,903,761
10	—	—	—	—	—	—	—	211,915,431

All Variables with Four Categories

J	2	3	4	5	6	10	20	30
$\prod_{j=1}^{J} L_j$	16	64	256	1,024	4,096	1,048,576	1.1×10^{12}	1.15×10^{18}
K					Latent Class Model			
2	13*	19	25	31	37	61	121	181
3	20*	29	38	47	56	92	182	272
4	—	39	51	63	75	123	243	363
5	—	49	64	79	94	154	304	454
6	—	59	77	95	113	185	365	545
7	—	69*	90	111	132	216	426	636
8	—	—	103	127	151	247	487	727
9	—	—	116	143	170	278	548	818
10	—	—	129	159	189	309	609	909
					GOM Model			
2	14	21	28	35	42	70	140	210
3	23*	36	50	65	81	155	410	765
4	—	55	82	115	155	405	2,010	5,815
5	—	79*	129	200	299	1,150	10,925	46,825
6	—	—	197	341	569	3,182	53,489	325,171
7	—	—	293*	566	1,049	8,217	230,649	1,948,421
8	—	—	—	911	1,859	19,687	888,509	10,296,191
9	—	—	—	1,421*	3,164	44,027	3,108,644	48,904,301
10	—	—	—	—	5,184*	92,677	10,015,604	211,916,031

*Number of parameters $\geq \prod_{j=1}^{J} L_j$; hence the model is not identified.

349

(51) are compared with the number of parameters required for 2, 3, 4, 5, 6, 10, 20, and 30 binary variables, and for 2, 3, 4, 5, 6, 10, 20, and 30 multinomial variables for the GOM and latent class models with K classes. For every J, the number of parameters identified increases linearly for the latent class model but approximately exponentially for the GOM model. Hence the GOM model reaches a limit to identifiability at smaller K values than the latent class model. Comparison of results for binary and four-category variables indicates that (a) the limits for each J for four-category variables are the square of the limits for binary variables, (b) the number of parameters in the latent class model identified for each J for four-category variables is approximately three times the number for binary variables, (c) the number of parameters in the GOM model identified for four-category variables is less than three times the number for binary variables when J is small but converges at large values of J and K. For binary variables for $J = 10$, the number of parameters that can be theoretically identified indicates a maximum $K = 4$ for the GOM model and $K = 93$ for the latent class model. For $J = 20$, the maximum is $K = 8$ for the GOM model and $K = 49{,}932$ for the latent class model. For $J = 30$, the maximum is $K = 11$ for the GOM model and $K = 34{,}636{,}833$ for the latent class model. For $J = 6$, the maximum is $K = 4$ for the GOM model and $K = 9$ for the latent class model. Thus, GOM models with $J = 20$ variables are roughly equivalent in complexity (i.e., K values) to latent class models with $J = 6$ variables. At the other extreme, the differences are smaller. For $J = 5$, the maximum is $K = 2$ for the GOM model and $K = 5$ for the latent class model. The minimum number of variables is $J = 3$ for the latent class model and $J = 4$ for the GOM model. Thus, the "operating ranges" of the two procedures are different: The latent class model is best for 3 to 6 variables, and the GOM model is best for 7 or more.

In (35) and (51) many equations are required to fit parameters. There are seldom that many independent equations, because for large J (e.g., 20+) for any reasonably sized sample, many moments will be functionally dependent. Thus, for higher-order models, the number of independent moments that can be determined for an additional class is limited to the number of g_{ik} estimated.

Empirical comparison of the GOM model and the CLC model. Table 3 illustrates the application of the GOM model and the CLC model to a common data set on 33 psychiatric symptoms in the epidemiological catchment area (ECA) study (Woodbury et al. 1990). Both models were based on (29c), where, for the CLC model, the g_{ik} are forced to be 0 or 1.

The GOM λ_{kjl} represent clinically distinct patterns because individual heterogeneity is isolated in the g_{ik}; i.e., variation not common to individuals is not forced into the λ_{kjl}. The CLC model is difficult to interpret because all persons assigned to the kth class are assumed to be identical so that information represented by the GOM model in the unconstrained g_{ik} is forced into the λ_{kjl} estimates in the CLC model. Individual heterogeneity can only be represented by adding classes; i.e., K will generally be greater for the CLC model than for the GOM model.

This data set also illustrates the effect of complex sample design on parameter estimates. Skinner, Holmes, and Smith (1986) discuss how principal component analysis and other multivariate models (e.g., factor analysis) can be distorted in a complex sample because the covariance matrix differs from that for a simple random sample because of design effects. Since design effects reflect the observation plan, and not the phenomena, this produces artifacts. In the GOM model each person is a stratum of size one (i.e., conditional upon his g_{ik}). Hence, the λ_{kjl} are not distorted by design effects. Design effects can be represented in the g_{ik} distribution by postweighting the g_{ik} to produce weighted g_{ik} moments appropriate for the population.

The ECA data set was used to assess these effects by simulating a sample design using a diagnostic threshold to screen cases (Woodbury et al. 1990). By applying screens, one systematically sampled cases. The effects on the CLC model were complex, and the fitted models did not lead to clinically meaningful classes. In the GOM model, the λ_{kjl} were robust to systematic sampling.

4. STRUCTURAL GENERALIZATIONS OF THE GOM MODEL

4.1. *Representation of Structural Equation Systems (General)*

Multivariate structural dependencies may be represented as simultaneous equation systems with cross-equation parameter constraints. Estimation requires evaluating the joint distribution func-

TABLE 3
Comparison of the λ_{kjl} Estimated for CLC and GOM Models with $K=6$, ECA Data, 7,183 Cases, 33 Psychiatric Symptoms

Psychiatric Symptom	Marginal Frequency (%)	Latent Class Model Latent Classes						Grade-of-Membership Analysis GOM Classes					
		1	2	3	4	5	6	1	2	3	4	5	6
Sad for two weeks	4.1	37.9	34.8	2.4	2.6	16.5	1.0	100.0	0.0	0.0	0.0	0.0	0.0
Sad for two years	1.2	13.1	10.4	0.7	0.0	12.9	0.3	39.6	0.0	0.0	0.0	0.0	0.0
Fainting	0.3	3.0	0.9	3.5	0.0	0.0	0.2	0.0	30.8	0.0	0.0	0.0	0.0
Shortness of breath	1.2	6.1	16.0	17.1	0.9	0.0	0.4	0.0	100.0	0.0	0.0	0.0	0.0
Palpitations	2.1	12.6	16.6	19.6	1.9	22.1	0.8	0.0	100.0	0.0	0.0	0.0	0.0
Felt dizzy	2.3	12.4	19.9	15.2	2.8	0.0	1.1	0.0	100.0	0.0	0.0	0.0	0.0
Feel weak	1.4	6.1	18.5	16.9	2.5	1.9	0.5	0.0	100.0	0.0	0.0	0.0	0.0
Nervous person	23.6	67.9	86.3	68.7	34.1	39.0	17.0	100.0	100.0	100.0	0.0	0.0	0.0
Fright attack	1.8	7.3	30.9	100.0	0.0	0.0	0.0	0.0	100.0	0.0	0.0	0.0	0.0
Phobias													
Eating in public	1.1	1.9	25.1	0.9	5.3	0.0	0.2	0.0	100.0	0.0	0.0	0.0	0.0
Speaking in small group	1.5	2.4	18.9	15.9	8.1	0.8	0.5	0.0	100.0	0.0	0.0	0.0	0.0
Speaking to strangers	1.9	2.9	39.7	4.7	10.5	0.0	0.5	0.0	100.0	0.0	0.0	0.0	0.0
Fear of being alone	1.4	4.5	32.0	5.1	3.9	5.4	0.3	0.0	80.5	0.0	0.0	37.9	0.0
Tunnels and bridges	3.6	1.8	50.9	17.2	30.0	0.0	0.6	0.0	0.0	0.0	100.0	0.0	0.0
Crowds	2.7	4.4	48.4	22.8	16.0	0.0	0.5	0.0	100.0	0.0	0.0	0.0	0.0
Public transportation	4.0	2.8	55.6	17.9	30.6	0.0	0.9	0.0	100.0	0.0	100.0	0.0	0.0

Outside house alone	1.3	3.7	23.5	0.0	6.8	0.0	0.4	0.0	100.0	0.0	0.0	0.0	0.0
Heights	7.7	5.2	54.3	17.1	47.9	0.0	3.4	0.0	0.0	0.0	100.0	0.0	0.0
Closed place	2.9	2.6	43.7	2.9	17.7	6.5	0.9	0.0	100.0	0.0	100.0	0.0	0.0
Storms	4.7	3.9	46.0	23.0	26.5	6.1	1.9	0.0	0.0	0.0	100.0	0.0	0.0
Water	4.4	4.0	35.4	32.7	30.5	6.5	1.4	0.0	0.0	0.0	100.0	0.0	0.0
Bugs	9.0	13.0	55.5	23.9	52.4	13.2	3.7	0.0	0.0	0.0	100.0	0.0	0.0
Animals	2.0	2.9	25.6	0.7	11.5	0.0	0.8	0.0	0.0	0.0	91.6	0.0	0.0
Crying spells	4.9	22.5	32.1	9.2	5.7	100.0	2.2	0.0	0.0	0.0	0.0	100.0	0.0
Felt hopeless	4.0	29.5	26.5	5.6	3.1	100.0	1.1	0.0	0.0	0.0	0.0	100.0	0.0
Change in weight or appetite	6.1	32.9	48.4	26.2	6.5	11.0	2.8	100.0	0.0	0.0	0.0	0.0	0.0
Sleeping more or less	10.7	52.6	64.9	24.9	16.9	36.0	5.2	100.0	0.0	0.0	0.0	0.0	0.0
Talking or moving slower	5.7	37.8	72.9	5.1	6.4	5.4	1.7	100.0	0.0	0.0	0.0	0.0	0.0
Interest in sex much less	2.2	13.6	23.3	9.2	3.6	1.4	0.9	63.0	0.0	0.0	0.0	0.0	0.0
More tired	7.4	48.7	61.6	5.2	6.8	2.8	2.8	100.0	0.0	0.0	0.0	0.0	0.0
Felt worthless, sinful, or guilty	2.8	25.0	32.8	0.6	1.6	16.8	0.7	100.0	0.0	0.0	0.0	0.0	0.0
Difficulty concentrating or thinking	5.2	38.9	53.9	6.6	4.2	11.8	1.5	100.0	0.0	0.0	0.0	0.0	0.0
Thoughts of death or suicide	9.3	41.9	63.3	24.7	15.1	36.4	4.5	0.0	0.0	0.0	0.0	100.0	0.0

tion and isolating the variables into (at least) two classes: endogenous variables, whose behavior is determined within the system, and exogenous variables. These equations are written for endogenous variables, η, and for exogenous variables, ξ, as

$$\beta\,\eta = \Gamma\,\xi + \zeta, \tag{55}$$

where β and Γ are $(N \times N)$ and $(N \times P)$ matrices of coefficients describing (a) the interrelations of N endogenous variables η, where elements on the diagonal of β are unity and β is nonsingular, and (b) the dependency of N endogenous variables η on P exogenous variables ξ (Dillon and Goldstein 1984). More generally, η and ξ are latent variables related to the observed endogenous (y) and exogenous (x) variables by

$$\mathbf{x} = \Lambda_x\,\xi + \delta, \tag{56}$$

$$\mathbf{y} = \Lambda_y\,\eta + \epsilon. \tag{57}$$

In LISREL and LISCOMP models, coefficient matrices Λ_x, Λ_y, β, Γ, and ϕ (the covariance matrix of ξ) are estimated by ML, assuming that the joint distribution function for observed variables $\mathbf{x}$ and $\mathbf{y}$ is described by a partitioned covariance matrix:

$$\mathbf{S}_T = \begin{pmatrix} \mathbf{S}_{yy} : \mathbf{S}_{xy} \\ \cdots \cdots \\ \mathbf{S}_{yx} : \mathbf{S}_{xx} \end{pmatrix} = \begin{pmatrix} \Lambda_y\,\beta^{-1}\,(\Gamma\phi\Gamma' + \Psi)\,[\beta^{-1}]'\,\Lambda'_y + \theta_\epsilon : \Lambda_y\,\beta^{-1}\,\Gamma\phi\Lambda'_x \\ \cdots \cdots \cdots \cdots \cdots \cdots \cdots \cdots \cdots \cdots \cdots \cdots \cdots \\ \Lambda_x\,\phi\Gamma'[\beta^{-1}]'\,\Lambda'_y \qquad\qquad : \Lambda_x\phi\Lambda'_x + \theta_\delta \end{pmatrix} . \tag{58}$$

LISREL requires that the distribution function be well described by the second-order moments, where $\mathbf{S}_{xx}$ is the sample covariance matrix for exogenous variables described by a standard factor model, $\mathbf{S}_{yx}$ is the cross-covariance matrix representing the regression of η on ξ, and $\mathbf{S}_{yy}$ represents the covariance matrix of $\mathbf{y}$ described as a quadratic form involving both Γ and β. The coefficients for the measurement models are included in each segment. The LISREL model is a two-component model, consisting of (a) a structural equation model (55) and (b) measurement models for exogenous variables (56) and endogenous variables (57).

4.2. *The GOM Representation of Structural Equations*

The GOM equivalent to (55) for distributions with unique moments up to degree J can be generated. In (58) the estimate of $\mathbf{S}_{xx}$ does not involve information on $\mathbf{y}$ or on its joint distribution with $\mathbf{x}$. However, the parameters of $\mathbf{S}_{xx}$ (i.e., Λ_x, $\boldsymbol{\phi}$, and $\boldsymbol{\theta}_\delta$) are also parameters of $\mathbf{S}_{yx}$ and $\mathbf{S}_{yy}$, so they are estimated simultaneously with Λ_y, $\boldsymbol{\beta}$, $\boldsymbol{\Gamma}$, $\boldsymbol{\Psi}$, and $\boldsymbol{\theta}_\epsilon$.

To estimate the GOM structural model, we must modify (29c). We define M sets of discrete variables, $\mathbf{Y}_m$, such that $\mathbf{Y}_1$ is causally or temporally prior to $\mathbf{Y}_2, \ldots, \mathbf{Y}_M$, and $\mathbf{Y}_2$ is causally prior to $\mathbf{Y}_3, \ldots,$ $\mathbf{Y}_M$, etc. The set $\mathbf{Y}_m$ contains J_m variables, where the jth has L_{mj} response levels, denoted $y_{ijl}^{(m)}$. For simplicity, we use superscripted parentheses to index model stages or partitioned matrices that correspond to model stages. Define, for $m = 1$,

$$\boldsymbol{\Pi}_1 = \mathrm{E}(\mathbf{Y}_1) = \mathbf{G}_{11}\,\boldsymbol{\Lambda}_{11}, \tag{59}$$

where $\mathrm{E}(\cdot)$ denotes mathematical expectation, or, in scalar terms with K_1 classes,

$$\pi_{ijl}^{(1)} = \mathrm{E}(y_{ijl}^{(1)}) = \sum_{k=1}^{K_1} g_{ik}^{(1,1)}\,\lambda_{kjl}^{(1,1)}. \tag{60}$$

This is the *measurement* model (i.e., (56)) for the exogenous variables, $\mathbf{Y}_1$. Thus, for $\mathbf{Y}_1$, the $g_{ik}^{(1,1)}$ correspond to the latent factor scores $\boldsymbol{\xi}$, and the $\lambda_{kjl}^{(1,1)}$ correspond to the elements of Λ_x. Since neither the exogenous variables, $y_{ijl}^{(1)}$, nor the latent state variables, $g_{ik}^{(1,1)}$, are normally distributed, $e_{ijl}^{(1)} = y_{ijl}^{(1)} - \pi_{ijl}^{(1)}$, which corresponds to $\boldsymbol{\delta}$, is not normal.

We generalize (2) so that after introducing exogenous latent variables, we can introduce endogenous variables yet maintain $\Sigma_k\,g_{ik} = 1.0$ at both stages. To do this we replace (29c) with

$$L = \prod_i \prod_j \prod_l \left(\frac{\sum_k g_{ik}\,\lambda_{kjl}}{\sum_k (g_{ik}\sum_l \lambda_{kjl})} \right)^{y_{ijl}}, \tag{61}$$

which is derived (Woodbury et al. 1990) from (29c) using empirical Bayes arguments. The constraint $\Sigma_l\lambda_{kjl} = 1$ is not required in (61).

This allows us to derive normalizations for the g_{ik} for each *stage* of the model. If we rewrite (59) (with subscripts suppressed) as

$$E(\mathbf{Y}) = \mathbf{U}\,\mathbf{V}, \tag{62}$$

or, in scalar terms, as

$$E(y_{ijl}) = \sum_{k=1}^{K} u_{ik} v_{kjl}, \tag{63}$$

where parameters $\mathbf{U}$ and $\mathbf{V}$ are related to $\mathbf{G}$ and Λ by the normalization, then

$$\mathbf{U} = \mathbf{G}\,\mathbf{D}^{-1} \quad \text{and} \quad \mathbf{V} = \mathbf{D}\,\Lambda, \tag{64}$$

where $\mathbf{D}$ is a diagonal matrix with kth diagonal element

$$d_{kk} = \sum_{i} g_{ik}/I = \bar{g}_{k}. \tag{65}$$

Thus, $\mathbf{U}$ and $\mathbf{V}$ vary from $\mathbf{G}$ and Λ only by the normalizing factor $\bar{g}_{k} = \sum_{i} g_{ik}/I$, i.e., by the average of the g_{ik} values for the kth class.

To estimate $\mathbf{U}$ and $\mathbf{V}$ we need an identifiability constraint, because $\sum_{l} \lambda_{kjl} = 1.0$ is no longer enforced on (61). We use

$$L = \prod_{i}\prod_{j} \exp\{(-y_{ij+} \sum_{k} u_{ik} \sum_{l} v_{kjl}\} \prod_{l} (\sum_{k} u_{ik} v_{kjl})^{y_{ijl}}/y_{ijl}! \tag{66}$$

maximized with the constraint (which follows from (65)) that

$$\sum_{i} u_{ik} = I \tag{67}$$

and where y_{ij+} is an indicator that a response was obtained on x_{ij}; i.e.,

$$y_{ij+} = \sum_{l} y_{ijl}. \tag{68}$$

If x_{ij} is missing, $y_{ij+} = 0$ and the contribution of x_{ij} to (66) is unity; i.e., the variable is ignored. Alternately, if x_{ij} is present, such that $x_{ij} = l$, then $y_{ij+} = 1$ and $y_{ijl} = 1$:

$$\mathrm{Pr}(x_{ij} = l \mid y_{ij+} = 1) = \frac{\sum_{k} u_{ik} v_{kjl}}{\sum_{k}(u_{ik} \sum_{l} v_{kjl})}, \tag{69}$$

which is the same as (61). Thus (66) is the marginal likelihood that generates (61) by conditioning on $\{y_{ij+}\}$.

From $\mathbf{U}$ and $\mathbf{V}$ we use the normalization in (67) to obtain

$$\mathbf{G}^{*} = \mathbf{U}\,\mathbf{C} \quad \text{and} \quad \Lambda^{*} = \mathbf{C}^{-1}\,\mathbf{V}, \tag{70}$$

where $\mathbf{C}$ is a diagonal matrix with kth diagonal element

$$c_{kk} = \sum_j \sum_l v_{kjl}/J. \qquad (71)$$

Asterisks on $\mathbf{G}^*$ and $\boldsymbol{\Lambda}^*$ in (70) indicate that parameters are obtained with the normalization

$$g_{ik} = g_{ik}^* / \sum_m g_{im}^*, \qquad (72)$$

$$\lambda_{kjl} = \lambda_{kjl}^* / \sum_m \lambda_{kjm}^*. \qquad (73)$$

Thus, the model in (59),

$$E(\mathbf{Y}) = \mathbf{G}\,\boldsymbol{\Lambda}, \qquad (74)$$

is replaced by

$$E(\mathbf{Y}) = \mathbf{G}^*\,\boldsymbol{\Lambda}^*, \qquad (75)$$

which differs by the normalization in (72) and (73). From (70), $\mathbf{U}$ and $\mathbf{V}$ are the parameter matrices used in optimization. For calculation we reparameterize the first stage as

$$E(\mathbf{Y}_1) = \mathbf{U}_1\,\mathbf{V}_{11}. \qquad (76)$$

The second stage is

$$E(\mathbf{Y}_2) = \mathbf{U}_1\,\mathbf{V}_{12} + \mathbf{U}_2\,\mathbf{V}_{22}. \qquad (77)$$

The third stage is

$$E(\mathbf{Y}_3) = \mathbf{U}_1\,\mathbf{V}_{13} + \mathbf{U}_2\,\mathbf{V}_{23} + \mathbf{U}_3\,\mathbf{V}_{33}, \qquad (78)$$

with obvious generalizations for additional stages.

The general multistage model in (62) can be partitioned as

$$\mathbf{Y} = [\mathbf{Y}_1 \vdots \mathbf{Y}_2 \vdots \mathbf{Y}_3 \vdots \cdots \vdots \mathbf{Y}_M] \qquad (79)$$

$$\mathbf{U} = [\mathbf{U}_1 \vdots \mathbf{U}_2 \vdots \mathbf{U}_3 \vdots \cdots \vdots \mathbf{U}_M] \qquad (80)$$

$$\mathbf{V} = \begin{bmatrix} \mathbf{V}_{11}\,\mathbf{V}_{12}\,\mathbf{V}_{13}\cdots\,\mathbf{V}_{1M} \\ 0\;\;\mathbf{V}_{22}\,\mathbf{V}_{23}\cdots\,\mathbf{V}_{2M} \\ 0\;\;\;\;0\;\;\mathbf{V}_{33}\cdots\,\mathbf{V}_{3M} \\ \vdots\;\;\;\;\vdots\;\;\;\;\vdots\;\;\ddots\;\;\vdots \\ 0\;\;\;\;0\;\;\;\;0\;\cdots\,\mathbf{V}_{MM} \end{bmatrix}. \qquad (81)$$

The scalar form (63) is substituted into (66) for joint ML estimation. Let K_m denote the number of classes introduced at stage m, and let $K^{(m)}$ denote $K_1 + \ldots + K_m$. $\mathbf{U}_m$ has dimension $I \times K_m$, $m = 1, \ldots,$

M. Also $L_m = \Sigma_j L_{mj}$, where L_{mj} is the number of responses to the jth variable in $\mathbf{Y}_m$. It follows that $\mathbf{V}_{mn}$ is $K_m \times L_n$. Once the $\mathbf{U}_m$ and $\mathbf{V}_{mn}$ are estimated, the $\mathbf{G}_{nm}$ and Λ_{mn} are obtained from equations (70) through (73), so that equations (76) through (78) are, after renormalization,

$$E(\mathbf{Y}_1) = \mathbf{G}_{11} \Lambda_{11}, \tag{82}$$

$$E(\mathbf{Y}_2) = \mathbf{G}_{21} \Lambda_{12} + \mathbf{G}_{22} \Lambda_{22}, \tag{83}$$

$$E(\mathbf{Y}_3) = \mathbf{G}_{31} \Lambda_{13} + \mathbf{G}_{32} \Lambda_{23} + \mathbf{G}_{33} \Lambda_{33}. \tag{84}$$

The stage-specific GOM scores are

$$\mathbf{G}^{(1)} = \mathbf{G}_{11}, \tag{85}$$

$$\mathbf{G}^{(2)} = [\mathbf{G}_{21} \vdots \mathbf{G}_{22}], \tag{86}$$

$$\mathbf{G}^{(3)} = [\mathbf{G}_{31} \vdots \mathbf{G}_{32} \vdots \mathbf{G}_{33}] \tag{87}$$

and, in general,

$$\mathbf{G}^{(m)} = [\mathbf{G}_{m1} \vdots \ldots \vdots \mathbf{G}_{mm}], \tag{88}$$

where $\mathbf{G}^{(m)}$ has dimension $I \times K^{(m)}$ and contains the m sets of GOM scores obtained at stage m. Because of renormalization, the GOM scores for each stage change when an additional stage is introduced. The Λ characterize the GOM classes in much the same way that the factors in factor analysis are named from patterns in the factor loadings matrix (Singer 1989).

In the LISREL model, since the individual scores are not directly informative (all information is assumed to be in the covariance matrix), extraction of the latent scores for the individual cases is usually done *after* estimation of the structural coefficients in a conditional Bayesian step. In the GOM model the latent scores ($\mathbf{G}$) are obtained simultaneously as parameters with the structural coefficients because they contain information on higher-order moments affecting the solution; i.e., they describe all order dependencies (up to J) between the various stages. This is a higher-order structure than LISREL. For large problems, this structure is complex, so we summarize specific features of it. We discuss two such structures. The first represents the $(K^{(1)} \times K^{(2)})$–order relations of $\mathbf{G}^{(1)}$ to $\mathbf{G}^{(2)}$ and the $(K^{(2)} \times K^{(3)})$–order relations of $\mathbf{G}^{(2)}$ to $\mathbf{G}^{(3)}$, where $\mathbf{G}^{(m)}$ refers to the mth stage of the analysis. The second is a structural equation model directly analogous to the LISREL model in (55).

4.3. *The GOM Model of State Variable Changes*

Let $\mathbf{T}^{(1,2)} = \{t_{kl}\}$, where t_{kl} is the flow from class k to class l in (5). It follows from (3) and (4) that

$$\mathbf{G}^{(2)} = \mathbf{G}^{(1)} \mathbf{T}^{(1,2)} + \mathbf{E}^{(1,2)}, \tag{89}$$

or, with partitioned matrices,

$$[\mathbf{G}_{21} \vdots \mathbf{G}_{22}] = \mathbf{G}_{11} [\mathbf{T}_1^{(1,2)} \vdots \mathbf{T}_2^{(1,2)}] + \mathbf{E}_1^{(1,2)} \vdots \mathbf{E}_2^{(1,2)}], \tag{90}$$

or

$$\mathbf{G}_{21} = \mathbf{G}_{11} \mathbf{T}_1^{(1,2)} + \mathbf{E}_1^{(1,2)}, \tag{91}$$

$$\mathbf{G}_{22} = \mathbf{G}_{11} \mathbf{T}_2^{(1,2)} + \mathbf{E}_2^{(1,2)}. \tag{92}$$

The $K_1 \times K_2$ matrix $\mathbf{T}_2^{(1,2)}$ is a matrix of coefficients that describe transitions from the K_1 classes in stage 1 to the K_2 classes introduced in stage 2.

To relate scores from the third (and subsequent) stages to scores from prior stages, we generalize (89):

$$\mathbf{G}^{(m)} = \mathbf{G}^{(n)} \mathbf{T}^{(n,m)} + \mathbf{E}^{(n,m)}, \tag{93}$$

where $n < m$ and

$$\mathbf{T}^{(n,m)} = [\mathbf{T}_1^{(n,m)} \vdots \ldots \vdots \mathbf{T}_m^{(n,m)}], \tag{94}$$

$$\mathbf{E}^{(n,m)} = [\mathbf{E}_1^{(n,m)} \vdots \ldots \vdots \mathbf{E}_m^{(n,m)}]. \tag{95}$$

The diagonals of $\mathbf{T}^{(n,m)}$ indicate persistence in the set of $K^{(n)}$ scores. The rightmost blocks, $\mathbf{T}_m^{(n,m)}$, indicate flow from the $K^{(n)}$ classes in stage n to the K_m classes introduced in stage m.

We can model different processes. The $\mathbf{G}$ matrices above assume *one* set of I observations. We can define processes in which, for M sets of repeated observations, there are M sets of g_{ik}, $\mathbf{G}_m$, $m=1, \ldots, M$, but only one set of λ_{kjl}, Λ_{11}, e.g., if a common set of measures is repeated over time on an individual ($\mathbf{Y}_m = \mathbf{Y}_1, m=1, \ldots, M$). In this case, we require that $\Lambda_{mm} = \Lambda_{11}, m=1, \ldots, M$, for each set of replicates and estimate

$$\mathbf{Y}_m = \mathbf{G}_m \Lambda_{11} + \mathbf{E}_m. \tag{96}$$

Λ_{11} must define a simplex of high enough dimensionality to encompass all g_{ik} trajectories over time. All M sets of variables are assumed to be exogenous (i.e., the dimensionality and structure of the space is assumed to be invariant over time), with temporal variation manifested only at the individual level. This is similar to deleting $\mathbf{U}_1 \mathbf{V}_{12}$ from (77) or to deleting the structural equation (55) from LISREL. We can write a "mixed" model with both replicates and repeated measurements, i.e., certain g_{ik} trajectories for a fixed set of Λ elements and certain g_{ik} trajectories for sets of Λ elements estimated conditionally.

We can use the procedure to explore the structure of processes. If innovation processes are statistically independent, the process has first-order temporal dependence if $\mathbf{Y}_{m-1}$ and $\mathbf{Y}_{m+1}$ are independent given $\mathbf{Y}_m$ or, for $m=2$, if $\mathbf{V}_{13} = 0$ in (78). In general, for an lth-order process, $\mathbf{V}_{nm} = \mathbf{0}$ in (81), when $n < m-l$.

The $\mathbf{V}$ in (81) define an upper-triangular block matrix in which all order relations between two time periods exist. Given that simultaneous effects are represented within each $\mathbf{Y}_m$ and that temporal dependence is represented by the relation of $\mathbf{Y}_m$ to $\mathbf{Y}_{m-l}$, the lower off-diagonal portion of $\mathbf{V}$ is zero, which indicates that future system states do not affect past system states.

Though *causality* dictates that the lower off-diagonal portion of $\mathbf{V}$ be zero, observationally it may not be. There is no requirement that different $\mathbf{Y}_m$ contain the same set of variables; new observations of a process may involve variables not previously measured. New states may provide information about *past* states not measured before, e.g., left censoring. If estimates of the lower off-diagonal portion of $\mathbf{V}$ are generated, current observations can be used to reconstruct the past behavior of the system. The upper-triangular portion of $\mathbf{V}$ can be used to forecast system states forward in time. The lower off-diagonal portion of $\mathbf{V}$ could provide updating information in forward forecasting to determine if the information on past states is "correct."

4.4. *The GOM Structural Equation Model*

The model in section 4.3 is applicable if we have sets of measurements repeated over time. In other cases, the structure of the process is constrained. Let $\mathbf{G} \equiv \mathbf{G}^{(M)}$ be the M-component matrix of GOM scores for an M-stage model. The structural equation model is

$$G = GB + E, \tag{97}$$

where $\mathbf{B}$ is blocked upper triangular with an identity in the first block and zero elements ($b_{ii} = 0$) on the remainder of the main diagonal; i.e., for $M = 3$,

$$\mathbf{B} = \begin{bmatrix} \mathbf{I}_{11} & : \mathbf{B}_{12} & : \mathbf{B}_{13} \\ 0 & : \mathbf{B}_{22} & : \mathbf{B}_{23} \\ 0 & : 0 & : \mathbf{B}_{33} \end{bmatrix}. \tag{98}$$

Thus,

$$\mathbf{G}_{32} = \mathbf{G}_{31}\,\mathbf{B}_{12} + \mathbf{G}_{32}\,\mathbf{B}_{22} + \mathbf{E}_{32}, \tag{99}$$

or

$$\mathbf{G}_{32}\,(\mathbf{I} - \mathbf{B}_{22}) = \mathbf{G}_{31}\,\mathbf{B}_{12} + \mathbf{E}_{32}, \tag{100}$$

which, except for transposition, has the same form as the LISREL structural equation (55) where $\boldsymbol{\beta} = (\mathbf{I} - \mathbf{B}_{22})$ and $\boldsymbol{\Gamma} = \mathbf{B}_{12}$. The equation for $\mathbf{G}_{33}$ is written

$$\mathbf{G}_{33}\,(\mathbf{I} - \mathbf{B}_{33}) = \mathbf{G}_{31}\,\mathbf{B}_{13} + \mathbf{G}_{32}\,\mathbf{B}_{23} + \mathbf{E}_{33}. \tag{101}$$

Then $\mathbf{B} = \{b_{kl}\}$ is

$$b_{kl} = E(m_{ikl})/E(g_{ik}), \tag{102}$$

where m_{ikl} differs from g_{ikl} in (8) because of the constraint that $m_{ikl} = 0$ for $k = l$ and for k indexing a later stage than l. These represent the causal structure for $\mathbf{B}$. Additional zeroes can be imposed to represent other structures. To estimate m_{ikl} we use a minimum entropy algorithm, subject to

$$\sum_l m_{ikl} \leq g_{ik} \quad \text{and} \quad \sum_k m_{ikl} \leq g_{il}. \tag{103}$$

This is applied hierarchically to reflect the greater influence of temporally and causally more-proximate sets of variables. Specifically, the joint memberships supporting $\mathbf{B}_{22}$ were estimated prior to those supporting $\mathbf{B}_{12}$; and the joint memberships supporting $\mathbf{B}_{33}$ were estimated prior to $\mathbf{B}_{23}$, which, in turn, were estimated prior to $\mathbf{B}_{13}$. This hierarchical approach maximizes the coefficients in $\mathbf{B}_{mm}$ relative to $\mathbf{B}_{nm}$, for $n < m$. In particular, the coefficients in $\mathbf{B}_{1m}$ are minimized, reflecting the assumption that the causally most-remote variables have the smallest influence.

5. EXAMPLE

5.1. *Data*

To illustrate the structural equation model in (97), we need a data set with adequate measures to define multiple structural domains. We used the 1982 and 1984 National Long Term Care Survey (NLTCS), whose sample design and instrumentation are described elsewhere (e.g., Manton 1988). Briefly, in 1982 a list sample of 35,018 persons was drawn from Medicare records. Thus, the sample is representative of all Medicare-eligible elderly persons (those aged 65 and older). A second-stage screening procedure was used to select 6,393 persons with chronic disability (90 days or more) on one or more of nine activities of daily living (ADL) or seven instrumental activities of daily living (IADL). In 1982, persons in the community who did not have chronic disability (26,623) and institutional residents (1,992) were *not* interviewed. All persons chronically disabled or in institutions in 1982 were automatically reinterviewed in 1984. In addition, 12,100 (of the 26,623) who were elderly but not disabled in 1982 and 4,916 who reached age 65 in the interval were screened. Those found to be chronically disabled in 1984 received a detailed interview. This produced 12,200 respondents for the two sets of community interviews. We selected from the total set of respondents all persons ($I = 1,343$) using Medicare Home Health Agency (HHA) Services in a 12-month period after the 1982 and 1984 interview dates. This is a chronically disabled population who remained community residents despite disability.

Health and functional status are described by 56 variables indicating the presence of 29 medical conditions and 27 limitations in ADL, IADL, or physical functioning. A second set of 34 variables describes resources, attitudes, and behaviors. A third set of 17 variables describes acute and long-term care (LTC) utilization and expenditures.

5.2. *Model*

Figure 1 outlines the relation between and among variables classed according to a priori criteria and ordered from top to bottom by causal stages. The model posits that health and functional status determine health-service utilization and that the influence of health

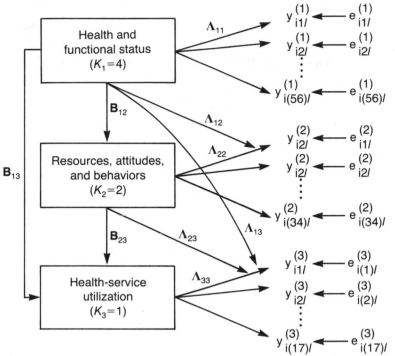

FIGURE 1. Causal structure of health-service utilization model.

on utilization is mediated by resources, attitudes, and behaviors. The relation of the latent variables to their indicators (the measurement model) is represented by Λ_{11}, Λ_{22}, and Λ_{33}. The relation of the variables in subsequent stages to the classes determined in prior stages is designated by Λ_{12}, Λ_{13}, and Λ_{23}. These are conditional estimates with the prior g_{ik} held fixed, i.e., through functional dependence on the prior u_{ik} (equations (82)–(84)).

Changes in the latent fuzzy classes are indicated by the $\mathbf{B}_{12}$, $\mathbf{B}_{13}$, and $\mathbf{B}_{23}$ matrices. Parameters were estimated by ML using (66), subject to (79)–(81). We used equations (70)–(73) to convert the $\mathbf{U}$-$\mathbf{V}$ estimates to the $\mathbf{G}$-Λ form. This model determines the degree to which the use of services is explained by prior groups of variables in a simultaneous equation system with two levels of endogeneity.

To keep the example manageable while presenting a realistic description of the 107 variables, we selected a model structure with $K = 7$ classes: four in stage 1, two in stage 2, and one in stage 3. We did not evaluate alternate models with different numbers of classes at each stage. The U-V likelihood in (66), compared with a null model with $K = 1$, yielded a χ^2 statistic of 32,188.5 with 10,157 df, indicating that the model is statistically highly significant. In addition, the ratio $\chi^2/df = 3.7$ indicates that the average model improvement per df is large compared with the minimum ratio of 2.0 proposed by Akaike (1974). Thus, we can have confidence in the model. Below, the seven classes are shown to be substantively meaningful and yield interpretable coefficients.

5.3. Results

Measurement models for exogenous and endogenous sets of variables. For exogenous health variables $j = 1$ to 56, the scalar form of (82) is

$$E(y_{ijl}) = g_{i1}^{(1,1)} \lambda_{1jl}^{(1,1)} + g_{i2}^{(1,1)} \lambda_{2jl}^{(1,1)} + g_{i3}^{(1,1)} \lambda_{3jl}^{(1,1)} + g_{i4}^{(1,1)} \lambda_{4jl}^{(1,1)}. \quad (104)$$

Equation (104) represents the GOM equivalent of the measurement model for exogenous variables in LISREL. The four classes can be described as (1) persons who are lightly impaired, (2) persons with hip and other fractures, (3) persons with cardiopulmonary problems, and (4) persons who are frail and who have multiple medical problems. The λ_{kjl} relating the four latent fuzzy classes to the 56 health and functioning measures are in Table 4. The four classes are described by comparing each column of the λ_{kjl} to the marginal proportion. The λ_{kjl} that are larger than the marginal positively characterize the type (e.g., Singer 1989). A small or zero λ_{kjl} represents a nonassociation.

Class 1, lightly impaired, has no large λ_{kjl} for ADLs, few IADLs, and only moderate physical impairment. Class 2 has significant mobility, bathing, and toileting problems, problems climbing stairs, and problems with several other physical functions. This class has the highest incidence of hip fractures (19.7 percent) and other fractures (27.3 percent). Class 3 has light ADL impairments, a number of IADL and physical functioning impairments, and a wide range of cardiopulmonary problems: for example, heart attack (39.6 percent), hypertension (97.8 percent), chronic heart problems (100 percent), bronchitis (49.9 percent), emphysema (27.4 percent), and asthma (29.4 percent). Class 4 is very frail and has a number of

TABLE 4

Marginal and Conditional Probabilities (%) of Outcome Levels for 56 Health and Functional Status Variables, by Four GOM Classes, Λ_{11} Coefficients for the Model in Figure 1

	Marginal Frequency	Class			
		1	2	3	4
Activities of Daily Living					
Needs help with					
1. Eating	15.6	0.0	0.0	0.0	100.0
2. Getting in/out of bed	52.6	0.0	100.0	3.3	100.0
3. Getting about inside	64.3	6.9	100.0	36.6	100.0
4. Dressing	41.6	0.0	82.1	0.0	100.0
5. Bathing	70.3	10.7	100.0	80.3	100.0
Mobility restriction					
6. Using toilet	44.5	0.0	100.0	0.0	100.0
7. Bedfast	3.1	0.0	0.0	0.0	15.9
8. No inside activity	5.1	0.0	0.0	0.0	27.3
9. Wheelchairfast	10.5	0.0	13.5	0.0	36.3
Instrumental Activities of Daily Living					
Needs help with					
10. Heavy work	89.4	58.2	100.0	100.0	100.0
11. Light work	48.0	0.0	100.0	26.4	100.0
12. Laundry	68.3	5.5	100.0	100.0	100.0
13. Cooking	56.8	0.0	100.0	71.1	100.0
14. Grocery shopping	82.1	26.5	100.0	100.0	100.0
15. Getting about outside	83.3	40.3	100.0	100.0	100.0
16. Traveling	80.3	27.6	100.0	100.0	96.8
17. Managing money	44.2	0.0	11.1	63.4	100.0
18. Taking medicine	43.9	0.0	21.3	42.4	100.0
19. Telephoning	27.4	0.0	0.0	0.0	100.0
Instrumental Activities of Daily Living 2					
20. Difficulty climbing one flight of stairs					
No	6.1	19.5	0.0	0.0	0.0
Some	19.4	58.0	0.0	0.0	8.8
Very	33.4	22.5	29.5	65.5	0.0
Cannot	41.1	0.0	70.5	34.5	91.2
21. Difficulty bending for socks					
No	27.9	80.8	0.0	0.0	0.0
Some	24.1	19.3	20.7	48.5	0.0

TABLE 4 Continued

	Marginal Frequency	Class			
		1	2	3	4
Very	21.8	0.0	40.7	51.5	0.0
Cannot	26.3	0.0	39.2	0.0	100.0
22. Difficulty holding 10-pound package					
No	11.6	37.5	0.0	0.0	0.0
Some	12.0	39.0	0.0	0.0	0.0
Very	14.5	23.4	12.8	17.2	0.0
Cannot	61.9	0.0	87.2	82.8	100.0
23. Difficulty reaching over head					
No	43.4	97.7	63.0	0.0	0.0
Some	22.4	2.3	29.0	49.9	4.2
Very	18.0	0.0	8.0	38.2	28.1
Cannot	16.2	0.0	0.0	11.9	67.7
24. Difficulty combing hair					
No	54.9	100.0	74.8	0.0	0.0
Some	19.1	0.0	17.4	70.4	0.0
Very	11.7	0.0	7.8	29.6	19.6
Cannot	14.4	0.0	0.0	0.0	80.4
25. Difficulty washing hair					
No	31.7	90.9	0.0	0.0	0.0
Some	13.0	9.1	9.8	42.0	0.0
Very	12.1	0.0	15.7	47.5	0.0
Cannot	43.3	0.0	74.6	10.5	100.0
26. Difficulty grasping small objects					
No	57.7	98.3	76.7	20.2	0.0
Some	21.6	1.7	23.3	47.5	21.3
Very	13.2	0.0	0.0	32.3	35.3
Cannot	7.4	0.0	0.0	0.0	43.4
27. See well enough to read newspaper	64.9	87.6	100.0	41.6	9.6
Medical Conditions					
28. Rheumatism/arthritis	70.8	57.5	66.0	100.0	59.6
29. Paralysis	16.8	0.0	14.7	0.0	66.3
30. Permanent stiffness	26.0	5.5	13.7	52.8	43.8
31. Multiple sclerosis	1.0	0.7	0.0	0.0	3.9
32. Cerebral palsy	0.7	0.3	0.0	0.0	2.8
33. Epilepsy	1.0	0.0	1.0	1.4	1.9
34. Parkinson's disease	4.0	0.0	2.7	3.2	11.8
35. Glaucoma	9.2	9.9	9.9	4.1	12.9

36. Diabetes	23.5	11.1	6.4	55.5	28.7
37. Cancer	11.0	7.0	13.9	10.6	13.6
38. Constipation	36.5	11.4	17.6	79.8	52.7
39. Trouble sleeping	43.6	16.2	19.4	100.0	36.9
40. Headache	17.4	0.0	0.0	70.4	16.3
41. Obesity	17.1	14.9	12.0	41.9	1.2
42. Arteriosclerosis	34.6	9.2	0.0	80.8	71.0
43. Mental retardation	2.6	0.0	0.0	0.0	13.0
44. Dementia	13.9	0.0	0.0	0.0	72.1
45. Heart attack	11.1	2.2	0.0	39.6	5.4
46. Other heart problem	35.2	8.4	0.0	100.0	35.3
47. Hypertension	46.7	30.7	20.9	97.8	45.6
48. Stroke	15.8	5.9	0.0	0.0	62.9
49. Circulation trouble	56.4	25.1	15.7	100.0	88.5
50. Pneumonia	9.2	4.3	0.0	22.2	12.8
51. Bronchitis	12.6	0.0	0.0	49.9	8.8
52. Influenza	13.2	7.4	8.1	31.1	9.2
53. Emphysema	12.1	7.3	5.9	27.4	10.7
54. Asthma	7.5	0.0	0.0	29.4	5.5
55. Broken hip	5.4	0.1	19.7	0.0	2.0
56. Other broken bones	8.5	0.0	27.3	0.0	3.8

Source: 1982 and 1984 National Long Term Care Survey.

neurological problems: for example dementia (72.1 percent) and stroke (62.9 percent).

The *average* contribution of each of the four classes to each of the 56 variables can be represented by substituting the average $g_{ik}^{(1,1)}$ in equation (104):

$$E(y_{ijl}) = .301 \times \lambda_{1jl}^{(1,1)} + .265 \times \lambda_{2jl}^{(1,1)} + .221 \times \lambda_{3jl}^{(1,1)} + .213 \times \lambda_{4jl}^{(1,1)}. \tag{105}$$

The normalization in these equations is $\Sigma_1^4 g_{ik} = 1.0$. All four classes contribute strongly to the 56 functional and health measures.

The scalar form of the 34 equations representing the measurement model for the mediating resource variables is

$$E(y_{ijl}) = g_{i1}^{(2,1)} \lambda_{1jl}^{(1,2)} + g_{i2}^{(2,1)} \lambda_{2jl}^{(1,2)} + g_{i3}^{(2,1)} \lambda_{3jl}^{(1,2)} + g_{i4}^{(2,1)} \lambda_{4jl}^{(1,2)} + g_{i1}^{(2,2)} \lambda_{1jl}^{(2,2)} + g_{i2}^{(2,2)} \lambda_{2jl}^{(2,2)}, \tag{106}$$

where the $\lambda^{(1,2)}$ are columns of Λ_{12} in (83), the $g^{(2,1)}$ are rows of G_{21}, the $g^{(2,2)}$ are rows of G_{22}, and the $\lambda^{(2,2)}$ are columns of Λ_{22}. This is a measurement model for the 34 second-stage variables with two components of variation, one due to the 56 exogenous variables and one due to the 34 mediating variables, conditioned on the exogenous variables. These two components define two fuzzy classes. This is logically similar to constructing the covariance matrix S_{yy} in LISREL from factors both in the space of the exogenous variables (i.e., $\Lambda\phi\Lambda'$) and from factors in the residual space. The λ_{kjl} for the six classes are in Table 5.

The λ_{kjl} for classes 1–4 represent the association of the 34 mediating characteristics with the four prior latent health classes. The λ_{kjl} for classes 5 and 6 are response probabilities that show how the 34 resource variables determine the two second-stage classes. Both classes 5 and 6 had a hospital stay in the last year, are unlikely to agree that a person should stay out of a nursing home, and are unlikely to be satisfied with their own living quarters. Class 5 is a white, urban dweller who owns his or her home, has private health insurance, and has a spouse as a primary helper. Class 6 is a black, large-city dweller who lives in an apartment near other elderly persons, receives food stamps, participates in Medicaid, and has nonrelatives as primary helpers. Class 5 has the highest risk of using a urinary catheter or colostomy bag and of losing his or her temper.

The λ_{kjl} for the first four classes suggest that they are related to past nursing home use (i.e., classes 2 and 4), incontinence, desire to go to a nursing home (and being on a waiting list), hearing, behavioral, and other problems (class 4). Class 3, with the most acute illness, is most likely to live in a *non*metropolitan area.

Substituting the average g_{ik} in (106) yields

$$
\begin{aligned}
E(y_{ijl}) = {} & .281 \times \lambda_{1jl}^{(1,2)} + .252\, \lambda_{2jl}^{(1,2)} + .202\, \lambda_{3jl}^{(1,2)} \\
& + .197\, \lambda_{4jl}^{(1,2)} + .033\, \lambda_{1jl}^{(2,2)} + .035\, \lambda_{2jl}^{(2,2)},
\end{aligned}
\tag{107}
$$

using the normalization $\Sigma_{k=1}^{6} g_{ik} = 1$. Coefficients for classes 1–4 represent their *average* contribution to the 34 resource variables. Compared with (104), the effects for classes 1–4 decreased 7 percent, 5 percent, 9 percent, and 8 percent, respectively. Only 6.8 percent of the mediating variables' membership is in classes 5 and 6. The remaining 93.2 percent is in the four classes derived from the 56 exogenous health status variables. That is, exogenous health inputs are strongly related to these mediating resource variables.

In Table 6, the λ_{kjl} in the measurement model (84) for 17 health

TABLE 5

Marginal and Conditional Probabilities (%) of Outcome Levels for 34 Mediating Variables—the Λ_{12} Probabilities for Classes 1–4 and the Λ_{22} Probabilities for Classes 5–6

	Marginal Frequency	Class					
		1	2	3	4	5	6
1. Type of area							
Open country	8.9	0.0	1.0	28.5	14.0	10.3	0.0
Farm	4.4	0.6	0.0	12.4	10.4	0.0	0.0
Small city	39.1	49.0	44.6	52.0	38.5	0.0	0.0
Medium city	22.2	30.5	34.4	7.1	22.9	3.7	13.5
Suburban	8.5	6.7	10.6	0.0	2.5	55.9	6.5
Large city	16.9	13.2	9.4	0.0	11.7	30.1	80.1
2. Living quarters							
House	63.9	87.4	100.0	76.1	100.0	70.5	0.0
Duplex	8.1	7.5	0.0	0.0	0.0	29.6	14.5
Apartment	22.0	0.0	0.0	0.0	0.0	0.0	79.3
Other	6.0	5.2	0.0	23.9	0.0	0.0	6.2
3. Satisfaction with living quarters							
Very satisfied	47.3	59.9	78.1	30.3	21.8	0.0	0.0
Satisfied	44.3	40.2	21.9	64.5	75.2	55.9	46.0
Not satisfied	8.4	0.0	0.0	5.2	3.0	44.1	54.0
4. Elderly people live around these quarters	10.0	0.0	0.0	0.0	0.0	0.0	100.0
5. Person should stay out of nursing home	94.0	93.4	100.0	100.0	87.7	64.5	52.0
6. Ever been nursing home patient	15.5	6.7	40.3	0.0	19.8	0.0	2.8
7. On a nursing home waiting list	2.1	1.0	2.6	0.0	6.1	0.0	0.0

TABLE 5 Continued

	Marginal Frequency	Class					
		1	2	3	4	5	6
8. Had hospital stay in last year	70.1	44.6	77.2	80.6	61.9	100.0	100.0
9. Use urinary catheter or colostomy bag	9.9	0.0	0.0	0.0	40.9	76.0	0.0
10. You care for catheter or bag	1.4	0.0	0.0	0.0	0.0	36.9	0.0
11. Incontinent	32.4	0.0	8.8	48.8	96.2	47.3	0.0
Relationship of helper(s)							
12. Spouse	33.2	0.0	0.0	0.0	0.0	100.0	0.0
13. Offspring	47.4	35.2	41.1	100.0	100.0	0.0	0.0
14. Other relative	33.2	18.3	69.0	68.0	56.6	0.0	0.0
15. Friend	13.9	0.0	36.2	0.0	0.0	0.0	100.0
16. Other	59.5	13.2	100.0	16.4	77.3	0.0	100.0
17. Medicaid paid for health care in last year	22.6	0.0	0.0	0.0	0.0	0.0	100.0
Performance/behavior							
18. Unable to speak	8.3	0.0	0.0	0.0	48.9	0.0	0.0
19. Unable to hear and comprehend	12.4	0.0	0.0	0.0	61.7	0.0	0.0
20. Loses temper	11.2	4.0	0.0	8.9	22.0	100.0	0.6
21. Loses way	4.5	0.0	0.0	6.8	14.2	1.6	11.2
22. Takes money	1.7	0.0	0.0	0.0	8.7	0.0	0.0
23. Forgetful	20.1	5.2	0.0	68.2	34.5	0.0	5.8
24. Score on mini-mental state							
0	0.7	0.0	0.0	0.0	4.2	0.0	2.5
1	0.4	0.0	0.0	0.0	3.4	0.0	0.0
2	0.7	0.0	0.0	0.0	0.0	0.0	9.7

3	0.8	2.5	0.0	0.0	0.0	0.0	0.0
4	2.5	0.0	0.0	0.0	12.8	0.0	14.8
5	4.7	0.0	0.0	0.0	40.7	0.0	0.0
6	6.0	1.9	0.0	0.0	28.8	0.0	31.1
7	10.1	8.6	7.2	14.3	4.3	0.0	35.8
8	19.2	12.5	19.2	48.8	0.0	12.9	6.0
9	26.1	23.8	30.6	37.0	5.8	49.0	0.0
10	29.0	50.7	43.1	0.0	0.0	38.1	0.0
Resources							
25. Current medical participant	24.0	0.0	0.0	0.0	0.0	0.0	100.0
26. Other public assistance	2.0	0.0	2.1	0.0	0.0	16.0	27.1
27. CHAMPUS	0.8	0.6	0.0	0.0	0.0	16.0	0.0
28. Other health insurance	64.3	79.2	100.0	53.2	50.9	100.0	0.0
29. Owns home	60.5	100.0	100.0	100.0	100.0	100.0	0.0
30. Food stamps	11.7	0.0	0.0	0.0	0.0	0.0	100.0
31. Other children	72.9	67.7	54.3	100.0	82.5	100.0	0.0
32. Supportive housing	39.3	19.9	82.7	9.0	35.9	0.0	100.0
33. Race							
White	87.5	100.0	100.0	100.0	82.2	100.0	0.0
Black	11.3	0.0	0.0	0.0	11.6	0.0	97.5
Other	1.2	0.0	0.0	0.0	6.2	0.0	2.5
34. Metropolitan status							
Metropolitan	71.9	81.8	93.3	17.7	61.6	100.0	100.0
Nonmetropolitan	28.1	18.2	6.7	82.3	38.4	0.0	0.0

Source: 1982 and 1984 National Long Term Care Survey.

TABLE 6

Marginal and Conditional Probabilities (%) of Outcome Levels for 17 Health-Service Utilization Variables: The Λ_{13} Probabilities for Classes 1–4, the Λ_{23} Probabilities for Classes 5–6, and the Λ_{33} Probabilities for Class 7

	Marginal Frequency	Class						
		1	2	3	4	5	6	7
1. Total out-of-pocket payment to helpers								
Unknown	31.0	0.0	61.7	0.0	45.5	0.0	75.4	0.0
$0	48.6	78.7	0.0	100.0	30.6	100.0	0.0	89.2
$1–$39	8.7	17.8	7.8	0.0	0.0	0.0	24.7	0.0
$40–$124	4.7	1.1	15.1	0.0	2.3	0.0	0.0	10.9
$125–$399	3.4	2.4	6.6	0.0	10.0	0.0	0.0	0.0
$400+	3.7	0.0	8.9	0.0	11.6	0.0	0.0	0.0
2. Number of helpers								
0	11.0	64.7	0.0	0.0	0.0	0.0	86.6	0.0
1	42.8	0.0	0.0	0.0	0.0	100.0	0.0	0.0
2	26.7	23.2	58.8	60.1	39.2	0.0	13.5	95.1
3	11.5	12.2	26.7	22.0	31.2	0.0	0.0	0.0
4+	8.0	0.0	14.5	18.0	29.7	0.0	0.0	4.9
3. Number of helper-days per week								
0	17.0	61.4	0.0	0.0	0.0	0.0	67.1	0.0
1–5	15.9	38.6	45.3	0.0	0.0	0.0	33.0	51.3
6–7	37.7	0.0	0.0	0.0	0.0	100.0	0.0	0.0
8–12	13.4	0.0	26.5	72.2	18.2	0.0	0.0	48.7
13+	16.0	0.0	28.2	27.8	81.8	0.0	0.0	0.0

Services received							
4. Home nursing service	39.2	0.0	91.1	0.0	92.5	0.0	100.0	0.0
5. Therapist in last month	12.1	0.0	38.8	0.0	15.1	0.0	11.9	0.0
6. Mental health professional in last month	0.7	0.0	0.0	0.0	0.7	0.0	15.1	0.0
7. Emergency room visit in last month	8.2	0.0	0.0	12.8	0.0	85.8	61.4	0.0
8. Other MD office visit	45.8	43.0	32.7	100.0	0.0	100.0	12.8	0.0
9. MD home visit	5.4	0.0	10.7	0.0	12.3	0.0	15.6	0.0
10. Rx in last month	85.8	79.4	81.4	100.0	92.9	100.0	77.3	0.0
11. Medicare hospital reimbursement								
None	19.0	0.0	0.0	0.0	0.0	0.0	0.0	100.0
<$3,000	19.2	39.2	5.5	43.1	45.6	0.0	0.0	0.0
$3,000 to $5,699	20.6	35.0	34.4	30.5	35.2	0.0	0.0	0.0
$5,700 to $10,199	20.0	25.8	34.8	26.4	19.2	25.2	0.0	0.0
$10,200+	21.2	0.0	25.3	0.0	0.0	74.8	100.0	0.0
12. Medicare SNF and other long-stay reimbursement								
None	93.5	98.9	81.1	100.0	96.0	67.4	100.0	100.0
<$890	1.8	0.0	0.0	0.0	2.2	32.6	0.0	0.0
$890 to $1,279	1.5	0.1	6.3	0.0	0.0	0.0	0.0	0.0
$1,280 to $2,929	1.8	0.0	7.7	0.0	0.0	0.0	0.0	0.0
$2,930+	1.5	0.0	5.0	0.0	1.8	0.0	0.0	0.0
13. Medicare HHA reimbursement								
<$250	21.8	0.0	0.0	0.0	0.0	0.0	0.0	100.0
$250 to $629	23.9	87.5	25.3	72.3	15.2	0.0	0.0	0.0
$630 to $1,479	23.2	0.0	0.0	0.0	0.0	100.0	83.1	0.0
$1,480 to $2,939	17.2	12.5	46.3	27.7	22.5	0.0	16.9	0.0
$2,940+	13.9	0.0	28.5	0.0	62.4	0.0	0.0	0.0

TABLE 6 Continued

	Marginal Frequency	Class						
		1	2	3	4	5	6	7
14. Number of medicare HHA visits								
1–5	19.0	0.0	0.0	0.0	0.0	0.0	0.0	100.0
6–14	22.9	82.6	29.3	56.6	14.4	0.0	0.0	0.0
15–34	25.8	0.0	0.0	0.0	0.0	100.0	96.2	0.0
35–74	18.2	17.4	43.2	43.4	23.4	0.0	3.8	0.0
75+	14.2	0.0	27.5	0.0	62.2	0.0	0.0	0.0
15. Length of medicare hospital stays (in days)								
None	18.8	0.0	0.0	0.0	0.0	0.0	0.0	100.0
1–10	16.6	39.0	0.0	37.0	48.9	0.0	0.0	0.0
11–20	22.9	57.4	36.6	16.1	27.9	0.0	12.9	0.0
21–30	12.4	3.6	21.4	36.9	7.5	20.6	0.0	0.0
31+	29.3	0.0	42.1	10.0	15.9	79.4	87.1	0.0
16. Length of medicare SNF stays (in days)								
None	91.5	98.9	76.4	100.0	97.7	61.5	85.4	100.0
1–14	1.9	0.0	0.0	0.0	0.0	38.5	0.0	0.0
15–30	2.2	0.0	7.2	0.0	0.0	0.0	14.6	0.0
31–60	2.7	1.1	10.4	0.0	0.0	0.0	0.0	0.0
61+	1.8	0.0	6.0	0.0	2.3	0.0	0.0	0.0
17. Length of medicare HHA stays (in days)								
1–30	25.8	0.0	0.0	0.0	0.0	0.0	0.0	100.0
31–60	23.2	70.5	0.0	45.1	0.0	50.0	38.6	0.0
61–119	22.4	23.9	24.9	24.9	21.5	39.9	51.4	0.0
120–210	14.9	0.0	47.5	17.4	23.5	10.1	10.0	0.0
211+	13.8	5.6	27.6	12.6	55.0	0.0	0.0	0.0

Source: 1982 and 1984 National Long Term Care Surveys.

service and expenditure variables are presented. The λ_{kjl} for the 17 variables on the four exogenous health classes, the two mediating classes, and class 7 show how each class relates to the 17 variables. This generalizes a LISREL measurement model by composing observed variables from three independent components. The system of 17 equations is

$$E(y_{ijl}) = g_{i1}^{(3,1)} \lambda_{1jl}^{(1,3)} + g_{i2}^{(3,1)} \lambda_{2jl}^{(1,3)} + g_{i3}^{(3,1)} \lambda_{3jl}^{(1,3)} + g_{i4}^{(3,1)} \lambda_{4jl}^{(1,3)}$$
$$+ g_{i1}^{(3,2)} \lambda_{1jl}^{(2,3)} + g_{i2}^{(3,2)} \lambda_{2jl}^{(2,3)} + g_{i1}^{(3,3)} \lambda_{1jl}^{(3,3)}. \tag{108}$$

The λ_{kjl} for class 7 indicate that this group uses no Medicare services, few acute care services, and has small out-of-pocket expenses for helpers. However, helpers provide from 1–5 to 8–12 days of help per week. Thus, this class relies on informal, home-based LTC services.

In contrast, classes 5 and 6 used a lot of acute services: 74.8 percent of class 5 and 100 percent of class 6 required over \$10,200 in Medicare hospital reimbursement, and 79.4 percent of class 5 and 87.1 percent of class 6 were hospitalized over 31 days. Both classes 5 and 6 were moderate users of HHA services, but not of SNF (skilled nursing facilities). Classes 2 and 4 are the biggest users of SNF, HHA visits, and home helpers, and they are moderate users of hospitals. Classes 1 and 3 did not use SNF, but they did use the hospital, HHA visits, and home helpers.

The average contributions of the seven classes to the 17 service measures are

$$E(y_{ijl}) = .270 \times \lambda_{1jl}^{(1,3)} + .244 \, \lambda_{2jl}^{(1,3)} + .195 \, \lambda_{3jl}^{(1,3)} + .190 \, \lambda_{4jl}^{(1,3)}$$
$$+ .047 \, \lambda_{1jl}^{(2,3)} + .040 \, \lambda_{2jl}^{(2,3)} + .014 \, \lambda_{1jl}^{(3,3)}, \tag{109}$$

using the normalization $\Sigma_{k=1}^{7} g_{ik} = 1$. The parameters of this third-stage model describe the relations among a set of variables grouped and ordered to reflect predictors of the use of, and expenditure for, medical services.

Structural equations. Table 7 presents structural parameters for the model, the $\bar{g}_k$ for each class, and the relative determination by each class of classes introduced at the same or later stages.

Net of the exogenous (health and functional) variables, the two classes for the mediating variables have a strong joint dependency or feedback: 34.3 percent of class 6, the high-service-use, low-

TABLE 7

Structural Equation Parameters (%) Indicating Dependence of GOM Classes at Each Stage and on All GOM Classes Introduced at Previous Stages, The **B** Matrix

Class	Class						
	1	2	3	4	5	6	7
1	100.00	0.00	0.00	0.00	3.23	3.97	0.57
					(18.38)	(26.99)	(11.32)
2	0.00	100.00	0.00	0.00	4.32	2.04	0.38
					(22.18)	(12.55)	(6.77)
3	0.00	0.00	100.00	0.00	3.26	2.86	0.25
					(13.41)	(14.10)	(3.54)
4	0.00	0.00	0.00	100.00	4.32	2.50	0.32
					(17.33)	(12.01)	(4.51)
5	0.00	0.00	0.00	0.00	0.00	28.70	11.01
						(34.34)	(38.22)
6	0.00	0.00	0.00	0.00	34.34	0.00	12.28
					(28.70)		(35.64)
7	0.00	0.00	0.00	0.00	0.00	0.00	0.00
E (g_{ik}) (%)	26.97	24.39	19.54	19.02	4.75	3.97	1.37
Pr$(g_{ik} > 0)$ (%)	70.79	78.70	79.30	63.22	71.33	64.41	44.01
E$(g_{ik} \mid g_{ik} > 0)$ (%)	38.37	30.99	24.64	30.09	6.66	6.16	3.11

Note: Figure in parenthesis under each off-diagonal entry is the product $[b_{kl} \times E(g_{ik})/ E(g_{il})] \times 100\%$. This gives the percentage contribution of each row class to the column class, taking account of both the structural coefficient and the size of the row class.

socioeconomic-resource group, is determined jointly with class 5 (both reflecting urban residence and high-service-use states). The dependency of class 5 on class 6 is also strong (28.7 percent). This means that the social and other characteristics in the two second-stage classes strongly determine service use *beyond* differences in health.

The joint dependency of these two classes suggests that high levels of services are consumed either by persons with high levels of personal economic resources *and* private supplementary (to Medicare) insurance or by persons who are poor and have supplementation of Medicare services through Medicaid. It appears, for groups with high service needs, that Medicare services are inadequate and require supplementation through either private sources or Medicaid. The strong relation of these classes suggests that persons tend to move from reliance on private resources to dependence on Medicaid—i.e., they tend to spend-down. The partial dependence between the classes reflects gradation within each class. For example, class 5 persons ideally (i.e., with high g_{ik} values) have large amounts of private resources. However, not all persons will be ideally situated, though they may have some limited resources that allow them to remain independent of Medicaid services for some time.

These two classes represent factors strongly independent of the health inputs (classes 1–4), suggesting that use of the acute medical and home health services associated with these classes is not solely determined by medical needs. That is, conditional upon medical needs there are social, economic, and other variables (including areal access to health care represented by the urban residence proxies) that determine the amounts of services received. This suggests inefficiency or inequality in the system, i.e., that health service distribution is not determined solely by health needs.

Class 7 is strongly dependent on classes 5 and 6 (73.8 percent), moderately dependent on class 1 (11.3 percent), and least dependent on classes 2–4 (14.8 percent). Although the mean g_{ik} for class 7 is small (1.37 percent), 591 persons (44 percent) had nonzero memberships in this class with a conditional mean of 3.11 percent. Class 7 represents an additional component of informal care services independent of both health inputs (classes 1–4) *and* socioeconomic resources (classes 5–6). In effect, there is additional informal care provided by the family for persons not requiring large amounts of medical services. It is most determined by classes 5 and 6, suggesting that it supplements formal services.

The structural parameters in Table 7 exactly reproduce the $\bar{g}_k$ using (97), with $\mathbf{E} = \mathbf{0}$. This is because there is sufficient joint membership, m_{ikl}, to satisfy the equality constraints in (103) for classes 5–7: 44 percent to 71 percent of the cases have nonzero g_{ik} on classes 5–7, with $\bar{g}_k$ of 6.66 percent, 6.16 percent, and 3.11 percent, respectively. Few have a g_{ik} score above 20 percent on classes 5–7. Substantively, there is a continuum between the high acute service use of classes 5 and 6 and the low service use of class 7, and the sample is better characterized along the continuum than at its extremes.

6. DISCUSSION

In this paper we presented a multivariate procedure for describing structural equation systems for discrete variables. This procedure described states of individuals by latent fuzzy classes. Fuzzy classes are generalizations of discrete classes in which individual coefficients, or grades of membership, are estimated to represent how well a person's attributes are described by the classes.

The GOM structure was constrained by modifying the ML function so that the parameter space represented the causal ordering of variables. The model was used to estimate parameters from an elderly subsample from the 1982–1984 NLTCS. The structural equation model was estimated for a three-stage model of health-service utilization where errors in variables operate at all levels. The coefficients for simultaneous sets of equations for discrete response variables using full-information procedures were presented and discussed.

From applications to many data sets, we have found the estimation procedure to be robust. If new cases fall within the interior of the K-1–dimensional simplex, the λ_{kjl} estimates do not vary when samples are supplemented. Though, for some multivariate procedures, one sees "flat" likelihoods with multiple solutions, estimation of the information matrix for coefficients shows that the GOM model's standard errors for the λ_{kjl} are generally small, suggesting that the overall likelihood is not flat in reasonable applications (e.g., with 30 or more variables and 1,000 or more cases, the size of data sets often seen in national surveys, large federal demonstrations, and many multicenter clinical trials).

However, even when data sets are small, one can use a procedure that produces well-behaved results. That is, one can use a trial partition "start" that is substantively related to the classes of interest (e.g., age and chronic health problems). If information in the data is equivocal, the solution will be "biased" towards the informative trial partition. If sample information is strong, then the effects of the trial partition on the solution will be overwhelmed. This produces reasonable solutions even in limited data and is in the spirit of biased estimation when the conditioning of classical estimators is poor (e.g., in ridge regression or Marquardt's procedures).

REFERENCES

Akaike, H. 1974. "A New Look at the Statistical Model Identification." *IEEE Transactions on Automatic Control* AC-19:716–23.

Anderson, T. W., and Y. Amemiya. 1988. "The Asymptotic Normal Distribution of Estimators in Factor Analysis Under General Conditions." *Annals of Statistics* 16:759–71.

Blackman, R. B., and J. W. Tukey. 1958. "The Measurement of Power Spectra from the Point of View of Communications Engineering—Part 1." *Bell System Technical Journal* 37:185–282.

Bollen, K. A. 1989. *Structural Equations with Latent Variables*. New York: Wiley.

Christoffersson, A. 1975. "Factor Analysis of Dichotomized Variables." *Psychometrika* 40:5–32.

Clive, J., M. A. Woodbury, I. C. Siegler. 1983. "Fuzzy and Crisp Set-Theoretic-Based Classification of Health and Disease." *Journal of Medical Systems* 7:317–22.

Davidson, J., M. A. Woodbury, S. Zisook, and E. L. Giller. 1989. "Classification of Depression by Grade of Membership: A Confirmatory Study." *Psychological Medicine* 19:987–98.

Dempster, A. P. 1969. *Elements of Continuous Multivariate Analysis*. Reading, MA: Addison-Wesley.

Dillon, W. R., and M. Goldstein. 1984. *Multivariate Analysis: Methods of Application*. New York: Wiley.

Eaton, W. W., A. McCutcheon, A. Dryman, and A. Sorenson. 1989. "Latent Class Analysis of Anxiety and Depression." *Sociological Methods and Research* 18:104–25.

Everitt, B. S. 1984. *An Introduction to Latent Variable Models*. London: Chapman and Hall.

Johnston, J. 1984. *Econometric Methods*. New York: McGraw-Hill.

Jöreskog, K. G. 1969. "A General Approach to Confirmatory Maximum Likelihood Factor Analysis." *Psychometrika* 34:183–202.

Jöreskog, K. G., and D. Sörbom. 1979. *Advances in Factor Analysis and Structural Equation Models*. Cambridge, MA: Abt.

———. 1986. *A Preprocessor for LISREL*. Mooresville, IN: Scientific Software.

———. 1988. *LISREL 7: A Guide to the Program and Applications*. Chicago: SPSS Inc.

Kaufmann, A., and M. M. Gupta. 1985. *Introduction to Fuzzy Arithmetic: Theory and Applications*. New York: Van Nostrand Reinhold.

Kiefer, J., and J. Wolfowitz. 1956. "Consistency of the Maximum Likelihood Estimator in the Presence of Infinitely Many Parameters." *Annals of Mathematical Statistics* 27:887–906.

Kuhn, H. W., and A. W. Tucker. 1951. "Nonlinear Programming." Pp. 481–92 in *Proceedings of the Second Berkeley Symposium on Mathematical Statistics and Probability*. Berkeley: University of California Press.

Kullback, S., and R. A. Leibler. 1951. "On Information and Sufficiency." *Annals of Mathematical Statistics* 22:79–86.

Lawley, D. N., and A. E. Maxwell. 1971. *Factor Analysis as a Statistical Method*. New York: Elsevier.

Lazarsfeld, P. F., and N. W. Henry. 1968. *Latent Structure Analysis*. Boston: Houghton Mifflin.

Lipster, R., and A. Shiryayev. 1977. *Statistics of Random Processes.* Vol. 1, *General Theory.* New York: Springer-Verlag.

Madansky, A. 1959. "Partitioning Methods in Latent Class Analysis." Report P-1644. Santa Monica: RAND Corp.

Malinvaud, E. 1970. *Statistical Methods of Econometrics.* Amsterdam: North-Holland.

Manton, K. G. 1988. "A Longitudinal Study of Functional Change and Mortality in the United States." *Journal of Gerontology* 43:153–61.

Manton, K. G., M. A. Woodbury, and E. Stallard. 1991. "Statistical and Measurement Issues in Assessing the Welfare Status of Aged Individuals and Populations." *Journal of Econometrics* 50:151–81.

Marini, M. M., and B. Singer. 1988. "Causality in the Social Sciences." Pp. 347–409 in *Sociological Methodology 1988,* edited by C. C. Clogg. Washington, DC: American Sociological Association.

Muthén, B. 1978. "Contributions to Factor Analysis of Dichotomous Variables." *Psychometrika* 43:551–60.

———. 1987. *LISCOMP: Analysis of Linear Structural Equations with a Comprehensive Measurement Model.* Mooresville, IN: Scientific Software.

———. 1989. "Dichotomous Factor Analysis of Symptom Data." *Sociological Methods and Research* 18:19–65.

Muthén, B., and A. Christoffersson. 1981. "Simultaneous Factor Analysis of Dichotomous Variables in Several Groups." *Psychometrika* 46:407–19.

Orchard, T., and M. A. Woodbury. 1972. "A Missing Information Principle: Theory and Applications." Pp. 679–715 in *Proceedings of the Sixth Berkeley Symposium on Mathematical Statistics and Probability.* Vol. 1. Berkeley: University of California Press.

Saris, W. E., M. de Pijper, and J. Mulder. 1978. "Optimal Procedures for Estimation of Factor Scores." *Sociological Methods and Research* 7:85–106.

Scott, D. W. 1985. "Theory and Application." *Journal of the American Statistical Association* 80:348–54.

Self, S. G., and K. Y. Liang. 1987. "Asymptotic Properties of Maximum Likelihood Estimators and Likelihood Ratio Tests Under Nonstandard Conditions." *Journal of the American Statistical Association* 82:605–10.

Shah, B. V. 1990. *RTI Program Description: Grade-of-Membership Analysis.* Research Triangle Park, NC: Research Triangle Institute.

Singer, B. H. 1989. "Grade of Membership Representations: Concepts and Problems." Pp. 317–34 in *Festschrift for Samuel Karlin,* edited by T. W. Anderson, K. B. Athreya, and D. Iglehardt. Orlando: Academic Press.

Skinner, C. J., D. J. Holmes, and T. M. Smith. 1986. "The Effect of Sample Design on Principal Component Analysis." *Journal of the American Statistical Association* 81:789–98.

Terrell, G. R., and D. W. Scott. 1985. "Oversmoothed Nonparametric Density Estimates." *Journal of the American Statistical Association* 80:209–14.

Tolley, H. D., and K. G. Manton. 1990. "Testing for the Number of Pure Types of a Fuzzy Partition Model." Unpublished manuscript.

———. 1991. "Large Sample Properties of a Fuzzy Partition." *Journal of Statistical Mathematics.*

U.S. Department of Health and Human Services. 1988. *Overview and Use of the Public Use Data Files of the 1982 and 1984 National Long Term Care Surveys.* PB-881-72267. Springfield, VA: National Technical Information Service.

Woodbury, M. A. 1963. "The Stochastic Model of Mental Testing Theory and an Application." *Psychometrika* 28:391–94.

Woodbury, M. A., and J. Clive. 1974. "Clinical Pure Types as a Fuzzy Partition." *Journal of Cybernetics* 4:111–21.

Woodbury, M. A., J. Clive, and A. Garson. 1978. "Mathematical Typology: A Grade of Membership Technique for Obtaining Disease Definition." *Computers and Biomedical Research* 11:277–98.

Woodbury, M. A., and K. G. Manton. 1982. "A New Procedure for Analysis of Medical Classification." *Methods of Information in Medicine* 21:210–20.

Woodbury, M. A., K. G. Manton, and H. D. Tolley. 1990. "Empirical Comparisons of Discrete Mixture and Grade of Membership Models: Procedures to Classify Health Behavior and Health Service Use." Unpublished manuscript.

Zadeh, L. A. 1965. "Fuzzy Sets." *Information Control* 8:338–53.

———. 1968. "Probability Measures of Fuzzy Events." *Journal of Mathematical Analysis and Applications* 10:421–27.

Erratum

In *Sociological Methodology 1977* (published by Jossey-Bass), there was an error on page 65 of the chapter "Estimation in Panel Models: Results on Pooling Cross-Sections and Time Series" by Michael T. Hannan and Alice A. Young. The equation just above equation (15) should read

$$\hat{\sigma}_{\mu}^{2} = \sum_{i=1}^{N} (\hat{\mu}_{i} - \sum_{i=1}^{N} \hat{\mu}_{i}/N)^{2}/N.$$

The authors thank Kenneth C. Land for calling this to their attention.

NAME INDEX

Achen, C. H., 100, 113, 127, 130–31, 134, 144
Agresti, A., 282, 317
Aitchison, J., 280, 317
Aitkin, M., 283, 317
Akaike, H., 364, 378
Alba, R. D., 29n, 32
Allison, P. D., 124, 142, 144, 145
Alwin, D. F., 63, 84, 86, 87, 89, 90, 91, 92, 92n, 94, 96, 97, 99, 100, 100n, 101, 102, 103, 103n, 104, 105, 112, 113, 116, 117
Amemiya, Y., 266, 276, 322, 344, 378
Anderson, D., 283, 317
Anderson, J. G., 1, 32
Anderson, T. W., 124, 125n, 144, 255, 266, 276, 322, 344, 378
Andrews, F. M., 87, 90–91, 92, 113
Andrich, D., 101n, 113
Anselin, L., 222, 223, 236n, 236–38, 237n, 240, 242, 244, 245, 246
Arabie, P., 4, 16, 32
Arminger, G., 125, 146, 250, 252, 253, 261, 264, 276
Asher, H. B., 126, 145

Bainbridge, W. S., 239, 246
Barb, K. H., 87, 114
Barker, K., 37n
Bartholomew, D. J., 90, 114
Basmann, R. L., 230, 247
Baughman, J. L., 37n
Beach, L. R., 42, 42n, 43, 62, 63
Belson, W. A., 41, 62

Bendig, A. W., 87, 89, 92, 114
Benesh, C., 37n
Benson, P. H., 84, 114
Bentler, P. M., 99n, 104, 105, 110n, 114, 250, 252, 253, 254, 255, 258, 259, 266, 267, 271, 276, 277, 278
Berent, M. K., 105n, 116
Birkett, N. J., 90, 114
Bishop, G. F., 39, 62
Bishop, Y. M. M., 148, 177, 306, 317
Blackman, R. B., 343, 379
Blau, J. R., 238, 247
Block, J., 92, 114
Bock, R. D., 282, 301, 302, 304, 305, 306, 317
Bollen, K. A., 87, 114, 221n, 250, 276, 322, 379
Boorman, S., 2, 4, 16, 32, 35
Borgatti, S. P., 4, 4n, 13n, 17, 28n, 32, 33
Borjas, G., 188, 219
Bourdon, R. D., 92, 116
Boyd, J. P., 32, 33
Bradburn, N. M., 41, 44, 56n, 62, 65, 85n, 114
Brady, M. L., 37n
Brandt, D., 120n, 146
Breault, K. D., 238, 247
Breiger, R. L., 1, 2, 4, 16, 32, 35, 147n, 171, 177
Breland, H. M., Jr., 146
Brenner, M., 40, 62
Breusch, T. S., 154, 156, 161, 177
Briggs, C. L., 40, 62

385

SUBJECT INDEX

THE MORA

THE MORAL ANIMAL

*Evolutionary Psychology
and Everyday Life*

ROBERT WRIGHT

LITTLE, BROWN AND COMPANY

A *Little, Brown* Book

First published in the United States by Pantheon Books, 1994
This edition published by Little, Brown, 1995

Copyright © Robert Wright, 1994

The moral right of the author has been asserted.

A CIP catalogue record for this book
is available from the British Library.

ISBN 0 316 87501 5

Printed in England by Clays Ltd, St Ives plc

Little, Brown and Company (UK)
Brettenham House
Lancaster Place
London WC2E 7EN

For Lisa

Without thinking what he was doing, he took another drink of brandy. As the liquid touched his tongue he remembered his child, coming in out of the glare: the sullen unhappy knowledge-able face. He said, "Oh God, help her. Damn me, I deserve it, but let her soul live for ever." This was the love he should have felt for every soul in the world: all the fear and the wish to save concentrated unjustly on the one child. He began to weep; it was as if he had to watch her from the shore drown slowly because he had forgotten how to swim. He thought: This is what I should feel all the time for everyone . . .

– Graham Greene, *The Power and the Glory*

Contents

THE MORAL ANIMAL

Introduction: **DARWIN AND US**

The Origin of Species contains almost no mention of the human species. The threats the book posed—to the biblical account of our creation, to the comforting belief that we are more than mere animals—were clear enough; Charles Darwin had nothing to gain by amplifying them. Near the end of the final chapter he simply suggested that, through the study of evolution, "light will be thrown on the origin of man and his history." And, in the same paragraph, he ventured that "in the distant future" the study of psychology "will be based on a new foundation."[1]

Distant was right. In 1960, 101 years after the *Origin* appeared, the historian John C. Greene observed, "With respect to the origin of man's distinctively human attributes, Darwin would be disappointed to find matters little advanced beyond his own speculations in *The Descent of Man*. He would be discouraged to hear J. S. Weiner of the Anthropology Laboratory at Oxford University describe this subject as 'one large baffling topic on which our evolutionary insight remains meagre.' . . . In the current emphasis on man's uniqueness as a culture-transmitting animal Darwin might sense a tendency to return to the pre-evolutionary idea of an absolute distinction between man and other animals."[2]

A few years after Greene spoke, a revolution started. Between 1963 and 1974, four biologists—William Hamilton, George Williams, Robert Trivers, and John Maynard Smith—laid down a series of ideas that, taken together, refine and extend the theory of natural selection. These ideas have radically deepened the insight of evolutionary biologists into the social behavior of animals, including us.

At first, the relevance of the new ideas to our species was hazy. Biologists spoke confidently about the mathematics of self-sacrifice among ants, about the hidden logic of courtship among birds; but about human behavior they spoke conjecturally, if at all. Even the two epoch-marking books that synthesized and publicized the new ideas—E. O. Wilson's *Sociobiology* (1975) and Richard Dawkins's *The Selfish Gene* (1976)—said relatively little about humans. Dawkins steered almost entirely clear of the subject, and Wilson confined his discussion of our species to a final, slender, admittedly speculative chapter—28 pages out of 575.

Since the mid-1970s, the human angle has gotten much clearer. A small but growing group of scholars has taken what Wilson called "the new synthesis" and carried it into the social sciences with the aim of overhauling them. These scholars have applied the new, improved Darwinian theory to the human species, and then tested their applications with freshly gathered data. And along with their inevitable failures, they have had great success. Though they still consider themselves an embattled minority (an identity they seem sometimes to secretly enjoy), signs of their rising stature are clear. Venerable journals in anthropology, psychology, and psychiatry are publishing articles by authors who ten years ago were consigned to upstart journals of an expressly Darwinian bent. Slowly but unmistakably, a new worldview is emerging.

Here "worldview" is meant quite literally. The new Darwinian synthesis is, like quantum physics or molecular biology, a body of scientific theory and fact; but, unlike them, it is also a way of seeing everyday life. Once truly grasped (and it is much easier to grasp than either of them) it can entirely alter one's perception of social reality.

The questions addressed by the new view range from the mundane to the spiritual and touch on just about everything that matters: romance, love, sex (Are men and/or women really built for monogamy? What circumstances can make them more so or less so?); friendship and enmity (What is the evolutionary logic behind office politics—or, for that matter, politics in general?); selfishness, self-sacrifice, guilt (Why did natural selection give us that vast guilt repository known as the conscience? Is it truly a guide to "moral" behavior?); social status and social climbing (Is hierarchy inherent in human society?); the differing inclinations of men and women in areas such as friendship and ambition (Are we prisoners of our gender?); racism, xenophobia, war (Why do we so easily exclude large groups of people from the reach of our sympathy?); deception, self-deception, and the unconscious mind (Is intellectual honesty possible?); various psychopathologies (Is getting depressed, neurotic, or paranoid "natural"—and, if so, does that make it any more acceptable?); the love-hate relationship between siblings (Why isn't it pure love?); the tremendous capacity of parents to inflict psychic damage on their children (Whose interests do they have at heart?); and so on.

A QUIET REVOLUTION

The new Darwinian social scientists are fighting a doctrine that has dominated their fields for much of this century: the idea that biology doesn't much matter—that the uniquely malleable human mind, together with the unique force of culture, has severed our behavior from its evolutionary roots; that there is no inherent human nature driving human events, but that, rather, our essential nature is to be driven. As Emile Durkheim, the father of modern sociology, wrote at the turn of the century: human nature is "merely the indeterminate material that the social factor molds and transforms." History shows, said Durkheim, that even such deeply felt emotions as sexual jealousy, a father's love of his child, or the child's love of the father, are "far from being inherent in human nature." The mind, in this view, is basically passive—it is a basin into which, as a person matures, the local culture is gradually poured; if the mind sets any limits at all on the content of culture, they are exceedingly broad. The anthropologist Robert Lowie wrote in 1917 that "the principles of psychology are as incapable of accounting for the phenomena of culture as is gravitation to account for architectural styles."[3] Even psychologists—who might be expected to argue on behalf of the human mind—have often depicted it as little more than a blank slate. Behaviorism, which dominated psychology for a good part of this century, consists largely of the idea that people tend habitually to do what they are rewarded for doing and not do what they are punished for doing; thus is the formless mind given form. In B. F. Skinner's 1948 utopian novel *Walden II*, envy, jealousy, and other antisocial impulses were being eliminated via a strict regime of positive and negative reinforcements.

This view of human nature—as something that barely exists and doesn't much matter—is known among modern Darwinian social scientists as "the standard social science model."[4] Many of them learned it as undergraduates, and some of them spent years under its sway before beginning to question it. After a certain amount of questioning, they began to rebel.

In many ways, what is now happening fits Thomas Kuhn's description of a "paradigm shift" in his well-known book *The Structure of Scientific Revolutions*. A group of mainly young scholars have challenged the settled worldview of their elders, met with bitter resistance, persevered, and begun to flourish. Yet however classic this generational conflict may seem, it features a couple of distinctive ironies.

To begin with, it is, as revolutions go, inconspicuous. The various revolutionaries stubbornly refuse to call themselves by a single, simple name, the sort of thing that would fit easily onto a fluttering banner. They once had such a name—"sociobiology," Wilson's apt and useful term. But Wilson's book drew so much fire, provoked so many charges of malign political intent, so much caricature of sociobiology's substance, that the word became tainted. Most practitioners of the field he defined now prefer to avoid his label.[5] Though bound by allegiance to a compact and coherent set of doctrines, they go by different names: behavioral ecologists, Darwinian anthropologists, evolutionary psychologists, evolutionary psychiatrists. People sometimes ask: What ever happened to sociobiology? The answer is that it went underground, where it has been eating away at the foundations of academic orthodoxy.

The second irony of this revolution is tied to the first. Many features of the new view that the old guard most dislikes and fears are not, in fact, features of the new view. From the beginning, attacks on sociobiology were reflexive—reactions less to Wilson's book than to past books of a Darwinian cast. Evolutionary theory, after all, has a long and largely sordid history of application to human affairs. After being mingled with political philosophy around the turn of the century to form the vague ideology known as "social Darwinism," it played into the hands of racists, fascists, and the most heartless sort of capitalists. It also, around that time, spawned some simplistic ideas about the hereditary basis of behavior—ideas that, conveniently, fed these very political misuses of Darwinism. The resulting aura—of crudeness, both intellectual and ideological—continues to cling to Darwinism in the minds of many academics and laypersons. (Some people think the term Darwinism *means* social Darwinism.) Hence many misconceptions about the new Darwinian paradigm.

INVISIBLE UNITIES

For example: the new Darwinism is often mistaken for an exercise in social division. Around the turn of the century, anthropologists spoke casually of the "lower races," of "savages" who were beyond moral improvement. To the uncritical observer, such attitudes seemed to fit easily enough into a Darwinian framework, as would later supremacist doctrines, including Hitler's. But today's Darwinian anthropologists, in scanning the world's peoples, focus less on surface differences among cultures than on deep unities. Beneath the global crazy quilt of rituals and customs, they see recurring patterns in the structure of family, friendship, politics, courtship, morality. They believe the evolutionary design of human beings explains these patterns: why people in all cultures worry about social status (often more than they realize); why people in all cultures not only gossip, but gossip about the same kinds of things; why in all cultures men and women seem different in a few basic ways; why people every-

7

where feel guilt, and feel it in broadly predictable circumstances; why people everywhere have a deep sense of justice, so that the axioms "One good turn deserves another" and "An eye for an eye, a tooth for a tooth" shape human life everywhere on this planet.

In a way, it's not surprising that the rediscovery of human nature has taken so long. Being everywhere we look, it tends to elude us. We take for granted such bedrock elements of life as gratitude, shame, remorse, pride, honor, retribution, empathy, love, and so on—just as we take for granted the air we breathe, the tendency of dropped objects to fall, and other standard features of living on this planet.[6] But things didn't have to be this way. We could live on a planet where social life featured none of the above. We could live on a planet where some ethnic groups felt some of the above and others felt others. But we don't. The more closely Darwinian anthropologists look at the world's peoples, the more they are struck by the dense and intricate web of human nature by which all are bound. And the more they see how the web was woven.

Even when the new Darwinians *do* focus on differences—whether among groups of people or among people within groups—they are not generally inclined to explain them in terms of genetic differences. Darwinian anthropologists see the world's undeniably diverse cultures as products of a single human nature responding to widely varying circumstances; evolutionary theory reveals previously invisible links between the circumstances and the cultures (explaining, for example, why some cultures have dowry and others don't). And evolutionary psychologists, contrary to common expectation, subscribe to a cardinal doctrine of twentieth-century psychology and psychiatry: the potency of early social environment in shaping the adult mind. Indeed, a few are preoccupied with this subject, determined to uncover basic laws of psychological development and convinced that they can do so only with Darwinian tools. If we want to know, say, how levels of ambition or of insecurity get adjusted by early experience, we must first ask why natural selection made them adjustable.

This isn't to say that human behavior is infinitely malleable. In tracing the channels of environmental influence, most evolutionary psychologists see some firm banks. The utopian spirit of B. F. Skinner's behaviorism, the sense that a human being can become any sort of animal at all with proper conditioning, is not faring well these days. Still, neither is the idea that the grimmest parts of the human experience are wholly immutable, grounded in "instincts" and "innate drives"; nor the idea that psychological differences among people boil down mainly to genetic differences. They boil down to the *genes*, of course (where else could rules for mental development ultimately reside?), but not necessarily to *differences* in genes. A guiding assumption of many evolutionary psychologists, for reasons we'll come to, is that the most radical differences among people are the ones most likely to be traceable to environment.

In a sense, evolutionary psychologists are trying to discern a second level of human nature, a deeper unity within the species. First the anthropologist notes recurring themes in culture after culture: a thirst for social approval, a capacity for guilt. You might call these, and many other such universals, "the knobs of human nature." Then the psychologist notes that the exact tunings of the knobs seem to differ from person to person. One person's "thirst for approval" knob is set in the comfort zone, down around (relatively) "self-assured," and another person's is up in the excruciating "massively insecure" zone; one person's guilt knob is set low and another person's is painfully high. So the psychologist asks: How do these knobs get set? Genetic differences among individuals surely play a role, but perhaps a larger role is played by genetic commonalities: by a generic, species-wide developmental program that absorbs information from the social environment and adjusts the maturing mind accordingly. Oddly, future progress in grasping the importance of environment will probably come from thinking about genes.

Thus, human nature comes in two forms, both of which have a natural tendency to get ignored. First, there's the kind that's so pervasively apparent as to be taken for granted (guilt, for example). Second, there's the kind whose very function is to generate differences among people as they grow up, and thus naturally conceals itself (a developmental program that *calibrates* guilt). Human nature consists of knobs and of mechanisms for tuning the knobs, and both are invisible in their own way.

There is another source of invisibility, another reason human nature has been slow to come to light: the basic evolutionary logic common to people everywhere is opaque to introspection. Natural selection appears to have hidden our true selves from our conscious selves. As Freud saw, we are oblivious to our deepest motivations— but in ways more chronic and complete (and even, in some cases, more grotesque) than he imagined.

DARWINIAN SELF-HELP

Though this book will touch on many behavioral sciences—anthropology, psychiatry, sociology, political science—evolutionary psychology will be at its center. This young and still inchoate discipline, with its partly fulfilled promise of creating a whole new science of mind, lets us now ask a question that couldn't have been profitably asked in 1859, after the *Origin* appeared, nor in 1959: What does the theory of natural selection have to offer ordinary human beings?

For example: Can a Darwinian understanding of human nature help people reach their goals in life? Indeed, can it help them choose their goals? Can it help distinguish between practical and impractical goals? More profoundly, can it help in deciding which goals are worthy? That is, does knowing how evolution has shaped our basic moral impulses help us decide which impulses we should consider legitimate?

The answers, in my opinion, are: yes, yes, yes, yes, and, finally, yes. The preceding sentence will annoy, if not outrage, many people in the field. (Believe me. I've shown it to some of them.) They have long had to labor under the burden of Darwinism's past moral and political misuses, and they would like to keep the realms of science and value separate. You can't derive basic moral values from natural selection, they say, or indeed from any of nature's workings. If you do, you're committing what philosophers call "the naturalistic fallacy"—the unwarranted inference of "ought" from "is."

I agree: nature isn't a moral authority, and we needn't adopt any "values" that seem implicit in its workings—such as "might makes right." Still, a true understanding of human nature will inevitably affect moral thought deeply and, as I will try to show, legitimately.

This book, with its relevance to questions of everyday life, will have some features of a self-help book. But it will lack many. The next several hundred pages aren't loaded with pithy advice and warm reassurance. A Darwinian viewpoint won't hugely simplify your life, and in some ways will complicate it, by shining harsh light on morally dubious behaviors to which we are prone and whose dubiousness evolution has conveniently hidden from us. The few crisp and upbeat prescriptions I can glean from the new Darwinian paradigm are more than matched by the stubborn and weighty trade-offs, dilemmas, and conundrums it illuminates.

But you can't deny the intensity of the illumination—at least you won't, I hope, be denying it by the end of the book. Although one of my aims is to find practical applications of evolutionary psychology, the prior and central aim is to cover the basic principles of evolutionary psychology—to show how elegantly the theory of natural selection, as understood today, reveals the contours of the human mind. This book is, first, a sales pitch for a new science; only secondarily is it a sales pitch for a new basis of political and moral philosophy.

I've taken pains to keep these two issues separate, to distinguish between the new Darwinism's claims about the human mind and my own claims about the practical emanations of the new Darwinism. Many people who buy the first set of claims, the scientific set, will no doubt reject much of the second set, the philosophical set. But I think few people who buy the first set will deny its relevance to the second set. It is hard, on the one hand, to agree that the new paradigm is by far the most powerful lens through which to look at the human species and then to set the lens aside when examining the human predicament. The human species *is* the human predicament.

DARWIN, SMILES, AND MILL

The Origin of Species wasn't the only seminal book published in England in 1859. There was also the best-selling and genre-christening *Self-Help*, written by the journalist Samuel Smiles. And then there was *On Liberty*, by John Stuart Mill. As it happens, these two books nicely frame the question of what Darwin's book will ultimately come to mean.

Self-Help didn't stress getting in touch with your feelings, extricating yourself from sour relationships, tapping into harmonic cosmic forces, or the various other things that have since given self-help books an air of self-absorption and facile comfort. It preached essential Victorian virtues: civility, integrity, industry, perseverance, and, undergirding them all, iron self-control. A man, Smiles believed, can achieve almost anything "by the exercise of his own free powers of action and self-denial." But he must be ever "armed against the temptation of low indulgences," and must not "defile his body by sensuality, nor his mind by servile thoughts."[7]

On Liberty, by contrast, was a strong polemic against the stifling Victorian insistence on self-restraint and moral conformity. Mill indicted Christianity, with its "horror of sensuality," and complained that " 'thou shalt not' predominates unduly over 'thou shalt.' " He found especially deadening the Calvinist branch, with its belief that, "human nature being radically corrupt, there is no redemption for any one until human nature is killed within him." Mill took a sunnier view of human nature, and suggested that Christianity do the same. "[I]f it be any part of religion to believe that man was made by a good Being, it is more consistent with that faith to believe, that this Being gave all human faculties that they might be cultivated and unfolded, not rooted out and consumed, and that he takes delight in every nearer approach made by his creatures to the ideal conception embodied in them, every increase in any of their capabilities of comprehension, of action, or of enjoyment."[8]

Characteristically, Mill had hit on an important question: Are people inherently bad? Those who believe so have tended, like Samuel Smiles, to be morally conservative—to stress self-denial, abstinence, taming the beast within. Those who believe not have tended, like Mill, to be morally liberal, fairly relaxed about how people choose to behave. Evolutionary psychology, young though it is, has already shed much light on this debate. Its findings are at once comforting and unsettling.

Altruism, compassion, empathy, love, conscience, the sense of justice—all of these things, the things that hold society together, the things that allow our species to think so highly of itself, can now confidently be said to have a firm genetic basis. That's the good news. The bad news is that, although these things are in some ways blessings for humanity as a whole, they didn't evolve for the "good of the species" and aren't reliably employed to that end. Quite the contrary: it is now clearer than ever how (and precisely *why*) the moral sentiments are used with brutal flexibility, switched on and off in keeping with self-interest; and how naturally oblivious we often are to this switching. In the new view, human beings are a species splendid in their array of moral equipment, tragic in their propensity to misuse it, and pathetic in their constitutional ignorance of the misuse. The title of this book is not wholly without irony.

Thus, for all the emphasis in popular treatments of sociobiology on the "biological basis of altruism," and for all its genuine importance, the idea that John Stuart Mill ridiculed—of a corrupt human nature, of "original sin"—doesn't deserve such summary dismissal. And for that reason, I believe, neither does moral conservatism. Indeed, I believe some—*some*—of the conservative norms that prevailed in Victorian England reflect, if obliquely, a surer grasp of human nature than has prevailed in the social sciences for most of this century; and that *some* of the resurgent moral conservatism of the past decade, especially in the realm of sex, rests on an implicit rediscovery of truths about human nature that have long been denied.

If modern Darwinism indeed has some morally conservative emanations, does that mean it has politically conservative emanations? This is a tricky and important question. It's easy enough, and correct, to dismiss social Darwinism as a spasm of malicious confusion. But the question of innate human goodness casts a political shadow that can't be so casually disregarded, for linkage between ideology and views on human nature has a long and distinguished history. Over the past two centuries, as the meanings of political "liberalism" and "conservatism" have changed almost beyond recognition, one distinction between the two has endured: political liberals (such as Mill, in his day) tend to take a rosier view of human nature than conservatives, and to favor a looser moral climate.

Still, it isn't clear that this connection between morals and politics is truly necessary, especially in a modern context. To the extent that the new Darwinian paradigm has reasonably distinct political implications—and as a general rule it just doesn't—they are about as often to the left as to the right. In some ways they are radically to the left.

13

(Though Karl Marx would find much to dislike in the new paradigm, he would find parts of it very appealing.) What's more, the new paradigm suggests reasons a modern political liberal might subscribe to some morally conservative doctrines as a matter of ideological consistency. At the same time, it suggests that a conservative moral agenda may at times profit from liberal social policies.

DARWINIZING DARWIN

In making the case for a Darwinian outlook, I will use, as Exhibit A, Charles Darwin. His thoughts, emotions, and behavior will illustrate the principles of evolutionary psychology. In 1876, in the first paragraph of his autobiography, Darwin wrote, "I have attempted to write the following account of myself, as if I were a dead man in another world looking back at my own life." (He added, with characteristic grim detachment, "Nor have I found this difficult, for life is nearly over with me.")[9] I like to think that if Darwin were looking back today, with the penetrating hindsight afforded by the new Darwinism, he would see his life somewhat as I'll be depicting it.

Darwin's life will serve as more than illustration. It will be a miniature test of the explanatory power of the modern, refined version of his theory of natural selection. Advocates of evolutionary theory—including him, including me—have long claimed that it is so powerful as to explain the nature of all living things. If we're right, the life of any human being, selected at random, should assume new clarity when looked at from this viewpoint. Well, Darwin hasn't exactly been selected at random, but he'll do as a guinea pig. My claim is that his life—and his social environment, Victorian England—make more sense when looked at from a Darwinian vantage point than from any competing perspective. In this respect, he and his milieu are like all other organic phenomena.

Darwin doesn't *seem* like other organic phenomena. The things that come to mind when we think of natural selection—the ruthless pursuit of genetic self-interest, survival of the fiercest—don't come to mind when we think of Darwin. By all accounts, he was enormously civil and humane (except, perhaps, when circumstance made it hard to be both; he could grow agitated while denouncing slavery, and he might lose his temper if he saw a coachman abusing a horse).[10] His gentleness of manner and his utter lack of pretense, well marked from his youth, were uncorrupted by fame. "[O]f all eminent men that I have ever seen he is beyond comparison the most attractive to me," observed the literary critic Leslie Stephen. "There is something almost pathetic in his simplicity and friendliness."[11] Darwin was, to borrow a phrase from the title of *Self-Help*'s last chapter, a "true gentleman."

Darwin read *Self-Help*. But he needn't have. By then (age fifty-one) he was already a walking embodiment of Smiles's dictum that life is a battle against "moral ignorance, selfishness, and vice." Indeed, one common view is that Darwin was decent to a fault—that, if he needed a self-help book, it was a self-help book of the late-twentieth-century variety, something about how to feel good about yourself, how to look out for number one. The late John Bowlby, one of Darwin's most perceptive biographers, believed that Darwin suffered from "nagging self-contempt" and an "overactive conscience." Bowlby wrote: "While there is so much to admire in the absence of pretension and in the strong moral principles that were an integral part of Darwin's character and that, with much else, endeared him to relatives, friends and colleagues, these qualities were unfortunately developed prematurely and to excessive degree."[12]

Darwin's "excessive" humility and morality, his extreme lack of brutishness, are what make him so valuable as a test case. I will try to show that natural selection, however seemingly alien to his character, can account for it. It is true that Darwin was as gentle, humane, and decent a man as you can reasonably hope to find on this planet. But it is also true that he was fundamentally no different from the rest of us. Even Charles Darwin was an animal.

Part One: **SEX, ROMANCE, AND LOVE**

Chapter 1: **DARWIN COMES OF AGE**

*As for an English lady, I have almost forgotten what she is.—
something very angelic and good.*
                                        —Letter from the HMS *Beagle* (1835)[1]

Boys growing up in nineteenth-century England weren't generally
advised to seek sexual excitement. And they weren't advised to do
things that might lead them to think about seeking it. The Victorian
physician William Acton, in his book *The Functions and Disorders
of the Reproductive Organs,* warned about exposing a boy to the
"classical works" of literature. "He reads in them of the pleasures,
nothing of the penalties, of sexual indulgences. He is not intuitively
aware that, if the sexual desires are excited, it will require greater
power of will to master them than falls to the lot of most lads; that
if indulged in, the man will and must pay the penalty for the errors
of the boy; that for one that escapes, ten will suffer; that an awful
risk attends abnormal substitutes for sexual intercourse; and that self-
indulgence, long pursued, tends ultimately, if carried far enough, to
early death or self-destruction."[2]

Acton's book was published in 1857, during the mid-Victorian period whose moral tenor it exudes. But sexual repression had long been in the air—before Victoria's ascent to the throne in 1837, even before the date more loosely used to bracket the Victorian era, 1830. Indeed, at the turn of the century, the Evangelical movement that so nourished the new moral austerity was well under way.[3] As G. M. Young noted in *Portrait of an Age*, a boy born in England in 1810— the year after Darwin's birth—"found himself at every turn controlled, and animated, by the imponderable pressure of the Evangelical discipline. . . . " This was not a matter only of sexual restraint, but of restraint generally—an all-out vigilance against indulgence. The boy would learn, as Young put it, that "the world is very evil. An unguarded look, a word, a gesture, a picture, or a novel, might plant a seed of corruption in the most innocent heart. . . . "[4] Another student of Victorianism has described "a life of constant struggle— both to resist temptation and to master the desires of the ego"; by "an elaborate practice of self-discipline, one had to lay the foundation of good habits and acquire the power of self-control."[5]

It was this view that Samuel Smiles, born three years after Darwin, would package in *Self-Help*. As the book's wide success attests, the Evangelical outlook spread well beyond the walls of the Methodist churches that were its wellspring, into the homes of Anglicans, Unitarians, and even agnostics.[6] The Darwin household is a good example. It was Unitarian (and Darwin's father was a freethinker, if a quiet one), yet Darwin absorbed the puritanical strain of his time. It is visible in his burdensome conscience and in the astringent code of conduct he championed. Long after he had given up his faith, he wrote that "the highest stage in moral culture at which we can arrive, is when we recognise that we ought to control our thoughts, and [as Tennyson said] 'not even in inmost thought to think again the sins that made the past so pleasant to us.' Whatever makes any bad action familiar to the mind, renders its performance by so much the easier. As Marcus Aurelius long ago said, 'Such as are thy habitual thoughts, such also will be the character of thy mind; for the soul is dyed by the thoughts.' "[7]

Though Darwin's youth and life were in some ways eccentric, in this one sense they were typical of his era: he lived amid tremendous moral gravity. His world was a place where questions of right and wrong were seen at every turn. What's more, it was a place where these questions seemed answerable—absolutely answerable—though the answers were sometimes painful to bear. It was a world very different from ours, and Darwin's work would do much to make the difference.

AN UNLIKELY HERO

The original career plan for Charles Darwin was to be a doctor. His father, he recalled, felt sure "that I should make a successful physician—meaning by this, one who got many patients." The senior Darwin, himself a successful physician, "maintained that the chief element of success was exciting confidence; but what he saw in me which convinced him that I should create confidence I know not." Nonetheless, Charles at age sixteen dutifully left the cozy family estate in Shrewsbury and, accompanied by his older brother, Erasmus, headed for the University of Edinburgh to study medicine.

Enthusiasm for this calling failed to materialize. At Edinburgh Darwin paid grudging attention to course work, avoided the operating theater (watching surgery, in the days before chloroform, wasn't his cup of tea), and spent much time on extracurricular pursuits: trawling with fishermen to gather oysters, which he then dissected; taking taxidermy lessons to complement his newfound love of hunting; walking and talking with a sponge expert named Robert Grant, who ardently believed in evolution—but didn't, of course, know how it works.

Darwin's father sensed a certain vocational drift and, Charles recalled, "was very properly vehement against my turning an idle sporting man, which then seemed my probable destination."[8] Hence Plan B. Dr. Darwin proposed a career in the clergy.

This may seem strange guidance, coming from a man who didn't believe in God, given to a son who wasn't glaringly devout and who had a more obvious calling in zoology. But Darwin's father was a practical man. And in those days zoology and theology were two sides of one coin. If all living things were God's handiwork, then the study of their ingenious design was the study of God's genius. The most noted proponent of this view was William Paley, author of the 1802 book *Natural Theology; or, evidences of the existence and attributes of the Deity, collected from the appearances of nature*. In it Paley argued that, just as a watch implies a watchmaker, a world full of intricately designed organisms, precisely suited to their tasks, implies a designer.[9] (He was right. The question is whether the designer is a farseeing God or an unconscious process.)

The workaday upshot of natural theology was that a country parson could, without guilt, spend much of his time studying and writing about nature. Hence, perhaps, Darwin's fairly favorable, if not especially spiritual, reaction to the prospect of donning the cloth. "I asked for some time to consider, as from what little I had heard and thought on the subject I had scruples about declaring my belief in all the dogmas of the Church of England; though otherwise I liked the thought of being a country clergyman." He did some reading on divinity and "as I did not then in the least doubt the strict and literal truth of every word in the Bible, I soon persuaded myself that our Creed must be fully accepted." To prepare for the clergy, Darwin went to Cambridge University, where he read his Paley and was "charmed and convinced by the long line of argumentation."[10]

Not for long. Just after finishing at Cambridge, Darwin encountered a strange opportunity: to serve as naturalist aboard the HMS *Beagle*. The rest, of course, is history. Though Darwin didn't conceive of natural selection aboard the *Beagle*, his study of wildlife around the world convinced him that evolution had taken place, and alerted him to some of its most suggestive properties. Two years after the end of the ship's five-year voyage, he saw how evolution works. Darwin's plans to enter the clergy would not survive this insight. As if to provide future biographers with ample symbolism, he had brought along on the voyage his favorite volume of verse, *Paradise Lost*.[11]

As Darwin left England's shores, there was no glaring reason to think people would be writing books about him a century and a half later. His youth, ventured one biographer, in a fairly common judgment, had been "unmarked by the slightest trace of genius."[12] Of course, such claims are always suspect, as the early inauspiciousness of great minds makes for good reading. And this particular claim deserves special doubt, as it rests largely on Darwin's self-appraisals, which didn't tend toward inflation. Darwin reports that he couldn't master foreign languages, and struggled with mathematics, and "was considered by all my masters and by my Father as a very ordinary boy, rather below the common standard in intellect." Maybe, maybe not. Perhaps more stock should be placed in another of his appraisals, about his knack for winning the friendship of men "so much older than me and higher in academical position": "I infer that there must have been something in me a little superior to the common run of youths."[13]

Anyway, the absence of blinding intellectual flash isn't the only thing that has led some biographers to deem Darwin "an unlikely survivor in the immortality stakes."[14] There is also the sense that he just wasn't a formidable man. He was so decent, so sweet, so lacking in untrammeled ambition. And he was something of a country boy, a bit insular and simple. One writer has asked, "Why was it given to Darwin, less ambitious, less imaginative, and less learned than many of his colleagues, to discover the theory sought after by others so assiduously? How did it come about that one so limited intellectually and insensitive culturally should have devised a theory so massive in structure and sweeping in significance?"[15]

One way to answer that question is by contesting its assessment of Darwin (an exercise we'll get to), but an easier way is to contest its assessment of his theory. The idea of natural selection, while indeed "sweeping in significance," is not really "massive in structure." It is a small and simple theory, and it didn't take a huge intellect to conceive it. Thomas Henry Huxley, Darwin's good friend, staunch defender, and fluent popularizer, supposedly chastised himself upon comprehending the theory, exclaiming, "How extremely stupid not to have thought of that!"[16]

All the theory of natural selection says is the following. If within a species there is variation among individuals in their hereditary traits, and some traits are more conducive to survival and reproduction than others, then those traits will (obviously) become more widespread within the population. The result (obviously) is that the species' aggregate pool of hereditary traits changes. And there you have it.

Of course, the change may seem negligible within any given generation. If long necks help animals reach precious leaves, and shorter-necked animals therefore die before reproducing, the species' average neck size barely grows. Still, if variation in neck size arises freshly with new generations (through sexual recombination or genetic mutation, we now know), so that natural selection continues to have a range of neck sizes to "choose" from, then average neck size will keep creeping upward. Eventually, a species that started out with horselike necks will have giraffe-like necks. It will, in other words, be a new species.

Darwin once summed up natural selection in ten words: "[M]ultiply, vary, let the strongest live and the weakest die."[17] Here "strongest," as he well knew, means not just brawniest, but best adapted to the environment, whether through camouflage, cleverness, or anything else that aids survival and reproduction.* The word *fittest* (a coinage Darwin didn't make but did accept) is typically used in place of *strongest,* signifying this broader conception—an organism's "fitness" to the task of transmitting its genes to the next generation, within its particular environment. "Fitness" is the thing that natural selection, in continually redesigning species, perpetually "seeks" to maximize. Fitness is what made us what we are today.

If this seems easy to believe, you probably aren't getting the picture. Your entire body—much more complexly harmonious than any product of human design—was created by hundreds of thousands of incremental advances, and *each increment was an accident;* each tiny step between your ancestral bacterium and you *just happened* to help some intermediate ancestor more profusely get its genes into the next generation. Creationists sometimes say that the odds of a person being produced through random genetic change are about equal to those of a monkey typing the works of Shakespeare. Well, yes. Not the complete works, maybe, but certainly some long, recognizable stretches.

Still, things this unlikely can, through the logic of natural selec-

---

*Actually, Darwin divided the "survival" and "reproductive" aspects of the process. Traits leading to successful mating he attributed to "sexual selection," as distinct from natural selection. But these days, natural selection is often defined broadly, to encompass both aspects: the preservation of traits that are in any way conducive to getting an organism's genes into the next generation.

tion, be rendered plausible. Suppose a single ape gets some lucky break—gene XL, say, which imbues parents with an ounce of extra love for their offspring, love that translates into slightly more assiduous nurturing. In the life of any one ape, that gene probably won't be crucial. But suppose that, *on average*, the offspring of apes with the XL gene are 1 percent more likely to survive to maturity than the offspring of apes without it. So long as this thin advantage holds, the fraction of apes with gene XL will tend to grow, and the fraction without it will tend to shrink, generation by generation by generation. The eventual culmination of this trend is a population in which all animals have the XL gene. The gene, at that point, will have reached "fixation"; a slightly higher degree of parental love will be "species typical" now than before.

Okay, so one lucky break thus flourishes. But how likely is it that the luck will persist—that the *next* random genetic change will *further* increase the amount of parental love? How likely is the "XL" mutation to be followed by an "XXL" mutation? Not at all likely in the case of any one ape. But within the population there are now scads of apes with the XL gene. If any one of them, or any one of their offspring, or grand-offspring, happens to luck out and get the XXL gene, the gene will have a good chance of spreading, if slowly, through the population. Of course, in the meantime, lots more apes will probably get various less auspicious genes, and some of those genes may extinguish the lineage in which they appear. Well, that's life.

Thus does natural selection beat the odds—by not really beating them. The thing that is massively more probable than the charmed lineages that populate the world today—an uncharmed lineage, which reaches a dead end through an unlucky break—happened a massively larger number of times. The dustbin of genetic history overflows with failed experiments, long strings of code that were as vibrant as Shakespearean verse *until* that fateful burst of gibberish. Their disposal is the price paid for design by trial and error. But so long as that price can be paid—so long as natural selection has enough generations to work on, and can cast aside scores of failed experiments for every one it preserves—its creations can be awesome. Natural selection is an inanimate process, devoid of consciousness, yet is a tireless refiner, an ingenious craftsman.*

Every organ inside you is testament to its art—your heart, your lungs, your stomach. All these are "adaptations"—fine products of inadvertent design, mechanisms that are here because they have in the past contributed to your ancestors' fitness. And all are species-typical. Though one person's lungs may differ from another's, sometimes for genetic reasons, almost all the genes involved in lung construction are the same in you as in your next-door neighbor, as in an Eskimo, as in a pygmy. The evolutionary psychologists John Tooby and Leda Cosmides have noted that every page of *Gray's Anatomy* applies to all peoples in the world. Why, they have gone on to ask, should the anatomy of the mind be any different? The working thesis of evolutionary psychology is that the various "mental organs" constituting the human mind—such as an organ inclining people to love their offspring—are species-typical.[18] Evolutionary psychologists are pursuing what is known in the trade as "the psychic unity of humankind."

CLIMATE CONTROL

Between us and the australopithecine, which walked upright but had an ape-sized brain, stand a few million years: 100,000, maybe 200,000 generations. That may not sound like much. But it has taken only around 5,000 generations to turn a wolf into a chihuahua—and, at the same time, along a separate line, into a Saint Bernard. Of course, dogs evolved by artificial, not natural, selection. But as Darwin stressed, the two are essentially the same; in both cases traits are weeded out of a population by criteria that persist for many generations. And in both cases, if the "selective pressure" is strong enough—if genes are weeded out fast enough—evolution can proceed briskly.

One might wonder how the selective pressure could have been

---

*In this book I will sometimes talk about what natural selection "wants" or "intends," or about what "values" are implicit in its workings. I'll always use quotation marks, since these are just metaphors. But the metaphors are worth using, I believe, because they help us come to moral terms with Darwinism.

very strong during recent human evolution. After all, what usually generates the pressure is a hostile environment—droughts, ice ages, tough predators, scarce prey—and as human evolution has proceeded, the relevance of these things has abated. The invention of tools, of fire, the advent of planning and cooperative hunting—these brought growing control over the environment, growing insulation from the whims of nature. How, then, did ape brains turn into human brains in a few million years?

Much of the answer seems to be that the environment of human evolution has been human (or prehuman) beings.[19] The various members of a Stone Age society were each other's rivals in the contest to fill the next generation with genes. What's more, they were each other's tools in that contest. Spreading their genes depended on dealing with their neighbors: sometimes helping them, sometimes ignoring them, sometimes exploiting them, sometimes liking them, sometimes hating them—and having a sense for which people warrant which sort of treatment, and when they warrant it. The evolution of human beings has consisted largely of adaptation to one another.

Since each adaptation, having fixed itself in the population, thus changes the social environment, adaptation only invites more adaptation. Once all parents have the XXL gene, it gives no parent an edge in the ongoing contest to create the most viable and prolific offspring. The arms race continues. In this case, it's an arms race of love. Often, it's not.

It is fashionable in some circles to downplay the whole idea of adaptation, of coherent evolutionary design. Popularizers of biological thought often emphasize not the role of fitness in evolutionary change but the role of randomness and happenstance. Some climate shift may come out of the blue and extinguish unlucky species of flora and fauna, changing the whole context of evolution for any species lucky enough to survive the calamity. A roll of the cosmic dice and suddenly all bets are off. Certainly that happens, and this is indeed one sense in which "randomness" greatly affects evolution. There are other senses as well. For example, new traits on which natural selection passes judgment seem to be randomly generated.[20]

But none of the "randomness" in natural selection should be allowed to obscure its central feature: that the overriding criterion of organic design is fitness. Yes, the dice do get rerolled, and the context of evolution changes. A feature that is adaptive today may not be adaptive tomorrow. So natural selection often finds itself amending outmoded features. This ongoing adjustment to circumstance can give organic life a certain jerry-built quality. (It's the reason people have back trouble; if you were designing a walking organism from scratch rather than incrementally adapting a former tree-dweller, you would never have built such bad backs.) Nonetheless, changes in circumstance are typically gradual enough for evolution to keep pace (even if it has to break into a trot now and then, when selective pressure becomes severe), and it often does so ingeniously.

And all along the way, its definition of good design remains the same. The thousands and thousands of genes that influence human behavior—genes that build the brain and govern neurotransmitters and other hormones, thus defining our "mental organs"—are here for a reason. And the reason is that they goaded our ancestors into getting their genes into the next generation. If the theory of natural selection is correct, then essentially everything about the human mind should be intelligible in these terms. The basic ways we feel about each other, the basic kinds of things we think about each other and say to each other, are with us today by virtue of their past contribution to genetic fitness.

DARWIN'S SEX LIFE

No human behavior affects the transmission of genes more obviously than sex. So no parts of human psychology are clearer candidates for evolutionary explanation than the states of mind that lead to sex: raw lust, dreamy infatuation, sturdy (or at least sturdy-feeling) love, and so on—the basic forces amid which people all over the world, including Charles Darwin, have come of age.

When Darwin left England he was twenty-two and, presumably, flooded with the hormones that young men are, by design, flooded with. He had been sweet on a couple of local girls, especially the pretty, popular, and highly coquettish Fanny Owen. He once let her shoot a hunting gun, and she looked so charming, gamely pretending its kick hadn't hurt her shoulder, that he would recall the incident decades later with evident fondness.[21] From Cambridge he conducted a tenuous flirtation with her by mail, but it isn't clear that he ever so much as kissed her.

While Darwin was at Cambridge, prostitutes were available, not to mention the occasional lower-class girl who might settle for less explicit payment. But university proctors prowled the streets near campus, ready to arrest women who could plausibly be accused of "streetwalking." Darwin had been warned by his brother never to be seen with girls. His closest known connection with illicit sex is when he sent money to a friend who had dropped out of school after siring a bastard.[22] Darwin may well have left the shores of England a virgin.[23] And the next five years, spent mainly on a ninety-foot ship with six dozen males, wouldn't provide many opportunities to change that status, at least not through conventional channels.

For that matter, sex wouldn't be abundantly available on his return either. This was, after all, Victorian England. Prostitutes could be had in London (where Darwin would take up residence), but sex with a "respectable" woman, a woman of Darwin's class, was more elusive—close to impossible in the absence of extreme measures, such as marriage.

The great gulf between these two forms of sex is one of the most famous elements of Victorian sexual morality—the "Madonna-whore" dichotomy. There were two kinds of women: the kind a bachelor would later marry and the kind he might now enjoy, the kind worthy of love and the kind that warranted only lust. A second moral attitude commonly traced to the Victorian age is the sexual double standard. Though this attribution is misleading, since Victorian moralists so strongly discouraged sexual license in men *and* women, it's true that a Victorian man's sexual extravagance raised fewer eyebrows than a woman's. It's also true that this distinction was closely linked to the Madonna-whore dichotomy. The great punishment awaiting a sexually adventurous Victorian woman was permanent consignment to the latter half of the dichotomy, which would greatly restrict her range of available husbands.

There is a tendency these days to reject and scoff at these aspects of Victorian morality. Rejecting them is fine, but to scoff at them is to overestimate our own moral advancement. The fact is that many men still speak openly about "sluts" and their proper use: great for recreation, but not for marriage. And even men (such as well-educated liberal ones) who wouldn't dream of talking like that may in fact act like that. Women sometimes complain about seemingly enlightened men who lavish respectful attention on them but then, after sex on the first or second date, never call again, as if early sex had turned the woman into a pariah. Similarly, while the double standard has waned in this century, it is still strong enough for women to complain about. Understanding the Victorian sexual climate can take us some distance toward understanding today's sexual climate.

The intellectual grounding of Victorian sexual morality was explicit: women and men are inherently different, most importantly in the libido department. Even Victorians who railed against male philandering stressed the difference. Dr. Acton wrote: "I should say that the majority of women (happily for them) are not very much troubled with sexual feeling of any kind. What men are habitually, women are only exceptionally. It is too true, I admit, as the divorce courts show, that there are some few women who have sexual desires so strong that they surpass those of men." This "nymphomania" is "a form of insanity." Still, "there can be no doubt that sexual feeling in the female is in the majority of cases in abeyance . . . and even if roused (which in many instances it never can be) is very moderate compared with that of the male." One problem, said Dr. Acton, was that many young men are misled by the sight of "loose or, at least, low and vulgar women." They thus enter marriage with exaggerated notions of its sexual content. They don't understand that "the best mothers, wives, and managers of households, know little or nothing of sexual indulgences. Love of home, children, and domestic duties, are the only passions they feel."[24]

Some women who consider themselves excellent wives and mothers may hold a different opinion. And they may have strong supporting evidence. Still, the idea that there are *some* differences between the typical male and female sexual appetite, and that the male appetite is less finicky, draws much support from the new Darwinian paradigm. For that matter, it draws support from lots of other places. The recently popular premise that men and women are basically identical in nature seems to have fewer and fewer defenders. It is no longer, for example, a cardinal doctrine of feminism. A whole school of feminists—the "difference feminists," or "essentialists"—now accept that men and women are deeply different. What exactly "deeply" means is something they're often vague about, and many would rather not utter the word *genes* in this context. Until they do, they will likely remain in a state of disorientation, aware that the early feminist doctrine of innate sexual symmetry was incorrect (and that it may have in some ways harmed women) yet afraid to honestly explore the alternative.

If the new Darwinian view of sexuality did nothing more than endorse the coalescing conventional wisdom that men are a pretty libidinous group, it would be of meager value. But in fact it sheds light not just on animal impulses, like lust, but on the subtler contours of consciousness. "Sexual psychology," to an evolutionary psychologist, includes everything from an adolescent's fluctuating self-esteem to the aesthetic judgments men and women make about each other to the moral judgments they make about each other, and, for that matter, the moral judgments they make about members of their own sex. Two good examples are the Madonna-whore dichotomy and the sexual double standard. Both now appear to have roots in human nature—in mental mechanisms that people use to evaluate each other.

This calls for a couple of disclaimers. First, to say something is a product of natural selection is not to say that it is unchangeable; just about any manifestation of human nature can be changed, given an apt alteration of the environment—though the required alteration will in some cases be prohibitively drastic. Second, to say that something is "natural" is not to say that it is good. There is no reason to adopt natural selection's "values" as our own. But presumably if we want to pursue values that are at odds with natural selection's, we need to know what we're up against. If we want to change some disconcertingly stubborn parts of our moral code, it would help to know where they come from. And where they *ultimately* come from is human nature, however complexly that nature is refracted by the many layers of circumstance and cultural inheritance through which it passes. No, there is no "double-standard gene." But yes, to understand the double standard we must understand our genes and how

31

they affect our thoughts. We must understand the process that selected those genes and the strange criteria it used.

We'll spend the next few chapters exploring that process as it
has shaped sexual psychology. Then, thus fortified, we'll return to
Victorian morality, and to Darwin's own mind, and the mind
of the woman he married. All of which will enable us to see our
own situation—courtship and marriage at the end of the twentieth
century—with new clarity.

Chapter 2: **MALE AND FEMALE**

In the most distinct classes of the animal kingdom, with mammals, birds, reptiles, fishes, insects, and even crustaceans, the differences between the sexes follow almost exactly the same rules; the males are almost always the wooers. . . .
— *The Descent of Man* (1871)[1]

Darwin was wrong about sex.

He wasn't wrong about the males being the wooers. His reading of the basic characters of the two sexes holds up well today. "The female, . . . with the rarest exception, is less eager than the male. . . . [S]he is coy, and may often be seen endeavouring for a long time to escape from the male. Every one who has attended to the habits of animals will be able to call to mind instances of this kind. . . . The exertion of some choice on the part of the female seems almost as general a law as the eagerness of the male."[2]

Nor was Darwin wrong about the *consequences* of this asymmetrical interest. He saw that female reticence left males competing with one another for scarce reproductive opportunities, and thus explained why males so often have built-in weapons—the horns of stags, the hornlike mandibles of stag beetles, the fierce canines of chimpanzees.[3] Males not hereditarily equipped for combat with other

33

males have been excluded from sex, and their traits have thus been discarded by natural selection.

Darwin also saw that the choosiness of females gives great moment to their choices. If they prefer to mate with particular kinds of males, those kinds will proliferate. Hence the ornamentation of so many male animals—a lizard's inflatable throat sack, brightly colored during the mating season; the immense, cumbersome tail of the peacock; and, again, the stag's horns, which seem more elaborate than the needs of combat alone would dictate.[4] These decorations have evolved not because they aid in daily survival—if anything, they complicate it—but because they can so charm a female as to outweigh the everyday burdens they bring. (How it came to be in the genetic interest of females to be charmed by such things is another story, and a point of subtle disagreement among biologists.)[5]

Both of these variants of natural selection—combat among males and discernment by females—Darwin called "sexual selection." He took great pride in the idea, and justifiably so. Sexual selection is a nonobvious extension of his general theory that accounts for seeming exceptions to it (like garish colors that virtually say "Kill me" to predators), and that has not just endured over time but grown in scope.

What Darwin was wrong about was the evolutionary *cause* of female coyness and male eagerness. He saw that this imbalance of interest creates competition among males for precious reproductive slots, and he saw the consequences of this competition; but he didn't see what had created the imbalance. His attempt late in life to explain the phenomenon was unsuccessful.[6] And, in fairness to him, whole generations of biologists would do no better.

Now that there is a consensus on the solution, the long failure to find it seems puzzling. It's a very simple solution. In this sense, sex is typical of many behaviors illuminated by natural selection; though the illumination has gotten truly powerful only within the last three decades, it could in principle have done so a century earlier, so plainly does it follow from Darwin's view of life. There is some subtle logic involved, so Darwin can be forgiven for not having seen the full scope of his theory. Still, if he were around today to hear evolutionary biologists talk about sex, he might well sink into one of his self-effacing funks, exclaiming at his obtuseness in not getting the picture sooner.

PLAYING GOD

The first step toward understanding the basic imbalance of the sexes is to assume hypothetically the role natural selection plays in designing a species. Take the human species, for example. Suppose you're in charge of installing, in the minds of human (or prehuman) beings, rules of behavior that will guide them through life, the object of the game being to maximize each person's genetic legacy. To oversimplify a bit: you're supposed to make each person behave in such a way that he or she is likely to have lots of offspring—offspring, moreover, who themselves have lots of offspring.

Obviously, this isn't the way natural selection actually works. It doesn't consciously design organisms. It doesn't consciously do anything. It blindly preserves hereditary traits that happen to enhance survival and reproduction.* Still, natural selection works *as if* it were consciously designing organisms, so pretending you're in charge of organism design is a legitimate way to figure out which tendencies evolution is likely to have ingrained in people and other animals. In fact, this is what evolutionary biologists spend a good deal of time doing: looking at a trait—mental or otherwise—and figuring out what, if any, engineering challenge it is a solution to.

When playing the Administrator of Evolution, and trying to maximize genetic legacy, you quickly discover that this goal implies different tendencies for men and women. Men can reproduce hundreds of times a year, assuming they can persuade enough women to cooperate, and assuming there aren't any laws against polygamy—which there assuredly weren't in the environment where much of our evolution took place. Women, on the other hand, can't reproduce more often than once a year. The asymmetry lies partly in the high price of eggs; in all species they're bigger and rarer than minuscule,

---

*Actually, one premise of the new Darwinian paradigm is that natural selection's guiding light is a bit more complex than "survival and reproduction." But that nuance won't matter until chapter seven.

mass-produced sperm. (That, in fact, is biology's official definition of a female: the one with the larger sex cells.) But the asymmetry is exaggerated by the details of mammalian reproduction; the egg's lengthy conversion into an organism happens inside the female, and she can't handle many projects at once.

So, while there are various reasons why it could make Darwinian sense for a woman to mate with more than one man (maybe the first man was infertile, for example), there comes a time when having more sex just isn't worth the trouble. Better to get some rest or grab a bite to eat. For a man, unless he's really on the brink of collapse or starvation, that time never comes. Each new partner offers a very real chance to get more genes into the next generation—a much more valuable prospect, in the Darwinian calculus, than a nap or a meal. As the evolutionary psychologists Martin Daly and Margo Wilson have succinctly put it: for males "there is always the possibility of doing better."[7]

There's a sense in which a female can do better, too, but it has to do with quality, not quantity. Giving birth to a child involves a huge commitment of time, not to mention energy, and nature has put a low ceiling on how many such enterprises she can undertake. So each child, from her (genetic) point of view, is an extremely precious gene machine. Its ability to survive and then, in turn, produce its own young gene machines is of mammoth importance. It makes Darwinian sense, then, for a woman to be selective about the man who is going to help her build each gene machine. She should size up an aspiring partner before letting him in on the investment, asking herself what he'll bring to the project. This question then entails a number of subquestions that, in the human species especially, are more numerous and subtle than you might guess.

Before we go into these questions, a couple of points must be made. One is that the woman needn't literally ask them, or even be aware of them. Much of the relevant history of our species took place before our ancestors were smart enough to ask much of anything. And even in the more recent past, after the arrival of language and self-awareness, there has been no reason for every evolved behavioral tendency to fall under conscious control. In fact, sometimes it is emphatically *not* in our genetic interest to be aware of exactly what

we are doing or why. (Hence Freud, who was definitely onto something, though some evolutionary psychologists would say he didn't
know exactly what.) In the case of sexual attraction, at any rate,
everyday experience suggests that natural selection has wielded its
influence largely via the emotional spigots that turn on and off such
feelings as tentative attraction, fierce passion, and swoon-inducing
infatuation. A woman doesn't typically size up a man and think: "He
seems like a worthy contributor to my genetic legacy." She just sizes
him up and feels attracted to him—or doesn't. All the "thinking"
has been done—unconsciously, metaphorically—by natural selection. Genes leading to attractions that wound up being good for her
ancestors' genetic legacies have flourished, and those leading to less
productive attractions have not.

Understanding the often unconscious nature of genetic control is
the first step toward understanding that—in many realms, not just
sex—we're all puppets, and our best hope for even partial liberation
is to try to decipher the logic of the puppeteer. The full scope of the
logic will take some time to explain, but I don't think I'm spoiling
the end of the movie by noting here that the puppeteer seems to have
exactly zero regard for the happiness of the puppets.

The second point to grasp before pondering how natural selection
has "decided" to shape the sexual preferences of women (and of men)
is that it isn't foresightful. Evolution is guided by the environment
in which it takes place, and environments change. Natural selection
had no way of anticipating, for example, that someday people would
use contraception, and that their passions would thus lead them into
time-consuming and energy-sapping sex that was sure to be fruitless;
or that X-rated videotapes would come along and lead indiscrimi-
nately lustful men to spend leisure time watching them rather than
pursuing real, live women who might get their genes to the next
generation.

This isn't to say that there's anything wrong with "unproductive"
sexual recreation. Just because natural selection created us doesn't
mean we have to slavishly follow its peculiar agenda. (If anything,
we might be tempted to spite it for all the ridiculous baggage it's
saddled us with.) The point is just that it isn't correct to say that
people's minds are designed to maximize their fitness, their genetic

legacy. What the theory of natural selection says, rather, is that people's minds were designed to maximize fitness *in the environment in which those minds evolved.* This environment is known as the EEA—the environment of evolutionary adaptation.[8] Or, more memorably: the "ancestral environment." Throughout this book, the ancestral environment will lurk in the background. At times, in pondering whether some mental trait is an evolutionary adaptation, I will ask whether it seems to be in the "genetic interest" of its bearer. For example: Would indiscriminate lust be in the genetic interest of men? But this is just a kind of shorthand. The question, properly put, is always whether a trait would be in the "genetic interest" of someone in the EEA, not in modern America or Victorian England or anywhere else. Only traits that would have propelled the genes responsible for them through the generations in our ancestral social environment should, in theory, be part of human nature today.[9]

What was the ancestral environment like? The closest thing to a twentieth-century example is a hunter-gatherer society, such as the !Kung San of the Kalahari Desert in Africa, the Inuit (Eskimos) of the Arctic region, or the Ache of Paraguay. Inconveniently, hunter-gatherer societies are quite different from one another, rendering simple generalization about the crucible of human evolution difficult. This diversity is a reminder that the idea of a single EEA is actually a fiction, a composite drawing; our ancestral social environment no doubt changed much in the course of human evolution.[10] Still, there are recurring themes among contemporary hunter-gatherer societies, and they suggest that some features probably stayed fairly constant during much of the evolution of the human mind. For example: people grew up near close kin in small villages where everyone knew everyone else and strangers didn't show up very often. People got married—monogamously or polygamously—and a female typically was married by the time she was old enough to be fertile.

This much, at any rate, is a safe bet: whatever the ancestral environment was like, it wasn't much like the environment we're in now. We aren't designed to stand on crowded subway platforms, or to live in suburbs next door to people we never talk to, or to get hired or fired, or to watch the evening news. This disjunction between the contexts of our design and of our lives is probably responsible for much psychopathology, as well as much suffering of a less dramatic sort. (And, like the importance of unconscious motivation, it is an observation for which Freud gets some credit; it is central to his *Civilization and Its Discontents*.)

To figure out what women are inclined to seek in a man, and vice versa, we'll need to think more carefully about our ancestral social environment(s). And, as we'll see, thinking about the ancestral environment also helps explain why females in our species are less sexually reserved than females in many other species. But for purposes of making the single, largest point of this chapter—that, whatever the typical level of reserve for females in our species, it is higher than the level for males—the particular environment doesn't much matter. For this point depends only on the premise that an individual female can, over a lifetime, have many fewer offspring than an individual male. And that has been the case, basically, forever: since before our ancestors were human, before they were primates, before they were mammals—way, way back through the evolution of our brain, down to its reptilian core. Female snakes may not be very smart, but they're smart enough to know, unconsciously, at least, that there are some males it's not a good idea to mate with.

Darwin's failure, then, was a failure to see what a deeply precious commodity females are. He saw that their coyness had made them precious, but he didn't see that they were *inherently* precious—precious by virtue of their biological role in reproduction, and the resulting slow rate of female reproduction. Natural selection had seen this—or, at least, had "seen" it—and female coyness is the result of this implicit comprehension.

ENLIGHTENMENT DAWNS

The first large and clear step toward human comprehension of this logic was made in 1948 by the British geneticist A. J. Bateman. Bateman took fruit flies and ran them through a dating game. He would place five males and five females in a chamber, let them follow their hearts, and then, by examining the traits of the next generation, figure out which offspring belonged to which parents. He found a clear pattern. Whereas almost all females had about the same number of offspring, regardless of whether they mated with one, two, or three males, male legacies differed according to a simple rule: the more females you mate with, the more offspring you have. Bateman saw the import: natural selection encourages "an undiscriminating eagerness in the males and a discriminating passivity in the females."[11]

Bateman's insight long lay essentially unappreciated. It took nearly three decades, and several evolutionary biologists, to give it the things it lacked: full and rigorous elaboration on the one hand, and publicity on the other.

The first part—the rigor—came from two biologists who are good examples of how erroneous some stereotypes about Darwinism are. In the 1970s, opposition to sociobiology often took the form of charges that its practitioners were closet reactionaries, racists, fascists, etcetera. It is hard to imagine two people less vulnerable to such charges than George Williams and Robert Trivers, and it is hard to name anyone who did more than they to lay the foundations of the new paradigm.

Williams, a professor emeritus at the State University of New York, has worked hard to dispel vestiges of social Darwinism, with its underlying assumption that natural selection is a process somehow worthy of obedience or emulation. Many biologists share his view, and stress that we can't derive our moral values from its "values." But Williams goes further. Natural selection, he says, is an "evil" process, so great is the pain and death it thrives on, so deep is the selfishness it engenders.

Trivers, who was an untenured professor at Harvard when the new paradigm was taking shape and is now at Rutgers University, is much less inclined than Williams toward moral philosophy. But he evinces an emphatic failure to buy the right-wing values associated with social Darwinism. He speaks proudly of his friendship with the late Black Panther leader Huey Newton (with whom he once co-authored an article on human psychology). He rails against the bias of the judicial system. He sees conservative conspiracies where some people don't.

In 1966 Williams published his landmark work, *Adaptation and Natural Selection: A Critique of Some Current Evolutionary Thought.*

Slowly this book has acquired a nearly holy stature in its field. It is a basic text for biologists who think about social behavior, including human social behavior, in light of the new Darwinism.[12] Williams's book dispelled confusions that had long plagued the study of social behavior, and it laid down foundational insights that would support whole edifices of work on the subjects of friendship and sex. In both cases Trivers would be instrumental in building the edifices.

Williams amplified and extended the logic behind Bateman's 1948 paper. He cast the issue of male versus female genetic interests in terms of the "sacrifice" required for reproduction. For a male mammal, the necessary sacrifice is close to zero. His "essential role may end with copulation, which involves a negligible expenditure of energy and materials on his part, and only a momentary lapse of attention from matters of direct concern to his safety and well-being." With little to lose and much to gain, males can profit, in the currency of natural selection, by harboring "an aggressive and immediate willingness to mate with as many females as may be available." For the female, on the other hand, "copulation may mean a commitment to a prolonged burden, in both the mechanical and physiological sense, and its many attendant stresses and dangers." Thus, it is in her genetic interest to "assume the burdens of reproduction" only when circumstances seem propitious. And "one of the most important circumstances is the inseminating male"; since "unusually fit fathers tend to have unusually fit offspring," it is "to the female's advantage to be able to pick the most fit male available. . . . "[13]

Hence courtship: "the advertisement, by a male, of how fit he is." And just as "it is to his advantage to pretend to be highly fit whether he is or not," it is to the female's advantage to spot false advertising. So natural selection creates "a skilled salesmanship among the males and an equally well-developed sales resistance and discrimination among the females."[14] In other words: males should, in theory, tend to be show-offs.

A few years later, Trivers used the ideas of Bateman and Williams to create a full-blown theory that ever since has been shedding light on the psychology of men and women. Trivers began by replacing Williams's concept of "sacrifice" with "investment." The difference may seem slight, but nuances can start intellectual avalanches, and this one did. The term *investment*, linked to economics, comes with a ready-made analytical framework.

In a now-famous paper published in 1972, Trivers formally defined "parental investment" as "any investment by the parent in an individual offspring that increases the offspring's chance of surviving (and hence [the offspring's] reproductive success) at the cost of the parent's ability to invest in other offspring."[15] Parental investment includes the time and energy consumed in producing an egg or a sperm, achieving fertilization, gestating or incubating the egg, and rearing the offspring. Plainly, females will generally make the higher investment up until birth, and, less plainly but in fact typically, this disparity continues after birth.

By quantifying the imbalance of investment between mother and father in a given species, Trivers suggested, we could better understand many things—for example, the extent of male eagerness and female coyness, the intensity of sexual selection, and many subtle aspects of courtship and parenthood, fidelity and infidelity. Trivers saw that in our species the imbalance of investment is not as stark as in many others. And he correctly suspected that (as we'll see in the next chapter) the result is much psychological complexity.

At last, with Trivers's paper "Parental Investment and Sexual Selection," the flower had bloomed; a simple extension of Darwin's theory—so simple that Darwin would have grasped it in a minute—had been glimpsed in 1948, clearly articulated in 1966, and was now, in 1972, given full form.[16] Still, the concept of parental investment lacked one thing: publicity. It was E. O. Wilson's book *Sociobiology* (1975) and Richard Dawkins's *The Selfish Gene* (1976) that gave Trivers's work a large and diverse audience, getting scores of psychologists and anthropologists to think about human sexuality in modern Darwinian terms. The resulting insights are likely to keep accumulating for a long time.

TESTING THE THEORY

Theories are a dime a dozen. Even strikingly elegant theories, which, like the theory of parental investment, seem able to explain much with little, often turn out to be worthless. There is justice in the complaint (from creationists, among others) that some theories about the evolution of animal traits are "just so stories"—plausible, but nothing more. Still, it is possible to separate the merely plausible from the compelling. In some sciences, testing theories is so straightforward that it is only a slight exaggeration (though it is always, in a certain strict sense, an exaggeration) to talk of theories being "proved." In others, corroboration is roundabout—an ongoing, gradual process by which confidence approaches the threshold of consensus, or fails to. Studying the evolutionary roots of human nature, or of anything else, is a science of the second sort. About each theory we ask a series of questions, and the answers nourish belief or doubt or ambivalence.

One question about the theory of parental investment is whether human behavior in fact complies with it in even the most basic ways. Are women more choosy about sex partners than men? (This is not to be confused with the very different question, to which we'll return, of which sex, if either, is choosier about *marriage* partners.) Certainly there is plenty of folk wisdom suggesting as much. More concretely, there's the fact that prostitution—sex with someone you don't know and don't care to know—is a service sought overwhelmingly by males, now as in Victorian England. Similarly, virtually all pornography that relies sheerly on visual stimulation—pictures or films of anonymous people, spiritless flesh—is consumed by males. And various studies have shown men to be, on average, much more open to casual, anonymous sex than women. In one experiment, three fourths of the men approached by an unknown woman on a college campus agreed to have sex with her, whereas none of the women approached by an unknown man were willing.[17]

It used to be common for doubters to complain that this sort of evidence, drawn from Western society, reflects only its warped values. This tack has been problematic since 1979, when Donald Symons published *The Evolution of Human Sexuality,* the first comprehensive anthropological survey of human sexual behavior from the new Darwinian perspective. Drawing on cultures East and West, industrial and preliterate, Symons demonstrated the great breadth of the patterns implied by the theory of parental investment: women tend to be relatively selective about sex partners; men tend to be less so, and tend to find sex with a wide variety of partners an extraordinarily appealing concept.

One culture Symons discussed is about as far from Western influence as possible: the indigenous culture of the Trobriand Islands in Melanesia. The prehistoric migration that populated these islands broke off from the migrations that peopled Europe at least tens of thousands of years ago, and possibly more than 100,000 years ago. The Trobrianders' ancestral culture was separated from Europe's ancestral culture even earlier than was that of Native Americans.[18] And indeed, when visited by the great anthropologist Bronislaw Malinowski in 1915, the islands proved startlingly remote from the currents of Western thought. The natives, it seemed, hadn't even gotten the connection between sex and reproduction. When one seafaring Trobriander returned from a voyage of several years to find his wife with two children, Malinowski was tactful enough not to suggest that she had been unfaithful. And "when I discussed the matter with others, suggesting that one at least of these children could not be his, my interlocutors did not understand what I meant."[19]

Some anthropologists have doubted that the Trobrianders could have been so ignorant. And although Malinowski's account of this issue seems to have the ring of authority, there is no way of knowing whether he got the story straight. But it is important to understand that he could, in principle, be right. The evolution of human sexual psychology seems to have preceded the discovery by humans of what sex is for. Lust and other such feelings are natural selection's way of getting us to act as if we wanted lots of offspring and knew how to get them, whether or not we actually do.[20] Had natural selection *not* worked this way—had it instead harnessed human intelligence so that our pursuit of fitness was entirely conscious and calculated—then life would be very different. Husbands and wives would, for example, spend no time having extramarital affairs with contraception; they would either scrap the contraception or scrap the sex.

Another un-Western thing about Trobriand culture was the lack of Victorian anxiety about premarital sex. By early adolescence, both girls and boys were encouraged to mate with a series of partners to their liking. (This freedom is found in some other preindustrial societies, though the experimentation typically ends, and marriage begins, before a girl reaches fertility.) But Malinowski left no doubt about which sex was choosier. "[T]here is nothing roundabout in a Trobriand wooing. . . . Simply and directly a meeting is asked for with the avowed intention of sexual gratification. If the invitation is accepted, the satisfaction of the boy's desire eliminates the romantic frame of mind, the craving for the unattainable and mysterious. If he is rejected, there is not much room for personal tragedy, for he is accustomed from childhood to having his sexual impulses thwarted by some girl, and he knows that another intrigue cures this type of ill surely and swiftly. . . . " And: "In the course of every love affair the man has constantly to give small presents to the woman. To the natives the need of one-sided payment is self-evident. This custom implies that sexual intercourse, even where there is mutual attachment, is a service rendered by the female to the male."[21]

There were certainly cultural forces reinforcing coyness among Trobriand women. Though a young woman was encouraged to have an active sex life, her advances would be frowned on if too overt and common because of the "small sense of personal worth that such urgent solicitation implies."[22] But is there any reason to believe this norm was anything other than a culturally mediated reflection of deeper genetic logic? Can anyone find a single culture in which women with unrestrained sexual appetites *aren't* viewed as more aberrant than comparably libidinous men? If not, isn't it an astonishing coincidence that all peoples have independently arrived at roughly the same cultural destination, with no genetic encouragement? Or is it the case that this universal cultural element was present half a million or more years ago, before the species began splitting up? That seems a long time for an essentially arbitrary value to endure, without being extinguished in a single culture.

This exercise holds a couple of important lessons. First: one good reason to suspect an evolutionary explanation for something—some mental trait or mechanism of mental development—is that it's universal, found everywhere, even in cultures that are as far apart as two cultures can be.[23] Second: the general difficulty of explaining such universality in utterly cultural terms is an example of how the Darwinian view, though not *proved* right in the sense that mathematical theorems are proved right, can still be the view that, by the rules of science, wins; its chain of explanation is shorter than the alternative chain and has fewer dubious links; it is a simpler and more potent theory. If we accept even the three meager assertions made so far— (1) that the theory of natural selection straightforwardly implies the "fitness" of women who are choosy about sexual partners and of men who often aren't; (2) that this choosiness and unchoosiness, respectively, is observed worldwide; and (3) that this universality can't be explained with equal simplicity by a competing, purely cultural, theory—if we accept these things, and if we're playing by the rules of science, we have to endorse the Darwinian explanation: male license and (relative) female reserve are to some extent innate.

Still, it is always good to have more evidence. Though absolute "proof" may not be possible in science, varying degrees of confidence are. And while evolutionary explanations rarely attain the 99.99 percent confidence sometimes found in physics or chemistry, it's always nice to raise the level from, say, 70 to 97 percent.

One way to strengthen an evolutionary explanation is to show that its logic is obeyed generally. If women are choosy about sex because they can have fewer kids than men (by virtue of investing more in them), and if females in the animal kingdom generally can have fewer offspring than males, then female animals in general should be choosier than males. Evolutionary theories can generate falsifiable predictions, as good scientific theories are expected to do, even though evolutionary biologists don't have the luxury of rerunning evolution in their labs, with some of its variables controlled, and predicting the outcome.

This particular prediction has been abundantly confirmed. In species after species, females are coy and males are not. Indeed, males are so dim in their sexual discernment that they may pursue things other than females. Among some kinds of frogs, mistaken homosexual courtship is so common that a "release call" is used by males who find themselves in the clutches of another male to notify him that they're both wasting their time.[24] Male snakes, for their part, have been known to spend a while with dead females before moving on to a live prospect.[25] And male turkeys will avidly court a stuffed replica of a female turkey. In fact, a replica of a female turkey's head suspended fifteen inches from the ground will generally do the trick. The male circles the head, does its ritual displays, and then (confident, presumably, that its performance has been impressive) rises into the air and comes down in the proximity of the female's backside, which turns out not to exist. The more virile males will show such interest even when a wooden head is used, and a few can summon lust for a wooden head with no eyes or beak.[26]

Of course, such experiments only confirm in vivid form what Darwin had much earlier said was obvious: males are very eager. This raises a much-cited problem with testing evolutionary explanations: the odd sense in which a theory's "predictions" are confirmed. Darwin didn't sit in his study and say, "My theory implies coy, picky females and mindlessly lustful males," and then take a walk to see if he could find examples. On the contrary, the many examples are what prompted him to wonder which implication of natural selection had created them—a question not correctly answered until midway through the following century, after even more examples had piled up. This tendency for Darwinian "predictions" to come after their evident fulfillment has been a chronic gripe of Darwin's critics. People who doubt the theory of natural selection, or just resist its application to human behavior, complain about the retrofitting of fresh predictions to preexisting results. This is often what they have in mind when they say evolutionary biologists spend their time dreaming up "just so stories" to explain everything they see.

In a sense, dreaming up plausible stories *is* what evolutionary biologists do. But that's not by itself a damning indictment. The power of a theory, such as the theory of parental investment, is gauged by how much data it explains and how simply, regardless of when the data surfaced. After Copernicus showed that assuming the Earth to revolve around the Sun accounted elegantly for the otherwise perplexing patterns that stars trace in the sky, it would have been beside the point to say, "But you cheated. You knew about the patterns all along." Some "just so stories" are plainly better than others, and they win. Besides, how much choice do evolutionary biologists have? There's not much they can do about the fact that the database on animal life began accumulating millennia before Darwin's theory.

But there is one thing they can do. Often a Darwinian theory generates, in addition to the pseudopredictions that the theory was in fact designed to explain, additional predictions—real predictions, untested predictions, which can be used to further evaluate the theory. (Darwin elliptically outlined this method in 1838, at age twenty-nine—more than twenty years before *The Origin of Species* was published. He wrote in his notebook: "The line of argument pursued throughout my theory is to establish a point as a probability by induction, & to apply it as hypothesis to other points. & see whether it will solve them.")[27] The theory of parental investment is a good example. For there are a few oddball species, as Williams noted in 1966, in which the male's investment in the offspring roughly matches, or even exceeds, the female's. If the theory of parental investment is right, these species should defy sex stereotypes.

Consider seahorses, and their near relative, the pipefish. Here the male plays a role like a female kangaroo's: he takes the eggs into a pouch and plugs them into his bloodstream for nutrition. The female can thus start on another round of reproduction while the male is playing nurse. This may not mean that she can have more offspring than he over a lifetime—after all, it took her a while to produce the eggs in the first place. Still, the parental investment isn't grossly imbalanced in the usual direction. And, predictably, female pipefish and seahorses tend to take an active role in courtship, seeking out the males and initiating the mating ritual.[28]

Some birds, such as the phalarope (including the two species known as sea snipes), exhibit a similarly abnormal distribution of parental investment. The males sit on the eggs, leaving the females free to go get some wild oats sown. Again, we see the expected departure from stereotype. It is the phalarope *females* who are larger and more colorful—a sign that sexual selection is working in reverse, as females compete for males. One biologist observed that the females, in classically male fashion, "quarrel and display among themselves" while the males patiently incubate the eggs.[29]

If the truth be told, Williams knew that these species defy stereotype when he wrote in 1966. But subsequent investigation has confirmed his "prediction" more broadly. Extensive parental investment by males has been shown to have the expected consequences in other birds, in the Panamanian poison-arrow frog, in a water bug whose males cart fertilized eggs around on their backs, and in the (ironically named, it turns out) Mormon cricket. So far Williams's prediction has encountered no serious trouble.[30]

APES AND US

There is another major form of evolutionary evidence bearing on differences between men and women: our nearest relatives. The great apes—chimpanzees, pygmy chimps (also called bonobos), gorillas, and orangutans—are not, of course, our ancestors; all have evolved since their path diverged from ours. Still, those forks in the road have come between eight million years ago (for chimps and bonobos) and sixteen million years ago (for orangutans).[31] That's not long, as these things go. (A reference point: The australopithecine, our presumed ancestor, whose skull was ape-sized but who walked upright, appeared between six and four million years ago, shortly after the chimpanzee off-ramp. *Homo erectus*—the species that had brains midway in size between ours and apes', and used them to discover fire—took shape around 1.5 million years ago.)[32]

The great apes' nearness to us on the evolutionary tree legitimizes a kind of detective game. It's possible—though hardly certain—that when a trait is shared by all of them and by us, the reason is common descent. In other words: the trait existed in our common, sixteen-million-year-old proto-ape ancestor, and has been in all our lineages ever since. The logic is roughly the same as tracking down four distant cousins, finding that they all have brown eyes, and inferring that at least one of their two common great-great-grandparents had brown eyes. It's far from being an airtight conclusion, but it has more credence than it had when you had seen only one of the cousins.[33]

Lots of traits are shared by us and the great apes. For many of the traits—five-fingered hands, say—pointing this out isn't worth the trouble; no one doubts the genetic basis of human hands anyway. But in the case of human mental traits whose genetic substratum is still debated—such as the differing sexual appetites of men and women—this inter-ape comparison can be useful. Besides, it's worth taking a minute to get acquainted with our nearest relatives. Who knows how much of our psyche we share by common descent with some or all of them?

Orangutan males are drifters. They wander in solitude, looking for females, who tend to be stationary, each in her own home range. A male may settle down long enough to monopolize one, two, or even more of these ranges, though vast monopolies are discouraged by the attendant need to fend off vast numbers of rivals. Once the mission is accomplished, and the resident female gives birth, the male is likely to disappear. He may return years later, when pregnancy is again possible.[34] In the meantime, he doesn't bother to write.

For a gorilla male, the goal is to become leader of a pack comprising several adult females, their young offspring, and maybe a few young adult males. As dominant male, he will get sole sexual access to the females; the young males generally mind their manners (though a leader may, as he ages and his strength ebbs, share females with them).[35] On the downside, the leader does have to confront any male interlopers, each of which aims to make off with one or more of his females and thus is in an assertive mood.

The life of the male chimpanzee is also combative. He strives to climb a male hierarchy that is long and fluid compared to a gorilla hierarchy. And, again, the dominant male—working tirelessly to protect his rank through assault, intimidation, and cunning—gets first dibs on any females, a prerogative he enforces with special vigor when they're ovulating.[36]

Pygmy chimps, or bonobos (they're actually a distinct species from chimpanzees), may be the most erotic of all primates. Their sex comes in many forms and often serves purposes other than reproduction. Periodic homosexual behavior, such as genital rubbings between females, seems to be a way of saying, "Let's be friends." Still, broadly speaking, the bonobos' sociosexual outline mirrors that of the common chimpanzees: a pronounced male hierarchy that helps determine access to females.[37]

Amid the great variety of social structure in these species, the basic theme of this chapter stands out, at least in minimal form: males seem very eager for sex and work hard to find it; females work less hard. This isn't to say the females don't like sex. They love it, and may initiate it. And, intriguingly, the females of the species most closely related to humans—chimpanzees and bonobos—seem particularly amenable to a wild sex life, including a variety of partners. Still, female apes don't do what male apes do: search high and low, risking life and limb, to find sex, and to find as much of it, with as many different partners, as possible; it has a way of finding them.

FEMALE CHOICE

That female apes are, on balance, more reticent than male apes doesn't necessarily mean that they actively screen their prospective partners. To be sure, the partners get screened; those who dominate other males mate, while those who get dominated may not. This competition is exactly what Darwin had in mind in defining one of the two kinds of sexual selection, and these species (like our own) illustrate how it favors the evolution of big, mean males. But what about the other kind of sexual selection? Does the female participate in the screening, choosing the male that seems the most auspicious contributor to her project?

Female choice is notoriously hard to spot, and signs of its long-term effect are often ambiguous. Are males larger and stronger than females just because tougher males have bested their rivals and gotten to mate? Or, in addition, have females come to prefer tough males, since females with this genetically ingrained preference have had tougher and therefore more prolific sons, whose many daughters then inherited their grandmother's taste?

Notwithstanding such difficulties, it's fairly safe to say that in one sense or another, females are choosy in all the great ape species. A female gorilla, for example, though generally confined to sex with a single, dominant male, normally emigrates in the course of her lifetime. When an alien male approaches her pack, engaging its leader in mutual threats and maybe even a fight, she will, if sufficiently impressed, decide to follow him.[38]

In the case of chimps, the matter is more subtle. The dominant, or alpha, male can have any female he wants, but that's not necessarily because she prefers him; he shuts off alternatives by frightening other males. He can frighten her too, so that any spurning of low-ranking males may reflect only her fear. (Indeed, the spurning has been known to disappear when the alpha isn't looking.)[39] But there is a wholly different kind of chimp mating—a sustained, private consortship that may be a prototype for human courtship. A male and female chimp will leave the community for days or even weeks. And although the female may be forcibly abducted if she resists an invitation, there are times when she successfully resists, and times when she chooses to go peacefully, even though nearby males would gladly aid her in any resistance.[40]

Actually, even going unpeacefully can involve a kind of choice. Female orangutans are a good example. They do often seem to exercise positive choice, favoring some males over others. But sometimes they resist a mating and are forcibly subdued and—insofar as this word can be applied to nonhumans—raped. There is evidence that the rapists, often adolescents, usually fail to impregnate.[41] But suppose that they succeed with some regularity. Then a female, in sheerly Darwinian terms, is better off mating with a good rapist, a big, strong, sexually aggressive male; her male offspring will then be more likely to be big, strong, and sexually aggressive (assuming sexual aggressiveness varies at least in part because of genetic differences)—and therefore prolific. So female resistance should be favored by natural selection as a way to avoid having a son who is an inept rapist (assuming it doesn't bring injury to the female).

This isn't to say that a female primate, her protests notwithstanding, "really wants it," as human males have been known to assume. On the contrary, the more an orangutan "really wants it," the less she'll resist, and the less powerful a screening device her reticence will be. What natural selection "wants" and what any individual wants needn't be the same, and in this case they're somewhat at odds. The point is simply that, even when females demonstrate no clear preference for certain kinds of males, they may be, in practical terms, preferring a certain kind of male. And this de facto discretion may be de jure. It may be an adaptation, favored by natural selection precisely *because* it has this filtering effect.

In the broadest sense, the same logic could apply in any primate species. Once females in general begin putting up the slightest resistance, then a female that puts up a little extra resistance is exhibiting a valuable trait. For whatever it takes to penetrate resistance, the sons of strong resisters are more likely to have it than the sons of weak resisters. (This assumes, again, that the relative possession by different males of "whatever it takes" reflects underlying genetic differences.) Thus, in sheerly Darwinian terms, coyness becomes its own reward. And this is true regardless of whether the male's means of approach is physical or verbal.

ANIMALS AND THE UNCONSCIOUS

A common reaction to the new Darwinian view of sex is that it makes perfect sense as an explanation for animal behavior—which is to say, for the behavior of *nonhuman* animals. People may chuckle appreciatively at a male turkey that tries to mate with a poor rendition of a female's head, but if you then point out that many a human male regularly gets aroused after looking at two-dimensional representations of a nude woman, they don't see the connection. After all, the man surely knows that it's only a photo he's looking at; his behavior may be pathetic, but it isn't comic.

And maybe it isn't. But if he "knows" it's a photo, why is he getting so excited? And why are women so seldom whipped up into an onanistic frenzy by pictures of men?

Resistance to lumping humans and turkeys under one set of Darwinian rules has its points. Yes, our behavior is under more subtle, presumably more "conscious," control than is turkey behavior. Men can decide not to get aroused by something—or, at least, can decide not to look at something they know will arouse them. Sometimes they even stick with those decisions. And although turkeys can make what look like comparable "choices" (a turkey hounded by a shotgun-wielding man may decide that now isn't the time for romance), it is plainly true that the complexity and subtlety of options available to a human are unrivaled in the animal kingdom. So too is the human's considered pursuit of very long-run goals.

It all feels very rational, and in some ways it is. But that doesn't mean it isn't in the service of Darwinian ends. To a layperson, it may seem natural that the evolution of reflective, self-conscious brains would liberate us from the base dictates of our evolutionary past. To an evolutionary biologist, what seems natural is roughly the opposite: that human brains evolved not to insulate us from the mandate to survive and reproduce, but to follow it more effectively, if more pliably; that as we evolve from a species whose males forcibly abduct females into a species whose males whisper sweet nothings, the whispering will be governed by the same logic as the abduction—it is a means of manipulating females to male ends, and its form serves this function. The basic emanations of natural selection are refracted from the older, inner parts of our brain all the way out to its freshest tissue. Indeed, the freshest tissue would never have appeared if it didn't toe natural selection's bottom line.

Of course, a lot *has* happened since our ancestors parted ways with the great apes' ancestors, and one can imagine a change in evolutionary context that would have removed our lineage from the logic that so imbalances the romantic interests of male and female in most species. Don't forget about the seahorses, sea snipes, Panamanian poison-arrow frogs, and Mormon crickets, with their reversed sex roles. And, less dramatically, but a bit closer to home, there are the gibbons, another of our primate cousins, whose ancestors waved good-bye to ours about twenty million years ago. At some point in gibbon evolution, circumstances began to encourage much male parental investment. The males regularly stick around and help provide for the kids. In one gibbon species the males actually carry the infants, something male apes aren't exactly known for. And talk about marital harmony: gibbon couples sing a loud duet in the morning, pointedly advertising their familial stability for the information of would-be home-wreckers.[42]

Well, human males too have been known to carry around infants, and to stay with their families. Is it possible that at some time over the last few million years something happened to us rather like what happened to the gibbons? Have male and female sexual appetites converged at least enough to make monogamous marriage a reasonable goal?

Chapter 3: **MEN AND WOMEN**

Judging from the social habits of man as he now exists, and from most savages being polygamists, the most probable view is that primeval man aboriginally lived in small communities, each with as many wives as he could support and obtain, whom he would have jealously guarded against all other men. Or he may have lived with several wives by himself, like the Gorilla. . . .
—The Descent of Man (1871)[1]

One of the more upbeat ideas to have emerged from an evolutionary view of sex is that human beings are a "pair-bonding" species. In its most extreme form, the claim is that men and women are designed for a lifetime of deep, monogamous love. This claim has not emerged from close scrutiny in pristine condition.

The pair-bond hypothesis was popularized by Desmond Morris in his 1967 book *The Naked Ape*. This book, along with a few other 1960s books (Robert Ardrey's *The Territorial Imperative*, for example), represent a would-be watershed in the history of evolutionary thought. That they found large readerships signaled a new openness to Darwinism, an encouraging dissipation of the fallout from its past political misuses. But there was no way, in the end, that these books could start a Darwinian renaissance within academia. The problem was simple: they didn't make sense.

One example surfaced early in Morris's pair-bonding argument. He was trying to explain why human females are generally faithful to their mates. This is indeed a good question (if you believe they are, that is). For high fidelity would place women in a distinct minority within the animal kingdom. Though female animals are generally less licentious than males, the females of many species are far from prudes, and this is particularly true of our nearest ape relatives. Female chimpanzees and bonobos are, at times, veritable sex machines. In explaining how women came to be so virtuous, Morris referred to the sexual division of labor in an early hunter-gatherer economy. "To begin with," he wrote, "the males had to be sure that their females were going to be faithful to them when they left them alone to go hunting. So the females had to develop a pairing tendency."[2]

Stop right there. It was in the reproductive interests of the *males* for the *females* to develop a tendency toward fidelity? So natural selection obliged the males by making the necessary changes in the females? Morris never got around to explaining how, exactly, natural selection would perform this generous feat.

Maybe it's unfair to single Morris out for blame. He was a victim of his times. The trouble was an atmosphere of loose, hyperteleological thinking. One gets the impression, reading Morris's book, and Ardrey's books, of a natural selection that peers into the future, decides what needs to be done to make things generally better for the species, and takes the necessary steps. But natural selection doesn't work that way. It doesn't peer ahead, and it doesn't try to make things generally better. Every single, tiny, blindly taken step either happens to make sense in immediate terms of genetic self-interest or it doesn't. And if it doesn't, you won't be reading about it a million years later. This was an essential message of George Williams's 1966 book, a message that had barely begun to take hold when Morris's book appeared.

One key to good evolutionary analysis, Williams stressed, is to focus on the fate of the gene in question. If a woman's "fidelity gene" (or her "infidelity gene") shapes her behavior in a way that helps get copies of *itself* into future generations in large numbers, then that gene will by definition flourish. Whether the gene, in the process, gets mixed in with her husband's genes or with the mailman's genes is by itself irrelevant. As far as natural selection is concerned, one vehicle is as good as the next. (Of course, when we talk about "a gene" for anything—fidelity, infidelity, altruism, cruelty—we are usefully oversimplifying; complex traits result from the interaction of numerous genes, each of which, typically, was selected for its incremental addition to fitness.)

A new wave of evolutionists has used this stricter view of natural selection to think with greater care about the question that rightly interested Morris: Are human males and females born to form enduring bonds with one another? The answer is hardly an unqualified yes for either sex. Still, it is closer to a yes for both sexes than it is in the case of, say, chimpanzees. In every human culture on the anthropological record, marriage—whether monogamous or polygamous, permanent or temporary—is the norm, and the family is the atom of social organization. Fathers everywhere feel love for their children, and that's a lot more than you can say for chimp fathers and bonobo fathers, who don't seem to have much of a clue as to which youngsters are theirs. This love leads fathers to help feed and defend their children, and teach them useful things.[3]

At some point, in other words, extensive *male parental investment* entered our evolutionary lineage. We are, as they say in the zoology literature, high in MPI. We're not so high that male parental investment typically rivals female parental investment, but we're a lot higher than the average primate. We indeed have something important in common with the gibbons.

High MPI has in some ways made the everyday goals of male and female humans dovetail, and, as any two parents know, it can give them a periodic source of common and profound joy. But high MPI has also created whole new ways for male and female aims to diverge, during both courtship and marriage. In Robert Trivers's 1972 paper on parental investment, he remarked, "One can, in effect, treat the sexes as if they were different species, the opposite sex being a resource relevant to producing maximum surviving offspring."[4] Trivers was making a specific analytical point, not a sweeping rhetorical one. But to a distressing extent—and an extent that was unclear before his paper—this metaphor does capture the overall situation; even with high MPI, and in some ways because of it, a basic underlying dynamic between men and women is mutual exploitation. They seem, at times, designed to make each other miserable.

WHY WE'RE HIGH IN MPI

There is no shortage of clues as to why men are inclined to help rear their young. In our recent evolutionary past lie several factors that can make parental investment worthwhile from the point of view of the male's genes.[5] In other words, because of these factors, genes inclining a male to love his offspring—to worry about them, defend them, provide for them, educate them—could flourish at the expense of genes that counseled continued remoteness.

One factor is the vulnerability of offspring. Following the generic male sexual strategy—roaming around, seducing and abandoning everything in sight—won't do a male's genes much good if the resulting offspring get eaten. That seems to be one reason so many bird species are monogamous, or at least relatively monogamous. Eggs left alone while the mother went out and hunted worms wouldn't last long. When our ancestors moved from the forests out onto the savanna, they had to cope with fleet predators. And this was hardly the only new danger to the young. As the species got smarter and its posture more upright, female anatomy faced a paradox: walking upright implied a narrow pelvis, and thus a narrow birth canal, but the heads of babies were larger than ever. This is presumably why human infants are born prematurely in comparison to other primates. From early on, baby chimps can cling to their mother while she walks around, her hands unencumbered. Human babies, though, seriously compromise a mother's food gathering. For many months, they're mounds of helpless flesh: tiger bait.

Meanwhile, as the genetic payoff of male investment was growing, the cost of investment was dropping. Hunting seems to have figured heavily in our evolution. With men securing handy, dense packages of protein, feeding a family was practical. It is probably no coincidence that monogamy is more common among carnivorous mammals than among vegetarians.

On top of all of this, as the human brain got bigger, it probably depended more on early cultural programming. Children with two parents may have had an educational edge over children with only one.

Characteristically, natural selection appears to have taken this cost-benefit calculus and transmuted it into feeling—in particular, the sensation of love. And not just love for the *child;* the first step toward becoming a solid parental unit is for the man and woman to develop a strong mutual attraction. The genetic payoff of having two parents devoted to a child's welfare is the reason men and women can fall into swoons over one another, including swoons of great duration.

Until recently, this claim was heresy. "Romantic love" was thought to be an invention of Western culture; there were reports of cultures in which choice of mate had nothing to do with affection, and sex carried no emotional weight. But lately anthropologists mindful of the Darwinian logic behind attachment have taken a second look, and such reports are falling into doubt.[6] Love between man and woman appears to have an innate basis. In this sense, the "pair-bonding" hypothesis stands supported, though not for all the reasons Desmond Morris imagined.

At the same time, the term *pair bonding*—and for that matter, the term *love*—conveys a sense of permanence and symmetry that, as any casual observer of our species can see, is not always warranted. To fully appreciate how large is the gap between idealized love and the version of love natural to people, we need to do what Trivers did in his 1972 paper: focus not on the emotion itself, but on the abstract evolutionary logic it embodies. What are the respective genetic interests of males and females in a species with internal fertilization, an extended period of gestation, prolonged infant dependence on mother's milk, and fairly high male parental investment? Seeing these interests clearly is the only way to appreciate how evolution not only invented romantic love, but, from the beginning, corrupted it.

WHAT DO WOMEN WANT?

For a species low in male parental investment, the basic dynamic of courtship, as we've seen, is pretty simple: the male really wants sex; the female isn't so sure.[7] She may want time to (unconsciously) assess the quality of his genes, whether by inspecting him or by letting him battle with other males for her favor. She may also pause to weigh the chances that he carries disease. And she may try to extract a precopulation gift, taking advantage of the high demand for her eggs. This "nuptial offering"—which technically constitutes a tiny male parental investment, since it nourishes her and her eggs—is seen in a variety of species, ranging from primates to black-tipped hanging flies. (The female hanging fly insists on having a dead insect to eat during sex. If she finishes it before the male is finished, she may head off in search of another meal, leaving him high and dry. If she isn't so quick, the male may repossess the leftovers for subsequent dates.)[8] These various female concerns can usually be addressed fairly quickly; there's no reason for courtship to drag on for weeks.

But now throw high MPI into the equation—male investment not just at the time of sex, but extending up to and well beyond birth. Suddenly the female is concerned not only with the male's genetic investment, or with a free meal, but with what he'll bring to the offspring after it materializes. In 1989 the evolutionary psychologist David Buss published a pioneering study of mate preferences in thirty-seven cultures around the world. He found that in every culture, females placed more emphasis than males on a potential mate's financial prospects.[9]

That doesn't mean women have a specific, evolved preference for *wealthy* men. Most hunter-gatherer societies have very little in the way of accumulated resources and private property. Whether this accurately reflects the ancestral environment is controversial; hunter-gatherers have, over the last few millennia, been shoved off of rich land into marginal habitats and thus may not, in this respect, be representative of our ancestors. But if indeed all men in the ancestral environment were about equally affluent (that is, not very), women may be innately attuned not so much to a man's wealth as to his social status; among hunter-gatherers, status often translates into power—influence over the divvying up of resources, such as meat after a big kill. In modern societies, in any event, wealth, status, and power often go hand in hand, and seem to make an attractive package in the eyes of the average woman.

Ambition and industry also seem to strike many women as auspicious—and Buss found that this pattern, too, is broadly international.[10] Of course, ambition and industriousness are things a female might look for even in a low-MPI species, as indices of genetic quality. Not so, however, for her assessment of the male's *willingness* to invest. A female in a high-MPI species may seek signs of generosity, trustworthiness, and, especially, an enduring commitment to her in particular. It is a truism that flowers and other tokens of affection are more prized by women than by men.

Why should women be so suspicious of men? After all, aren't males in a high-MPI species designed to settle down, buy a house, and mow the lawn every weekend? Here arises the first problem with terms like *love* and *pair bonding*. Males in high-MPI species are, paradoxically, capable of greater treachery than males in low-MPI species. For the "optimal male course," as Trivers noted, is a "mixed strategy."[11] Even if long-term investment is their main aim, seduction and abandonment can make genetic sense, provided it doesn't take too much, in time and other resources, from the offspring in which the male *does* invest. The bastard youngsters may thrive even without paternal investment; they may, for that matter, attract investment from some poor sap who is under the impression that they're his. So males in a high-MPI species should, in theory, be ever alert for opportunistic sex.

Of course, so should males in a low-MPI species. But this doesn't amount to exploitation, since the female has no chance of getting much more from another male. In a high-MPI species, she does, and a failure to get it from any male can be quite costly.

The result of these conflicting aims—the female aversion to exploitation, the male affinity for exploiting—is an evolutionary arms race. Natural selection may favor males that are good at deceiving females about their future devotion and favor females that are good at spotting deception; and the better one side gets, the better the other side gets. It's a vicious spiral of treachery and wariness—even if, in a sufficiently subtle species, it may assume the form of soft kisses, murmured endearments, and ingenuous demurrals.

At least it's a vicious spiral *in theory*. Moving beyond all this theoretical speculation and into the realm of concrete evidence— actually glimpsing the seamy underside of kisses and endearments—

is tricky. Evolutionary psychologists have made only meager progress. True, one study found that males, markedly more than females, report depicting themselves as more kind, sincere, and trustworthy than they actually are.[12] But that sort of false advertising may be only half the story, and the other half is much harder to get at. As Trivers didn't note in his 1972 paper, but did note four years later, one effective way to deceive someone is to believe what you're saying. In this context, that means being blinded by love—to feel deep affection for a woman who, after a few months of sex, may grow markedly less adorable.[13] This, indeed, is the great moral escape hatch for men who persist in a pattern of elaborate seduction and crisp, if anguished, abandonment. "I loved her at the time," they can movingly recall, if pressed on the matter.

This isn't to say that a man's affections are chronically delusional, that every swoon is tactical self-deception. Sometimes men *do* make good on their vows of eternal devotion. Besides, in one sense, an out-and-out lie is impossible. There's no way of knowing in mid-swoon, either at the conscious or unconscious level, what the future holds. Maybe some more genetically auspicious mate will show up three years from now; then again, maybe the man will suffer some grave misfortune that renders him unmarketable, turning his spouse into his only reproductive hope. But, in the face of uncertainty as to how much commitment lies ahead, natural selection would likely err on the side of exaggeration, so long as it makes sex more likely and doesn't bring counterbalancing costs.

There probably would have been *some* such costs in the intimate social environment of our evolution. Leaving town, or at least village, wasn't a simple matter back then, so blatantly false promises might quickly catch up with a man—in the form of lowered credibility or even shortened life span; the anthropological archives contain stories about men who take vengeance on behalf of a betrayed sister or daughter.[14]

Also, the supply of potentially betrayable women wasn't nearly what it is in the modern world. As Donald Symons has noted, in the average hunter-gatherer society, every man who can snare a wife does, and virtually every woman is married by the time she's fertile. There probably was no thriving singles scene in the ancestral environment, except one involving adolescent girls during the fruitless phase between first menstruation and fertility. Symons believes that the lifestyle of the modern philandering bachelor—seducing and abandoning available women year after year after year, without making any of them targets for ongoing investment—is not a distinct, evolved sexual strategy. It is just what happens when you take the male mind, with its preference for varied sex partners, and put it in a big city replete with contraceptive technology.

Still, even if the ancestral environment wasn't full of single women sitting alone after one-night stands muttering "Men are scum," there were reasons to guard against males who exaggerate commitment. Divorce can happen in hunter-gatherer societies; men do up and leave after fathering a child or two, and may even move to another village. And polygamy is often an option. A man may vow that his bride will stay at the center of his life, and then, once married, spend half his time trying to woo another wife—or, worse still, succeed, and divert resources away from his first wife's children. Given such prospects, a woman's genes would be well served by her early and careful scrutiny of a man's likely devotion. In any event, the gauging of a man's commitment does seem to be part of human female psychology; and male psychology does seem inclined to sometimes encourage a false reading.

That male commitment is in limited supply—that each man has only so much time and energy to invest in offspring—is one reason females in our species defy stereotypes prevalent elsewhere in the animal kingdom. Females in *low*-MPI species—that is, in most sexual species—have no great rivalry with one another. Even if dozens of them have their hearts set on a single, genetically optimal male, he can, and gladly will, fulfill their dreams; copulation doesn't take long. But in a high-MPI species such as ours, where a female's ideal is to *monopolize* her dream mate—steer his social and material resources toward her offspring—competition with other females is inevitable. In other words: high male parental investment makes sexual selection work in two directions at once. Not only have males evolved to compete for scarce female eggs; females have evolved to compete for scarce male investment.

Sexual selection, to be sure, seems to have been more intense among men than among women. And it has favored different sorts of traits in the two. After all, the things women do to gain investment from men are different from the things men do to gain sexual access to women. (Women aren't—to take the most obvious example— designed for physical combat with each other, as men are.) The point is simply that, whatever each sex must do to get what it wants from the other, both sexes should be inclined to do it with zest. Females in a high-MPI species will hardly be passive and guileless. And they will sometimes be the natural enemies of one another.

WHAT DO MEN WANT?

It would be misleading to say that males in a high-male-parental-investment species are selective about mates, but in theory they are at least *selectively* selective. They will, on the one hand, have sex with just about anything that moves, given an easy chance, like males in a low-MPI species. On the other hand, when it comes to finding a female for a long-term joint venture, discretion makes sense; males can undertake only so many ventures over a lifetime, so the genes that the partner brings to the project—genes for robustness, brains, whatever—are worth scrutinizing.

The distinction was nicely drawn by a study in which both men and women were asked about the minimal level of intelligence they would accept in a person they were "dating." The average response, for both male and female, was: average intelligence. They were also asked how smart a person would have to be before they would con-sent to sexual relations. The women said: Oh, in that case, markedly *above* average. The men said: Oh, in that case, markedly *below* average.[15]

Otherwise, the responses of male and female moved in lockstep. A partner they were "steadily dating" would have to be much smarter than average, and a marriageable partner would have to be smarter still. This finding, published in 1990, confirmed a prediction Trivers had made in his 1972 paper on parental investment. In a high-MPI species, he wrote, "a male would be selected to differentiate between a female he will only impregnate and a female with whom he will also raise young. Toward the former he should be more eager for sex and less discriminating in choice of sex partner than the female toward him, but toward the latter he should be about as discriminating as she toward him."[16]

As Trivers knew, the nature of the discrimination, if not its intensity, should still differ between male and female. Though both seek general genetic quality, tastes may in other ways diverge. Just as women have special reason to focus on a man's ability to provide resources, men have special reason to focus on the ability to produce babies. That means, among other things, caring greatly about the age of a potential mate, since fertility declines until menopause, when it falls off abruptly. The last thing evolutionary psychologists would expect to find is that a plainly postmenopausal woman is sexually attractive to the average man. They don't find it. (According to Bronislaw Malinowski, Trobriand Islanders considered sex with an old woman "indecorous, ludicrous, and unaesthetic.")[17] Even before menopause, age matters, especially in a long-term mate; the younger a woman, the more children she can bear. In every one of Buss's thirty-seven cultures, males preferred younger mates (and females preferred older mates).

The importance of youth in a female mate may help explain the extreme male concern with physical attractiveness in a spouse (a concern that Buss also documented in all thirty-seven cultures). The generic "beautiful woman"—yes, she has actually been assembled, in a study that collated the seemingly diverse tastes of different men—has large eyes and a small nose. Since her eyes will look smaller and her nose larger as she ages, these components of "beauty" are also marks of youth, and thus of fertility.[18] Women can afford to be more open-minded about looks; an oldish man, unlike an oldish woman, is probably fertile.

Another reason for the relative flexibility of females on the question of facial attractiveness may be that a woman has other things to (consciously or unconsciously) worry about. Such as: Will he provide for the kids? When people see a beautiful woman with an ugly man, they typically assume he has lots of money or status. Researchers have actually gone to the trouble of showing that people make this inference, and that the inference is often correct.[19]

When it comes to assessing character—to figuring out if you can *trust* a mate—a male's discernment may again differ from a female's, because the kind of treachery that threatens his genes is different from the kind that threatens hers. Whereas the woman's natural fear is the withdrawal of his investment, his natural fear is that the investment is misplaced. Not long for this world are the genes of a man who spends his time rearing children who aren't his. Trivers noted in 1972 that, in a species with high male parental investment and internal fertilization, "adaptations should evolve to help guarantee that the female's offspring are also his own."[20]

All of this may sound highly theoretical—and of course it is. But this theory, unlike the theory about male love sometimes being finely crafted self-delusion, is readily tested. Years after Trivers suggested that anticuckoldry technology might be built into men, Martin Daly and Margo Wilson found some. They realized that if indeed a man's great Darwinian peril is cuckoldry, and a woman's is desertion, then male and female jealousy should differ.[21] Male jealousy should focus on *sexual* infidelity, and males should be quite unforgiving of it; a female, though she'll hardly applaud a partner's extracurricular activities, since they consume time and divert resources, should be more concerned with *emotional* infidelity—the sort of magnetic commitment to another woman that could eventually lead to a much larger diversion of resources.

These predictions have been confirmed—by eons of folk wisdom and, over the past few decades, by considerable data. What drives men craziest is the thought of their mate in bed with another man; they don't dwell as much as women do on any attendant emotional attachment, or the possible loss of the mate's time and attention. Wives, for their part, do find the sheerly sexual infidelity of husbands traumatic, and do respond harshly to it, but the long-run effect is often a self-improvement campaign: lose weight, wear makeup, "win him back." Husbands tend to respond to infidelity with rage; and even after it subsides, they often have trouble contemplating a continued relationship with the infidel.[22]

Looking back, Daly and Wilson saw that this basic pattern had been recorded (though not stressed) by psychologists before the theory of parental investment came along to explain it. But evolutionary psychologists have now confirmed the pattern in new and excruciating detail. David Buss placed electrodes on men and women and had them envision their mates doing various disturbing things. When men imagined sexual infidelity, their heart rates took leaps of a magnitude typically induced by three successive cups of coffee. They sweated. Their brows wrinkled. When they imagined instead a budding emotional attachment, they calmed down, though not quite to their normal level. For women, things were reversed: envisioning *emotional* infidelity—redirected love, not supplementary sex—brought the deeper physiological distress.[23]

The logic behind male jealousy isn't what it used to be. These days some adulterous women use contraception and thus don't, in fact, dupe their husbands into spending two decades shepherding another man's genes. But the weakening of the logic doesn't seem to have weakened the jealousy. For the average husband, the fact that his wife inserted a diaphragm before copulating with her tennis instructor will not be a major source of consolation.

The classic example of an adaptation that has outlived its logic is the sweet tooth. Our fondness for sweetness was designed for an environment in which fruit existed but candy didn't. Now that a sweet tooth can bring obesity, people try to control their cravings, and sometimes they succeed. But their methods are usually roundabout, and few people find them easy; the basic sense that sweetness feels good is almost unalterable (except by, say, repeatedly pairing a sweet taste with a painful shock). Similarly, the basic impulse toward jealousy is very hard to erase. Still, people can muster some control over the impulse, and, moreover, can muster much control over some forms of its expression, such as violence, given a sufficiently powerful reason. Prison, for example.

WHAT ELSE DO WOMEN WANT?

Before further exploring the grave imprint that cuckoldry has left on the male psyche, we might ask why it would exist. Why would a woman cheat on a man, if that won't increase the number of her progeny—and if, moreover, she thus risks incurring the wrath, and losing the investment, of her mate? What reward could justify such a gamble? There are more possible answers to this question than you might imagine.

First, there is what biologists call "resource extraction." If female humans, like female hanging flies, can get gifts in exchange for sex, then the more sex partners, the more gifts. Our closest primate relatives act out this logic. Female bonobos are often willing to provide sex in exchange for a hunk of meat. Among common chimpanzees, the food-for-sex swap is less explicit but is evident; male chimps are more likely to give meat to a female when she exhibits the red vaginal swelling that signifies ovulation.[24]

Human females, of course, *don't* advertise their ovulation. One theory about this "cryptic ovulation" sees it as an adaptation designed to expand the period during which they can extract resources. Men may lavish gifts on them well before or past ovulation and receive sex in return, blissfully oblivious to the fruitlessness of their conquest. Nisa, a woman in a !Kung San hunter-gatherer village, spoke candidly with an anthropologist about the material rewards of multiple sex partners. "One man can give you very little. One man gives you only one kind of food to eat. But when you have lovers, one brings you something and another brings you something else. One comes at night with meat, another with money, another with beads. Your husband also does things and gives them to you."[25]

Another reason women might copulate with more than one man—and another advantage of concealed ovulation—is to leave several men under the impression that they *might* be the father of particular offspring. Across primate species, there is a rough correlation between a male's kindness to youngsters and the chances that he is their father. The dominant male gorilla, with his celestial sexual stature, can rest pretty much assured that the youngsters in his troop are his; and, although not demonstrative by comparison with a human father, he is indulgent of them and reliably protective. At the other end of the spectrum, male langur monkeys kill infants sired by others as a kind of sexual icebreaker, a prelude to pairing up with the (former) mother.[26] What better way to return her to ovulation—by putting an emphatic end to her breast-feeding—and to focus her energies on the offspring to come?

Anyone tempted to launch into a sweeping indictment of langur morality should first note that infanticide on grounds of infidelity has been acceptable in various human societies. In two societies men have been known to demand, upon marrying women with a past, that their babies be killed.[27] And among the Ache hunter-gatherers of Paraguay, men sometimes collectively decide to kill a newly fatherless child. Even leaving murder aside, life can be hard on children without a devoted father. Ache children raised by stepfathers after their biological fathers die are half as likely to live to age fifteen as children whose parents stay alive and together.[28] For a woman in the ancestral environment, then, the benefits of multiple sex partners could have ranged from their not killing her youngster to their defending or otherwise aiding her youngster.

This logic doesn't depend on the sex partners' consciously mulling it over. Male gorillas and langurs, like the Trobriand Islanders as depicted by Malinowski, are not conscious of biological paternity. Still, the behavior of males in all three cases reflects an implicit recognition. Genes making males unconsciously sensitive to cues that certain youngsters may or may not be carrying their genes have flourished. A gene that says, or at least whispers, "Be nice to children if you've had a fair amount of sex with their mothers" will do better than a gene that says, "Steal food from children even if you were having regular sex with their mothers months before birth."

This "seeds of confusion" theory of female promiscuity has been championed by the anthropologist Sarah Blaffer Hrdy. Hrdy has described herself as a feminist sociobiologist, and she may take a more than scientific interest in arguing that female primates tend to be "highly competitive . . . sexually assertive individuals."[29] Then again, male Darwinians may get a certain thrill from saying males are built for lifelong sex-a-thons. Scientific theories spring from many sources. The only question in the end is whether they work.

Both of these theories of female promiscuity—"resource extraction" and "seeds of confusion"—could in principle apply to a mateless woman as well as a married one. Indeed, both would make sense for a species with little or no male parental investment, and thus may help explain the extreme promiscuity of female chimpanzees and bonobos. But there is a third theory that grows uniquely out of the dynamics of male parental investment, and thus has special application to wives: the "best of both worlds" theory.

In a high-MPI species, the female seeks two things: good genes and high ongoing investment. She may not find them in the same package. One solution would be to trick a devoted but not especially brawny or brainy mate into raising the offspring of another male. Again, cryptic ovulation would come in handy, as a treachery facilitator. It's fairly easy for a man to keep rivals from impregnating his mate if her brief phase of fertility is plainly visible; but if she appears equally fertile all month, surveillance becomes a problem. This is exactly the confusion a female would want to create if her goal is to draw investment from one man and genes from another.[30] Of course, the female may not consciously "want" this "goal." And she may not be consciously aware of when she's ovulating. But at some level she may be keeping track.

Theories involving so much subconscious subterfuge may sound too clever by half, especially to people not steeped in the cynical logic of natural selection. But there is some evidence that women are more sexually active around ovulation.[31] And two studies have found that women going to a singles bar wear more jewelry and makeup when near ovulation.[32] These adornments, it seems, have the advertising value of a chimpanzee's pink genital swelling, attracting a number of men for the woman to choose from. And these decked-out women did indeed tend to have more physical contact with men in the course of the evening.

Another study, by the British biologists R. Robin Baker and Mark Bellis, found that women who cheat on their mates are more likely to do so around ovulation. This suggests that often the secret lover's genes, not just his resources, are indeed what they're after.[33]

Whatever the reason(s) women cheat on their mates (or, as biologists value-neutrally put it, have "extra-pair copulations"), there's no denying that they do. Blood tests show that in some urban areas more than one fourth of the children may be sired by someone other than the father of record. And even in a !Kung San village, which, like the ancestral environment, is so intimate as to make covert liaison tricky, one in fifty children was found to have misassigned paternity.[34] Female infidelity appears to have a long history.

Indeed, if female infidelity *weren't* a long-standing part of life in this species, why would distinctively maniacal male jealousy have evolved? At the same time, that men so often invest heavily in the children of their mates suggests that cuckoldry hasn't been rampant;

if it had, genes encouraging this investment would long ago have run into a dead end.[35] The minds of men are an evolutionary record of the past behavior of women. And vice versa.

If a "psychological" record seems too vague, consider a more plainly physiological bit of data: human testicles—or, more exactly, the ratio of average testes weight to average male body weight. Chimpanzees and other species with high relative testes weights have "multimale breeding systems," in which females are quite promiscuous.[36] Species with low relative testes weights are either monogamous (gibbons, for example) or polygynous (gorillas), with one male monopolizing several families. (*Polygamous* is the more general term, denoting a male *or* a female that has more than one mate.) The explanation is simple. When females commonly breed with many different males, male genes can profit by producing lots of semen for their transportation. Which male gets his DNA into a given egg may be a question of sheer volume, as competing hordes of sperm do subterranean battle. A species' testicles are thus a record of its females' sexual adventure over the ages. In our species, relative testes weight falls between that of the chimpanzee and the gorilla, suggesting that women, while not nearly as wild as chimpanzee females, are, by nature, somewhat adventurous.

Of course, adventurous doesn't mean unfaithful. Maybe women in the ancestral environment had their wild, unattached periods— during which fairly weighty testicles paid off for men—as well as their devoted, monogamous periods. Then again, maybe not. Consider a truer record of female infidelity: variable sperm density. You might think that the number of sperm cells in a husband's ejaculate would depend only on how long it's been since he last had sex. Wrong. According to work by Baker and Bellis, the quantity of sperm depends heavily on the amount of time a man's mate has been out of his sight lately.[37] The more chances a woman has had to collect sperm from other males, the more profusely her mate sends in his own troops. Again: that natural selection designed such a clever weapon is evidence of something for the weapon to combat.

It is also evidence that natural selection is fully capable of designing equally clever psychological weapons, ranging from furious jealousy to the seemingly paradoxical tendency of some men to be sexually aroused by the thought of their mate in bed with another man. Or, more generally: the tendency of men to view women as possessions. In a 1992 paper called "The Man Who Mistook His Wife for a Chattel," Wilson and Daly wrote that "men lay claim to particular women as songbirds lay claim to territories, as lions lay claim to a kill, or as people of both sexes lay claim to valuables. . . . [R]eferring to man's view of woman as 'proprietary' is more than a metaphor: Some of the same mental algorithms are apparently activated in the marital and mercantile spheres."[38]

The theoretical upshot of all this is another evolutionary arms race. As men grow more attuned to the threat of cuckoldry, women should get better at convincing a man that their adoration borders on awe, their fidelity on the saintly. And they may partly convince themselves too, just for good measure. Indeed, given the calamitous fallout from infidelity uncovered—likely desertion by the offended male, and possible violence—female self-deception may be finely honed. It could be adaptive for a married woman to not *feel* chronically concerned with sex, even if her unconscious mind is keeping track of prospects and will notify her when ardor is warranted.

THE MADONNA-WHORE DICHOTOMY

Anticuckoldry technology could come in handy not just when a man has a mate, but earlier, in choosing her. If available females differ in their promiscuity, and if the more promiscuous ones tend to make less faithful wives, natural selection might incline men to discriminate accordingly. Promiscuous women would be welcome as short-term sex partners—indeed, preferable, in some ways, since they can be had with less effort. But they would make poor wife material, a dubious conduit for male parental investment.

What emotional mechanisms—what complex of attractions and aversions—would natural selection use to get males to uncomprehendingly follow this logic? As Donald Symons has noted, one candidate is the famed Madonna-whore dichotomy, the tendency of men to think in terms of "two kinds of women"—the kind they respect and the kind they just sleep with.[39]

One can imagine courtship as, among other things, a process of placing a woman in one category or the other. The test would run roughly as follows. If you find a woman who appears genetically suitable for investment, start spending lots of time with her. If she seems quite taken by you, and yet remains sexually aloof, stick with her. If, on the other hand, she seems eager for sex right away, then by all means oblige her. But if the sex does come that easily, you might want to shift from investment mode into exploitation mode. Her eagerness could mean she'll always be an easy seduction—not a desirable quality in a wife.

Of course, in the case of any particular woman, sexual eagerness may *not* mean she'll always be an easy seduction; maybe she just finds this one man irresistible. But if there is any general correlation between the speed with which a woman succumbs to a man and her likelihood of later cheating on him, then that speed is a statistically valid cue to a matter of great genetic consequence. Faced with the complexity and frequent unpredictability of human behavior, natural selection plays the odds.

Just to add a trifle more ruthlessness to this strategy: the male may actually *encourage* the early sex for which he will ultimately punish the woman. What better way to check for the sort of self-restraint that is so precious in a woman whose children you may invest in? And, if self-restraint proves lacking, what faster way to get the wild oats sown before moving on to worthier terrain?

In its extreme, pathological form—the Madonna-whore *complex*—this dichotomization of women leaves a man unable to have sex with his wife, so holy does she seem. Obviously, this degree of worship isn't likely to have been favored by natural selection. But the more common, more moderate version of the Madonna-whore distinction has the earmarks of an efficient adaptation. It leads men to shower worshipful devotion on the sexually reserved women they want to invest in—exactly the sort of devotion these women will demand before allowing sex. And it lets men guiltlessly exploit the women they don't want to invest in, by consigning them to a category that merits contempt. This general category—the category of reduced, sometimes almost subhuman, moral status—is, as we'll see, a favorite tool of natural selection's; it is put to especially effective use during wars.

In polite company, men sometimes deny that they think differently of a woman who has slept with them casually. And wisely so. To admit that they do would sound morally reactionary. (Even to admit as much to themselves might make it hard to earnestly assure such a woman that they'll still respect her in the morning—sometimes a vital part of foreplay.)

As many modern wives can attest, sleeping with a man early in courtship doesn't doom the prospect of long-term commitment. A man's (largely unconscious) assessment of a woman's likely fidelity presumably involves many things—her reputation, how she looks at other men, how honest she seems generally. And anyway, even in theory the male mind shouldn't be designed to make virginity a prerequisite for investment. The chances of finding a virgin wife vary from man to man and from culture to culture—and to judge by some hunter-gatherer societies, they would have been quite low in the ancestral environment. Presumably males are designed to do the best they can under the circumstances. Though in prudish Victorian England some men may have insisted on virgin wives, the term *Madonnawhore dichotomy* is actually a misnomer for what is surely a more flexible mental tendency.[40]

Still, the flexibility is bounded. There is some level of female promiscuity above which male parental investment plainly makes no genetic sense. If a woman seems to have an unbreakable habit of sleeping with a different man each week, the fact that all women in that culture do the same thing doesn't make her any more logical a spouse. In such a society, men should in theory give up entirely on concentrated parental investment and focus solely on trying to mate with as many women as possible. That is, they should act like chimpanzees.

VICTORIAN SAMOANS

The Madonna-whore dichotomy has long been dismissed as an aberration, another pathological product of Western culture. In particular, the Victorians, with their extraordinary emphasis on virginity and their professed disdain for illicit sex, are held responsible for nourishing, even inventing, the pathology. If only men in Darwin's day had been more relaxed about sex, like the men in non-Western, sexually liberated societies. How different things would be now!

The trouble is, those idyllic, non-Western societies seem to have existed only in the minds of a few misguided, if influential, academics. The classic example is Margaret Mead, one of several prominent anthropologists who early this century reacted to the political misuses of Darwinism by stressing the malleability of the human species and asserting the near absence of human nature. Mead's best-known book, *Coming of Age in Samoa,* created a sensation upon its appearance in 1928. She seemed to have found a culture nearly devoid of many Western evils: status hierarchies, intense competition, and all kinds of needless anxieties about sex. Here in Samoa, Mead wrote, girls postpone marriage "through as many years of casual love-making as possible." Romantic love "as it occurs in our civilisation," bound up with ideas of "exclusiveness, jealousy and undeviating fidelity," simply "does not occur in Samoa."[41] What a wonderful place!

It is hard to exaggerate the influence of Mead's findings on twentieth-century thought. Claims about human nature are always precarious, vulnerable to the discovery of even a single culture in which its elements are fundamentally lacking. For much of this century, such claims have been ritually met with a single question: "What about Samoa?"

In 1983 the anthropologist Derek Freeman published a book called *Margaret Mead and Samoa: The Making and Unmaking of an Anthropological Myth.* Freeman had spent nearly six years in Samoa (Mead had spent nine months, and hadn't spoken the language when she arrived), and was well versed in accounts of its earlier history, before Western contact had much changed it. His book left Mead's reputation as a great anthropologist in serious disarray. He depicted her as a naïf, a twenty-three-year-old idealist who went to Samoa steeped in fashionable cultural determinism, chose not to live among the natives, and then, dependent for her data on scheduled interviews, was duped by Samoan girls who made a game of misleading her. Freeman assaulted Mead's data broadly—the supposed dearth of status competition, the simple bliss of Samoan adolescence—but for present purposes what matters is the sex: the purportedly minor significance of jealousy and male possessiveness, the seeming indifference of men to the Madonna-whore dichotomy.

Actually, on close examination, Mead's point-by-point findings turn out to be less radical than her glossy, well-publicized generalizations. She conceded that Samoan males took a certain pride in the conquest of a virgin. She also noted that each tribe had a ceremonial virgin—a girl of good breeding, often a chief's daughter, who was carefully guarded until, upon marriage, she was manually deflowered, with the blood from her hymen proving her purity. But this girl, Mead insisted, was an aberration, "excepted" from the "free and easy experimentation" that was the norm. Parents of lower rank "complacently ignore" their daughters' sexual experimentation.[42] Mead granted, almost under her breath, that a virginity test was "theoretically" performed "at weddings of people of all ranks," but she dismissed the ceremony as easily and often evaded.

Freeman raised the volume of Mead's more hushed observations and pointed out some things she had failed entirely to note. The value of virgins was so great in the eyes of marriageable men, he wrote, that an adolescent female of any social rank was monitored by her brothers, who would "upbraid, and sometimes beat" her if they found her with "a boy suspected of having designs on her virginity." As for the suspected boy, he was "liable to be assaulted with great ferocity." Young men who fared poorly in the mating game sometimes secured a mate by sneaking in at night, forcibly deflowering a woman, and then threatening to disclose her corruption unless she agreed to marriage (perhaps in the form of elopement, the surest way to avoid a virginity test). A woman found on her wedding day not to be a virgin was publicly denounced with a term meaning, roughly, "whore." In Samoan lore, one deflowered woman is described as a "wanton woman, like an empty shell exposed by the ebbing tide!" A song performed at defloration ceremonies went like this: "All others have failed to achieve entry, all others have failed to achieve entry. . . . He is first by being foremost, being first he is foremost; O to be foremost!"[43] These are not the hallmarks of a sexually liberated culture.

It now appears that some of the supposed Western aberrations that Mead found lacking in Samoa had if anything been *suppressed* by Western influence. Missionaries, Freeman noted, had made virginity testing less public—performed in a house, behind a screen. In "former days," as Mead herself wrote, if the tribe's ceremonial virgin was found at her wedding to be less than virginal, "her female relatives fell upon and beat her with stones, disfiguring and sometimes fatally injuring the girl who had shamed their house."[44]

So too with the Samoan jealousy that, Mead stressed, was so muted by Western standards: Westerners may have done the muting. Mead noted that a husband who caught his wife in adultery might be appeased by a harmless ritual that, as she depicted it, would end in an air of bonhomie. The male offender would bring men of his family, sit outside the victimized husband's house in supplication, offering finery in recompense, until forgiveness was forthcoming and everyone buried the hatchet over dinner. Of course, "in olden days," Mead observed, the offended man might "take a club and together with his relatives go out and kill those who sit without."[45]

That violence became less frequent under Christian influence is, of course, a testament to human malleability. But if we are ever to fathom the complex parameters of that malleability, we must be clear about which is the core disposition and which is the modifying influence. Time and again, Mead, along with her whole cohort of mid-twentieth-century cultural determinists, got things backwards.

Darwinism helps set the record straight. A new generation of Darwinian anthropologists is combing old ethnographies and conducting new field studies, finding things past anthropologists didn't stress, or even notice. Many candidates for "human nature" are emerging. And one of the more viable is the Madonna-whore dichotomy. In exotic cultures from Samoa to Mangaia to the land of the Ache in South America, a reputation for extreme promiscuity is something men actively avoid in a long-term mate.[46] And an analysis of folklore reveals the "good girl/bad girl" polarity to be a chronically recurring image—in the Far East, in Islamic states, in Europe, even in pre-Columbian America.[47]

Meanwhile, in the psychology laboratory, David Buss has found evidence that men do dichotomize between short-term and long-term mates. Cues suggesting promiscuity (a low-cut dress, perhaps, or aggressive body language) make a woman more attractive as a short-term mate and less attractive as a long-term mate. Cues suggesting a lack of sexual experience work the other way around.[48]

For now, the hypothesis that the Madonna-whore dichotomy has at least some inherent basis rests on strong theoretical expectation and considerable, though hardly exhaustive, anthropological and psychological evidence. There is also, of course, the testimony of experienced mothers from many eras who have warned their daughters what will happen if a man gets the impression that they're "that kind of girl": he won't "respect" them anymore.

FAST AND SLOW WOMEN

The Madonna-whore distinction is a dichotomy imposed on a continuum. In real life, women aren't either "fast" or "slow"; they are promiscuous to various degrees, ranging from not at all to quite. So the question of why some women are of one type and others of the other has no meaning. But there is meaning in the question of why women are nearer one end of the spectrum than the other—why women differ in their general degree of sexual reserve. And for that matter, what about men? Why do some men seem capable of unswerving monogamy, and others so inclined to depart from that ideal to various degrees? Is this difference—between Madonnas and whores, between dads and cads—in the genes? The answer is a definite yes. But the only reason the answer is definite is that the phrase "in the genes" is so ambiguous as to be essentially meaningless.

Let's start with the popular conception of "in the genes." Are some women, from the moment their father's sperm meets their mother's egg, all but destined to be Madonnas, while others are almost certain to be whores? Are some men equally bound to be cads, and others dads?

For both men and women, the answer is: unlikely, but not impossible. As a rule, two extremely different alternative traits will not both be preserved by natural selection. One or the other is usually at least slightly more conducive to genetic proliferation. However marginal its edge, it should win out, given enough time.[49] That's why almost all of the genes in you are also in the average inhabitant of any land in the world. But there is something called "frequency-dependent" selection, in which the value of a trait declines as it becomes more common, so that natural selection places a ceiling on its predominance, thus leaving room for the alternative.

Consider the bluegill sunfish.[50] The average bluegill male grows up, builds a bunch of nests, waits for females to lay eggs, then fertilizes the eggs and guards them. He is an upstanding member of the community. But he may have as many as 150 nests to tend, a fact that leaves him vulnerable to a second, less responsible kind of male, a drifter. The drifter sneaks around, surreptitiously fertilizes eggs, and then darts off, leaving them to be tended by their duped custodian. At a certain stage in life, drifters even don the color and behavior of females to mask their covert operations.

You can see how the balance between drifters and their victims is maintained. The drifters must do fairly well in reproductive terms; otherwise they wouldn't be around. But as this success makes their fraction of the population grow, the success itself diminishes, because the relative supply of upstanding, exploitable males—the drifters' meal ticket—shrinks. This is a situation in which success is its own punishment. The more drifters there are, the fewer offspring per drifter there are.

In theory, the drifter fraction of the population should grow until the average drifter is having as many offspring as the average upstanding bluegill. At that point, any shift in the fraction—growth or shrinkage—will change the value of the two strategies in a way that tends to reverse the shift. This equilibrium is known as an "evolutionarily stable" state, a term coined by the British biologist John Maynard Smith, who, during the 1970s, fully developed the idea of frequency-dependent selection.[51] Bluegill drifters, presumably, long ago reached their evolutionarily stable fraction of the population, which seems to be about one fifth.

The dynamics of sexual treachery are different for humans than for bluegill sunfish, in part because of the mammalian penchant for internal fertilization. But Richard Dawkins has shown, with an abstract analysis applicable to our species, that Maynard Smith's logic can, in principle, fit us too. In other words: one can imagine a situation in which neither coy nor fast women, and neither cads nor dads, have a monopoly on the ideal strategy. Rather, the success of each strategy varies with the prevalence of the three other strategies, and the population tends toward equilibrium. For example, with one set of assumptions, Dawkins found that five-sixths of the females would be coy, and five-eighths of the males would be faithful.[52]

Now, having comprehended this fact, you are advised to forget it. Don't just forget the fractions themselves, which, obviously, grow out of arbitrary assumptions within a highly artificial model. Forget the whole idea that each individual would be firmly bound to one strategy or the other.

As Maynard Smith and Dawkins have noted, evolution equilibrates to an equally stable state if you assume that the magic proportions are found *within* individuals—that is, if each female is coy on five-sixths of her mating opportunities, and each male is coy on five-eighths of his. And that's true even if the fractions are *randomly* realized—if each person just rolls dice on each encounter to decide what to do. Imagine how much more effective it is for the person to ponder each situation (consciously or unconsciously) and make an informed guess as to which strategy is more propitious under the circumstances.

Or imagine a different kind of flexibility: a developmental program that, during childhood, assesses the local social environment and then, by adulthood, inclines the person toward the strategy more likely to pay off. To put this in bluegill terms: imagine a male that during its early years checks out the local environment, calculates the prevalence of exploitable, upstanding males, and *then* decides—or, at least, "decides"—whether to become a drifter. This plasticity should eventually dominate the population, pushing the two more rigid strategies into oblivion.

The moral of the story is that limberness, given the opportunity, usually wins out over stiffness. In fact, limberness seems to have won a partial victory even in the bluegill sunfish, which isn't exactly known for its highly developed cerebral cortex. Though some genes incline a male bluegill to one strategy, and others to the other, the inclination isn't complete; the male absorbs local data before "deciding" which strategy to adopt.[53] Obviously, when you move from fish to us, the likely extent of flexibility grows. We have huge brains whose whole reason for being is deft adjustment to variable conditions. Given the many things about a person's social environment that can alter the value of being a Madonna versus a whore, a cad versus a dad— including the way other people react to the person's particular assets and liabilities—natural selection would be uncharacteristically obtuse not to favor genes that build brains sensitive to these things.

So too in many other realms. The value of being a given "type" of person—cooperative, say, or stingy—has depended, during evolution, on things that vary from time to time, place to place, person to person. Genes that irrevocably committed our ancestors to one personality type should in theory have lost out to genes that let the personality solidify gracefully.

This is not a matter of consensus. There are in the literature a few articles with titles like "The Evolution of the 'Con Artist.' "[54] And, to return to the realm of Madonnas and whores, there is a theory that some women are innately inclined to pursue a "sexy son" strategy: they mate promiscuously with sexually attractive men (handsome, brainy, brawny, and so on), risking the high male parental investment they might extract if more Madonnaish but gaining the likelihood that any sons will be, like their fathers, attractive and therefore prolific. Such theories are interesting, but they all face the same obstacle: with con artists as with promiscuous women, however effective the strategy, it is even more effective when flexible—when it can be abandoned amid signs of likely failure.[55] And the human brain is a pretty flexible thing.

To stress this flexibility isn't to say that all people are born psychologically identical, that all differences in personality emerge from environment. There plainly are important genetic differences for such traits as nervousness and extroversion. The "heritability" of these traits is around .4; that is, about 40 percent of individual differences in these traits can be explained by genetic differences. (By comparison, the heritability of height is around .9; about 10 percent of the difference in height among individuals is due to nutritional and other environmental differences.) The question is *why* the undoubtedly important genetic variation in personality exists. Do different degrees of genetic disposition toward extroversion represent different personality "types," each of which has stabilized after a very elaborate process of frequency-dependent selection? (Though frequency dependence is classically analyzed in terms of two or three distinct strategies, it could also yield a more finely graded array.) Or are the differing genetic dispositions just "noise"—some incidental by-product of evolution, not specifically favored by natural selection? No one knows, and evolutionary psychologists differ in their suspicions.[56] What they agree on is that a big part of the story of personality differences is the evolution of malleability, what they call "developmental plasticity."

This emphasis on psychological development doesn't leave us back where social scientists were twenty-five years ago, attributing everything they saw to often unspecified "environmental forces." A primary—perhaps *the* primary—promise of evolutionary psychology is to help specify the forces, to generate good theories of personality development. In other words: evolutionary psychology can help us see not only the "knobs" of human nature, but also how the knobs are tuned. It not only shows us that (and why) men in all cultures are quite attracted to sexual variety, but can suggest what circumstances make some men more obsessed with it than others; it not only shows us that (and why) women in all cultures are more sexually reserved, but promises to help us figure out how some women come to defy this stereotype.

A good example lies in Robert Trivers's 1972 paper on parental investment. Trivers noted two patterns that social scientists had already uncovered: (1) the more attractive an adolescent girl, the more likely she is to "marry up"—marry a man of higher socioeconomic status; and (2) the more sexually active an adolescent girl, the less likely she is to marry up.

To begin with, these two patterns make Darwinian sense independently. A wealthy, high-status male often has a broad range of aspiring wives to choose from. So he tends to choose a good-looking woman who is also relatively Madonnaish. Trivers took the analysis further. Is it possible, he asked, "that females adjust their reproductive strategies in adolescence to their own assets"?[57] In other words, maybe adolescent girls who get early social feedback affirming their beauty make the most of it, becoming sexually reserved and thus encouraging long-term investment by high-status males who are looking for pretty Madonnas. Less attractive women, with less chance to hit the jackpot via sexual reserve, become more promiscuous, extracting small chunks of resources from a series of males. Though this promiscuity may somewhat lower their values as wives, it wouldn't, in the ancestral environment, have doomed their chances of finding a husband. In the average hunter-gatherer society, almost any fertile woman can find a husband, even if he's far from ideal, or she has to share him with another woman.

DARWINISM AND PUBLIC POLICY

The Trivers scenario doesn't imply a *conscious* decision by attractive women to guard their jewels (though that may play a role, and, what's more, parents may be genetically inclined to encourage a daughter's sexual reserve with special force when she is pretty). By the same token, we aren't necessarily talking about unattractive women who "realize" they can't be choosy and start having sex on less than ideal Darwinian terms. The mechanism at work might well be subconscious, a gradual molding of sexual strategy—read: "moral values"—by adolescent experience.

Theories like this one matter. There has been much talk about the problem of unwed motherhood among teenagers, especially poor teenagers. But no one really knows how sexual habits get shaped, or how firmly fixed they then are. There is much talk about boosting "self-esteem," but little understanding of what self-esteem is, what it's for, or what it does.

Evolutionary psychology can't yet confidently provide the missing basis for these discussions. But the problem isn't a shortage of plausible theories; it's a shortage of studies to test the theories. The Trivers theory has sat in limbo for two decades. In 1992, one psychologist did find what the theory predicts—a correlation between a woman's self-perception and her sexual habits: the less attractive she thinks she is, the more sex partners she has had. But another scholar didn't find the predicted correlation—and, more to the point, *neither* study was conducted specifically to test Trivers's theory, of which both scholars were unaware.[58] For now, this is the state of evolutionary psychology: so much fertile terrain, so few farmers.

Eventually, the main drift of Trivers's theory, if not the theory itself, will likely be vindicated. That is: women's sexual strategies probably depend on the likely (genetic) profitability of each strategy, given prevailing circumstances. But those circumstances go beyond what Trivers stressed—a particular woman's desirability. Another factor is the general availability of male parental investment. This factor surely fluctuated in the ancestral environment. For example, a village that had just invaded a neighboring village might have a suddenly elevated ratio of women to men—not just because of male casualties, but because victorious warriors commonly kill or vanquish enemy men and keep their women.[59] Overnight, a young woman's prospects for receiving a man's undivided investment could thus plummet. Famine, or sudden abundance, might also alter investment patterns. Given these currents of change, any genes that helped women navigate them would, in theory, have flourished.

There is tentative evidence that they did. According to a study by the anthropologist Elizabeth Cashdan, women who perceive men in general as pursuing no-obligation sex are more likely to wear provocative clothes and have sex often than women who see men as generally willing to invest in offspring.[60] Though some of these women may be conscious of the connection between local conditions and their lifestyle, that isn't necessary. Women surrounded by men who are unwilling or unable to serve as devoted fathers may simply feel a deepened attraction to sex without commitment—feel, in other words, a relaxation of "moral" constraint. And perhaps if market conditions suddenly improve—if the male to female ratio rises, or if men for some other reason shift toward a high-investment strategy—women's sexual attractions, and moral sensibilities, shift accordingly.

All of this is necessarily speculative at this early stage in evolutionary psychology's growth. But already we can see the sort of light that will increasingly be shed. For example, "self-esteem" almost

g onto male parental investment drops. There are plenty of middle-
ed women who, especially if they're financially secure, can take or
ave their husbands. Still, there is no Darwinian force *driving* them
leave their husbands, nothing about leaving him that will sharply
dvance their genetic interests. The thing most likely to drive a post-
enopausal woman out of a marriage is her husband's malicious
arital discontent. Many a woman seeks divorce, but that doesn't
ean *her* genes are ultimately the problem.

Among all the data on contemporary marriage, two items stand
ut as especially telling. First is the 1992 study which found that the
usband's dissatisfaction with a marriage is the single strongest predictor of divorce.[66] Second is that men are much more likely than
women to remarry after a divorce.[67] The second fact—and the biological force behind the second fact—is probably a good part of the
reason for the first.

Objections to this sort of analysis are predictable: "But people
leave marriages for *emotional* reasons. They don't add up the number
of their children and pull out their calculators. Men are driven away
by dull, nagging wives, or by the profound soul-searching of a midlife crisis. Women are driven out by abusive or indifferent husbands,
or lured away by a sensitive, caring man."

All true. But, again: emotions are just evolution's executioners.
Beneath all the thoughts and feelings and temperamental differences
that marriage counselors spend their time sensitively assessing are the
stratagems of the genes—cold, hard equations composed of simple
variables: social status, age of spouse, number of children, their ages,
outside opportunities, and so on. Is the wife *really* duller and more
nagging than she was twenty years ago? Possibly, but it's also possible
that the husband's tolerance for nagging has dropped now that she's
forty-five and has no reproductive future. And the promotion he just
got, which has already drawn some admiring glances from a young
woman at work, hasn't helped. Similarly, we might ask the young
childless wife who finds her husband intolerably insensitive why the
insensitivity wasn't so oppressive a year ago, before he lost his job
and she met the kindly, affluent bachelor who seems to be flirting
with her. Of course, maybe her husband's abuses are quite real, in
which case they signal his disaffection, and perhaps his impending

certainly isn't the same, either in its sources or in its effects, for boys
and girls. For teenage girls, feedback reflecting great beauty may, as
Trivers suggested, bring high self-esteem, which in turn encourages
sexual restraint. For boys, extremely high self-esteem could well have
the opposite effect: it may lead them to seek with particular intensity
the short-term sexual conquests that are, in fact, more open to a good-
looking, high-status male. In many high schools, a handsome, star
athlete is referred to, only half-jokingly, as a "stud." And, for those
who insist on scientific verification of the obvious: good-looking
men do have more sex partners than the average man.[61] (Women
report putting more emphasis on a sex partner's looks when they
don't expect the relationship to last; they are apparently willing,
unconsciously, to trade off parental investment for good genes.)[62]

Once a high-self-esteem male is married, he may not be notable
for his devotion. Presumably his various assets still make philandering
a viable lifestyle, even if it's now covert. (And you never know when
an outside escapade will take on a life of its own, and lead to desertion.) Men with more moderate self-esteem may make more committed, if otherwise less desirable, husbands. With fewer chances at
extramarital dalliance, and perhaps more insecurity about their own
mate's fidelity, they may focus their energy and attention toward
family. Meanwhile, men with *extremely* low self-esteem, given continued frustration with women, may eventually resort to rape. There
is ongoing debate within evolutionary psychology over whether rape
is an adaptation, a designed strategy that any boy might grow up to
adopt, given sufficiently discouraging feedback from his social environment. Certainly rape surfaces in a wide variety of cultures, and
often under the expected circumstances: when men have had trouble
finding attractive women by legitimate means. One (non-Darwinian)
study found the typical rapist to possess "deep-seated doubts about
his adequacy and competency as a person. He lacks a sense of confidence in himself as a man in both sexual and nonsexual areas."[63]

A second sort of light shed by the new Darwinian paradigm may
illuminate links between poverty and sexual morality. Women living
in an environment where few men have the ability and/or desire to
support a family might naturally grow amenable to sex without commitment. (Often in history—including Victorian England—women

in the "lower classes" have had a reputation for loose morals.)[64] It is too soon to assert this confidently, or to infer that inner-city sexual mores would change markedly if income levels did. But it is noteworthy, at least, that evolutionary psychology, with its emphasis on the role of environment, may wind up highlighting the social costs of poverty, and thus at times lend strength to liberal policy prescriptions, defying old stereotypes of Darwinism as right-wing.

Of course, one could argue that various policy implications ensue from any given theory. And one can dream up wholly different kinds of Darwinian theories about how sexual strategies get shaped.[65] The one thing one *can't* do, I submit, is argue that evolutionary psychology is irrelevant to the whole discussion. The idea that natural selection, acutely attentive to the most subtle elements of design in the lowliest animals, should build huge, exquisitely pliable brains and not make them highly sensitive to environmental cues regarding sex, status, and various other things known to figure centrally in our reproductive prospects—that idea is literally incredible. If we want to know when and how a person's character begins to assume distinct shape, if we want to know how resistant to change the character will subsequently be, we have to look to Darwin. We don't yet know the answers, but we know where they'll come from, and that knowledge helps us phrase the questions more sharply.

THE FAMILY THAT STAYS TOGETHER

Much of the attention paid to the "short-term" sexual strategies of women—whether unattached women willing to settle for a one-night stand, or attached women sneaking out on a mate—is fairly recent. Sociobiological discussion during the 1970s, at least in its popular form, tended to depict men as wild, libidinous creatures who roamed the landscape looking for women to dupe and exploit; women were often depicted as dupes and exploitees. The shift in focus is due largely to the growing number of female Darwinian social scientists, who have patiently explained to their male colleagues how a woman's psyche looks from the inside.

Even after this restoration of balance, there remains one important sense in which men and women will tend to be, respectively, exploiter

and exploited. As a marriage progresses, the tempt... should—in the *average* case—shift toward the man. T... as people sometimes assume, that the Darwinian c... breakup are greater for the woman. True, if she has ... and her marriage dissolves, that child may suffer—wh... she can't find a husband willing to commit to a woman... man's child, or because she finds one who neglects or... child. But, in Darwinian terms, this cost is borne eq... deserting husband; the child who will thus suffer is h... after all.

The big difference between men and women comes ... the *benefits* side of the desertion ledger. What can each ... from a breakup in the way of future reproductive payof... band can, in principle, find an eighteen-year-old woman w... five years of reproduction ahead. The wife—even asid... trouble she'll have finding a husband if she already has ... cannot possibly find a mate who will give her twenty-five y... of reproductive potential. This difference in outside oppo... negligible at first, when both husband and wife are youn... they age, it grows.

Circumstance can subdue or heighten it. A poor, low-st... band may not have a chance to desert and may, indeed, pr... wife with reason to desert, especially if she has no children... thus find another mate readily. A husband who rises in st... wealth, on the other hand, will thus strengthen his incentive t... while weakening his wife's. But all other things being equal, ... husband's restlessness that will tend to grow as the years pa...

All this talk of "desertion" may be misleading. Though ... is available in many hunter-gatherer cultures, so is polygyny;... ancestral environment, gaining a second wife didn't necessarily ... leaving the first. And so long as it didn't, there was no good... winian reason to desert. Staying near offspring, giving protectio... guidance, would have made more genetic sense. Thus, males m... designed less for opportune desertion than for opportune polyg... But in the modern environment, with institutionalized monog... a polygynous impulse will find other outlets, such as divorce. ...

As a mother's children grow self-sufficient, the urgency of h...

departure—and merit just the sort of preemptive strike the wife is now mustering.

Once you start seeing everyday feelings and thoughts as genetic weapons, marital spats take on new meaning. Even the ones that aren't momentous enough to bring divorce are seen as incremental renegotiations of contract. The husband who on his honeymoon said he didn't want an "old-fashioned wife" now sarcastically suggests that it wouldn't be too taxing for her to cook dinner once in a while. The threat is as clear as it is implicit: I'm willing and able to break the contract if you're not willing to renegotiate.

PAIR BONDS REVISITED

All told, things are not looking good for Desmond Morris's version of the pair-bond hypothesis. We do not seem to be too much like our famously, just about unswervingly, monogamous primate relatives, the gibbons, to which we have been optimistically compared. This should come as no great surprise. Gibbons aren't very social. Each family lives on a large home range—sometimes more than a hundred acres—that buffers it from extramarital dalliances. And gibbons chase off any intruders that might want to steal or borrow a mate.[68] We, by contrast, have evolved in large social groups that are rife with genetically profitable alternatives to fidelity.

We do have, to be sure, the earmarks of high male parental investment. For hundreds of thousands of years, and maybe longer, natural selection has been inclining males to love their children, thus giving them a feeling females had been enjoying for the previous several hundred million years of mammalian evolution. Natural selection has also, during that time, been inclining men and women to love each other (or, at least, to "love" each other, with the meaning of that word varying greatly, and seldom approaching the constancy of devotion it reaches between parent and offspring). Still, love or no love, gibbons we aren't.

So what *are* we? Just how far from being naturally monogamous is our species? Biologists often answer this question anatomically. We've already seen anatomical evidence—testes weight and the fluctuations in sperm density—suggesting that human females are not devoutly monogamous by nature. There is also anatomical evidence bearing on the question of precisely how far from monogamous males naturally are. As Darwin noted, in highly polygynous species the contrast in body size between male and female—the "sexual dimorphism"—is great. Some males monopolize several females, while other males get shut out of the genetic sweepstakes altogether, so there is immense evolutionary value in being a big male, capable of intimidating other males. Male gorillas, who mate with lots of females if they win lots of fights and no females if they win none, are gargantuan—twice as heavy as females. Among the monogamous gibbons, small males breed about as prolifically as bigger ones, and sexual dimorphism is almost imperceptible. The upshot is that sexual dimorphism is a good index of the intensity of sexual selection among males, which in turn reflects how polygynous a species is. When placed on the spectrum of sexual dimorphism, humans get a "mildly polygynous" rating.[69] We're much less dimorphic than gorillas, a bit less than chimps, and markedly more than gibbons.

One problem with this logic is that competition among human, and even prehuman, males has been largely mental. Men don't have the long canine teeth that male chimps use to fight for alpha rank and thus supreme mating rights. But men do employ various stratagems to raise their social status, and thus their attractiveness. So some, and maybe much, of the polygyny in our evolutionary past would be reflected not in gross physiology but in distinctively male mental traits. If anything, the less than dramatic difference in size between men and women paints an overly flattering picture of men's monogamous tendencies.[70]

How have societies over the years coped with the basic sexual asymmetry in human nature? Asymmetrically. A huge majority—980 of the 1,154 past or present societies for which anthropologists have data—have permitted a man to have more than one wife.[71] And that number includes most of the world's hunter-gatherer societies, societies that are the closest thing we have to a living example of the context of human evolution.

The more zealous champions of the pair-bond thesis have been known to minimize this fact. Desmond Morris, hell-bent on proving the natural monogamy of our species, insisted in *The Naked Ape* that the only societies worth paying much attention to are modern industrial societies, which, coincidentally, fall into the 15 percent of societies that have been avowedly monogamous. "[A]ny society that has failed to advance has in some sense failed, 'gone wrong,' " he wrote. "Something has happened to it to hold it back, something that is working against the natural tendencies of the species. . . . " So "the small, backward, and unsuccessful societies can largely be ignored." In sum, said Morris (who was writing back when Western divorce rates were about half what they are now): "whatever obscure, backward tribal units are doing today, the mainstream of our species expresses its pair-bonding character in its most extreme form, namely long-term monogamous matings."[72]

Well, that's one way to get rid of unsightly, inconvenient data: declare them aberrant, even though they vastly outnumber the "mainstream" data.

Actually, there *is* a sense in which polygynous marriage has not been the historical norm. For 43 percent of the 980 polygynous cultures, polygyny is classified as "occasional." And even where it is "common," multiple wives are generally reserved for a relatively few men who can afford them or qualify for them via formal rank. For eons and eons, most marriages have been monogamous, even though most societies haven't been.

Still, the anthropological record suggests that polygyny is natural in the sense that men given the opportunity to have more than one wife are strongly inclined to seize it. The record also suggests something else: that polygyny has its virtues as a way of handling the basic imbalance between what men and women want. In our culture, when a man whose wife has given him a few children grows restless and "falls in love" with a younger woman, we say: Okay, you can marry her, but we insist that you desert your first wife and that a stigma be placed on your kids and that, if you don't make much money, your kids and former wife suffer miserably. Some other cultures have tended to say: Okay, you can marry her, but only if you can really afford a second family; and you can't desert your first family, and there won't be any stigma placed on your kids.

Maybe some of today's nominally monogamous societies, those in which half of all marriages actually fail, should just go whole hog. Maybe we should fully erase the already fading stigma of divorce.

Maybe we should simply make sure that men who stray from their families remain legally responsible for them, and keep supporting them in the manner to which they had become accustomed. Maybe we should, in short, permit polygyny. A lot of presently divorced women, and their children, might be better off.

The only way to intelligently address this option is to first ask a simple question (one that turns out to have a counterintuitive answer): How did a strict cultural insistence on monogamy, which seems to go against the grain of human nature, and several millennia ago was almost unheard of, ever come to be?

Chapter 4: **THE MARRIAGE MARKET**

It is hardly possible to read Mr. M'Lennan's work and not admit that almost all civilised nations still retain some traces of such rude habits as the forcible capture of wives. What ancient nation, as the same author asks, can be named that was originally monogamous?

—The Descent of Man (1871)[1]

Something about the world doesn't seem to make sense. On the one hand, it is run mostly by men. On the other hand, in most parts of it, polygamy is illegal. If men really are the sort of animals described in the two previous chapters, why did they let this happen?

Sometimes this paradox gets explained away as a compromise between the male and female natures. In an old-fashioned, Victorian-style marriage, men get routine subservience in exchange for keeping their wanderlust more or less under control. The wives cook, clean, take orders, and put up with all the unpleasant aspects of a regular male presence. In return, the husbands graciously agree to stick around.

This theory, however appealing, is beside the point. Granted, within any monogamous marriage there is compromise. And within any two-man prison cell there is compromise. But that doesn't mean prisons were invented by a compromise among criminals. Compromise between men and women is the way monogamy endures (when it does), but it's no explanation of how monogamy got here.

The first step toward answering the "Why monogamy" question is to understand that, for some monogamous societies on the anthropological record—including many hunter-gatherer cultures—the question isn't all that perplexing. These societies have hovered right around the subsistence level. In such a society, where little is stowed away for a rainy day, a man who stretches his resources between two families may end up with few or no surviving children. And even if he were willing to gamble on a second family, he'd have trouble attracting a second wife. Why should she settle for half of a poor man if she can have all of one? Out of love? But how often will love malfunction so badly? Its very purpose, remember, is to attract her to men who will be good for her progeny. Besides, why should her family—and in preindustrial societies families often shape a bride's "choice" forcefully and pragmatically—tolerate such foolishness?

Roughly the same logic holds if a society is somewhat above the subsistence level but all men are about equally above it. A woman who chooses half a husband over a whole one is still settling for much less in the way of material well-being.

The general principle is that economic equality among men—especially, but not only, if near the subsistence level—tends to short-circuit polygyny. This tendency by itself dispels a good part of the monogamy mystery, for more than half of the known monogamous societies have been classified as "nonstratified" by anthropologists.[2] What really demand explanation are the six dozen societies in the history of the world, including the modern industrial nations, that have been monogamous yet economically stratified. These are true freaks of nature.

The paradox of monogamy amid uneven affluence has been stressed especially by Richard Alexander, one of the first biologists to broadly apply the new paradigm to human behavior. When monogamy is found in subsistence-level cultures, Alexander calls it "ecologically imposed." When it appears in more affluent, more stratified cultures, he calls it "socially imposed."[3] The question is why society imposed it.

The term *socially imposed* may offend some people's romantic ideals. It seems to imply that, in the absence of bigamy laws, women would flock toward money, gleefully signing on as second or third wife so long as there was enough of it to go around. Nor is the term *flock* used lightly here. There is a tendency for polygyny to occur in bird species whose males control territories of sharply differing quality or quantity. Some female birds are quite happy to share a male so long as he has a lot more real estate than any male they could have monopolized.[4] Most human females would like to think they are guided by a more ethereal sort of love, and that they have somewhat more pride than a long-billed marsh wren.

And of course they do. Even in polygynous cultures, women are often less than eager to share a man. But, typically, they would rather do that than live in poverty with the undivided attention of a ne'er-do-well. It is easy for well-educated, upper-class women to scoff at the idea that any self-respecting woman would willingly suffer the degradation of polygyny, or to deny that women place great emphasis on a husband's income. But upper-class women seldom even *meet* a man with a low income, much less face the prospect of marrying one. Their milieu is so economically homogeneous that they don't have to worry about finding a minimally adequate provider; they can refocus their search, and spend their time pondering a prospective mate's taste in music and literature. (And these tastes are themselves cues to a man's socioeconomic status. This is a reminder that the Darwinian evaluation of a mate needn't be *consciously* Darwinian.)

In favor of Alexander's belief that there's something artificial about highly stratified yet monogamous societies is the fact that polygyny tends to lurk stubbornly beneath their surface. Though being a mistress is even today considered at least mildly scandalous, a number of women seem to prefer that role to the alternative: a greater commitment from a man of lesser means—or, perhaps, a commitment from no man.

Since Alexander began stressing the two kinds of monogamous societies, his distinction has drawn a second, more subtle, kind of support. The anthropologists Steven J. C. Gaulin and James S. Boster have shown that dowry—a transfer of assets from the bride's to the groom's family—is found almost exclusively in societies with socially imposed monogamy. Thirty-seven percent of these stratified nonpolygynous societies have had dowry, whereas 2 percent of all nonstratified nonpolygynous societies have. (For polygynous societies the figure is around 1 percent.)[5] Or, to put it another way: although only 7 percent of societies on record have had socially imposed monogamy, they account for 77 percent of societies with a dowry tradition. This suggests that dowry is the product of a market disequilibrium, a blockage of marital commerce; monogamy, by limiting each man to a single wife, makes wealthy men artificially precious commodities, and dowry is the price paid for them. Presumably, if polygyny were legalized, the market would right itself more straightforwardly: males with the most money (and perhaps with the most charm and the ruggedest physiques and whatever else might partly outweigh considerations of wealth) would, rather than fetch large dowries, have multiple wives.

WINNERS AND LOSERS

If we adopt this way of looking at things—if we abandon a Western ethnocentric perspective and hypothetically accept the Darwinian view that men (consciously or unconsciously) want as many sex-providing and child-making machines as they can comfortably afford, and women (consciously or unconsciously) want to maximize the resources available to their children—then we may have the key to explaining why monogamy is with us today: whereas a polygynous society is often depicted as something men would love and women would hate, there is really no natural consensus on the matter within either sex. Obviously, women who are married to a poor man and would rather have half of a rich one aren't well served by the institution of monogamy. And, obviously, the poor husband they would gladly desert wouldn't be well served by polygyny.

Nor are these superficially ironic preferences confined to people near the bottom of the income scale. Indeed, in sheerly Darwinian terms, *most* men are probably better off in a monogamous system and *most* women worse off. This is an important point, and warrants a brief illustrative detour.

Consider a crude and offensive but analytically useful model of the marital marketplace. One thousand men and one thousand women are ranked in terms of their desirability as mates. Okay, okay: there isn't, in real life, full agreement on such things. But there are clear patterns. Few women would prefer an unemployed and rudderless man to an ambitious and successful one, all other things being even roughly equal; and few men would choose an obese, unattractive, and dull woman over a shapely, beautiful, sharp one. For the sake of intellectual progress, let's simplemindedly collapse these and other aspects of attraction into a single dimension.

Suppose these 2,000 people live in a monogamous society and each woman is engaged to marry the man who shares her ranking. She'd like to marry a higher-ranking man, but they're all taken by competitors who outrank her. The men too would like to marry up, but for the same reason can't. Now, before any of these engaged couples gets married, let's legalize polygyny and magically banish its stigma. And let's suppose that at least one woman who is mildly more desirable than average—a quite attractive but not overly bright woman with a ranking of, say, 400—dumps her fiancé (male #400, a shoe salesman) and agrees to become the second wife of a successful lawyer (male #40). This isn't wildly implausible—forsaking a family income of around $40,000 a year, some of which she would have to earn herself by working part-time at a Pizza Hut, for maybe $100,000 a year and no job requirement (not to mention the fact that male #40 is a better dancer than male #400).[6]

Even this first trickle of polygynous upward mobility makes most women better off and most men worse off. All 600 women who ranked below the deserter move up one notch to fill the vacuum; they still get a husband all to themselves, and a better husband at that. Meanwhile 599 men wind up with a wife slightly inferior to their former fiancées—and one man now gets no wife at all. Granted: in real life, the women wouldn't move up in lockstep. Very early in the process, you'd find a woman who, pondering the various intangibles of attraction, would stand by her man. But in real life, you'd probably have more than a trickle of upward mobility in the first place. The basic point stands: many, many women, even many women *who will choose not to share a husband*, have their options expanded when all women are free to share a husband.[7] By the same token, many, many men can suffer at the hands of polygyny.

All told, then, institutionalized monogamy, though often viewed as a big victory for egalitarianism and for women, is emphatically not egalitarian in its effects on women. Polygyny would much more evenly distribute the assets of males among them. It is easy—and wise—for beautiful, vivacious wives of charming, athletic corporate titans to dismiss polygyny as a violation of the basic rights of women. But married women living in poverty—or women without a husband or child, and desirous of both—could be excused for wondering just which women's rights are protected by monogamy. The only under-privileged citizens who should favor monogamy are men. It is what gives them access to a supply of women that would otherwise drift up the social scale.

So neither gender, as a whole, belongs on either side of the im-aginary bargaining table that yielded the tradition of monogamy. Monogamy is neither a minus for men collectively nor a plus for women collectively; within both sexes, interests naturally collide. More plausibly, the grand, historic compromise was cut between more fortunate and less fortunate men. For them, the institution of monogamy does represent a genuine compromise: the most fortunate men still get the most desirable women, but they have to limit them-selves to one apiece. This explanation of monogamy—as a divvying up of sexual property among men—has the virtue of consistency with the fact that opened this chapter: namely, that it is men who usually control sheerly political power, and men who, historically, have cut most of the big political deals.

This is not to say, of course, that men ever sat down and ham-mered out the one-woman-per-man compromise. The idea, rather, is that polygyny has tended to disappear in response to egalitarian values—not values of equality between the sexes, but of equality among men. And maybe "egalitarian values" is too polite a way of putting it. As political power became distributed more evenly, the hoarding of women by upper-class men simply became untenable. Few things are more anxiety-producing for an elite governing class than gobs of sex-starved and childless men with at least a modicum of political power.

This thesis remains only a thesis.[8] But reality at least loosely fits it. Laura Betzig has shown that in preindustrial societies, extreme polygyny often goes hand in hand with extreme political hierarchy, and reaches its zenith under the most despotic regimes. (Among the Zulu, whose king might monopolize more than a hundred women, coughing, spitting, or sneezing at his dining table was punishable by death.) And the allocation of sexual resources by political status has often been fine-grained and explicit. In Inca society, the four political offices from petty chief to chief were allotted ceilings of seven, eight, fifteen, and thirty women, respectively.[9] It stands to reason that as political power became more widely disbursed, so did wives. And the ultimate widths are one-man-one-vote and one-man-one-wife. Both characterize most of today's industrialized nations.

Right or wrong, this theory of the origin of modern institutionalized monogamy is an example of what Darwinism has to offer historians. Darwinism does not, of course, explain history *as* evolution; natural selection doesn't work nearly fast enough to drive ongoing change at the level of culture and politics. But natural selection did shape the minds that *do* drive cultural and political change. And understanding how it shaped those minds may afford fresh insight into the forces of history. In 1985 the eminent social historian Lawrence Stone published an essay that stressed the epic significance of the early Christian emphasis on the fidelity of husbands and the permanence of marriage. After reviewing a couple of theories as to how this cultural innovation spread, he concluded that the answer "remains obscure."[10] Perhaps a Darwinian explanation—that, given human nature, monogamy is a straightforward expression of political equality among men—deserved at least a mention. It may be no accident that Christianity, which served as a vehicle for monogamy politically as well as intellectually, has often pitched its message to poor and powerless men.[11]

WHAT'S WRONG WITH POLYGYNY?

This Darwinian analysis of marriage complicates the choice between monogamy and polygyny. For it shows that the choice isn't between equality and inequality. The choice is between equality among men and equality among women. A tough call.

There are several conceivable reasons to vote for equality among men (that is, monogamy). One is to dodge the wrath of the various feminists who will not be convinced that polygyny liberates down-trodden women. Another is that monogamy is the only system that, theoretically at least, can provide a mate for just about everyone. But the most powerful reason is that leaving lots of men without wives and children is not just inegalitarian; it's dangerous.

The ultimate source of the danger is sexual selection among males. Men have long competed for access to the scarcer sexual resource, women. And the costs of losing the contest are so high (genetic oblivion) that natural selection has inclined them to compete with special ferocity. In all cultures, men wreak more violence, including murder, than women. (Indeed, across the animal kingdom, males are the more belligerent sex, *except* in those species, such as phalaropes, where male parental investment is so high females can reproduce more often than males.) Even when the violence isn't against a sexual rival, it often boils down to sexual competition. A trivial dustup may escalate until one man kills another to "save face"—to earn the sort of raw respect that, in the ancestral environment, could have raised status and brought sexual rewards.[12]

Fortunately, male violence can be dampened by circumstance. And one circumstance is a mate. We would expect womanless men to compete with special ferocity, and they do. An unmarried man between twenty-four and thirty-five years of age is about three times as likely to murder another male as is a married man the same age. Some of this difference no doubt reflects the kinds of men that do and don't get married to begin with, but Martin Daly and Margo Wilson have argued cogently that a good part of the difference may lie in "the pacifying effect of marriage."[13]

Murder isn't the only thing an "unpacified" man is more likely to do. He is also more likely to incur various risks—committing robbery, for example—to gain the resources that may attract women. He is more likely to rape. More diffusely, a high-risk, criminal life often entails the abuse of drugs and alcohol, which may then compound the problem by further diminishing his chances of ever earning enough money to attract women by legitimate means.[14]

This is perhaps the best argument for monogamous marriage, with its egalitarian effects on men: inequality among males is more socially destructive—in ways that harm women *and* men—than in-equality among women. A polygynous nation, in which large num-bers of low-income men remain mateless, is not the kind of country many of us would want to live in.

Unfortunately, this is the sort of country we already live in. The United States is no longer a nation of institutionalized monogamy. It is a nation of serial monogamy. And serial monogamy in some ways amounts to polygyny.[15] Johnny Carson, like many wealthy, high-status males, spent his career monopolizing long stretches of the reproductive years of a series of young women. Somewhere out there is a man who wanted a family and a beautiful wife and, if it hadn't been for Johnny Carson, would have married one of these women. And if this man has managed to find another woman, she was similarly snatched from the jaws of some other man. And so on—a domino effect: a scarcity of fertile females trickles down the social scale.

As abstractly theoretical as this sounds, it really can't help but happen. There are only about twenty-five years of fertility per woman. When some men dominate more than twenty-five years' worth of fertility, some man, somewhere, must do with less. And when, on top of all the serial husbands, you add the young men who live with a woman for five years before deciding not to marry her, and then do it again (perhaps finally, at age thirty-five, marrying a twenty-eight-year-old), the net effect could be significant. Whereas in 1960 the fraction of the population age forty or older that had never married was about the same for men and women, by 1990 the fraction was markedly larger for men than for women.[16]

It is not crazy to think that there are homeless alcoholics and rapists who, had they come of age in a pre-1960s social climate, amid more equally distributed female resources, would have early on found a wife and adopted a lower-risk, less destructive lifestyle. Anyway, you don't have to buy this illustration to buy the point itself: if polygyny would indeed have pernicious effects on society's less for-tunate men, and indirectly on the rest of us, then it isn't enough to just oppose legalized polygyny. (Legalized polygyny wasn't a loom-ing political threat last time I checked, anyway.) We have to worry about the de facto polygyny that already exists. We have to ask not whether monogamy can be saved, but whether it can be restored. And we might be enthusiastically joined in this inquiry not only by discontented wifeless men, but by a large number of discontented former wives—especially the ones who had the bad fortune to marry someone less wealthy than Johnny Carson.

DARWINISM AND MORAL IDEALS

This view of marriage is a textbook example of how Darwinism can and can't legitimately enter moral discourse. What it can't do is furnish us with basic moral values. Whether, for example, we want to live in an egalitarian society is a choice for us to make; natural selection's indifference to the suffering of the weak is not something we need emulate. Nor should we care whether murder, robbery, and rape are in some sense "natural." It is for us to decide how abhorrent we find such things and how hard we want to fight them.

But once we've made such choices, once we *have* moral ideals, Darwinism can help us figure out which social institutions best serve them. In this case, a Darwinian outlook shows the prevailing marital institution, serial monogamy, to be in many ways equivalent to polygyny. As such, this institution is seen to have inegalitarian effects on men, working against the disadvantaged. Darwinism also highlights the costs of this inequality—violence, theft, rape.

In this light, old moral debates assume a new cast. For example, the tendency of political conservatives to monopolize the argument for "family values" starts to look odd. Liberals, concerned about the destitute, and about the "root causes" of crime and poverty, might logically develop a certain fondness for "family values." For a drop in the divorce rate, by making more young women accessible to low-income men, might keep an appreciable number of men from falling into crime, drug addiction, and, sometimes, homelessness.

Of course, given the material opportunities that polygyny (even de facto polygyny) may afford poor women, one can also imagine a liberal argument *against* monogamy. One can even imagine a liberal *feminist* argument against monogamy. And, in any event, one can see that a Darwinian feminism will be a more complicated feminism.

Viewed in Darwinian terms, "women" are not a naturally coherent interest group; there is no single sisterhood.[17]

There is one other kind of fallout from current marital norms that comes into focus through the new paradigm: the toll taken on children. Martin Daly and Margo Wilson have written, "Perhaps the most obvious prediction from a Darwinian view of parental motives is this: Substitute parents will generally tend to care less profoundly for children than natural parents." Thus, "children reared by people other than their natural parents will be more often exploited and otherwise at risk. Parental investment is a precious resource, and selection must favor those parental psyches that do not squander it on nonrelatives."[18]

To some Darwinians, this expectation might seem so strong as to render its verification a waste of time. But Daly and Wilson took the trouble. What they found surprised even them. In America in 1976, a child living with one or more substitute parents was about one hundred times more likely to be fatally abused than a child living with natural parents. In a Canadian city in the 1980s, a child two years of age or younger was seventy times more likely to be killed by a parent if living with a stepparent and natural parent than if living with two natural parents. Of course, murdered children are a tiny fraction of the children living with stepparents; the divorce and re-marriage of a mother is hardly a child's death warrant. But consider the more common problem of nonfatal abuse. Children under ten were, depending on their age and the particular study in question, between three and forty times more likely to suffer parental abuse if living with a stepparent and a natural parent than if living with two natural parents.[19]

It is fair to infer that many less dramatic, undocumented forms of parental indifference follow this rough pattern. After all, the whole reason natural selection *invented* paternal love was to bestow benefits on offspring. Though biologists call these benefits "investment," that doesn't mean they're strictly material, wholly sustainable through monthly checks. Fathers give their children all kinds of tutelage and guidance (more, often, than either father or child realizes) and guard them against all kinds of threats. A mother alone simply can't pick up the slack. A stepfather almost surely won't pick up much, if any of it. In Darwinian terms, a young stepchild is an obstacle to fitness, a drain on resources.

There are ways to fool mother nature, to induce parents to love children that aren't theirs. (Hence cuckoldry.) After all, people can't telepathically sense that a child is carrying their genes. Instead, they rely on cues that, in the ancestral environment, would have signified as much. If a woman feeds and cuddles an infant day after day, she may grow to love the child, and so may a man who has been sleeping with her for years. This sort of bonding is what makes adopted children lovable and nannies loving. But both theory and casual observation suggest that, the older a child is when first seen by the substitute parent, the less likely deep attachment is. And a large majority of children who acquire stepfathers are past infancy.

One can imagine arguments among reasonable and humane people over whether a strongly monogamous society is better than a strongly polygynous one. But this much seems less controversial: whenever marital institutions—in either kind of society—are allowed to dissolve, so that divorce and unwed motherhood are rampant, and many children no longer live with both natural parents, there will ensue a massive waste of the most precious evolutionary resource: love. Whatever the relative merits of monogamy and polygyny, what we have now—serial monogamy, de facto polygyny—is, in an important sense, the worst of all worlds.

PURSUING MORAL IDEALS

Obviously, Darwinism won't always simplify moral and political debate. In this case, by stressing the tension between equality among men and among women, it actually complicates the question of which marital institutions best serve our ideals. Still, the tension was always there; at least now it's in the open, and debate can proceed in stronger light. Further, once we *have* decided, with help from the new paradigm, which institutions best serve our moral ideals, Darwinism can make its second kind of contribution to moral discourse: it can help us figure out what sorts of forces—which moral norms, which social policies—help nourish those institutions.

And here comes another irony in the "family values" debate: conservatives may be surprised to hear that one of the best ways to strengthen monogamous marriage is to more equally distribute income.[20] Young single women will feel less inclined to tempt husband A away from wife A if bachelor B has just as much money. And husband A, if he's not drawing flirtatious looks from young women, may feel more content with wife A, and less inclined to notice her wrinkles. This dynamic presumably helps explain why monogamous marriage has often taken root in societies with little economic stratification.

One standard conservative argument against antipoverty policies is their cost: taxes burden the affluent and, by reducing their incentive to work, lower overall economic output. But if one goal of the policy is to bolster monogamy, then making the affluent less affluent is a welcome side effect. Monogamy is threatened not just by poverty in an absolute sense but also by the relative wealth of the wealthy. That reducing this wealth cuts overall economic output may, of course, still be regrettable; but once we add more stable marriages to the benefits of income redistribution, the regret should lose a bit of its sting.

One might imagine that this whole analysis is steadily losing its relevance. After all, as more women enter the workforce, they can better afford to premise their marital decisions on something other than the man's income. But remember: we're dealing with women's deep romantic attractions, not just their conscious calculation, and these feelings were forged in a different environment. To judge by hunter-gatherer societies, males during human evolution controlled most of the material resources. And even in the poorest of these societies, where disparities in male wealth are hard to detect, a father's social status often translates subtly into advantages for offspring, material and otherwise, in ways that a mother's social status doesn't.[21] Though a modern woman can of course reflect on her wealth and her independently earned status, and try to gauge marital decisions accordingly, that doesn't mean she can easily override the deep aesthetic impulses that had such value in the ancestral environment. In fact, modern women manifestly do not override them. Evolutionary psychologists have shown that the tendency of women to place greater emphasis than men on a mate's financial prospects persists regardless of the income or expected income of the women in question.[22]

So long as a society remains economically stratified, the challenge of reconciling lifelong monogamy with human nature will be large. Incentives and disincentives (moral and/or legal) may be necessary. One way to see what sorts of incentives can work is to look at an economically stratified society where they worked. Say, for example, Victorian England. To search for the peculiarities of Victorian morality that helped marriages succeed (at least in the minimal sense of not dissolving) isn't to say we should adopt those peculiarities ourselves. One can see the "wisdom" of some moral tenet—see how it achieves certain goals by implicitly recognizing deep truths about human nature—without finding it, on balance, worth the side effects. But seeing the wisdom is still a good way to appreciate the contours of the challenge it met. Looking at a Victorian marriage—Charles and Emma Darwin's—from a Darwinian point of view is worth the effort.

Before we return to Darwin's life, one caution is in order. So far we've been analyzing the human mind in the abstract; we've talked about "species-typical" adaptations designed to maximize fitness. When we shift our focus from the whole species to any one individual, we should *not* expect that person to chronically maximize fitness, to optimally convey his or her genes to future generations. And the reason goes beyond the one that has so far been stressed: that most human beings don't live in an environment much like the one for which their minds were designed. Environments—even the environments for which organisms *are* designed—are unpredictable. That is why behavioral flexibility evolved in the first place. And unpredictability, by its nature, cannot be mastered. As John Tooby and Leda Cosmides have put it, "Natural selection cannot directly 'see' an individual organism in a specific situation and cause behavior to be adaptively tailored."[23]

The best that natural selection can do is give us adaptations— "mental organs" or "mental modules"—that play the odds. It can give males a "love of offspring" module, and make that module sensitive to the likelihood that the offspring in question is indeed the man's. But the adaptation cannot be foolproof. Natural selection can give women an "attracted to muscles" module, or an "attracted to status" module, and, what's more, it can make the strength of those attractions depend on all kinds of germane factors; but even a highly flexible module can't guarantee that these attractions translate into viable and prolific offspring.

As Tooby and Cosmides say, human beings aren't general purpose "fitness maximizers." They are "adaptation executers."[24] The adaptations may or may not bring good results in any given case, and success is especially spotty in environments other than a small hunter-gatherer village. So as we look at Charles Darwin, the question isn't: Can we conceive of things he could have done to have more viable, prolific offspring than he had? The question is: Is his behavior intelligible as the product of a mind that consists of a bundle of adaptations?

Chapter 5: **DARWIN'S MARRIAGE**

Like a child that has something it loves beyond measure, I long to dwell on the words my own *dear Emma.... My own dear Emma, I kiss the hands with all humbleness and gratitude, which have so filled up for me the cup of happiness ... but do dear Emma, remember life is short, and two months is the sixth part of the year.*

—Darwin in November 1838, in a letter to his fiancée, urging an early wedding

Sexual desire makes saliva to flow ... curious association.
—Darwin in his scientific notebook, same month, same year[1]

In the decade of Darwin's marriage, the 1830s, the number of British couples filing for divorce averaged four per year. This is in some ways a misleading statistic. It probably reflects, in part, the tendency of men back then to die before reaching the climax of their midlife crises. (A misnomer; often the wife's middle age, more than the man's, brings on the crisis.) And it certainly reflects the fact that getting a divorce required—literally—an act of Parliament. Marriages also ended in other ways, especially through privately arranged separations. Still, there's no denying that marriage back then was, by and large, for keeps, especially within Darwin's upper-middle-class social stratum. And marriage stayed that way for half a century after 1857, the year the Divorce Act made breaking up easier to do.[2] There was something about Victorian morality conducive to staying married.

There is no telling how much misery was generated in Victorian England by unhappy, unendable marriages. But it may well not exceed the misery generated by modern marital dissolution.[3] In any case, we do know of some Victorian marriages that seem to have been successful. Among these is the marriage of Charles and Emma Darwin. Their devotion was mutual and seems, if anything, to have strengthened with time. They created seven children who lived to adulthood, and none of them penned nasty memoirs about tyrannical parents ("Darwin Dearest"). Their daughter Henrietta called their marriage a "perfect union."[4] Their son Francis wrote of his father: "In his relationship towards my mother, his tender and sympathetic nature was shown in its most beautiful aspect. In her presence he found his happiness, and through her, his life,—which might have been overshadowed by gloom,—became one of content and quiet gladness."[5] Viewed from today, the marriage of Charles and Emma Darwin appears almost idyllic in its geniality, tranquility, and sheer durability.

DARWIN'S PROSPECTS

On the Victorian marriage market, Darwin must have been a fairly desirable commodity. He had a winning disposition, a respectable education, a family tradition that augured well for his career, and, in any event, his looming inheritance. He wasn't notably handsome, but so what? The Victorians were very clear about their division of aesthetic labor, and it was consistent with evolutionary psychology: good financial prospects made for an attractive husband, and good looks made for an attractive wife. In the large correspondence between Darwin and his sisters—while he was at college, or, later, on the *Beagle*—there is much talk of romance, as his sisters report gossip and relay any reconnaissance work they've done on his behalf. Almost invariably, men are gauged by their ability to provide materially for a woman, while women are seen as providing a pleasant visual and auditory environment for a man. Newly betrothed women, and the women who qualify as prospects for Charles, are "pretty" or "charming" or, at the very least, "pleasant." "I am sure you would like her," Charles's sister Catherine wrote of one candidate. "She is so very merry and pleasant, and I think very pretty." Newly betrothed men, on the other hand, are either of means or not of means. Susan Darwin wrote to her brother during his voyage: "Your charming Cousin Lucy Galton is engaged to marry Mr. Moilliet: the eldest son of a *very fat* Mrs. Moilliet. . . . The young Gentleman has a good fortune, so of course the match gives great satisfaction."[6]

The *Beagle*'s voyage lasted longer than expected, and Darwin wound up spending five years—the heart of his twenties—away from England. But, like undistinguished looks, advancing age was something men didn't have to worry greatly about. Women of Darwin's class often spent their early twenties on prominent display, hoping to catch a man while in their prime. Men often spent their twenties as Darwin did—singlemindedly pursuing the sort of professional stature (and/or money) that might later attract a woman in her prime. There was no rush. It was considered natural for a woman to marry a markedly older man, whereas a Victorian man who married a much older woman was cause for dismay. While Darwin was aboard the *Beagle*, his sister Catherine reported that cousin Robert Wedgwood, who was around Darwin's age, had "fallen vehemently and desperately in love with Miss Crewe, who is 50 years old, and blind of one eye." His sister Susan chimed in sarcastically, "just 20 years difference in their ages!" And sister Caroline: "a woman more than old enough to be his Mother." Catherine had a theory: "She is a clever woman, and must have entrapped him by her artifices; & she has the remains of great beauty to help her."[7] In other words: the man's age-detection system was functioning as designed, but he happened upon a woman whose enduring beauty—that is, youthful appearance—fooled it.

The realm within which the young Darwin was likely to find a mate was not vast. From adolescence on, the likely candidates came from two well-to-do families not far from the Darwin home in Shrewsbury. There was the ever-popular Fanny Owen—"the prettiest, plumpest, Charming" Fanny Owen, as Darwin described her during college.[8] And then there were the three youngest daughters of Josiah Wedgwood II, Darwin's maternal uncle: Charlotte, Fanny, and Emma.[9]

As of the *Beagle*'s departure, no one seems to have picked Emma as the frontrunner for Charles's affections—though his sister Caroline, in a letter sent to him around then, did note in passing that "Emma is looking very pretty & chats very pleasantly."[10] (What more could a man ask for?) As fate would have it, the other three candidates dropped out of the running in short order.

First to go was Emma's sister Charlotte. In January of 1832, she wrote Darwin to announce her unexpected engagement to a man who, she admitted, had "only a very small income now" but stood to inherit much upon his grandmother's death, and, anyway, had "high principles & kind nature which gives me a feeling of security. . . ."[11] (Translation: resources in the offing, and a reliable willingness to invest them parentally.) Charlotte had, in truth, probably been a dark horse as far as Charles was concerned. Though she had impressed both him and his brother Erasmus—they referred to her as "the incomparable"—she was more than a decade older than Charles; Erasmus was probably more smitten by her (as he seems to have been by a series of women, none of whom he managed to marry).

More unsettling than Charlotte's fate, probably, was the almost simultaneous news that the beguiling Fanny Owen was also to take the plunge. Fanny's father wrote to Charles of the news, plainly disappointed that the groom was "now not very rich & indeed probably never will be."[12] On the other hand, her husband was a man of status, serving briefly in Parliament.

Darwin, responding to all this matrimonial news in a letter to his sister Caroline, made no pretense of happiness. "Well it may be all very delightful to those concerned, but as I like unmarried women better than those in the blessed state, I vote it a bore."[13]

The vision that Darwin's sisters had of his future—becoming a country parson and settling down with a good wife—was not growing more likely as potential wives fell by the wayside. Catherine surveyed the remains, Emma and Fanny Wedgwood, and gave the nod to Fanny. She wrote to Charles that she hoped Fanny would still be single when he returned—"a nice little invaluable Wife she would be."[14] We'll never know. She fell ill and died within a month, at age twenty-six. With three of the four contenders either married or buried, the odds shifted decisively in Emma's favor.

If Charles had long-standing designs on Emma, he hid them well. He had predicted, as Catherine recalled, that upon his return he would find Erasmus "tied neck and heels to Emma Wedgwood, and heartily sick of her." In 1832, Catherine wrote to Charles that "I am much amused at your prophecy, and I think it may possibly have a good effect, and prevent its own fulfillment."[15] Erasmus continued to show interest in Emma, but she was still available when the *Beagle* returned to England in 1836. In fact, you might say she was emphatically available. She had been a carefree twenty-three when the *Beagle* set sail, and over the next couple of years had gotten several marriage proposals. But now she was a year and a half from thirty and spending much time at home caring for her invalid mother; she wasn't getting quite the exposure she had once gotten.[16] In preparation for Darwin's arrival, she wrote to her sister-in-law, she was reading a book on South America "to get up a little knowledge for him."[17]

There was cause to wonder whether "a little knowledge" would be enough to keep Charles's attention focused on childhood friends. Upon returning, he possessed something that women in all cultures and at all times seem to have prized in men: status. He had always had high social standing by virtue of his family's rank, but now he had a prominence all his own. From the *Beagle*, Darwin had sent back fossils, organic specimens, and acute observations on geology that had won a large scientific audience. He now rubbed elbows with the great naturalists of the day. By the spring of 1837, he had settled into London, in bachelor's quarters a few doors down from his brother Erasmus, and was in social demand.

A person of greater vanity and less certain purpose might have been drawn into a time-sapping social whirl—a corruption that the gregarious Erasmus would have been delighted to abet. Certainly Darwin was aware of his growing stature ("I was quite a lion there," he reported of a visit to Cambridge). But he was too measured and earnest a man to be a mingler by nature. As often as not, he saw fit to forgo large gatherings. He would, he told his mentor, Professor John Henslow, "prefer paying you a quiet visit to meeting all the world at a great Dinner." A note of demurral to Charles Babbage, the mathematician who designed the "analytical engine," forerunner of the digital computer, began, "My dear Mr. Babbage, I am very much obliged to you for sending me cards for your parties, but I am afraid of accepting them, for I should meet some people there, to whom I have sworn by all the saints in Heaven, I never go out. . . ."[18]

With the time thus saved, Darwin embarked on a remarkable burst of accomplishment. Within two years of his return to England, he: (1) edited his shipboard journal into a publishable volume (which reads nicely, sold well, and is today in print, further abridged, under the title *Voyage of the Beagle*); (2) skillfully extracted a thousand-pound subsidy from the Chancellor of the Exchequer for publication of *The Zoology of the Voyage of H.M.S. Beagle* and lined up contributors to it; (3) consolidated his place in British science by presenting half a dozen papers, ranging from a sketch of a new species of American ostrich (named *Rhea darwinii* by the Zoological Society of London) to a new theory about the formation of topsoil ("every particle of earth forming the bed from which the turf in old pasture land springs, has passed through the intestines of worms");[19] (4) went on a geological expedition to Scotland; (5) hobnobbed with eminences at the exclusive men's club the Athenaeum; (6) was elected secretary of the Geological Society of London (a post he accepted reluctantly, fearing its demand on his time); (7) compiled scientific notebooks—on subjects ranging from the "species question" to religion to human moral faculties—of such high intellectual density that they would serve as the basis for his largest works in the ensuing four decades; and (8) thought up the theory of natural selection.

CHOOSING MARRIAGE

It was toward the end of this phase—a few months before natural selection dawned on him—that Darwin decided to marry. Not necessarily anyone in particular; it isn't clear that he had Emma Wedgwood even remotely in mind, and one common view is that she wasn't at the center of his thinking on the subject. In a remarkable deliberative memorandum, apparently composed around July of 1838, he decided the matter of marriage in the abstract.

The document has two columns, one labeled *Marry*, one labeled *Not Marry*, and above them, circled, are the words "This is the Question." On the pro-marriage side of the equation were "Children—(if it Please God)—Constant companion, (&friend in old age) who will feel interested in one,—object to be beloved & played with."

After reflection of unknown length, he modified the foregoing sentence with "better than a dog anyhow." He continued: "Home, & someone to take care of house— Charms of music & female chitchat— These things good for one's health.— *but terrible loss of time.*" Without warning, Darwin had, from the pro-marriage column, swerved uncontrollably into a major anti-marriage factor, so major that he underlined it. This issue—the infringement of marriage on his time, especially his work time—was addressed at greater length in the appropriate, *Not Marry* column. Not marrying, he wrote, would preserve "Freedom to go where one like—choice of Society & *little of it.*—Conversation of clever men at clubs—not forced to visit relatives, & to bend in every trifle—to have the expense & anxiety of children—Perhaps quarelling—*Loss of time.*—cannot read in the Evenings—fatness & idleness—Anxiety & responsibility— less money for books &c—if many children forced to gain one's bread."

Yet the pro-marriage forces carried the day, with this train of thought at the end of the *Marry* column: "My God, it is intolerable to think of spending ones whole life, like a neuter bee, working, working, & nothing after all.—No, no won't do.—Imagine living all one's day solitarily in smoky dirty London House.—Only picture to yourself a nice soft wife on a sofa with good fire, & books & music perhaps." After recording these images he wrote: "Marry-Mary[sic]-Marry Q.E.D."

Darwin's decision had to survive one more wave of doubt. The backlash began innocently enough, as Darwin wrote, "It being proved necessary to Marry, When? Soon or Late." But this question incited that final spasm of panic with which many grooms are familiar. Brides are familiar with it too, of course, but their doubt seems more often to be whether their choice of a lifelong mate is the right one. For men, as Darwin's memo attests, the panic isn't essentially related to any particular prospective mate; it is the *concept* of a lifelong mate that is at some level frightening. For—in a monogamous society, at least—it dampens the prospects for intimacy with all those other women that a man's genes urge him to find and get to know (however briefly).

This isn't to say that the premarital panic fixes itself coarsely on images of would-be sex partners; the subconscious can be more subtle than that. Still, there is, somewhat reliably among men who are about to pledge themselves to one woman for life, a dread of impending entrapment, a sense that the days of adventure are over. "Eheu!!" Darwin wrote, with one final shudder in the face of lifelong commitment. "I never should know French,—or see the Continent—or go to America, or go up in a Balloon, or take solitary trip in Wales—poor slave—you will be worse than a negro." But then, fatefully, he mustered the necessary resolve. "Never mind my boy—Cheer up—One cannot live this solitary life, with groggy old age, friendless & cold, & childless staring one in ones face, already beginning to wrinkle.—Never mind, trust to chance—keep a sharp look out—There is many a happy slave—" End of document.[20]

CHOOSING EMMA

Darwin had written an earlier deliberative memorandum, probably in April, in which he rambled on about career paths—teach at Cambridge? in geology? in zoology? or "Work at transmission of Species"?—and pondered the marriage question inconclusively.[21] There is no way of knowing what drove him to reopen the question and this time settle it. But it's intriguing that, of the six entries made between April and July in his sporadically kept personal journal, two say he was feeling "unwell." Unwellness was to become a way of life for Darwin, a fact he may already have suspected. It is ironic that hints of mortality can draw a man into marriage, for often it is these same hints, much later, that drive him out, to seek fresh proof of his virility. But the irony dissolves when reduced to ultimate cause: both the impulses to profess lifelong love to a woman and to wander lie within a man by virtue of how often, in his ancestors, they led to progeny. In that sense, both are an apt antidote to mortality, though in the end futile (except from the genes' point of view), and, in the latter case—wandering—often destructive as well.

Anyway, on a less philosophical plane: Darwin may have sensed that he would before long need a devoted helpmate and nurse. And perhaps he even had a glimmer of spending many years working, in patient and needy solitude, on a big book about evolution. As Darwin's health had gotten worse, his grasp of that subject had gotten better. He opened his first notebook on "transmutation of Species" in June or July of 1837, and his second in early 1838.[22] By the time he was rigorously mulling marriage, he had gone some of the way toward natural selection. He believed that one key to evolution lay in initially slight hereditary difference; that when a species is divided into two populations by, say, a body of water, what are at first merely two variants of the species grow apart until they qualify as new and distinct species.[23] All that remained—the hard part—was to figure out what guided that divergence. In July of 1838, he finished his second species notebook and opened his third, the one that would bring him the answer. And he may, as he penned his fateful marriage memorandum that same month, have had a sense of impending success.

In late September, the solution came. Darwin had just read Thomas Malthus's famous essay on population, which noted that a human population's natural rate of growth will tend to outstrip the food supply unless checked. Darwin recalled in his autobiography: "[B]eing well prepared to appreciate the struggle for existence which everywhere goes on from long-continued observation of the habits of animals and plants, it at once struck me that under these circumstances favourable variations would tend to be preserved, and unfavourable ones to be destroyed. The result of this would be the formation of new species. Here, then, I had at last got a theory by which to work."[24] Under the heading of September 28, Darwin jotted in his notebook some lines about Malthus and then, without explicitly describing natural selection, surveyed its effects: "One may say there is a force like a hundred thousand wedges trying [to] force every kind of adapted structure into the gaps in the economy of Nature, or rather forming gaps by thrusting out weaker ones. The final cause of all this wedgings, must be to sort out proper structure & adapt it to change."[25]

The direction of Darwin's professional life was set, and now he fixed the course of his personal life. Six weeks after writing this passage, on Sunday, November 11 ("The Day of Days!" he wrote in his personal journal), he proposed to Emma Wedgwood.

Viewed in the simplest Darwinian terms, Darwin's attraction to Emma seems strange. He was now a high-status and well-to-do man in his late twenties. Presumably he could have had a young and beautiful wife. Emma was a year older than he and, though not unattractive (at least in the eyes of her portrait painter), was not thought beautiful. Why would Darwin do anything so maladaptive as to marry a plain woman who had already exhausted more than a decade of her reproductive potential?

First of all, this simple equation—rich, high-status male equals young, beautiful wife—is a bit crude. There are many factors that make for a genetically auspicious mate, including intelligence, trust-worthiness, and various sorts of compatibility.[26] Moreover, the selection of a spouse is also the selection of a parent for one's offspring. Emma's sturdiness of character foreshadowed the attentiveness she would bring to her children. One of her daughters recalled: "Her sympathy, and the serenity of her temper, made her children feel absolutely at their ease with her, and sure of comfort in every trouble great or small, whilst her unselfishness made them know that she would never find anything a burden, and that they could go to her with all the many little needs of a child for help or explanation."[27]

Besides, if the issue is how "valuable" a wife Darwin should be expected to seek, the question isn't, strictly speaking, how marketable a mate he was, but how marketable he had been given the impression he was. By adolescence, if not earlier, people are getting feedback about their market value, feedback that shapes their self-esteem and thus affects how high they aim their sights. Darwin doesn't seem to have emerged from adolescence feeling like an alpha male. Though large, he was meek, not much of a fighter. And, as one of his daughters noted, he considered his face "repellently plain."[28]

Of course, all of this was rendered less relevant by later achievement. Darwin may not have had high status as a teenager, but he got it later, and status per se can compensate, in the eyes of women, for mediocre looks and a lack of brute strength. Yet his insecurity seems to have persisted—as, indeed, insecurities formed in adolescence often do. The question is why.

Maybe the developmental mechanism that fine-tuned Darwin's insecurity was a vestige of evolution, an adaptation that would have tended to raise fitness in the ancestral environment but no longer does. In many hunter-gatherer societies, the male dominance hier-

who will send me to my lessons, and make me better, I trust, in every respect. . . ."[34]

DARWIN GETS EXCITED

To say that Darwin carefully and rationally selected his wife isn't to say that he wasn't in love with her. By the time of their wedding day, his letters to Emma were so laden with emotion as to raise a question: How did his feelings accelerate so rapidly? As of July, he is, depending on your interpretation of the evidence, either (a) not even dreaming of marrying her in particular; or (b) dithering violently over whether to marry her. In late July, he pays her a visit, and they have a long talk. On his next visit, three and a half months later, he pops the question. Now, suddenly, he is in ecstasy, writing florid letters about how he waits anxiously for the day's mail in the hope it will hold a letter from her; how he lies awake at night thinking of their future together; how "I long for the day when we shall enter the house together; how glorious it will be to see you seated by the fire of our own house."[35] What has happened to this man?

At the risk of seeming to harp on a single theme, I direct your attention again to the subject of genes. In particular: the differing genetic interests of a man and a woman who have never had sex with one another. Pre-sex, a woman's genes often call for wary evaluation. Affection should not too quickly become overwhelming passion. The male's genetic interest, meanwhile, often lies in speeding things up, saying things that will melt the woman's reserve. High on the list of these things are intimations of deep affection and eternal devotion. And nothing produces more convincing intimations then *feelings* of affection and devotion.

This logic may be amplified by various circumstances, and one of them is how much sex the man has been getting up until now. As Martin Daly and Margo Wilson have observed, "any creature that is recognizably on track toward complete reproductive failure" should, in theory, try with increasing intensity to change this trajectory.[36] That is: natural selection probably would not have been kind to the genes of men whose quest for sex wasn't accelerated by its prolonged absence. So far as anyone knows, Darwin went through his bachelor

years without ever having sexual intercourse.[37] How little does it take
to arouse a man who has been so long deprived? When the *Beagle*
docked in Peru, Darwin saw elegant ladies shrouded in veils that
exposed only one eye. "But then," he wrote, "that one eye is so
black and brilliant and has such powers of motion and expression
that its effect is very powerful."[38] It is not surprising that when Emma
Wedgwood was placed within reach—her whole face visible, and her
body soon to be his—Darwin began to salivate. (Literally, it would
seem. See Darwin's journal excerpt at the head of this chapter.)

It is hard to estimate the exact ratio of love to lust in Darwin's
heart as the wedding approached; their relative reproductive value
during our evolutionary past has varied widely from moment to moment (as it still does) and from millennium to millennium. A few
weeks before the wedding, Darwin mused in one of his scientific
notebooks, "What passes in a man's mind when he says he loves a
person . . . it is blind feeling, something like sexual feelings—love
being an emotion does it regard—is it influenced by—other emotions?"[39] Like many passages in Darwin's notebooks, this is cryptic,
but in mentioning love and sexual feelings in the same breath, and
in suggesting that love may be subterraneanly rooted in other feelings,
it seems headed in the general direction of a modern Darwinian view
of human psychology. And it suggests (as does his mention of sali-
vation) that he was, at that point, experiencing more than one kind
of feeling toward Emma.

What was Emma feeling? If indeed the male's intense interest in
impending sex is often matched by lingering female wariness, she
might be expected to feel somewhat less ardor than Darwin. There
are all kinds of factors that could change things in any one case, of
course, but this is the generic expectation: more female than male
ambivalence about consummation. Thus the Victorian postponement
of sex until marriage should theoretically have shifted power toward
women during the engagement. While the man had cause to be eager
for the wedding day (compared to today's men, at least), the woman
had cause to pause and reflect (compared to today's women, at least).

Emma complied with theory. Weeks into the engagement, she
suggested that the wedding be put off until spring, whereas Darwin

was pushing for winter. She cited the feelings of her sister Sarah Elizabeth, who, fifteen years her senior and still unwed, had mixed emotions about the event. But Emma added candidly, in a letter to Darwin's sister Catherine, "besides which I should wish it myself." She urged, "Do dear Catty clog the wheels a little slow."[40]

Darwin, enlisting some lush prose ("hope deferred does make my heart quite sick to call you in truth my wife"), kept the honeymoon from receding. But even after the wedding date was firm, he seems to have been left a bit insecure by Emma's reluctance, and perhaps by her overall tenor; her letters are warm, but they're far from effusive. Darwin wrote: "I earnestly pray, you may never regret the great, & I will add very good, deed, you are to perform on *the* Tuesday." Emma tried to reassure him, but she wasn't under the same magical spell he was under: "You need not fear my own dear Charles that I shall not be quite as happy as you are & I shall always look upon the event of the 29th as a most happy one on my part though perhaps not so great or so good as you do."[41] Ouch.

Now, all of this may reflect wholly on the peculiar dynamics between Charles and Emma, and not at all on the Victorian linkage of marriage with consummation. Emma was never an overly sentimental woman.[42] And, anyway, she may have begun having doubts about Charles's health, doubts that would have been warranted. Still, the basic point is probably valid in the aggregate: if it is harder to drag men to the altar today than it used to be, one reason is that they don't have to stop there on the way to the bedroom.

AFTER THE HONEYMOON

Consummation can alter the balance of affection. Though the average woman is more selective in unleashing her ardor than the average man, she should, in theory, be less inclined to rein it in once it has left the gate. Having deemed a man worthy of joining in her epic parental investment, she typically has a strong genetic interest in keeping him involved. Again, Emma's behavior matches expectations. Within the first few months of their marriage she wrote: "I cannot tell him how happy he makes me and how dearly I love him and thank him for all his affection which makes the happiness of my life more and more every day."[43]

Whether a man's devotion will be nourished by consummation is a less certain matter. Maybe his professions of affection were self-delusion; maybe, once his mate is pregnant, a better deal will come along. But in Darwin's case, the early signs were good. Months after his wedding day (and weeks after the conception of his first child), Darwin, writing in his notebook, groped for an evolutionary explanation of why a man's acts of "kindness to wife and children would give him pleasure, without any regard to his own interest," which suggests that his affection for Emma still felt deep.[44]

Perhaps this is not surprising. The tactical value of a woman's sexual reserve isn't just that men desperately want sex and to get it may say anything, even *believe* anything—including "I want to spend my whole life with you." If a Madonna-whore switch is indeed built into the male brain, then a woman's early reticence can lastingly affect a man's view of her. He is more likely to respect her in the morning—and perhaps for many years to come—if she doesn't weaken under his advances. He may *say* "I love you" to various women he yearns for, and he may mean it; but he may be more likely to keep meaning it if he doesn't get them right away. There may have been a bit of wisdom in the Victorian disapproval of premarital sex.

Even beyond this disapproval, Victorian culture was finely calibrated to excite the "Madonna" part of a man's mind and numb the "whore" part. The Victorians themselves called their attitude toward females "woman worship." The woman was a redeemer—innocence and purity incarnate; she could tame the animal in a man and rescue his spirit from the deadening world of work. But she could only do this in a domestic context, under the blessing of marriage, and after a long, chaste courtship. The secret was to have, as the title of one Victorian poem put it, an "Angel in the House."[45]

The idea wasn't just that men were supposed to at some point quit sowing wild oats, get hitched, and worship their wives. They were supposed to not sow the wild oats in the first place. Though the double standard for promiscuity prevailed in nineteenth-century Britain as elsewhere, it was battled by the more austere guardians of

Victorian morality (including Dr. Acton), who preached not just extramarital, but also premarital, abstinence for men. In *The Victorian Frame of Mind* Walter Houghton writes, "To keep body and mind untainted, the boy was taught to view women as objects of the greatest respect and even awe." Though he was supposed to give all women this respect, a certain kind of woman warranted something more. "He was to consider nice women (like his sister and his mother, like his future bride) as creatures more like angels than human beings— an image wonderfully calculated not only to dissociate love from sex, but to turn love into worship, and worship of purity."[46]

When Houghton says "calculated," he means it. One author in 1850 expressed the virtue of male premarital chastity as follows: "Where should we find that reverence for the female sex, that tenderness towards the feelings, that deep devotion of the heart to them, which is the beautiful and purifying part of love? Is it not certain that all of [the] delicate and chivalric which still pervades our sentiments towards women, may be traced to *repressed*, and therefore hallowed and elevated passion? . . . And what, in these days, can preserve chastity, save some relic of chivalrous devotion? Are we not all aware that a young man can have no safeguard against sensuality and low intrigue, like an early, virtuous, and passionate attachment?"[47]

Aside from the word *repressed*, which probably mischaracterizes the psychodynamics, this passage is plausible enough. It implies that a man's passion can be "hallowed and elevated" if not quenched too readily—that a chaste courtship, in other words, helps move a woman into the "Madonna" part of his mind.

This is not the only reason that a chaste courtship may encourage marriage. Recall how different the ancestral environment was from the modern environment. In particular: there were no condoms, diaphragms, or birth-control pills. So if an adult couple paired up, slept together for a year or two, and produced no baby, the chances were good that one of them wasn't fertile. No way of telling which one, of course; but for both of them there was little to lose and much to gain by dissolving the partnership and finding a new mate. The adaptation expected to arise from this logic is a "mate-ejection module"—a mental mechanism, in both male and female, that would encourage souring on a mate after lots of sex without issue.[48]

This is a quite speculative theory, but it has some circumstantial evidence on its side. In cultures around the world, barren marriages are among the most likely to break up.[49] (Though cases where barrenness is cited as the cause of breakup don't quite get at the crux of this theory: the *unconsciously* motivated alienation from a mate.) And, as many husbands and wives can attest, the birth of a child often cements a marital bond, if obliquely; the love of spouse is partly diverted to the child and then refracted diffusely onto the family as a whole, mate included. It is a different *kind* of love for the spouse, but it's sturdy in its own way. In the absence of this roundabout recharge, love of spouse may tend to disappear entirely—by design.

Darwin once worried that contraceptive technology would "spread to unmarried women & would destroy chastity on which the family bond depends; & the weakening of this bond would be the greatest of all possible evils to mankind."[50] He surely didn't grasp all the plausible Darwinian reasons that contraception and the attendant premarital sex might indeed discourage marriage. He didn't suspect the deep basis of the Madonna-whore dichotomy or the possible existence of a "mate-ejection module." And even today, we're far from certain about these things. (The established correlations between premarital sex and divorce, and between premarital cohabitation and divorce, are suggestive but ambiguous.)[51] Still, it is harder now than it would have been thirty years ago to dismiss Darwin's fear as the rantings of an aging Victorian.

Contraception isn't the only technology that may affect the structure of family life. Women who breast-feed often report a weakened sex drive—and with good Darwinian cause, since they're usually incapable of conception. Husbands, meanwhile, sometimes fail to find a breast-feeding wife sexually exciting, presumably for the same ultimate reason. Thus bottle-feeding may make wives both more lustful and more attractive. Whether this is, on balance, good for family cohesion is hard to say. (Does it more often tempt wives into extramarital affairs or distract husbands from having them?) In any event, this logic may make sense of Dr. Acton's otherwise comical-sounding claim that "the best mothers, wives, and managers of house-holds, know little or nothing of sexual indulgences. Love of home, children, and domestic duties, are the only passions they feel." In Victorian England, when so many wives spent so many of their fertile years either pregnant or nursing, their passion may indeed have spent much time in abeyance.[52]

Even if a succession of babies helps keep both partners devoted, the interests of husband and wife may diverge as time goes by. The older the children (the less urgently needful of paternal investment), and the older the wife, the less support a man's devotion gets from his evolutionary heritage. More and more of the harvest has been reaped; the ground is less and less fertile; it may be time to move on.[53] Of course, whether the husband feels this impulse strongly may depend on how likely it is to bear fruit. A dashing and wealthy man may get the kinds of glances from women that fuel it; a poor and disfigured man may not. Still, the strength of the impulse will tend to be greater in the husband than in the wife.

Though the shifting balance of attraction between husband and wife is seldom described this explicitly, it is often reflected more obliquely—in novels, in aphorisms, in the folk wisdom offered up as advice to bride and groom. Professor Henslow, a fifteen-year veteran of the blessed state, wrote to Darwin shortly before his marriage: "All the advice, which I need not give you, is, to remember that as you take your wife for better for worse, be careful to value the better & care nothing for the worse." He added: "It is the neglect of this little particular which makes the marriage state of so many men worse than their single blessedness."[54] In other words, just remember one simple rule: don't stop loving your wife, as men seem inclined to do.

Emma, meanwhile, was getting advice not about overlooking Charles's flaws, but about concealing any flaws of her own, especially those that make a woman look old and haggard. An aunt (perhaps mindful of Emma's noted lack of fashion consciousness) wrote: "If you do pay a little more, be always dressed in good taste; do not despise those little cares which give everyone more pleasing looks, because you know you have married a man who is above caring for such little things. No man is above caring for them. . . . I have seen it even in my half-blind husband."[55]

The logic of male intolerance typically remains opaque to all concerned. A man souring on a mate doesn't think, "My reproductive potential is best served by getting out of this marriage, so for entirely selfish reasons I'll do so." Awareness of his selfishness would only impede its pursuit. It's much simpler for the feelings that got him into the marriage to simply stage a slow but massive retreat.

The increasingly severe view that a restless husband may take of an aging wife was well illustrated by Charles Dickens, one of the few upper-class Victorians who actually got out of a marriage (by separation, not divorce). Dickens, who was elected to membership in London's Athenaeum Club on the same day in 1838 as Darwin, had then been married for two years to the woman he called his "better half." Two decades later—now much more famous, and thus commanding the attention of many young women—he was having trouble seeing her brighter side. It now seemed to him that she lived in a "fatal atmosphere which slays every one to whom she should be dearest." Dickens wrote to a friend: "I believe that no two people were ever created with such an impossibility of interest, sympathy, confidence, sentiment, tender union of any kind between them, as there is between my wife and me." (If so, mightn't he have discussed this with her *before* she bore him ten children?) "To his eyes," a chronicler of their marriage has written, his wife "had become unresponsive, grudging, inert, close to inhuman."[56]

Emma Darwin, like Catherine Dickens, grew old and shapeless. And Charles Darwin, like Charles Dickens, rose markedly in stature after his wedding. But there's no evidence that Darwin ever saw Emma as close to inhuman. What accounts for the difference?

Chapter 6: **THE DARWIN PLAN FOR MARITAL BLISS**

She has been my greatest blessing, and I can declare that in my whole life I have never heard her utter one word which I had rather have been unsaid. . . . She has been my wise adviser and cheerful comforter throughout life, which without her would have been during a very long period a miserable one from ill-health. She has earned the love and admiration of every soul near her.

—*Autobiography* (1876)[1]

In his pursuit of a lasting and fulfilling marriage, Charles Darwin possessed several distinct advantages.

To begin with, there was his chronic ill health. Nine years into marriage, while visiting his ailing father, and while ailing himself, he wrote to Emma of how he "yearned" for her, as "without you, when sick I feel most desolate." He closed the letter: "I do long to be with you & under your protection for then I feel safe."[2] After three decades of marriage, Emma would observe that "nothing marries one so completely as sickness."[3] This reflection may have been more bitter than sweet; Darwin's illness was a lifelong burden for her, and she couldn't have grasped its full weight until well after the wedding. But, whether or not it gave her second thoughts about the marriage, it meant that, for much of Darwin's married life, he wasn't a very marketable commodity. And in marriage, an unmarketable commodity—male or female—is often a contented one, with little if any sexual restlessness.

A complementary asset that Darwin brought to his marriage was hearty subscription to the Victorian ideal of woman as spiritual salvation. In his premarital deliberative soliloquies, he had imagined an "angel" who would keep him industrious yet not let him suffocate in his work. He got that, and a nurse too. And, for good measure, the chasteness of the courtship may have helped keep Emma filed under "Madonna" in Darwin's mind. Something did. "I marvel at my good fortune," he wrote toward the end of his life, "that she, so infinitely my superior in every single moral quality, consented to be my wife."[4]

A third advantage was residential geography. The Darwins lived, gibbon-like, on an eighteen-acre parcel, two hours by coach from London and its young female distractions. Male sexual fantasies tend to be essentially visual in nature, whereas female fantasies more often include tender touching, soft murmurs, and other hints of future investment. Not surprisingly, male fantasies, and male sexual arousal, are also more easily activated by sheerly visual cues, by the mere sight of anonymous flesh.[5] So visual isolation is an especially good way to keep a man from thinking the thoughts that could lead to marital discontent, infidelity, or both.

Isolation is hard to come by these days, and not just because attractive young women no longer stay in their homes, barefoot and pregnant. Images of beautiful women are everywhere we look. The fact that they're two-dimensional doesn't mean they're inconsequential. Natural selection had no way of "anticipating" the invention of photography. In the ancestral environment, distinct images of many beautiful young women would have signified a (genetically) profitable alternative to monogamy, and it would have been adaptive for feelings to shift accordingly. One evolutionary psychologist has found that men shown pictures of *Playboy* models later describe themselves as less in love with their wives than do men shown other images. (Women shown pictures from *Playgirl* felt no such attitude adjustment toward spouses.)[6]

The Darwins also had the blessing of fecundity. A marriage that produces a steady stream of children, and has the resources to care for them, may dampen the wanderlust of both women and men. Wandering takes time and energy, both of which can be well invested in those endearing little vehicles of genetic transmission. That divorce does grow less likely as more children are born is sometimes taken to mean that couples choose to endure the pain of matrimony "for the sake of children." No doubt this happens. But it's at least possible that evolution has inclined us to love a mate more deeply when marriage proves fruitful.[7] In either event, couples who say they'll stay married but won't have children may well prove wrong on one count or the other.[8]

We can now roughly sketch a Charles Darwin plan for marital bliss: have a chaste courtship, marry an angel, move to the country not long after the wedding, have tons of kids, and sink into a deeply debilitating illness. A heartfelt commitment to your work probably helps too, especially when the work doesn't entail business trips.

MARRIAGE TIPS FOR MEN

From the point of view of the average, late-twentieth-century man, the Darwin plan doesn't get high marks for feasibility. Perhaps some more practicable keys to lifelong monogamy can be gleaned from Darwin's life. Let's start with his three-step approach to marriage: (1) decide, rationally and systematically, to get married; (2) find someone who in most practical ways meets your needs; (3) marry her.

One biographer has chastised Darwin for this formulaic approach, complaining that "there is an emotional emptiness about his ponderings on marriage."[9] Maybe so. But it's worth noting that Darwin was a loving husband and father for around half a century. Any men who would like to fill this role might profit from looking closely at the "emotional emptiness" of Darwin's ruminations on marriage. They may hold a lesson transplantable to modern times.

Namely: lasting love is something a person has to *decide* to experience. Lifelong monogamous devotion is just not natural—not for women even, and emphatically not for men. It requires what, for lack of a better term, we can call an act of will. Hence the aptness of Darwin's apparent separation of the marriage question from the marriage-partner question. That he made up his mind—firmly, in the end—to get married and to make the most of his marriage was as important as his choice of mate.

This isn't to say that a young man can't hope to be seized by love. Darwin himself got fairly worked up by his wedding day. But whether the sheer fury of a man's feelings accurately gauges their likely endurance is another question. The ardor will surely fade, sooner or later, and the marriage will then live or die on respect, practical compatibility, simple affection, and (these days, especially) determination. With the help of these things, something worthy of the label "love" can last until death. But it will be a different kind of love from the kind that began the marriage. Will it be a richer love, a deeper love, a more spiritual love? Opinions vary. But it's certainly a more impressive love.

A corollary of the above is that marriages aren't made in heaven. One great spur to divorce is the belief of many men (and no few women) that somehow they just married the "wrong" person and next time they'll get it "right." Not likely. Divorce statistics support Samuel Johnson's characterization of a man's decision to remarry as "the triumph of hope over experience."[10]

John Stuart Mill held a similarly sober view. Mill insisted on *tolerance* of moral diversity, and stressed the long-term value of experimentation by society's nonconformists, but he didn't recommend moral adventurism as a lifestyle. Beneath the radicalism of *On Liberty* lay Mill's belief in keeping our impulses under firm cerebral control. "Most persons have but a very moderate capacity of happiness," he wrote in a letter. "Expecting . . . in marriage a far greater degree of happiness than they commonly find: and knowing not that the fault is in their own scanty capabilities of happiness—they fancy they should have been happier with some one else." His advice to the unhappy: sit still until the feeling passes. "[I]f they remain united, the feeling of disappointment after a time goes off, and they pass their lives together with fully as much happiness as they could find either singly or in any other union, without having undergone the wearing of repeated and unsuccessful experiments."[11]

Many men—and some, but fewer, women—would enjoy the opening stages of those experiments. But in the end they might find that the glimpse of lasting joy the second time around was just another delusion sponsored by their genes, whose primary goal, remember, is to make us prolific, not lastingly happy (and which, anyway, aren't operating in the environment of our design; in a modern society, where polygamy is illegal, a polygamous impulse can do more emotional damage to all concerned—notably offspring—than natural selection "intended"). The question then becomes whether the fleeting fun of greener pastures outweighs the pain caused by leaving the golden-brown ones. This isn't a simple question, much less a question whose answer is easy to impose on one's yearnings. But more often than many people (men in particular) care to admit, the answer is no.

And, anyway, there is debate over whether a minute-by-minute summation of pleasure and pain should settle the issue. Maybe the cumulative coherence of a life counts for something. Men from many generations have testified that over the long haul, a life shared with another person and several little people, for all its diverse frustrations, brings rewards of a sort unattainable through other means. Of course, we shouldn't give infinite weight to the testimony of old married men. For every one of them who claims to have had a fulfilling life, there is at least one bachelor claiming to be enjoying his series of conquests. But it's noteworthy that a number of these old men went through early phases of sexual liberty and concede that they enjoyed them. None of those making the other side of the argument can say they know what it's like to create a family and stay with it until the end.

John Stuart Mill made this point in a larger context. Even Mill, who, as the foremost publicist of utilitarianism, insisted that "pleasure, and freedom from pain, are the only things desirable as ends," didn't mean that the way it sounds. He believed that the pleasure and pain of all people affected by your actions (emphatically including any people your marriage created) belong in your moral calculus. Further, Mill stressed not just quantity of pleasure but quality, attaching special value to pleasures involving the "higher faculties." He wrote: "Few human creatures would consent to be changed into any of the lower animals, for a promise of the fullest allowance of a beast's pleasures. . . . It is better to be a human being dissatisfied than a pig satisfied; better to be Socrates dissatisfied than a fool satisfied. And if the fool, or the pig, is of a different opinion, it is because they only know their own side of the question. The other party to the comparison knows both sides."[12]

DIVORCE THEN AND NOW

Since Darwin's day, the incentive structure surrounding marriage has been transformed—indeed, inverted. Back then men had several good reasons to get married (sex, love, and societal pressure) and a good reason to stay married (they had no choice). Today an unmarried man can get sex, with or without love, regularly and respectably. And if for some reason he does stumble into matrimony, there's no cause for alarm; when the thrill is gone, he can just move out of the house and resume an active sex life without raising local eyebrows. The ensuing divorce is fairly simple. Whereas Victorian marriage was enticing and ultimately entrapping, modern marriage is unnecessary and eminently escapable.

This change had begun by the turn of the century, and it reached dramatic proportions after midcentury. The American divorce rate, which was level during the 1950s and early 1960s, doubled between 1966 and 1978, reaching its present level. Meanwhile, as escape from marriage became simple and commonplace, the incentive for men (and, in a probably less dramatic way, for women) to enter one was being dulled. Between 1970 and 1988, though the average age of a woman upon (first) marriage was rising, the number of eighteen-year-old girls who reported having had intercourse grew from 39 to 70 percent. For fifteen-year-olds it went from one in twenty to one in four.[13] The number of unmarried couples living together in the United States grew from half a million in 1970 to nearly three million in 1990.

Hence the double whammy: as easy divorce creates a growing population of formerly married women, easy sex creates a growing population of never-married women. Between 1970 and 1990, the number of American women aged thirty-five to thirty-nine who had never been married rose from one in twenty to one in ten.[14] And of women in that age group who *have* gotten married, about a third have also gotten divorced.[15]

For men, the figures are even more severe. One in seven men aged thirty-five to thirty-nine has never married; as we've seen, serial monogamy tends to leave more men than women in that condition.[16] Still, women may be the bigger losers here. They are more likely than men to want children, and a forty-year-old unmarried childless woman, unlike her male counterpart, is watching her chances of parenthood head briskly toward zero. And as for the relative fortunes of *formerly* married men and women: in the United States, divorce brings the average man a marked increase in standard of living, while his wife, along with her children, suffers the opposite.[17]

The Divorce Act of 1857, which helped legitimize marital breakup in England, was welcomed by many feminists. Among them was John Stuart Mill's wife, Harriet Taylor Mill, who, until the death of her first husband, had been trapped in a marriage she detested. Mrs. Mill, who seems never to have been a great enthusiast for sexual intercourse, had painfully come to believe "that all men, with the exception of a few lofty minded, are sensualists more or less" and that "women on the contrary are quite exempt from this trait." To any wife who shared her distaste for sex, Victorian marriage could seem like a series of rapes punctuated by dread. She favored divorce on demand for the sake of women.

Mill too favored divorce on demand (*assuming* the couple had no children). But his view of the matter differed from hers. He saw wedding vows as a constraint less on the wife than on the husband. The strict marriage laws of the day, Mill observed, with great insight into the likely origins of institutionalized monogamy, had been written "*by* sensualists, *for* sensualists, and *to bind* sensualists."[18] He was not alone in this view. Behind opposition to the Divorce Act of 1857 was a fear that it would turn men into serial monogamists. Gladstone opposed the bill because, he said, it "would lead to the degradation of woman."[19] (Or, as an Irish woman would put it more than a century later: "A woman voting for divorce is like a turkey voting for Christmas.")[20] The effects of easy divorce have been complex, but in many ways the evidence supports Gladstone. Divorce is very often a raw deal for women.

There's no point in trying to turn back the clock, no point in trying to sustain marriages by making the alternative virtually illegal. Studies show that the one thing harder on children than divorce is for parents to stay together even though locked in mortal combat.

But surely there shouldn't be a financial *incentive* for a man to get divorced; divorce shouldn't *raise* his personal standard of living, as it now usually does. In fact, it seems only fair to lower his standard of living—not necessarily to punish him, but because that's often the only way to keep the living standards of his wife and children from plunging, given the inefficiencies of two households compared to one. If financially secure, women can often be happy rearing children without a man—happier than they were with him, sometimes, and happier even than he'll be after he's gotten used to the grass on the other side of the fence.

R-E-S-P-E-C-T

There is a difference of opinion over how much "respect" women get in the modern moral climate. Men think they get lots. The portion of American men saying women are better respected than in the past went from 40 percent in 1970 to 62 percent in 1990. Women disagree. In a 1970 survey, they were most likely to call men "basically kind, gentle, and thoughtful," but a 1990 survey conducted by the same pollster found women most likely to describe men as valuing only their own opinions, trying to keep women down, preoccupied with getting women into bed, and not paying attention to household affairs.[21]

Respect is an ambiguous word. Maybe those men who consider women well "respected" mean that women have been accepted at work as worthy colleagues. And maybe women are indeed getting more of this kind of respect. But if by *respect* you mean what the Victorians meant when they urged respect for women—not treating them as objects of sexual conquest—then respect has probably dropped since 1970 (and it certainly has since 1960). One interpretation of the above numbers is that women would like to have more of this second kind of respect.

There's no clear reason for a sharp trade-off between the two; no reason that feminists of the late 1960s and early 1970s, in insisting on the first kind of respect, had to undermine the second (which, actually, they said they also wanted). But, as things happened, they did. They preached the innate symmetry of the sexes in all major arenas, including sex. Many young women took the doctrine of symmetry to mean they could follow their sexual attractions and disregard any vague visceral wariness: sleep with any man they liked, without fear that his sexual interest didn't signify comparable affection, without fear that sex might be more emotionally entangling for her than for him. (Some feminists practiced casual sex almost out of a sense of ideological commitment.) Men, for their part, used the doctrine of symmetry to ease themselves off the moral hook. Now they could sleep around without worrying about the emotional fallout; women were just like them, so no special consideration was necessary. In this they were, and are, aided by women who actively resist special moral consideration as patronizing (which it sometimes is, and certainly was in Victorian England).

Lawmakers, meanwhile, took sexual symmetry to mean that women needed no special legal protection.[22] In many states, the 1970s brought "no-fault" divorce and the automatically equal division of a couple's assets—even if one spouse, usually the wife, hasn't been on a career track and thus faces bleaker prospects. The lifelong alimony that a divorced woman could once expect may now be replaced by a few years of "rehabilitative maintenance" payments, which are supposed to give her time to launch her career recovery—a recovery that, in fact, will extend beyond a few years if she has a few children to tend. In trying to get a more equitable deal, it won't help to point out that the cause of the breakup was her husband's rampant philandering, or his sudden, brutal intolerance. These things, after all, are nobody's fault. The no-fault philosophy is one reason divorce is literally a profitable enterprise for men. (The other reason is lax enforcement of the man's financial obligations.) The height of the no-fault vogue has now passed, and state legislatures have undone some of the damage, but not all.

The feminist doctrine of innate sexual symmetry wasn't the only culprit, or even, initially, the main one. Sexual and marital norms had been changing for a long time, for many reasons, ranging from contraceptive technology to communications technology, from residential patterns to recreational trends. So why dwell on feminism?

Partly because of the sheer irony that (perfectly laudable) attempts to stop one kind of exploitation of women aided another kind. Partly, too, because, though feminists didn't single-handedly create the problem, some of them have helped sustain it. Until very recently, fear of feminist backlash was far and away the main obstacle to an honest discussion of differences between the sexes. Feminists have written articles and books denouncing "biological determinism" without bothering to understand biology or determinism. And the increasing, if belated, feminist discussion of sex differences is sometimes vague and disingenuous; there is a tendency to describe differences that are plausibly explicable in Darwinian terms while dodging the question of whether they are innate.[23]

UNHAPPILY MARRIED WOMEN

The "Darwin plan" for staying married—and, indeed, the general thrust of this chapter so far—may seem to presuppose a simple picture: women love marriage, men don't. Obviously, life is more complicated than that. Some women don't want to get married, and many more, once married, are far from bliss. If this chapter has stressed the *male* mind's incongruence with monogamous marriage (and it has), it's not because I think the female mind is a perpetual font of adulation and fidelity. It's because I think the male mind is the largest single obstacle to lifelong monogamy—and certainly the largest such obstacle that emerges distinctly from the new Darwinian paradigm.

The incongruence between the *female* mind and modern marriage is less simple and clear-cut (and, in the end, less disruptive). The clash isn't so much with monogamy itself as with the social and economic setting of modern monogamy. In the typical hunter-gatherer society, women have both a working life and a home life, and reconciling the two isn't hard. When they go out to gather food, child care is barely an issue; their children may go with them or, instead, stay with aunts, uncles, grandparents, cousins. And when mothers, back from work, do care for children, the context is social, even communal. The anthropologist Marjorie Shostak, after living in an African hunter-gatherer village, wrote: "The isolated mother burdened with bored small children is not a scene that has parallels in !Kung daily life."[24]

Most modern mothers seem to find themselves well to one side or the other of the (reasonably) happy medium that a hunter-gatherer woman naturally strikes. They may work forty or fifty hours a week, worry about the quality of day care, and feel vaguely guilty. Or they may be full-time housewives who rear their children alone and are driven nearly mad by monotony. Some housewives, of course, manage to build a solid social infrastructure even amid the transience and anonymity of the typical modern neighborhood. But the unhappiness of the many women who don't is virtually inevitable. It's no surprise that modern feminism gathered such momentum during the 1960s, after post–World War II suburbanization (and so much else) had diluted the sense of neighborhood community and pulled the extended family apart; women weren't designed to be suburban housewives.

The generic suburban habitat of the fifties was more "natural" for men. Like many hunter-gatherer fathers, vintage suburban husbands spent a little time with their children and a lot of time out bonding with males, in work, play, or ritual.[25] For that matter, many Victorian men (though not Darwin) had the same setup. Although lifelong monogamy per se is less natural for men than for women, one form that monogamous marriage has often taken, and still often takes, may be harder on women than on men.

But that's not the same as saying that the female mind threatens modern monogamy more than, or as much as, the male mind. A mother's discontent seems not to translate into breakup as naturally as a father's. The ultimate reason is that, in the ancestral environment, seeking a new husband once there were children was seldom a genetically winning proposition.

To make modern monogamy "work"—in the sense both of enduring and of leaving husband and wife fairly happy—is a challenge of overwhelming complexity. A successful overhaul might well entail tampering with the very structure of modern residential and vocational life. Any aspiring tamperers would do well to ponder the social environment in which human beings evolved.

People weren't, of course, designed to be relentlessly happy in the ancestral environment; there, as here, anxiety was a chronic motivator, and happiness was the always pursued, often receding, goal. Still, people *were* designed not to go crazy in the ancestral environment.

THE EMMA PLAN

Notwithstanding the discontents of modern marriage, many women aspire to find a lifelong mate and have children. Given that the current climate doesn't favor this goal, what are they to do? We've talked about how men might behave if they want marriage to be a sturdier institution. But giving men marriage tips is a little like offering Vikings a free booklet titled "How Not to Pillage." If women are closer than men to being naturally monogamous, and often suffer from divorce, maybe they are a more logical locus for reform. As George Williams and Robert Trivers discovered, much of human sexual psychology flows from the scarceness of eggs relative to sperm. This scarcity gives women more power—in individual relationships, and in shaping the moral fabric—than they sometimes realize.

Sometimes they do realize it. Women who would like a husband and children have been known to try the Emma Wedgwood plan for landing a man. In its most extreme form, the plan runs as follows: if you want to hear vows of eternal devotion right up to your wedding day—and if you want to make sure there *is* a wedding day—don't sleep with your man until the honeymoon.

The idea here isn't just that, as the saying goes, a man won't buy the cow if he can get the milk for free. If the Madonna-whore dichotomy is indeed rooted firmly in the male mind, then early sex with a woman may tend to stifle any budding feelings of love for her. And, if there are such things as "mate-ejection modules" in the human mind, sustained sex without issue may bring—in the man *or* the woman—a cooling toward the other.

Many women find the Emma strategy abhorrent. To "trap" a man, some say, is beneath their dignity; if he has to be coerced into marriage, they'd rather do without him. Others say the Emma approach is reactionary and sexist, a revival of the hoary demand that women carry the moral burden of self-control for the sake of the social order. Still others say this approach seems to presume that sexual restraint for a woman is easy, which it often is not. These are all valid reactions.

There is one other common complaint about the Emma strategy: it doesn't work. These days much sex is available to men for little commitment. Not as much as a few years ago, maybe, but enough so that, if any one woman cuts off the supply, alternatives abound. Prim women sit at home alone and bask in their purity. Around Valentine's Day of 1992, the *New York Times* quoted a twenty-eight-year-old single woman who "lamented the lack of romance and courtship." She said, "Guys still figure if you don't come across, someone else will. It's like there's no incentive to wait until you get to know each other better."[26]

This, too, is a valid point, and a good reason why a one-woman austerity crusade isn't likely to bring great rewards. Still, some women have found that a move *of some distance* toward austerity may make sense.[27] If a man isn't interested enough in a woman, as a human being, to endure, say, two months of merely affectionate contact before graduating to lust, he's unlikely to stick around for long in any event. Some women have decided not to waste the time—which, needless to say, is more precious for them than for men.

This mild version of the Emma approach can be self-reinforcing. As more women discover the value of a short cooling-off period, it becomes easier for each of them to impose a longer one. If an eight-week wait is common, then a ten-week wait won't put a woman at much of a competitive disadvantage. Don't expect this trend to reach Victorian extremes. Women, after all, do like sex. But expect the trend, which seems already to be under way, to continue. Much of today's incipiently conservative sexual climate may come from a fear of sexually transmitted diseases; but, to judge by the increasingly clear opinion of many women that men are basically pigs, a part of the new climate may come from women rationally pursuing self-interest in recognition of harsh truths about human nature. And one generally safe bet is that people will continue to pursue their self-interest as they see it. In this case, evolutionary psychology helps them see it.

A THEORY OF MORAL CHANGE

There is another reason trends in sexual morality—whether toward or away from sexual reserve—may be self-sustaining. If men and women are indeed designed to tailor their sexual strategies to local market conditions, the norm among each sex depends on the norm among the other. We've already seen evidence, from David Buss and others, that when men deem a woman promiscuous, they treat her accordingly—as a short-term conquest, not a long-term prize. We've also seen evidence, from Elizabeth Cashdan, that women who perceive males to be generally pursuing short-term strategies are themselves more likely to look and act promiscuous: to wear sexy clothes and have sex often.[28] One can imagine these two tendencies getting locked in a spiral of positive feedback, leading to what the Victorians would have called ongoing moral decline. A proliferation of low-cut dresses and come-hither looks might send the visual cues that discourage male commitment; and as men, thus discouraged, grow less deferential toward women, and more overtly sexual, low-cut dresses might further proliferate. (Even come-hither looks that show up on billboards, or in the pages of *Playboy*, might have some effect.)[29]

If things should for some reason begin moving in the other direction, *toward* male parental investment, the trend could be sustained by the same dynamic of mutual reinforcement. The more Madonnaish the women, the more daddish and less caddish the men, and thus the more Madonnaish the women, and so on.

To call this theory speculative would almost be an understatement. It has the added disadvantage of being (like many theories of cultural change) hard to test directly. But it does rest on theories of individual psychology that are themselves testable. The Buss and Cashdan studies amount to a preliminary test, and so far the two pillars of the theory hold up. The theory also has the virtue of helping to explain why trends in sexual morality persist for so long. Just as Victorian prudishness, at its high-water mark, was the culmination of a century-long trend, it seems to have then receded for a long, long time.

Why does the long, slow swing of the pendulum ever reverse? The possible reasons range from changes in technology (contraceptive, for example) to changes in demographics.[30] It's possible too that the pendulum may tend to reverse when a large fraction of one sex or the other (or both) finds its deepest interests not being served and begins to consciously reevaluate its lifestyle. In 1977 Lawrence Stone observed, "The historical record suggests that the likelihood of this period of extreme sexual permissiveness continuing for very long without generating a strong backlash is not very great. It is an ironic thought that just at the moment when some thinkers are heralding the advent of the perfect marriage based on full satisfaction of the sexual, emotional and creative needs of both husband and wife, the proportion of marital breakdowns, as measured by the divorce rate, is rising rapidly."[31] Since he wrote, women, who have much leverage over sexual morality, have, in apparently growing numbers, asked basic questions about the wisdom of highly casual sex. Whether we are entering a period of long growth in moral conservatism is impossible to say. But modern society doesn't exude an overwhelming sense of satisfaction with the status quo.

VICTORIA'S SECRET

Many judgments have been rendered about Victorian sexual morality. One is that it was horribly and painfully repressive. Another is that it was well suited to the task of preserving marriage. Darwinism affirms these two judgments and unites them. Once you have seen the odds against lifelong monogamous marriage, especially in an economically stratified society—in other words, once you have seen human nature—it is hard to imagine anything short of harsh repression preserving the institution.

But Victorianism went well beyond simple, general repression. Its particular inhibitions were strikingly well-tailored to the task at hand.

Perhaps the greatest threat to lasting marriage—the temptation of aging, affluent, or high-status men to desert their wives for a younger model—was met with great social firepower. Though Charles Dickens did manage, amid great controversy and at real social cost, to leave his wife, he forever confined contact with his mistress to secret meetings. To admit that his desertion was, in fact, a desertion would have been to draw a censure he wasn't willing to face.

It's true that some husbands spent time in one or another of London's many brothels (and housemaids sometimes served as sexual outlets for men of the upper classes). But it's also true that male infidelity may not threaten marriage so long as it doesn't lead to desertion; women, more easily than men, can reconcile themselves to living with a mate who has cheated. And one way to ensure that male infidelity doesn't lead to desertion is to confine it to, well, whores. We can safely bet that few Victorian men sat at the breakfast table daydreaming about leaving their wives for the prostitute they had enjoyed the night before; and we can speculate with some confidence that part of the reason is a Madonna-whore dichotomy planted deeply in the male psyche.

If a Victorian man did more directly threaten the institution of monogamy, if he committed adultery with "respectable" women, the risk was great. Darwin's physician, Edward Lane, was accused in court by a patient's husband of committing adultery with the patient. In those days, this sort of case was so scandalous that the *Times* of London carried daily coverage. Darwin followed it closely. Perhaps conveniently, he doubted Lane's guilt ("I never heard a sensual expression from him"), and he worried about Lane's future: "I fear it will ruin him."[32] It probably would have, if the judge hadn't exonerated him.

Of course, in keeping with the double standard, female adulterers drew even stronger censure than their male counterparts. Both Lane and his patient were married, yet her diary recounted a post-tryst conversation between them that allocated blame in the following proportions. "I entreated him to believe that since my marriage I had never before in the smallest degree transgressed. He consoled me for what I had done, and conjured me to forgive myself."[33] (Lane's lawyer convinced the court that her diary was a mad fantasy, but even if so, it reflects prevailing morality.)

The double standard may not be fair, but it does have a kind of rationale. Adultery per se is a greater threat to monogamy when the wife commits it. (Again: the average man will have much more trouble than the average woman continuing a marriage with a mate known to have been unfaithful.) And if the husband of an adulterer does for some reason stay in the marriage, he may start treating the children less warmly, now that doubts about their paternity have arisen.

Conducting this sort of brisk, clinical appraisal of Victorian morality is risky. People are inclined to misunderstand. So let's be clear: clinical isn't the same as prescriptive; this is *not* an argument on behalf of the double standard, or any other particular aspect of Victorian morality.

Indeed, whatever contribution the double standard may have once made to marital stability by offering a vent for male lust, times have changed. These days a high-powered businessman doesn't confine his extramarital affairs to prostitutes, or to maids and secretaries whose cultural backgrounds make them unlikely wives. With women more widely in the workplace, he will meet young single women at the office, or on a business trip, who are exactly the sort he might marry if he had it to do all over again; and he *can* do it all over again. Whereas extramarital activity in the nineteenth century, and often in the 1950s, was a sheerly sexual outlet for an otherwise committed husband, today it is often a slippery slope toward desertion. The double standard may have once bolstered monogamy, but these days it brings divorce.

Even aside from the question of whether Victorian morality would "work" today, there is the question of whether any benefits would justify its many peculiar costs. Some Victorian men and women felt desperately trapped by marriage. (Although when marriages seem inescapable, almost literally unthinkable, people may dwell less on shortcomings.) And prevailing morality made it hard for some women to guiltlessly enjoy even marital sex—not to mention the fact that Victorian men weren't known for their sexual sensitivity. Life was also hard for women who wanted to be more than ornaments, more than an "Angel in the House." The Darwin sisters reported to Charles with some concern about brother Erasmus's budding, if ambiguous, friendship with the author Harriet Martineau, who didn't fit meekly into the feminine mold. Darwin, upon meeting her, had this impression: "She was very agreeable and managed to talk on a most wonderful number of subjects, considering the limited time. I was astonished to find how little ugly she is, but as it appears to me, she is overwhelmed with her own projects, her own thoughts and own abilities. Erasmus palliated all this, by maintaining one ought not to look at her as a woman."[34] This sort of remark is one of many reasons we shouldn't try to recreate Victorian sexual morality wholesale.

There no doubt are other moral systems that could succeed in sustaining monogamous marriage. But it seems likely that any such system will, like Victorianism, entail real costs. And although we can certainly strive for a morality that distributes costs *evenly* between men and women (and evenly among men and among women), distributing the costs *identically* is less likely. Men and women are different, and the threats that their evolved minds pose to marriage are different. The sanctions with which an efficient morality combats these threats will thus be different for the two sexes.

If we are really serious about restoring the institution of monogamy, *combat*, it seems, will indeed be the operative word. In 1966, one American scholar, looking back at the sense of shame surrounding the sexual impulse among Victorian men, discerned "a pitiable alienation on the part of a whole class of men from their own sexuality."[35] He's certainly right about the alienation. But the "pitiable" part is another question. At the other end of the spectrum from "alienation" is "indulgence"—obedience to our sexual impulses as if they were the voice of the Noble Savage, a voice that could restore us to some state of primitive bliss which, in fact, never was. A quarter-century of indulging these impulses has helped bring a world featuring, among other things: lots of fatherless children; lots of embittered women; lots of complaints about date rape and sexual harassment; and the frequent sight of lonely men renting X-rated videotapes while lonely women abound. It seems harder these days to declare the Victorian war against male lust "pitiable." Pitiable compared to what? Samuel Smiles may seem to have been asking a lot when he talked about spending one's life "armed against the temptation of low indulgences," but the alternative isn't obviously preferable.

WHERE DO MORAL CODES COME FROM?

The intermittently moralistic tone of this chapter is in a sense ironic. Yes, on the one hand, the new Darwinian paradigm does suggest that any institution as "unnatural" as monogamous marriage may be hard to sustain without a strong (that is, repressive) moral code. But the new paradigm also has a countervailing effect: nourishing a certain moral relativism—if not, indeed, an outright cynicism about moral codes in general.

The closest thing to a generic Darwinian view of how moral codes arise is this: people tend to pass the sorts of moral judgments that help move their genes into the next generation (or, at least, the kinds of judgments that would have furthered that cause in the environment of our evolution). Thus a moral code is an informal compromise among competing spheres of genetic self-interest, each acting to mold the code to its own ends, using any levers at its disposal.[36]

Consider the sexual double standard. The most obvious Darwinian explanation is that men were designed, on the one hand, to be sexually loose themselves yet, on the other, to relegate sexually loose women ("whores") to low moral status—even, remarkably, as those same men encourage those same women to be sexually loose. Thus, to the extent that men shape the moral code, it may include a double standard. Yet on closer inspection, this quintessentially male judgment is seen to draw natural support from other circles: the parents of young, pretty girls, who encourage their daughters to save their favors for Mr. Right (that is, to remain attractive targets for male parental investment), and who tell their daughters it's "wrong" to do otherwise; the daughters themselves, who, while saving their virtue for a high bidder, self-servingly and moralistically disparage the competing, low-rent alternatives; happily married women who consider an atmosphere of promiscuity a clear and present danger to their marriage (that is, to continued high investment in their offspring). There is a virtual genetic conspiracy to depict sexually loose women as evil. Meanwhile, there is relative tolerance for male philandering, and not only because some males (especially attractive or rich ones) may themselves like the idea. Wives, too, by finding a husband's from the proposal of weak hypotheses; the way weak hypotheses get strong is by being proposed and then mercilessly scrutinized. And if Kitcher is suggesting only that we label speculative hypotheses as such, no one has any objection to that. Indeed, thanks to people like Kitcher (and this isn't meant sarcastically), many Darwinians are now masters of careful qualification.

Which brings us to the second problem with Kitcher's argument: the suggestion that Darwinian social scientists, but not social scientists generally, should proceed with great caution. The unspoken assumption is that incorrect Darwinian theories about behavior will tend to be more pernicious than incorrect *non*-Darwinian theories about behavior. But why should that be so? One long-standard and utterly non-Darwinian doctrine of psychology—that there are no important innate mental differences between men and women bearing on courtship and sex—seems to have caused a fair amount of suffering over the past few decades. And it depended on the lowest imaginable "standards of evidence"—no real evidence whatsoever, not to mention the blatant and arrogant disregard of folk wisdom in every culture on the planet. For some reason, though, Kitcher isn't upset about this; he seems to think that theories involving genes can have bad effects but theories not involving genes can't.

A more reliable generalization would seem to be that incorrect theories are more likely than correct theories to have bad effects. And if, as is often the case, we don't know for sure which theories are right and which are wrong, our best bet is to go with the ones that seem most likely to be right. The premise of this book is that evolutionary psychology, in spite of its youth, is now far and away the most likely source of theories about the human mind that will turn out to be right—and that, indeed, many of its specific theories already have fairly firm grounding.

Not all threats to the honest exploration of human nature come from the enemies of Darwinism. Within the new paradigm, truth sometimes gets sugarcoated. It is often tempting, for example, to downplay differences between men and women. Regarding the more polygamous nature of men, politically sensitive Darwinian social scientists may say things like: "Remember, these are only statistical generalizations, and any one person may diverge greatly from the

desertion more shattering than his mere infidelity, reinforce the double standard.

If you buy this way of looking at moral codes, you won't expect them to serve the interests of society at large. They emerge from an informal political process that presumably gives extra weight to powerful people; they are quite unlikely to represent everyone's interests equally (though more likely to do so, perhaps, in a society with free speech and economic equality). And there's definitely no reason to assume that existing moral codes reflect some higher truth apprehended via divine inspiration or detached philosophical inquiry.

Indeed, Darwinism can help highlight the contrast between the moral codes we have and the sort that a detached philosopher might arrive at. For example: though the double standard's harsh treatment of female promiscuity may be a natural by-product of human nature, an ethical philosopher might well argue that sexual license is more often *morally* dubious in the case of the man. Consider an unmarried man and an unmarried woman on their first date. The man is more likely than the woman to exaggerate emotional commitment (consciously or unconsciously) and obtain sex under these false pretenses. And, if he does so, his warmth is then more likely than hers to fade. This is far, far from a hard and fast rule; human behavior is very complex, situations and individuals vary greatly, and members of both sexes get emotionally chewed up in all kinds of ways. Still, as a gross generalization, it is probably fair to say that single men cause more pain to partners of short duration through dishonesty than single women do. So long as women don't sleep with already mated men, their sexual looseness typically harms others obliquely and diffusely, if at all. Thus, if you believe, as most people seem to, that it is immoral to cause others pain by implicitly or explicitly misleading them, you might be more inclined to condemn the sexual looseness of men than of women.

That, at any rate, would be my inclination. If in this chapter I seemed to suggest that women practice sexual restraint, the advice wasn't meant to carry any overtone of obligation. It was self-help, not moral philosophy.

This may sound paradoxical: one can, from a Darwinian vantage point, advise sexual restraint for women, roughly echoing traditional moral exhortation, while at the same time decrying the moral censure of women who don't take the advice. But you might as well get used to the paradox, for it's part of a more general Darwinian slant on morality.

On the one hand, a Darwinian may treat existing morality with suspicion. On the other hand, traditional morality often embodies a certain utilitarian wisdom. After all, the pursuit of genetic interest sometimes, though not always, coincides with the pursuit of happiness. Those mothers who urge their daughters to "save themselves" may at one level be counseling ruthless genetic self-interest, but they are, on another level, concerned for the long-term happiness of their daughters. So too for the daughters who follow mother's advice, believing it will help them become lastingly married and have children: yes, the reason they want childen is because their genes "want" them to want children; nonetheless, the fact remains that they *do* want children, and may well, in fact, have more fulfilling lives if they get them. Though there's nothing inherently good about genetic self-interest, there's nothing inherently wrong with it either. When it does conduce to happiness (which it won't always), and doesn't gravely hurt anyone else, why fight it?

For the Darwinian inclined toward moral philosophy, then, the object of the game is to examine traditional morality under the assumption that it is laden with practical, life-enhancing wisdom, yet is also laced with self-serving and philosophically indefensible pronouncements about the absolute "immorality" of this or that. Mothers may be wise to counsel restraint in their daughters—and, for that matter, wise to condemn competing girls who aren't so restrained. But the claim that these condemnations have *moral* force may be just a bit of genetically orchestrated sophistry.

Extricating the wisdom from the sophistry will be the great and hard task of moral philosophers in the decades to come, assuming that more than a few of them ever get around to appreciating the new paradigm. It is a task, in any event, to which we'll return toward the end of this book, after the origins of the most fundamental moral impulses have become apparent.

SUGARCOATED SCIENCE

One common reaction to discussions of morality in light of the new Darwinism is: Aren't we getting a little ahead of the game here Evolutionary psychology is just getting started. It has produced som theories with powerful support (an innate difference in male a female jealousy); some with fair-to-middling support (the Madonn whore dichotomy); and many more that are sheer, if plausible, sp ulation (the "mate ejection" module). Is this body of theories re capable of supporting sweeping pronouncements about Victorian any other, morality?

Philip Kitcher, a philosopher who in the 1980s established hir as sociobiology's preeminent critic, has carried this doubt a step ther. He believes Darwinians should tread carefully not just in m moral or political extensions from their inchoate science (exten most of them avoid anyway, thanks to the scorching a few re in the 1970s), but in making the science in the first place. Af even if they don't cross the line between science and values, so else will; theories about human nature will inevitably be support this or that doctrine of morality or social policy. An theories turn out to be wrong, they may have done a lot of in the meanwhile. Social science, Kitcher notes, is differe physics or chemistry. If we embrace "an incorrect view of th of a distant galaxy," then "the mistake will not prove tr contrast, if we are wrong about the bases of human social if we abandon the goal of a fair distribution of the benefits and of society because we accept faulty hypotheses about ours our evolutionary history, then the consequences of a scientif may be grave indeed." Thus, "When scientific claims bear of social policy, the standards of evidence and of self-criti be extremely high."[37]

There are two problems here. First, "self-criticism" p an essential part of science. Criticism from colleagues— *collective* self-criticism—is. It is what keeps the "stand; dence" high. And this collective self-criticism can't even a hypothesis is put forward. Presumably Kitcher isn't sug we short-circuit this algorithm of scientific progress b

Emma and Charles Darwin around the time of their wedding. Evolutionary psychology sheds light on various aspects of their relationship, including Emma's relative coolness toward impending marriage. She wrote to Charles, "I shall always look upon the event of the 29th as a most happy one on my part though perhaps not so great or so good as you do."

Above: George Williams in the early 1960s. Williams helped formulate the theory that explains why in most species males are sexually assertive and females more reserved. He also saw a way to test the theory; if it is correct, then this pattern should be weak, or even reversed, in species whose males invest heavily in offspring. *Left:* A male seahorse gives birth after incubating eggs that the female laid in his pouch.

Above: The biologists Robert Trivers and John Maynard Smith in India in 1980.
Below: A !Kung San father and daughter. In all human cultures, males invest
heavily in offspring—less heavily than seahorse males, perhaps, but more heavily
than males in the primate species most closely related to us. This male parental
investment, Trivers has observed, helps explain much about human sexual
psychology, including the kinds of duplicity to which men and women are prone.

!Kung San women collecting food. Hunter-gatherer societies are the closest thing we have to a real-life model of the social context of human evolution. These societies reconcile motherhood and work fairly simply, whether, as here, by bringing children to work or by using kin and friends for babysitting. The anthropologist Marjorie Shostak, who took this picture, wrote, "The isolated mother burdened with bored small children is not a scene that has parallels in !Kung daily life." Her remark illustrates a general point that may account for much current suffering: the human mind wasn't designed for the modern world.

Honeypot ants of the genus *Myrmecocystus,* hanging from the roof of an underground nest, their abdomens swollen with liquid food. During dry spells, these living storage bins provide nourishment for their relatives. Darwin successfully explained the utter altruism of sterile insect castes such as the honeypot, but in very vague terms. Only with the theory of kin selection in the early 1960s did biologists see that Darwin's logic could be used to explain self-sacrifice in many species, including ours.